Bargain Book

W9-ANT-705

Rich Indians

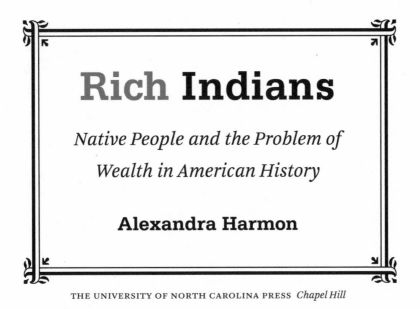

Rich **Indians**

Native People and the Problem of
Wealth in American History

Alexandra Harmon

THE UNIVERSITY OF NORTH CAROLINA PRESS *Chapel Hill*

© 2010 The University of North Carolina Press
All rights reserved

Designed and set in Arnhem and Serifa by Rebecca Evans

Manufactured in the United States of America

The paper in this book meets the guidelines for permanence
and durability of the Committee on Production Guidelines for
Book Longevity of the Council on Library Resources.

The University of North Carolina Press has been a
member of the Green Press Initiative since 2003.

Library of Congress Cataloging-in-Publication Data
Harmon, Alexandra, 1945–
Rich Indians: Native people and the problem of
wealth in American history / Alexandra Harmon.
p. cm.   Includes bibliographical references and index.
ISBN 978-0-8078-3423-7 (cloth: alk. paper)
1. Indians of North America — Economic conditions. 2. Indians of
North America — Social conditions. 3. Indians of North America —
Social life and customs. 4. Rich people — United States — History.
5. Wealth — Social aspects — United States — History. 6. Wealth —
Moral and ethical aspects — United States — History. 7. Social
change — United States — History. 8. United States — Ethnic
relations. 9. United States — Economic conditions. I. Title.
E98.E2H37 2010   973.04′97 — dc22   2010018368

14 13 12 11 10   5 4 3 2 1

Contents

Illustrations

Acknowledgments

This book has been a decade in the making partly because I was shy about consulting with other scholars as I planned and launched into research. But when I did seek help identifying sources or analyzing them, and when I asked colleagues to read drafts, many people gave generously of their time, expertise, and encouragement. I am profoundly grateful to them all and want to acknowledge the important ways they supported a long, challenging project.

I am especially indebted to Richard Johnson, Frederick Hoxie, Sven Beckert, David Kleit, Jeff Ostler, Brian Hosmer, Colleen O'Neill, Paul Rosier, and Jessica Cattelino for reading chapter drafts. The final versions benefited from their frank, incisive, fair-minded critiques and valuable suggestions. John Findlay, Ben Schmidt, Linda Nash, and other members of the University of Washington history faculty research group also offered useful comments on an early draft of chapter one.

I had capable research assistance from Beatrice Marx, Jen Seltz, and Christopher Herbert. Richard Johnson, Colleen Boyd, David Getches, Luana Ross, and Dan Hart supplied me with significant specific sources. And I thank Clara Sue Kidwell for the warm hospitality she extended during my sojourn in Norman, Oklahoma, for research.

A grant from the Institute for Ethnic Studies in the United States at the University of Washington covered some early research expenses. I was fortunate as well to receive a fellowship from the University of Washington's Simpson Center for the Humanities, affording a brief leave from teaching and stimulating discussions with other fellows at a crucial time in my research. I have also had the support and encouragement of my colleagues in the American Indian Studies department, particularly our chair, Tom Colonnese.

Librarians, archivists, curators, and historical society staff are essential partners in a historical research project, and I had the help of many such hardworking people at the National Archives, University of Washington Libraries,

Oklahoma Historical Society, University of Oklahoma Western History Collections, Library of Congress, New York State Historical Association, and Denver Public Library.

It was my good fortune to meet University of North Carolina Press acquisitions editor Mark Simpson-Vos just as the time came to seek a publisher. His belief in the value of the project gave me needed confidence as I made last revisions. Mark, Ron Maner, René Hayden, and other press staff have moved the manuscript expeditiously toward production, responding promptly and encouragingly to my questions and offering wise, welcome advice.

Rich Indians

Introduction

The late 1990s were a heady time for believers in the bounty of American capitalism. Bullish investors stampeded into the stock market, and share values inflated rapidly in the heat of their frenzy. Week after week, the media announced ballooning personal fortunes, especially from new information technology ventures. Although most people in the United States got no financial boost from the boom, the fortunate ones seemed to show what was possible in an expanding economy. They could gleefully rake in wealth without incurring much public censure.

Political scientist Andrew Hacker observed in the *New York Times* that "Americans know the rich are getting richer" yet appear ambivalent about "the upward flow of money. . . . Even those unsettled by the shift in wealth seem hesitant about framing the discussion in moral terms." When contemplating the hyperinflated incomes of celebrities, they focus "less on whether greed is good or bad than on . . . when or which superpayments may be deserved." Hacker himself did not impute greed or amorality to lavishly paid individuals. In fact, Americans' reluctance to define extreme wealth as a moral problem made sense to him. "For many political and economic reasons," Hacker wrote, "the 1990's have surpassed the 1980's in creating opportunities for becoming rich. And those who do, much like the rest of us, see no reason to refuse what comes their way."[1]

The temperature of the economy cooled abruptly in the next decade, and many high-flying speculators lost altitude, but the "upward flow of money" continued. Not only did the wealthiest people add to their wealth at an extraordinary rate, but politicians advocated or acquiesced in legislation that increased the trend's momentum. Once again some analysts noted that expressions of moral indignation or concern about social justice were muted. Economist Paul Krugman had an ear cocked for sermons about selfishness but heard few. No crusade for reform followed a Congressional Budget Office announcement that the largest family incomes rose 140 percent, while middle bracket incomes climbed only 9 percent between 1979 and 1997. "You might have expected the concentration . . . at the top to provoke populist demands to soak the rich," Krugman suggested. Instead, the response was "a drive to reduce taxes on the rich." Fellow columnist David Brooks also noticed a shortage of unease about policies that directed ever more money into pockets already overflowing. He asked rhetorically why there was little opposition to the repeal of an estate tax "explicitly for the mega-upper class." His answer: *Income resentment is not a strong emotion in much of America. . . . Many Americans admire the rich.*"[2]

From Seattle, an epicenter of the so-called dot-com business boom, I followed the developments these pundits analyzed, and I shared their perception that critical commentary couched in ethical or ideological principles was scarce, at least in mainstream media. Most reports of soaring private fortunes seemed celebratory. I hoped to hear debate about the compatibility of headlong profit-seeking and extreme income disparities with other national ideals, but my wish went unfulfilled. The surge of moneymaking did not arouse much public soul-searching.

At the same time, I followed a story of growing affluence in another demographic minority and noticed discourse of a different sort. American Indians—barely more than one percent of the U.S. population—had launched enterprises that were earning them millions of dollars and avid interest from journalists. A sizable number of Indians responded to this turn of events with calls for sober reflection on the values that ought to motivate their economic activity. One was Marty Firerider, an Anishinaabe man in San Diego, where Indian tribes were banking fabulous profits from casinos. Firerider lamented that some of the prospering tribes had "turned a blind eye to the needs of their Indian neighbors." "Indian country is threatened with disunity," he warned, "because with wealth come greed and power. . . . Acquiring or possessing more than what one needs (self greed) is not the Indian way."[3]

Non-Indian commentators invoked principles of morality and social justice as well. When California tribes balked at raising the share of casino proceeds they contributed to state coffers, Governor Arnold Schwarzenegger accused them of duplicity as well as "tremendous greed."[4] In the name of equity, U.S. Senator Slade Gorton proposed to cut federal aid for tribes with the most lucrative enterprises. Some Indians countered by impugning the motives and integrity of these politicians. Schwarzenegger's complaint that Indians with billions in income were not paying their fair share struck a reader of *Indian*

Country Today as all-too-familiar "racialist" language. To tribal representatives, Gorton's suggestion that it was "time to redistribute Federal funds from the wealthier tribes to the poorer ones" was hypocritical. They reportedly asked, "Since when are tax-cutting Republicans interested in redistributing wealth?" The proposed move in this case, they added, would perpetuate the broken promises and "outright theft" that stained the record of White people's dealings with Indians.[5]

In the reactions to Indians' new and growing wealth, moral judgments of economic behavior merged with ideas about Indians. Whether the ostensible subject was revenue sharing or the moral acceptability of a revenue source, conceptions of Indianness underlay the positions people took. Normative generalizations about Indian propensities—often paired with contrasting characterizations of non-Indians—were common. Some Indians detected and resented a widespread assumption that making money was inconsistent with Indian traits. One groused in a letter to the *Denver Post* that "many Americans seem to believe Indians must be poor and helpless in order to be Indian." Conversely, when Hopi voters rejected a proposed tribal casino, an *Indian Country Today* correspondent explained that it was "the Hopi way" to shun "excessive wealth and material possessions."[6]

Thus, remarkable Indian financial gains triggered unusual public discussion of economic ethics, and the discourse plainly owed its distinctiveness to the moneymakers' Indian identity. If the prospering people had not been Indians, the discourse might have been as unconcerned with social ideals as the buzz surrounding dot-com millionaires. However, when it seemed that Indians could also be millionaires, many people tried to sort out their thoughts on ambition and on Indians simultaneously. In the process, they articulated and debated some values or principles that might guide economic activity. Notions of fairness, individual rights, and responsibility to others colored their statements about money matters. A recurrent issue was whether American ideals required that Indians and their fellow citizens conduct economic activities by the same rules.

Enterprising Indians stirred so much discussion partly because they seemed novel in the 1990s. From media coverage of rising tribal revenues, which seldom failed to mention Indians' history of pervasive poverty, Americans could reasonably infer that well-heeled Indians were a new phenomenon. But some octogenarians knew better; they could recall reports in the 1920s that Osage Indians were the world's richest people. As a history scholar, I also knew about wealthy Indians in the past. While still a novice historian, I had seen Indian names on an early twentieth-century list of rich ranchers in Washington State.

Later I learned of Cherokees and Creeks whose immense landholdings in the 1890s earned them condemnation as immoral monopolists.

This book began with my desire to know more about the controversy surrounding those big Cherokee and Creek landholders. What did fellow tribe members have to say about individuals who accumulated extensive property? How did Indians—rich and poor—respond to denunciations of the rich ones? What social ideals or norms of conduct did Indians and non-Indians invoke when discussing the acquisitive Indians? What ideas about Indians were reflected in and propagated by such commentary? What were the practical consequences of the controversy? Did racial ideology in particular affect its outcome?[7]

The distinctive discourse about thriving present-day Indian entrepreneurs inspired me to extend my inquiry to additional occasions in the past when Indians were conspicuously affluent. It seemed all but certain that they, too, would have provoked public discussion of right and wrong in economic affairs. Indians and Euro-Americans have a long history of articulating their respective principles or ideals by comparing themselves to each other. Non-Indians have often imagined Indian practices as the antithesis of American ideals, although some have credited Indians with virtues that other Americans have lost or failed to embrace.[8] Meanwhile, Indians, by contrasting their ideals to the words and deeds of non-Indians, have also developed characterizations of themselves and other peoples.[9] The subjects of comparison have necessarily included economic conduct. Moreover, the desire to control wealth has given Indians and non-Indians their most common and compelling motivation to deal with each other. Therefore, if and when Indians had substantial wealth, debate about the morality of Indian and Euro-American economic conduct was apt to flare up.

Debates of that sort are not only a noteworthy aspect of Indians' history; they are also significant episodes in Americans' long struggle with the consequences of their nation's origins in settler colonialism. European colonization, which was above all an economic quest, initiated a process of assessing whether and how the economic aims of immigrants and indigenous peoples could be reconciled. Recent reactions to lucrative Indian businesses indicate that the process is continuing. The discursive aspect of that process has had momentous practical ramifications for both groups. It has been integral to the endeavor of giving meaning to the words "American" and "Indian." As anthropologist Patrick Wolfe observes, words have served as a vital defense against the erasure of indigenes as distinct peoples. In a "settler-colonial economy" where natives are "superfluous," "survival is a matter of not being assimilated," and often "the sanctions practically available to the native are ideological ones."[10]

Hoping for fresh perspectives on some of the moral or ideological questions that came with European colonization of an inhabited continent, I resolved to investigate responses to notable instances of Indian affluence. The result is a set of seven stories with a common hypothesis: accumulations of wealth in Indian hands have presented both Euro-Americans and Indians with circumstances that obliged them to rethink their own economic aims and ethics, critique each other's aims, and choose in practice to prioritize some aims or ideals over others. Those thoughts on wealth, property rights, and the objectives of economic activity have been entangled with ideas about Indians. Reactions to Indian wealth have reflected and affected ideologies of race and nationality as well as economic ideologies. By examining controversies about affluent Indians in successive periods, we can see the changing interplay of those ideologies, other sociocultural motivations, and material conditions. We can also learn why controversy has swirled around enterprising Indians long after Indians acceded to capitalism's hegemony.

This book's seven chapters consider nearly as many geographical areas and Indian peoples as time periods and phases of American economic history: the Powhatan chiefdom in the first years of the Virginia colony, some individual Mohawks and Creeks in the eighteenth century, Indian nations of the Southeast in the early 1800s, the relocated southeastern groups during the Gilded Age, Osages in the Roaring Twenties, communities from Alaska to Maine during the tribal renaissance of the 1970s, and tribes that have drawn gamblers to casinos across the United States since the 1990s. In their times, all these Indians engaged the attention of substantial audiences, and most have since had attention from scholars. At least three of the featured groups are stock characters in American history courses and texts, familiar even to scholars who do not specialize in Indians. My decision to analyze well-known people and high-profile historical episodes followed from my concern with public discourse. Certain Indians have attracted historians' notice in part because documentation of their activities is plentiful, and documentation is plentiful because of circumstances that stimulated public discourse, including—not infrequently—the Indians' control of considerable wealth.[11]

In only one of the instances I studied was there serious doubt that the Indians had claim to significant wealth: when founders of the Jamestown colony and native inhabitants of the Chesapeake area were taking the measure of each other's resources, both of them hoping for relations that would improve their own fortunes. Chapter one analyzes that doubt, showing that Englishmen and Powhatans assessed their relative prosperity and judged each other's economic conduct by the different standards of their dissimilar cultures. The essay concludes with a brief chronicle of the Powhatans' eventual descent into unambiguous poverty—a decline that seemed to some Britons to portend the outcome of all Indian encounters with colonists and thus contributed to the expectation of poverty Indians would defy when they did get rich.

Well into the eighteenth century, most of North America was still the domain of indigenous people who had not met the Powhatans' fate, and British colonies needed such people as trading partners and allies. Because the need was mutual, and because leadership in both populations depended on access to wealth, rich individuals familiar with Indian and colonial cultures had the material and social means to wield influence among natives and colonists. The second chapter considers questions posed at the time by the careers of four Indians who obtained and used wealth much as colonial gentry did. Could such persons secure the respect of the gentry as well as Indians, and thus function as protectors of the Indian nations' autonomy and resources? Could Indian and colonial societies coexist and conduct relations through leaders from both societies who would recognize each other by their economic conduct as people of merit and comparable rank?

Those questions were moot by the 1820s. The rapid growth of the United States had weakened the colonial elite as well as native nations that stood in the way of the expanding republic. When some tribes pinned their hopes of keeping their homelands on the adoption of Euro-American economic practices and prospered as a result, they provoked debates about urgent new moral issues, which are the subject of the third chapter. Members of the so-called Civilized Tribes scrutinized each other's conduct for signs of greed while Whites in the States argued fiercely about which was the greater threat to the principles of American civilization—the presence of autonomous Indian societies that held their land in common, or the dishonor that Americans would incur by driving the Indians from their land.

Half a century later, when private concentrations of wealth had reached unprecedented proportions in the relocated Civilized Tribes and in the United States, Euro-Americans and tribe members engaged in parallel deliberations about the merits and perils of self-interested individual enterprise. At the same time, as chapter four shows, tribe members and U.S. citizens also debated each other, and a decisive issue in that debate was whether fundamental differences between Indians and non-Indians required disparate responses to greed in their respective societies.

Not long afterward, greed became an issue in a different way for nearby Osage Indians. Chapter five is set on Osage land in the 1920s, where a bonanza from oil wells enabled many of the Indians to buy whatever they wanted and attracted a plague of covetous vendors, lenders, and scam artists. At a time when millions of other prospering Americans were encouraged to indulge their appetite for consumer goods as never before, the question arose again whether Indians' distinctive characteristics or status called for enforcement of a separate norm.

The wealth at issue in the sixth chapter came after fifty years in which government officials and social scientists repeatedly publicized the poverty afflicting Indian communities and tried ineffectively to alleviate it. By securing access to some valuable resources in the 1970s, Indian tribes unsettled the prevalent belief that they were chronic economic failures or victims. Their surprising successes and an ensuing backlash revived and reframed the question asked in earlier eras: whether Indians and non-Indians did or should live by the same rules of economic relations.

Six stories about six distinct time periods make it possible to see continuity and change in the issues raised by Indian wealth. For instance, some themes of the controversy that erupted in the 1970s have carried over to the present century, and they run through recent commentary on tribal casino profits. The final portion of the book examines the most recent commentary for recurrent questions debated in earlier eras, and it spots several. Is it correct to characterize the Indians under discussion as rich? Are the affluent people actually Indians? Is the wealth fairly distributed? Is it bound to corrupt its possessors? Does it make them powerful, or is it an indication of excessive power? Are non-Indians likely to expropriate it?

Two concepts central to this study—economic culture and morality—require explication. As a term for shared, socially perpetuated ways of thinking and acting, "culture" is problematic. Outside of anthropology, where that connotation of culture defines a major field of study, the word's meanings are numerous and vague. Even cultural anthropologists have discovered that predicaments come with their use of the concept. Yet it is impractical to analyze relations between people from Europe or their descendants and the people they called Indians without employing the ubiquitous concept of culture. For the purposes of this book, I conceive of culture as James Axtell defines it: an idealized, fluid pattern of meanings, values, and norms that members of a society share to differing degrees, and reveal in their non-instinctive behavior and symbolism. The modifier "economic" focuses attention on patterns of meanings, values, and norms pertaining to the production, distribution, and use of material resources, income, wealth, or commodities and on the human relations associated with those activities.[12]

When I say that morality has been an issue in controversies about Indian economic culture, I mean morality in the broadest philosophical sense of the term. Although popular usage cheapens the meaning of the word by associating it primarily with sexual conduct, "morality" denotes systems or principles for classifying all sorts of behavior as good or bad, acceptable or unacceptable, ethical or irresponsible. The studies in this volume show that Indian affluence caused Indians and non-Indians to ponder a variety of questions about right and wrong. Whether riches themselves or particular rich people were good or bad was often the least of their concerns.

Sources for the stories I tell differ in kind from essay to essay. For evidence and analysis of economic culture and evidence of discourse about Indian practices, the earlier essays rely largely on secondary literature and published primary documents, while later essays draw heavily on such primary sources as government records, newspapers, and other periodicals. The factors that account for this difference include disparities in the extent of existing scholarship on the various subjects and disparities in the amounts and sorts of records that document pertinent public discourse. For example, there is ample scholarship on the prosperous individual Indians featured in chapter two but far less on the Osages who are the subject of chapter five. Sources also reflect the nature of the controversy under examination and the types of forums where it played out. News media did not host the debates of the seventeenth and eighteenth centuries, but by the mid-twentieth century, print and broadcast media were important forums for Indians as well as non-Indians. The foundation of the last three chapters is therefore a generous sampling of discourse in newspapers, magazines, and television.

It is an understatement to say histories of prosperous Indians are uncommon. In adopting that unusual focus, I had in mind some shortcomings of existing scholarship. For one thing, simply by concentrating on Indian economic strategies and dilemmas, this book expands a catalog of literature that is much too slim. Although it is exceptional for a history of Indians not to describe the economic consequences of colonial invasions, works that take Indian economic life as their central subject—particularly life since the nineteenth century—are still comparatively and regrettably scarce.

When historical accounts do foreground Indian economic affairs, a common theme is a conflict of cultures that worked in Euro-Americans' favor, leading to Indians' impoverishment. In some recent works describing Indian accommodations to Euro-American economic dominance, we can read about Indians who apparently embraced the colonizers' acquisitive individualism.[13] Few histories, however, identify material affluence as one of the challenges Indians have faced, let alone emphasize that Indian affluence could trouble non-Indians in sundry ways.[14] Such a bias in historical scholarship is understandable, since poor Indians have been far more numerous than rich ones, and good fortune has seldom lasted long for Indians. But it is precisely because stories of wealthy Indians deviate from the familiar chronicle of economic decline that they deserve to be told. As historian Philip Deloria has shown, Indians who defy expectations about Indians prompt us to articulate prevalent conceptions of Indians and reconsider them in light of Indians' actual experiences and conduct. The result can be a revelation of processes obscured by habitual ways of framing Indian history.[15] As presumed rarities or anomalies, prosperous Indians have defied the expectations of contemporaries and historians. Their stories, including the reactions they provoked, should afford new insights about Indians and the non-Indians who dealt with them.

Historians' neglect of prosperous Indians may be due in part to a common assumption that the self-interested pursuit and retention of wealth was not an indigenous American value. There are scholars bent on refuting this assumption, but three of them say their efforts have made little headway against a persistent false myth that "indigenous populations historically did not view property as private, or that they shared communally the various factors of economic development."[16] Although the myth's influence on historical scholarship is weaker than this complaint suggests, the debunkers identify a seductive paradigm that has drawn historians' gaze away from enterprising Indians. The paradigm contrasts an egalitarian, spiritual, traditionalist Indian ethos with a competitive, materialistic, activist non-Indian ethos.[17]

Paradoxically, when historians have noticed Indians exhibiting a supposedly un-Indian interest in acquiring wealth, they have seldom probed deeply for explanations. Their apparent assumption is that exposure to enterprising foreigners with alluring possessions awakened a natural human desire for what others have. Accepting economists' premise that the calculated pursuit of economic advantage is rationality, some historians have concentrated on determining when Indians abandoned nonrational conceptions of their economic relations with Europeans in favor of a pragmatic concern with maximizing gain. But Indian desires for wealth require more analysis than that. It explains little to assert, as a Hollywood director did when discussing his film about corporate takeovers, that "people have been greedy since the Bible."[18] People have promoted, condoned, or tolerated acquisitive behavior in some societies or circumstances more than others.[19] If "rational" means based on reasoning or in accordance with reason, an economic order may be rational whether it encourages or discourages the accumulation of wealth. History can elucidate circumstances that have encouraged acquisitiveness and ideas that Indians have brought to bear in response.

Another argument for studying wealthy Indians takes a cue from historians who study wealthy White Americans. Steve Fraser and Gary Gerstle deem it important to learn how the wealthy have "formulated the ideological justifications for their empowerment," because the ideology of the rich has often passed as the predominant ideology of a society or nation. In his history of New York City's bourgeoisie, Sven Beckert shows how the well-to-do achieved a dominance that made their interests and ideas seem to be "those of most Americans." Beckert traces the evolution of a class culture and creed as well as class members' consolidation of economic and political power.[20] Tracing the interrelationship of wealth, culture, creed, and power in Indian societies is similarly important. Just as it has paid muckrakers to follow the money when deciphering American power relations, it should pay historians to track wealth in Indian nations.

Since scarcity can enhance an item's ascribed worth, this book's emphasis on the moral premises of economic culture should add to its value, for histories with that emphasis are nearly as rare as histories of rich Indians. Historians seldom remind us, as Ethan Yorgason has, that an economy constitutes "a system of meaning [or] . . . a moral order."[21] Economic life proceeds according to, or sometimes contrary to, rules of social relationship that reflect notions of fairness and humans' obligations in the world. Yet scholars of economic history have generally followed the discipline of economics in emphasizing impersonal systems, institutions, and quantitative analysis at the expense of inquiries into the moral philosophies that inspire and gain validation from economic custom. Although some social and labor historians have highlighted the beliefs of economic actors, it is common in economic history to study institutions and processes without exploring the "meanings, values, and norms" underlying them.[22]

The attention of this book to Indian views of Indians is also rarer than it should be. Studies of Euro-American ideas about Indians are numerous. I would say they are a dime a dozen if they were not worth much more than that to historical scholarship. However, many of them misleadingly if unintentionally suggest that non-Indian conceptions of Indians developed with little or no Indian input. In reality, Indians have taken active part in processes that generated common images of Indians. They have monitored and worked to affect representations of Indians, sometimes by exploiting stereotypes for their own purposes, sometimes by appearing in Euro-American forums or employing Euro-American media to project alternative images of Indians.[23] Histories documenting such efforts are still scarce. With this volume, their number grows by one. While beliefs about Indians were shaping Euro-American reactions to rich Indians and being reshaped in turn by the Indians' affluence, Indians' thoughts about Indianness were also affecting and reflecting their responses to affluence in their own ranks. The two conceptualization processes did not unfold in isolation from each other; rather, they informed each other.

It is a premise of this book that the reciprocal influences of Indian and non-Indian ideas have extended to the subject of economic relations and wealth. Whether or not non-Indians acknowledged Indians' ideas, they reacted to them when responding to Indian conduct. A historical examination of American thought regarding economic morality is therefore incomplete unless it includes Indian thought.[24] Admittedly, Euro-Americans have had more power than Indians to define the issues and set the terms of discourse on economic culture. The issues examined in this book arose from developments that non-Indians set in motion, and as their numbers grew, non-Indians continually created conditions to which Indians had to respond. Yet Euro-Americans could not wholly preempt discourse grounded in distinctive Indian values, and Euro-American ideas would have developed differently in the absence of Indians.

By emphasizing intercultural discourse about wealth, this book also defies Indian economic history's regrettable isolation from the rest of economic history. As a rule, Indians are peripheral characters in studies of American economic life. They are often missing altogether. In 2009, historian Paul Rosier searched textbooks, monographs, and journals of American economic history for references to Indians and found exceedingly few. Rosier's findings confirm what economics professor Linda Barrington wrote seven years earlier: "Native American economic history is still quite underrepresented in the standard economic history curriculum."[25]

Economic history's disregard of Indians is due in part to lingering effects of a discredited historical division of academic labor. Until recent decades, historians largely conceded the study of Indians to anthropologists. Anthropologists, says Patricia Albers, maintained that Indian economies were "driven by cultural logics radically different" from the logics of European market commercialism and American industrialism.[26] Meanwhile, economic historians followed the lead of economists in taking the development of modern market industrialism as their subject.[27] Both anthropologists and historians therefore came to believe that key concepts of economic history were "not easily transferable" to aboriginal peoples of North America.[28] Although many economic historians now see the benefits of crossing disciplinary boundaries,[29] few have yet ventured into Indian history, perhaps wary not only of encountering people whose economic logic is foreign, but also of having to rely on the work of scholars in a discipline that seems foreign. Due to anthropology's long monopoly on Indian scholarship, for example, it is difficult to write about Indians without consulting ethnographies produced years ago, which purport to describe bounded aboriginal societies unaffected by European colonization and thus contravene history's premise of universal change.

Now that scholars of all disciplines acknowledge the historicity of Indian societies and no longer relegate them to a timeless "ethnographic present," it behooves us to find ways of overcoming the legacy of Indians' exclusion from much of American economic history. Differences between indigenous and colonial or capitalist economies did not prevent economic relations between Indians and non-Indians in the past; nor should differences in academic culture discourage scholars from venturing across the boundaries between disciplines.

A field that bridges the divide between history and anthropology is ethnohistory, in which scholars employ both ethnological and historical methods, usually to describe and explain culture change in homogeneous subaltern groups.[30] Indian tribes are typical subjects of ethnohistory.[31] Although I aimed to understand the changing economic culture of heterogeneous, hegemonic Euro-American society as well as Indian societies, I followed ethnohistorians' example by turning for insights to the findings of anthropologists, particularly economic anthropologists, and they helped me articulate some guiding assumptions of this study.

Most fundamentally, anthropology affirms that wealth is a human invention and thus subject to continual reinvention. Although wealth is also a universal concept, its meanings are culturally and historically specific. Even money, despite its function as a standardized medium of exchange, takes on multiple meanings by time and place.[32] The leading dictionary definition of wealth—all goods and resources that have exchange or use value—does not tell us what people have valued.[33] It follows that words such as "rich" and "poor" are not self-defining either. Intercultural dialogues about economic issues oblige those involved to define their terms.

Societies differ, too, in the significance they assign to the acquisition, accumulation, uses, and distribution of wealth.[34] Concepts of wealth and notions of economic morality reflect and affect how people structure their relationships to each other and to outsiders. The character of relations between distinct peoples has therefore depended in part on the compatibility of their beliefs and customs related to wealth. In addition, differences in access to wealth affect and reflect the structure of relations. For example, ethnic and racial categories, which are often the basis for relations of domination, have developed and persisted in the service of economic objectives.[35]

Anthropologists tell us, too, that there is considerable variation in the degree to which people distinguish economics from other aspects of life, but there is never strict separation. In small "tribal" societies, economic strategy has typically been embedded in relations with kin and friendly associates. In the present world of nation-states, by contrast, it has become normal to conceive of economic relations as a distinct realm of life with its own laws of operation.[36] Yet a maxim offered by Manning Nash applies in both settings: "Economic activity derives its meaning from the general values of the society, and people engage in economic activity for rewards often extrinsic to the economy itself." The objectives of economic activity are inseparable from needs and aspirations of other sorts, such as status and power. An observation of Maurice Bloch and Jonathan Parry is also relevant: every society has "a conception of the relationship of the acquisitive individual to a social or cosmic order that transcends the individual."[37]

In other words, humans everywhere think about economic matters on multiple levels. They may think in metaphors that link wealth and economic relations to basic biological or emotional aspects of life.[38] Even in societies where designated "rational" decision-makers or worldwide market networks largely set the parameters of economic choice, people may understand and explain many of their day-to-day choices with reference to a different value system. People may even function effectively for some purposes in an economic system whose guiding principles they do not share or fully comprehend.[39] As historian Benjamin Heber Johnson observes, "Capitalism is a powerful but contingent force that competes with other ways of understanding economic life."[40]

Finally, anthropologists argue persuasively that the premises, concepts, and methodology of modern economic thought are products of a particular time and cultural tradition. Today's "Western notion" of economic rationality may be far-reaching, but it is not culture-neutral.[41] I have tried to keep this insight in mind for all periods of American history, taking the logic of non-Indians' economic culture no more for granted than the logic of Indians' culture. Ethnographies—problematic as their reconstructions of culture often are—have helped me in this respect. The best of them not only recite how society members procured, produced, distributed, and used material resources and other wealth; they also venture to explain how that economic behavior reflected and reinforced such features of society as kinship, religion, prestige, and power relations. Ethnographies suggested questions to ask about Euro-American actors as well as Indians in several of my case studies. How did they define wealth? How did they explain and legitimate their acquisition or accumulation of wealth? What purposes did their pursuit, possession, or control of wealth serve? What obligations did they feel to others as they engaged in economic activity? That is, what were their notions of economic justice? On what basis and by what processes did they allocate wealth? What power relations did these patterns reflect and effect?

Where I did not find answers to such questions in other scholars' work, I looked for records showing how people of the various groups responded to each other's economic conduct. An axiom in history and related fields of study is that "meaning is a matter of comparison." Perceived differences prompt comparisons and reactions that make meaning apparent, both to the people reacting and to historians.[42] When confronted with the unfamiliar, people become more conscious of their own expectations and more apt to articulate or manifest their tacit assumptions, values, and motivations. Thus, confronted with markedly prosperous Indians, Indians and non-Indians have expressed feelings and ideas that otherwise might not have surfaced—not that their statements always represented true feelings or precluded their holding contradictory views. Espoused values frequently do not match those exhibited in behavior. In addition, surprise and novelty call for improvisation. Therefore, rather than revealing a customary structure of meanings and norms, reactions to novelty may represent alterations of that structure.[43] In examining what people said and did about affluent Indians, I have tried to distinguish the innovative or aberrant from the customary, but I have not deemed it essential to make a confident determination, because my primary aim has been to discover the meanings people ascribed to a notable phenomenon at the time.

The undertaking has been worth the time and effort invested if, as I hope, this book casts new light on what settler colonialism has meant for Indians and non-Indians. At the center of each story I tell is the well-known power struggle that colonization initiated, and the outcomes in the particular cases will not surprise most readers. But the diverse characters, their dilemmas, their motives, and their capabilities may be surprising. Their stories reveal facets of the power struggle that are not readily apparent from other ways of looking at American and American Indian history. Taken together, the separate stories suggest the outline of a larger tale.

Repeatedly, since people of European origin took up residence among

Indians, some people in both groups have construed Indians' possession of substantial wealth as a problem. In the course of grappling with the problem, they have compared, debated, and sometimes reconsidered the basic premises of their economic practices. Fueling their debates was a need to answer a fundamental question posed by European colonization and United States expansion in North America: whether the economic aims and cultures of indigenous peoples and colonizers were compatible or reconcilable. Although it might seem, in retrospect, that the answer was evident soon after colonial settlement began, the question arose anew with each instance of conspicuous Indian prosperity. Reframed as the historical context changed, the question could not be answered without attention to moral or ethical issues. Nor could those issues be separated from the process of investing the word "Indian" with meaning. Ideas about Indians determined which principles or ideological tenets people invoked, and economic ideologies informed their ideas about Indians. Unfortunately for Indians, the meanings and the moral precepts that ultimately counted most were those proposed by Euro-Americans. Wealth did not afford Indians the power to say which conceptions of Indians and which principles would determine the nature of their relations with Euro-Americans.

These seven stories do not minimize the covetousness of many Euro-Americans or the self-serving nature of their commentary on wealthy Indians. But the plots are more complicated than the familiar one of Indians' victimization and dispossession at the hands of Whites. When we view Indian-White relations through the prism of both peoples' efforts to define, control, and allocate wealth, we do not see clearly demarcated bands of people, with greedy Whites at one edge of a limited spectrum, and poor but generous Indians at the other. Instead, the refracted light reveals a broader, fuzzier spectrum of skin colors and behaviors that includes Euro-Americans who championed Indian property rights and Indians who sought additional wealth for selfish ends. We can see that racist justifications of Indians' dispossession had tremendous power but never gained an undisputed hold on Euro-American minds. Not only did a heritage of divergent ideals and contradictory images of Indians ensure that the ideology of White entitlement would have rivals, but also Euro-American advocates of economic progress were not always able to suppress their own countervailing moral impulses.[44] We can also see that some Indians came to approve of acquisitive individualism as a force for their people's "advancement" even while other Indians embraced a contrasting economic ethos as essential to their cherished Indianness.

Many people have told the story of the struggle for America's wealth as the triumph of a White supremacist ideology that excused Europeans' confiscation of Indian land and resources. Like Lumbee legal scholar Robert A. Williams, they stress that "identification of the Indian as incommensurable other ... resolved a number of acute problems for the West's ... project of colonization of the New World, which required a justification for its conquests of other peoples' lands." Certainly that assertion summarizes a body of compelling scholarship.[45] The colonial project did require and tend to validate a conception of Indians that largely absolved settlers of blame for Indians' deprivation. Colonists' economic aspirations powerfully motivated them to believe that Indians were incapable of thriving in a rich land as "civilized" people could. In the course of reconciling their self-conception as instruments of progress and universal prosperity with their identity as colonizers, Euro-Americans fashioned an economic culture that had no room for Indians as they imagined them. However, Euro-Americans' ascendancy did not put a stop to conversation on that issue. Indians and their sympathizers would have more to say about it, again and again. And their perseverance was not entirely in vain.

[1]

"Savages," Rich and Poor

As the colony of Virginia approached its hundredth anniversary, Robert Beverley took up pen and ink to write the story of that British outpost in North America, his birthplace and home. His account contrasted the colonists' economic culture with that of the indigenous people. Before English settlers came, Beverley asserted, natives of Virginia had nothing they considered riches except "trifles" made of shell. "It was the *English* alone that taught them first to put a value on their Skins and Furs, and to make a Trade of them." Although Beverley was unsure whether that lesson had corrupted the people he called Indians or perpetuated their primitive innocence, he knew they had not prospered along with the colony. As of 1705, the Indians—formerly happy "in their simple State of Nature, and in their enjoyment of Plenty, without the Curse of Labour"—were in a sorry state. The cause of the change was plain: "The *English* have taken away great part of their Country, and consequently made every thing less plenty amongst them. They have introduc'd Drunkenness and Luxury amongst them, which have multiply'd their Wants, and put them upon desiring a thousand things, they never dreamt of before."[1]

At least one of these assertions would surely have brought confirming nods from the Indians Berkeley wrote about: immigrants from England *had* "made every thing less plenty" for them. From the James River north to the Potomac River, a coastal plain that sustained thousands of their ancestors was now occupied largely by foreigners. Beyond the frontiers of immigrant occupation, large indigenous populations still controlled territory rich in the necessities of life and in commodities the English would buy.[2] But the wretched condition of Indians in the colony's shadow suggested that natives of America were fated to lose economic ground as colonists gained it.

Another British writer explicitly posited this relationship between colonial prosperity and Indian poverty. During travels through North Carolina in 1701, John Lawson saw Europeans making "good Use of the Advantages . . . offer'd" there, thus "raising themselves to great Estates." Many had "become rich, and . . . supply'd with all Things necessary for Trade, and genteel Living." Most of the natives Lawson met seemed pitiably poor by comparison. "All other Nations of *Indians*," he concluded, "are observ'd to partake of the same Fate, where the *Europeans* come."[3] Lawson not only echoed an observation that many of his contemporaries made; he also articulated a belief that would have a long life in the minds of non-Indians and Indians alike: if Indians were not poor when Europeans came, they became poor thereafter.

That belief developed as a consequence of events in times and places besides seventeenth-century Virginia, but some of its original and vital roots were there, in the native towns and early English settlements around Chesapeake Bay. Virginia Company adventurers set up residence on a tributary of the bay more than a decade before Britons planted lasting colonies anywhere else in North America, and the nearby Indians were the first to be stripped of their country—their principal wealth—by English intruders. That precedent is one reason to begin a study of bicultural perspectives on Indian wealth with the establishment of Jamestown, Virginia.

Did the Indians around Jamestown have substantial wealth in 1607, either by the colonists' standard or by their own reckoning? The answer to that question was of considerable import for both groups, but it was not easy to come by. Cultural blinders and the circumstances of their interaction limited the two peoples' ability to determine their relative affluence. Initially, however, everyone concerned had grounds to answer the question affirmatively, and that is an additional reason to examine the colonial encounter in Virginia.

Robert Beverley's contradictory characterization of the aboriginal economy provides a foretaste of what we will see. Whether or not native people needed the English to teach them the commercial value of their natural resources, as Beverley alleged, they did enjoy a "plenty" of sorts in 1607, and a pressing issue for both groups was whether they would relate to each other in a way that undermined or bolstered that prosperity. In other words, significant Indian wealth was at stake in the intercultural negotiations that followed the English intrusion. An inseparable issue was whose economic culture would prevail in the region.

It would take years to decide those issues, partly because the Indians had a lengthy advantage over the colonists in food production, but also because the colonists first had to revise their conceptions of wealth and their strategy for obtaining it in the American setting. Indeed, native/newcomer relations prompted both peoples to adjust their notions of what constituted wealth and their sense of relative affluence. To study that adjustment process is to see a complex interplay of economic motivations, economic thought, moral choices, and ideas about Indians at a seminal moment in American history.

Similar economic motivations focused the two peoples' initial interest in each other. For colonists, appraising the Indians' resources and economic competence was a top-priority task; it was vital to carrying out the colonial mission of generating wealth.[4] The Virginia Company men said they would be pleased to find inhabitants who were rich in commodities prized by Europeans and eager to exchange some of that wealth for English goods. The inhabitants they found, contrary to Beverley's claim, did have and care about riches of several kinds. Native people of the Chesapeake region not only prized some substances that qualified as wealth in England, but, like the English, they sustained a political and social hierarchy with the acquisition, accumulation, and exchange of valuables. Furthermore, they considered the English a probable source of additional wealth. Thus, while the colonists were assessing the Indians' economic status, Indians were measuring their prosperity against that of the intruders, and both groups hoped to improve their fortunes by drawing their new neighbors' resources and desirable possessions into their own exchange networks. At first, both groups also had realistic hopes of gaining materially from relations with each other, and each had cause to feel richer than the other in important respects.

Nevertheless, the English deemed the Indians' economic culture inferior to their own in essential ways, and such disdain was apparently reciprocated. Any possibility of reversing those negative judgments vanished when the colonists finally learned that land was the local resource whose acquisition could enrich them. Thereafter, relations between natives and newcomers worked increasingly to the natives' disadvantage, and a common British preconception of indigenous Americans as people without property became a self-fulfilling prophecy. Before the colonial venture was a century old, Virginians had considerable basis in local experience for thinking that Indians were, and inevitably would be, poor. Disparaging Indians' morals, including their supposedly irrational desire for "Luxury," served to excuse the colony's ruinous effect on the indigenous economy. Indians' dismal destiny was attributed largely to a defective culture, conceived as sinful savagery.

It was May 1607 when three ships belonging to the Virginia Company of London dropped anchor in a wide river winding through the country that natives called Tsenacomoco.[5] From the writings of men who stepped off those vessels and from the works of subsequent historians, we know the indigenous people of Tsenacomoco as Powhatan Indians.[6] But there are many things we cannot know about seventeenth-century Powhatans. Because they left no written accounts of themselves, because the century's events drove them and their descendants to the margins of a colonial society that ignored their view of history, and because their language fell out of use before linguists could record it, we have scant evidence from which to infer how Powhatans thought about most aspects of life, including economic affairs.[7] We are dependent to a discomfiting degree on tall tales and amateur ethnography penned by chauvinistic and self-serving Englishmen, including reports that historian Joyce Chaplin ridicules as "absurd transcriptions" of purported speeches by "ventriloquized" Indians.[8]

The scarcity of evidence has not kept some hardy modern scholars from venturing to describe the economic culture of Tsenacomoco's aboriginal communities. The most prolific and experienced re-creator of Powhatan life and history is Helen Rountree, an anthropologist. By reading the early English accounts in light of limited archaeological evidence, environmental data, anthropological theory, and information on Indians of the larger region, especially Algonquian language speakers, Rountree has formulated a characterization of Powhatan economic life in the early 1600s that other ethnohistorians find plausible in most respects.[9]

In flat, wooded terrain laced by rivers that flowed to Chesapeake Bay, Powhatans usually fed themselves well by hunting, fishing, collecting wild plants, and cultivating a variety of edible crops. At numerous cleared townsites, amid bountiful cornfields and smaller gardens, they erected bark- or mat-covered houses for extended families. Beyond their towns stretched mature forests of hardwood trees. Because stone was scarce and iron unknown, the people had to craft tools, buildings, canoes, and clothing using less durable materials. What they made with implements such as sharpened reeds, turkey spurs, bird bills, beaver teeth, and shells seemed ingenious but primitive to Europeans, who had worked with iron and steel for countless generations.

According to Rountree, "'wealth' among the Powhatans consisted of foodstuffs and hides. It was not easily inheritable, and it was accessible to all, since the land was owned in common" and all able persons had procurement skills appropriate to their gender. In a country "so rich" and a society with "little or no economic specialization," Rountree suggests, "everyone had a chance to prosper." Even so, some people prospered considerably more than others. A few "ruling families" enjoyed "a truly noble lifestyle," with privileges that included an abundance of high-status food and possessions.

Echoing the terminology of the English colonists, Rountree explains that a noble lifestyle was possible because the rulers or chiefs—called *weroances* if male—received tribute from their subjects. Some tribute took the form of labor in weroances' fields and a portion of the crops from commoners' fields. A ruling family would therefore control a supply of corn—"the most prestigious food"—even "in late winter and early spring, when most people's stores were gone." Tribute also included items prized for qualities other than mundane utility—beauty, permanence, scarcity, and presumed spiritual power. Most such "nonperishable luxury goods"—copper, pearls, antimony ore, shell beads, and a root that supplied pigment and medicine—originated in lands beyond Tsenacomoco. Because weroances managed their communities' relations with outsiders, the exotic riches generally came into Powhatan hands via those men.[10]

Although ethnohistorian Frederic Gleach questions whether tribute is the appropriate term, he agrees with Rountree and other analysts that Powhatans channeled wealth of several types to their chiefs. The resulting accumulations had many possible functions. Besides satisfying the personal needs or vanity of noble families and their close associates, weroances' treasuries provided the means to recruit or reward followers and allies, entertain visiting dignitaries, and relieve food scarcity by trading luxuries for corn from communities with staples to spare.[11]

Based partly on a few English observations, especially an account that a weroance deposited precious items in a "gods house," anthropologists hypothesize that Powhatan religious ideas determined the meanings and distribution of exotic valuables, if not all wealth. Gleach, for one, flatly asserts that Powhatans regarded copper, shell beads, and other "luxury goods" as "objects of sacred power." They directed such objects to the weroance, who had power to "socialize" them for ceremonial use or redistribution. Stephen Potter similarly surmises that Powhatans conceived of weroances as intermediaries between their society and other realms, including the sacred. By entrusting chiefs with riches and surplus food for use in rituals and diplomacy, they ensured the well-being of their community.[12]

If the anthropologists are correct, Powhatan ideology did not construe the chiefs' control of wealth as self-interested acquisitiveness or greed. David Murray imagines an alternative explanation for the weroances' appropriation of corn that commoners grew—an explanation stressing "the redistributive aspects and the relations of kinship and reciprocity that bind ruler and ruled." Murray cites Henry Spelman, who lived in Powhatan towns as a youth and saw the paramount weroance fling beads to people as they planted corn for him.

The weroance "is therefore a figure of bounty," Murray proposes, "even at the very moment the people are working to produce what will later be his bounty to distribute to them at harvest time." Gleach favors a similar interpretation of the evidence. Powhatans gave their allegiance to a person who could dispense food and wealth, he argues. The weroance's generosity and the tribute that enabled him to be generous attested to his "high moral position."[13]

This conception of leaders is typical of societies where households carry out all productive functions, as they did in Tsenacomoco. Kin relations are the model for other economic relations. Although their kinship and economic systems differ, such "tribal" societies invariably idealize mutual caretaking and generosity, and they structure relations to enforce those ideals. That ethos does not preclude hierarchy. Even communities with modest material resources may acquire and stockpile things in excess of subsistence needs, and if the surplus funnels to a production leader, the conditions for a self-perpetuating unequal distribution of wealth arise. The leader has the wherewithal to be generous, but his beneficiaries reciprocate or induce his benevolence with offerings of their own, and he thus receives a disproportionate share of circulating wealth. The people conceive of their ruler's treasury as family wealth that he can use to meet their needs. He may claim that the common welfare depends on his putting some of the wealth to such seemingly personal uses as display, but he does so by appealing to the ideals of mutual support and generosity among kin. "Everywhere in the world," anthropologist Marshall Sahlins observes tartly, "the indigenous category for exploitation is 'reciprocity.'"[14]

We cannot trust seventeenth-century Englishmen to tell us whether the allocation of wealth in Tsenacomoco was exploitation, let alone whether Powhatan commoners viewed it as such. Colonists saw indigenous societies through a distorting lens of English ideas and aims. The lack of a common language further limited what they could learn. Additionally, and perhaps most important, the colonists' mission in America influenced how they depicted Powhatan society in correspondence and publications. Nonetheless, their writings do supply convincing evidence that they had entered the domain of a formidable weroance who presided over an extensive "family" of communities and had a claim on much of the region's wealth.

Colonists knew the man's "proper" name was Wahunsonacock, but they more often called him Powhatan—a name they heard he had taken from the town that was his "principall place of dwelling." Before the English arrived, Wahunsonacock had reportedly increased, from six to thirty or more, the number of local weroances who paid him homage, in some instances by conquest or coercion.[15] During a two-year stay at Jamestown, William Strachey came to share other colonists' perception that Wahunsonacock was a powerful and wealthy overlord. "Every Weroance knowes his owne Meetes and lymitts to fish fowle or hunt in," Strachey wrote in 1612, "but they hold all of the great Weroance Powhatan, vnto whome they paie 8. parts of 10. tribute of all the Commodities which their Country yeildeth . . . ; for what he Comaundeth they dare not disobey in the least thing." English correspondents rendered the great weroance's native title—*mamanitowock*—variously as "Prince," "King," and even "Emperour."[16] We may question whether colonists accurately gauged the nature of the mamanitowock's power or understood how the Indians conceived of the treasure he amassed, but we can trust that they saw a man who occupied an exalted rank in his society, and they correctly deduced that his status was inseparable from his control of significant wealth. Among Powhatans, a command of exceptional wealth apparently indicated and sustained the power that entitled some men to rule.

Colonists equated Wahunsonacock with a king or prince because the same was true in their society: rank and wealth were reciprocal constituents of a person's social identity. To be sure, the English had forms and measures of wealth unknown to Powhatans; but in their homeland as in Tsenacomoco, wealth was both an indicator and a necessity of elevated status. Moreover, the English expected, or said they wanted, their aristocrats to observe a patriarchal role and socio-economic ethic much like those attributed here to Powhatan chiefs. But high-ranking Britons also acquired and exchanged wealth in ways that deviated substantially from the kinship model.

Wealth was an elemental concept in early seventeenth-century England, though one that had multiple and indefinite meanings. In addition to simply connoting abundance, the word denoted a variety of esteemed substances, objects, and privileges. Although it could refer to the aggregate of a nation's assets, it more often conjured thoughts of things an individual might possess "for his or her satisfaction." By the late 1500s, the wealth of well-endowed Britons could be measured in land, livestock, and manors, but also in elegant clothing, carriages, fine furniture, pearls, ivory, diamonds, or precious metals.[17] Much English wealth consisted of commodities procured or produced for distribution through institutionalized marketing networks that had no counterpart in Tsenacomoco. The most prized of all resources—land—was not yet such a commodity because sundry persons usually had rights of various kinds in a single tract, and none had unlimited transferable rights. However, a busy market in land rights was developing, and the value of realty as well as other types of wealth could be expressed in money. Money was concentrated in cities, where there was also a growing class of people who specialized in buying and selling commodities.[18]

The growth of that commercial class was one sign of rising tension between ideology and economic practices. Religion supplied most of the language and rules pertaining to economic relations, and religious orthodoxy abjured personal enrichment as a central life goal. Medieval Christian theologians had taught that God stocked the earth with finite wealth and expected his children to share it, though not equally. The greater portion of wealth was meant for persons high in earthly hierarchies, to whom God had delegated the governance of human affairs. In theory, riches were a means to fulfill the obligations of superior status rather than a means of attaining high rank. As in Tsenacomoco, one ostensible obligation of high-ranking persons was to use the wealth entrusted to them for the good of the community.[19]

At the turn of the sixteenth century, this ideology still structured economic relations for much of England's population. A majority of people lived in intimate communities, accepted the stations that providence had assigned them, and opted, when possible, for the predictability of the established order rather than the risks that would come with moving to new places or occupations. Even a person who did strive for greater wealth was likely to profess that moral considerations took precedence over economic self-interest. When William Strachey contemplated his sojourn in Virginia, which he undertook "in hope of recouping his fortune," he mused, "What is the travayle for all the pompe, the treasure, the pleasaure, and whatsoever belongeth to this life, compared to the Riches of the Soule."[20]

However, the circumstantial foundation of these beliefs about wealth was eroding by the early 1600s. Rapid population growth late in the preceding century had triggered price inflation and shifts in land and income distribution. Commercial trade had expanded dramatically. In the words of Wallace Notestein, the English "had become an adventurous people, seeking out customers and selling goods in far ports." According to Joyce Youings, as merchants imported new goods from distant destinations, Queen Elizabeth's subjects "discovered expectations of material comfort previously undreamed of."[21] For these and other reasons, economic relations had grown more complex and competitive in the Elizabethan era. While many people suffered great distress as a result, others found new ways to prosper. By adding to his wealth, a man could even raise his status significantly within his lifetime. Rather than the "harmonious equilibrium" of the medieval ideal, says J. C. K. Cornwall, England was "a scenario of conflicting interests." Although an enterprising man might pledge allegiance to the traditional social order and a moral economy driven by obligations to family and community, his conduct often suggested that hopes of private material gain determined his choices.[22]

The Virginia colonization project—a private venture intended to realize a profit for investors—attracted people who saw these trends and were inclined to respond by taking economic risks.[23] Some were the sons of aristocrats or gentry, in many cases precluded by birth order from inheriting their fathers' estates. Others were men of lower-class origin who sought a social and economic prospect more heartening than they expected in England. (Except John Smith, a yeoman by birth and upbringing, the authors of surviving eyewitness accounts were acknowledged gentlemen.) [24] All were willing to wager something of value for a chance to extract wealth from an unfamiliar land across the ocean. Most were eager for material gain to a degree still suspect, though increasingly common, in their homeland.[25] No doubt they concurred that a list of the colony's "Principal and Maine Endes" should begin with the Christian duty to spread the faith—"to preach and baptize . . . a number of poore and miserable soules, wrapt up unto death, in almost *invincible ignorance*."[26] But in practice, they subordinated that goal to mercenary pursuits.

The colonizers also acted on a desire to replicate lucrative Spanish exploits in the New World and to preempt Spain's acquisition of more American territory. All England had heard about the hoards of gold and jewels that Mexicans and Peruvians surrendered to their Spanish conquerors. John Smith remarked of the Spaniards, "We see daily their mountaines of wealth (sprong from the plants of their generous indeauours)" in the New World. That example inspired many Englishmen to dream of earning personal and national glory by accomplishing similar feats, especially by discovering other New World lands replete with gold, silver, and gems.[27]

Under the influence of such dreams, English seafarers scouted the American coast north of Florida and announced that closer inspection would be worthwhile. A particularly tantalizing narrative appeared in the 1589 edition of a book entitled *The Principal Navigations*: three stranded sailors making their way north to Cape Breton had encountered kings wearing enormous rubies and ordinary people carrying out household tasks with utensils made of gold. Although compiler Richard Hakluyt omitted this tale from later editions because of "certain incredibilities," Virginia Company recruits could read or hear other reports from North America that conjured images of streams and hills glistening with precious ore.[28] Arthur Barlowe's account of a 1584 sojourn at Roanoke, not far south of Tsenacomoco, itemized the jewelry adorning native nobles, including a "plate of golde" on a "king's" head. Of course, Barlow cautioned, the plate could have been copper, "for being vnpolished we knew not what metall it should be."[29] But even after close inspections repeatedly confirmed the wisdom of Barlow's caution, English prospectors clung to their hopes of finding mineral wealth free for the taking. John Smith wrote with scorn of that ambition's effect on his fellow colonists: "There was no talk, no hope, no work, but dig gold, wash gold, refine gold, load gold, such a bruit of gold."[30]

Advocates of colonization insisted that a colony could produce wealth whether or not it proved to be a source of precious metals. In 1609, the Virginia Company council advised a new governor and his deputy to try three "principall waies of enrichinge the Colonies" besides discovering mines or a westward sea route to Asia: they could trade, collect tribute, and work their own men.[31] Meanwhile, Robert Johnson drummed up support for the enterprise by assuring potential investors and colonists that Virginia's economic resources included not only "mineralles" but an "aboundance of fish," "plentie of woods (the wants of England)," "strong" soil, and "many kindes of rich furres." "If bare nature be so amiable," he rhapsodized, "what may we hope, when Arte and Nature both shall ioyne." Johnson also repeated the company line that trade was a likely means of recouping the investment in colonization. Not only could the colonists ship products of Virginia to England and other nations, but they could find a market for English goods among the native Americans. In a short time, Britons' "little Northerne corner of the world" could become "the richest Store-house and Staple for Marchandise in all Europe."[32]

Two of the colonists' strategies for generating wealth—trade and tribute— banked on untested assumptions about the people already living in the region christened Virginia. For trade to prove lucrative, the native inhabitants' assets or resources and their desires had to complement English assets and aspirations. But as Richard Hakluyt the Elder observed, the plan to sell American natives "a thousand kinds of . . . wrought wares" assumed a demand for English goods that might not materialize. "If the people be content to live naked and to content themselves with few things of mere necessity," Hakluyt wrote in 1585, "then in vain seemeth our voyage, unless this nature may be altered. . . . If the people . . . be clothed, and desire to live in the abundance of all such things as Europe doth, and have at home all the same in plenty, yet we cannot have traffic with them, by means they want not anything that we can yield them."[33] Likewise, collecting tribute would be profitable only if the indigenous people had things to deliver that Europeans valued. In sum, the colonizers expected the thrust and results of their venture to hinge on whether Indians were rich or poor, zealous for material gain or indifferent to it. Twenty years after Hakluyt wrote, Virginia Company personnel still had much to learn on that subject.

While hoping to come upon a country and perhaps a population rich in gold and silver, the men and boys who sailed for Virginia in 1607 were prepared for the possibility of finding poor people instead. Exploration literature had primed them to expect "savages," and that word designated people who were poor by most English measures. Savages purportedly lacked the institutions, technology, and God-given enlightenment of civilized Europeans, including sophisticated property relations. Thus, Strachey left for Virginia in 1609 thinking, "We goe to laye amongest a simple and barbarous People." Images of simple, economically ignorant or innocent people had pervaded European accounts of America, beginning with Christopher Columbus's report that the islanders at his first landfall were "very poor in everything."[34] Many chronicles of subsequent exploration contrasted the opulence of the New World's natural resources with the poverty or nakedness of its human occupants.[35]

Once in Virginia, company men reported signs consistent with their high hopes as well as their low expectations. After a first visit to the town of Pamunkey, one of them (probably Captain Gabriel Archer) wrote, "This Wyroans Pamaunche I holde to inhabite a Rych land of Copper and pearle. . . . They weare it in their eares, about their neckes in Long lynckes, and in broade plates on their heades. . . . The kyng had a Chaine of pearle about his neck thrice Double, the third parte of them as bygg as pease, which I could not valew lesse worth then .3. or .400.[li] had the pearle ben taken from the muskle as it ought to be. . . . [He] hath (as the rest likewise) many ryche furres."[36] But the same man also advised, "The Comodityes of this Country, what they are in Esse, is not much to be regarded, the inhabitantes having no comerce with any nation, no respect of profitt, neither is there scarce that we call meum et tuum among them save only the kinges know their owne territoryes, & the people their severall gardens."[37]

If readers in London could not tell from colonists' communications whether the Indians of Virginia had the wealth or will to play a useful role in the colonial enterprise, obtuseness was not to blame. Initial reports from Jamestown provided conflicting assessments of natives' prosperity, commercial savvy, and economic aims. Some, like Archer's statement that they scarcely knew the meaning of "mine and yours," were formulaic depictions of savages as Europeans had long imagined them. Others afforded views of an economy not so easily classed as primitive. Colonists' assessments were contradictory and ambiguous for several reasons besides the difficulty of deciphering an alien culture. Their own thinking about wealth was contradictory and ambivalent, they wrote with varying motives, and their perspectives on Powhatan behavior varied, not only from person to person, but as circumstances changed.

In the main, however, the early investigators described native people who lived amid rich resources but were oblivious to their value and thus possessed nothing approaching the wealth of England.

Certainly, colonists did see fewer signs or sorts of wealth in Tsenacomoco than in England. No stone or brick mansions dominated the landscape. No local waterway teemed with ships disgorging spices, wines, silks, or bullion and taking on grain, woolens, pewter, or ironware. Neither fine damasks and brocades nor ivory combs and emerald rings adorned the bodies of native nobles. During exploratory visits to Powhatan towns, some Virginia Company men surely thought, as Thomas Hariot had when sizing up inhabitants of nearby Roanoke, "In respect of us they are a people poore . . . for want of skill and iudgement in the knowledge and use of things."[38]

Nevertheless, people "poore" for lack of English inventions were not necessarily destitute of valuables, and reports from Virginia usually assured readers that the "savages" did indeed possess commodities valued in Europe. The writers maintained that Virginia was fully capable of enriching its residents, and they supported the contention in part with references to Indian possessions. Of course, they had to talk up the region's economic potential, lest their homeland backers lose heart and forsake them. Some of their optimistic claims were therefore bravado or outright fantasy. A letter that new governor Thomas Dale sent home in 1614, when the colony had yet to prove profitable, was patent boosterism. "I can assure you," Dale trumpeted, "no Country of the world affords more assured hopes of infinite riches, which both by mine owne peoples discovery, and the relation of the Savages . . . assureth me."[39] But hyperbole aside, Dale was speaking for many people under his jurisdiction. They did believe there was abundant exploitable wealth around them, some of it in the hands of natives.

Aware of America's previous isolation from eastern hemisphere trade networks, colonists expected Indians' stock of wealth to be parochial and possibly limited to natural products of the country. Though hardly cultural relativists, colonial leaders also realized, as Hariot did, that there would be an indigenous scale of values. In fact, they counted on Indians' ignorance of values in Europe as a basis for trading at their own profit. They therefore took stock of local products that Europeans would prize and simultaneously tried to determine what the native people prized. William Strachey—a more clear-eyed or candid commentator than most—listed corn, copper, pearls, and beads as things the natives valued "according to their owne estymation." But then, apparently thinking of wealth as abundance of any desirable items, Strachey added, "To saye triuth, their victuall is their chief riches."[40] Other observers identified peltry as the Indians' principal treasure. "They have a great abundance of skins for very rich furs," a captured sailor told his Spanish interrogators, "especially sable martens, and the King has houses full of them, and they are his wealth." Some fellow Britons, meanwhile, rejoiced to see "the better sort" of Indians bedecked with pearls.[41]

A statement that the better sort had pearls and furs reflected a circular thought process by which Englishmen identified Powhatan wealth and a Powhatan elite. Colonists were predisposed to classify as wealth the types of possessions found solely or largely among high-ranking persons and, conversely, to recognize such persons by the distinctive nature of their property. In England, after all, property was a signifier of rank as well as a necessary means to sustain one's rank. And colonists did hope that Virginia natives would have a recognizable social and political hierarchy. Spanish experience in Mexico and Peru seemed to show that a European monarch could easily rule hierarchical native societies by subordinating or supplanting the local sovereigns and the lesser lords through whom they ruled.[42] Thus, taking inventory of Powhatan valuables was part of an effort to identify a Powhatan aristocracy. While assuming that the allocation of special goods indicated who the aristocrats were, colonists also identified such goods as the society's wealth because they assumed that aristocrats would possess greater wealth than common people.

To explain how they recognized native nobility, English observers cited behavior as well as material signs. Focusing on men and women who took unmistakably commanding roles in public formalities, they paired descriptions of stately or haughty deportment with lists of the dignitaries' showy possessions. Besides coteries of attendants and larger-than-ordinary houses, certain clothing and accessories appeared to be Powhatan emblems of rank.[43] Thomas Hariot had told colonists what to look for. His caption for John White's drawing of a "cheiff Lorde of Roanoac" read, "In token of authoritye, and honor, they wear a chaine of great pearles, or copper beades or smoothe bones abowt their necks, and a plate of copper hinge upon a stringe, from the navel unto the midds of their thighes."[44] William Strachey relied entirely on words to prove that he had seen a Powhatan "queen." Although not so handsome as other native females, he wrote, the woman "with a kynd of pride [could] take vpon her a shew of greatnes." She commanded servants to lift her from a boat to a pallet spread with fine mats, "her self Covered with a faire white drest deare-skyn."

> When she rose, she had a Mayde who fetch't her a frontall of white
> Corrall, and pendants of great (but imperfect coulored, and worse
> drilled) pearles, which she putt into her eares, and a Chayne with long

lynckes of Copper . . . which came twice or thrice double about her neck, and . . . thus attyred with some variety of feathers, and flowers stuck in their hayres, they seem as debonayre, quaynt, and well pleased, as (I wis) a daughter of the howse of Austria behoung with all her Iewells, Likewise her Mayd fetch't her a Mantell . . . made of blew feathers, so arteficially and thick sowed togither, that yt showes like a deepe purple Satten, and is very smooth and sleek.[45]

Strachey did not have to spell out for an English audience his assumption that deerskins, pendants, chains, and mantles were savage marks of nobility as well as savage wealth.

Like English nobles, the native elite seemed to recognize an obligation to expend wealth in lavish hospitality. Lavish is the word for receptions that colony officials enjoyed during early visits to native towns. With elaborate decorum, weroances bestowed food and drink on their guests in prodigious amounts.[46] When Captain Christopher Newport came to pay his respects to the mamanitowock, two or three hundred people escorted the officer's party into town.

Powhatan strained himself to the utmost of his greatness to entertain them . . . with the most plenty of victuals he could provide to feast them. He sat upon his bed of mats, his pillow of leather embroidered after their rude manner with pearl and white beads, his attire a fair robe of skins as large as an Irish mantle. At his head and feet a handsome young woman. On each side of his house sat twenty of his concubines, their heads and shoulders painted red, with a great chain of white beads about each of their necks. Before those sat his chiefest men in like order in his arbor-like house, and more than forty platters of fine bread stood as a guard in two files on each side the door.[47]

Along with such evidence that Powhatans had a rich aristocracy, colonists did note contrary signs. Some native finery—fire-smudged pearls or dead "rats" suspended from ears—seemed far from fine by English standards.[48] High-ranking persons displayed fewer and less ornate marks of distinction in Tsenacomoco than in England. Their houses were larger than others in native towns but not sumptuous, and their clothing was distinctive only on ceremonial occasions. Also, despite their apparent command of numerous servants, weroances performed the same subsistence tasks as "the common sort" did. Such unaristocratic practices prompted a few English witnesses to scoff at native rulers' air of superiority or puzzle about the servile responses it elicited,

Two nearly contemporaneous depictions of Matoaka, also known as Pocahontas,
reflect ambivalent early English evaluations of the Powhatan elite. The engraving on the
left, based on art and accounts by English eyewitnesses, is one of many published images in
which ostensible American Indian aristocrats lack the rich garb that identified English nobility. From "The Abduction of Pocahontas by Captain Argall," engraved by Theodore de Bry and
sons. Courtesy of Wisconsin Historical Society, image 23857. The other portrait, made in
1617 while Matoaka was in London billed as the daughter of an emperor, reflects the
importance her hosts attached to symbolizing her royalty and the wealth of her
father's realm by dressing her in expensive European garments.

even from colonists. Referring to Wahunsonacock, Strachey mused, "And sure
yt is to be wondered at, how such a barbarous and vncivill Prynce, should take
into him (adorned and set forth with no greater outward ornament and mu-
nificence) a forme and ostentacion of such Maiestie as he expresseth, which
oftentimes strykes awe and sufficient wonder into our people."[49]

At times, Englishmen griped that even the richest Powhatans' wealth was
mundane and meager by comparison with the legendary treasure of Aztec and
Inca emperors. When colonists realized that royal diadems were low-quality
copper and flecks of silver on painted skin were merely antimony, their disappointment expressed itself as disdain for the natives' store of wealth.[50] Disdain
is evident in a tally of the loot that fell to colonists who attacked Kecoughtan
in 1610: "The Governour and his women fled . . . but left his poore baggage,
and treasure to the spoyle of our Souldiers, which was only a few Baskets of
old Wheate, and some other of Pease and Beanes, a little Tobacco, and some

few womens Girdles of Silke, of the Grasse-silke."[51] And when profitable trade eluded the colony, company officers tried shifting the blame to the natives by belittling what they had to offer. That was John Smith's response to complaints from England about colonists' failure to find riches such as Spain and Portugal had gleaned in the Americas: "Had those fruitful countries been as savage, as barbarous, as ill peopled, as little planted, labored, and manured as Virginia their proper labors it is likely would have produced as small profit as ours. . . . But we chanced in a land even as God made it, where we found only an idle, improvident, scattered people, ignorant of the knowledge of gold and silver or any commodities and careless of anything but from hand to mouth except baubles of no worth; nothing to encourage us but what accidentally we found nature afforded."[52]

Belittling Powhatan wealth was also a tactic of men bent on trading profitably for that wealth, but the operative value of native possessions was set by what the English actually paid for them. Exchanges established the immediate relative worth of the resources at colonists' and Indians' command. The preconceptions and aims that skewed initial English appraisals of Powhatan wealth could not obscure some realities of economic relations with the Indians. From records of exchanges, we can deduce those realities and tell how Powhatans assessed the colonists' affluence. We can see that early tallies of wealth and resources did not appear to favor the newcomers. For at least a decade, the natives' advantage in supplies of food, productive land, and productive personnel was undeniable. Much of that time they had a near-monopoly on food, giving added meaning to Strachey's comment that victuals were their chief riches. To obtain those indispensable riches, the English surrendered more of their own assets than many thought wise. The balance of resources was unstable, however, and supply ships from England could tilt it in the colonists' direction, changing the local values of Powhatan and English assets. Eventually, colonists reversed the ratio of Indian and colonial wealth for good by acquiring arable land, profiting from its use, and thus attracting many more of their countrymen.

From the beginning, colonists counseled each other to act as if they saw little of value among Powhatan possessions.[53] The first contingent of settlers strived specifically to hide their desire for copper and pearls, lest native people realize they could ask a great deal in exchange for those coveted items. Two years into the venture, directors of the reorganized colony instructed Deputy Governor Thomas Gates to ensure that commerce with the Indians would be profitable "by seeminge to make little estimacion of trade with them and by pretendinge to be so able to consist within your selves that you neede care for nothinge of theires, but rather that you doe them a curtesy to spare such necessaries as they want as . . . iron tooles, or copper." The directors then admitted that such dissembling was probably futile. English goods had already lost value among natives, who knew how ardently the colonists cared for something of theirs—their corn—precisely because the colonists could not "consist within" themselves. "If you hope to winne them and to provide for your selves by trade you will be deceaved," the instructions said, "for already your copper is embased by your abundance and neglect of prising it and they will never feede you but for feare."[54]

In numerous negotiations and exchanges, contrary to company policy, colonists and crewmen from supply ships betrayed their esteem for commodities at the natives' command. When their own larders were adequately stocked, colonists particularly prized the pelts of otter, beaver, raccoon, and bear that natives could supply in profusion. But when the cupboards were bare, nothing was more precious than food; and the indigenous people were far richer in food than the denizens of Jamestown. Even in bad growing seasons, some Powhatans seemed to have maize and vegetables to spare as well as turkeys, venison, and fish. Strachey was not the only colonist to observe, perhaps wistfully, "They be all of them huge eaters." For failure to organize effective methods of producing and procuring food on their own, the colonists could seldom eat adequately, let alone hugely. They endured repeated periods of hunger.[55] In 1609, John Smith conceded that the well-fed people of Pamunkey were richer in that vital respect than Jamestown residents. One account has him saying to the ruler of that native town, "Opechancanough, last yeare you kindly fraughted our ship, but now you have invited me to starve with hunger. You know my want, and I your plenty, of which by some meanes I must have part." Another chronicler commented, "Men may think it strange there should be such a stir for a little corn, but had it been gold with more ease we might have got it; and had it wanted the whole colony had starved." The decline in the local value of English copper was due in part to such circumstances. As Strachey explained it in 1612, "The English are now content, to receave in Exchaunge a few measures of Corne for a great deale of that mettell (valuing yt according to the extreeme price yt beares with them, not to the estymacion which yt hath with vs)."[56]

Even after colonists made greater efforts to grow their own food, lean times were common, and treasure hunters more often headed for the Indians' fields of golden corn than for potential fields of gold ore. As late as 1625, Virginia officials lamented "the present extreame povertie and consumpcon of the Plantacion being for want of the accustomed yearly supplies." Although no settlers would have doubted that the English people as a whole were richer than a small nation of savages, many must have wondered whether the superiority of the English economy was obvious in Tsenacomoco. Writing to an English nobleman in 1619, colony secretary John Pory declared, "All our riches for the present doe consiste in Tobacco" and then promptly offered a correction: "Our principall wealth (I should have said) consisteth in servants." Finally, to prove that the colonists were not "the veriest beggers in the worlde," Pory resorted to describing the silk garments of Jamestown's "cowekeeper" and a recent female immigrant.[57]

Pory's inventory of colonists' wealth was a plea for respect in England. To win native people's respect, the colonists counted heavily on displays of wealth emanating from England. Thomas Hariot had explained the strategy in the 1580s: "By howe much they upon due consideration shall finde our manner of knowledges and craftes to exceede theirs in perfecttion, and speed for doing or execution, by so much the more is it probable that they shoulde desire our friendships & love, and have the greater respect for pleasing and obeying us."[58] The message for those considering investment in a colonial venture was that savages would surely deem English products more perfect than their own and would crave those products along with English love.

The Indians near Jamestown met this expectation in one respect: they did seem to crave some English products. But that simple fact tells us little about their appraisal of the colonists' wealth or their own comparative prosperity. Although there is ample support for Strachey's claim that Powhatans were "much desirous of" iron tools and glass beads from England, it is wise to down a grain of salt while reading the assertions of colonists or modern authors that the Indians deemed the English much richer than they. We do not even know whether Powhatan Algonquian had a word equivalent to the connotation of "rich" in that claim.[59] It would be foolish to conclude solely from the Indians' appetite for imported goods, as Britons commonly did, that the economic superiority of the colonists' home country was evident to all. The pale foreigners' access to some impressive forms of wealth was undeniable. They had fearsome weapons and other alluring articles as well as an unmistakable high opinion of themselves. But they were not numerous, and in critical respects they were pathetically needy.[60] Accordingly, the native people, and their paramount weroance in particular, initially responded to the colonists' presence as if they saw a group whose resources and needs complemented theirs and thus could be grounds for mutually beneficial relations—just what the English ostensibly had hoped.

It is possible to imagine even more specifically, and with some confidence, how Powhatans evaluated colonists' economic status and conduct. Their mental processes would have been similar in nature to those occurring in English heads. That is, Indians tried first to fit new things, people, and actions into familiar conceptual categories. They measured the foreigners' prosperity by local standards and looked for signs that English economic motives and values were like theirs. They also applied their usual criteria for identifying people of high rank—a step in managing relations that would have seemed as necessary to them as to the colonists. "I esteeme you a great werowans," Wahunsonacock reportedly told Christopher Newport. If so, he made this classification not only because John Smith had disingenuously told him that Newport was a supreme ruler, but also because colonists evidently deferred to the ship captain, and because Newport came bearing gifts befitting a weroance's treasury.[61]

Englishmen who commanded large sailing vessels, wore elaborate garments, wielded guns and swords, or laid out presents of glass beads and metal hatchets appeared rich in the sense that a weroance and his family were: they controlled objects that Powhatans construed as embodiments of special power. But in other respects, the colonists—even the gentry—could hardly have seemed affluent. For example, the all-male first colonial contingent was probably a strange and perhaps pitiful sight to people who esteemed women as the producers of corn, an essential form of wealth. Women enabled a Powhatan family to prosper, and the richest households were polygynous. "The custum of ye cuntry," Henry Spelman related, "is to haue many wiues and to buye them, so that he which haue most copper and Beads may haue most wiues."[62]

The English settlers were also poor in Powhatan eyes for lack of farming, hunting, and foraging territory—the fundamental source of prosperity in the Powhatan world. Until 1610, the colonists had no more land to use than the natives allowed them, either affirmatively or passively.[63] The first place the Englishmen chose to occupy was a swampy peninsula, vacant because it was an unhealthful site for year-round habitation. Residents of the little colonial compound could rarely supply their own food, and no one was poorer than a man without the means to feed himself and his family. In fact, the colonists were bereft of such means so often that most could not sustain life for long. The company ships deposited just over one hundred people at the Jamestown site in 1607; six months later only thirty-eight were alive. By 1624, 6,040 of the 7,289 people who had left England for Virginia were dead, many from starvation or its accompanying threats to life. Colonists made sporadic vain efforts to hide their hunger and devastating mortality rate from the Indians, but they repeatedly begged, bought, extorted, and stole natives' corn. More than once, according to John Smith, Englishmen's arrogance goaded a weroance into pointing out their dependence on natives for survival.[64]

Some colonists said the Indians, awed by marvelous mechanical inventions and manufactured items from Europe, assumed the English had help from potent gods. Even if that was an accurate rendering of Indian thoughts, it does not necessarily follow that Powhatans lost faith in their own power to prosper. If nothing else, the suffering at Jamestown would have suggested that the English deities' power had critical limits.[65]

Colonists could try to counter their needy appearance by describing the wealth of their homeland and pointing to incoming ships and cargo as evidence, but native people had little basis for visualizing an opulent kingdom across the water. To enlighten them on this score, company agents took a few Indians to England. Wahunsonacock's adviser Namontack made the round-trip in 1608, as did a man named Tomocomo in 1617. According to a clergyman in England, Tomocomo was amazed "at the sight of so much Corne and Trees in his comming from Plimmouth to London, the Virginians imagining that defect thereof here had brought us thither." The record does not reveal, however, whether these or other returning Indian voyagers communicated the desired message to people at home, let alone whether their audiences believed their outlandish descriptions of the place they had seen.[66]

No doubt Powhatans would have conceded that their "gods"—the powers or powerful beings for which colonists used that name—did not guarantee them continuous good fortune. Crops could fail in dry years, for example. Indeed, Jamestown's founding coincided with a prolonged drought. Famine and possibly deadly disease had thinned Powhatan ranks not long before the foreigners arrived—a factor Strachey did not consider when attributing Virginia's low population density to Indians' economic backwardness.[67] However, Tsenacomoco was capable of providing many thousands of people with a good living, and it usually did. Native inhabitants ordinarily had numerous blessings to count. They met their needs for food and shelter with moderate exertion; their houses were easy to construct and weatherproof; their diet was nutritious and varied. In most years, the food they delivered to the weroance was food they could spare, but it also represented the security of belonging to a community whose leader would feed and protect them in harder times. The "riches" that flowed to and from the weroance symbolized their well-being.[68]

In sum, Powhatans had ample cause to consider themselves prosperous when Virginia Company ships first sailed into Chesapeake Bay, and early relations with the newcomers would have done little to dispel such a belief, notwithstanding native people's admiration for some English possessions. On the contrary, by lavishing food on English visitors and delivering many baskets of corn to hungry Jamestown residents, local weroances manifested their people's prosperity. The gifts they bestowed on and received from leading colonists also confirmed that Powhatans could command respect from foreigners who had access to wealth. And since the food and furs that Powhatans gave or traded were commonplace in comparison to the wondrous objects they stood to receive in return, relations with the colonists promised to enhance Powhatans' feeling of prosperity.

On balance, relations did fulfill this promise for a while; at least they enabled native people to obtain new things of impressive beauty or utility. The most precious English goods piled up in "temples" and weroances' houses. Within a year or two, Strachey heard, Wahunsonacock had "gathered into his store a great quantitie and number . . . [of] Swords, besides Axes, and Pollaxes, Chissels, Howes . . . , with an infinite treasure of Copper." When Captain Newport staged a coronation of Wahunsonacock that was meant to make him the English king's vassal, the ceremony included gifts to the mamanitowock of a "basin, ewer, bed, bedstead, clothes, and such costly novelties." Furthermore, Smith grumbled, instead of prompting Wahunsonacock to humble himself before his richer English lord, "this stately kind of soliciting made him so much overvalue himself that he respected us as much as nothing at all." Even lowlier Powhatans obtained wonders from Europe, some by providing services to colonists who repaid them in goods, many by pairing with individual colonists or sailors to trade. It is unclear whether commoners passed their acquisitions on to the weroance, but in any case, early exchanges with the foreigners may have promoted a sense of growing community affluence.[69]

In particular, contacts with the English brought Powhatans unprecedented amounts of copper—a substance they had long revered. Most of the added supply did make its way into the mamanitowock's coffers. Strachey construed this accumulation as evidence of Wahunsonacock's lust for wealth and power. The great weroance, he complained, "doth . . . monopolize all the Copper brought into Virginia by the English; and whereas the English are now content, to receave in Exchaunge a few measures of Corne for a great deale of that mettell. . . . Powhatan doth againe vent some smale quantety thereof to his neighbour Nations for 100. tymes the value, reserving . . . for himself a plentifull quantety." Strachey probably discerned correctly that Wahunsonacock was intent not only on building his store of riches but also on increasing his political capital and military capacity. As the principal distributor of English copper to other Indians of the tidewater plain, the mamanitowock could extend his influence to outlying communities and recruit fighters for clashes with enemies. Strachey expected him to use the supply he reserved "to levy men withall, when he shall fynd cause to vse them against vs." Whatever his motive, Wahunsonacock was richer in copper and perhaps in politically useful social bonds after two years of English presence than before.[70]

Enriching relations with the English did not last, however. In fits and starts, interspersed with serious setbacks, the colonists gained leverage until the balance of economic power tipped decisively in their favor. For native people as a whole, the consequences were ruinous. In 1607, they had enough essential resources that the paramount weroance allegedly did not begrudge the Virginia Company pioneers a marshy hunting area for their camp or fort.[71] Even ten years later, when Wahunsonacock's brother Opechancanough presented George Yeardley with a spacious tract of land, he did not expect to impoverish himself or his followers.[72] But within a few more decades, indigenous communities on the coastal plain lost enough of their land base to jeopardize their self-sufficiency, and before the end of the century, most were painfully poor by any measure of well-being.

Numerous histories relate the developments that transformed the hapless English colony, at Indians' expense, from an investor's nightmare to an enterprising planter's dreamscape. Some begin the account around 1614, when new governing officers coaxed colonists to greater industry by assigning them plots of company land for individual gardens. The next pivotal step was John Rolfe's demonstration that he could raise sweet Caribbean tobacco on his acreage and sell it in Europe at a handsome profit. After a few more years, a fusion of privatization and profits powered a classic commercial boom. As surviving original colonists completed their ten-year commitment to the company, the directors authorized them to establish private estates, which they planted in tobacco.[73] The company also lured new immigrants to Virginia with a promise of land or a share of the crops they raised. Tobacco exports were twenty times greater in 1618 than in 1616, and by 1621, the number of settlers was more than twice as large as in 1618. Where there had been sixty half-dead adventurers ready to abandon the colony in 1611, there were more than 2,300 men, women, and children who had come determined to farm.[74]

Before this turn of events — before the reconstituted Virginia Company resolved to create an agricultural province and reap profits from land sales — the colony's success did not necessarily hinge on impoverishing indigenous people. But with the emergence of the new strategy between 1612 and 1619, there was no more talk in company councils of filling investors' purses with money by filling Indian homes with English manufactures and clothing Indian bodies in English fabrics. The colonial enterprise then became a clear and present danger to the prosperity of nearby native communities.[75]

This summary of occurrences and circumstances that assured Virginia's survival does not explain how colonists acquired the land where they raised their economic fortunes by raising tobacco. Due to the skimpy record, a definitive, tract-by-tract explication is not possible. But available evidence indicates that the English, proceeding on the debated assumption that they were entitled to land in Virginia, took control of particular tracts by doing whatever a situation permitted or required—sometimes squatting on unoccupied ground, sometimes compensating Indians in the area, sometimes resorting to brute force, sometimes doing more than one of these things.

From the first Virginia Company charter, it appears that masterminds of the colonial project did not wonder whether or how they could claim land in Powhatan territory. The king purported to grant what the colonists needed. He promised letters patent to an area one hundred miles square and specified that the rights conveyed would extend to soil, waters, forests, mines, minerals, and other commodities found there. Implicit in this assertion of the English monarch's sovereignty in Virginia was a notion that the indigenous inhabitants had no property rights English law would recognize. Land was ostensibly available for the taking. That thought pleased Virginia Company members. For the life of the corporate body, they maintained that the Indians lacked legal title to the country targeted for colonization.[76]

However, once a few score colonists found themselves in a country with several thousand native occupants, if not sooner, they knew it would be harder to take actual possession of the land than to execute a deed of possession in distant London. Some of them also felt the need to frame a justification of their plans that went beyond a bald declaration of their monarch's sovereignty. Protestant gentlemen wanted to think of themselves as morally superior to papist Spaniards, whose treatment of Indians had earned them censure in England. And after a century of European intellectual debate about the rights of indigenous Americans, England was home to its share of thinkers who disagreed with the Crown's position on Indians' legal claim to land.[77] In London, Pastor Robert Gray pointed out that the first objection to an English colonial venture would be "by what right or warrant we can enter in the land of these Savages, take away their rightfull inheritance from them, and plant ourselves in their places, being unwronged or unprovoked by them."[78] Strachey must have had such doubts in mind when he pledged that colonists would give good value for ground used in furtherance of their venture. "What Iniury can yt be to people of any Nation," he asked rhetorically, "for *Christians* to come vnto their Portes, Havens, or Territoryes, when the Law of Nations (which is the lawe of god and man) doth priveledge all men to doe so, which admitts yt lawfull, to trade with any manner of People." But he conceded that Christians should offer something in exchange for land, as they would for the other things they wanted from Indians. "Even every foote of Land which we shall take vnto our vse," Strachey wrote, "we will bargayne and buy of them for copper, hatchetts, and such like commodityes . . . , and thus we will commune and entreat with them, truck and barter our Commodityes for theirs, and theirs for ours."[79]

Three years after Strachey wrote, on the eve of John Rolfe's experiment in tobacco farming, colonists occupied land at ten places along a thirty-five-mile stretch of river between Jamestown and the fall line. How many of those tracts had they actually "bargayned" and bought of Indians? Apparently, a minority. Legal scholar Stuart Banner, in the course of a broader argument that colonists in North America did acknowledge Indians' landownership by paying them for some tracts, mentions just two early purchases in Virginia. In 1610, Virginia Company officials declared themselves justified in taking land for several reasons, but "'chieflie because *Paspehay*, one of their Kings, sold unto us for copper, land to inherit and inhabite.'" The next year, Governor Dale claimed to have bought other land from the Indians. Strachey also heard that Wahunsonacock had conveyed "his birthright," the "Country Powhatan," to Captain Francis West in 1609.[80] Helen Rountree, however, assumes from the scattered and cryptic evidence that the English squatted in most places, then intimidated any native people who objected, sometimes appeasing them belatedly with gifts. In several instances, the English ran Indian occupants off at gunpoint. Either way, it is clear that colonists did not acquire many of their initial plantation sites by paying a price negotiated with willing native sellers.[81]

On some occasions, the English also seized other vital resources, especially corn, from Indians with whom there had been none of the mutually gratifying "trucking" that Strachey envisioned. John Smith, who led several expeditions to extract corn from Indians by force of arms or other coercive tactics, accused more recent immigrants of tormenting Indians in the vicinity of Powhatan town "by stealing their corne, robbing their gardens" and "breaking their houses."[82]

Colonists and their overseers offered few excuses for specific moves to take land or food in defiance of native people's wishes, but their writings as a whole reveal how they rationalized this appropriation of resources until an Indian uprising in 1622 provided a particularly compelling sanction. They devoted less effort to proving their own righteousness than to pointing out Indian transgressions, finding fault with the Indians' character, and citing Powhatans' ignorance or disobedience of God's economic commandments to humanity.

One of the Indians' alleged sins was avarice. Knowing from their own impulses that greed was a common human failing, Englishmen readily spotted it among the "savages." In their view, covetousness could explain why Powhatans craved European goods, stole from colonists, and allegedly buried valuables to hide them from each other.[83] Wahunsonacock's wealth, power, and privilege bespoke wicked greed as well. Strachey, who wrote with unusual candor about colonists' cupidity, suggested avarice as a reason for the paramount weroance's cache of treasure and control of the copper trade. By making his subjects pay him "tribute of all the Commodities which their Country yeildeth," Strachey declared, the Indian ruler "robbes the poore in effect of all they have even to the deares Skyn wherewith they cover them from Could."[84] Virginia Company directors disingenuously explained their plan to collect tribute as a response to that abusive exploitation: they would free the mamanitowock's subjects from his burdensome exactions.

Another rationale for appropriating Powhatan resources focused not on a sin to which Englishmen were also prone, but on faults supposedly peculiar to Indians, especially deficiencies in economic culture. In fact, colonists saw Powhatan practices that belied their accusations of greed but incurred their disapproval nonetheless. Smith said a native would not sell anything to English acquaintances "till [he] had first received their presents, and what they had that [he] liked." The weroance secreted treasures in a "howse . . . frequented only by Priests," and when he died, the priests presided over ceremonies where much of that treasure was destroyed or interred with the corpse.[85] In these and other ways, native people seemed careless of the wealth at their command. The English regarded that apparent improvidence as perverse, especially when extended to land and its potential fruits. In their own small island kingdom, which was far more thickly settled than Tsenacomoco, religious leaders taught that God expected them to exploit in full the earth's capacity to serve human needs. If the Indians were not developing the resources of their country as God intended, a more industrious, godly people could rightfully carry out the divine plan. Clergyman Samuel Purchas, for instance, defended English colonization plans with a reference to "God in wisedome having enriched the Savage Countries, that those riches might be attractive for Christian suters, which there may sowe spirituals and reape temporals."[86]

Here, the conception of indigenous Americans as simple and barbarous savages served colonists' economic purposes. Unlike civilized people, savages converted few of nature's inchoate riches to divinely ordained uses and so did not preempt English use of those resources. Colonists would not be depriving Virginia's natives of a "rightfull inheritance" if those natives had made no meaningful efforts to claim their legacy. Accordingly, the Reverend William Symonds, preaching to people bound for Virginia in 1609, ridiculed the idea that Indians owned the vast lands they had barely touched. The English, he said, intended to plant "a peaceable Colony in a waste country, where the people doe live but like Deere." Just as Christians could lawfully make the wild deer's habitat serve human needs, they could occupy and cultivate land that "wild" people wasted.[87]

Tsenacomoco's many towns, gardens, and productive cornfields discredited the image of Indians that Symonds sketched. Candid witnesses admitted that Powhatans worked to make the land yield crops and respected cultivators' right to the ground they improved. "Each household knoweth their own lands and gardens, and most live of their own labors," John Smith reported. When colonists decided in particular circumstances to pay for Powhatan land, they effectively acknowledged the property rights of Indian farmers and homebuilders. However, they kept the arguments about savagery and waste in reserve for use as needed.[88] Thus Strachey, while noting elsewhere that every weroance knew the boundaries of his hunting and fishing territory, depicted the lush Virginia landscape as largely unclaimed. One reason for the small human footprint, he proposed, was the Indians' "Ignoraunce in not fynding out yet the use of many things necessary and beneficiall to Nature, which their Country yet plentefully and naturally affourdes." His comment echoed Smith's explanation for the absence of large cities in Tsenacomoco: "To nourish so many together they have yet no means, because they make so small a benefit of their land, be it never so fertile." Although he made statements to the contrary, Smith also parroted the common English claim that the native people had left the land "even as God made it."[89] In other words, greedy though they were, the "savages" of Virginia were insufficiently inclined and equipped to develop the wealth in their midst.[90]

To explain why colonists appropriated some native townsites and cultivated fields without giving something in return, English leaders might charge the Indians with other breaches of a civilized moral code. A Virginia Company brief on the subject in 1610 alluded to unspecified Powhatan violations of the law of nations.[91] If attacked without just cause by such "human beasts," colonists could not only defend themselves but also counterattack and enjoy the spoils of war in good conscience. Since the English did meet with sporadic attacks from their first days in Tsenacomoco, their forcible seizures of land were soon a cause as well as a consequence of such armed conflict, which became chronic within two years.[92]

The Indians in turn may have intended their aggression as punishment for unacceptable behavior. Seth Mallios argues that colonists provoked Powhatans to violence by breaking local rules of reciprocity, which he calls rules of a classic "gift economy." To people whose model for economic relations was kinship obligations, English failures to meet those obligations would indeed have been grave offenses. With ritual gift-giving and assurances of goodwill, the weroances had signaled their acceptance of the outsiders as figurative kin—a precondition of friendly relations. They would then have expected their new "relatives" to reciprocate with gifts and to exchange resources on the basis of need and supply rather than hard-nosed commercial calculations.[93] For Powhatans, the social bonds between peoples were more important than the commodities they could offer each other. By behaving contrary to such expectations, the English risked reverting to the status of other strangers—that is, presumptive enemies.

The best interpretation of John Smith's famous captivity story supports this hypothesis. It characterizes a speech attributed to Wahunsonacock as a bid to incorporate the colonists in the Powhatan network of fictive kin, with appurtenant benefits and obligations. Before releasing Smith, the mamanitowock reportedly pronounced the Englishman his son and offered Smith's people provisions, protection, and the town of Capahowasick on the understanding that they would supply their Powhatan "father" with copper and hatchets.[94]

An oft-told tale of Wahunsonacock's refusal to barter also reveals a man who viewed familial reciprocity as the proper basis for intercommunity exchanges. Smith may not have translated the great weroance's words expertly or quoted them precisely, but he had no cause to fabricate the story that Wahunsonacock balked at "pedling . . . trade for trifles." "Hee seeming to despise the nature of a Merchant, did scorne to sell," Smith related; "but we freely should give him, and he liberally would requite us." This anecdote captures the essence of an invitation to establish relations modeled on kinship—to make gifts instead of trading commodities judged equivalent in economic value. Generosity, compassion, and need would be the ostensible reasons to exchange goods, not cold calculations by people with no personal relationship. In one account of the talk, Wahunsonacock bid Newport, "Lay me down all your commodities togither, and what I like I will take, and in recompence give you that I thinke fitting their value." To Englishmen such as Smith and Newport, greed seemed a likely impetus for the mamanitowock's proposal to take whatever he fancied without specifying what he would give in return. And we cannot rule out greed as one of Wahunsonacock's motivations. But selfishly or not, he was asking the English officer to show goodwill by playing the role of a generous relative. Newport's gifts, like those Wahunsonacock made in return, would confirm the giver's status as a symbolic family head, able and willing to share the wealth entrusted to him with a metaphorical brother.[95]

When the English withheld things that Indians requested, when they failed to accept and requite Wahunsonacock's or others' gifts, when they haggled about the value of their goods, and when they employed strong-arm methods of obtaining corn from native towns, did Powhatans view such behavior as immoral? To use that term would impose an English mode of thought on people who may have had a different conception of aberrant conduct. But behavior that did not meet Powhatan expectations of reciprocity or conform to protocol for intercommunity relations was certainly objectionable and probably insulting to the mamanitowock.[96] Sure enough, English behavior did earn them rebukes consistent with this conjecture. In 1608, after the Powhatan ruler had offered him a town to govern, John Smith understood Wahunsonacock to say, "Captaine Smith, I never used anie of Werowances so kindlie as your self; yet from you, I receave the least kindnesse of anie. . . . None doth denie to laie at my feet, or do, what I desire, but onelie you; of whom I can have nothing but what you regard not: and yet you wil have whatsoever you demand." Similarly, the mamanitowock's adviser Uttamatomakkin reportedly complained to Smith while in England, "You gave Powhatan a white Dog, which Powhatan fed as himself; but your King gave me nothing, and I am better than your white Dog."[97]

We can accept the theory that Powhatans resented the colonists' failure to reciprocate "kindnesses" without romanticizing the Indians as generous innocents baffled by the foreigners' stinginess. Smith boasted about unmasking several malevolent Indian deceptions and surviving some deadly traps they set. Inflated as those tales may be, they are credible evidence that Powhatan leaders matched or exceeded the English in wariness and cunning. While agreeing that Wahunsonacock hoped for a customary familial relationship with the English, historian Camilla Townsend thinks the mamanitowock—shrewd political operator that he was—would also have been alert for Machiavellian English schemes. "Very likely," Townsend suggests, "he surmised that they had come with the intention of extracting goods . . . and conceivably even lands from him. That was certainly why he himself conquered other tribes." In fact, the Powhatan ruler said something in 1609 that Smith rendered as, "Many do informe me, your comming is not for trade, but to invade my people and possesse my Country." Even so, after grilling the captive Smith for days in 1607, Wahunsonacock apparently gambled that "he could keep the [English] coat-wearers isolated and contained, and then through trade with them gain a monopoly of access to the valuable weapons and metal cutting tools they brought."[98]

It was not for inability to comprehend each other's expectations that

English/Powhatan relations turned violent. In fact, Smith soon grasped the basics of the native ethic, and other spokesmen for the colony may have done so as well. Smith even invoked the ethic when it would serve his purpose. He could understand the Indians' disgruntlement with English behavior, not only because people in both societies worked at surmounting the language barrier, but also because the psychology of the Powhatan moral economy was not altogether foreign to an Englishman of Smith's era. Participants in the colonial venture may have had an individualistic commercial bent, but English aristocrats still played—or at least claimed—a role more akin to the mamanitowock's paternalism. Like Wahunsonacock the patriarch, an English lord would have disdained the haggling "nature of a Merchant" as inconsistent with his dignity and his ascribed stewardship of inherited wealth. And like Wahunsonacock the ruler, an English monarch affirmed his status by conferring largesse and receiving the gifts of subordinates or foreign dignitaries. Newport, Smith, and other agents of the colony made gifts to weroances for the same reason as weroances gifted them: to show the giver's power and to put the recipients in their social and political debt, if not their economic debt.

Thus, key men in the colony did sense what Wahunsonacock and his people expected of them; they simply were not inclined to abide by Powhatan principles when other workable options suited the colonial project better. Smith reported using words that Wahunsonacock could have understood as consonant with a familial relationship: he identified Newport as "father" of the English "children" at Jamestown.[99] But he was not promising that Newport or any other English leader would treat the mamanitowock like a brother patriarch rather than a subject.[100] If the settlement in Virginia were to be a paying enterprise, the asserted needs of an Indian "brother" could not determine how resources would change hands or be apportioned in the long run. Colonists had come with the intention of operating according to English law and rules of the emerging economic culture that gave rise to their venture. Remaining in America as subjects of an Indian "emperor" was not an option they would consider. Instead, company officials instructed Deputy Governor Thomas Gates in May of 1609 that the colonists should rule the Indians.

> You should make Powhaton your tributary and all his weroances. Every
> provincial lord should pay you a certain measure of corn at each harvest,
> likewise dye and skins . . . according to his proporcion in greatenes
> of territory and men; by which meanes you shall quietly drawe to your
> selves an annuall revenue of every commodity growinge in that countrey
> and this tribute payd to you, for which you shall deliver them from the

exeacions of Powhaton which are now burdensome . . . ; shall also be a meanes of clearinge much ground of wood and of reducing them to la- boure and trade seinge for this rent onely they shall enjoye their howses, and the rest of their travell quietly and many other commodities and blessings of which they are yet insensible.[101]

For their part, Powhatans did not need a tutorial on the English ideology of colonialism in order to see that the foreigners rejected the terms on which Wahunsonacock offered them a place in his chiefdom. Even before Gates re- ceived his instructions, the paramount weroance sensed that the colonists aimed instead to subordinate him to their distant mamanitowock. That is undoubtedly why he neither bowed to receive the crown that Captain New- port brought in 1608 nor generously requited the other gifts presented at his supposed coronation.[102] Furthermore, many in Wahunsonacock's realm felt the force of English determination to acquire local resources whether or not native people consented. Anger at these and other insults surfaced in Indian acts of retaliation that fed colonists' fears and suspicions, until people in both groups thought they had reason for war.

"War with the natives" was ongoing from 1609 to 1614, Virginia's General Assembly recalled in 1621, and colonists avenged every English death at Indian hands, whether by killing, or by seizing crops, burning houses, and spoiling fish weirs.[103] The conflict subsided in 1614 when John Rolfe's marriage to Wahunsonacock's daughter Matoaka, nicknamed Pocahontas, established an undeniable familial tie between Virginians and Powhatans. But English xeno- phobia remained irksome, unrelenting English demands for corn were alarm- ing, and the implications of the colonists' lust for land, excited by tobacco profits and heightened by tobacco's rapid depletion of the soil, were eventually hard to miss.

Faced with growing threats to their welfare, Powhatans staged a daring coordinated attack on the colony in 1622, slaying almost 350 men, women, and children, and indirectly causing the death of several hundred more from ensuing famine and disease. For the next several years, Virginia in general fit one colonist's doleful description of his personal state—a "plantation of sor- rowes, . . . plentifull in nothing but want and wanting nothing but plenty."[104] Rather than destroying the English colony, however, the Indian uprising pro- voked a reaction that accelerated the Powhatans' loss of resources and power. Colonists no longer voiced doubts about the morality of taking over land in Tsenacomoco; rather, they construed the Indians' resort to violence as just cause to uproot and destroy the savages without mercy. A company spokesman proclaimed, "We, who hitherto have had possession of no more ground then their waste, and our purchase . . . may now by right of Warre, and law of Nations, invade the Country, and destroy them who sought to destroy us. . . . Now their cleared grounds in all their villages (which are situate in the fruitfullest places of the land) shall be inhabited by us." "Armies of settlers," writes Alden Vaughan, "set out to destroy every vestige of Indian presence in the areas between the James and York rivers and beyond." On instructions from company officials, they torched houses, smashed canoes, interrupted communal hunts, yanked out fish traps, and confiscated crops.[105]

The long-term consequences of the 1622 uprising were thus a greater calamity for Powhatans than for the colony. England could and did send replacements for dead colonists; the Indians had no reinforcements waiting in the wings. As native towns lost population to English weapons and disease (and lost battles in part because they lost population), they could not hold onto the land from which their most important wealth came.[106] In 1625, Vaughan notes, "several minor chiefs mortgaged to the colony all their lands, some nearly the size of an English shire, in exchange for wheat." Conditions were not favorable for paying off the loan and redeeming the collateral. Less than three years later, Governor Samuel Argall informed the company that the Indians were too poor to pay either their debts or their tribute.[107]

While Powhatan power and prosperity eroded, the fortunes of some colonists swelled. The state of war handed decision-making in the colony to tough-minded soldiers and aggressive planters, many of whom exploited the conditions to line their own pockets. Warlords profited from trafficking in the spoils of their semi-annual raids on native towns, especially corn and land.[108] By planting the land in tobacco instead of food crops, drawing fearful settlers off isolated farms to work in "great men's" protected fields, and feeding those workers confiscated Indian corn, ruthless and well-connected colonists added rapidly to their wealth.[109] Some of them, catering to tobacco farming's voracious appetite for laborers, invested successfully in imported human cargoes — enslaved Africans as well as indentured Britons. The men who became rich that way were a small fraction of the colonial population. For every prospering planter there were scores of people toiling under various terms of servitude to increase the planters' assets instead of their own. But at last, it seemed, the English had discovered the formula for economic success in Virginia: land plus labor generated tobacco, and tobacco was nearly as good as gold.[110]

The little colony was not yet so secure or self-sufficient that it could expand without regard to its adverse effects on Indian communities. Wahunsonacock's successor as mamanitowock, Opechancanough, was a proud man and experienced warrior, capable of orchestrating another deadly rebellion if English incursions threatened to leave the Indians bereft of resources altogether.[111] Indeed, that is what he did in 1644. But the second coordinated Powhatan effort to cow the foreigners and perhaps expel them was as futile as the first. It provoked two years of intermittent retaliatory raids, which culminated in Opechancanough's capture and death at the hands of a colonial jailer. The victorious English then compelled the new paramount weroance, Necotowance, to endorse a treaty ceding all Indian territory south of the York River, even the lands of communities no longer submitting to Powhatan rule. Although the treaty reserved an area for Indian occupation, a letter from Virginia in 1649 informed Londoners that "since the Massacree, the *Savages* have been driven far away, many destroyed of them, their Towns and houses ruinated, their cleer grounds possessed by the English to sow Wheat in." Necotowance, heading a party of only five "petty Kings," acknowledged the English ascendancy by tendering a tribute of beaver pelts to the English monarch, giving colonists blanket permission to pass through his dominions, forbidding his people to enter the colony except as his emissaries, and granting colonists license to kill Indian trespassers.[112]

These concessions did not appease the English craving for land. According to the anonymous correspondent of 1649, even officers on the ships that called at Jamestown sought property in Virginia.[113] At times, the newcomers' land acquisitions were clearly Indian losses; at other times, the equation was not so straightforward. Some native communities, reduced in size due to war and deprivation or anxious to distance themselves from abrasive settlers, made additional land available to colonists simply by vacating it. In other instances, Indians concluded that selling land was a sensible course of action. Notwithstanding the Virginia Company's position or an English court's ruling that the "heathens" lacked authority to convey title, governors and colonists saw the pragmatic wisdom of compensating them for giving up ground.[114] Hard-pressed Indians with shrinking populations could thus exchange land for English goods that now seemed more necessary than some of their fields and forests.[115]

For decades after the 1640s, colonial officials periodically professed concern about the attrition of the Indian land base. Landless Indians could not raise corn for colonists. Bitter and desperate, they might resort to violence and theft. The governor and legislative assembly therefore enacted measures meant to preserve essential acreage for cooperative native groups.[116] Although their motives were often less noble than compassion for Indians, officials even enforced such measures on occasion, ordering unauthorized colonists to vacate tribal land or compensate Indians whose houses they destroyed.[117] As late as 1690, after English conflict with Iroquoians on Virginia's frontier spread to tribes in the coastal plain, the colonial council expressed fear that settlers were endangering the peace when they obtained patents from Indians "by Subtile and Crafty Contrivances." Located at great distances from each other, new English plantations were vulnerable to nearby Indians, "a people of noe Faith or Creditt, who at their Pleasure may Cutt of a Family, and pretend it to be done by Strange Indians." It was important, the council emphasized, "that the Indians may not have Just reason to Complaine of being Cheated of their Lands Contrary to the Articles of Peace Agreed & Concluded with them."[118]

Some government acts and pronouncements of this sort were responses to Indians who said they were being forced into "narrow Streights, and places That they Cannot Subsist, Either by plantinge, or huntinge." Yet restrictions on land transfers, even when observed, were hardly a solution to native people's economic woes. In 1688, the legislative assembly received a petition from Indian communities at Pamunkey Neck and south of the Blackwater River, proposing to grant the English their surplus land "not only as a means of protection to the petitioners, but also as a relief to them in their indigent condition." "As each chiefdom's lands decreased," Helen Rountree summarizes, "the core Indian people became poorer."[119]

Virginians did not have to overpower and dispossess all Indians of the greater Chesapeake region in order to augment their own estates. While systematically reducing Powhatan communities to impotence and poverty, colonists allied with more distant native groups for mutual economic advantage. The principal advantage for the English, as it turned out, was the money to be made selling furs obtained from the remote Indians. A few daring men pioneered this trade when they invested their war booty in ships and goods, sailed to native towns in the upper Chesapeake watershed, and returned with cargoes of beaver skins. Rumors circulated that the skins had sold in England for a profit of 3,000 percent. The commerce that flourished as a result was an essential pillar of the colonial economy in the mid-1600s.[120] For Indians who supplied the beaver and other pelts, the trade had two advantages. It not only gave them desirable imported goods and a middleman's leverage in dealings with Indians farther inland, but it also gave the English a reason to leave them in possession of hunting lands. Thus, while Wahunsonacock's former subjects suffered dispossession and humiliating decline, Susquehannocks and other native peoples to the north and west could take pride in their wealth and power for the time being.[121]

According to Frederick Fausz, warfare eventually doomed this economic symbiosis and the Indian fur suppliers' prosperity. Susquehannocks and their English allies battled Senecas and their Dutch allies for primacy in the beaver trade, thereby undermining the trade's profitability. But Virginia's fur trade alliances had probably sealed their own doom anyway by giving the colony decades of peace with Indians on its frontiers. Peace lured new immigrants, who demanded new land to cultivate and looked for it in the apparently vacant areas that sustained the fur-bearing animals. The clashing interests of native hunters and encroaching settlers sparked more warfare in the 1670s, and Indians again were the losers. "After 1677," writes Fausz, "no Indian group native to the region would possess the population, the power, or the products to influence key events in the coastal plain."[122]

The Indians' disadvantage was obvious to Durand of Dauphiné, who scouted Virginia as a potential destination for fellow French Huguenots in 1687 and 1688. Like the first English colonists, folks at home would especially want to know the economic conditions and prospects of people in America. Durand's report on White Virginians' economic culture, though hardly flattering, implied that greater wealth was easily within their power to attain.

> The land is so rich & so fertile that when a man has fifty acres of ground, two men-servants, a maid & some cattle, neither he nor his wife do anything but visit among their neighbors. . . . Money is rarely used, except by the people of quality. They barter with tobacco as though it were specie. With it they buy land, they rent it, they buy cattle, & as they can get anything they need in exchange for this commodity, they become so lazy that they send to England for clothes, linen, hats, women's dresses, shoes, iron tools, nails, & even wooden furniture, although their own wood is very fine to work on, & they have loads of it.[123]

The economic practices of the native "savages," however, were significantly more peculiar and negligent. "The men in the village wear only a shabby shirt of blue or white linen," Durand wrote, "& from the time they put it on they do not remove it until it falls in rags, for they never wash anything. . . . The men do nothing but hunt, & fish, while the women plant Indian corn. The crop belongs to the community, each taking whatever he needs." As far as Durand could tell, the Indians' only treasures were rosary beads from France, which "the wealthiest" draped in profusion on their arms and necks.[124]

A local Christian minister, writing in the same decade, claimed to know that the Indians were resigned to a humble economic status. "They think we have one God, and they another," he explained, "and that ours is better and stronger than theirs, because wee are better provided for, with meat, drink, and cloaths etc."[125] He was probably correct that native people—even the feather and "coronet"-wearing ones he identified as nobles—were worse provided for than the great colonial planters or merchants. On the other hand, there were many people in the colony whose material wealth Indians had little reason to envy. The large majority of non-Indians possessed no greater array of tangible assets than the typical resident of an Indian town, and many did not even have a right to the products of their labor. Virtually all began life in Virginia, and many ended it, residing in "a mean abode" of one room with a dirt floor and thatch roof. Even the frame houses to which some colonists graduated were dark, overcrowded, underheated, and so insubstantial that they lasted but a few years. Furnishings were meager in the extreme; most families slept on the floor and did without a table. Indentured servants would have a chance to farm their own land only if they survived years of grueling labor, and slaves from Africa lacked even that hope.[126]

By the 1680s, some Indians could be found among the slaves, servants, and other penurious laborers of Virginia. But most descendants of Powhatans were still in separate communities, on land designated for Indians, garnering subsistence much as their ancestors had. In the fields remaining to them, native women still grew corn and vegetables. Men hunted and foraged where the English permitted. Many people made baskets, mats, pipes, pottery, wooden trays, or tanned deerskin for sale to colonists who paid in strings of beads known as peake or wampumpeake. Deer continued to provide the stuff of everyday clothing; garments of English cloth were for ceremonial meetings with the English. Houses in the traditional style afforded ample space not only to sleep, but also to store the occupants' few possessions. When visitors came, Indians could usually offer "roasted game, wild fruits, fish and a kind of food, made of coarse and fresh meal." And because the common native people still paid tribute to hereditary leaders (who, in at least one instance, also received costly gifts from the English king), a few eminent Indians still had the wherewithal to dress elaborately, command a retinue of attendants, and entertain generously on special occasions.[127]

To the people who persisted in it, this increasingly precarious aboriginal way of life must have had more to recommend it than the squalid life of the colonial underclass. The proud Powhatans, Rountree writes, were reluctant to call themselves poor. But comfortably endowed European observers would have deemed such reluctance irrational. How could Indians not consider themselves poor when their stock of European goods amounted only to a few "matchcoates, hoes, and axes"? How could they think themselves rich when they wore necklaces of shell money rather than gold or silver? How could they pretend to be prosperous when they annually confirmed their submission to the English monarch with a trifling tribute of twenty beaver pelts?[128] If Indians could not see their poverty, it was further proof that they were savages, adhering blindly to an obsolescent way of life whose moral failings had doomed them to replacement by a superior civilization.

Midway through the eighteenth century, a well-educated British immigrant to Virginia remarked that the Indians there were "living examples of the primitive savages" mentioned in the Bible. "Every small town is a petty kingdom," Hugh Jones wrote, "governed by an absolute monarch, assisted and advised by his great men, selected out of the gravest, oldest, bravest, and richest; if I may allow their dear-skins, peak and poenoak (black and white shells with holes, which they wear on strings about their arms and necks) to be wealth."[129] The resemblance between these remarks and descriptions of Indian society by founders of the Virginia colony might suggest that neither the Indian political economy nor English views of Indians had changed in a century and a half. But the contrary is the case, as this account of colonists and Powhatans reveals. Between 1607 and the 1750s, there had been significant change in the economic relations of natives and immigrants, with important consequences for the groups' conceptions of themselves and each other.

In a colony whose architects had predicted a mutually enriching trade with the Indians, a few people had prospered for a while by swapping European goods for animal pelts or "peak."[130] But scarcely ten years after the first colonists cut logs for a fortified settlement, British Virginians staked the survival of their enterprise on acquiring land where they could raise an inedible plant that sold well in Europe. Meanwhile, Powhatan Indians added English tools, guns, metal, and cloth to the items they counted as wealth, and some were willing at times to make land available for the foreigners who could supply such valuables. Unfortunately for Powhatans, the colonists' modest toeholds became the basis for a fateful demographic and economic shift. The more residents the colony attracted and the more Indian land they took, the fewer were the assets available to Indians whose welfare had been predicated on access to a wide array of resources in an extensive country. Thus, the beleaguered native population dwindled as immigrant numbers grew. In a colony that once depended on Indians to supply residents with food, Europeans eventually gained the means to feed themselves and had no further need of Indian farmers or hunters. During Jamestown's early years, famished colonists had defected to villages where Powhatans served visitors more bread and venison than they could possibly eat. As those years slipped further into the past, some of the villagers' hungry descendants sent their children to colonists' homes where they would work as servants and eat what their employers deigned to supply.[131]

On the eve of the colony's centennial, an upper-class European visitor would still have seen a comparatively poor place, and for reasons that were ironically like colonists' reasons for calling the native people poor in 1607. Virginia lacked valuable minerals, local production of wealth was modest, local trade was limited in scope and volume, the population was scattered, there were no cities, and most residents' personal possessions were few and simple. One English visitor described colonists in the late 1680s much as the first colonists had described the "savages." Virginia, wrote the Reverend John Clayton, is "a place where plenty makes poverty" because "evry one can live at ease & therefore they scorne & hate to worke to advantage themselves so are poor wth abundance." Yet Clayton, like other commentators of the time, saw an important contrast between the "coveteousnesse" that drove fellow Britons to claim and develop American land and the lethargy or indifference to gain of the "Aborigines," who seemed to do little more than hunt, eat, and sleep, taking "no care for the future."[132]

Six decades later, the Indians reminded Hugh Jones of biblical savages because the perception of Indians as economically careless hunters endured. It was an image with roots older than John Smith's condescending comment that Powhatans left the land as God made it. But the trope of the poor savage had taken on significant added meaning for Virginians by Hugh Jones's time. Because of colonists' refocused and heightened desire to control regional sources of wealth — especially land — and because of the decisive shift in their power to realize their desires, their depictions of Indians' poverty and economic incompetence were more confident and more consistent in the 1750s than in 1607. The trope of savagery could be deployed more usefully than ever in the service of colonial interests. It excused the English for enriching themselves at Indians' expense and glorified colonists' economic priorities while obscuring some unflattering facts: Virginians' collective wealth was meager compared with that of the motherland, the great majority of Virginians were as poor as ordinary Indians, and the richest Virginians' estates were hardly a match for those of English aristocrats.

The English had come to Virginia bent on gaining wealth, and although they denied any intention of making native people poorer, they carried ideas from which they could concoct a rationale for taking native resources and offering little more in exchange than a lowly place in an English empire. Yet the first colonists' condition and behavior did not initially make that imperialist ideology clear to the indigenous people, let alone reveal the power that would someday enable them to effect the Indians' dispossession. Native people had reason to think themselves well-off by comparison to the newcomers, and they did not try to dislodge the colony until it was too late. Instead, Powhatan leaders offered to incorporate the small tribe of Britons into the existing regional network of productive groups interlinked by relations of reciprocity. Like the colonists, they hoped for deference from their strange new neighbors. Ultimately, it was the shift in the power to control vital resources that determined who deferred to whom. And when the Indians eventually acknowledged the English king as their figurative father, they did not acquire a wealthy protector who used his control of wealth to meet their needs; they became the king's neglected and ever-poorer stepchildren.

In the mid-eighteenth century, Virginia was one of thirteen North American colonies planted by English migrants. Economic culture varied from colony to colony, as did the indigenous economies on colony borders. But colonists everywhere took an interest in whether the natives were rich or poor, commerce-minded or not. At the same time, native people made their own evaluations of the foreigners' economic condition and ethics. In nearly every case, because colonists were dependent at first on assistance from and trade with indigenous people, both groups had reason to hope for economic advantages from their relations, and some Indians realized those hopes for a time. But the dialectic of land acquisition and population change that beggared Powhatan communities as Virginia thrived had counterparts in other areas of English colonization. From the colonists' vantage point, Indians appeared to be fated for poverty.

Could Indians defy that fate? If so, how? Would prosperity hinge on fundamental change in their philosophy of economic relations? What repercussions would affluence have? Would it warrant a different image and forecast for Indian societies? Could wealth be a basis for significant and enduring Indian power? These were questions that people in diverse places would confront and answer in a variety of ways during the two and a half centuries to follow.

[2]

Indian Gentry

After the American War for Independence ended and the smoke of battle cleared, many people looked to recover property lost in the fray. Among them was Joseph Brant, a renowned loyalist fighter. In 1785, Brant took his search across the Atlantic to ministries and palaces of the British monarchy. His decorous deportment impressed the ladies and gentlemen who wined, dined, and lauded him at banquets, balls, and drawing room receptions. But when Brant asked the Prince of Wales whether promises "made . . . by certain persons . . . during the late war" entitled him to an officer's wages, he apparently sensed disapproval of the inquiry. He sent a follow-up note to a royal secretary, offering to drop the subject. If the propriety of payment was in doubt, Brant wrote, he did not want it. Recompense for his service was not his idea in the first place; his only motivation for joining the fight was his forefathers' "sacred" covenant with the king. "However," he added, "the English gave me pay and a commission from the Commander-in-Chief, which I gladly received as a mark of attention, though I never asked for it."[1]

Paradoxically, British officials may have taken this show of high-minded indifference to money as proof that Joseph Brant deserved further monetary "marks of attention." He returned to America not only with funds to cover his losses in the war—more than one thousand pounds—but also with a captain's half pay and special pension. That compensation and a grant of land underwrote the prosperity he enjoyed for the remaining two decades of his life.[2] Visitors to his home in Ontario marveled at its elegant furnishings and the excellent meals that liveried servants set before numerous guests. Jeromus Johnson had the impression that Brant's wealth was a point of pride with him. Upon meeting Johnson in 1797, Brant extended "a pressing invitation to call and see him at his residence . . . ; stated that he had large possessions," including many Black slaves, "and could make his friends very comfortable." Yet, more than once Brant disavowed any desire for riches beyond what he needed to live decently. He was a Mohawk Indian, he stressed, and Indians did not crave material riches.[3]

The sincerity of Brant's disclaimer was a subject of heated debate during his lifetime, and scholars have not settled the issue.[4] But sincere or not, the disclaimer is significant for what it suggests about Brant's self-conception, his social aspirations, and their historical context. It is the rhetoric of an ambitious man who expected his words and behavior to elevate him in the estimation of British Americans as well as Indians. By disavowing selfish economic motives, Brant expressed an ideal of his Mohawk forebears and contemporaries, but he also appealed to an ideal that his non-Indian audience and patrons endorsed. His talk of a distinctive Indian ethos belied a belief that prosperous, high-ranking members of Euro-American and Indian societies could admire and associate with each other because they shared some fundamental values and espoused a similar code of conduct.

Joseph Brant's belief had a basis in two interrelated phenomena of the eighteenth century. Throughout Britain's North American colonies, political power and social preeminence were reserved for people with "superior wealth," preferably accompanied by "polished manners, classical learning, and a reputation for honor and integrity." "Everywhere it was the same," observes Gordon Wood: "those who had the property and power to exert influence in any way—whether by lending money, doing favors, or supplying employment—created obligations and dependencies that could be turned into political authority."[5] Meanwhile, members of indigenous societies likewise deferred to individuals who acquired wealth and used it in acts of patronage and generosity. Joseph Brant and his sister Molly were such individuals. So were two Muskogee Indians, also known as Creeks—the formidable statesman Alexander McGillivray and a willful businesswoman named Coosaponakeesa, also called Mary.

By adopting economic practices, material tastes, and decorum identified with the "better sort" of non-Indians, these four Indians, and a number of others, equipped themselves to associate and negotiate with colonial leaders at a time when the colonies needed to appease native nations. In the dual role of tribal representative and benefactor, they obtained and distributed wealth, gaining influence as a consequence. Such adroit Indian intermediaries were key participants in the process of structuring relations between indigenous and immigrant societies. On that basis, they could reasonably believe their cultural hybridity would assure them and their nations of non-Indians' continuing respect.

The Indians who amassed exceptional wealth and used it to enhance their social importance gave contemporaries cause to rethink assumptions about the relationship of access to wealth and personal merit. Was there a correlation in these instances? The affluent Indians' political role influenced observers' answers to this question. In the context of an expanding, intensifying, multinational contest for American resources, the term "Indians" referred to distinct peoples who held extensive lands—a form of wealth that everyone coveted and many would fight to obtain or keep. When wealthy individuals of indigenous descent became advocates for Indian landownership and sovereignty, questions about their personal virtue became less important than their political cause. And as the non-Indian population swelled and spread, Euro-Americans increasingly held that cause in contempt. With contempt for Indian nations came contempt for the affluent Indians' bid to associate as equals with elite Whites.

Because Britain's North American colonies did not attract nobility from the homeland, gentry claimed the top rank in colonial society. Genteel status was more social than legal, and not necessarily inherited. It required evidence of superior breeding—dignified bearing, gracious manners, "refined" tastes, erudition, liberality—as well as the financial means to indulge good taste, be a generous host, and render public service without concern for the cost. Although Britons thought they saw physical differences between common people and their betters, it was education, affluence, and comportment rather than biology that determined gentility.[6]

So it could seem to many a non-Indian that Joseph Brant, even with his tawny skin and black eyes, was a gentleman.[7] General Peter B. Porter told Brant's first biographer that the Mohawk man "was punctilious in the observance of the rules of honor and etiquette practised among individuals of that [leading] caste in their social relations." A Reverend Doctor Miller praised Brant for the "most respectful sentiments of his intellectual character, his personal dignity, and his capacity to appear well in any society." The clergyman confessed surprise "at the simple, easy, polished, and even court-like manners [Brant] was capable of assuming."[8] The reason for Miller's surprise, though unstated, is no mystery: he had assumed that Indians lacked genteel qualities. Aaron Burr made the same assumption until he hosted a dinner for Brant at Philadelphia in 1797; but afterward he wrote a letter urging his daughter to entertain the famous Mohawk, who was heading to New York where she lived.

Brant "is a man of education," gushed Burr, "speaks and writes the English perfectly—and has seen much of Europe and America. . . . He is not one of those Indians who drink rum, but is quite a gentleman . . . who understands and practices what belongs to propriety and good breeding."[9]

By the standards of Burr's peers in Philadelphia and New York, Joseph Brant was not especially wealthy, as was usual and a virtual necessity for gentlemen. But in the western reaches of Ontario, where non-Indian settlement was recent, and in the new Indian communities along the Grand River there, Brant's income and assets did make him a rich man. That access to wealth was a basis for influence among fellow Mohawks and other Indians, but it also enabled him to acquire the classy possessions, enjoy the leisure activities, and extend the lavish hospitality that Euro-Americans associated with gentility.[10]

Brant's wealth and his social relations with upper-crust Whites were remarkable for an Indian of his day, as Burr's comments suggest, but they were not unique. Some other Indians received White visitors at comfortable estates and called at elegant non-Indian homes, confident that their guests and hosts recognized them as people of high rank. In a memoir of travels through the colonies, physician Alexander Hamilton described without apparent condescension a stop in 1744 at a Narragansett Indian's residence, "commonly called King George's house or palace": "He possesses twenty or thirty 1000 acres of very fine levell land round this house, upon which he has many tennants and has, of his own, a good stock of horses and other cattle. This King lives after the English mode. . . . His queen goes in a high modish dress in her silks, hoops, stays, and dresses like an English woman. He educates his children to the belles letters and is himself a very complaisant mannerly man. We pai'd him a visit, and he treated us with a glass of good wine."[11] And in 1790, New York City patricians rolled out the welcome mat for the *isti atcagagi thlucco* (Great Beloved Man) of the Creek Indians, Alexander McGillivray. McGillivray in turn welcomed respectable Whites to his plantations north of Georgia, impressing them with his amenities, magnanimity, manners, and learning.[12]

The affluence of these Indians originated in eighteenth-century developments that affected Indians throughout eastern North America, with diverse results. Changes in English colonial society—particularly a surge in commercial enterprise and status-conscious consumption—had roots, parallels, and repercussions in native communities.[13] The burgeoning commerce enriched numerous Indians as well as non-Indians. Indian beneficiaries owed their new wealth directly or indirectly to intercourse with colonists, many of whom thrived on dealings with indigenous nations beyond the colonial enclaves. In this unscripted drama of intercultural relations, there was a rewarding role for individuals who mastered congruent aspects of both cultures, especially the practice of earning esteem by acquiring and strategically dispensing wealth.

The audacious Coosaponakeesa—known to colonists successively as Mary Musgrove, Mary Mathews, and Mary Bosomworth—achieved such mastery. Exploiting her prestigious Muskogee lineage, the teachings of British relatives, and proceeds of her commercial trade with Indians, Coosaponakeesa made herself indispensable to mid-century interactions between important Creek Indian communities and authorities in colonial Georgia. As an acknowledgment of her role, she expected and received property on a par with the richest Georgians.

Although exceptional in some ways, Coosaponakeesa personified relations that were common in the 1700s and hardly novel by then. Mutually solicited relations between eminent Indians and non-Indians had a history reaching back more than two hundred years. From the first encounters of Europeans and indigenous Americans, high-ranking persons sought to deal with their counterparts, as the paramount Powhatan chief and Virginia Company officers did. Once they had identified each other, they tried to determine whether they had things to offer each other that made further exchanges desirable. Successful efforts could result in military alliances and trade partnerships. On occasion, as when the English gentleman John Rolfe married Wahunsonacock's daughter Pocahontas, leaders symbolized and served their peoples' complementary interests with a social merger.

Conditions that encouraged such collaboration did not endure where English colonization was dense and settlers wanted land more than they wanted neighboring natives' products or protection. Thus, in the eyes of Virginians, Powhatan rulers lost stature as their "empire" lost wars, population, and control of vital resources.[14] But relations with Indians farther inland were a different matter. Throughout the 1700s, colonial leaders and other ambitious colonists had incentives to befriend various western Indians. English colonies on the Atlantic Coast continued to need allies in the competition with France, Spain, and each other for North American resources. Native populations west of the Appalachian Mountains warranted respect for their size and martial prowess. The likelihood of lucrative trade was also a compelling reason to curry the favor of leading men and women in Indian country. Their followers had access to commodities that sold briskly in the colonies and overseas, particularly animal pelts and captive native enemies.[15] The Indians often had corresponding grounds to want cordial relations with colonial officials. They too needed allies, and they liked much of the merchandise that colonists offered to trade.[16]

Toward the end of the 1600s, reciprocal interest in trading brought ambitious White residents of Virginia and the Carolinas together with Indians of the populous societies to the west. South Carolinians saw the potential value of trade with so-called Creek Indians shortly after a delegation from that loose, multiethnic confederacy visited the new colony to propose an alliance.[17] Before the 1680s ended, Charlestown had become a hub of British commerce with Creeks and more distant Indians. After that, a desire for regular exchange dictated the sites of other towns in the region, both non-Indian and Indian. The "savage Indians covet a Christian Neighbourhood for the advantage of Trade," an Irish visitor remarked in 1737. Coveting the advantage of Indians' trade, the founders of Georgia identified a location convenient for "savage" customers and created the "Christian neighbourhood" of Augusta in 1736. It was a smart business move. Creeks and Cherokees converged on the new marketplace, as did traders from Charlestown. A band of Chickasaws in Carolina, already far from their nation's territory in the Mississippi Valley, relocated to the environs of Augusta.[18]

Social bonds, especially between high-ranking persons, were a prerequisite of these trade relations. Personal acquaintance and professions of affinity were particularly important to the Indians, who conceived of trade as a replication or extension of the reciprocity that relatives owed each other. Like Powhatans when the English colonists arrived, Creeks and their native neighbors conditioned trading partnerships on a sense of kinship, which could be established symbolically and had to be periodically confirmed by ceremonial gifting. An exchange of gifts between leaders could signify the kinship of their respective peoples.[19]

Market-minded non-Indians reinterpreted these native conventions, regularly characterizing the Indians who expected presents as beggars, bribe-takers, or debtors; but they observed the conventions for several reasons.[20] By showing concern for Indians' material needs, colonists elicited the desired pledges of fraternal loyalty in trade and war.[21] To the Scots who dominated the southern colonial Indian trade, such ritual gift-giving was familiar and meant much the same as it did to Indians. Moreover, non-Indian businessmen shared Indians' preference for dealing on a regular basis with relatives or friends. Britain's transition to a more impersonal market economy was well under way by then; but in the colonies, Edwin Perkins notes, the "distribution of goods and services was uniformly a . . . highly personal form of . . . activity."[22]

Among Indians even more than in the colonies, social relationships determined the routes that valued items took as they passed from hand to hand. In order to secure a strategic place along a route from tribal hunting ground to colonial seaport, a British trader was well advised to join a prominent native family. Men who set up shop among southern Indians seldom ignored such advice. While touring northern Florida in 1774, naturalist William Bartram found that virtually all the traders in Indian towns had local female companions. Obtaining the women's "friendship in matters of trade and commerce" was wise, Bartram judged. "Upon principles of reciprocity, there are but few instances of their neglecting or betraying the interests and views of their temporary husbands; they labour and watch constantly to promote their private interests, and detect and prevent any plots or evil designs which may threaten their persons, or operate against their trade or business."[23] Arranging such conjugal matches was usually the prerogative of the high-ranking Indians who presided over relations with outsiders.[24]

By the early 1700s, an untidy web of personal ties linked merchants in southern colonies to Indians and intermarried traders in communities from the Appalachians to the Mississippi River.[25] New wealth moved both ways along strands of the web. At the far eastern end, riches accumulated swiftly in White hands. Creeks and other Indians supplied North Carolina, South Carolina, and Georgia with their most lucrative early exports: deerskins and human captives. Profits on hides averaged 400 to 600 percent. No wonder a recruitment brochure assured prospective emigrants to South Carolina that they could "grow very Rich, in a few Years . . . from a small Beginning" if they brought "Stocks of Goods . . . to furnish the Inhabitants, and *Indian* Traders."[26] By investing some of their proceeds in plantations and slave labor, merchants and traders also facilitated their settlements' expansion and economic growth.[27]

While Britons thought they had the best of bargains with Indians, Creeks believed trade relations worked to their advantage. In exchange for hides and captives obtained in the prestigious activities of hunting and war, men could get desirable things that no natives made: guns and ammunition, metal tools, iron cookware, textiles, fabric clothing, and jewelry.[28] Accordingly, Creek hunting and raiding intensified, and the Indians' wealth in exotic goods increased rapidly. Those gains would not have admitted them to the ranks of England's rich and powerful, but in the estimation of historian David Corkran, the Creek confederacy was soon "a fiercely acquisitive and affluent . . . society."[29]

The basis of that affluence became shaky as commercial traders hooked hunter-warriors on credit and rum. A generation after trade with Carolinians began, debts and dependence on European commodities determined many Creek choices in economic and diplomatic affairs. Headmen from two Creek towns told Tobias Fitch in 1725, "We hope that your King will not Stop the White mens bringing goods among us, for unless You Supply us with goods and Ammunition we are no people Neither shal we be able to pay Debts unless we Can be Supply'd with Amunition from You."[30] Yet Indians also said on many later occasions that they were much wealthier than their forebears, thanks to relations with Whites. At a meeting with Georgia's governor in 1757, a Creek spokesman declared, "Our fathers were poor, but you have made us rich. This we often tell our young people. We desire them to hold you fast by the hand as the surest means to continue secure in their present happiness."[31] As late as 1774, Bartram found the "Lower Creeks or Seminoles" living in prosperity that he attributed mainly to their supply of marketable natural resources. They occupied a vast territory, he reported, with "a superabundance of the necessaries and conveniences of life. The hides of deer, bears, tigers and wolves, together with honey, wax and other productions of the country, purchase their cloathing, equipage and domestic utensils from the Whites. They seem to be free from want and desires."[32]

Some individuals gained considerably more than others from the commerce linking Indians to European markets. The colonists who profited are easy to identify, whether the measure of their gain is economic, political, or social. Historian Tom Hatley found that "traders and the merchants who backed them were at the top of the income ladder" in South Carolina. "Factors, or agents, of Charlestown trading houses could make nearly twice the wage" of plantation overseers, and deerskin buyers who did not affiliate with merchants might do even better. By converting some of their income to real property and slave labor, many in the business attained gentry standing and membership in the colonial power elite. For decades, hope of joining them inspired other men to risk money, and sometimes their lives, in the Indian trade.[33]

Coosaponakeesa and her Creek husband, Johnny Musgrove, were among those who invested in merchandise to barter for deerskins and consequently added to their wealth. Although their assumption of the trader's role was uncommon for Indians, they did know other Creeks who acquired more than a few personal items of European make. Coosaponakeesa's cousin Malatchi made many such acquisitions as a result of representing a major Creek town in relations with colonists. When he journeyed to a French fort in 1755 to receive "great Presents," both the South Carolina officials from whom he had regularly accepted gifts and other Indians took notice of his apparent cupidity.[34]

The motivation of ambitious colonists and the measures of their success will seem obvious to modern readers. Profit-oriented enterprise and quests for personal wealth hardly need explanation today. Nor did they need much explanation at the time in Georgia or the Carolinas, even though many colonists urged allegiance to an older, less mercenary value system.[35] But the mo-

tives of Indians like Malatchi require more analysis. Lasting personal enrichment and ever-increasing wealth creation were not customary aims of Creek
economic relations; quite the contrary. Creeks and neighboring Indians had
no for-profit institutions equivalent to British merchant houses or joint stock
companies. Most Indians participated in the peltry trade as consumers whose
communities frowned on accumulation. Even so, some individuals did come
to control exceptional amounts of the wealth that entered their country from
the colonies. Those Indians owed their apparent affluence to the interplay of
European political-economic strategies and traditional native ways of earning
respect, especially giving valuables away.

It was evident to British traders and colonial officials that disparate ideals, mores, or aims guided European and Indian conduct in economic affairs.
James Adair, who made a living in the 1700s selling hides purchased from
Chickasaws and other Indians, contrasted "the community of goods prevailing" among them with the self-serving mindset of fellow traders. He likened
the Indians' economic ethic to primitive Christianity, romanticizing both in
the process. "They are so hospitable, kind-hearted, and free," he wrote, "that
they would share with those of their own tribe, the last part of their provisions even to a single ear of corn; and to others, if they called when they were
eating. . . . An open generous temper is a standing virtue among them; to be
narrow-hearted, especially to those in want, or to any of their own family, is
accounted a great crime, and to reflect scandal on the rest of the tribe." "Martial virtue, and not riches is their invariable standard for preferment," Adair
also remarked, "for they neither esteem, nor despise any of their people one
jot more or less, on account of riches or dress." Countless other Europeans
attested to Indians' egalitarianism, contempt for the possessive rich, and disgust at the disparities of wealth in colonial society.[36]

Nevertheless, and ironically, Britons often interpreted Indians' behavior in
light of their own yen for wealth. Like other humans, they assumed, Indians
would naturally be tempted by riches and inclined to want what richer people
had. That assumption seemed to explain Indians' desire for European goods.
Appealing to a presumably inherent selfishness was therefore a central element of imperial strategy in Indian affairs. When a military officer remarked
to South Carolina's governor in 1756, "Indians are a commodity that are to be
bought and sold," he was not referring to slaves, but to bribery.[37]

On the premise that Indians could be bought, traders and officials bestowed
European goods on individuals who seemed willing and able to promote colonial interests, both commercial and geopolitical. The ideal recipients were
native men and women with ready-made followings—the people colonists re-

ferred to as kings, queens, emperors, headmen, head warriors, or chiefs. Accustomed to receiving material tokens of respect from outsiders and distributing gratuities as incentives or rewards to followers, headmen or chiefs were obvious conduits for the gifts with which Europeans sought to purchase the allegiance or acquiescence of entire tribes.[38] Colonial records are replete with entries like the one in the South Carolina government's books for 23 November 1751: "Presents Given to the Cherokee Indians . . . : For the Raven a scarlet Coat, Wastcoat and Breches, ruffled Shirt, gold-laced Hat, Shoes, Buckles, Buttons, Stockins and Gartring, Saddle, one of the best Guns, Cutlass, a Blanket and Knife, a Peice of Stroud, 5 Yards of Callico, ten Yards of Em[bossed] Serge." To each lesser chief went a gun, coat, shirt, flax, hat, and boots. These were personal gifts above and beyond the guns, ammunition, blankets, knives, pipes, tobacco, kettles, pots, mirrors, wire, cloth, beads, needles, thread, earbobs, cadiz, garters, ribbons, scissors, buttons, combs, and trunks the Cherokee delegation received for the people at home.[39]

At other times, the flow of presents could bypass a headman, giving someone else the means to attract a following. Europeans often found it hard to tell which Indians were of high rank. Occasionally, an undifferentiated throng of Indians appeared in a colonial town seeking tangible signs of the Whites' regard for them and concern for their well-being. George Chicken reported that he was trying to discourage such invasions when he told a Cherokee audience in 1725, "I desired that when ever they sent any of their people abt business to the English that they might be head Warriours, that We might know how to Use them, and those were the people among them that We must take the most Notice of."[40] But in some instances, Europeans unwittingly conferred bounty on men of modest stature or on challengers to existing leadership.

Snubbing established chiefs could also be a deliberate European stratagem. If colonists could not find tractable Indians with clout, they tried to create new leaders by channeling goods to cooperative individuals. Other Indians were apt to construe the gifts lavished on a man (and they usually *were* men) as signs of the foreigners' respect for him. And once a man seemed likely to receive periodic awards of European commodities, others had reason to curry his favor by deferring to his guidance. Traders, too, might promote the political fortunes of selected commoners by providing them with the material means to act like headmen.[41]

Bypassed headmen protested such breaches of protocol. In 1725, a Creek chief complained that any "young Fellow . . . goes Down and Tell[s] a Find [fine] Story they [get] a Commission and then they Come here and they are head Men and at the Same Time No more [fit] for it than Doges."[42] Thirty years later, South Carolina councilor and merchant Edmond Atkin heard the same refrain from "old men" concerned "that . . . Traders, who confine their kindness and Civility almost wholly to the Young Hunters for the sake of the deerskins, shew Slights to them which lessen them in the Eyes of their People." The consequences of this practice for Indians concerned Atkin less than its effects on England's rivalry with France. Certain traders, he lamented, were imposing "their own Favourites or Friends upon the Government as Leading Men, for the sake of Presents; by which means many Indians receive valuable Presents, who have really very little Influence in their Nation. . . . In the mean while many of the old Creek Chiefs who bear great Sway among the Young Men, being unable to perform such a Journey, are forc'd to cringe to the French who live among them, for the sake of a few necessaries."[43]

Such complaints suggest that an Indian who received exceptional new wealth could not only unseat a poorer headman; he or she could also arouse envy and incur censure for neglecting obligations to less fortunate people. The Yamacraw headman Tomochichi faced charges that he was not passing English presents on to others.[44] South Carolina governor James Glen learned in 1753 that grumbling was rife among Cherokees after their "Emperour . . . received rich Presents" for ceding land to colonists. And one trader heard a warrior mutter that gifts had made some headmen "hearty in their [English] Interest" while "we that are (the Back of the House People) or the People in general might go naked, and of course very miserable."[45]

The alleged avarice of some headmen and the indignation of people who received fewer gifts seem at odds with Adair's statement that Indians did not covet riches because riches played no part in winning them respect. Indeed, a second Adair observation suggests that the first was an oversimplified and romanticized interpretation of Indian values. Indians, including "the young warriors," Adair noted, were so fond of "European ornaments" that they loaded their limbs and clothing with brass and silver "in proportion to their ability of purchasing them."[46] Considered in light of testimony that headmen rewarded young men's achievements with items for personal adornment and other luxuries, this love of ornaments implies more than vanity or an appreciation of beauty. Even before the advent of trade with Europeans, native people took pride in acquiring, receiving, or conferring precious articles because that attested to their competence or indicated others' admiration for them. European goods simply joined the class of items whose receipt or transmittal could signify a person's social merit. Obtaining and distributing glass beads, brass buttons, or wool blankets was another way to represent one's accomplishments, sense others' respect, and earn respect. As Hatley says of Cherokees who sold deerskins, Indians "used new goods to express their older roles with new emphasis."[47]

Adair's assertion that preferment in Indian societies did not depend on wealth was neither an error nor a falsehood; it was just misleadingly incomplete. Generosity did earn praise and influence in communities where Adair traded; hoarding property earned scorn. These norms were institutionalized in rituals that dismantled personal collections of wealth. At annual renewal ceremonies, for example, people destroyed most of their household belongings; at a funeral, they buried cherished possessions with the body.[48] But because the voluntary transfer of wealth from one person to another could express esteem and confirm the giver's status, the desire to receive wealth and control a sizable quantity of it was not inconsistent with the veneration of generosity, and that desire could be intense.[49]

In other words, to explain southeastern Indians' zeal to acquire English imports, we need not infer that apostles of British materialism had corrupted or converted them. Rationales for acquiring riches were inherent in the Indians' own system of meanings. Adair himself reported at one point, "They wish some of their honest warriors to have these things [the Whites have], as they would know how to use them aright, without placing their happiness, or merit, in keeping them, which would be of great service to the poor, by diffusing them with a liberal hand."[50] Given their desire to earn respect by "diffusing" goods to the poor, few Indians would have engaged in trade with the stated aim of adding over the long term to their material net worth, but many were beguiled nonetheless by opportunities to obtain more goods. As instruments for establishing vital social relations and symbolizing desirable personal qualities, the new riches from Europe were precious indeed.

Thus, in the world of the 1700s that Indians shared with Europeans, access to wealth and knowledge of wealth's diverse meanings could make someone important, and importance could ensure access to wealth. Wealth spoke to and for Indians as well as non-Indians, although the messages differed in key respects and did not always translate accurately. Both Indians and Whites judged rectitude in part by a person's methods of obtaining and using wealth, but determining whether everyone applied the same criteria was difficult. For instance, Indians said they measured the kindness of gift-givers by ability to give, not by the economic value of the gifts, and British leaders occasionally echoed that claim.[51] But the distinction was difficult to maintain as Indians and Britons used commodities to communicate their intentions and desires. Upon making an unusually lavish offering to Chickasaws in 1756, the governor of South Carolina said, "These Presents are great; by them you must judge of the Greatness of my Love for you." And because the Indians thought the governor was rich, they would consider him less than loving if his presents were not great.[52]

Coosaponakeesa understood the relationship of wealth to rank, influence, and social approval in both cultures. So it seems, at least, from the way she made herself important to colonists and Indians alike. Her influence both derived from and enabled control of trade goods and land. Goods and land in turn served as marks of high status and the means to maintain that status. Coosaponakeesa's claims to land, money, and patrician rank galled some British officials, but they were afraid for years to alienate the Creeks who endorsed those claims. By exploiting the officials' fear, Coosaponakeesa compelled the leadership of Georgia in effect to recognize her as both an Indian aristocrat and a wealthy member of colonial society.

According to most historians and her own autobiographical writings, Coosaponakeesa embodied the status-conscious social ties that facilitated exchanges and alliances between colonists and leading Indians. Her mother was reputedly a close relative—probably a sister or cousin—of a headman so influential that Georgia's governor referred to him as "the great Brim, who was called Emperor of the Creeks by the Spaniards."[53] Her father was a British trader whose union or dalliance with a high-born Muskogee woman must have aided his business. While young, Coosaponakeesa received a Christian education and the name Mary from an English family in South Carolina, possibly relatives. Her first husband was the son and namesake of Colonel John Musgrove, a colonial trade commissioner who had fathered Johnny by an Indian woman. Several historians think it likely that Brim arranged the marriage in 1716, when Coosaponakeesa or Mary was sixteen or seventeen, in order to seal a peace and trade pact with South Carolinians.[54]

Probably after a few years among the Creeks, Mary and Johnny Musgrove settled on a South Carolina plantation, where they raised livestock and traded British goods to other Indians. In 1732, they accepted an invitation to open a trading house among the Yamacraws, a community composed primarily of relocated Lower Creeks, near the Savannah River. Their Yamacraw post was soon a high-volume operation, taking in as much as one-sixth the total skins handled by Charlestown merchants.[55]

The Musgroves had scarcely erected and stocked their shelves before a boatload of Britons disembarked nearby, intent on creating the colony of Georgia. Mary's approval of the colonial project probably helped to ensure Yamacraw cooperation, on the understanding that she would remain the Indians' local source of trade goods.[56] Johnny and Mary provided other assistance to the new settlers, who were in turn a new source of wealth for the Musgroves. Because they presided over a plantation where servants and slaves raised cattle and corn, the Musgroves could sell colonists essential foodstuffs. Their ability to host and interpret for Indian leaders was also worth a lot to Georgia's founders. In return for accompanying an Indian delegation to England, Johnny received 100 pounds and 500 acres of colony land. Thus, as traders, planters, mediators, and interpreters, the Musgroves had access to plentiful economic resources. When Johnny died in 1735, his widow was reputedly the richest person in the region, native or not.[57]

Mary's economic fortunes took a turn for the worse in the next decade. A free-spending new husband, his disabling illness and early death, expenditures to help the Georgians in war with neighboring Spaniards, poaching from her cattle ranch, and a Yamasee raid on her unattended inland trading post nearly bankrupted Mary by 1742. She managed nonetheless to maintain or enhance her importance as a businesswoman, landholder, and confidante of eminent men, both British and Indian. Her access to trade goods, the hospitality she provided for Indian delegations, her family connection to "Emperor" Brim, and her facility with spoken and written English lent Mary continuing stature among Creeks. At the same time, officers of the infant colony relied on her to reassure Indians about their intentions, dispense goods symbolizing British friendship, and enlist warriors to fight the Spanish.[58] Alexander Heron, the commander of colonial troops, proclaimed Mary's importance in a 1747 letter to the deputy secretary of state:

I have had personal Knowledge of her Merit since my first Arrival in this Country and am highly Sensible of the Singular Service she has done her Country (a great part at the Expence of her own private Fortune) . . . And since Malatchi the Emperor's Arrival here, I am more than ever Convinced that she is looked upon by the whole Creek Nation as their Natural princess, and any Injury done to her will be Equally Resented as if done to the whole Nation. . . . For I assure you Sir, She is a Woman of such Consequence that if she is driven to the necessity of Flying to her Indian Friends for Bread it will be morally impossible for me to Maintain his Majestys peace & Authority amongst them.[59]

Heron fretted that Mary might fly to her Indian friends because his superiors in the colonial hierarchy were unwilling to honor requests she had made. Especially troublesome was a request for recognition of her title to land that Creek leaders had granted her. The Georgians had not initially concerned themselves with the legal basis for Mary's use of land because her ranch and store were outside the strip they acquired by a treaty with Creek headmen.[60] But in 1737, Tomochichi announced his intent to grant Mary the original Yamacraw townsite adjoining the colonial settlement of Savannah. The next year, leading men from four Creek towns informed General James Oglethorpe that they too wanted Mary to have the Yamacraw tract. And when the Indians asked colonial officials to record her title to that land, probably at the suggestion of Mary and her new spouse, they triggered alarms in Savannah and London.[61] Georgia's trustees, who had decided to mete out land to colonists in modest-sized parcels, feared anarchy if Englishmen could marry Indians and thus, through their wives, obtain vast acreage from Indians directly. The authorities were therefore loath to agree that Coosaponakeesa—Mary Mathews to them—had taken title to land in their midst without their approval. Their dispute with her lasted twenty years. Time and again during those two decades, Georgians found they needed Mary to smooth their relations with Creeks. Time and again, Creek leaders made it known that relations would be anything but smooth unless colonial officials acknowledged her right to land and treated her as the equal of high-ranking Britons.

Mary's taste in husbands encouraged British detractors to dismiss her claim of high rank and her expectation of deference. Her second husband, Jacob Mathews, was her former indentured servant. Two years after he died, she wed a young Englishman of somewhat higher status and even loftier aspirations—recently ordained Anglican rector Thomas Bosomworth. Many colonists thought the match was ludicrous but suppressed their titters to attend a lavish nuptial celebration hosted by the Savannah court president. William Stephens wrote in his journal that he spread specially constructed tables with "all such kind of provisions as this place could afford, boyled Roasted and Baked, brought ready dressed," and "nothing happen'd in the whole Company (large as it was) that gave any offence."[62] But the Reverend Bosomworth—his desire to be rich apparently greater than his desire to be righteous—soon gave offense to many of his countrymen by forsaking his pastoral duties and promoting his wife's economic interests with unsettling impertinence.

In 1747, the Bosomworths renewed and buttressed Mary's demand for English recognition of her title to the land conveyed by Indian leaders. They produced documentation that Creek chiefs had reaffirmed their grant of the Yamacraw tract and given additional tracts—three coastal islands—to Mary and Thomas.[63] Meanwhile, managers of the colony incurred further debts to Mary when she advanced the supplies that Thomas's brother carried on an official mission to the Creeks. As months passed without a favorable response either to the Bosomworths' requests for repayment or to their claims of landownership, Georgians' relations with Creek leaders deteriorated. People on both sides accused each other of scandalously unprincipled conduct. Mary characterized the English position as stinginess—a damning rebuke among Creeks. Colonial officials called her a liar who affected concern for Indians' welfare while advancing her own selfish interests. Malatchi, who had succeeded Brim as *mico* or headman of Coweta, bristled at the colonists' shabby treatment of his "sister" Coosaponakeesa.[64]

Mistrust prompted the antagonists to give each other more cause for mistrust. The mounting tensions climaxed in August of 1749, when Malatchi and his retinue came uninvited to Savannah, ostensibly seeking assurance that the English meant no harm to Mary Bosomworth. Town officers nearly panicked at news that more Indians were on their way. There ensued a month-long series of confrontations in which Mary's character and status were central bones of contention. Determined to break her power over their conduct of Indian affairs, colonial officers publicly humiliated her, jailed her for a time, and attempted to undermine Indians' faith in her with allegations that she planned to appropriate presents meant for them.

Mary's humiliation briefly damaged her reputation in Creek country as well as Georgia, but she soon regained standing and leverage with key Indians. By skillfully playing on their gratitude for the goods and hospitality she had provided, on their desire for European gifts, and on Georgia's need for Creek friendship, she foiled several more English attempts to talk or trick headmen into disavowing her and her land claim. At a conference in 1750 with an agent for Governor John Reynolds, chiefs from Upper Creek towns endorsed Mary's petition because "Malatchi and Mrs. Bosomworth had agreed Together about the Lands and as Malatchi was a very Great man they did not want to have any further disputes between the two nations, but allowed the validity of Malatchi's title in favour of Mrs. Bosomworth." Subsequently, Lower Creek headmen also "declared with one voice that . . . they gave the Lands to Mrs. Bosomworth as an Indian and one of themselves by whom they had often been kindly received when they came to Savannah."[65]

Mary reminded Malatchi and the other headmen that the English refusal to acknowledge her role in the colony's survival was an insult to a kinswoman. This grievance was a cause of chronic discord between Creeks and Georgians until 1759, when a new governor finally conceded that Mary's pleas had some merit. Although her importance to Georgians had diminished by then, many sympathized with her, and others feared her. Embittered, she might again foment trouble among Indians and even among Whites; mollified, she could be a useful ally in the rivalry with French colonies to the west. Therefore, even though Governor Henry Ellis finally persuaded Creek headmen to entrust the disputed lands to the Crown and thus claimed victory in the legal contest, he obtained permission to grant St. Catherine Island back to the Bosomworths. The English government also reimbursed Mary's outlay for supplies in 1747 and added £2,100 as compensation for her long service to the colony. By accepting this compromise, Mary abandoned her struggle to make English property law serve the purposes of an Indian aristocrat as well as an aspiring British gentlewoman. However, the settlement established the Bosomworths, by one scholar's calculation, as "the largest landholders in Georgia and among the richest of colonists."[66]

In the long run, the most consequential matter at issue in the Bosomworth affair was not Mary's ultimate net worth or her social standing; it was whether Britons or Indians would control allocation of the resource they both treasured most—land. On one side, officers of the colony claimed exclusive power to acquire land from Indians and dispense it to colonists. They cited English legal doctrine that an individual right to land could come only from the sovereign. Under the colonial charter, they had responsibility for safeguarding that aspect of their king's sovereignty in Georgia. Mary's contention that she and her husband could acquire title to land directly from Creek headmen was tantamount to sedition. In the words of one official, the Indians, Mary, and her husbands had demanded "an unallowable Sovereignty."[67]

On the other side, Creek headmen—strangers to English legal and political doctrine—believed the land was theirs to confer on Coosaponaseeka or any other person they chose. Just as General Oglethorpe had recognized the Creek chiefs' authority to donate or assign land for a colony, the governor and council had to recognize that the chiefs could grant Creek land to one of their own. Although Creek property concepts are not clear from the headmen's recorded statements, their disdain for the English legal argument is unambiguous.[68] At a climactic point during the showdown of 1749, Malatchi declared hotly that the Georgians owed their toehold on the coast entirely to Mary, who was there "before the Squire (meaning General Oglethorpe) brought any White People; that She gave them liberty to Settle; that the Lands they now lived on were held under her; that all the lands they should Settle on, should be held from her, for that She was the Queen and Head of their Nation."[69]

Malatchi's declaration shows that the dispute about control of land—important as it was—did not eclipse the issue of Mary's social status and national affiliation. Nor should historians allow it to do so. Indeed, the land and sovereignty issue was intertwined with the argument regarding Mary's place in regional social hierarchies. Was Coosaponakeesa, alias Mary Bosomworth,

Creek "royalty?" Or was she an ordinary British subject, bound by law not only to obey the king but also to subsume her identity in that of her husband? Could she only be one or the other, not both? There was much debate on this topic during the 1749 ruckus in Savannah.

The colonial councilors announced that they regarded Mrs. Bosomworth—the daughter and wife of Englishmen—as legally English. In the presence of Malatchi and other headmen, Mary vehemently demurred, "declaring herself to be Empress and Queen of the Upper and Lower Creeks." Asked to say again whether "she was not a Subject of the King of Great Britain," she replied grandiosely that "she owed him no Allegiance otherwise, than in Alliance, being herself a sovereign." Five days later, the trustees took a nastier tack in their effort to discredit her, alleging that the first colonists found her "in mean and low Circumstances, being only Cloathed with a Red Stroud Petticoat and . . . Shift," and saying flatly that "Squire" Oglethorpe by his sponsorship and "extraordinary presents . . . made her the Woman she now appears to be."[70] But Malatchi insisted with Mary on identifying her as a Creek noblewoman. Although he explained the Creeks' conception of her land tenure in varying terms over time, he steadfastly denied that Mary's paternal ancestry, marriage, or adaptation to English ways made her a common Englishwoman. "My Sister, Mrs. Bosomworth," Malatchi told officials in South Carolina, "I do not look upon as a white Person. She is an Indian, intitled to all the Rights and Privileges of an Indian, and . . . to the Lands she possessed."[71]

The positions of the parties to this debate certainly served their respective economic interests, but that alone does not explain why colonial authorities insisted on identifying Mary Bosomworth as English or why she disagreed. If the absence of English references to her as Indian is factored in, evidence is plentiful that Whites saw no salient reason to classify Mary as Indian even before she gave officials an economic and governmental reason to declare her English. When mentioning her in correspondence and journals, colonists and British visitors did not use the term "Indian." Instead, they referred to her simply as "Mrs. Musgrove," "Mrs. Mathews," "Mrs. Bosomworth" or as "wife" to each man. In letters to those men, she was termed "your lady." Thus, Britons implicitly differentiated Mary from the people they did label Indians. One rare allusion to her Muskogee lineage, in the journal of an Austrian immigrant, described her as "Daughter of an *English* Man by an *Indian* Woman" but went on to emphasize that she was "a very good Christian, and gave the *Indians* some Notions of the Holy Scriptures."[72] Overall, the documentary record suggests that Mary's method of earning a livelihood, her Christian faith, her husbands' and father's nationality, and her fluency in English determined her affiliation in colonists' eyes. Her Indian ancestry or physical traits had little or no relevance.[73] In the Indians' matrilineal kinship system, however, parentage did determine the classification we might designate today as ethnicity or nationality. To the people that colonists knew as Creeks, Mary was indisputably Creek because her mother was.[74]

Creek though she was, Mary pursued wealth with determination worthy of an ambitious English subject, and at times the dispute about her social status focused on what that pursuit meant about her moral character. A case for selfishness was not hard to make. Although Mary used many of the resources at her disposal in public service, which included the gifts and sustenance she supplied to Indians, hers was not an altruistic quest for wealth. There are clues, for example, that she planned to subdivide and sell part of the land received from the Indian headmen.[75] No doubt some Creeks thought her more greedy than generous and accordingly held her in lower esteem than she claimed. She also lost Indian support for a time when colonists insinuated that she planned to keep gifts intended for distribution.

But Mary's acquisitiveness and entrepreneurship are not proof that she chose to repudiate Indian economic mores and live by English mores instead. It is just as reasonable to infer that she thought English and Indian practices and ethics were either congruent or reconcilable. In both societies, receipt and control of wealth could signify and enhance estimable status and influence, which were certainly among Mary's aspirations. By acquiring wealth through means learned from Britons but dispensing much of it as proper for a high-ranking Creek, she expected to command respect from all the people she knew. She had devised a strategy to make herself important in everyone's eyes. It was a strategy that worked well so long as Britons were constrained to stay on friendly terms with Creeks.

Admittedly, Mary's choice of husbands and places of residence suggest a preference for English society. And when she was among colonists, making a living as she had seen some of them do, their example or encouragement gave her license to take actions atypical of her indigenous kin, such as claiming "ownership" of more land than she could personally put to use. But it would be rash to conclude that Mary consciously substituted a British code of conduct for the ethos of her Indian relatives. Like the goods coming from Europe, some of the colonists' customs could seem to Creeks like new tools for achieving old goals, not for dismantling the indigenous culture. A decision to emulate colonists in specific respects was not a renunciation of Creek identity.

Mary's cousin Malatchi also showed exceptional interest in adding to his personal wealth, yet it is doubtful that anyone claimed he was therefore any less Muskogee.[76] James Adair heard that Malatchi was the first Creek to bequeath his property to surviving kin instead of taking it with him to the grave. Such a move could mean that Malatchi—perhaps at Mary's urging—knowingly chose an English alternative to a Creek custom.[77] But one departure from custom does not signal a rejection of all values that Creeks held dear. When meeting with the English in his capacity as *mico*, Malatchi dressed as they did and adopted an air of "courtly politeness," which made it possible for council president Stephens to imagine that Malatchi "had been bred in some European Court."[78] Yet the headman's dignity was standard chiefly conduct for a Creek. Chances are that he also made sense of his decision to conserve and pass down his possessions by reference to norms he would have identified as Creek.[79] Perhaps he saw himself meeting his obligation to sustain relatives, and his definition of relatives would certainly have reflected Creek social structure, not English. Similarly, his "sister" Coosaponaseeka could reasonably believe that she need not disavow all Creek ideals in order to live among Britons as a rich woman.

Like many of Mary's British contemporaries, some scholars have assumed that Jacob Mathews and Thomas Bosomworth instigated and managed their wife's campaign for recognition in Georgia as a landowner, government creditor, and Creek noblewoman.[80] But the notion that Mary would passively allow either husband to create and exploit a new persona for her is implausible; it gives insufficient weight to the evidence of her strong will, independent actions, and previous experience in business and regional diplomacy. It also reflects a conception of gender roles that Creeks did not share. In England, married women were economically subordinate to their husbands, who alone held legal title to a couple's property.[81] Conversely, married women in Creek communities had full control of houses, household effects, domesticated animals, and cultivated land.[82] Whether Mary's domestic partnerships operated on a Creek model or an English one is a matter for speculation. But the well-documented force of her personality makes it hard to picture her on the short end of the power balance in her family. Mathews may have counseled his wife to seek title under English law, thinking that formal title was a prerequisite of subdivision and sale to colonists. Bosomworth may have been responsible for some strategic planning and campaign rhetoric, such as the references to Mary as a queen and empress. Clearly, however, both men counted on their association with Mary to boost their own wealth and status more than she counted on them to boost hers. It is unlikely that they saw her as a common widow and economic simpleton whom they could reinvent as Queen of the Creeks. Instead, each saw a woman of wealth and importance who could enrich him and thus promote him from servant or vicar to planter and, eventually, to gentleman. Unfortunately for Mary and her Creek kin, that happened only when she conceded the supremacy of English property law.[83]

About the time that Mary Bosomworth's settlement with Georgia fulfilled her third husband's hopes for a prestigious estate, a young Mohawk woman settled *her* hopes for prosperity and prestige on union with a British man. Like Mary Bosomworth, Mary Brant had kin ties to Indians that her non-Indian mate could exploit for his own purposes, including the enlargement of his personal estate. But unlike Bosomworth, Mary Brant—more often called Molly— was less affluent and initially less influential than her husband.[84] It would be crude and anachronistic to suggest that Molly merely saw William Johnson as her ticket to wealth and power. Strong mutual affection reportedly sustained their fifteen-year partnership. It is fair to say, however, that access to Johnson's wealth gave Molly the means to earn added respect from Indians, which in turn won her the respect and financial support of Johnson's British peers. As a colonial gentleman's consort, Molly became an especially powerful Mohawk matron in a period when the interests and identifying traits of Indian and non-Indian elites still seemed largely compatible.

Since the 1600s, Mohawks had achieved impressive prosperity in much the same way as Creeks. They and five other Iroquois nations had leveraged their military prowess, their strategic location between rival French and British colonies, and the rivals' desire for their trade.[85] Like their Indian forebears and Creek contemporaries, eighteenth-century Iroquois conceived of reciprocity as the basis for economic relations, and they idealized generosity. However, in the words of historian Alan Taylor, their "wants exceeded those of their ancestors." After decades of bartering furs for European goods, they had become consumers dependent on a flow of imported commodities. During Molly Brant's youth, the Iroquois maintained their consumer economy through a tenuous alliance with the British in New York, who acknowledged the Six Nations' sovereignty and services with regular gifts as well as trade.[86] France's defeat in the Seven Years' War left the Iroquois economy at Britain's mercy after 1763, just as land-hungry colonists were pushing into the Mohawk Valley from the east, but Mohawks compensated for their dwindling leverage and trade revenues by selling or leasing rights to some of their lands.[87] Trade was still conducted as it had been for generations. Vital goods reached Mohawk homes primarily through the hands of a few civil leaders, called *sachems*, whose largesse proved and secured their power. By the 1760s, the hands that passed out the goods were often those of William Johnson and Molly Brant.[88]

Molly was about seven years older than her brother Joseph Brant. Because records of their lineage are as sparse as those for Coosaponakeesa, scholars still debate whether Molly and Joseph were born into the hereditary Mohawk elite. Historians agree, however, that the siblings' widowed mother Margaret married a sachem named Brant Canagaraduncka when Molly was a teenager. An artful sachem like Brant had several ways of acquiring wealth, including gifts from colonial governments. Margaret, meanwhile, may have capitalized on the new market for ginseng, a locally abundant plant. Perhaps for those reasons, the blended family was one of the most affluent at the "castle" or town of Canajoharie. Some of their economic choices and apparent values reflected Mohawks' lengthy contact with Europeans. They were Anglican Christians living in a single-family house built and furnished in the English style.[89]

Molly met William Johnson because he was a friend and political ally of her stepfather. Middle-aged and widowed by the time he courted young Molly, Johnson had been in the area since coming from Ireland in 1738 to manage an uncle's land. His knack for getting along with Indians was soon evident. He won their goodwill by conferring gifts, buying furs, mastering Iroquois ceremonial protocol, and keeping promises. He cultivated personal connections to Mohawk leaders. Mohawks dubbed him Warraghiyagey, variously translated to denote a man who does important business.[90] By parlaying trade revenue into a landed estate and by astute military leadership during the war with France, Johnson also earned a good name for himself in British ruling circles. His ability to please Mohawk sachems, enlist Indian warriors in British fights, and simultaneously build his own fortune impressed the king, who made him a baronet in 1755 and superintendent of Indian affairs for a northern colonial district in 1756. When business or official duties took him to Canajoharie, Johnson stayed at the home of Brant Canagaraduncka. Sometime in 1759, Molly moved from Canagaraduncka's house to Johnson's, ten miles downriver. Her new residence—a two-story stone structure in Georgian style—was the center of a bustling manorial estate worthy of an English gentleman.[91]

On one hand, William Johnson's pursuit and use of wealth conformed to a venerable British model of economic relations. His endeavors had the implicit aim of replicating the economic and social order in his homeland. A scion of minor Anglo-Irish gentry, he aspired to an even higher place in that familiar hierarchy, and he needed greater wealth to attain his goal. By actions befitting a British aristocrat—extending aid and protection to social inferiors, taking advantage of the resulting influence to augment his economic resources, and wielding those resources so as to enhance his influence further—Johnson did become one of the richest, most powerful men on the colonial frontier. The vast landholdings he amassed and doled out to tenants were both a basis of his power and a sign of his rank among Europeans.[92] Like other wealthy colonists, Sir William also advertised his genteel status by stocking his sumptuous houses with physical proof of his wealth and good taste: costly imported mahogany furniture, elaborately framed portraits, deluxe draperies, books, crystal, china, and silver table settings.[93]

On the other hand, Johnson smoothed his route to affluence and power by also learning and following some Indian rules of social-economic morality. This was a pragmatic accommodation to the proximity and power of the Iroquois nations, but it was not disingenuous mimicry. Johnson respected Indians and their ethic of reciprocity. He understood how reciprocal exchanges with them engendered and confirmed trust, comradeship, and mutual obligation. He was undoubtedly the source of the observation his brother Warren recorded: "If an Indian takes you for a Mate, or friend, he will doe any thing for you, & Expects the same from you; but must have the greatest opinion of you before they commence Such a friendship."[94] By using his resources with these Indian notions of propriety in mind, Sir William won the "greatest opinion" and abiding fealty of many Mohawks and their native allies. Records document how frequently he showed them, by acts of charity and hospitality, that he would "doe any thing" for his friends. He made them gifts not only from the goods and money his English superiors provided but also from his personal store of wealth.[95] In return, according to Johnson, Indian friends insisted that he accept their gifts, including more than one valuable tract of land. He was also able to purchase tribal lands for his private use and for non-Indian peers. By the time of his death, he had accumulated more real estate than any colonist in North America except William Penn.[96]

Thus, while Mohawks could conceive of Johnson as an especially fortunate and generous sachem (and did confer that title on him), he could regard himself as a British squire whose dependents happened to include Indians.[97] But there was no convenient analogue in British society for the status that Indian women expected vis-à-vis eminent men, including Johnson. Unlike women in England or Ireland, Iroquois matrons had an acknowledged role in decisions about war, peace, and the disposition of vital resources. When Johnson balked at discussing military issues with the matrons, Indian men tried to set him straight. One explained that women were properly present at war councils, "being of much estimation among Us, in that we proceed from them, & they provide our Warriors with provisions when they go abroad."[98] Nor did the Indians permit Johnson to flout women's authority over Iroquois land, foodstuffs, and houses. In 1763, a Mohawk sachem insisted that Warraghiyagey ask the women as well as the men to approve a land sale because the women were "the

Truest Owners being the persons who labour on the Lands, and therefore are esteemed in that light."[99] Consequently, when Johnson made Molly Brant his "housekeeper"—his wife in Mohawk eyes—he was well aware that she could promote his interests at Indian councils. It is unclear whether he also foresaw that she would use his material resources to enhance her standing among Mohawks and thus eventually compel Johnson's British peers to acknowledge her importance.[100]

Molly warmed quickly to the opportunities for influence that her partnership with Johnson presented. She took charge of providing for the baronet's endless stream of house guests, who included many Indians. At Johnson Hall, the spacious mansion he built in 1763, Sir William hosted conferences with tribal delegations whose care and feeding was largely Molly's responsibility. To that end, she purchased quantities of blankets, clothing, and rum on Johnson's account. She also met requests for material aid that individual Indians directed specifically to her.[101] Isabel Kelsay, Joseph Brant's biographer, vividly explains the effect of Molly's benevolence on her standing among Indians. "The more meals Molly served, the more blankets and shirts she handed out, the more drams she poured, the more small gifts of cash she made to indigent and begging Indians, the more orders on merchants she authorized, the greater her influence grew." Many acquaintances and observers attested to that influence. The generous mistress of Johnson Hall, they agreed, had "great sway" in the Iroquois nations.[102]

While filling the role of a prosperous Mohawk matron attentive to her people's needs, Molly Brant also conducted herself in ways that met the approval of genteel non-Indians. Several of Johnson's distinguished White visitors described her as a comely, sensible woman who performed with poise the gentlewoman's role of gracious hostess. Her decorum was such that Lady Susan O'Brien considered her "well-bred" and "pleasant." According to at least one source, Molly spoke English well and was literate in Mohawk if not in English. She directed the labor of many indentured servants and slaves, thus defying the stereotype of the overworked Indian "squaw." She also had a patrician's taste for personal finery and expensive home furnishings. Although she usually dressed in Mohawk style, non-Indians recognized the fabrics she used as "the finest of their kind."[103]

Johnson's death in 1774 reduced but did not eliminate the wealth Molly could dispense to Indian friends and constituents. By will, the baronet passed much of his real estate and nearly half his money to a son from his first marriage, but he did not neglect his "prudent & faithfull Housekeeper Mary Brant" or the children she had borne him. To Molly he bequeathed a slave, two hundred pounds in currency, and a life estate in some of the land the Mohawks had given him. In addition, he did not presume to allocate the contents of Molly's room at Johnson Hall. Each of her eight surviving children received cash, more than a thousand acres of land, and a share of their father's slaves and clothing.[104] When the widow Brant and her brood returned to Canajoharie, they brought an accumulation of wealth no family there could match. Three years later, forced by warfare to flee in a hurry, Molly left behind belongings numerous and luxurious enough to arouse the envy of all but the richest Whites: fine blankets and featherbeds, silver flatware and mugs, china plates and cups, an expensive chaise, silk cloaks, satin gowns in the French style, laced hats, a violin, music books, and hundreds of silver buckles and brooches. On his errand to England after the war, Joseph requested and received more money to cover her losses than his.[105]

Molly apparently used some of her inheritance to stock up on trade goods. Tench Tilghman, touring Iroquois country in 1775 to determine the Indians' view of the colonial independence movement, found "the favourite Mistress of the late Sr. William" carrying on "a small Trade" with Mohawks around Canajoharie. Although Tilghman saw Molly then as a "poor Creature . . . 'fallen from her high Estate,'" and she seemed to agree, he also remarked, "The Indians pay her great respect." She had their respect not only because of her long-time affiliation with Warraghiyagey and her status as a Turtle clan matron, but also because she remained a generous host and benefactor.[106]

Molly Brant expected continuing respect from Sir William's White friends as well. Those British friends did show her respect, especially when she made herself useful to the Crown during the Revolutionary War, first by passing intelligence to and from the Iroquois, and later by defusing the anger of Indians who suspected their English allies of stinginess and misplaced favoritism. In exchange for Molly's vital services, royal officials and loyalist merchants pledged to support her. The costs of doing that were considerable because, in addition to caring for a big family, she felt "obliged to keep . . . open house for all those Indians that [had] any weight in the 6 Nations confederacy," which was "pretty expensive to her." She helped herself to such a volume of goods from British stores that accusations of greed circulated behind her back; but most of the goods were destined for distribution to Indians from whom she wanted continuing allegiance.[107]

Although Molly Brant's extraordinary political clout waned when the war ended, tangible expressions of British gratitude enabled her to live in genteel fashion among non-Indians until she died in 1796. From the royal government, she received land, two suitably comfortable houses in the new settlement of Kingston, and a substantial military pension. She was a charter member and active parishioner of the local Anglican church. The willingness of high-ranking non-Indians to associate with her is also evident from her children's life stories. Five of Molly's daughters married men in the colonial upper crust—a physician, a legislator, and three military officers. (The sixth daughter remained single, even though she was reputedly "handsome . . . & a perfect Lady.")[108]

William Johnson and Molly Brant groomed their children for admission to the region's most powerful and prosperous elite—the colonial gentry—by sending them to school, providing them with substantial property, and introducing them to the "better sort" of Whites. The daughters, graced with Christian educations and manners pleasing to refined Britons, could join the Anglo-American gentry simply by attracting and accepting well-bred White suitors, whose status they then shared. The sons could not attain genteel status by marriage; they had to earn it by fulfilling a public role prescribed for respectable British men, and such roles required money as well as appropriate education. Johnson therefore asked a merchant colleague to mentor Peter, their oldest child, and Molly pointed her orphaned younger son George in a similar direction. Neither boy became a prosperous gentleman, however. Peter, who did show aptitude and enthusiasm for business matters, died in battle in 1777; George apparently opted to live among Indians, leaving few tracks for historians to follow.[109] But Molly and William had another protegé, who proved to be a bright and long-lived student of elite British culture: Molly's brother Joseph. Although Joseph Brant rose to the top in Mohawk ranks rather than the colonial hierarchy, his cultivated gentility was a significant factor in his belief and in the perception of many Whites that he was a suitable Indian liaison to colonial leaders.

During Joseph's childhood in Canajoharie, Mohawk relatives prepared him for the prescribed male roles of hunter and warrior. He was a teenager when his new brother-in-law arranged for his education in the ways of the British gentry. At Sir William's request, a school that would later become Dartmouth College admitted Joseph and concentrated during his short stay there on developing his English proficiency. Johnson saw to it afterward that the young man had government employment and a commission in the colonial army. Sir William was probably responsible as well for Joseph's acceptance in the fraternity of Freemasonry, which claimed as members many of colonial society's prominent men.[110] Brant did not pair this social climbing with a renunciation of his Mohawk training or tastes. He earned the reputation for ferocity in battle that Iroquois men prized, and he often dressed the part of the Mohawk warrior—in

When Joseph Brant sat for this portrait by Ezra Ames in 1806, he had achieved the material prosperity that enabled him to indulge a taste for such luxuries as imported furniture, silver and china table settings, fine wine, and European art, yet he reportedly retained his preference for Mohawk-style dress. Courtesy of Fenimore Art Museum, Cooperstown, N.Y.

leggings and moccasins, brass armbands, and earbobs rather than knee pants, buckled shoes, and cocked hats. But thanks to Johnson's example, he also acquired, and was eventually able to indulge, a taste for symmetrical Georgian mansions, upholstered chairs, fine wines, silk and lace, delicate porcelain tea cups, and imported musical instruments. Alan Taylor calls the elegant house where Brant spent his later years a "stage to perform his hybridity as an Indian gentleman."[111]

The most important lesson William Johnson imparted was a way of thinking about land and rights to land. By the time Joseph Brant was a sachem known to Mohawks as Thayendanegea, he understood how non-Indians commodified land and derived power from its ownership.[112] For that reason among others, he was well equipped to negotiate on Indians' behalf with agents of colonial expansion. Tapped for that role many times after the war, he advocated a strategy that his Irish mentor would have approved: ceding surplus Indian territory to Whites, but retaining land on which Indians could support themselves as non-Indians did. Selling land to Whites was a sensible option, Brant maintained, if the buyers paid what the land was worth to them and Indians held onto crucial acreage, putting it to gainful use.

For his ability to make Whites pay well, Brant won respect from Indians as well as non-Indians. Mississaugas asked him to serve as their spokesman when they negotiated a land cession in 1798. "They say that Brant is fittest to be their Chief," a colonial agent explained, "because he alone knows the value of Land." John Norton, a self-described Scot-Cherokee adopted by the Mohawks at Grand River, also lauded Brant's astute bargaining. According to Norton, Brant "obtained a much higher price for a few Townships of Land, which he disposed of in behalf of the Five Nations, than had ever been paid to the Aborigine of America."[113]

For the wealth and power that accrued to Brant in the course of his offices as negotiator, some Indians and non-Indians also resented him. Many readily believed rumors that he took a hefty commission for arranging the sale of some Grand River reserve lands—a sale he rationalized as necessary and sensible because hunting had declined, and the Indians needed money more than territory devoid of game. Brant's management of another land sale exposed him to charges of embezzlement. When defending himself successfully against those charges, he claimed that opportunities to make money at his people's expense did not tempt him because he had his own private land, where he could generate income enough to meet his needs.[114]

Brant did not say then, but he surely thought, that his needs as a leader and representative of Mohawks included access to much more wealth than common Indians or Whites required. Although he may have appeared to want a growing stock of property for its own sake, he could explain that he merely sought the wherewithal to fulfill a sachem's responsibility to visitors and needy followers. What Brant craved most was the prestige and influence that followed—in colonial capitals as well as Indian country—from controlling valued commodities and bestowing them on others. To feed the craving, he acted shrewdly on the knowledge that land had become the most valuable commodity of all for Indians as for non-Indians. Moravian missionary John Heckewelder saw this during a stop at Grand River in 1798. The famous Mohawk sachem, he observed, "sells land to the white people, or permits them to settle on it, at his discretion, and on the terms which he is pleased to prescribe; and all the settlers are in a kind of vassalage to him."[115] Joseph Brant, the sachem Thayendanegea, had learned well from William Johnson's example.

Unlike William Johnson or Coosaponakeesa's father, most White men took little or no trouble to educate children they had by Indian women. Even if they tried, many could not overcome the expectation in matrilineal native societies that a mother and her blood kin would teach her children.[116] Yet Johnson was not the only colonial patriarch who equipped his biracial offspring to join the emergent American gentry. Lachlan McGillivray did the same. A Scot who reached colonial Georgia's social and economic summit by way of his trading post in Creek country, McGillivray envisioned a lucrative career in business for his son Alexander. Had it not been for the American Revolution, that vision might have become reality. Like Joseph Brant and William Johnson's son Peter, Alexander McGillivray was a smart lad who readily absorbed lessons in economic culture from his British kin. When the colonial rebellion began in 1775, Alexander was a budding merchant-planter. During the war, however, he cast his lot with his mother's Upper Creek people. And although his subsequent commercial activity enriched and empowered him, he maintained that his practices were consistent with Creek ideals.

In early boyhood, Alexander McGillivray's education was probably the responsibility of his mother Sehoy and her relatives at Little Tallassee, where Lachlan had a store and plantation.[117] But when Lachlan moved to Augusta in 1755—if his biographer is correct—he took his six-year-old son with him, then sent the boy a year later to study with a Scottish cousin in Charlestown.[118] While Alexander was in South Carolina, his father acquired several dozen slaves, several thousand acres of land in Georgia (two hundred in Alexander's name), and appointments to government office. By virtue of his wealth and public roles, Lachlan McGillivray—husband of a Creek, father of three Creek children, and host of myriad Creek visitors to Georgia—had become a pillar of Georgia's nascent genteel establishment.

When Alexander returned to Georgia at age seventeen, he had ample opportunity to see how the colony's elite lived and ample grounds to expect that he would join them. He resided with his father on a princely new plantation near Savannah, witnessing real estate transactions and deals that added rapidly to Lachlan's wealth. Alexander's appearance and speech did not advertise his Creek ancestry. After meeting him several years later, Abigail Adams wrote, "I should never suspect him to be of that Nation, as he is not very dark" and "speaks English like a Native."[119] Under Lachlan's will, Alexander stood to inherit one thousand pounds, at least two hundred acres, and one-fifth of the remainder of an estate whose estimated value was more than twenty-one thousand pounds. But if the son expected to follow his father's steps, the War for Independence forced a change of plans. Lachlan, a loyalist, escaped wrathful rebels by retreating with his portable wealth to Scotland. Alexander, like several hundred other loyalists, took refuge in Creek territory.[120]

Alexander McGillivray's star then rose swiftly in the Creek firmament. It got a boost from his distinguished lineage: his mother belonged to the powerful Wind clan, and his uncle Red Shoes was a preeminent Creek headman.

Historian Michael Green points out that McGillivray "had clan kinsmen in influential positions throughout the Nation, bound by clan obligations and encouraged by clan loyalties to be receptive to him and his ideas." Creeks were also receptive because Alexander had what it took in the 1780s to manage their all-important relations with Euro-Americans: familiarity with merchants and colonial officials, fluency in English, innate shrewdness, and daring. At the war's end, his status among Creeks, though not uncontested, was likely higher than the rank he could have attained among Georgians. Even if the revolutionaries had not confiscated his property in Georgia, he probably would have stayed away. By his account, the Creeks' cause had become his cause.[121]

McGillivray's stated aim as a *mico* or "beloved man" in his native nation was to preserve Creek territory, autonomy, and economic well-being. Like Mohawks in the same period, his people faced the conjoined threats of dependency on the declining peltry trade and Euro-Americans' growing demand for land. A skillful self-promoter, McGillivray led agents of the United States to believe that Creeks would back any course of responsive action he recommended. Accordingly, American leaders, intent by 1790 on avoiding war with Indians while persuading them to cede land, paid McGillivray close and seemingly deferential attention.[122] He was much on George Washington's mind in 1789, when the new U.S. president advised his southern military commissioners, "Mr. McGilivrey is stated to possess great abilities an[d] unlimited influence over the Creek nation and part of the Cherokees." Washington's information came from Secretary of War Henry Knox, who cited McGillivray's "english Education," great "abilities and ambition," and "unbounded" resentment of Georgia "for confiscating his Father's estate, and the estates of his other friends . . . several of whom reside with him among the Creeks." Knox saved the most important information about the Creek *mico* for last. McGillivray, he noted, "is said to be a partner of a trading house, which has the monopoly of the trade of the Creeks."[123]

Knox and other Americans had an exaggerated estimate of McGillivray's power over Creeks, who jealously guarded their local communities' autonomy and their individual freedom from coercive governance.[124] Nonetheless, McGillivray did have uncommon ability to secure Creek compliance with his wishes, in part because he was the principal conduit of the trade goods they needed for personal use and for the exchanges that structured their social and political relations. In 1784, he had become an agent and probably a partner of the Florida-based trading firm Panton, Leslie and Company. When he subsequently accepted appointment as commissary for Florida's Spanish government, McGillivray gained a near-monopoly on the flow of goods, guns, and ammunition to Creek country. Michael Green explains:

> Every town had a Panton, Leslie and Company trader who did business on a license issued by McGillivray, subject to a body of regulations which McGillivray, as a Creek headman, helped to write, and which McGillivray, as Spanish commissary, enforced. In his Spanish capacity McGillivray also distributed the king's presents. . . . But what he gave he could also withhold. . . . Headmen aligned with McGillivray's opponents had trouble arming their hunters and warriors. While McGillivray's largesse, direct and indirect, was an important source of power, the threat of its discontinuation was even more important.[125]

As outsiders competed for influence with McGillivray, a number of them dangled economic bait in his line of vision. Not only did the Spanish and U.S. governments offer pay, but Georgia officials talked of conditionally restoring his father's estate, and land speculators proposed to cut him in on profits if he would endorse their venture.[126] To some of his critics—Indian and non-Indian—McGillivray appeared all-too susceptible to such bribery, especially after word leaked out in 1790 that the United States had rewarded him under the table for signing a treaty in New York. The payoff was a military commission, an annual salary of $1,200, and an exclusive right to import $60,000 worth of American goods into Creek country each year, duty-free. Not long afterward, U.S. officials thought they had proof that McGillivray valued money more than honor when he accepted additional pay from Spain despite a treaty clause binding Creeks to forsake their Spanish friends.[127]

McGillivray's lifestyle could also be construed as proof of his ambition for private wealth. At a time when most Creeks raised crops on a few acres and built nothing sturdier than wattle-and-daub shelters with earthen floors, he had several large plantations and at least two substantial houses, one of them on his father's former estate at Little Tallassee. To work the land and tend his abundant livestock, he kept about sixty slaves and hired a White overseer. He may also have had slaves in Spanish territory. He always traveled with two servants. Genteel visitors to his home found nothing lacking in the quality and quantity of the food and drink provided; the wines and spirits were choice imports. Moreover, by historian Claudio Saunt's calculation, McGillivray's annual salaries in 1792 totaled 200 times more than a typical Creek hunter could earn selling skins.[128]

Nevertheless, like Joseph Brant, McGillivray protested often and eloquently that he was not mercenary—that instead, he had sacrificed income or property for the good of his mother's people. To assure his colleagues at Panton, Leslie and Company that the firm could depend on his integrity, he said his part in the trade did "not spring entirely from motives of interest" but reflected a desire for his "poor, abandoned compatriots" to have "all the advantages that seem . . . possible." In another letter, he explained, "I have no family which obliges me to accumulate possessions; for although I have some negroes and a few dependents, since I cannot use wealth in this country and expect never to leave it, all that I want is a decent living." Three months before the 1790 treaty with the United States, McGillivray declared that he would "certainly be opulent and independent" if the Americans did return his "rich estates"; yet even though his means at the time fell "far short of abundance," he would refuse any offer that came with conditions unacceptable to his "friends." Shortly after the treaty, he wrote to a Spanish officer, "Being in general little influenced by personal considerations I did not stipulate anything . . . with respect to my estates in Georgia and South Carolina. . . . It is a well known fact that I am not greedy." A charge of greed, he implied in other correspondence, was more appropriately leveled at some of his Creek critics, who did not scruple to sell Creek land if that would satisfy their unceasing quest for presents.[129]

To Saunt, who has documented the appearance of an acquisitive economic ethos among Creeks, these protestations smack of hypocrisy. Other scholars give them credence. Biographer John Caughey points out that McGillivray served for years as a poorly paid Spanish agent without requesting a raise, spurned an offer from Georgia to return his father's property because it was conditioned on his turning his back on the Spanish, did not try to wring the maximum possible monetary inducement from the Americans who wanted his signature on a treaty, and did not solicit added pay from Spain after the treaty. Michael Green suggests that money motivated McGillivray much less than power or recognition. Emoluments from the United States and Spain, Green reasons, were probably important to him not because he wanted the money, but because he wanted the entrée to government chambers that came with his salaried positions.[130]

Like Joseph Brant, McGillivray understood that control of land was another possible basis for the prestige and authority he desired. If nothing else, the experience of responding to repeated American demands for Creek territory taught him that the new republic valued Indian land more than it valued Indians' trade. In the treaty negotiations of 1790, he said he agreed with U.S. representatives that Creeks should make use of their land as Whites did instead of claiming vast undeveloped tracts for hunting. Perhaps he planned to shift his own economic focus from trade to landownership and development. He showed in other actions that he was not categorically opposed to speculating in real estate.[131] But if he had lived long enough to put his money where his mouth was in 1790, his model of land use would have been that of slave-owning White planters in his region, rather than that of the neo-feudal landlords Brant saw in the North.[132] Because McGillivray died a few years later, posterity can only guess at the principles or impulses that would have guided his economic strategy after 1812, when a U.S. victory in war against Britain and rebellious Creeks dimmed Indian hopes of preventing American expansion.[133]

As in the case of Joseph Brant, we cannot know for certain whether Alexander McGillivray could hold a mirror to his face, look himself in the eye and say, without suppressing a smirk or shifting his gaze, that he never wanted great riches. We can be confident, however, that he wanted respect. He wanted it from people who said they respected men for showing that economic gain motivated them less than preserving personal honor. The people he had in mind included non-Indians as well as Indians. After all, White Americans expected their high-ranking citizens to exhibit some of the same virtues that Indians sought in leaders—liberality, unstinting hospitality, and selfless public service.[134] The challenge for McGillivray was that plentiful wealth was required to make liberality, hospitality, and public influence possible; yet neither Indians nor Whites would approve if he seemed crassly concerned with accumulating more wealth.[135]

McGillivray's strategy for maximizing his importance was stunningly effective for a decade, but if he had lived beyond that, success would have been hard to sustain. Creeks were not oblivious to the possibility that a selfish or self-aggrandizing man would abuse their system of allocating wealth and power. They could see that McGillivray drew political strength from their own weakness—their dependency on trade goods—and from their practice of deferring to benefactors. Not surprisingly, therefore, Creek resistance to McGillivray's power was growing by the time he died.[136] The respect that Whites paid McGillivray was also unreliable. If Americans believed money could buy McGillivray's cooperation, they were unlikely to admire him any more than he admired the Creeks he could bribe with gifts. More important, Americans' respect was conditioned on McGillivray's presumed ability to bring the Creek confederacy into the United States' orbit. Their respect would dissipate if he wielded his power as they hoped—that is, if he persuaded Creeks to relinquish land—because he would thereby contribute to a significant loss of Creek power and, with it, his own power.

In the second half of the eighteenth century, eastern North America was a theater of dramatic interactions between indigenous nations and the colonies planted by European states. Those dramas had starring roles for adept intermediaries. Access to wealth helped Alexander McGillivray, William Johnson, Molly Brant, Joseph Brant, and Coosaponakeesa or Mary Musgrove Bosomworth land such roles, which in turn afforded access to more wealth and a means of influencing other actors. Yet each of these ambitious individuals aspired to be more than a rich intercultural mediator. Each hoped for recognition in both immigrant and native societies as a person of "the better sort."

For William Johnson, admission to the upper echelon of colonial society was a realistic hope. Indeed, thanks to his genteel British origins, his head for business, his appointment to public office, and his extensive land acquisitions, Johnson did attain the colonies' highest social rank. His simultaneous climb to a comparable status among the Iroquois was a credit to his perceptiveness and his convincing performance of a sachem's traditional role. Indians saw that Sir William not only had power to secure wealth but also understood the importance of faithfully meeting his friends' needs for some of that wealth.

From a present-day standpoint, the hopes of Coosaponakeesa, Joseph Brant, Molly Brant, and Alexander McGillivray seem more quixotic because they were identified as Indians, and we know that supremacist Euro-Americans eventually gained the power to dominate and demote Indians. In the 1700s, however, the relative status of Indians and non-Indians still seemed negotiable, at least to these four self-assured individuals of indigenous descent. They were acquainted with influential gentry such as Johnson and apparently thought they could fill much the same role to the satisfaction of Whites as well as Indians. The professed ethos of leadership in British colonial society seemed congruent in essential respects with the ethos of Indian leadership. A person who acquired wealth and shared much of it could imagine that he or she displayed both the virtues of an Indian leader and some ideals of a high-ranking Briton.

Because the Brants, McGillivray, and Coosaponakeesa disseminated large amounts of wealth as Indian ethics required, they did earn respect from many Indians. But they also departed from indigenous tradition in ways that raised questions about their devotion to indigenous values. Systematically developing a fund of personal wealth and luxuries, as the two Creeks and Joseph Brant did, was not a prerequisite for authority in either Iroquois or Creek society. Many leaders in both Indian confederacies were richer than their neighbors only in wisdom and courage.[137] Nor was there a tradition in their nations of acquiring land with intent to lease or sell it for gain, as Coosaponakeesa, McGillivray, and Joseph Brant did or planned to do. Yet all four people could have explained their conduct as consistent with a native leader's traditional obligation to meet followers' material needs. They were simply meeting new needs with new forms of wealth and new ways of obtaining wealth. Thus, Coosaponakeesa, the Brants, and McGillivray cast themselves as appropriate successors to the ancestral Indian elite, and many Indians found them believable.

All four succeeded, too, in getting genteel Whites to identify them as persons of high standing and quality. The prevailing concept of gentility made that accomplishment possible. If asked how they knew gentility when they saw it, Euro-Americans would not have relied solely or even primarily on real estate ownership, fine clothing, and luxurious home furnishings. They would also have emphasized dignified bearing, polite speech, liberality, and the will and ability to assume costly civic responsibilities. Non-Indian descriptions of the Brants, McGillivray, and Coosaponakeesa mention all those traits.[138] Of course, the surprise of meeting a mannerly, propertied Indian—so unlike the stereotypical savage—may have caused some Whites to overstate the degree of gentility they saw. And the four individuals' formidable negotiating skills probably added an incentive to speak well of them, since it reflected poorly on one's character to negotiate with an ignoble adversary. But Whites' descriptions of a regal Coosaponakeesa, a courteous Joseph Brant, a poised Molly Brant, and a hospitable Alexander McGillivray are plausible because they describe traits that Indians also prized in their leaders.

The idea that an Indian could attain gentility was compatible with other trends in Euro-American thought. Resentment of hereditary aristocrats and well-known instances of social mobility had led many colonists to believe that a classic education could enable a person to move into the gentry from a lower class.[139] This belief particularly benefited McGillivray, whose erudition was at least as impressive as William Johnson's. The Brants and Mary Musgrove did not have formal education of the same caliber, but they were literate and familiar with some European intellectual traditions, especially Christianity. Additionally, Britons schooled in Enlightenment thought were inclined to regard "Indian" more as a cultural category than a biological one. The seeds of nineteenth-century racism had sprouted in American soil by the late 1700s, largely where colonists had resorted to meeting labor needs with enslaved Africans, but also where many Indians and Whites had shed each other's blood. Still, a significant proportion of Whites did not see aboriginal ancestry per se as a hindrance to an Indian's advancement from "savagery" to a respectable civilized state.[140] Attributing nobility to selected Indians also served the purpose of patriots who contrasted the decadence of Europe's hereditary aristocrats with the natural nobility of accomplished Americans. After all, who was more American than Indians?

As the 1700s drew to a close, an additional factor probably disposed some old-school gentry to credit people such as McGillivray or the Brants with genteel attributes. They feared that Americans were losing sight of gentility's meaning. Economic expansion was adding new names to the list of rich Americans, especially after the Revolution, and the nouveaux riches were eager to claim high rank. People with older pedigrees felt called to justify their claim of distinction on grounds other than the size of their fortunes. When they praised dignified, hospitable Indians who articulated an ethic of economic self-sacrifice, they implicitly faulted the White upstarts for crass commercialism. Insisting that gentility rested in noble character traits rather than wealth, they resisted the leveling of the old social hierarchy with an argument for the inclusion of some Indians.[141]

Not that it was a certification of spotless character to be identified as a gentleman or lady as well as a sachem, matron, or beloved man. The role that ambitious Indians assumed was a delicate balancing act, and there were spectators on both sides who fully expected to see them fall into shame or villainy. If they leaned too far in the direction of pursuing riches, they could expect scorn from Indians who considered it "foolish and demeaning to labor beyond what they needed to subsist."[142] Whites who saw an Indian as keen on building a personal fortune might cater to that ambition while demanding reciprocal favors that threatened the indigenous nation's interests. Ironically, aspiring Indian gentry were also likely to face accusations of vulgar cupidity from the same Whites who tried to bribe them, and to suffer sabotage from Indians who envied the honors and powers that Whites bestowed.[143]

Mary Bosomworth, the Brants, and Alexander McGillivray did hear charges of greed and corruption coming from both sides of the high-wire they walked. Impressive personal capabilities enabled them to shrug off these challenges and maintain their eminence, but circumstances were also right at the time for their feats of cultural hybridity. Conditions called for people with their attributes, talents, resources, and strategic vision. Before the American Revolution, European colonies needed Indians' trade, and their military support or neutrality, and Indians needed European goods. Indians west of the Appalachians still had autonomy and control of vast undeveloped lands. Even as late as the 1790s, no one in North America knew what the long-term relationship between such autonomous native societies and colonial nation-states would be. Whites could not yet determine the relationship unilaterally. In that context, the services of bicultural people such as the Brants, McGillivray, and

Coosaponakeesa—orchestrating and mediating Indians' relations with non-Indians—were arguably more important than at any other time in American history.[144]

Performing that public service did not prevent the intermediaries from serving selfish interests at the same time. They could play to Indians' admiration for generosity with the aim of building their personal wealth and influence. But it was not greed, corruption, extravagance, or improvident generosity on their part that ultimately queered the relations of Indian gentry with upper-class Whites and undermined their power to affect the course of events on American soil. Rather, it was as advocates of Indian sovereignty and landownership that they most offended Whites, and it was the growing White power to take Indian land that would ultimately doom the well-to-do Indians' strategy for ensuring their peoples' autonomy and prosperity.[145]

The dispute about Mary Bosomworth's land was a harbinger of the irreconcilable conflict to come. Joseph Brant foresaw the problem because Mohawks, facing a decline in the fur trade, had granted Whites the use of some land with an expectation of reciprocal support, only to find that the new occupants would neither share the land's bounty nor give Indians access to the land conveyed.[146] Alexander McGillivray recognized the problem when Whites encroached on Creek territory from the east. He saw their hunger for Indian land, their disdain for Indian ways of using the land, and their expectation that Indians would pay trade debts in land. A well-founded belief that land-hungry Euro-Americans could not be trusted to respect Indian territory or Indian channels of authority largely explains the decision that the Brants, McGillivray, and many other Indians made to side with the British government in the Revolutionary War. They thought the colonial rebels were less likely than the king to respect Indian landownership or the leadership of affluent Indians who had land of their own to protect.[147]

Events following the rebel victory confirmed the Indian loyalists' perspicacity. Branded by many Americans as wicked enemies of the republic—a righteous republic whose survival supposedly depended on widespread White landownership—Indians of all ranks in the trans-Appalachian West would soon find that the new United States had no use for them.[148]

3

Civilized Indian Nations

In 1835, President Andrew Jackson, professing a desire to put Indians "be-yond the reach of the moral evils . . . hastening . . . [their] destruction," urged Cherokees to move west of the Mississippi River. Several of their brethren had recently agreed to terms for such a move. The sooner the rest of the nation approved that arrangement with the American government, the sooner Chero-kees could begin a "career of improvement and prosperity." Although Jackson purported to know that a large portion of the Indians had "acquired little or no property in the soil itself, or in any article of personal property which can be useful to them," he assured them that the new pact afforded "due protection to private rights."[1]

Eighteen months later, despite strenuous Cherokee opposition, the U.S. Senate approved the relocation plan, formalized as the Treaty of New Echota. In a plea for reconsideration signed by 2,209 Cherokees, Chief John Ross con-tested Jackson's claim of solicitude for property rights. "By this instrument," he charged, "we are despoiled of our private possessions, the indefeasible property of individuals." Now that "unprincipled men" had done their dirty work, Cherokee hopes for justice rested on the consciences of honorable American lawmakers. And there was reason for hope, Ross indicated, because "our cause is your own . . . ; it is based upon your own principles, which we have learned from yourselves. . . . The result is manifest. The wildness of the forest has given place to comfortable dwellings and cultivated fields." "To you we address our reiterated prayers," the petition implored; "spare the wreck of our prosperity!"[2]

If the people who elected Chief Ross shared his principles, as his appeal suggested, there was indeed an affinity between Cherokee and American economic ideals. Ross had embraced values and practices that most Americans espoused. Moreover, he did so in circumstances remarkably similar to those that shaped Andrew Jackson's approach to economic affairs. Jackson and Ross were the son and grandson, respectively, of British immigrants to southern colonies in North America. As orphaned young men of meager means, Andrew Jackson and Daniel Ross had moved to the Tennessee frontier at about the same time. There, Jackson vaulted into the region's elite by engaging in commercial trade, obtaining land, and running a plantation with slave labor. The elder Ross likewise prospered as a trader-cum-slave-owning planter, and he passed his knack for lucrative activity on to his son. John Ross and Andrew Jackson were also alike in wanting political power even more ardently than profits and property. Once they did attain high office, both pledged to protect the liberties of humble people from arrogant men bent on appropriating their nations' wealth.[3] Despite all they had in common, however, the two men became implacable adversaries after Jackson resolved to rid Tennessee of its Cherokee neighbors. As the child of a Cherokee woman, Ross was a Cherokee, and he shared that people's determination to remain in the ancestral homeland.

If a single factor had to account for the antagonism between Jackson and Ross and their respective constituencies, it would be nationalism. In the 1830s, when Jackson finally realized his dream of evicting Cherokees and other Indians from the South, American nationalists triumphed over tribal nationalists. However, both species of nationalism grew from and nourished economic ambitions; and those ambitions, like the careers of Ross and Jackson, coincided in many respects. Contrary to Jackson's contention that a difference in economic culture necessitated Indians' relocation, the banishment of Cherokees, Choctaws, Chickasaws, and Creeks was a response to competition between peoples with comparable economic agendas and comparable enterprising classes. At bottom, American efforts to expel the tribes and the tribes' efforts to avoid expulsion were motivated by desires for the same resources and for prosperity achieved by similar means, including profitable private ventures. Standard bearers for the Indian nations aimed to glean wealth in the same places and ways as men who rallied Americans behind the banner of Indian removal. They explained their aims by invoking shared ideals.

Thus, Andrew Jackson and John Ross represented opposing sides of a debate about more than whether the Cherokees should relocate or whether the United States would displace all the indigenous peoples in the way of its expansion. At issue as well were some of the new American republic's defining values. Jackson spoke for many compatriots when he said that an essential disparity between key precepts of American life and Indian proclivities required the races' separation. Ross had ample non-Indian help disputing this allegation. He and numerous allies insisted that the real question was whether their opponents would honor a set of moral tenets they had all endorsed.

During the long controversy about Indian removal, many people did acknowledge an increasing resemblance between the southern indigenous societies and American society, especially in economic practices. Indian spokesmen and their White supporters cited this trend as a basis for coexistence and even for hope that Indian nations could eventually merge with the United States. They also argued that bedrock American legal and moral tenets required respect for Indians' property rights. But proponents of removal construed the tribes' land tenure system as a negation of property rights. Even when Indians made their livings as non-Indians did, the Whites who wanted them gone insisted that tribal economic culture differed fundamentally and intolerably from the American way. Indians, they maintained, were unwilling or unable to abandon a primitive communal life centered on hunting. Consequently, Indians languished in poverty while failing to realize the economic potential of their lands. Some Americans also said that the political economy of the tribes was unacceptably alien in another respect: a few shrewd men with inordinate appetites for wealth and power held sway there, resisting relocation because it threatened their selfish interests and aristocratic prerogatives. It did not trouble the critics that they were faulting Indians both for too little and for too much economic ambition. They effectively denied any contradiction by characterizing the rich tribe members as more White than Indian.

While the removal debate prompted White Americans and Indians to critique each other's economic orientations, it also focused debaters' attention on the conduct of their fellow citizens. The controversy arose as a surge of wealth-seeking activity fed, and in turn gained strength from, a rapid transformation of the American economy. Growing numbers of people in the States and in the Indian tribes were bent on adding significantly to their wealth, often by methods that seemed contrary to time-honored communitarian ideals. The zeal for profit-making also coincided with changes in tribal and U.S. governance, giving Indians as well as Americans reason to ponder the relationship of private riches to political power. Thus, for everyone concerned, the removal controversy was an opportunity to articulate and evaluate the premises that guided or might guide their economic relations.

The opportunity was not entirely squandered. Commentary on political-economic morality had prominent place in discourse about Indian removal. It masqueraded at times as religious or legal opinion, and it was subordinated at other times to pronouncements regarding racial traits. But thoughts about the ethics of seeking and deploying wealth were never far below the surface of interested parties' minds, and many of those thoughts found expression in letters, speeches, or publications bearing on "the Indian question." Tribal citizens as well as Americans took positions on issues such as the desirability of self-interested economic enterprise, the moral constraints on government in economic matters, and the corrupting influence of wealth in political arenas.

This does not mean that southern Indians' fate hung on the resolution of a principled debate about economic ethics. With coveted resources and the powers of several governments at stake, adversaries in the removal dispute were determined to prevail, not to find common philosophical ground. Regarding each other as dangerous and dishonest, they fought hyperbole with hyperbole and, in many instances, with hypocrisy. The discourse about morality reflected this polarization and animosity. To hear the antagonists tell it, their opponents were guilty of sins that imperiled the very foundations of a democratic nation. Ironically, the evils they named most often—excessive materialism and greed—were logical extremes of the economic ethos that spokesmen on both sides endorsed.

Psychologists would probably find a process called projection at work in the dispute, for there is evidence that some of the people who leveled charges of avarice were themselves prone to acquisitive behavior. People who fear or disapprove their own impulses are often quick to see them reflected in the behavior of others. When foes in the removal controversy studied each other and thought they saw familiar demons, many became passionate crusaders, counting on a righteous stance to deter attacks on their integrity. Historians have argued that so-called Jacksonians, most of whom favored Indians' expulsion, were especially apt to project their own sinful inclinations onto adversaries; and several prominent Jacksonian advocates of Indian removal were undoubtedly proverbial black pots decrying sooty kettles.[4] Even scrupulous Christians on the other side of the debate avoided some worthwhile soul-searching while denouncing the immorality of involuntary removal. Although they deplored the sins that acquisitive people were prone to commit, they strived to bring Indian economic culture into conformity with the market-oriented individualism that increasingly characterized American society. Lacking the power or will to discourage materialism except by sermons, they chastised those who put selfish worldly aims before virtue, but they also allied with people who probably deserved that scolding. During most of the debate about Indian policy, the people they accused of greed were White Americans, who answered in kind. But when tribe members eventually took opposing positions on the wisdom of moving west, they turned their accusations of avarice on each other as well. Desire for riches, they charged, had corrupted some Indians just as it had corrupted Whites in the United States.

Various historians have described how a culture of economic individualism and progress took hold in the early American republic, devaluing the modest material measures of well-being that prevailed in colonial agrarian society, justifying a general scramble for wealth, and enhancing the status of successful businessmen.[5] Other histories explain the contemporaneous developments that prompted many southern Indians to engage in new commercial activities and accumulate property, in some cases attaining a deluxe standard of living as well as leadership positions in their tribes.[6] But specialized scholarship can give the impression that these two revolutions in economic culture are separate stories. In fact, they not only occurred at the same time and took similar directions, they were interconnected.

The concurrent changes in Indian and non-Indian societies, though hardly mirror images of each other, were alike in key respects and rooted in the same phenomenon—the ascendance of economic endeavors geared to expanding markets. During the early decades of the nineteenth century, Americans by the thousands broke away from eastern farming communities and took up land in new areas of settlement, hoping to brighten their economic prospects. Meanwhile, Cherokees, Choctaws, Chickasaws, and Creeks left their clustered homes and contiguous cornfields in order to develop scattered cropland on their own. A large majority of the dispersing people, non-Indian as well as Indian, remained or became small-scale farmers producing mainly for their own subsistence. To realize more than a basic competence, a person had either to acquire command of extensive fertile land and subservient laborers or to sell popular goods or services. Pecuniary ambitions motivated many more Whites than Indians, but across the South, some citizens of the indigenous nations did become business owners. By marketing livestock, cash crops, merchandise, shipping and travel services, or interests in land, the luckiest of ambitious tribe members and Whites grew rich simultaneously.[7]

Euro-Americans set the models, the pace, and many of the conditions for these parallel developments. A feverish desire for gain had infected some residents of the British colonies prior to the Revolutionary War, although it was neither prevalent nor always welcome among small farmers, who were a majority of the colonial population.[8] Independence promoted the fever's spread by opening the West to migrants and land acquisitions. As transportation improvements followed, farmers who might formerly have left home seeking only land enough for self-support now hoped to profit from crop sales or speculation in real estate. After the War of 1812, as Americans annexed great swaths of new territory and commerce expanded, febrile visions of personal gain became epidemic. By the 1820s, foreign visitors generally agreed that Americans were a "restless, fortune-seeking people."[9]

Had they not been able to acquire vast territory from Indians, Americans probably would have viewed their economic opportunities differently. Land that Indians yielded up was the seed capital for a variety of Euro-American fortunes.[10] The perceived abundance of obtainable lands also fostered an energizing mythology of material progress. "Great numbers of early national Americans were convinced that their potential for material prosperity was unequaled anywhere else on earth," Cathy Matson writes, because they began to envision "the hinterlands less as a terrain filling with self-sufficient farms than as 'the greatest factory of American raw materials.'"[11]

Optimists pictured U.S. prosperity as the sum of individual economic achievements, which faced few apparent obstacles. In 1819, New York luminary C. D. Colden crowed, "While we have so many millions of acres of uncultivated land, it is impossible that any portion of our population should want employment." Myriad Americans shared his faith that their immense, expanding land base was insurance against the poverty and economic inequity disgracing Europe.[12] They were wrong, of course. The nostrum for get-rich fever was not evenly distributed. A relative handful of people—speculators, large-scale planters, importers and exporters, financiers—cornered much of the land supply. In the absence of a hereditary aristocracy, those people claimed the highest ranks of the country's social hierarchy.[13]

While United States territory was growing, and because it was growing, the territories of nearby Indian nations shrank. In the South, demand for new land and efforts to displace native occupants increased with the revenues of cotton producers. Americans not only badgered Indians to cede territory but also made it difficult in numerous ways for them to use land as they wished. Headmen gave in repeatedly to such pressure until, by 1820, the remaining acreage of each large southern tribe was smaller than the total amount it had relinquished.[14]

It is a dark irony that the primary incentive for White Americans to disperse in search of prosperity was an abundance of land, while southern Indians' main reason for dispersing was a shortage of land. Choctaws, Chickasaws, Creeks, and Cherokees had long prized and managed territory as much for the game it harbored as for the arable ground it encompassed—all the more so once they were dependent on goods purchased with deerskin.[15] Because commercial hunting required large tracts of uncultivated territory, it became a precarious livelihood when deer populations dwindled and tribesmen had to pay mounting trade debts by selling land. As their trade income and homelands shrank, many Indians adopted modes of production that seemed to work for non-Indians, particularly stock-raising and farming on separate homesteads.[16]

According to the Cherokee John Ridge, his nation's hunting-based economy was a thing of the past by 1826. In reply to an inquiry that year from statesman and ethnologist Albert Gallatin, Ridge wrote, "I don't know of one Cherokee who depends on the chase for subsistence." Instead, nearly all tribe members were farming. "A few," Ridge made a point of saying, "have grown cotton for the market & have realised good profits."[17] Another literate Cherokee was even more effusive about the tribe's transition to a market-oriented economy based in agriculture. On the nation's plains, David Brown reported in 1825, "numberless herds of cattle are dispersed . . . ; horses are plenty, and are used for servile purposes; numerous flocks of sheep, goats, and swine cover the valleys and hills."

> The natives carry on considerable trade with the adjoining States; and some of them export cotton, in boats, down the Tennessee to the Mississippi, and down that river to New Orleans. Apple and peach orchards are quite common, and gardens are cultivated, and much attention paid to them; butter and cheeses are seen on Cherokee tables. There are many public roads in the nation, and houses of entertainment kept by natives. . . . Cotton and woollen cloths are manufactured here; blankets, of various dimensions, manufactured by Cherokee hands, are very common; almost every family in the nation grows cotton for its own consumption. Industry and commercial enterprise are extending themselves in every part; nearly all the merchants in the nation are native Cherokees. . . . Indolence is discountenanced. . . . We are out of debt, and our public revenue is in a flourishing condition.[18]

Economic reorientation arguably brought greater prosperity to Cherokees than to Choctaws, Chickasaws, or Creeks—at least the Cherokee transition inspired the largest volume of sanguine commentary and historical documentation. But people in all four native nations took to raising cattle, clearing larger fields for family farms, growing cotton as well as corn, marketing produce, and doing business with their own merchants.[19]

In the tribes as in the United States, rewards of the new economic activities were unevenly distributed. While most Indians labored just to meet basic

Built in 1804 by James Vann and inherited by his son Joseph, the luxurious plantation house at Springplace contributed to the fame of the wealthiest Cherokee men in the early nineteenth century. Maintained and furnished according to the Vanns' rich tastes, the house is now a Georgia State Historic Site. Photograph by Alexandra Harmon, 2001.

needs, a few generated income enough to live in exceptional comfort. Outward signs of a family's affluence included spacious fenced fields of marketable crops worked by dark-skinned slaves, expensive clothing, large houses with glass windows, fine furniture, and servants who set the dinner table with porcelain, silver, and imported delicacies.[20] Missionary Samuel Worcester knew by sight how wealth was apportioned in the Cherokee Nation. Although Cherokee houses "are not *generally* well furnished," he wrote circa 1829, "a few are furnished even elegantly."[21] Other observers specified the luxuries that rich citizens of southern tribes enjoyed. John Norton, traveling from Mohawk country, stopped in 1809 at the house of "a wealthy Cherokee." "By trade and agriculture," Norton explained, the man "acquired a considerable property. He has *many negroes* and white servants to attend to the labours of the field, and a capacious building." Norton also marveled at the immense estate of James Vann, a Cherokee trader who "possessed at his death a *hundred negroes* employed on different plantations, besides a great sum in specie, and numerous herds of cattle; horses and hogs."[22]

The Vann estate, which passed from James to his son Joe, continued to dazzle visitors and Cherokees long after Norton's visit.[23] In 1836, Cherokee leaders, seeking restitution for property seized by Georgians, told Congress that Joseph Vann, "a native Cherokee, was a man of great wealth, had about eight hundred acres of land in cultivation; had made exstensive [*sic*] improvements, consisting, in part, of a brick house, costing about ten thousand dollars, mills, kitchens, negro houses, and other buildings. He had fine gardens, and extensive apple and peach orchards. His business was so extensive, he was compelled to employ an overseer and other agents." Federal appraisers ultimately awarded Vann the munificent sum of $26,979.25 to compensate for his loss of the plantation described to lawmakers, and they assigned a value of $10,459.85 to another spread in Tennessee where Vann took refuge before heading west with other banished Cherokees.[24]

Joe Vann's great wealth assured him of attention from later generations and historians as well. He has shared the spotlight with Cherokee contemporaries such as John Ross and Major Ridge, whose fame owes more to their political roles than to their wealth. But when ranked by the dollar value of their assets in the 1830s, Ross and Ridge do not fall far behind Vann. Appraisers pegged the property that Ross lost to invading Whites at $23,665.75. He deemed that figure much too low, but it was high enough, his biographer states, to make him "one of the five wealthiest men in the Cherokee nation, a distinction he shared with his brother Lewis and his friend Major Ridge."[25] An estate of that size also made Ross richer than most White southerners. Even three decades later, only 5.6 percent of people in the South had assets valued at more than $10,000.[26]

Postremoval appraisals do not account for human property that Vann, Ross, Ridge, and approximately 200 other Cherokees possessed. Vann's inventory of 110 slaves was the nation's largest. The tally of the runner-up was one hundred, but most Cherokee slaveowners had fewer than fifty slaves, and John Ross had about twenty at the time of removal. If, as missionary Cyrus Kingsbury estimated, field hands were worth $400 to $500 and skilled "negroes" fetched as much as $1,000 in 1825, then human chattel added at least $10,000 to John Ross's net worth and more than $50,000 to Joe Vann's.[27] Economic historian Lee Soltow calculated that possession of just twenty slaves placed an American among the top 8 percent of owners in 1830. A little over 1 percent owned more than fifty people, and only .004 percent were in a class with Joe Vann. Such numbers lend credibility to statements from contemporary observers that the richest Cherokees lived as well as or better than wealthy Whites in the region.[28]

Rich Cherokees had counterparts in the Creek, Choctaw, and Chickasaw nations. During the 1820s, rumors circulated that the Creek chief Big Warrior had bequeathed "six-score" slaves and $50,000 to his son.[29] One Choctaw with a Midas touch—Peter Pitchlynn—had two sections of improved land, fifty cattle, other livestock, and a corn harvest that sold for the equivalent of $18,000 in 1832. According to his biographer, Pitchlynn "converted some of the cash into slaves, purchasing five Negro girls ranging in age from eleven to thirteen years old and in price from $275 to $450. On other occasions, he made similar transactions in partnership with his father, and by October he owned or had an interest in forty-five Negroes." Fellow Choctaws Greenwood Leflore and David Folsom also each had flourishing plantations and thousands of dollars invested in slaves. Chickasaws known for their wealth included George Colbert, who operated ferries, stagecoaches, and roadside stands. Colbert reportedly sold a private land reserve for $40,000.[30]

Accounting for such well-endowed Indians is a different proposition than accounting for wealthy Whites of the same period. The eagerness and ability of many Americans to get rich does not puzzle scholars of the so-called market revolution. They and other historians trace Americans' reverence for private property and self-interested economic activity back at least to early English settlement in America. Although a lingering medieval ethos caused many of those settlers to doubt that commercial pursuits were honorable, their colonies were meant to make money, and their successful leaders knew how to turn a profit.[31] Colonists were also eager to acquire property because social ranks were unsettled in the New World, and a substantial estate could confer desirable status.[32] These seeds of acquisitiveness found room to grow during the 1700s as commerce expanded, more consumer goods became available, and enterprise seemed to promise greater material rewards for increasing numbers of people. A common heritage of antimaterialist ideals was not forgotten, but Americans began the 1800s with ample social and ideological impetus to seek private wealth.[33]

The same cannot be said of Cherokees, Choctaws, Chickasaws, and Creeks. The commercial practices and personal habits that enabled the Vanns and Big Warriors of their day to amass personal fortunes did not have obvious roots in tribal histories. When scholars look for such roots, they see recent growths grafted onto cultures that disdained possessiveness. They describe indigenous people who were unfamiliar with self-centered materialism or profit-oriented commerce. As late as the mid-1700s, they say, virtually everyone in the southern tribes idealized generosity, relied on networks of reciprocating kin and friends for their security, and prompted each other in ritualized ways to share the means of subsistence and distribute accumulated property.[34]

For evidence of Indian values in the early nineteenth century, scholars are indebted partly to amateur ethnographers of the time. One was George

Stiggins, a Virginian of Scottish and Natchez Indian descent who served in the 1830s as U.S. agent to the Creek Nation, where he had in-laws. Stiggins reported that headmen bore responsibility for publicly reprimanding persons "of bad repute," and a scolding was especially "acrimonious should there be an instance of a person . . . so churlish of his eatables as to be inhospitable . . . , such a niggardly person is termed by them a (no body)." Stiggins seldom saw such churlishness. Instead, Creeks were "ingeneral [*sic*] disinterested to a degree of negligence either in the distribution of their provisions to eat or the means for the acquisition of it or wealth." But Creeks also told Stiggins, apologetically, that thieves were no longer rare in their towns; exposure to the wealth and behavior of Whites had corrupted some Indians. Before that, "being raised poor and habituated to that life . . . they felt no anxiety for the goods or property of another, so they had no excitement to perpetrate acts of thievery for the acquisition of a thing that they did not crave nor know the want of."[35]

Many historians likewise blame (or credit) Whites for the appearance of acquisitive Indians. Some seem to assume that the mere sight of Europeans' marvelous possessions whetted Indian appetites for wealth and aroused natural desires to be as rich as the newcomers. Others simply note the high proportion of acquisitive tribe members who had White fathers, as if kinship or even "blood" is sufficient explanation for such a tendency. Scholars also commonly assert, without closer examination, that aboriginal principles eroded as Whites encouraged possessiveness.[36] But the turn of many Indians toward economic individualism requires more careful, compelling explanation. The transition to a new model of economic relations was a complex process.

When retracing this process, it is wise to bear in mind that seemingly unselfish Indian behavior did not indicate a lack of desire for riches. Regarding Creeks' customary readiness to share their possessions, Stiggins said, "It is not that their passions are indifferent either to the case of wealth or possession of property, for they are very fond of possessing property if they make no more use of it than the possessing of it." And indeed, contrary to an impression prevalent among Euro-Americans, southern Indians had not held all goods in common before encountering non-Indians. They recognized personal possessory rights to such things as hides, clothing, jewelry, weapons, tools, and cultivated plots of land. Furthermore, individuals reveled in acquiring and displaying ornaments and prestigious items. Men gained status by bringing riches home from war or hunts. And although it was customary to destroy or bury valuables when owners died, there was even precedent for the transmission of property from chiefs to male heirs.[37]

In other words, it was not a taste for wealth that Indians had to develop in order to be more like enterprising Whites; it was the habit of amassing property, and either retaining it or putting it to use in the generation of additional wealth that would stay within a limited family circle. Customs that encouraged people to distribute their possessions had to lose potency, and the advantages of keeping property for the long term had to outweigh the social disadvantages. According to Theda Perdue, a master scholar of southeastern Indian history, that process began when the individual exploits of hunters and warriors gained importance as a consequence of European commercial activity in the region.[38] Commerce with Whites also added to the cachet of a person who showed mercenary cunning, for there was no rule against trying to get the better of an outsider. Reciprocity was due only to kin.[39]

Indian hunters and warriors may have exulted in their ability to acquire brass bracelets and ruffled shirts, but very few began laying in supplies of bracelets and shirts for profitable resale. Moreover, southern tribes did not expect a man to be the sole source of his wife's and children's economic security, as Euro-Americans did. Instead, they counted on clan loyalties and the ethic of reciprocity to see them through times of scarcity. In sum, not many Indians made it their principal business before 1800 to exploit opportunities for profit and thus to build a family estate. Yet Major Ridge, Peter Pitchlynn, and George Colbert—to name a few—did just that; and many compatriots soon followed suit.

How did tribe members learn economic practices so different from those of their indigenous ancestors? They learned from non-Indians whose ideology justified the pursuit of private property and profit but was ambiguous enough for interpretations consonant with some Indian customs and ideals. They learned from commercial traders, agents of non-Indian governments, protocapitalist White relatives and neighbors, and industrious Christian missionaries, expecting to put their lessons to use in the service of tribal objectives. An account of their economic education will help to make sense of their part in the discourse on economic morality that accompanied the removal controversy.

Hundreds of non-Indian traders had contact with the southern tribes before the early 1800s, but the number who inspired Indians to emulate them was comparatively small, and the number who trained Indians to manage businesses and property was smaller still. Nonetheless, traders were the principal progenitors—some literal, some figurative—of the tribes' wealthy elite. Traders made their cultural influence felt in several ways. Some large firms identified well-connected tribe members and granted them extra credit, or engaged them as merchandise distributors. With such privileges came advice on the conduct necessary to preserve them. Individual traders also gained access to customers by taking on native partners—an arrangement that could amount to an apprenticeship in Whites' business methods.[40] But the most common and effective mentors of early Indian entrepreneurs were traders who established permanent residence and kin ties among Indians—men such as Scottish immigrant Robert Grearson. In the late 1790s, U.S. Indian agent Benjamin Hawkins found Grearson at home in Creek country, where he had a profitable trading post, a Creek wife, five "halfbreed" children, "large possessions, negros, cattle and horses." At the agent's suggestion, Grearson also opened a cotton cloth "manufactory" with female Creek employees. But in Hawkins's view, the Scot's most notable achievement was making his "whole family" respect him.[41]

Men like Grearson and the offspring who followed their lead are conspicuous in the historical record and probably account for historian William McLoughlin's assertion that intermarried White men "tended to bring up their children to act and think like whites." Theda Perdue, mindful of the record's bias, disagrees. Citing Hawkins's complaint that the traders were "almost all of them . . . as inattentive of their children as the Indians," Perdue infers that early White residents of Indian towns probably "lived like Indians, and they raised their children as Indians." Along with sociologist Duane Champagne, she thinks the children became "both white and red." Since a child customarily belonged to the mother's tribe and a maternal uncle usually educated her boys, that argument has substantial basis.[42]

Nevertheless, some exceptional White fathers had significant impact on the tribes' history because they did take responsibility for educating their children, and their children became pillars of the new economic elite. Louis Leflore, a Frenchman in business among the Choctaws, arranged for his Choctaw son to learn the ways of well-to-do Americans: he sent young Greenwood to live for five years with a wealthy White planter. The Briton John Pitchlynn, still a teenager when he settled in the Choctaw Nation, wed the Choctaw daughter of another White man and became the rich patriarch of a large brood to whom he conscientiously imparted the tenets of English culture. Daniel Ross, married to a Cherokee whose father and grandfather were Scottish traders, presided over a home "filled . . . with the latest American and English newspapers and an assortment of maps and books." Ross entrusted his children's instruction first to a private English tutor, then to schools in the States. While attending an academy in Tennessee, son John "boarded for a time with . . . one of the area's leading merchants and planters." A clerkship at a Tennessee trading firm rounded out John's education. By the time John Ross, Greenwood Leflore, Peter Pitchlynn, and many other bicultural children received bequests or valuable gifts from fathers raised in patrilineal cultures, they were prepared to manage property as their fathers did.[43]

Traders were not the only Whites residing in Indian country. Some of the others likewise coached Indians to procure and manage income-generating property. On his tour in 1809, John Norton met a young Cherokee he took at first to be a European. John Thompson, it turned out, was the son of a White U.S. government employee. No doubt the elder Thompson was pleased that his heir could boast of "an extensive improvement, abundance of cattle, several slaves . . . , some Anglo American Servants" and an American wife. Dozens of other southern tribe members were children of men stationed in the Indian nations as representatives of non-Indian governments—a role that did not preclude involvement in moneymaking ventures.[44]

Whether or not a federal agent had a knack for business, he was supposed to urge Indians in his bailiwick to adopt "civilized" economic practices. Benjamin Hawkins, a Carolina planter who could point to his own great wealth as an incentive to imitate Whites, took that assignment to heart when he became the first resident agent in the Creek Nation. Even though Hawkins declined to affiliate with Creeks by marriage, he claimed that his example, exhortations, and material aid induced many of them to create plantations on an American model.[45] In the same period, U.S. agent Return J. Meigs pressured Cherokees to take similar steps and made it clear that his government judged their competence by their material prosperity. Meigs urged Cherokee leaders to take pride in having "more money, more cattle, more horses, more and better cloathing than any other nation of Red men of equal numbers in America."[46]

Non-Indian officials provided an education in more sordid aspects of American economic culture when they strayed from the prescribed curriculum. Time and again, Indians saw representatives of federal and state governments make money by exploiting the power and access to resources that public office afforded. Cherokees watched, for instance, as U.S. agent Joseph McMinn allowed White friends to enrich themselves and their cronies by paying Indian emigrants far less for homes and farms than those improvements would fetch on resale. McMinn's friends included merchants who insisted that Indians take overvalued goods rather than cash in payment for their property. The agent allegedly arranged as well for confederates to lease ceded Indian land, then pocketed the rent instead of remitting it to the government.[47]

The tutelage of government employees is one of several reasons that a White parent or White ancestry was not a condition of success for Indian stu-

Although he was illiterate and did not speak English, the Cherokee known to Whites as Major Ridge opted to emulate the economic culture of familiar Euro-Americans. By middle age, he was a wealthy slave-owning commercial planter whose two-story frame house—surrounded by orchards and vineyards—had eight rooms, four brick fireplaces, glass windows, and a balcony with a glass door.

dents of American economic culture. Even so-called full-bloods could make a go of commercial farming, merchandising, or other businesses by following the examples or advice of acquaintances, Indian and White. James Taylor Carson names Choctaw chief Mushulatubbee and Greenwood Leflore's uncle, Robert Cole, as men with a talent and taste for making money, and with unbroken Indian lineage. In the case of illiterate, Cherokee-speaking Major Ridge, some reputed White ancestry was apparently unrelated to his education in business practices.[48]

To give his son and daughter the skills that helped him prosper, Ridge did not rely solely on home schooling. He also enrolled the children in Christian mission schools. Missionaries, too, endeavored to promote Indians' adoption of American economic culture, both in the classroom and by the example of mission operations. Although religious conversions were the evangelists' overriding concern, Protestant missionaries expected converts to make changes in daily conduct, and the conduct they urged was the kind a capitalist society required. Particularly after U.S. officials recruited churches to administer an Indian civilization fund that Congress established in 1819,·most mission sponsors concluded that their success depended on a "union of the arts of civilized life with moral and religious instruction." An essential condition of civilized life, as they defined it, was private property.[49]

Moravians founded the first mission among southern Indians when James Vann offered them land near his home in 1801. Other Protestant groups were slow to follow; but by the mid-1820s, Baptists, Methodists, Presbyterians, and the multi-denominational American Board of Commissioners for Foreign Missions (ABCFM) had stations scattered among Choctaws, Cherokees, Creeks, and Chickasaws. In Sunday sermons and schoolrooms, the missionaries described a god who looked with favor on industrious, thrifty people, rewarded them with prosperity, and expected them to honor each other's property rights.[50] To the deity's approval preachers added their own warm praise of efforts that brought Indians new wealth. When the *Missionary Herald* reported the results of a Choctaw property census, Reverend Cyrus Kingsbury contributed an introductory letter hailing his flock's "advance in dress, furniture, and all the comforts and conveniences of civilized life." "At the councils and other large meetings," he exulted, "the Indians . . . appear comfortably and decently and some of them richly clad. A great desire is manifested to obtain furniture for their houses, and some are already supplied in a manner not inferior to that of new settlers in our own country." Kingsbury's letter reached Indian eyes as a reprint in the Cherokee Nation's newspaper.[51]

As latecomers to Indian country, the missionaries often found themselves preaching their gospel of economic salvation to the converted. Many of the first children to attend their schools already appreciated the comforts that family wealth could buy (though some children of slaveowners did not appreciate the missionaries' insistence that no one deserved to enjoy wealth without hard work).[52] It was often the affluent Indians who facilitated the missions' establishment, as Vann did, and their motives were not primarily spiritual. With missions came economic opportunities for enterprising tribe members. The stations required supply roads, and roads benefited Indians who had products to market. An Indian grower might even sell produce to a mission if the residents could not fully provide for themselves. Missions and roads also attracted travelers whose needs a tribal businessman could supply. In addition, a few Indians valued missions for the paid employment they provided. In all these ways, resident Christian evangelists reinforced the lessons in economics that some Indians had already drawn from watching traders, government officials, and White commercial planters.[53]

With the hope that children of poor, "backward" Indians might also put their faith in self-interested enterprise, mission schools taught that hard work and thrift would lift a person from poverty to comfortable circumstances.[54] A corollary of this emphasis on self-support was disapproval of the unstinting hospitality and liberal gift-giving that Indians customarily practiced. The churchmen argued that such charity encouraged idleness. Seeking food and shelter from anyone but close kin was shameless begging. For fear that the children and their parents would expect gratuities from outsiders and not learn to rely on their own labor, Kingsbury hesitated to distribute donated clothing to his Choctaw pupils. "We wish ever to keep in mind," he cautioned, "that an injudicious bestowment of charity, increases the evil, it is designed to remedy. This is especially the case among savages."[55]

In the Christians' fine-tuned logic, begging was shameful, but coveting possessions was human nature and a necessary spur to productive effort. Accordingly, missionary teachers were not averse to molding pupils by appealing judiciously to presumed covetousness. They seemed to believe, as John Norton did, that "a little bribery used for the promotion of religion and industry may perhaps be excused, & leave us only to regret that the blindness of the bulk of Mankind sometimes may reduce us to that necessity." The principal challenge was to bribe in such a way as to "prevent the idle from squandering" what they received "& the avarice of others from being too much indulged." Staff at a Chickasaw mission thought they met such a challenge by rewarding children who paid "good attention to business" with chits valued at 6.25 cents, redeemable at mission stores for practical supplies.[56]

Admonitions from missionaries reached the ears of relatively few Indian children before the tribes' deportation in the 1830s. At the height of premoval evangelical efforts, when Cherokees, Choctaws, Chickasaws and Creeks were approximately 30,000 strong, the number of pupils in church-sponsored schools probably did not reach one thousand. Young tribe members who left home to study in the States, as John Ross and Ridge's son John did, were fewer still. Thus, the children deemed most in need of lessons on American culture were least likely to get them. Schools made sense primarily to families who already appreciated the economic value of knowing how to read, write, and crunch numbers.[57]

Children who arrived at mission schools speaking English and clothed like affluent Americans had experienced the world far differently than the children in moccasins and long shirts who spoke only Choctaw, Muskogee, Yuchi, or Cherokee. A process was under way by the 1820s that would sort people of the southern Indian nations into distinct classes. In contrast to the families who built spacious frame homes, furnished them in mahogany and chintz, invested in slaves, and cultivated relations with prosperous Whites, most of the Indians lived in small log cabins, plowed a few acres for corn and vegetables, raised just enough hogs and chickens to eat, and associated almost entirely with other Indians of modest means. Missionary Daniel Butrick bluntly noted this disparity in the Cherokee Nation. "There is a very great difference," he wrote in his journal, "between the highest and the lowest class."[58]

Disparate material circumstances seemed to reflect diverging value systems. Poorer Cherokees, taught as children to value social harmony and the support of kin above personal possessions, told agent Meigs that Whites' "enjoyments cost more than they are worth." When Meigs lamented that attitude in 1805, the Cherokee market revolution had yet to gather momentum. But two decades later, most tribe members still seemed oblivious to the advantages of Americans' economic culture. The "lowest class" struck Daniel Butrick then as "entirely ignorant of everything relating to another world."[59]

In contrast, some "high class" citizens of the tribes not only knew about "another world"—the American world that Butrick regarded as desirable—but preferred American practices to tribal traditions. Major Ridge's nephew Elias Boudinot was one such cultural convert. After several years at an ABCFM boarding school in Connecticut, where he assumed the name of an American benefactor and took a White wife, Boudinot was so bent on exchanging Cherokee for American culture that he castigated himself when he inadvertently witnessed an Indian ball game on the Sabbath. Boudinot's economic reorientation was evident in his decision as editor of the *Cherokee Phoenix* to publish an essay from the *Rochester Republican* entitled "How to Be Rich." Save a penny every day, the piece counseled, refrain from buying more furnishings than utility or comfort requires, and the interest accumulating on the money retained "would furnish your sitting room handsomely once in ten years."[60] Not only were the "ignorant full bloods" described by Butrick unable to read that article, printed only in English; they also had no sitting rooms to furnish.

There were signs of estrangement between people of the different cultural persuasions—a dissociation that caused some Indians to question the racial identity and national loyalty of tribe members who emulated and mingled with Whites. In 1813, so-called Red Stick Creeks took up arms against other Creeks partly out of anger at those who were accumulating wealth. A Red Stick chief explained that he saw his Creek enemies as people of the United States. And some acquisitive tribe members did appear at times to identify more with Whites than with Indians. John Ross, for instance, described himself to a missionary in 1819 as an American and a descendant of the Cherokee Nation. Using the pronoun "they" when referring to Cherokees, he also sounded like many White Americans when he said that most citizens of the tribe lived in a "crude state of nature."[61]

However, social relations in the tribes were more complex than such isolated bits of evidence suggest. Distinct culture groups were indeed forming, due in part to the common preference for marriage partners with compatible habits and values. As families with similar economic practices intermarried, procreated, and thus populated a distinct social circle, they reinforced traits that differentiated the people who accumulated property from those who did not. Each group disparaged some habits characteristic of the other group.[62] Nonetheless, peaceful coexistence was possible and even—many thought— desirable. For one thing, there was probably enough tribal land to meet tribe members' diverse aspirations. Market-oriented planters could each fence hundreds of acres without depriving subsistence farmers of their standard five or ten acres per family. More importantly, both culture groups derived benefits from sheltering together under the tribal umbrella. Tribal citizenship entitled the ambitious people to occupy as much land as they could develop. That right to free land inspired loyalty to the Indian nation—loyalty that gained strength when people of known Indian ancestry encountered racial bigotry among Whites outside tribal territory.[63] Once the four southern tribes formed governments that enacted laws to protect private property, as all of them did by the 1820s, enterprising people had more reason to stay on the Indian side of the political line.[64] For their part, Indian traditionalists looked to intermarried Whites, bicultural "mixed-bloods," and other Indians with American educations to provide some essential services, from interpreting at councils with U.S. officials and running interference with predatory Whites to selling liquor.[65]

Thus, the southern tribes were effectively becoming multicultural, stratified societies, composed of groups that differed in economic strategy and condition but agreed on the importance of preserving their nations. In 1818, when visiting Cherokee country on behalf of the ABCFM, Jeremiah Evarts sensed both the emerging class divisions and the national unity of the Cherokee population. Many in the tribe are of White descent, Evarts wrote,

> Yet all, who are partly Indians, are spoken of as Cherokees. The mixed breed can generally speak English, but some of them can neither understand nor speak that language at all. . . . The greater part . . . are as ignorant of evèry thing, which it is important for them to know, as the full-blooded Indians are. . . . Some of the half-breeds have large plantations, which they cultivate by the aid of slaves; but the fields of full-blooded Cherokees are generally small, and they do not carry on agriculture with much vigor and effect. . . . The greatest effect of introducing . . . the implements of civilized life, with English dress, and other things of small importance, has been to make some of the people most insatiably avaricious, leaving them as far from real civilization as before.[66]

As of 1818, those allegedly avaricious people were still the exception in the Cherokee Nation and other southern Indian populations. They numbered in the low hundreds, and were amassing property amid thousands of fellow citizens who prized social capital and a reputation for liberality more than stockpiled tangible possessions. If the nouveaux riches were to justify their practices and maintain mutually advantageous relations with other tribe members, they could not entirely ignore the values, moral sensibilities, and social cues of the less materialistic majority. Granted, some rich tribesmen apparently did thumb their noses at the expectation that they would distribute much of their wealth to needier Indians. Claudio Saunt sees evidence of that in the reported refusal of some Creek planters to feed hunters and warriors during "hungry years" that began in 1804.[67] But most of the rich people probably tried to reconcile their lifestyle in some respects with the venerable Indian ideals of generosity and reciprocity. At the same time, less acquisitive Indians worked to make sense of, or make good neighbors of, the rich.

It may have seemed plausible to view the new rich as successors of traditional headmen or chiefs, since the chiefs handled more wealth than commoners. In addition to overseeing public granaries, chiefs stocked up on the means to house and feed visitors and accepted gifts that acknowledged their patronage. They could legitimately keep "an inequitable amount" of what they received, Perdue notes, in order to meet obligations of their office. They thus controlled both personal and communal wealth, and the two "were not always distinguishable." After non-Indians began funneling presents, trade goods, payments for land, and tools for "civilized" pursuits to selected chiefs, some of those commingled treasuries grew very large. Like Alexander McGillivray, who accepted U.S. money under an agreement negotiated on behalf of fellow Creeks, favored chiefs could believe or pretend they were "fulfilling their traditional responsibility . . . to deal with outsiders and receive, in the name of the people, their largesse." As the range of Indians' economic activities broadened, some chiefs took charge of toll roads and ferry crossings that added to their revenues.[68] And if a chief dispensed what he received only to a small network of like-minded kin, who could say he was breaking with tradition?[69]

But the nineteenth-century new rich were not simply updated chiefs. The first tribe members to grow rich as businessmen also included people like James Vann who did not have a chief's role to exploit, and getting rich did not by itself promote a man from commoner to chief. Leaders had traditionally controlled wealth because they had people's respect, not the converse. Hence, for all his riches, Vann could not attract a following sufficient to unseat or neutralize the hereditary chiefs; and he was ultimately assassinated for plotting to gain power.[70] Nevertheless, the tradition of the benevolent headman created expectations that affluent people could not ignore if they wanted their

Indian neighbors' respect or cooperation. Many a member of the new upper economic stratum therefore provided generous aid to the less fortunate and extended hospitality to all comers, as the old chiefs had done.

Such magnanimity did not always come at the wealthy person's initiative. Traditionalists expected that someone who had plenty would share with those who did not, and they could make that expectation known in ways that brooked no denial. When rich young David Folsom and Greenwood Leflore got involved in Choctaw governance, James Taylor Carson relates, "the people were not shy about testing their new leaders' generosity." They descended by the score on the Leflore and Folsom homes, knowing that a good Choctaw would feed his visitors. And in 1840, the Cherokee ethic of hospitality was still so strong, according to Butrick, that people who had a claim "not merely on the pity, but the justice of those able to relieve them" would "use the imperative mode with as much boldness as the creditor when calling for his just due."[71] It is no wonder that John Ross and John Ridge, as they led opposing factions at the climax of the removal crisis, felt obliged to "keep an open house for Cherokees" and share their table with anyone who dropped in.[72]

Hospitality alone could not fool Indians into thinking of a mercenary man as worthy of deference. Indians were alert to selfishness and did not hesitate to name it when they saw it. At times, they meted out severe punishment to people who enriched themselves by dealing on the sly in common resources. Cherokees executed a chief named Doublehead, and Creeks assassinated their countryman William McIntosh, for taking money to arrange land cessions.[73] But in an era of new economic and political exigencies, it could be hard to tell whether a leader's actions were inconsistent with his customary responsibilities to the community. When Cherokee chiefs allocated tribal funds to pay individual members' trading debts, the biggest debts they covered were usually their own, yet they could argue with straight faces that everyone benefited from such a payout because it would quiet creditors who pressed them to raise additional money by selling more tribal land. The chiefs still drew no clear distinction between public and private assets.[74]

However, to some Indians who accumulated personal wealth as their nations' economies changed, a clear definition of public resources became increasingly desirable. To define and provide for the control of public resources was effectively to define and protect private assets as well. American officials insisted that progress and prosperity were possible only where individuals could acquire a wide array of property. Rather than the favors of paternalistic chiefs, it was the example of people who prospered by their own efforts that would inspire Indians to improve their lot. Connecticut-educated John Ridge endorsed this reasoning when he declared that the new class of rich Indians was cause for general satisfaction, not for accusations of greed. "It is true," Ridge admitted to an outsider in 1826, "that there are distinctions now existing & increasingly so—in the value of property possessed by individuals" in the Cherokee Nation, "but this only answers a good purpose, as a stimulus to those in the rear to equal their neighbors who have taken the lead." To help people "in the rear" see the stimulus, Ridge contributed a laudatory obituary to the *Cherokee Phoenix* for a woman named Oo-day-yee. "Unassisted by education, only in the knowledge of simple addition and subtraction which is within the reach of uncultivated minds," Ridge wrote, the deceased "by dint of application in farming and trading, had accumulated a very handsome property, consisting of household furniture, mill, waggon, horses & cattle, sheep, Negro Slaves and some money, all of which she has left to an only daughter and three grand children."[75]

In 1826, John Ridge saw a Cherokee Nation whose economic culture was coming to resemble that of the surrounding states in key respects. The historical record confirms Ridge's perception and documents similar trends in the other southern tribes.[76] Not only did most Cherokees, Choctaws, and Chickasaws rely by then on separate family farms for self-support, as most White Americans did; they also had exclusive rights to those farms, even though the land itself remained in tribal ownership. Many Creek communities still maintained common fields, yet separate Creek homesteads and valuable private estates were increasing in number.[77] One by one, the tribes adopted American ways of giving formal recognition and institutionalized protection to proprietary rights. In the Cherokee Nation, where this process began in 1808 and progressed furthest before removal, a judicial system was in place by the 1820s that served primarily as a forum for resolving disputes about contracts, debts, inheritance, and other economic relations familiar to Whites in the United States.[78]

Uneven distribution of property was another point of similarity between the Indian and American economies. The flow of wealth in the States was on a course that would direct 73 percent of it to 10 percent of the people by the 1860s.[79] Meanwhile, most of the wealth generated or acquired by members of the southern tribes was also collecting in a small number of large pools. Reliable statistics for the tribes are scarce, but scholars who have ventured to calculate the tribal distributions of wealth come up with percentages that are very close to those for the United States.[80]

What is more, the tribes' wealthiest class bore significant resemblance to the corresponding class of White southerners. John Ridge contentedly equated the Cherokee slaveholding class with its American counterpart. In the former, he remarked, "the principal value of property is retained and their farms are conducted in the same style as the southern white farms of equal ability in point of property."[81] Many non-Indians also saw the likeness between the Indian and American elites. After meeting a Cherokee delegation in 1824, Secretary of State John Quincy Adams jotted in his memoirs that the chiefs dressed as upper-class Americans did, and their manners were the same as any "well-bred country gentlemen." Delegates such as John Ross and Major Ridge met the criteria for southern gentry status summarized by historian Kenneth Startup: they had "a few hundred improved acres, a dozen or more slaves, . . . the wherewithal . . . to go about on horseback or in a carriage, a larger house than the local yeomen . . . , involvement in community affairs, and a bearing consistent with the ideal of a planter."[82]

Living standards were also similar for Indians and rural Americans of a lower class. When touring the South, Jeremiah Evarts pronounced the Indians' log cabins "not much inferior to those of the whites in the neighboring settlements." He later described the Cherokees as "peaceful agriculturists, better clothed, fed, and housed, than many of the peasantry, in most civilized countries."[83] Although Indians' clothing style was distinctive, they fashioned apparel from the same materials as non-Indians. By the standard of most New Englanders, Indian subsistence farmers were certainly poor, but so were many neighboring Whites. It was not hard to find Whites in the southeastern countryside whose stock of possessions was nearly as meager as the poorest Cherokees. Many small farmers in Tennessee, like the Cherokees, even recognized customary rights to common use of uncultivated lands.[84]

A third aspect of American economic life had a parallel in the tribes by the 1820s: it was possible to derive personal wealth from political power and political power from access to private wealth.[85] In this respect, John Ross's political rise resembled Andrew Jackson's rise to power in Tennessee. The young Jackson became rich enough to live as people expected of a public-spirited gentleman by seeking the patronage of men in the territorial elite, securing an office in the legal system, and learning through friends and work about opportunities to get land and money. He then used his material assets, ties to powerful people, and inside information to expand his influence as well as property holdings. He made himself the source of opportunities for would-be up-and-comers, as influential men had done for him. Despite later financial setbacks, Jackson faithfully followed the example of gentry in earlier generations: he was ever the generous host and magnanimous benefactor.[86]

John Ross adopted a similar strategy for gaining political influence while maintaining or enhancing his personal wealth. Although he did not face Jackson's steep climb from poverty, Ross moved into Cherokee government much the same way: he made himself useful to people already in office. He served the National Committee as an interpreter and learned the political ropes from popular chief Charles Hicks. While holding national offices himself, he became aware of business opportunities that he or friends could exploit, not the least of which were contracts to provision Cherokees when they finally had to go west. Ross's relations with constituents also had the marks of paternalism, as Jackson's did. His wealth enabled him not only to win tribe members' affection with hospitality, but also to subsidize some councils and delegations to Washington, D.C., thus convincing the Cherokee masses of his dedication to their interests.[87]

The archetypal leader in Jacksonian America was keen to make a profit and saw no harm in gaining personally from opportunities he spotted while in political office.[88] Astute as John Ross was at making money, he was perhaps too scrupulous or circumspect to be a Jacksonian politician of the most venal kind. At least he earned a firmer reputation for public-spirited integrity than Jackson and his cronies. Ross made a dramatic public show of incorruptibility when he exposed a Creek chief's attempt to bribe him, and he withstood multiple efforts to prove that he had lined his pockets with tribal funds.[89] Several other tribal leaders, however, operated much as the freewheeling, self-serving "Jackson men" did. When in the course of official duties they had a chance to enlarge their estates, they were inclined to accept. They also relished their ability to bestow economic favors on others, no doubt because of the power or prestige that followed.[90]

Take the Colberts of the Chickasaw Nation. Their patriotic defense of Chickasaw collective interests was symbiotically related to the advancement of their private economic interests. As English speakers who understood American motives, the Colberts were indispensable participants in treaty negotiations. Grateful for their services, older chiefs signed off on agreements that earmarked special benefits for the Colberts. And when the Colberts helped to write treaties that promoted Chickasaw-owned enterprise by excluding American businessmen from tribal territory, they felt no need to deny that they were the Chickasaws who would take the Americans' place.[91] Thus, in the Indian nations as in the United States, clever people could sometimes serve national and personal interests, including economic interests, through the same scheme. Because the resources of governing institutions were limited, public business often fell to men who could "get things done" by hook or by crook, and consequently might consider themselves entitled to some of the wealth or leverage they had secured.[92]

These parallel developments in the southern tribes and the United States—burgeoning private enterprise, class divisions with an economic basis, and temptations to profit from political office—brought questions about morality to the front and center of many minds. People in both settings proposed principles that should govern economic relations in their societies and publicly evaluated each other's behavior for consistency with those principles. As millions of Americans and several hundred Indians made personal enrichment their de facto priority, many of their contemporaries worried that other, worthier ideals were losing force. With corruption and schemes to profit at others' expense apparently on the increase, their nations' rectitude seemed on the decline.

In the United States, the widespread preoccupation with private gain made many people uneasy. For them, striving single-mindedly to get richer was hard to reconcile with important precepts of Christianity and with the attention to the common weal that the revered revolutionary generation espoused.[93] Teachers and preachers assured everyone that God considered industry a virtue and rewarded it with prosperity, but many Americans realized that it could be difficult to distinguish pious industriousness from actions aimed solely at satisfying selfish material desires.[94] Those who regretted that greed and sharp dealing were rampant generated a thick record of sermons and commentary.[95] Historians Oscar and Mary Handlin offered an amusing take on that public breast-beating in New England: "People incessantly engaged in buying and selling, in borrowing and lending, in swapping and haggling, nevertheless again and again voiced their anguish about the immorality of trade." Church congregations made up of merchants and their friends "nodded agreement as the clergy warned that greed, materialism and the obsession with gain led to corruption."[96] In the South, the cotton boom furnished clergy with material for numerous jeremiads about souls lost to the demons of envy and avarice. No doubt the speakers hoped to make some rich parishioners at least shift uneasily in the pews.[97]

As new money jingled in the pockets of wheeling and dealing Americans, some people recognized that the effect of wealth on political power was a subject in need of public attention. According to prevailing theory, it was the structural allocation of power that guided the allocation of wealth. The wide distribution of political power in a democracy was supposed to ensure near-universal access to wealth. Northerners therefore campaigned against the creation of new slave states on the grounds that slaveholders would use their added political power to establish economic monopolies. At the same time, however, rich Americans expected to have influence commensurate with their wealth, and usually got it. For that reason, some commentators observed, a small number of people holding large concentrations of wealth could wield disproportionate influence and potentially undermine the republic.[98]

To highlight the dilemmas posed by Americans' growing love of money, one social critic purported to examine the trend from the perspective of a "child of nature" — an Indian. In essays entitled *The Savage*, published around 1810, the pseudonymous Piomingo — supposedly a Creek who learned to write from a non-Indian disaffected with life in the States — surveyed America from Philadelphia, where he had recently taken up residence. "Wealth, in the present state of society," he lamented, "exercises a sovereign and independent influence and laughs at the laws or constitutions that would circumscribe its power." Americans were ruled by "a representative *plutocracy* or government of wealth." Plutocratic government was cause for concern, especially because the plutocrats obtained their wealth in conduct that had the effect of eradicating their "finer feelings and nobler sentiments." Piomingo pronounced it "nearly as hard for him who devotes his time to the acquisition of riches to be perfectly upright and honorable . . . as for a 'camel to go through the eye of a needle.'"[99]

While an American impersonating a Creek worried that love of money was eclipsing nobler impulses, many authentic Creeks and other southern Indians viewed developments in their homelands with similar anxiety. Some invoked an indigenous rule for living to explain their disapproval: acquisitive behavior was contrary to ancient instructions for harmonious social relations. Thus in 1817, when several White husbands of Cherokees leaped at a chance to get individual land under a new treaty with the United States, angry women urged the National Council to censure the men for being "only concerned how to increase their riches."[100] Those Cherokee women were not alone in charging that recipients of American economic favors had lost sight of their social obligations.[101] Americans sometimes dispensed with euphemisms and referred to the pecuniary bait they dangled before Indians as bribery, and Indians had come to know the meaning of that term when chiefs accepted such money on the sly and accumulated wealth instead of distributing it in traditional fashion.[102]

Tribal critics of selfish behavior were not all traditionalists, however. Some were advocates of economic Americanization who echoed the ethical admonitions of their missionary mentors. One was Elias Boudinot, editor of the *Cherokee Phoenix* from 1828 to 1832. Boudinot celebrated his people's growing stock of private property, but also reminded readers to prefer "a good conscience" over "the gilding, the trapping, the pride, and the pomp" of the rich. In 1828, he published two articles entitled "Money and Principles," which charged certain tribal officers with greed-driven disregard of proper official conduct. The rules of conduct, Boudinot cautioned, were meant to prevent an "aristocracy" from dominating Cherokee politics. A few months later, Boudinot added a general warning: "From . . . leaders, who pay more regard to the acquisition of wealth than the good and interest of our country, we have no reason to expect, any solid and permanent advantage."[103]

Like many of his readers, who included Americans as well as Cherokees, Boudinot had come to believe or preach that general prosperity was the result of individuals diligently seeking their own prosperity. And even when some individuals racked up far more wealth than others, often by cutthroat tactics, neither Indian nor American believers were apt to abandon that Lockean theory. Rather than suspecting their economic model had a basic flaw, they maintained that self-interest and community harmony were compatible, so long as no one wrecked another person's prospects and wealthy people used their bounty for the benefit of the larger society. Rich men had an obligation to take the same interest in the welfare of the poor as fathers took in their children's welfare. After all, a Christian should aim to live a virtuous life, not to heap riches upon riches. If by being virtuous a man did become rich, his wealth afforded additional means to do good.[104] That was the moral of an essay in the *Cherokee Phoenix* praising "Mr. Rothschild," a rich European, for partaking "of nothing that has the least semblance to extravagance, or even ordinary richness." The article, previously printed in the *Providence Literary Cadet*, rejoiced that Rothschild chose instead to expend "vast sums in meliorating the condition of the poor."[105]

The exemplary Mr. Rothschild observed two rules of economic life commended by most contemporary American moralists: he made the best of opportunities for gain, and he showed through charitable acts that his motives were not selfish.[106] To meet the same standard of morality, readers of the *Literary Cadet* or the *Cherokee Phoenix* had to strike a delicate balance. Furthermore, staying upright became increasingly difficult as winds of change buffeted individuals and eroded social structures designed to save them from falling into selfish ways. Yet people who did lean too far in the acquisitive direction might suffer nothing more than the jeers of onlookers because advocates of economic individualism, be they Americans or Cherokees, had few means besides moralizing rhetoric to discourage selfish choices.

Many people's choices did come under scrutiny as Americans and Indians debated whether to move the Indian nations beyond the western edge of the southern states. The decisive issue was to be the tribes' status vis-à-vis federal and state governments, but debaters also discussed the moral precepts that should govern economic relations and assessed each other's compliance. However, because stakes were high and mutual suspicions deep, the situation was hardly conducive to thoughtful dialogue on those subjects, let alone candid self-criticism.

Economic morality was a central concern of Whites who publicly opposed removal, and they were adamant that ejecting Indians from the South would not pass moral muster. Thousands of American women and men—northern churchgoers, for the most part—signed petitions and memorials pleading with their government to honor treaties that recognized the tribes' territorial boundaries. The nation's moral fiber, they declared, depended on keeping its promises and treating Indian landholdings with the same respect as other property.[107] The petitioners' rhetoric was passionate and alarmist because they sensed that Americans were increasingly liable to choose economic gain over righteousness when the two conflicted.

The leading spokesman for religiously motivated antiremoval Whites was Jeremiah Evarts, executive director of the American Board of Commissioners for Foreign Missions. Visions of a thoroughly moral America inspired Evarts's crusade, and self-restraint was the key to the morality he prescribed. His adversaries, Evarts believed, were politically ambitious people who pandered to people's selfish inclinations by glorifying unrestrained individual action taken in the name of progress and prosperity.[108] Their argument that it was fair to evict Indians so that enterprising Americans could develop the land was not only inconsistent with legal principles, it appealed to base desires. In a series of essays published under the pseudonym William Penn, and in memorials drafted for civic groups, Evarts countered the arguments for Indian removal—Cherokee removal, specifically—with points that ranged from pragmatic analysis of economic data and interpretation of the law to broad ethical exhortations.

Evarts ridiculed the complaint that the Cherokees' continuing presence in the South deprived Georgia of valuable land. Georgians were peeved about "a species of privation to which covetous men have always been exposed," he said tartly. Their "abuse of language" failed to disguise the ugly fact that they lusted after property whose owners declined to sell. Their contention that Indians wasted the land was equally disingenuous. "Georgia . . . has many millions of acres of unoccupied land," Evarts asserted. "When Georgia shall have a hundred souls to the square mile: (and her soil is capable of sustaining a larger number than that;) the Cherokees may have four times as many to the square mile as Georgia now contains."[109] Moreover, both natural justice and cherished principles of American law required recognition that the lands occupied by the tribes were their property. This line of argument appealed to publishers of the *North American Review*, who responded to the criticism of Indian land use patterns by asking, "How can one man assume the right of prescribing in what manner another man shall dispose of his own property? And how can there be one rule of morality and honesty for individuals, and another for communities?"[110]

Undeniably, Evarts conceded, the United States had power great enough to enforce a judgment that Americans could make better use of land than Indians. But might did not make economic right. Rather, because his nation was stronger and richer than the tribes, it had a solemn responsibility to deal justly with them. The "wealth of both the Indies" was not worth the moral integrity to be lost by robbing Indians of their patrimony. Besides, "Divine displeasure" would "not fail to punish a nation, that, unmindful of its engagements, and swayed by motives of temporary interest and narrow policy, disregard[ed] the cries of the oppressed."[111]

Although Evarts galvanized and drew hope from a grassroots petition drive of pious Americans, religious organizations did not unify in opposition to removal. Methodists in the Choctaw Nation and Baptist churches recommended Indian emigration as a pragmatic response to harassment by Whites.[112] Protestants stationed among the Cherokees under ABCFM auspices did eventually protest the plan to relocate the tribes, but countervailing economic considerations tugged at their minds, and they struggled to keep their moral balance. Tension between the ideals of Christian benevolence and self-reliant industry had always challenged them. Their responses had exposed them before to charges of uncharitable self-interest, and they knew their resistance to removal could be construed as yet more incriminating evidence.

On one hand, for fear of committing the sins of pride and greed, the missionaries had consciously tried to subordinate their economic agenda to their religious one. They had eschewed luxuries and even denied themselves comforts they would have enjoyed back home.[113] After 1820, Brainerd mission personnel could not hold private property there; they had either to consolidate private belongings with mission property or to send them away. Samuel Worcester once declined to keep a shipment of table linen that was "much nicer" than the Brainerd establishment should have. Deeming the souls of the poor as precious as those of the rich, missionaries had also tried to avoid favoring well-to-do tribe members. When Cherokees seemed to sneer at the appearance of Creeks whose "dress . . . bespoke the manners of the forest," Daniel Butrick told the Creeks "that I loved *them* as much as I did the Cherokees, and that their and our heavenly Father never despised any of his children for being poor."[114]

On the other hand, the missionaries came from communities where material progress and individualism were articles of a popular faith they shared. They had brought Indians not only the gospel of the Christ's resurrection but also the gospel of economic self-reliance and advancement.[115] Most of them went into the Indian "wilderness" with the teachings of the political economist Francis Wayland in mind. Wayland, a New England cleric who trained hundreds of men for the ministry, urged them to "teach economics to the heathen because it is the best thing to stimulate those emerging from barbarism." He held that "personal liberty and private property are the great principles of moral science and the social fabric." Founded on God's will, property was acquired "directly by the immediate gift of God."[116] So common and deepseated was the American association of wealth with blessedness that even for Daniel Butrick, who had no hope as a missionary of getting rich, gold was a metaphor for virtue. On an occasion when the malfeasance of some Cherokee law enforcement officers distressed him, a biblical lamentation came to mind, "O how is the gold become dim! How is the most fine gold changed!"[117]

What is more, gold or its financial equivalent was indispensable to the missionaries' undertaking. Some of the northern states' richest men were central players in the ABCFM, which could not sustain its network of missions without donations from wealthy persons.[118] Since private contributions did not cover the cost of operations, the ABCFM's board also accepted money from the United States Treasury. Rich tribe members were vital sources of support as well. Because the missionaries could not afford to alienate those Indian supporters, they had refrained from censuring some economic practices that offended their sense of decency. In particular, although they construed the use of slave labor as a symptom of greed, most of them had held their tongues rather than chastise Indian slaveowners. Finding that few Indians were interested in working for wages, some missionaries resorted to using enslaved laborers themselves.[119]

In addition, the grand evangelical project served the cause of American national expansion, which was in essence a drive for wealth. The larger missions were themselves conspicuous centers of economic enterprise.[120] Therefore, even before the removal controversy, missionaries faced charges or suspicions that their motives for gaining a foothold in Indian country were more worldly than godly. The Christians at Brainerd, for example, were aware that their station's prosperous appearance—its flourishing farm, blacksmith and mechanics, boarding school, and hostel for guests—"excited envy." Both Indians and Whites in the area told them so.[121]

Thus, for Butrick and his religious colleagues, the campaign to remove Indians from the South presented acute moral and political dilemmas intertwined with economic problems. One challenge was to protect investments in mission property without putting or seeming to put pecuniary concerns above spiritual ones. Church resistance to Indian removal, Butrick observed, would confirm Georgians' suspicions that the missionaries were "worldly designing men, having . . . temporal interests interwoven with those of the Cherokees, and therefore determined in opposition to their selling their country." After a man who favored removal won the presidency in 1828, a decision to resist also meant losing federal funds. But having assured the Indians that missionaries were cut from a different cloth than the Whites who schemed to take possession of tribal resources, Butrick was loath to make up the loss of federal money by requesting money from the Cherokee treasury. And when the resistance to removal finally collapsed, Butrick perceived another challenge to his notions of economic morality: his superiors resolved to get the highest possible payments for church assets located in Indian country. Butrick fretted that taking money for ABCFM property amounted to "robbing God."[122]

In conversations with Cherokee leaders about the threat of removal, Butrick insisted that his duty as a saver of souls was to remain indifferent to political issues facing the Indian nation. But privately, he railed at the greed that drove Americans to demand Indians' property and disguise the unprincipled nature of their suit. How dare such people pretend to be better human beings than the Indians! "While the white man can go and come without fear of robery [sic], oppression and murder, the poor Indian must watch night and day to preserve one little poney to plough his field, or one poor sow to nourish his family, or one creature of any kind, to furnish his meat. Or, if riding alone, he is in constant danger of having his horse torn from him, by the hands of ruffians. If seeking the fruit of his own soil, he is in danger of being seized, dragged to prison." "Wherever he goes, or which way soever he turns," Butrick lamented, the Indian "finds an American citizen with some dark and deep layed plan to rob him of his property . . . his all." Maybe the answer, Butrick mused with bitter irony, was to let the mistreated Indian go to "the western wilderness" after all, "& associate with the more virtuous Comanches. They, perhaps, without envy, can see him possess one little blanket, to wrap around him."[123]

Advocates of sending Indians to the western wilderness would have retorted that they and fellow Whites were unquestionably better humans than Indians; Indians had proved incapable of civilized economic relations. Although the rationale for replacing Indians with White settlers derived from a variant of American economic ideology that valued risk-taking and self-interested exploits more than frugality and charity, spokesmen for the cause insisted they were people of principle who had the common good in mind.[124] They saw nothing wrong with the avid pursuit of wealth, but they did see a grievous wrong when "aristocrats" deprived the common man of opportunities by monopolizing wealth and power. And that was the case in the Indian tribes, they said: aristocrats and would-be aristocrats had seized power there in order to fill their private coffers. Meanwhile, swayed by "selfish counsel," the U.S. government had tried to help the "unfortunate" Indians by adopting policies that were oppressing poor White citizens.[125]

Proremoval Whites scoffed at the suggestion that moral principles required the same respect for Indian claims to territory as fee ownership enjoyed in the United States. Citing the Lockean doctrine that property is the fruit of labor—in other words, that land and its resources belong by right to those who make them produce wealth—spokesmen for the removal campaign argued that Americans' interest in developing land trumped the interests of Indians who let so much ground go to waste. Indians' negligence was proof of an innate inability to use resources properly. Lewis Cass, a veteran U.S. Indian agent, professed to believe that the difficulty was "some insurmountable obstacle in the habits or temperament of the Indians," because he could think of no "branch of the human family . . . less provident in arrangement, less frugal in enjoyment, less industrious in acquiring" wealth. For that reason, Cass added, "The nature of the title, by which the Indians held their lands, is not easily reconciled to the principles by which the tenures of this description of property are regulated among civilized nations." George Gilmer, a one-time governor of Georgia, offered a similar, retrospective defense of the state's desire to be rid of Indians. "Our villifiers seemed . . . to have forgotten that . . . [the Indians] were without wealth, and were incapable of acquiring any; and that they had remained ignorant savages. . . . Their wealth was without money, and its greatest accumulation extended only to wigwams, skins, and canoes."[126]

Aware that educated Cherokees and their supporters were giving sympathetic northern audiences a different account of southern Indians' economic status, men like Cass and Gilmer had to admit their depiction did not apply to all tribe members; some enterprising people were present in the southern tribes. However, those people were not numerous, not honorable, and not even true Indians. Gilmer explained: "Whilst the unmixed Indians have remained what they ever were, and will ever be, until they finally pass away—the most thoughtless, listless, least lovely, of human beings—the half-breeds are making a show of civilization." To a correspondent's characterization of some Cherokee ambassadors as "polished gentlemen," Gilmer responded:

> What you say of the intelligence of the members of the Cherokee tribe who were in Washington City last winter, is partly true, and equally descriptive of many others. They are not Indians, however, but the children of white men, whose corrupt habits or vile passions have led them into connection with the Cherokee tribe. It is not surprising that the white men, and the children of white men, have availed themselves of the easy means of acquiring wealth, which the Cherokee territory has presented for thirty or forty years; nor that intelligence and spirited activity should increase with their increasing wealth; nor that, when wealth, intelligence, and industry are confined to the whites, and the children of white men, that the power over the tribe should become centered in the same hands. But that these causes are calculated to produce similar effects upon the Indians—the real aborigines—is disproved by every example among the thousands which the experience of the two last centuries has furnished in every part of this continent.[127]

Lewis Cass also conceded that some individual Cherokees had acquired property and a consequent appreciation of American institutions, but he insisted that "this change of opinion and condition" was largely "confined . . . to some of the *half-breeds* and their immediate connexions," who were not numerous enough "to affect our general proposition."[128]

Proponents of removal recognized that property holdings gave the "half-breeds" and their "connexions" a reason to resist removal. (They ignored the thousands of "real aborigines" who also owned and sought to keep farms.)[129] But they portrayed that desire to protect investments and businesses as the seemingly benign face of a sinister agenda. Intelligent, acquisitive tribe members were allegedly determined to monopolize wealth and power by depriving humbler Indians of the same, and relocation was a threat to the monopolists' income stream. That, in the view of U.S. agent Return Meigs, was the explanation for the Cherokee council's refusal to consider a land cession in 1822. "Their pretence of having obtained the sentiments of the people is a bubble," he contended, "for the populace are governed by a few leading men, who fabricate their political catechism. Indeed their government is an aristocracy, consisting of about 100 men . . . controlled by perhaps twenty speculating individuals; some . . . are making fortunes in trade by merchandise, a considerable portion of which merchandise is whiskey and other ardent spirits."[130]

Alabaman John Coffee was one of three treaty commissioners who blamed a similar cabal for Chickasaws' reluctance, in 1826, to sell their land and move. "The government seems to be in the hands principally of half-breeds and white men, who dictate to some of them, without regard to the interest of the poor Indians," Coffee charged. "The nation is fast declining in wealth and comforts generally, excepting a few half-breeds, who have been enlightened by education and otherwise, and who have settled on the road that leads through the nation, are gathering a harvest on that road, and who reap the greater part of the profits arising from the road and the annuities. It is, therefore, their interest to continue things as they now are."[131] In support of the argument that rich men held despotic sway over ordinary Indians, Governor Wilson Lumpkin of Georgia offered John Ross as Exhibit One. Ross, wrote Lumpkin, "has had the entire control and disbursement of millions of dollars, as *King* of the Cherokees, during the last twenty years. The control of this immense amount of money, in the absence of any enlightened supervision or *check* on his financial aspirations, is the key that unlocks the secret cause of his long career of absolute reign and power, as well as his great popularity, at home and abroad."[132]

Disregarding their own record of cultivating chiefs' taste for wealth by offering bribes and special economic privileges, President Andrew Jackson and other officials insisted that their interventions in tribal affairs and the treaties they proposed were aimed at protecting poor, unsophisticated Indians from grasping, "speculating," mostly White citizens of the tribes.[133] Historian Michael Rogin traces Jackson's image as a champion of the common man to these attacks on rich tribe members, and in retrospect, the effort to brand tribal chiefs as self-serving aristocrats does look typically Jacksonian. Democrats of that era warned repeatedly that privileged men were scheming to monopolize power in the States and turn it to their economic advantage.[134] The men who took the lead in demanding Indians' removal had sharp eyes for such conspiracies among their opponents, outside and inside the tribes. Lumpkin identified the true "moral criminals" in Indian affairs as "the white men who stimulate and excite these unlettered sons of the forest against their white neighbors. All this is done *'for the sake of filthy lucre.'*" On another occasion, Lumpkin asked rhetorically why "enlightened men engaged in the ruinous work of keeping" the Indians "back from entering the promised land?" His answer: "They will not let the people go until they fleece them of their last dollar."[135]

In the eyes of Jackson men, the patrician sponsors of Protestant missions were as suspect as any removal opponents. According to one scholar of Jackson's political ideology, a "sense of personal grievance" lay behind Old

Hickory's antagonism toward the Christian crusaders; he knew they considered him crude and morally tainted. Whatever the motives, advocates of removal did insinuate, as Daniel Butrick predicted, that missionaries with their network of valuable properties had an economic interest in abetting the Indian resistance. Some of them, Lumpkin alleged, "advanced their own circumstances and comfort, and improved their own conditions from what they had been accustomed to full as much as they improved the churches."[136]

To the claim that financial considerations motivated their fight against removal, both missionaries and tribal spokesmen responded that proponents of removal had more selfish economic reasons for their position. It was not hard to make that case. White southerners stood to gain in numerous ways from Indians' mass departure. In addition to the land that would open to White settlement, there were valuable homes and other improvements that well-to-do tribe members would vacate, recently discovered gold deposits in Cherokee country, and business niches that Whites could occupy when the enterprising Indians left.[137] Once removal became a certainty, Whites would also have opportunities to profit from the reluctant emigrants' need for supplies and transportation.[138]

Indians did not doubt that lust for land and profit was behind the campaign to move them. They had long since concluded that avarice motivated most Whites with whom they dealt. Relentless demands for their land were proof enough. Michael Green found a Creek name for Georgians that meant "people greedily grasping after the lands of the red people." And well before the state of Georgia sanctioned the seizure of Cherokee houses, farms, and ferries, tribal leaders pleaded with federal agents to protect them from the rapaciousness of Whites who wanted their land. Missionaries at Brainerd tried in vain to allay Chief Pathkiller's fear that Americans would leave Cherokees no place to live.[139] In fact, many tribe members remained unconvinced that pure benevolence had inspired the missionaries themselves to enter their nations. A rumor circulated that the Christians would demand real estate as pay for teaching Indian children; another foresaw that Indians' progress under the missionaries' tutelage would give the United States an excuse to pronounce them civilized and break the tribal land into private lots. Even when ABCFM ministers risked their liberty and property in support of Cherokees' bid to stay, some tribe members suspected them of taking bribes from Georgians.[140]

Anger at greedy Whites did not keep tribe members from seeing that greed in their own ranks might affect the outcome of the removal dispute. American money had induced their leaders to sell tribal territory before; it could do so again. In all four southern tribes, men who valued their own accumulations of private property had moved into positions of critical importance to tribal decision-making, and they might abandon the antiremoval cause if they ultimately concluded that they could do better economically by leaving for the West instead of refusing to move.[141]

Peter Pitchlynn's biographer speculates that an inclination to put personal interest ahead of tribal concerns may have been strong in men of dual ancestry who had distanced themselves culturally from Indians only to find that White Americans would not fully accept them.[142] But even if that psychological reflex did influence some mixed-blood responses to the possibility of removal, its influence was spotty. Acquisitive tribe members could find economic reasons both for and against emigrating. Incentives and disincentives varied over time and differed from tribe to tribe. Many big planters were as reluctant to move as traditionalists, and several historians agree with contemporaries who linked that reluctance to financial interests. Having taken advantage of their right to use large tracts of fertile land tax-free, the planters were sitting pretty in the East. Some also had businesses with White customers as well as Indians and doubted they could do as well in the sparsely settled West.[143]

Conversely, there were ways to make money by agreeing to move. For example, U.S. officials tried to make emigration worthwhile personally for Choctaw and Chickasaw treaty negotiators. To the Treaty of Dancing Rabbit Creek, which committed Choctaws to trade their land in Mississippi for western lands, the Americans added articles reserving valuable tracts for prominent families—at least 5,120 acres for the Pitchlynns—with the expectation that most recipients would realize tidy sums by selling their tracts and going west after all. Under fire from Indians unhappy with those provisions, Pitchlynn soon denounced the treaty and "piously accused [fellow Choctaw] David Folsom of being unable to withstand the temptation of land reservations." Later, Pitchlynn compensated for losing the fight against removal by exploiting new opportunities in the West. Wealthy Chickasaws profited not only by selling their business interests and the private lots they reserved in the removal treaty, but also by purchasing slaves with the proceeds and then collecting allowances to move the slaves west. Individuals in all four southern tribes also bid on federal contracts to supply and transport ejected Indians.[144]

The belief that selfish economic interests could influence tribe members' stands on removal fed suspicions and furious recriminations in the Cherokee Nation. Years before John Ridge, Elias Boudinot, and a handful of others signed the treaty providing for their nation's removal, Indians as well as U.S. agents noted that money-minded Cherokees were profiting from reimbursements for property they gave up when they moved west. Writing from Washington in 1829, a contributor to the *Phoenix* expressed dismay at reports that some fellow Cherokees were choosing to emigrate "under the promise of getting large sums for their improvements." Federal officials were equally unhappy that prospective emigrants were clearing new land in order to boost the amount the United States would pay to buy them out.[145] Yet those Cherokees who finally endorsed a removal treaty in 1835 found the federal and state governments solicitous of their property interests, making the bitter pill of exile easier for signers swallow.[146]

By negotiating a treaty without National Council authorization, Boudinot, Ridge, and their cohorts presented Cherokees with a question that was primarily political in nature. They contended that the autocratic John Ross had suppressed dissent and thus kept the Cherokee masses from learning that their fight to stay was futile.[147] Nevertheless, both the treaty signers and Ross also made economic morality a major issue in the exchange of insults that followed. As spokesman for the Cherokees who were determined to stay at almost any cost, Ross tried to discredit leaders of the treaty faction by alluding to their selfish economic ambitions. Their response was to turn the tables on Ross.

With some justification, Ridge and Boudinot thought Ross was telling Cherokees that graft motivated the treaty signers.[148] Boudinot sent Ross a lengthy self-defense. "Among the many charges that have been made against me and my associates during this unhappy controversy," he protested, "is that of being *interested persons*. This has been often repeated, and some have gone so far as to say that we have been *bought* or *bribed*." After denying any pecuniary interest in the treaty, Boudinot counterattacked:

> You have made such treaties, and you have seen such *special advantages* secured in them. . . . Instead of I being benefitted over my fellows, it is *you*. Any person need but look to the lists of valuations, to be convinced of this point. . . . It is well known that while you were adding one farm after another, and stretching your fences over hills and dales, from river to river, and through swamps and forests, no doubt, (for I can conceive no other substantial reason for such unusual conduct,) with a view to these very times; I say, while you were making these great preparations, which have now turned out to be a pecuniary advantage to you, I was here, toiling, at the most trying time of our difficulties, for the defence of our rights, in an arduous employment, and with a nominal salary of three hundred dollars only, entirely neglecting my own pecuniary interest.[149]

For his part, Boudinot was not averse to spreading rumors that "John Ross and his friends wished to get all the funds of the nation in their own hands, and this accounted for their repugnance to make a treaty at home in open council." Both he and his cousin John Ridge lit into the Ross party, which Ridge called "this unholy Aristocracy," for taking economic advantage of their lead role in negotiating earlier treaties.[150] Boudinot even claimed to detect a flawed moral code behind Ross's "extravagant demands" that the treaty of 1835 be amended to quadruple the payment for Cherokee lands. He chided, "Upon what principle could you have made the assertion . . . 'that the Cherokees had not suffered one half what their country was worth,' but upon the principle of valuing your nation in dollars and cents?" In contrast, because the treaty signers' aims were less material than patriotic, they did not try to wring the last possible dime from the United States. Why spend so much time trying to make a new treaty, Boudinot asked Ross, "to get . . . a full compensation for your gold mines, your marble quarries, your forests, your watercourses . . . while the canker is eating the very vitals of this nation? Perish your gold mines and your money, if, in pursuit of them, the moral credit of this people, their happiness and their existence are to be sacrificed."[151]

Ten years earlier, Boudinot had assured White audiences that "moral credit" was his most important aspiration in life. In a speech given, ironically, to drum up financial as well as moral support for the Cherokee acculturation strategy, he asked, "Who can prefer a little of his silver and gold, to the welfare of nations of his fellow beings? Human wealth perishes with our clay, but that wealth gained in charity still remains on earth, to enrich our names, when we are gone, and will be remembered in Heaven, when the miser and his coffers have mouldered together in their kindred earth." Now, with his reputation and possibly his life on the line because he had signed a treaty that most Cherokees repudiated, Boudinot anxiously maintained that he had not betrayed his vow of morality.[152] But his passing remark about his "nominal salary" and neglected "pecuniary interest," considered in light of evidence that leaders of the treaty faction shared the same economic culture as Ross, suggests that Boudinot and his associates did wish for greater economic opportunity than they expected under Ross's leadership in Georgia.[153]

Elias Boudinot and John Ross carried their written polemic about economic morality into the larger arena where Americans were still debating the justice of removing the Cherokees. In an "Answer to Inquiries from a Friend," which someone sent on to *Niles' Weekly Register*, Ross said he was trying to live by ethical standards that White Americans promoted but did not always observe. "I will own that it has been my pride," he wrote, "to implant in the bosoms of the people, and to cherish as my own, *the principles* of white men!" Ross apparently considered it unnecessary to explain that the White men he had in mind were not those who considered Indians incapable of principled self-improvement.[154]

When Ross, Boudinot, and Ridge addressed each other or White Americans on the subject of their personal integrity, the moral code they cited was not discernibly different from the one Jeremiah Evarts exhorted Americans to honor or, for that matter, the one Andrew Jackson claimed to follow. They all maintained that the material gains of enterprising persons were evidence of estimable conduct and conducive to national prosperity. They all said that an ethical ambitious person would draw the line at activity involving dishonesty or ruthless disregard for the rights of others. It is possible that Ross, Boudinot, and Ridge defended their integrity in other terms to traditionalist Indians, but the historical record does not document that. In their English writings and speeches, they offered themselves up for judgment by the ostensible, ambiguous standard of the American republic that was about to displace them.

Throughout the decade-long debate about Indian removal, charges of conduct inconsistent with moral principles flew back and forth within the American and Indian nations as well as between them. Greed and excessive materialism were the most common vices attributed to opponents in the debate. Antiremoval Americans decried proremoval Americans' avarice; proremoval Americans depicted antiremoval Americans as phony philanthropists with pecuniary motives of their own, who sought money from tribes and the federal government to fund their militant crusade.[155] Proremoval Americans painted John Ross and other acculturated tribal leaders as money-grubbers with aristocratic pretensions, but so did the tribe members who concluded that they or their nations would lose more by obstinacy than by negotiating removal treaties.[156] Indian proponents of removal treaties in turn faced accusations that mercenary self-interest underlay their position. And so it went. Rather than forcing a resolution of a dilemma inherent in the accumulation-oriented economic ethos of early American nationalists and some nationalist tribal leaders, the removal dispute allowed everyone involved to displace their concerns about economic morality onto their adversaries.

Historians have been unable to agree whether charges of greed should stick either to Ross or to the Boudinot-Ridge family and their cohorts.[157] No scholars have taken the aspersions cast on Ross's White allies seriously enough to investigate the balance sheets of the antiremoval organizations. But virtually all historians credit the allegations of greed and duplicity leveled at White southerners who agitated for removal. Because the people of Georgia, Alabama, and Mississippi proved ready to swoop in and snatch the banished Indians' nest eggs, state politicians' expressions of concern for the Indians rang false. "White inhabitants," Daniel Butrick testified, "stood with open arms to seize whatever property they could" when "8,000 people, many of whom were in good circumstances, and some rich, were rendered homeless" as troops enforced the New Echota treaty.[158] The evidence supports Butrick's allegation so convincingly that there is ample reason to call Wilson Lumpkin, George Gilmer, and Andrew Jackson liars for claiming that the common good, not opportunity for private gain, was the goal of their efforts to relocate the tribes.[159]

That claim is instructive, nonetheless, because it suggests that almost everyone who took sides in the debate about Indian removal was hoping to win with a clean conscience, or hoping at least for acknowledgment from peers that their position had moral justification. Just as significantly, there was substantial agreement on the test of a conscience's cleanliness, and people who tried to enrich themselves at others' expense did not meet it.[160] Thus, Lumpkin protested that he and fellow White southerners were not the ones deserving censure for sacrificing virtue in order to reap economic benefits; rather, the greatest depravity and turpitude belonged to "the combination of lawyers and politicians" who encouraged Ross and his party to resist the inevitable while consuming "all that could be extracted . . . in the way of fees for legal services."[161]

To buttress a moral case that many fellow Americans regarded as weak if not blatantly disingenuous, advocates of removal invoked beliefs about race that were rapidly gaining adherents in the United States—a tactic their prominent opponents largely eschewed. According to proremoval spokesmen, Indians were innately shiftless, improvident savages, inclined by nature to hunt rather than farm, and therefore destined to live in poverty. In the racial ideology that the removal campaign exploited, White Americans alone were paragons of enterprising ambition, which was a prerequisite of laudable productivity and progress. However, because ambition could also manifest itself as selfishness, the champions of removal found confirmation of their racist logic in the fact that many of the southern tribes' wealthy members had White ancestry. By that logic, attributing all wealth in the southern tribes to Whites made sense. The stereotype of Indians did not allow for enterprising ones.

In sum, by emulating Whites' economic strategies, Cherokees, Creeks, Choctaws, and Chickasaws had confirmed that their tribal lands could produce the kinds of wealth Americans craved. Even so, the Whites who called for the Indians' removal rationalized their campaign as a response to irreconcilable differences between Indian and American cultures, especially economic cultures. For a purported failure or inability to recognize the moral superiority of a civilization based on private property, the Indian nations faced demands that they forfeit their national territories and much of the property they had there.

When other Americans joined tribal spokesmen in condemning that demand, they framed the moral issues differently. Denying that it was impossible to reconcile Indian and American economic practices, they pointed to tribe members who had apparently accepted the common American belief in promoting the general welfare by encouraging the human desire for private wealth. The question they emphasized was not whether incompatible beliefs about property required the races' separation, but whether Americans would be true to the economic ethics they had urged Indians to embrace.

As opponents in the removal controversy charged each other with violations of a common moral code, they also discussed the obligations incumbent on people who subscribed to that code. But it was not a fruitful discussion. They did not agree on a definition of immoral selfishness, let alone how to correct it. Although they did not say so—and most may not have realized it—their actions were testimony to the tensions and contradictions inherent in an ideology that glorified efforts at self-enrichment. They could not act without choosing to honor some principles of their economic philosophy at the expense of others. It was a classic moral dilemma, and Americans and Indians responded with divergent choices—choices that put Indians in conflict with Americans but also put White Americans in conflict with White Americans and Indians in conflict with Indians.

[4]

Gilded Age Indians

By 1864, Sarah Bell Watie had lived more than four decades, and she knew
from experience that a desire for money could overwhelm nobler aspirations.
It might even prompt a person to put profit before the needs of kin or brothers-
in-arms. So when her husband complained by letter that a delivery of supplies
for his Confederate troops was late, Sarah surmised that the supplier was speculating. Her answering letter admonished, "I do not want you to do any thing
of that kind I would live on bread and water rather than have it said you had
speculated of your people. . . . if I thought you was working for nothing but to
fill our pocket it would trouble me a great deal but I know it is not else it would
have been filled before this time."[1]

It is possible that General Stand Watie deserved the nod to his integrity at
the end of Sarah's little sermon, but before the Civil War he had devoted considerable effort to filling his family's pocket. He had established a law practice,
opened a mercantile outlet, and developed a plantation where slaves raised
cash crops. Once the war was over and the slaves were freed, Watie allowed an
ambitious nephew—E. Cornelius Boudinot—to draw him into new commercial ventures, including a short-lived tobacco factory.[2]

After Stand Watie's death in 1871, Boudinot put Sarah on his list of potential partners for moneymaking activities, along with her brother Jim. In a quest
"to build up the fortune of the family again," Cornelius presented his aunt and
uncle with multiple proposals for investments that promised to yield immense
returns.[3] His feel for Uncle Jim's aims was accurate. James M. Bell was, in the
words of one historian, an "aggressive entrepreneur."[4] Bell in turn assumed
that his sister would welcome ways to make money. After all, she had sent
him letters bemoaning her shortage of funds and counseling him to establish

a reputation "as punctual to business." So in 1879, Bell invited Sister Sarah to claim a piece of the western lands he had targeted for colonization and urged her to act before other people snapped up the best parcels.[5] The project was one of several Bell and Boudinot schemes that ran afoul of public policy or alienated other family members, but opposition did not deter them. In Boudinot's case at least, it just seemed to spur a more dogged pursuit of the riches he had in sight.[6]

Boudinot and Bell chased money more avidly than most people Sarah Watie knew, but other relatives frankly yearned for wealth as well. In letters from North Carolina, a sister and niece lamented their modest incomes. The niece, Madeleine Shelton, wrote in 1876:

> Money here as everywhere, rules the day. One can be *a good respectable person*, but that is the highest position he can hope to attain without the almighty dollar. . . . Well, I guess what the matter with us is, our pride is too greate for our purse. . . . Would have been best if ambition had been smothered in us, than cultivated. My greatest sin is my love for money. I do not love it for it's self, but for the comforts and position it gives one in society. If I cannot go, and dress with the best of the country, I stay at home. Sis Cora has every wish gratified as far as money is capable of doing it. Everything brother Dave touches turns to gold.[7]

Did Sarah nod in knowing agreement or frown in disapproval as she read this? More than once, she expressed dismay at the greed that could possess people, but if she had qualms about her own relatives' economic aims, she left no clear evidence. To the contrary, she apparently expected her businessman brother to understand the revulsion she felt when watching a scramble for profit at the new town of Vinita. "I never could beleave that people were so selfish," said her note to Jim Bell in 1880, "but it growes here every day and I dont want to stay here and see so much of it." We are left to wonder whether Sarah regretted that Vinita was born of nephew Cornelius's speculation. It was Boudinot who had set the stage for the frenzy by staking out the townsite and persuading two railroads to make it their junction.[8]

Sarah Watie had good cause to believe that cutthroat wheeling and dealing was on the rise during her later years. Commercial projects and speculation were increasingly common in her world. The country around her was lightly populated as of 1880, yet it had several thousand residents like her brother and nephew, eager to exploit opportunities for personal gain. Those people were no different in that regard from millions of contemporaries throughout the United States. A passion for building family fortunes in business ventures seemed to grip many more Americans after the Civil War than before. However, Sarah's neighbors and relatives were different from those Americans in at least one crucial respect: they were citizens and residents of the Cherokee Nation, not the United States.

Four decades after leaving the American South under duress, Cherokees were well established on land west of Arkansas, in an area designated the Indian Territory. There they continued governing themselves. Other Indian exiles—Creeks, Choctaws, Chickasaws, and Seminoles—had located nearby and also resumed tribal life. All five of those so-called Civilized Tribes, to varying degrees, were experiencing the surge in get-rich schemes that disturbed Sarah Watie. Some schemers were non-Indians from the States, but others were Indians. The chickens of economic culture change had come home to roost in the tribes. Since the 1700s, many members had embraced the ethos of profit-making enterprise and private property accumulation that Euro-American society promoted but aboriginal ancestors disdained.[9] Perhaps Sarah's niece had this history in mind when wishing that her family's ambition had been smothered rather than cultivated. Encouraging people to strive for individual economic advantage had some discomfiting consequences.

Ambition was a problem for Madeleine Shelton because she craved more wealth than she could realistically expect to obtain. But in Sarah Watie's view, if we can believe her written words, the problem was that ambition could escalate to unacceptable selfishness. Other analysts warned that promoting private enterprise posed problems for the Five Tribes as communities, because some people were able to obtain far more wealth than others, often by means that jeopardized the long-term security of the less ambitious people. Even so, many in the tribes championed self-interested enterprise, arguing that it had general social benefits. Society's task, they maintained, was to thwart the most extreme form of ambition—heartless greed. The unanswered question was whether their societies, acting through tribal governments, were up to that task.

While the Five Tribes were contemplating the problematic aspects of economic individualism and debating possible ways to mitigate them, many people in the United States were doing the same. Historians affirm the contemporary perception that Americans in the late 1800s were bent more than ever before on maximizing their wealth. With the blessing of educators and clergymen who depicted personal economic freedom as a foundation of the republic, Americans increasingly focused on gratifying their desire for material prosperity, which intensified as the nation's economy grew.[10] But money-making ventures paid off much better for a tiny minority of people than for the vast majority, and the accumulated wealth of the most successful entrepreneurs grew to incomprehensible amounts. Some individuals also acquired larger stretches of the national domain than seemed consistent with republican ideals. The immensity of wealthy Americans' estates, fortunes, and power provoked extensive discourse about the moral principles that should govern economic conduct in the new industrial age.

The fact that these developments had parallels or manifestations in the Indian Territory did not escape Americans' notice. Indeed, rich tribe members and the tribes' widening distribution of wealth drew considerable attention from U.S. lawmakers, citizen activists, and journalists. But rather than equating the American and Indian situations, most non-Indian commentators attributed the rise of a wealthy tribal elite to peculiarities of Indian society and supposed racial traits. Accordingly, they advocated a singular solution: requiring the tribes to equalize shares of their collective wealth by allotting and privatizing the tribal lands. Many people expected privatization to facilitate the transfer of Indian property to Whites, yet the prospect troubled few Euro-Americans. Unlike the earlier Indian removal campaign, this drive to override the tribes' sovereignty did not provoke thousands of non-Indians to object on moral grounds; quite the contrary. Due to the arrogance that came with power and the ascendancy of an ideology that naturalized White superiority by the 1890s, most White Americans accepted without question their government's decision to compel a radical change in Indian property rights.

In the Five Tribes, meanwhile, the campaign for land allotment coincided with and incited further discussion about morality in economic affairs and, more specifically, about the sins and social contributions of the wealthy. But the campaign also skewed and ultimately preempted that tribal debate, because American advocates of allotment wanted to abolish the Indian governments as well. Tribe members were nearly united in their fear of losing sovereignty, and wealthy tribesmen led a defensive alliance, thereby partially deflecting questions about their commitment to other community ideals. When it became clear that resistance was futile, however, most of the wealthy accepted the redefinition of their property rights and counted on their familiarity with American legal and economic culture to compensate for the lost advantages of self-government. Many other tribe members, unable to accept the loss, signified their determination to remain Indians by reemphasizing their disdain for the culture of economic individualism. Once the Five Tribes were no longer acknowledged Indian nations with national land, their members had few reasons or means to overcome the difference in economic culture that alienated traditionalists from enterprising "progressives." Gone were the indigenous political structures that could have restrained the selfish individuals among them.

During the last quarter of the nineteenth century, wealth production took an impressive leap upward in eastern Indian Territory. Destructive tactics in the U.S. Civil War had plunged the tribes there into poverty, but signs of renewed enterprise were plentiful by 1880. In 1882, not long before Sarah Watie's death, editors of the Cherokee national newspaper crowed:

> The Cherokees, taken as a people in their corporate relations, are to-day the richest people under the sun—we say this without the least hesitations, or fear of successful contradiction—when numerically compared with other nations, they will not only make favorable showing with the best known governments of the world in opulence and power, but we think that in everything that constitutes a free, happy and successful people.... To be rich—to be opulent—to be powerful, an individual, a corporation, or a government, if you will, must possess certain things. They must, in the first place, be able to command money in quantities sufficient to meet every demand, or its equivalent, in substantial interests, or resources that can be made available in every time of need. These things we claim the Cherokees have, and have them in abundance.... Every acre is teeming with wealth, either in the richness of the soil, its mineral wealth, or in the exuberance of its spontaneous growths.... And the spirit of modern civilization, and modern Ethics is now permeating every member of our National autonomy.[11]

Ten years later, the Creek chief began his annual state of the nation message with the announcement, "We have now entered upon an era of prosperity never experienced in the past." Outside observers corroborated this claim, as have historians.[12]

The prosperity that cheered tribal chiefs and newspaper owners stemmed primarily from farming and ranching. In the Five Tribes' domains, the number of acres cultivated—many planted in cotton—rose by factors ranging from ten to thirty between 1865 and 1900. Cattle herds grew exponentially at the same time. Eastern Indian Territory, like other rural areas of the North American West, became a source of crops and animals for mills, slaughterhouses, and consumers in distant cities. That agricultural export economy supported a small but growing complement of merchandisers, tradesmen, and service professionals, many of whom located in towns that sprang up along transport routes.[13]

Concurrently, government officials and pundits in the United States saw reasons to boast about their own nation's economic growth and expanding prosperity. New transportation and communication networks spread across the continent, opening vast expanses to large-scale agriculture, stock-raising, and natural resource extraction. The growth of manufacturing and cities more than kept pace with rising production in rural areas. Historian Ray Ginger calculated that the country's "tangible assets . . . were perhaps two and a half times as great in 1900 as in 1877."[14]

These economic changes in the States and the Five Tribes were closely interrelated, and not simply because Euro-American wholesalers, merchants, exporters, and factories bought cotton, corn, and cattle raised in the Indian nations. Enterprising residents of the tribal enclaves had long done business in the surrounding states. Those residents included White people who were attracted to the Indian Territory by the economic possibilities they saw, many of which were contingent on marriage or other partnerships with tribe members.[15]

Commercial connections and migration between the States and the tribes increased in the 1870s and 1880s, especially when fingers of the U.S. railroad network reached into the tribal areas. Indian Territory products left for the States in trains that also brought the tribes American goods and American passengers who disembarked at Indian towns with eyes peeled for economic opportunity. In 1869, before the rails were laid, a U.S. Indian agent noted that the Five Tribes were "surrounded on three sides by States peopled with whites . . . energetic in their efforts to develop the resources of their own and neighboring States . . . , servitors of civilization demanding production from every available acre of land; and not long can a section of country of such magnitude, and so rich in all its resources, be held from their grasp."[16] The railroads subsequently made it easier for "energetic whites" to answer the siren call from the Indian side of the territorial boundary. Thousands of them took up residence there, both legally and illegally.[17]

The Creek chief Pleasant Porter later recalled, "Now, . . . the white people that came down to our country . . . wanted all these things" the Indians had— "a great deal of land" and "big lots of cattle." Once in Indian country, the Whites acted as if making money with ease was the "chief end and aim of existence," Porter complained, and they tempted the young Indian men "to do likewise."[18] Porter did not mention that he made money by collaborating with a White man in several business ventures or that other tribe members had encouraged people from the States to try their financial luck in the Indian Territory. Stand Watie's correspondence shows that his prominence, and possibly his reputation for listening with interest to business proposals, inspired out-siders to contact him about opportunities in the Cherokee Nation. One man wrote Watie after an acquaintance related a conversation he had had with the Cherokee general. Touting his own business savvy and claiming some Chero-kee ancestry, the writer offered to relocate from Missouri to the Cherokee Na-tion because he had heard "it was desirable by your commonwealth that every individual member of this Nation, however remote in blood relation, should identify himself locally, as well as otherwise, with the interests of that people, thereby contributing a mite, to the general strength and security of the whole." Another correspondent informed Watie that a Mr. Messingers had come to Cherokee country "on the representation . . . that a good chance could be had, to build a Mill, which would be profitable to him and you."[19]

Word of economic opportunities moved between the States and Indian Territory not only with letter carriers, travelers, and migrants, but also with newspapers and magazines produced in both places. The territory had enough literate residents to sustain several local papers, and major American periodi-cals also circulated there. According to a federal agent writing in 1889, people in the Five Tribes learned from U.S. news journals "that this is an age of self-endeavor, of advancement, of growth." And while Cherokees, Choctaws, or Creeks were perusing accounts of "self-endeavor" in the States, subscribers in the States were opening newspapers and magazines to find stories about burgeoning enterprise in Indian Territory.[20]

Although economic trends in the States and Five Tribes owed their simi-larity to commerce and communication between Indians and Americans, the similarity stopped short of replication. The tribal economies were not small-scale facsimiles of the U.S. economy. Corporate industrial capitalism and mushrooming cities—factors that drove American economic growth—were absent from the Indian nations until railroads bullied and bribed their way across the tribal lands in the 1870s.[21] Even then, most of the Indian Territory's new wealth was generated from farming and stock-raising at a time when ag-riculture, though expanding, was losing out to industry as Americans' greatest source of wealth.[22] For lack of substantial capital, Indian Territory did without banks until the 1890s. The tribal economies were also subject to political con-tingencies that did not affect other rural American jurisdictions: the tribes had acquired their lands by treaties that allowed the United States to control criti-cal economic conditions there. Federal officials not only assumed the power to interpret and enforce treaty clauses providing for railroad rights-of-way across the Indian lands; they also took tribal moneys in trust and invested them in railroads.[23]

In the view of many Americans, the tribal domains were economic backwaters. "The Indian on his reservation is pretty closely shut in either to farming or cattle raising," noted a contributor to the *New Englander and Yale Review* in 1889. "Jay Gould is reported to have compared that division of the M.K. & T.R.R. which lies in the Indian Territory to a tunnel 200 miles long, so far as any local business is concerned."[24] Railway development added a few corporations to the mix of players on the tribal scene, including firms that the tribes created or commissioned to cut crossties and mine coal for the railroads. Otherwise, eastern Indian Territory remained largely a country of corn and cotton fields, grazing ranges, and small towns, with not a major industrial complex or financial institution in sight.[25]

Nevertheless, the tribal and American economies had a feature in common that attested to the opportunities for lucrative activity they both afforded. Each had a small class of people who amassed extraordinary amounts of wealth. By means that reflected similar aspirations and comparable legal contexts, some individuals in the tribes and some in the States acquired so much property during the late 1800s that a tectonic shift in economic and political relations seemed under way. "Sixty years ago," wrote James Bryce, an Englishman who published his impressions of the United States in 1889, "there were no great fortunes in America, few large fortunes, no poverty. Now there is some poverty . . . , many large fortunes, and a greater number of gigantic fortunes than in any other country of the world."[26] A few years later, an observer of the Five Tribes claimed that wealthy landlords operated there "on a scale colossal enough to make the estates of the land barons of the Old World seem mere truck patches in comparison."[27]

This reference to Old World nobility was a stock rhetorical device of the time. "Business barons," "land barons," and "robber barons" were prevalent epithets for America's wealthiest entrepreneurs. Their displays of dazzling luxury, satirized by novelists Mark Twain and Charles Dudley Warner in *The Gilded Age*, seemed to rival the excesses of European aristocrats. But deriding ultra-rich capitalists as "barons" did not diminish Americans' fascination with them. Bryce called them "colossal millionaires who fill the public eye." He was amazed at the fuss made over their doings. Indeed, they were the great celebrities of the late nineteenth century. Their renown suggests to historian Alan Trachtenberg how most Americans viewed economic processes. "The prominence of names like Rockefeller, Carnegie, Hill, Huntington, Swift, and Armour [the era's great industrialists] indicates that business was still thought of as a field of personal competition, of heroic endeavor," says Trachtenberg. Supremely successful businessmen "represented themselves as the most prominent and potent figures in the society, princely in their mansions, their banquets, their excursions to pleasure resorts, their philanthropy and admonishments about success."[28]

Bryce attributed the appearance of American multimillionaires to rapid postwar development of the West—specifically, to new opportunities for land acquisition and speculation. His analysis validated an 1880 *New York Times* forecast that railway owners would make enormous fortunes from western land grants. The newspaper cited landholdings too enormous for most readers to imagine—25 to 50 million acres—and described the wealth of the top "money-getters" as "stupendous." Bryce hinted at the size of the most stupendous fortunes when he classified men with $5 to $15 million as mere "millionaires of the second order."[29]

No resident of Indian Territory could amass a fortune as immense as Bryce's "second order" millionaires did, let alone match the top-tier tycoons' wealth. Although the richest men in the Five Tribes presided over huge tracts of land, none of them had estates amounting to tens of millions of acres. Even so, the tribal populations included people wealthy enough to attract envious attention in the States and prompt an occasional comparison to the great American robber barons.[30] Cornelius Boudinot, interviewed for the *Chicago Daily Tribune* in 1873, volunteered that the richest man in the Indian Territory was "Old Bob Jones," a Choctaw owner of "several plantations on the Red River, and . . . worth $1,500,000."[31] In 1884, the *Indian Chieftain* newspaper, published at Vinita in the Cherokee Nation, ran a front-page story about the impressive aggregate wealth of Creek ranchers who had recently attended a cattlemen's convention in St. Louis. On the second page was additional coverage from the St. Louis *Globe-Democrat*, identifying one of the Creeks as "Col. F. B. Severs, the Jay Gould of the Nation."[32]

By then, Jay Gould, a New York financier with controlling stakes in rail lines through Indian Territory, was well-known to Cherokees and Creeks.[33] The *Cherokee Advocate* had reprinted a *Demorest's Monthly* article labeling Gould the most powerful human on earth thanks to his monopolies on transportation and communication networks and his "conscienceless" speculations.[34] *Advocate* editors assumed that their readers shared Americans' fascination with rich individuals, whether Indian or non-Indian. The paper catered to that fascination by carrying a *Kansas City Times* prediction that the wealth of Osage Indians—neighbors to the Cherokees—would soon tempt "run-down-at-the-heel" European noblemen to seek "American heiresses among the dusky bells [*sic*] of the Osage tribe." A Choctaw editor likewise deemed rich people newsworthy. He devoted space to a report that the Chickasaw governor was "erecting a large mansion," a credit to the "untiring energy" the governor had devoted to "private affairs."[35]

As notoriously rich persons "filled the public eye" in the United States and Indian Territory, the exceptional magnitude of their fortunes disturbed some spectators. Many Americans expressed fear that their most affluent countrymen now controlled too great a share of the nation's wealth, and Jay Gould was not the only one reviled for "conscienceless" greed. Members of the Five Tribes, for their part, did not confine accusations of greed to Americans like Gould; they found fault with homegrown "monopolists" as well. In the tribes and the States simultaneously, new outsized personal fortunes had brought attention to a disconcerting feature of a free-enterprise economy and set people to thinking about the ethics of trying to get rich.

Records of American discourse on the subject are abundant. Several historians have drawn on those records to describe the issue much as Nell Painter does: "Comparing the lavish lives of the aristocrats . . . with the poverty of the working masses, many thoughtful observers questioned the existence of immutable natural laws and worried instead that their society was out of joint." Although there had always been Americans who read the contrasting conditions of rich and poor as a sign that the republic was losing its virtue, their numbers grew, and indignant voices rang out more often in national forums as the century progressed.[36]

In 1881, Henry Demarest Lloyd, financial editor of the *Chicago Tribune*, persuaded *Atlantic Monthly* to publish his "Story of a Great Monopoly." Lloyd laid out data that moved him to describe the wealth and political pull of men like Gould as "sins against public and private faith on a scale impossible in the early days of republics and corporations." Shortly thereafter, John H. Reagan of Texas was denouncing such sins in Congress and forecasting a backlash from angry workers who saw their hard work going to "raise up a dozen Vanderbilts, with several hundred millions of dollars." William Moody chimed in with a widely read exposé of land monopolization. Before long, an accompanying chorus of journalists, politicians, educators, and even some businessmen was voicing concerns about extreme private wealth.[37] Backing them up and adding volume to the clamor, researchers published statistics showing that a very small percentage of the population held a very large portion of American wealth.[38] The morality and social role of the rich became an issue for people ranging from President Grover Cleveland, who said Americans were being trampled under the "iron heel" of trusts, to the Populists who endorsed an 1892 party platform alleging that "fruits of the toil of millions are boldly stolen to build up colossal fortunes for a few."[39]

The parallel public discourse in the Five Tribes left a sparser record, in part because the population of potential commentators was far smaller. The tribal commentary also focused more often on greed for land—the most common and politically significant form of wealth in the Indian Territory. Nonetheless, the likeness to discussion in the States was strong. In both places, the question on many minds was whether admirable enterprise had transmuted into pervasive, indecent selfishness that sullied the national character and invited civic disorder.

Taking an affirmative position on that question in 1895, a prominent Cherokee wrote under a pseudonym to the *Indian Chieftain*: "It is much to be regretted that a few of our citizens worship the dollar so much that they forget their poor neighbor has any rights in the country whatsoever. . . . The Cherokees have more greedy and avaricious people among them than any other race of people upon the globe."[40] By then, local newspapers had been publishing occasional jeremiads about rampant greed for at least two decades. An unnamed person contributed one to the *Cherokee Advocate* in 1874. "It displeases the old gentleman," he rumbled, "to see that some of his children are so greedy that they are not satisfied with what they need, and like the 'pale faces' would 'fall down and worship' the devil." Two years later, Principal Chief Charles Thompson said in his annual message to the Cherokee Nation, "I see in various portions of our country that there is greed and avariciousness manifested by some of our citizens to hold whole sections of land to the exclusion of other citizens, which . . . should not be permitted."[41]

As the number of mammoth landholdings in tribal territory grew, more Cherokees joined in condemning them as gluttonous. S. S. Stephens, who wanted the land meted out to all tribe members in equal lots, depicted the opposition as villainously selfish for taking possession of too much acreage and refusing to give up the excess. "How shall we designate such a ring?" Stephens asked in 1886. "Can we say you are brazen-faced and iron-fingered, vulture-hearted? Examine the . . . picture" of a big landholder, "and you will see the sharp fingers, pointed with gold, sinking deep into the heart of our nationality."[42]

Many such tirades, in the tribes as well as the States, warned of destructive conflict between social strata or classes—populations that seemed increasingly distinct and antagonistic due to disparities in wealth. Among relatively prosperous Americans, anxiety about class conflict intensified in the 1880s with a rash of strikes, riots, and violent state and industry reactions, dubbed the Great Upheaval. When labor organizers and Populist politicians spoke of enmity between the "plain" people who produced the country's wealth and the "idle rich" who confiscated it, they seemed to confirm that the fabric of society was unraveling.[43] In 1886, Josiah Strong, a Home Missionary minister, cited the "almost impassable gulf" between industrial employees and employers as one of several grave threats to the country's future.[44] And that divide was not the only one portending a national implosion. Many professionals, intellectuals, farmers, and craftsmen also declared their opposition to the capitalists, whom they accused of usurping power for selfish ends and denying other Americans opportunities that the nation's founders deemed essential for an enduring, genuine republic.[45]

People in the Five Tribes noticed more pronounced stratification of their societies as well, and many warned that internecine strife would follow.[46] Among them was Robert C. Childers, a Creek who grumbled that a rich man had "the advantage because of his wealth to graze his cattle on thousands of acres." The wealthy exerted undue influence over the distribution of land, Childers charged; but he predicted that the humble class of Indians would eventually unseat "the selfish money king and the avaracious [sic] politician."[47] In some places, "humble" Indians had already vented their anger at the "money kings" by killing animals and destroying other property belonging to large commercial operations.[48]

It was common (and not unfounded) to assume that the developing class conflict in the tribes coincided with an older rift between "traditionalists" and the "progressives" who had embraced American economic culture. After a visit to the Cherokee Nation in 1888, journalist Anna Laurens Dawes reported that only half of its citizens spoke English, thus "presenting the problem of a nation divided into two sharply opposed classes—the highly civilized class of the towns; and the peasant farmers of the open country, or 'natives,' as it is the fashion to call them, in amusing disregard of a common origin." An associate of James Bell differentiated his own "enterprising class" of Cherokees from "the Hog and Hominy class that cares for nothing further" in the way of material comforts.[49] More often, people called the two social strata "mixed-bloods" and "full-bloods," respectively, even though that categorization identified economic orientation more than ancestry.[50] Anna Dawes, for example, referred to "peasant farmers" as full-bloods and asserted that they knew nothing of ambition or progress; but she also cast doubt on her choice of terms by adding, "Nor is the admixture of white blood the only enterprising quality in these nations, as is sometimes somewhat superficially charged."[51]

In fact, disputes about economic strategy did not split the tribal memberships neatly into opposing camps of unambitious full-bloods and mercenary mixed-bloods. Some so-called full-bloods did strive to improve their economic

These images from the late 1800s attest to the disparity in material wealth that developed between the Civilized Tribes' business-minded classes and so-called full-bloods. While a small, crude log cabin was a typical dwelling for the majority of full-bloods, a big farmer and rancher such as William B. Moon could provide his family with the capacious comfort of a two-story frame house. Courtesy of Research Division of the Oklahoma Historical Society, images 1709 and 8821.

prospects, while many in the mixed-blood category condemned people who cared too much for their own material comfort.[52] Additionally, as Robert Childers noted, traditional and wealthy tribe members shared a devotion to tribal autonomy that prompted them to tolerate some differences in their economic practices and enabled them at times to agree on economic policy.[53] But Childers did not identify with either of those groups; instead, he claimed membership in a "third class" of Creeks who favored "civilization full and complete." Childers suggested that "complete civilization" would ensure universal opportunity to acquire and profit from property, and though he was in a middle class, he evidently counted himself among the "humble" Indians who were prepared to battle the "money kings" for such opportunity.[54]

Cornelius Boudinot similarly purported to exemplify a beleaguered Cherokee middle class—a population that William McLoughlin has since characterized as "a small bourgeoisie without power." When interviewed for the *Chicago Daily Tribune*, Boudinot contended that the critical struggle in his nation pitted people like him against an alliance of the tribe's richest and poorest members. Wealthy men, he complained, had commandeered the government, added the spoils of office to their coffers, and manipulated the impoverished full-bloods to direct their resentment at enterprising "half breeds" instead of the real villains.[55]

Even a three-class schematic of the tribal societies was oversimplified. Competition for resources made antagonists of people that Childers and Boudinot lumped in the upper class. There were two camps of Creek ranchers, for instance—those who wanted to maximize the land available for their own stock, and those who wanted land they could lease to Texas cattlemen.[56] The amorphous middle class divided on the issue of breaking tribal land into privately owned tracts, with people on each side portraying themselves as champions of the poor and their opponents as would-be "potentates."[57] A Cherokee "Committee of Safety" tried to banish James Bell for promoting land allotment and aiding "Rail Road Corporations Land Grabbers and Such arch Traitors as Cornelius Boudinot," but the committee undoubtedly included people who admired or envied successful businessmen, just as Bell did.[58]

In other words, much of the documented Indian animosity toward the rich came not from devotees of aboriginal communalism, but from individuals who craved lucrative opportunities and property themselves. Like their middle-class counterparts in the United States, they generally endorsed an ethos of economic individualism but faulted wealthier compatriots for failing to honor mitigating values.[59] They rationalized their own material ambitions in a way that middle-class Americans would have approved: by professing belief in the social value of profit-oriented enterprise and private property. Their faith rested on an assumption that every human has a natural desire for wealth, and on a second assumption that a continual increase in wealth is a universal desideratum of human societies. It followed, for them, that property rights were necessary and desirable instruments of progress—inducements to wealth-generating activity. If citizens could reap personal material rewards for investing labor, capital, or brainpower in productive ventures, their nation's cumulative wealth would grow vigorously.

Public figures in the tribes regularly articulated these beliefs. An 1873 *Cherokee Advocate* essay titled "Capital and Labor" opined that "the highest prosperity" consists "in the presence and possession of everything labor can produce and money can buy."

> It is honorable and creditable to want money. . . . The development of taste and intellect gives birth to new wants at every step, and to be indifferent to the means (which in great part is money,) by which alone such wants can be supplied, is an evidence of a low social condition, until, in following the downward grade, we find among savages no wants at all of any consequence. . . . Money to a man of common refinement, means a plenty of the best to eat and drink, for family and friends—rapid and easy conveyance from place to place—comfortable and tasteful dwellings, with neat and pleasant attachments within and without—well dressed and well-trained children—Literature,—music, &c. &c. . . . We believe such to be the present situation of Cherokees generally. They aspire to improvement, both of family and Nation. They appreciate the excellent uses of money.[60]

The following year, the National Party pledged that it would "favor the fostering of industry, the encouragement of enterprise, and the development of the resources of the [Cherokee] Nation," and would "use its influence to develop, especially, the agricultural and stock-growing interests." Even the rival Downing Party, which took a more populist tack and denounced large-scale ranchers for hogging land, declared itself "in favor of encouraging enterprise, industry, and education among all classes of our people."[61]

To judges of the Creek Supreme Court, it was self-evident that affording opportunity for private gain was a requisite of fostering productive industry. In an 1875 decision invalidating a tribal ban on the employment of U.S. citizens, they wrote, "It is a common right, created by devine [*sic*] authority for the benefit of man to say who shall cultivate his soil or perform any kind of [paid] labor." Creeks had adopted a constitution in order to secure "the blessing of . . . freedom," and freedom was "granted us to perform any duty that is our personal interest and advantage if the performance of such duty does not interfere with the rights and interest of others."[62] Even the Choctaw chief Coleman Cole, elected on the Full Blood Party ticket after pledging to protect communal ownership of key tribal resources, said that freedom to pursue personal economic interests was the best assurance of a prosperous society. "If we ascertain the most effectual means of promoting the wellfare of [our] nation," Cole advised legislators, "we have to inquire what constitutes the well being of an individual, because so far as we provide well for ourselves, for the ultimate and legitamate promotion of our own personal happiness and position in society, so far we increase the happiness, respectability and the importance in which we live, the prosperity of the nation at large and good to man kind."[63]

The assumptions underlying these Indian pronouncements were virtually the same as the predominant axioms of economic life in the United States. Drawn from the theories of Britons John Locke and Adam Smith, adapted to American conditions, and popularized in political oratory, sermons, school lessons, and literature, the axioms grounded an ideology that most Americans had come to regard as common sense. Francis Wayland, author of a widely read text on political economy, put a cardinal premise of the ideology in blunt terms. The two basic laws of creation, he declared, were "that every man must 'be allowed to gain all that he can,' and that 'having gained all that he can, he be allowed to use it as well.'"[64]

People who held those laws sacred could be found within all U.S. social ranks and political parties.[65] The *New York Times*, gently ridiculing a proposal to reduce "the excessive prevalence of millionaires" by limiting each person to assets worth $1 million, conjectured that "the vast majority" of Americans "would be more excited over a scheme that insured the getting of a million." Another tenet of the national creed, identified by historian John Cawelti, made this speculation plausible. "The argument ran like this: America is the land of opportunity; any individual willing to work hard can tap these opportunities; continuous growth and economic expansion are the best way of creating more opportunities; therefore, the pursuit of economic advancement is not only to the individual's advantage, but the best way to help others."[66] Substitute "the Choctaw Nation" for "America," and this becomes a paraphrase of Coleman Cole's message in 1878.

But what did it mean that some individuals experienced far greater "economic advancement" than others? Many commentators in the States and the Five Tribes offered essentially the same answer to this question: disparities of personal wealth had social utility. Americans cited several society-wide benefits associated with allowing exceptionally large private accumulations of wealth. Above all, in a nation with no privileged aristocracy, the feats of the top earners gave everyone an incentive to labor productively. As Abraham Lincoln reputedly said, "That some would be rich shows that others may become rich."[67] James Bryce explained Americans' esteem for the rich a bit differently: "When a man has won great wealth by the display of remarkable talents . . . , it is felt that his gifts are a credit to the nation." As citizens of a country that afforded all of them a chance to prosper by hard work, Americans could bask in their successful compatriots' reflected glory.[68]

In a variety of media and messages, wealthy businessmen got credit for other, more specific civic contributions. Besides inspiring competition that contributed to national progress, they modeled traits that enabled people to prosper. Believing that it required strength of character to succeed in profit-making activities, the entrepreneurs' admirers praised them as exemplars of socially desirable behavior. Francis Bowen, a dean of mainstream political economists, called the quest for wealth "a natural test of character, ability, and intelligence." Wealth "fairly earned," he intoned, was "usually coupled with sobriety, prudence, industry, and good sense."[69]

Millions of Americans would have nodded in reflexive agreement with another sentence from a Bowen treatise: "It is true that men are usually selfish in the pursuit of wealth; but it is a wise and benevolent arrangement of Providence, that even those who are thinking only of their own credit and advantage are led, unconsciously but surely, to benefit others."[70] An entrepreneur who generated wealth for his own pocket presumably created wealth for many other people as well. In addition to providing services and products people needed, his business paid employees and suppliers whose money, when spent, would support enterprises offering other goods and services. In defense of policies that made the great railroad fortunes possible, a social scientist and government advisor wrote, "Large as were the gains to the great corporations . . . and to Mr. Vanderbilt and his compeers, they were almost infinitesimal when compared with the gains of the public."[71] Even the best-selling author Henry George, accused of heresy for opposing private landownership, thought a capitalist should enjoy the full fruits of his activity on rented land because "by the additional value . . . created he has added that much to the common stock of wealth, and he ought to profit by it." Reasoning that "improvements" to the land "benefit the whole community," George said he "would do nothing to discourage them."[72]

There is philosophical accord between these words from American analysts and Robert Owen's apologia for the "opening up of large farms in the Five Nations." Owen, a Cherokee who served in the 1880s as U.S. agent for his tribe and others, conceded the possibility "that some individual will get more than he is entitled to." But he added, "The enterprising Indian is creating wealth for his community, and therefore contributing to progress." Robert Childers, too, sounded like an apt student of Francis Bowen when he urged fellow Creeks to allot their national land so that each person could have a deed to 400 acres rather than "one seventeen hundred thousandth interest" in a 7-million-acre tract under tribal ownership. "In event of the former, part of ones [sic] land could be deeded to purchasers who would pay more than $1.25 per acre and whose improvements would greatly enhance the value of the land yet unsold. This would settle up the country, bring capital, build up cities where we have cross road stores and invite railroads, manufacturers, etc., which would give employment to our people and markets for our productions."[73]

Faith in the righteousness of self-enriching ventures endured even though success did not reliably correspond to effort, talent, or other virtues. Most Americans accepted the moral logic of economic individualism despite the visibility of individuals who corralled huge shares of the national wealth simply by speculating or belonging to a rich family.[74] Occasionally, a public figure sidestepped the issue of unequal rewards for equal effort by resorting to the platitude that money was neither an exclusive nor a satisfactory measure of success and contentment. Oil magnate John D. Rockefeller—piously disparaging the kind of single-minded quest for profits that made him famous—remarked, "What people most seek cannot be bought with money."[75] But American moralists also said there was nothing wrong per se with wanting and accumulating money. Indeed, consistent with the maxim that prosperity was evidence of virtue, many social critics refrained from reproaching the rich and sought instead to reform the poor.[76] Commentary critical of wealthy people usually singled out those who lived in luxury while they denied charity to the blamelessly destitute. Many an editorial cautioned millionaires that they had a moral responsibility to use their fortunes for the good of society. In a sermon the New York Times deemed newsworthy but unsurprising, famous Protestant clergyman Henry Ward Beecher told an affluent audience, "Every rich man should hold himself bound to leave a memorial of his wealth to the community in which he amassed it and which aided him in his wealth-getting enterprises."[77]

Proposals to discourage the concentration of wealth by legislation circulated in the United States, but they were controversial, even when they did not repudiate the prevailing ideology. Advocates of government regulation, including the seemingly radical Populists, aimed mainly to prevent the monopolization of opportunity. They hoped to ensure (many would have said restore) conditions in which Americans could compete for wealth on equal terms. They did not propose to enforce equivalent results.[78] In contrast, backers of a strict laissez-faire policy contended that the playing field would level itself in time without legal action; the existing inequity was transitional and would give way to an economy that provided adequately for everyone, making vicious competition and greed obsolete.[79]

Whether government should take an active part in allocating wealth was also a topic of lively debate in the Five Tribes, and the opinions that saw print were ideological kin to American thought on the subject. The issue engaged Cherokees in 1882, for instance, when W. T. Adair proposed a national relief fund for a large indigent population that was "piteously and *grievously in need* of the means of subsistence." People on both sides of the debate agreed that the well-off should show concern for the poor, but they differed on the desirability of legislating benevolence. They also suggested reasons to suspect their opponents of selfish motives. Since the proposed aid would require a government purchase of grain, farmers with surplus corn to sell hardly seemed altruistic when they said the nation had a moral obligation to feed the poor. Conversely, a chronic shortage of hired hands cast doubt on the objectivity of ranchers' argument that charity would demoralize people who should learn instead to sell their labor.[80]

The subject of land allocation sparked more talk in the tribes about possible responses to unequal and hoarded wealth. Although each of the Five Tribes had decided that title to the national domain would remain forever in the tribe as a whole, each granted substantial property rights to citizens who created private estates by occupying and improving tracts of tribal land. Virtually every family did claim a plot of ground, but the size and value of claims varied greatly. Because an occupant could do with his claim almost everything that an American landowner could, a large or strategic landholding had the potential to make a person very prosperous. Tribal officials knew that monopolization of vital land was a possibility, and they feared the unrest it would cause among the numerous Indians who subsisted by tilling a few acres and pasturing stock on open areas. But many officials were profiting from their own expansive landholdings. Besides, the danger that enclosures would render some tribe members homeless or deprive them entirely of pasture seemed remote in most places until the 1880s, when people began to claim tracts of unprecedented size, often on former grazing commons.[81]

The factors that made enormous holdings possible—railroads, booming demand for cattle range, the invention of barbed-wire fencing, money and machinations of outside corporations, and the use of non-Indian tenants to take possession of land—posed a host of tough questions for the tribes. Issues of economic policy were entangled with urgent political and jurisdictional concerns, including the challenges presented by the explosive growth of non-member populations in tribal territory. Nonetheless, the subject of immoderate wealth accumulation received a generous share of specific attention. It inspired numerous letters and editorials in local newspapers, and those indicate that the question kindled debate in other forums across the Five Tribes. The fencing phenomenon disturbed the so-called full-blood element because they felt a proprietary attachment to the grazing commons. It also posed an intellectual challenge for tribe members who thought of private property rights in Lockean terms. Vast wire-bordered enclosures defied John Locke's labor-investment rationale for property rights when the claimants did nothing else to the land.

In 1882, aware of murmurs about the new practice of preempting grass-land with cheap wire fences, the Cherokee government newspaper staked out a laissez-faire position on the issue. "Many wants may be considered superfluous, while others as natural and necessary," observed editors of the *Advocate*, "but who has the right to pronounce judgment upon them? Of the simple and the primitive they are few—of the advanced and refined they are many. Shall the industrious and enterprising be stayed by those who are not?" That was surely not the intent of the tribal constitution's proscription against monopolies. "Privileges are only to be restrained and controlled, where mutual benefits might be enjoyed, or the exclusion of such might deprive, where they could be common, a neighbor of a participation."[82] Two years later, noting that large enclosures had provoked "a great deal of hard feeling" in the Cherokee and Chickasaw nations, the Choctaw Nation paper, *Indian Champion*, weighed in with a defense of property that would have gladdened Francis Wayland's heart:

> For centuries it has been the recognized right of one man, if he displays more energy and brains than another, to accumulate wealth. . . . There are four means of gaining wealth open to the people of the Territory— farming, stock-raising, the mercantile business, and one of the professions—and the government might as well say to the lawyer, who by his ability has obtained half of the business of the Nation, 'You have too much business and must divide,' as to say to the farmers, you must reduce your farms, or to the stockmen, you must reduce your herds— something that has yet been unheard.[83]

Among those with "hard feelings" about supersized farms and ranches was S. S. Stephens, a schoolteacher who argued in 1886, "The time has come for our government to limit the amount of accumulation of property" by allotting 160 acres to each Cherokee citizen. "Otherwise," he warned, "the work of absorption will go on, and the large fishes will eat up the small ones."[84] In subsequent years, many more citizens—and even tribal officials—spoke or wrote of a need to protect tribe members who had "neither the disposition, the means, or the chance to take the 'lions share' where greed is allowed full sway by law." But the commentators took divergent positions on whether allotting the land in equal portions would meet that need.[85] In 1892, the *Cherokee Advocate*, characterizing the issue as "a principle of justice between the Cherokee government and that portion of the people around whom it should throw an arm of protection," finally endorsed allotment as a means of foiling monopolies (although the immediate goal was probably to deflect a drive in Congress to force allotment on the tribe).[86] William P. Boudinot, also proclaiming his concern for the "more modest, less greedy, and by far the most deserving" people, took exception to the *Advocate*'s reasoning. He opposed allotment, he said, because he expected that the "selfish would make haste" to gobble up the good tracts. Instead, he recommended stricter controls on land use under the existing ownership and occupancy system.[87]

Boudinot argued further that there was no unjust monopolization of common resources so long as the strongest people did not "use their greater strength to crowd weaker ones back, fill themselves, then put the rest in bags for the future, not caring whether others starve."[88] By 1892, however, other editorialists thought such a state of affairs had already come to pass; the strong, having learned to manipulate the organs of tribal government in their interest, *were* crowding the weak back. As evidence of the monopolists' hold over the political process, one pseudonymous contributor to the *Muskogee Phoenix* cited his tribe's flat head tax. A married father of ten had to pay twelve times as much as a childless man, even if the former had only a tiny corn patch, while the latter's stock grazed "on a thousand hills, and the magnitude of his farms, in the aggregate, [ran] into thousands of acres, causing him to revel in wealth and affluence." "Is it not emphatically a rich man's government?" the writer asked."[89]

Pleasant Porter conceded that a man of his affluent class should curb his appetite for land if indulging it would threaten other Creeks' welfare. In an 1891 letter to Chief Isparhecher, whom he would succeed, Porter wrote, "As you know, I am one of those using a large portion of our public domain which has been and is a matter of great profit to me, yet because our law allows it

Pleasant Porter, son of a native Creek woman and a White adopted Creek man, served as chief of his nation from 1899 until 1907 during the allotment of tribal lands mandated by U.S. law. He exemplified many upper-class citizens of the Civilized Tribes in that he amassed wealth in business and in ranching on tribal lands, joined his tribe's numerous "full-bloods" in opposing allotment until resistance was futile, then accommodated the unwanted change without suffering economic setbacks. Courtesy of Research Division of the Oklahoma Historical Society, image 3180.

and others practice it, I do not feel that it is right or just that this profit should continue to me at the risk and expense of the whole people."[90] It is hard to know how honest Porter was being, either with Isparhecher or with himself. The sentiment he expressed was Creek orthodoxy, and tradition as well as the political strength of traditionalists like Isparhecher obliged Porter to endorse the prevailing moral code. But if Porter meant by his comments that he would stoutly defend the national ideal against apostate Creeks, he did not have a fair chance to prove it. The U.S. government would soon preempt the tribe's efforts to regulate the use of its land.

As large land claims stirred increasing controversy, the Indian governments did fashion regulatory responses, mostly consisting of limits on leases to outsiders and taxes on large cattle operations.[91] The ostensible purpose was to inhibit practices that could frustrate the policy of assuring every tribal citizen a place to live and raise food. But granting citizens the fruit of their individual investments was also accustomed policy by then, and tribal lawmakers did not plan to discourage or restrict private improvements to tribal land. In fact, since Americans were known to cite undeveloped Indian lands as evidence that tribes could afford to cede tracts for settlement by Whites, chiefs and councilors generally wanted to promote the development of vacant areas.[92]

That aim vied for primacy with the hope of many Indians that their government would require the land hogs to leave room for those whose appetite for land was more modest.

Tribal discussions of these competing considerations were freighted with implications for other critical issues, especially the tribes' status vis-à-vis the United States. Unlike the United States, the Five Tribes did not have the opportunity to consider independently how they should respond to selfish business practices or land monopolization. Americans with ominous objectives insisted on participating in the tribal debates. In fact, Americans had a major hand in launching and propelling those debates when they made monopolization an issue in their campaign for allotment of the Indian lands. Tribe members' thoughts on immoderate property accumulation could not help but reflect their reactions to the American campaign.

By the 1890s, that campaign had been under way for more than two decades. In 1873, the National Commercial Convention urged Congress to open the "exhaustless treasures" of the Indian Territory to "the surrounding and the incoming white population" by assigning each resident Indian family a homestead of specified size and selling surplus acreage.[93] Railway corporations were particularly eager for such a move because the treaties providing for their rights-of-way also promised them title to adjoining land if Indian title were ever extinguished.[94] The corporations easily enlisted residents of western states and development boosters in their fight. Over time, they also recruited allies among humanitarian activists, politicians, federal officials, and other groups with no immediate material interests at stake. Sundry tribe members abetted the cause as well, some knowingly and venally, some incidentally or in the belief that their communities' advancement depended on it.[95]

When civilian reformers pressed Congress early in the 1880s to authorize the allotment of all Indian reservations in the United States, correcting a skewed distribution of tribal wealth was not their stated goal. Rather, organizations such as the Indian Rights Association and the Women's National Indian Association, which united under the name Friends of the Indian, stressed that individual landownership would inspire Indians to adopt industrious habits and thus equip them to function in civilized society.[96] When focusing specifically on the five so-called Civilized Tribes, however, advocates of allotment repeatedly represented it as an antidote to avarice that had corrupted those societies.[97] They alleged from the beginning that the principal obstacle to privatization of Indian Territory land was the selfish resistance of persons who knew how to exploit tribal law and custom for their own enrichment. In 1886, the commissioner of Indian Affairs wrote, "It will not do to say, as the wealthy and influential leaders of the [Indian] nations contend, that their system of laws gives to every individual member of the tribe equal facilities to be independent and equal opportunity to possess himself of a homestead. Already the rich and choice lands are appropriated by those most enterprising and self seeking."[98]

After Congress excepted the Five Tribes from coverage of the General Allotment Act in 1887, American critics of that decision stepped up their vilification of the tribes' "enterprising and self seeking" members, portraying them as avaricious manipulators who took advantage of their dubious tribal ties and the naïveté of the Indian masses. An article in *Harper's New Monthly Magazine* claimed that simple-minded full-bloods were at the mercy of a few "short-sighted, selfish, venal leaders of slight Indian blood, who handle the large revenues of the tribe after the most modern method of 'practical politics.'" Speaking at the annual Friends of the Indian conference, Massachusetts senator Henry Dawes marshaled statistical evidence of greed in the Five Tribes. He alleged that a mere sixty-one Creeks together held 1 million of the tribe's 3 million acres. Another senator, Orville Platt of Connecticut, resorted to inflammatory rhetoric when arguing that allotment was the solution to such monopolization. "Probably nowhere else in the world since the time of the feudal barons has there been a condition of society demanding reformation equal to that now demanded in the Indian Territory," Platt fulminated in the *North American Review*. "As might be expected, the Indian citizen landholders control the Indian governments absolutely, and no law can be passed in Indian legislatures interfering with their greed." The "poor, shiftless, and ignorant" full-blood's "patrimony is absorbed by the rapacious white Indian or half-breed."[99]

Not surprisingly, such rhetoric drew defensive reactions not only from the people Platt termed "white Indians" and "half-breeds," but also from Indians he characterized as ignorant and politically impotent. An American plan to pair allotment with the dissolution of the tribal governments gave tribe members an added, urgent motivation to protest. Understandably, they were more concerned with defending their familiar system of landownership and allocation than with holding a candid, conclusive public debate about the morality or obligations of people who got rich in that system.

The defenders invoked sacrosanct tribal doctrine: the tradition of holding the land in common was necessary for and inseparable from the tribes' existence as sovereign, self-supporting peoples. The *Advocate* reminded Cherokees in 1876 that they had "land worth millions of dollars, and millions of dollars in cash—all depending upon the existence of our Government in which the title rests." Tribal ownership was the best protection against an ever-present threat from Euro-Americans who resented Indians' sovereignty and possession of valuable land. Viewing proposals for the subdivision and privatization of their territory in light of these time-honored truths, tribal leaders saw yet another scheme to rob them of their resources and independence.[100] A common response was to turn up the light on American greed and dim the light on acquisitiveness in tribal ranks, where it could be found among the leaders themselves.

Accordingly, even though the advocates of allotment included some Cherokees, Creeks, Choctaws, and Chickasaws, opponents billed the battle first and foremost as one between Indians and greedy White Americans.[101] A few Choctaws had urged "the mischievous project of sectionizing . . . their lands" as early as 1870, yet the wealthy chief Peter Pitchlynn directed his angriest invective at other backers of the plan. "Not only individuals are interested, whose mouths water for profitable speculations," Pitchlynn fumed, "but also some of the great railroad corporations which have so extraordinary an influence over Congress; and the Congress itself and the people of the United States are appealed to by the cry that the progress of the white race and the interests of trade and commercial intercourse require that our country shall be opened to settlement." Allotment and privatization would lead to speculation, taxation, and schemes to defraud allottees of their property. "These processes," Pitchlynn alleged with substantial basis, "have been so common that they may not unjustly be said to constitute a part of the settled policy of the United States."[102] In 1886, a Cherokee made the same point more acridly in the *Indian Chieftain*. "The graspings of this American people after wealth," he wrote, "are opposed to . . . our present land tenure system." How could allotment be anything but a means to take what belongs to Indians "and appropriate it to the greed of an avarice that will never be satisfied?"[103]

While tribal commentators said often that greed was an American trait, influential Americans maintained that apathy was Indians' dominant trait and the reason for the tribes' economic backwardness. Like defenders of the tribal governments, Americans generally believed that holding land in common was a defining feature of Indian societies, and for most Americans, that marked Indians as uncivilized people who lacked the enterprising spirit of their civilized superiors.[104] Both Americans and tribe members were vague or indecisive about whether their supposed contrasting economic propensities were due to natural dispositions or inherited tradition; but as they tried to bolster their own arguments or discredit their opposition, they all drew liberally on racial stereotypes.[105]

The popular American conception of Indians as change-resistant, primitive communists was older than the United States.[106] It had proved invulnerable to factual attacks during the antebellum crusade to remove the southern tribes from their original homelands. Even after the Civil War, people who knew of contrary examples invoked the concept unthinkingly or shamelessly to justify demands that the Indian Territory be opened to American settlers and business. When the Indian affairs commissioner called for allotment of all reservations in 1879, he pronounced the "system of title in common" pernicious, in that it "prevented individual advancement and repressed that spirit of rivalry and the desire to accumulate property for personal use or comfort which is the source of success and advancement in all white communities."[107] As this claim suggests, the identification of Indians with common ownership was tenacious in large part because it allowed Euro-Americans to define themselves by comparison as energetic agents of the progress that God or nature ordained. In the nationalist symbolism of the United States, Alan Trachtenberg observes, "'Indian' remained the utmost antithesis to an America dedicated to productivity, profit, and private property."[108]

Spokesmen for the Five Tribes tried to defend their system of landownership without accepting the associated image of Indians as unenterprising. For ammunition, they used both facts and stereotypes. On one hand, they peppered U.S. policymakers with information meant to show that private property rights were as important in their nations as in the States, and that these acted similarly as a force for civilization and progress. By retaining title to the land, the tribal governments did not squelch entrepreneurial spirit. This was the Cherokee Nation's pitch in a census report to Congress:

> The statements made to you that we, or any of the Indians, are communists, and hold property in common, are entirely erroneous. No people are more jealous of the personal right to property than Indians. The improvements on farms may be, and often are, sold; they may descend in families for generations, and so long as occupied cannot be invaded, nor for two years after abandonment. These farms and lots are practically just as much the property of the individuals as yours are. He who does not wish to keep can sell to all lawful citizens. The only difference between your land systems and ours is that the unoccupied surface of the earth is not a chattel to be sold and speculated in by men who do not use it. . . . We invite your attention to the fact that the five nations of the Indian Territory who have adopted this system have made the most rapid progress.[109]

On the other hand, tribe members often seemed to agree with Americans that common landownership not only preserved but virtually defined Indian societies, and some implied that it was a custom necessitated as much by Indian racial traits as by White greed and envy. In 1873, millionaire Robert M. Jones told a congressional committee that "the disposition of the Indian" largely explained why few of his fellow Choctaws had tried to accumulate wealth as he had. An 1885 communication to Congress from all five tribal governments stated, "Ownership of lands in common has been a part of their national policy from time immemorial. Indeed, the present secretary of the interior says, with literal truth, in his recent annual report, that this system 'is with them a religion, as well as a law of property.' It is based upon peculiarities and necessities of the race, which cannot be ignored, without the gravest perils to the people."[110] Tribal spokesmen thus made the paradoxical argument that their people had become full-fledged property owners yet continued to need a property system suited to Indian "peculiarities."

In their zeal to defend undivided landownership, spokesmen for the Five Tribes could also spout a mythology of opportunity as robust as the one Americans invoked to justify unfettered private property rights. Some of the Indians who complained at times about the spread of mammoth ranches bragged at other times about the near-utopian fairness of their property system. In answer to the monopoly-busting rationale for allotment, they said that holding the land in common ensured opportunity for all their people and basic security for the full-blood majority. By putting substantial unclaimed acreage to use, energetic individuals could prosper more than complacent or shiftless ones; but because every citizen could at least get land for a homestead, tribal ownership was proof against extremes of wealth and poverty. An 1876 "remonstrance" to Congress from four of the tribes claimed, "With us, while but few may attain to great wealth, all may attain to a decent competency, and none need be houseless or homeless paupers." This was the basis for Chief Joel Mayes's boast in 1891 that Cherokees had not only "the true system of government for the protection of the poor and helpless . . . , but the best government for all mankind."[111]

Tribal commentators hoped to enhance the effect of this flattering self-portrait by juxtaposing it with a contrasting depiction of American political economy in the Gilded Age. Although they often alluded to Americans' insatiable avarice and occasionally insinuated that avarice was innate in people of European descent, they more often emphasized that Americans' greedy behavior followed from a betrayal or corruption of the republic's original, laudable ideals. A contributor to the *Indian Chieftain* cited the Declaration of Independence for the principles that "every man born into the world naturally has a right to some land on which to stand and on which to make a living," and that "God created the world for every man, not for a few capitalists." By relinquishing collective control of their land, Americans had given free rein to selfish impulses and allowed individual gain to supersede higher social aims. Conversely, the tribal ownership system made it impossible for citizens to forget their obligations to the community or deny compatriots their democratic rights.[112] The Whites, in contrast, were "all in competition with each other," said Pleasant Porter. "The strong succeed, the weak fail," he scolded. "Then you build alms houses for the victims of your social and economic system of competition, and prisons for those who rebel against that system." In the Creek Nation, however, "a harmonious brotherhood" prevailed, "with no selfish competitions which affect injuriously the public interest."[113]

For the argument about cutthroat competition among Whites, tribal officials could find plenty of supporting data supplied by Americans themselves. Many people in the States were documenting and denouncing conditions inconsistent with the stated national policy of enabling "each citizen to obtain and use a portion of land for the satisfaction of his wants if he so desires." One writer reported that twenty-nine absentee landlords were in possession of an area as large as Ireland; another calculated that two-thirds of U.S. residents were tenants and a mere 10 percent of the population owned 90 percent of land values.[114]

The second part of the Indians' argument—that "selfish competitions" were unknown in the tribes—was harder to make with a straight face, especially by the 1890s. Tribal spokesmen were depicting their nations as egalitarian at a time when many people, including tribe members, were publicly discussing circumstances at odds with that image. Information was circulating that caused Pleasant Porter himself to lament, "We awake to find that the few of our people . . . are quietly possessing themselves of the lion's share of our common property," and a Cherokee candidate for chief to admit, "Under the present monopolization of the public domain which is hourly and daily increasing the rising generation is practically excluded from its benefits."[115]

Since the tribes' landownership system did not prevent members from developing the desire and ability to acquire extensive property, framing the allotment issue as a choice between egalitarian or stagnant Indian communalism and vibrant or ruthless Euro-American enterprise made little sense. Rather than abandoning their contrasting characterizations of Indian and American societies, however, people on both sides of the debate simply construed available data as consistent with those characterizations. Focusing on the economic actors' ancestry instead of tribal affiliations, they said they saw a correlation between economic penchants and racial identities. Then they cited that correlation, and particularly the traits imputed to Indians, as justification for their positions.

When the promoters of tribal land reform spotted tribe members who seemed bent on enriching themselves at other members' expense, they did not see Indians; they saw intermarried Whites and "almost white" people whose propensities they attributed to non-Indian progenitors.[116] For example, an essay in a popular magazine informed Americans that "mixed breeds" and "professional red men" controlled the Indian Territory's "rich and highly cultivated" farms and "opulent coal mines" because "the Indian," having "a repugnancy to toil," had invited Whites in to coax the wealth from their lands.[117] U.S. officials assumed that Whites with tribal citizenship also orchestrated the tribal governments for their own selfish ends.[118] Senator Platt expected no rebuttal to his charge in 1895 that "rapacious white Indians" were appropriating the full-bloods' patrimony. Even tribe members said it was so. Indian Territory newspapers received numerous letters alleging that the people who prevented "the poor ignorant full-blood" from grazing stock on tribal prairies were "half breeds" and intermarried Whites. "It is certain," declared the *Indian Chieftain* in 1895, "that if all the citizens of the tribe were full-bloods there would be no complaint of monopoly and would still be enough land for many generations to come for a people that are never so greedy as those of Anglo-Saxon mixture."[119]

Linking supposedly un-Indian economic practices to race was a useful line of argument for tribal opponents as well as American advocates of allotment. If the most acquisitive tribal citizens were not Indians at all, then tribe members could insist that Indians' less enterprising disposition necessitated common ownership, while Americans could continue to claim that common ownership kept the real Indians from developing an entrepreneurial spirit. Paradoxically, blaming the greediest deeds on "white Indians" or people "of Anglo-Saxon mixture" also helped to justify legislation altering the property interests of those individuals more drastically than Congress dared to do in the States.[120]

In 1893, U.S. lawmakers signaled their intent to force a reapportionment of Indian Territory lands. They created a three-man team known as the Dawes Commission to negotiate with the Five Tribes for the division of their lands into equal private parcels.[121] While Indian leaders tried to foil the American effort by refusing to bargain, the commission and a special Senate committee published reports describing the tribal regimes as so corrupt that "the interest of the Indian and whites alike" demanded radical change.[122] Congress responded first in 1896 with an act that directed the commission to compile rolls of tribe members, and then with the Curtis Act of 1898, which ordered allotment to proceed when the rolls were complete, whether or not the tribes agreed. Once every Indian had an allotment, surplus land would open to White settlement, and the tribal governments would cease to function. Lawmakers described the plan as a measure of justice not only for poor Indians but also for Americans in need of homes.[123]

Even though they would not have countenanced such meddling with the vested property rights of fellow Americans, congressmen who approved the Curtis Act had no trouble seeing it as morally defensible. A factor in their reasoning was their conception of an Indian tribe as a homogeneous racial or cultural group rather than a nation-state like the United States, defined primarily by a political compact and thus able to encompass people of diverse origins, ethnicities, and habits. According to this racial conception of the tribes, landholders and officeholders who seemed White had to be usurpers, even if they were tribal citizens. Sponsors of the Curtis Act argued that because the U.S. government had pledged in treaties to protect the tribal enclaves, it had a trustee's duty to rescue the true Indians from their parasitic oppressors.[124]

A handful of Americans detected and worked to expose dishonorable motives behind the push for allotment, especially before 1887. The National Indian Defense Association—an interracial agrarian populist group—identified railroads, land syndicates, and business monopolies as the interests that stood to gain the most. The association's White president, Thomas Bland, warned Congress against submitting to corporations whose motto was that "might makes right." He also disputed claims that allotment would realize the agrarian ideal—a society in which all members had means of self-support and a stake in the political order. Proallotment reformers wanted Indians to emulate Americans' enlightened selfishness, but Americans overemphasized the virtues of acquisitiveness, said Bland. As a result, economic power had concentrated to an extent that was morally and socially dangerous.[125] After Congress did mandate allotment and officials in the Five Tribes recommended compliance, the author of a *Harper's Weekly* article impugned their motives along with those of the federal commissioners, "squaw men," and "reckless and unprincipled" intruders who were intent "from the outset . . . upon the absorption of the red men's property by the whites."[126] Once the survey of lots was under way, a few other Americans noted that unprincipled residents of Indian Territory were maneuvering to exploit the new system as effectively as they had the old.[127]

However, Americans who decried allotment as a ploy to absorb Indians' property were few in number and short on political clout by the 1890s. Members of Congress and proallotment activists did not even make much effort to refute their critics. After declaring that "the more avaricious and unscrupulous" members of the Five Tribes had "acquired all the valuable land and left their fellow-citizens nothing but the poor land," one writer asked rhetorically, "Have we no right to equalize matters by giving to the poor Indian that of which he has been dispossessed, and taking from the rich that to which he is not entitled?" He did not seem to fear a negative reply from anyone of consequence.[128]

The contrast with the earlier American debate about Indian removal is striking. In the 1820s and 1830s, a host of churchgoing Whites across the northern states joined the Cherokees in charging that proponents of removal were motivated by ill-disguised lust for the Indians' productive land. Such greed, they warned, put the soul of the young republic in peril. Sixty years later, the Friends of the Indian—pious Christians as well—also made impassioned appeals for the fulfillment of republican ideals. But they were unmoved when leaders of the Five Tribes and a few White agrarian populists insisted that the pressure to allot tribal land was driven by envy and an undemocratic sense of White entitlement. Instead, the humanitarians of the Gilded Age convinced themselves that forced allotment would counteract greed and restore Indians' democratic rights.[129]

For example, when the Women's National Indian Association urged bold action to remedy the "grave situation" in the Indian Territory, it conceded, "Some property rights will be disturbed" by land allotment as "in any new order of things, and this fact may agitate and embitter many minds and may even lead to violence and danger." But such a risky step was necessary because "the less[er] interests, where a conflict cannot be avoided, must yield to the greater, the rights of the few to the needs of the whole number, and this principle, as seen in the law of eminent domain, already governs throughout our free Republic, and it well illustrates the divine statement that 'none of us liveth unto himself.'" Christian patriots would not object, "and to even the selfish patriot, if such a patriot is possible, there is the consoling fact, proved in all human history, that the best prosperity of the nation is the highest prosperity of each citizen. . . . Our republic now stands before the world as a government covenanted to give equally to all under it, with life, the liberty to pursue happiness." How could Friends of the Indian do anything but redouble their efforts to give every tribesman "law protection for all his rights, and the fullest opportunity freely to exploit all his gifts and talents?"[130]

Like members of the Women's National Indian Association, many Americans climbed on the allotment bandwagon believing it was bound for a land where more Indians and deserving non-Indians would have opportunities to prosper. Allotment seemed an elegantly simple solution to the problem of concentrated wealth in the tribes. As owners in common, tribe members had equal rights in the tribal estates; allotting and privatizing the land would merely enforce those rights and make them concrete. If some greedy people would thereby have to relinquish property interests, that was justice, not lawless confiscation. And if some land passed to Whites because tribal acreage exceeded the amount needed for Indian allotments, the cause of justice for victims of monopolization would be doubly served. Midwestern Knights of Labor chapters were among many groups around the United States that sent memorials to Congress urging the lawmakers to allot and open the Indian Territory so that speculators would cease their control of the land. To such agrarian populists, says historian Andrew Denson, Indian Territory allotment epitomized the effort "to secure justice for ordinary working people."[131]

If someone had told backers of the Curtis Act that their responses to concentrated wealth in the States and in the Indian tribes were contradictory, their reaction would probably have been puzzled denial. Comparing American and Indian property systems would have struck them as absurd. They maintained that the tribal elite's affluence was possible only because common ownership allowed aggressive people to appropriate land meant for vulnerable co-owners. Such misbegotten wealth was not entitled to the legal armor that protected American property owners from dispossession.[132]

And yet, it is also possible that the allotment plan appealed to the Friends of the Indian and to some in Congress, at least on a subliminal level, as a chance to correct the kinds of inequities they regretted in their own nation. Americans unhappy with a shortage of virtue among their fellow citizens have often imagined that Indians possess the missing desirable traits.[133] Could the idealists' enthusiasm for allotting the Five Tribes' lands have stemmed in part from a similar impulse? Friends of the Indian were no populists, but they surely shared other Americans' uneasiness about growing economic inequality in their nation, especially the monopolization of land. Did they project their concern onto the tribes, and did they expect allotment to assuage their uneasy feeling? Did they hope that providing every tribe member with a modest homestead would not only promote Indians' absorption as individuals into an American society of property owners, but would also remind Americans of their founding fathers' ideals? Minutes from the annual Friends of the Indian conference in 1901 suggest as much. They state that the Dawes Commission proceeded with great care when allotting the land in "the belief that a just and wise system of land tenure is the basis upon which the superstructure of a prosperous State must ultimately arise."[134]

Assembled at a bucolic resort in upstate New York—a populous state in an industrialized nation—the Friends of the Indian had reason to feel nostalgic about the republican dream of a society whose virtue rested on broad and equitable distribution of agricultural land.[135] But it was easier to strip greedy tribal landholders of excess acreage and topple tribal oligarchies than to rearrange power and property relations in the States. Proponents of Indian land allotment could construe it as evidence that the United States still stood for equality, or at least equal opportunity, notwithstanding the extremes of wealth and poverty that had developed by the eve of the twentieth century. Ironically, however, Congress could only implement that plan because the tribes' power and wealth were far from equal to U.S. power and wealth.

Few in the Five Tribes believed the blithe assertions that allotment would restrain greed and achieve economic justice. Many anticipated that well-intentioned reformers would fail to keep less benign Americans from prying allotted property out of Indians' hands. Many also expected allotment to inspire obnoxious behavior from some of their own.[136] How right they were! Allotment set the scene for legal and illegal actions effecting a massive transfer of Indian property into other hands by the 1930s. Historian and Oklahoma resident Angie Debo, whose exposé of those shady activities required considerable courage, called them "an orgy of plunder and exploitation probably unparalleled in American history."[137]

The exploiters included people on the tribal rolls. In 1894, a member of the commission that wrung allotment agreements from the Indian governments alleged, "The chief obstacle to our mission is the opposition of the barons (land & coal) and the politicians who are not willing to let go until they see an opportunity of obtaining more than their share of the common property."[138] The subsequent deeds of some Indian "barons" lend credibility to the commissioner's dim view of tribal politics. "As the United States closed in on the territory," says historian Erik Zissu, "the once healthy competition among diverse interests" within the tribes "turned malignant."[139] In the scramble to stake out final shares of the tribal domain, some tribe members ran roughshod over friends and neighbors. The most aggressively acquisitive people proved highly capable of manipulating the allotment process and the state legal system to their economic advantage. In reaction, a substantial portion of the full-blood class reaffirmed their distaste for a culture that prioritized individual gain.

They protested—violently, in some cases—and refused to participate in the allotment process.

The terms of allotment and the percentages of disaffected people varied from tribe to tribe. In the Choctaw Nation, the government of Green McCurtain negotiated an agreement with the Dawes Commission that survived a tribal referendum in 1898, even though members had voted overwhelmingly for antiallotment candidates two years before. In the Creek Nation, according to Chief Isparhecher, opposition to allotment remained almost unanimous while tribal representatives reluctantly negotiated with the federal commission.[140] Cherokee leaders, sensing that a majority of their citizens expected it, held out against federal pressure as long as possible, despite the fact that some in the English-speaking, educated class had advocated allotment for years. But everywhere, there was a sharp, growing rift between people who realized—either happily or wistfully—that allotment was now inevitable and people who refused to reconcile themselves to the new order.[141]

Even before the Curtis Act, "irreconcilables" in the Choctaw, Chickasaw, Creek, and Cherokee tribes joined to form the Four Mothers Society, which sustained and reinforced their belief that a traditional aversion to materialism made them more Indian than enterprising tribe members.[142] Once allotment was under way, thousands of the traditionalists declined to select land and even refused the papers documenting that agents had assigned them lots anyway. "It was soon apparent," remarks Debo, "that the sympathy expressed for the dispossessed fullbloods in the earlier Dawes reports had been misplaced, for their small holdings were as large as they cared to cultivate. When a piece of paper gave them the exclusive possession of some extra acres, they were willing to bestow it upon the first person who approached them."[143]

Some of the holdouts later testified at a Senate hearing that they had been involuntarily deprived of their property and thus impoverished, but the most important deprivation they had in mind was the loss of their undivided interests in a communal estate. Samuel Leslie, who identified himself as a full-blood Creek, tried to explain that he refused an allotment because he wanted to remain a co-owner of the tribe's entire land area. "I wanted my right and property interest, for I loved them," he said. "I love the old treaty, and I want it. . . . The full-blood Indian people don't want to lose their property or their rights, for the white man comes in our country and buys the land or they lease the land out. They have taken everything on that ground out there and the poor Indian hasn't anything left."[144] Feeling alienated not only from the "white man" who wanted to buy their land, but also from the tribal politicians and enterprising mixed-bloods who seemed willing to accept a change in the treaty, people like Leslie had come to believe that their reverence for the old common property system made them the real Indians.[145] Another holdout claimed, "Not a full-blood Indian ever voted" to change the treaty.[146]

Many in the "progressive" class saw nothing romantic or sensible about such obstinacy. The cause of the resisters is doomed, the *Indian Journal* announced in 1901. "They cannot compete with this white civilization which is so mighty, so selfish and so natural."[147] Other tribe members were equipped to compete in "white civilization," and many profited handsomely from the transition to private landownership. To be sure, some had to forfeit oversized spreads. In addition to ranchers who lost free access to thousands of acres, the losers included D. W. C. Duncan, who said he watched helplessly as an intermarried White citizen (himself displaced in the allotment process) filed on part of Duncan's 300-acre farm and left the seventy-six-year-old Cherokee Dartmouth graduate to eke out a living on just sixty acres.[148] But most of the so-called progressives began life as allottees in significantly better material circumstances than the subsistence farmers in the hills. At a minimum, by exercising their right to claim the homes and farms they already occupied, they could retain some of the best sites in the area for commercial activity.[149] Many devised ways to make out much better than that. Robert Owen, for instance, arranged that allotments carved out of his former landholding would go to people who stayed on small homesteads miles away while leasing their new tracts to Owen with an option to buy when the law allowed. As a consequence of such practices, a journalist reported in 1903, "nearly all of the large estates in the territory remain[ed] practically intact." Shrewd tribe members also prospered by platting new townsites or by joining the corps of "grafters" who collected rewards for guiding less savvy Indians through the new legal maze.[150]

A 1903 *Muskogee Phoenix* story shows how some tribe members intended to compete in a "white civilization." It reported the incorporation and capitalization of the Tribal Development Company in the Chickasaw Nation. The company's directors included a current Chickasaw governor and a former one, a U.S. attorney, a federal revenue inspector, a U.S. marshal, the president of the Chickasaw Nation bank, an unnamed "wealthy" young Chickasaw man, and the manager in Kansas of Central Coal and Coke Company. "The object," explained the article, "is to buy, sell, lease, sub-lease and abstract titles to real estate in the Indian Territory. The personnel of the company insures the full-blood element a safe medium through which to secure their allotments and will afford the outside investor a safe medium through which to secure Indian Territory investments."[151]

By 1907, the governments of the Five Tribes had dissolved as provided in the Curtis Act, and a new Oklahoma State government ruled the former tribal territories. That year, the Trans-Mississippi Commercial Congress met at Muskogee, the Creek capital. Moty Tiger, the last elected Creek chief, gave the welcome address. In the audience was Robert Owen, who had capitalized on his partial Cherokee ancestry and an upper-class education to secure a place in the Indian Territory elite after he arrived from Virginia as a young man.[152] Now, Owen was headed to Washington, D.C., as a senator from the new state. In that role, he would answer to a constituency composed of many more non-Indians than Indians, and Tiger was not optimistic that the result would be justice for Indians. Already Owen had joined in a call by White Oklahomans for legislation allowing the sale of Indian allotments, no doubt expecting to profit by dealing in such land himself. Still, Tiger had no choice but to direct his appeal for justice to a government controlled by men of Owen's bent; so he said, "The polished and educated man with the Indian blood in his veins who advocates the removal of restrictions from the lands of my ignorant people . . . is only reaching for gold to ease his itching palms, and our posterity will remember him only for his avarice and his treachery. . . . It is a fight between greed and conscience with this great government as arbiter, and upon the decision rests for generations, the fate of these untutored children of nature."[153]

When the "great government" of the United States decided that privatization of tribal land was to be the fate of "untutored" Indians, legislators did not think or admit they were choosing sides in a fight between greed and conscience. They declared their intent to meet their country's moral obligation to Indians—to promote Indian prosperity and opportunities for individual economic advancement—by a measure that would also serve the interests of ambitious Americans. Invoking an earlier era's notion of a moral economy, Congress ordered the equalization of Indian landholdings, but by the same stroke, it ensured the hegemony of freewheeling American capitalism in the tribal homelands. In doing so, lawmakers acted at the behest of an alliance that embodied the same contradiction—an alliance of Americans who favored a might-makes-right argument with humanitarians who cited moral imperatives for seizing control of the material basis for Indians' sovereignty. Sixty years earlier, the Indian removal issue had pitted moralists against White nationalists who demanded economic opportunity at Indians' expense, but in the campaign to dismantle the Five Tribes of Indian Territory, idealists and unabashed gold diggers found common cause.

Incongruous allies also waged the tribes' battle to prevent their destruction. For many years, people with divergent economic aims found common cause in the Indian nations. American schemes to deprive the tribes of sovereignty and resources threatened ambitious, acquisitive members as well as members whose indifference to building private wealth marked them in American eyes as backward Indians. By virtue of their ability to manage relations with Americans, the ambitious people gained disproportionate influence in the tribal governments—influence that some used to their personal economic advantage. But those people also needed followers among the traditionalists, who expected their governments to defend a model of economic relations that subordinated opportunities for individual gain to the ideal of collective security.

Debate about economic ethics was a necessary aspect of these uneasy tribal alliances. And because acquisitive tribe members had learned their enterprising ways from Americans, much of the debate was conducted in the same terms as a concurrent discussion about economic individualism in the United States. However, due to the presence and participation of Indians who had not embraced individualism, the tribal governments faced moral issues the U.S. government did not consider. In addition to weighing whether competing ideals of the American system could be reconciled—whether full freedom to strive for personal gain would ultimately frustrate the ideal of equal opportunity and freedom from exploitation—the tribes were called on to say whether and how they would honor the ideals of an older Indian economic culture.

They never arrived at answers. Before the United States cut them short in the 1890s, the tribal deliberations were desultory, in part because the educated Anglophones who dominated political discussion forums were divided, and in part because accommodating progressive and traditional ideals was not easy. It is telling that the enterprising people, when they did pledge to uphold traditional ideals, focused almost entirely on common landownership. They said little or nothing about the ideal of reciprocity that still inspired the traditionalists' economic relations. Nor did tribal officials or newspaper editors and readers appeal to the traditional moral principle that status in the community should depend on generous redistribution of wealth. Their silence on the subject is evidence that economic stratification in the tribes also reflected a significant cultural division, which the upper class had little desire or ability to bridge.[154] Extensive economic ties to outsiders, among other things, had weakened many tribe members' sense of interdependence. Nevertheless, tribal lawmakers and officials did take measures they could characterize as efforts to realize the dual ideals of fair economic opportunities and economic security for all.

U.S. lawmakers did the same, but only in the Indian Territory. For reasons that ranged from Machiavellian to sincerely if naïvely idealistic, they approved a redistribution of Indian property that purportedly enhanced poor Indians' security by enforcing the right to equal economic opportunity. Although wealth in the United States was increasingly concentrated, members of Congress did not accept populist demands for a federal government that would "ensure fair access to the benefits of modernity by acting for the majority rather than the wealthy minority." Yet, the same legislators usurped the power of Indian governments in the name of the same ideal—fair access to economic opportunities.[155] In thus applying one moral principle to Indian affairs, they chose to disregard others. While pretending to afford equal opportunity for all Indians, they broke a solemn promise to respect the tribes' sovereignty and thereby showed contempt for the tribe members' political liberty.

5

Osage Oil Owners

For several days in 1922, a curiously specific question preoccupied the House Committee on Indian Affairs: how much spending money Osage Indians should have. Under a law enacted the previous year, the U.S. government was holding most of the Osages' personal income in trust accounts and paying out just $4,000 per year—$1,000 per quarter—to each adult who did not have a certificate of competency.[1] Now a new bill in Congress would authorize officials to release additional cash if an Indian requested it for a worthy purpose. Osages could certainly afford added expenditures. Money was flowing into their accounts as fast as petroleum was gushing from the earth of their reservation in Oklahoma. However, $4,000 was a generous allowance. If Osages could get their hands on more than that, lawmakers asked, how would they learn to curb the extravagance that necessitated the original legislation?

Before Congress acted to restrain them, Osages had gone on a notorious spending spree, scandalizing and amusing observers with their many purchases of impractical luxuries. But did that justify federal control of their personal funds? At the 1922 hearings, a committee member suggested a reason for doubt. Addressing a non-Indian witness from Oklahoma, Representative Leatherwood prompted, "As a class [the Indians] spend their money just about like white men who get their money easily." "Just the same," the witness responded. "'Easy come and easy go?'" added Leatherwood. "Yes sir; that is about right," was the reply, "because there is a great deal of humanity about these Osages."[2] The implication of these remarks was clearer when a chief known as Bacon Rind made a similar point. Testifying through an interpreter, the chief said, "Any nationality of people would do the same thing the Osages are doing if they had the opportunity. Our children . . . have begun to realize the condition of the other people, see how they are dressed, and when they get to be 15 years old they want the best. They are our children; we hate to refuse them, the same with you people."[3] If the Indians' prodigal reaction to prosperity was standard human behavior, why were they alone subject to federal fiscal guardianship? Non-Indians could use their money as they pleased; Osages could not.

While acknowledging that the propensity to squander money could be found in all races, lawmakers resisted the conclusion that withholding the Osage funds was unfairly discriminatory. Although Congress, in 1925, did finally permit administrators to dole out extra cash to Indians who demonstrated special need, it rebuffed Osage pleas for unlimited access to the funds accruing in their names.[4] In his plea, Mekahwahtiankah told senators, "We do not like to be ruled by other people"; but Osage desires carried less weight in Congress than the argument that the United States owed the Indians protection from their own folly.[5] Representative W. W. Hastings declared that legislators had a duty "to try to preserve some of these Indians from being despoiled by the excessive use of money upon themselves." Never mind that Congress had recently allowed Indians elsewhere to make their own, possibly imprudent economic choices. "You have quite a different condition prevailing among these Osages," Hastings said. "Here is a tribe that has suddenly come into the possession of very great wealth."[6] The Osage bonanza required special measures.

The history of government controls on Osage money belies or complicates the adage that wealth is power. For Indians, power's relationship to wealth has been more like the proverbial relationship of chicken and egg. Each may be a prerequisite of the other, but chickens face extinction if they are not strong enough to preserve their eggs until chicks hatch and mature. People with limited power may occasionally produce or acquire considerable wealth, but power is a condition of retaining the wealth and wielding it influentially; and in the calculus of power, racial classifications and differences of economic culture have historically been important factors, affecting the equation in complex ways.

During negotiations with the U.S. government in the 1920s, when Osage Indians tried to tip the balance of power over their wealth in their direction, some of their notorious economic practices, attributed to race, carried decisive countervailing weight. Although they had undisputed rights to extraordinary wealth which gave them leverage at times, Osages were not able to secure all the privileges of other American property owners. At their richest hour, hundreds of Osages could not retain full control of their own money. Instead of buying them freedom from overbearing outsiders, copious oil revenue provided an excuse to institutionalize U.S. domination, which had become possible with the tribe's impoverishment a century earlier. Lawmakers and administrators responded to a twentieth-century turnaround in Osage fortunes by adopting rules and practices that perpetuated the power imbalance and confirmed the Indians' infantile legal status. To justify that response, they invoked notions of economic common sense or propriety along with a stereotype of Indians as people lacking in that common sense. Osage leaders, in need of allies to help fend off greedy neighbors and interlopers, invoked similar images of Indians at times, hoping the federal government would use its power benevolently.

Ironically, the sequence of events that made Osages rich began with a perilous loss of resources. In the early 1800s, when American settlers and Indian refugees thronged into their territory between the Missouri and Arkansas Rivers, the outnumbered Osages gradually ceded land to the United States until they were confined to a small tract in Kansas. Late in the 1860s, unable to prevent encroachment on that reserve, they accepted a U.S. plan to sell it. With part of the sale receipts, the Osage Tribe bought a corner of the Indian Territory from the Cherokees. The United States kept the remaining receipts—$8.5 million—in trust for the tribe. After several years of hunger and deprivation in their new location, Osages slowed and then halted their slide into poverty. They discovered that money could be had by renting their land, and in 1879, federal officials yielded to dogged Osage demands for quarterly per capita payments from the tribal trust account. After that, Osage families could count on cash income amounting to several hundred dollars a year.

Oil production on the reservation began in 1897, but it did not boost Osage incomes significantly at first. By then, tribe members faced American pressure to break their collective domain into modest-sized private lots. Most of them initially resisted, and they drew strength from the fact that the tribe owned the land outright. U.S. leaders interpreted treaties with the tribe as license for a paternal hand in Osage affairs, but their claim of authority to dispose of Osage land had a shaky basis because the reservation was not created from U.S. property. Consequently, when the Osages who favored allotment finally outnumbered those who opposed it, the tribe had leverage to exact federal approval of an unusually advantageous plan. Instead of losing land to Whites, as other tribes did when their reserved area exceeded the acreage needed for allotments, Osages would divide the entire reservation among tribe members alive in 1907. Subsurface resources would remain common property for twenty-five years more, and allottees would share equally in proceeds from the sale or lease of oil or minerals.[7] During those twenty-five years, especially after World War I stimulated demand for petroleum, oil leases earned huge sums for the Osages. Total revenues in 1923, for example, were more than $27.6 million.[8]

Osage Indians struck it rich at a time when, and because, non-Indian Americans also had reason to revel in their collective prosperity. The economy of the United States was growing like a hormone-gorged adolescent body. National income rose approximately 50 percent between 1900 and 1929. Although the new wealth did not reach every household—indeed, some scholars contend that it bypassed most of the population—millions of people felt more affluent than their parents and grandparents. Factories churned out an unprecedented quantity and variety of consumer goods.[9] Families of middling means could gratify wants that previous generations had suppressed or never expected to have, while people in upper income brackets conspicuously indulged a wider array of expensive desires.[10] "Can there be any real question," a prominent economic analyst asked in 1920, "that the material well-being of the people is increasing, not only steadily but rapidly?"[11] A decade later, historian Frederick Lewis Allen viewed the period from 1923 to 1929 as years of "unparalleled plenty."[12]

Merchants exploited this sense of plenty with the aid of professional advertisers, who tried imaginative new ways of enticing Americans to buy more goods and services. They promised fulfillment of the yearning "to be young and desirable, to be rich, to keep up with the Joneses, to be envied." Thus encouraged to spend, Americans were less and less inclined to live by the ethic of thrift their forebears had preached. Millions bought such erstwhile luxuries as pianos, household appliances, silk stockings, rayon shirts and dresses, cosmetics, and automobiles. Frederick Allen noted wryly that President Calvin Coolidge's "philosophy of hard work and frugal living and piety crowned with success might have been brought down from some Vermont attic where *McGuffy's Reader* gathered dust."[13]

The automobile became a prominent symbol of the new economy and its ethos of self-gratification. Between 1919 and 1929, the number of gasoline-powered vehicles on the roads tripled, from 7 to 23 million. At the early end of that time span, economist Albert Atwood concluded from available statistics that autos were no longer playthings solely for the rich; the most plausible explanation for the number of cars sold was that modest wage earners were buying them too. "Rockefeller and Morgan and their like are not the only persons who enjoy this exceedingly important form of wealth," Atwood exulted. "It is no exaggeration to say that the automobile alone has given millions of men the feeling of being capitalists, though these men toil with their hands."[14]

No matter how one defined "rich," Atwood continued, there were also enough rich people "to make the disposition of their incomes of very broad general interest." Indeed, what the well-heeled did with their money was grist for regular fare in tabloids and national magazines. Atwood remarked that almost daily newspaper articles were reminders of the many people with great wealth who spent it lavishly. He cited an article about "a Chicago highflyer . . . legally adjudged a spendthrift, after running through a trifle of $1,350,000 in one year" and one about "the widow of an automobile manufacturer," allowed by a probate court "to spend $500,000 a year on herself and two children."[15] A significant share of such publicity focused on people whose fortunes derived from oil.[16]

Those who wrote about the wealthy delighted in cataloguing what money could buy. They reported that affluence found expression in the purchase of ornate mansions, automobiles with enclosed seating, imported clothing, sojourns at exclusive resorts, and other pricey indulgences. Atwood maintained that the truly rich spent a small portion of their income on personal possessions and ostentatious display, but he doubted his ability to persuade readers of the *Saturday Evening Post*. "It is contrary to the popular conception," he conceded in 1924, "which can think of riches only in terms of fast motor cars, yachts, fine houses and the like." Many a publication reflected and perpetuated that popular conception.[17]

In fact, writers seldom missed a chance to show that the rich, especially the new rich, were prone to wildly impractical expenditures. An *American Magazine* essay spelled out the ways that a White Oklahoma farmer was apt to use his serendipitous oil income. "When his wealth comes . . . , he does not seem to know what to do with himself. First he looks about for something to buy. One man bought a dozen pairs of suspenders. . . . His needs and desires satisfied, the newly rich man usually buys next an expensive automobile and an imposing house. After that, registered dogs, perhaps, or blooded horses, fine cattle on a ranch. Sooner or later he is likely to indulge appetites for women, wine, and song."[18] Even Atwood acknowledged that "cases of glaring waste and luxury on the part of the rich" were "numerous" and offered a few juicy examples, such as "men who . . . spend $50,000 on changing the position of a fish pond." Envy and vicarious pleasure were detectable in more than one such account of the wealthy's wasteful ways.[19]

Many accounts also invoked the aphorism that money is the root of evil, particularly when the subject was people of lowly origin who had struck it rich. A *Saturday Evening Post* editorial warned that "sudden riches are inclined to . . . ruin the lives of those who thus find that fortune is only misfortune in

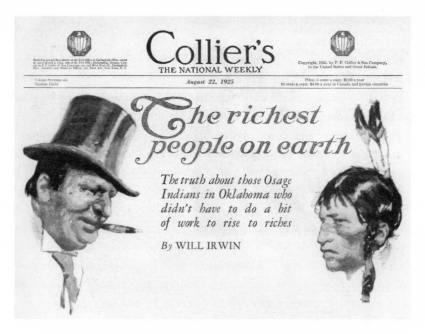

Collier's
THE NATIONAL WEEKLY
August 22, 1925

The richest people on earth

The truth about those Osage
Indians in Oklahoma who
didn't have to do a bit
of work to rise to riches

By WILL IRWIN

By 1925, national periodicals such as *Collier's* magazine accepted and promulgated
the notion that income from oil wells had made Osage Indians the world's richest people—
a turn of events that excited journalists not only because great Indian wealth seemed
improbable but also because some Osage uses of money would strike non-Indian
magazine readers as amusingly or shockingly inappropriate and profligate.

another guise." Cora Miley's evidence of that effect was her White Oklahoma
neighbors. Oil development had not only sullied their "pristine" farmland, she
wrote, but had also made meaningful work unnecessary, driven more than one
disoriented new millionaire to drink and drugs, and attracted a plague of beggars and con men.[20]

Osage Indians' oil-fueled ride to fortune and fame was thus in many respects a quintessential Roaring Twenties saga. There was no denying Osage
prosperity that decade or its source in the emerging car culture. After World
War I, a surging revenue stream lifted tribe members' personal income into
the highest census categories. An allotted Osage's share of annual oil money
jumped from $384 in 1916 to $2,719 in 1917. Three years later, at a time when
disposable per capita income in the United States was only $635, an Osage
headright was worth $8,090, and an owner of allotted land could add to that
wealth by leasing acreage to farmers or ranchers. The Office of Indian Affairs
reckoned that an Osage family of two adults and three children on the 1907
membership roll had income of more than $40,000 in 1920. By journalist Den-

nis McAuliffe's calculation, an allotted Osage in 1925 had buying power equivalent to a million dollars or more in the 1990s.[21]

The magnitude of Osages' income guaranteed them a prominent place in media coverage of postwar prosperity and its beneficiaries. Sky-high bids for Osage oil had prime news value, and oil money's effect on individual tribe members was an even more captivating subject. A typical headline in 1923 trumpeted, "Richest People Per Capita on Earth Get $8,290,100 for Oil Leases." Many a periodical carried articles like the one in *Harper's Monthly Magazine* for November 1920, predicting that the Osages would receive nearly $9,000 each that year—almost double their 1919 payment. Author William Shepherd estimated that a particular young woman—heir to seven full shares of the tribal wealth—would enjoy income "approximat[ing] President Wilson's salary." By delighting merchants "with their tremendous purchases," he added, "copper-hued citizens" of the tribe "shed their influence on towns as far distant as Tulsa and Oklahoma City, and Washington, D.C."[22]

As Shepherd's reference to Osage shoppers indicates, word of the tribe's great oil wealth triggered the usual scrutiny of wealthy people's purchases. Like well-to-do residents of New York's Park Avenue, Osages provided the reading public with opportunities to savor what the rich could own—modern brick houses, deluxe cars, modish clothing, fine jewelry, rugs, china vases, pianos, "talking machines," and radios.[23] An early list appeared in *The World's Work*, which labeled the Osages an "American Aristocracy": "Now the Osage, frequently accompanied by his gaily accoutred wife . . . honks up to the agency in his automobile. And this automobile is not a flivver, but usually a soft-cushioned touring car. . . . The home of the Osage to-day reflects this leisured prosperity. His taste goes to leather chairs and hardwood floors. Next to the automobile, the besetting passion of the Osage to-day is the phonograph, by means of which he is rapidly becoming acquainted with Caruso, Geraldine Farrar, and the most entrancing melodies of the latest Broadway musical shows."[24]

Osage watchers relished a report that one tribe member had managed in twenty-four hours to dish out $1,200 for a fur coat, $3,000 for a diamond ring, $5,000 for an automobile, $3,100 in loan repayments to her mother and sister, $7,000 for furniture, $600 to ship the furniture from Florida to California, $2,500 for a town lot, and $12,000 for additional real estate. Like other coverage of the new rich, a piece on the Osages was incomplete without mention of stunningly frivolous expenditures. "It is related," said one, "that when an Indian received his first money—a mere handful of change consisting of $2,500—he purchased a glittering hearse that had taken his vagrant fancy."

Literary Digest treated readers to a story about Osages who lined up, clutching wads of cash, for an airplane ride costing five dollars a minute, then readily agreed to stay aloft as long as the money in hand lasted.[25]

Rich Osages also had troubles enough to elicit the usual platitudes about money's association with evil. Evil made its presence known in the form of greedy, dishonest, and vicious outsiders, drawn to Indians with fat pocketbooks like wasps to meat. Observers detected evil, too, in a reputed high incidence of Indian alcohol and drug use, gluttony, and aimlessness. "Black gushing oil—heap big money—curses the Osage tribe of Indians to-day," lamented a *Literary Digest* item in 1926. "Murder, violence, unhappiness, run riot on the Oklahoma reservation." Osage country joined bloody Chicago, where gangsters battled to control the bootleg liquor trade, as a source of material for sermons about money's corrupting influence.[26]

While exemplifying some Roaring Twenties phenomena, the Osage oil rush story was also exceptional and singularly interesting because the main characters were Indians. Several factors made rich Indians seem especially newsworthy, including a common assumption that Indians were poor and an ongoing public debate about the validity of that assumption. Before Osage became a household name, the word "Indian" did not prompt Americans to think of someone in a costly car or Paris gown. The image that sprang more readily to mind was "Poor Lo," ragged relic of an obsolete hunting and gathering society.[27] Writers could therefore heighten the drama of the Osage tale by spinning it as an unexpected reversal of fortune. They could add color with references to brick houses springing up alongside tepees.

To some influential people, Osage income figures were potent evidence that the image of Poor Lo was a fallacy. Their contention that Indians were actually rich irked Charles de Young Elkus. "There is so much publicity about the 'rich Indian' and his constantly increasing wealth," the California civic leader complained in 1927, "that those who are unfamiliar with actual conditions are apt to be misled by glittering accounts of Indian prosperity . . . spread abroad by the Indian Bureau and its agents." Among other things, Elkus had in mind a recent statement from the assistant commissioner of Indian affairs: "The per capita wealth of the American Indian is nearly twice as great as the per capita wealth of the other citizens of this country." Government officials released such statistics, which the media reliably passed on, to show that Indians were poised for prosperity. The intended message was that Indians had benefited from the care of the federal guardians who were preparing them for citizenship. An Interior Department assertion that Indians' total assets exceeded $1 billion prompted a *Washington Star* correspondent to quip, "That lament, 'Lo the poor Indian,' might appropriately be revised to, 'Ho, the rich redskin.'" Edwin Slosson saw no need to make that even a tentative proposition. Writing for the *Independent* in 1920, Slosson proclaimed, "The American Indians are the wealthiest people in the world, the wealthiest that ever lived. No other race, however industrious, brilliant and economical, ever has become half so rich as they."[28]

People on the lookout for rich "redskins" sighted them in places besides Osage country. There was oil under the lands of other Indians, including neighbors of the Osages, and in the tribes where allotments carried mineral rights, a few individuals received royalties far greater than any Osage did. A Shawnee woman, in 1926, reportedly had "the largest daily income of any Indian in the United States"—approximately $1,200. According to other assessments, the title of richest Indian in the world belonged not to an Osage or a Shawnee but to a Creek man, Jackson Barnett. The press also publicized allegations that Indians of the Navajo and Flathead Reservations were sitting on resources worth many millions of dollars. And in 1925, "Chief Two Moon"—reputedly a "wealthy Indian medicine man from Waterbury, Connecticut"—intrigued people in Washington, D.C., as he made the rounds of monuments in his "palatial tour bus."[29]

Whether non-Indians expected most Indians to be rich or poor by then, their reactions to the rich ones reflected ideas that dominated Euro-American discourse about Indians in the early twentieth century. "Indians" connoted people who had lost their independence and historical means of subsistence in a doomed fight against advancing civilization. Common representations of Indians also depicted people who clung to an archaic culture, unable or unwilling to improve their condition by emulating White Americans' enterprise. Critics of federal policy portrayed Indians as a sidelined race, condemned to stagnation and impotence by bad laws and corrupt overseers.[30] When Indians became stupendously wealthy nonetheless, the supposed incongruity of their good fortune commanded attention and provoked responses reserved particularly for Indians.

It was fashionable to view Indians' oil wealth as a comical fluke. Lady Luck had played a prank on the aborigines and their conquerors alike. One travel writer's flippancy made it clear that she saw comedy in the situation. Dubbing Osage Indians "the Chosen People of Chance, the Anointed of Oil and Gas," Estelle Brown promised to relate "something of what happened when a prodigal fate suddenly showered on the unwashed heads of a blanket tribe of Indians well-nigh unlimited wealth and prosperity."[31] An *Outlook* essay hinted at the amusing irony in Chance's choice of the Osage for its oil and gas blessing:

> It may seem peculiar but at the time the Indians were rounded up . . . and transplanted on to what was then believed to be a desert district in Indian Territory it was thought that this was the end of the Indian. . . . But it didn't work out that way. Lo and behold! these same lands are to-day extremely rich in natural resources . . . , and the Indian, instead of starving to death . . . , now rides around in the best of motor cars and enjoys a steady income that turns bankers green with envy. . . . I learned, from first-hand information, of an Indian squaw with a blanket wrapped around her driving up to the Indian Commissioner, stepping out of the luxurious closed car, walking boldly into the Commissioner's office, and coming out with twenty-five one-thousand-dollar bills in her hand.[32]

The joke seemed all the funnier when observers saw signs that rich Osages were still uncivilized Indians at heart. *Harlow's Weekly* invited chuckles with a report that the Osage stomp dance "won additional fame" in 1920 "because some of the wealthy members of the nation attended, going to the dance from their homes by aeroplane." "The old rituals are observed at this dance," the article concluded, "but the means of conveying the dancers . . . have changed to such an extent in the past ten years as to make the occasion one which outrivals the ability of the fictionist to portray." Elmer Peterson coaxed smiles from readers of the *Independent* with a claim that it was common in Osage country "to find a circle of expensive automobiles surrounding an open camp-fire, where the bronzed and brightly blanketed owners are cooking meat in the primitive style." Peterson also presented as droll nonfiction the oft-told tale of an Indian who built a beautiful home but gave in to "wild instinct" at night when "he would take his blankets down to the living room and sleep on the hard floor before the fireplace, where the wraiths of his ancestors . . . danced out of the smoke to tell him the white man's lodge and the white man's black magic of the flowing ground-deeps were only the dreams of a fever."[33]

For Edwin Slosson, the serendipity that enabled a "wild" Indian home-owner to sleep on the floor of an elegant parlor was not a joke but a lesson in the regrettable arbitrariness of modern-day success. Indians' wealth was increasing, Slosson explained soberly, "not thru their own exertions for the most part, but chiefly from the incidental increase in the value of their lands and mineral deposits due to the enterprize of their white neighbors." Rather than a reward for investment and hard work, affluence in twentieth-century

America could be a matter of luck. But perhaps it was Indians' turn for a little luck, Slosson added:

> This billion and a half of property is mostly what the single-taxers call 'the unearned increment' which automatically accrues to the land owner whether or not he does anything to earn or to deserve it. The Indians have not earned it all and they deserved it only in the sense that the needy, improvident and incompetent always deserve the support and protection of the community in which they live. And if in our liberality we have overendowed them, if we have enabled them to accumulate more than we have ourselves, we should not regret it nor envy them their easy fortune for it is better to be over-generous than unjust.[34]

Slosson probably felt a need to defend Indians' right to their "unearned increment" because he sensed doubts about that right—others' doubts and perhaps his own. In fact, some Whites frankly proposed that Indian claims to oil wealth be annulled. The author of a letter to the *Independent* argued that a "Nordic," when faced with a rich Osage, was likely to think,

> [That] good-for-nothing redskin . . . wastrel is rich through no virtue of his own, but merely because the Government unfortunately located him upon oil land which we white folks have developed for him. If I had his wealth, I could do something with it worth while. . . . Only a careless government, would have given savage tribes subsoil rights in reservation lands, and only a government rich beyond need and sense would perpetuate them in the possession of assets which their white neighbors could use to better advantage. Their present arrangement, however moral it may be in theory, directly conduces to crime and needs revision almost as much as the white culprits need punishment.[35]

To prevent the crimes that resentful people might commit against Osages, the correspondent recommended legislation relieving the Indians of their unearned money.

The pseudonymous letter and Slosson's admonitions were part of a discourse about rich Indians that was largely divorced from discourse about other wealthy people. Although some newly rich Indians and Whites had behaviors and experiences in common—wasteful spending, idleness, and attractiveness to scoundrels, for example—few people noted the parallels. Public discussion proceeded as if moneyed Indians were a unique phenomenon fundamentally different from non-Indians with significant wealth. This conceptual segregation was symptomatic of a tendency to regard Indians as a subject distinct from others for most purposes—a tendency that continued in subsequent historical studies of the Roaring Twenties, where accounts of the Osage experience are virtually nonexistent.[36]

While paying occasional lip service to the premise that people of different races dealt in similar ways with sudden affluence, contemporary accounts of the Osage bonanza described a response that was in a class by itself. Observers plumbed their vocabularies for language strong enough to communicate what they saw. Federal inspector H. S. Traylor, reporting on a trip to Oklahoma in 1918, fulminated, "I never wholly appreciated the story of Sodom and Gomorrah . . . until I visited this Indian nation. All the forces of dissipation and evil are here found." Traylor was one of many who asserted that Osage profligacy was unrivaled. "The Osage Indian is to-day the prince of spendthrifts," travel writer Estelle Brown declared. "Judged by his improvidence, the Prodigal Son was simply a frugal person with an inherent fondness for husks." In 1920, George Vaux recommended that his colleagues on the Board of Indian Commissioners lobby for federal control of Osage annuities, saying, "I do not believe that the world can show a parallel to this situation."[37]

There was a marked contrast between such hyperbole and the more temperate language of essays about wealthy Whites. When Stuart Chase told *New Republic* readers how an average Park Avenue family spent $70,000 a year— $8,000 for food, $5,000 for jewelry, $4,000 on cars—his tone was coolly ironic, and value-laden terms were few. The *Los Angeles Daily Times* even drew a staid, if vaguely condescending portrait of new "negro oil magnates" from Oklahoma who toured California in 1922, looking for investment opportunities. It stressed that "every one" of the eleven men had "worked with his hands" to obtain the farmland he subsequently leased for oil wells, and every one "dressed in dark clothing and plain white linen. . . . Only two wore diamonds on their hand, and those were of modest size."[38]

Commentators had various ways of insinuating that rich Osages did not belong in the same category with other wealthy people. Providing numerous examples of outlandish extravagance was effective. Article upon article alleged that an Osage "buck" needed no better excuse than a flat tire to buy a new Cadillac, Osage "squaws" spent thousands per month for groceries, and Osage children could not be bothered to pick up coins they dropped. "The country collectively gulped," wrote Dennis McAuliffe in 1999, "upon learning that one Osage man spent $100 a week to feed his dogs." And a 1925 feature in *Collier's* magazine repeated the widely circulated claim that "Osage owners would leave the car out in the rain until the nickel tarnished; then they would turn it in for a new and shiny one."[39]

With a few additional words, commentators regularly linked Osages' exceptional extravagance to their Indian identity. In coverage of an oil lease auction or quarterly cash distribution, a casual mention of moccasins or scalp locks told readers that the reservation's rich residents were a very different breed from Philadelphia's upper crust. William Shepherd's description of a "huge" woman emerging from a chauffeured vehicle was typical: "She is blanketed, and her glistening hair is parted in the middle and brushed back above her ears. She has a bead necklace and a beaded bag, but you catch a flash of a silk stocking and you see that instead of moccasins she is wearing heelless, patent-leather slippers." The garb of the man behind her "is Indian to the last observable stitch, except for his hat." And if dress did not denote a rich Osage's Indianness, behavior could. A White Oklahoman told Elmer Peterson, "You'll seldom find them in their homes. They squat in the streets and watch, live in tents in the yard." Thanks to reportage of this kind, Osage country acquired a reputation as a place where "grand pianos often stood out on the lawns year around; priceless china and silverware sat on shelves while the Indians ate with their fingers, . . . expensive vases were used to keep vegetables in or as corn bins, and pigs were hauled in the back seats of . . . automobiles."[40]

Underlying such patronizing and derisive depictions was a belief that consumption should be appropriate for consumers' social stations and roles, which depended on more than annual income. Like humans everywhere, Americans relied in part on possessions to signal and spot group affiliations and status.[41] When people bought goods associated with a status higher than the one ascribed to their class, race, or ethnic group, they defied notions of propriety. That was true even after the mass-producing economy enabled the idle rich and wage workers alike to purchase radios, high-fashion garments, and automobiles. A contributor to *Harper's* magazine fretted, "We do not know how much respect to pay to the strangers we meet these days when the advertisements dress both rich and poor alike in the same stylish brand of collars." He proposed, tongue in cheek, that everyone wear a name tag indicating his or her income.[42]

Freewheeling Osage consumption bothered many non-Indians because it did not square with their conception of Indians' status. It was inconsistent with Indians' accustomed place on the fringe of the national social fabric. Most recorded commentary on Osages came from middle-class journalists and government officials whose audiences were their social peers. To those

Comely Osage women such as Mary Elkins Bowles graced several covers of *The American Indian* during its publication in Tulsa, Oklahoma, from 1926 to 1931. By featuring Osages in apparel worthy of fashionable White urban socialites and characterizing them as the equal of upper-class Whites in educational and cultural accomplishments, the magazine hoped to counter publicity depicting Osages' reaction to great wealth as irrational extravagance or uncivilized carelessness. *The American Indian* 3, no. 3 (March 1928).

writers, readers, and listeners, it was obvious that Osages—despite their ritzy cars, diamond rings, and fur coats—were not of a caliber equal to Boston bluebloods or even up-and-coming middle-class Whites. There were too many signs that Osages knew or cared little about the rules of elite behavior.

When Osages spent large sums on fleeting pleasures or impractical objects, they not only struck "respectable" Americans as overreaching, low-class upstarts; they also exposed themselves to censure that reflected stereotypes of Indians, both positive and negative. Critics reflexively construed Osage consumption as improvidence because improvidence was a deficiency expected of Indians. "Planning in advance," one magazine essay declared, "is not an Indian trait." The traits of oil-rich Indians, said another article, included "child-like credulity and almost total lack of economic concepts."[43] Conversely, the acquisitiveness and apparent vanity of free-spending Osages offended those who imagined Indians as communalists from a precommercial age, unconcerned with material riches. A contributor to *American Indian* magazine tried to affirm and update the association of Indians with unselfishness by emphasizing the good taste on display at an Osage Christmas giveaway. "You might expect some sort of an orgy when the 'World's Richest Nation' assembled for their great holiday dances and gift giving," the author posited, but "you couldn't find it. . . . If you sought the garish and gawdy in gifts or wrapping you were disappointed. Engraved cards, thoughtfully chosen gifts of real merit and artistically made parcels lent an air of distinction. . . . Beside the magnificence of their celebration, the Yule Log and Boar's Head pageantry of Merrie England's Christmas pomp, seems crude."[44] This public relations effort was largely futile. Three decades later, when Osage novelist and scholar John Joseph Mathews recalled the time of the great oil "frenzy," he thought sourly of "magazine . . . and Sunday supplement writers enjoying the bizarre impact of wealth on the Neolithic men, with the usual smugness and wisdom of the unlearned."[45]

If by unlearned, Mathews meant that non-Indians did not bother to determine whether Osage history and culture could explain the Indians' behavior during the "frenzy," he was correct. Did Osages think their spending was in accordance with sensible tribal traditions? Could apparent profligacy have served a prudent purpose in Osage society? Those questions do not appear to have occurred to the smug critics. Unfortunately, Mathews did not address them squarely either, even though he devoted countless hours to researching and recording ancestral Osage beliefs and practices.

Convinced that fierce winds of change had blown young tribe members far off the traditional course of life by the 1920s, Mathews felt an urgent need to preserve Osage memories of the old ways. In doing so, he added significantly to a meager stock of Osage ethnography. But because he did not investigate economic beliefs specifically, and because he did not intend to document new Osage beliefs, his work has little to say about whether Osages in the boom years were trying to abide by a traditional economic ethic.[46] Nor is there much other Osage testimony on the subject. Did their fondness for diamonds and gold hark back to indigenous forebears' custom of wearing abundant jewelry, or was it merely a manifestation of what the *Saturday Evening* Post termed humans' "pleasurable excitement in decorating ourselves for display"?[47] Were the modern Osages' prodigious food and clothing purchases consistent with a tribal history of admiring well-fed, well-dressed people for their superior survival skills, or is the urge to acquire food and clothing so inherently human that a cultural genealogy is irrelevant? The closest Mathews came to venturing an opinion about the lingering influence of ancestral values was an assertion that "the Indian never lost his Olympian indifference to money."[48] But a review of Osage history shows that this was an oversimplification. By the 1920s, the people known as Osages were so diverse in culture that Mathews's iconic Olympian Indian could not represent them all.

If many twentieth-century Osages had inherited elements of their aboriginal forebears' economic culture, that heritage probably did include both their zeal to acquire precious things and their notorious disinterest in conserving what they acquired. Drawing on reports by explorers, traders, soldiers, missionaries, and government agents, professional ethnographers have described an eighteenth- and nineteenth-century Osage society in which wealth was an important basis of personal prestige but was never hoarded. Even though people cooperated to procure food and tangible forms of wealth such as horses, some procured more than others and their status rose accordingly. In the words of ethnohistorian Willard Rollings, "Men who . . . kept their kin well fed were respected." Men also needed wealth to join the powerful priesthoods that directed Osages' ceremonial life. However, a person who stockpiled wealth forfeited others' respect. Sharing and caring generously for guests were social and economic imperatives. Fortunate Osages met the obligation to share and enhanced their social standing in large part by distributing their bounty as feasts and gifts. Such magnanimity did not have the effect of equalizing wealth, though, since the more numerous poor people honored benefactors with gifts of their own. For that reason, and because clans ensured that their neediest members had sustenance, neither great liberality nor low productivity left a person destitute. Survival as a group, which depended on unity, was paramount.[49] Mathews gave this moral code a romantic gloss when he wrote that "honor [was] of greater importance than wealth."[50]

To assume that the same ethic guided Osages of the oil boom generation would be rash for at least two reasons. First, when earlier Osages passed the wisdom of ancestors down to their children, they also cautioned that new knowledge could require new practices. Both Rollings and anthropologist Garrick Bailey draw that inference from Osage mythology and accounts of nineteenth-century religious practices. The "traditional Osages," Bailey states, were "strongly future oriented." They believed that the cosmos operated by dynamic rules and offered changing opportunities. Religious leaders had a duty to study the cosmic order continually so that Osages could conform to its evolving requirements.[51] During field work in the 1970s, Bailey concluded that Osages had transmitted this attitude about change to successive generations. In the 1920s, the great change facing Osages was the availability of immense wealth to most tribe members, regardless of their effort or status. Responding with prescribed resilience to that new circumstance would fulfill one ancestral ideal, but it might mean choosing to disregard other ideals.[52]

Second, whether or not they welcomed change, Osages had made alterations over time in their economic culture. Critical changes followed from their adaptations to the late-seventeenth-century appearance of pale foreigners who offered to trade desirable new things for peltry and horses. Osages responded by fighting successfully to dominate hunting areas, trade networks, and grazing lands in a vast stretch of the southern plains.[53] One consequence was a shift in the relative weight they gave to the two aims of tribal unity and individual attainment. With new riches obtained in trade, in battle, or from European patrons, more men had the means to gain stature in the accustomed way, and when they were unable or reluctant to displace established leaders, some opted instead to found new bands.[54] Subsequent developments exacerbated the strains on custom that came with this increased attention to acquiring wealth and decreased effort to preserve unity. Deadly diseases, warfare, and food shortages cut band populations, and the dispersed bands found it hard to sustain the system of priestly guidance that had historically unified Osages. Confinement to a reservation did not reverse this trend. Instead, the bands settled in separate areas of the reservation, where members continued to die at a high rate until there were too few men to fill the traditional religious leadership roles. By the 1880s, it was difficult to perform many of the rituals that expressed and perpetuated ancestral beliefs.[55] Over the next three decades, new factors, including systematic U.S. efforts to "civilize" Indians, further undermined the ancient institutions until, according to Bailey, "the traditional ceremonies had almost completely disappeared and most of the people were making a conscious effort to forget the 'old way.'"[56]

Even so, generosity was apparently one "old way" that many Osages did not want to forget. About 1885, with annuity and rental income making it possible to acquire and distribute property in growing amounts, they adopted a four-day Ponca ceremony that culminated in exuberant gift-giving.[57] Mathews captured the spirit of the event, known as I'n-lon-shka. "Sometimes a man who had little to give would become intoxicated with the image of himself as a generous giver, and filled with illusions of grandeur, he would trade all for the few moments when all eyes were on him and his song was being sung. . . . The poorer the recipient of some Nobody's generosity, the greater the 'ho-o-o-o-o-o-o-os' of praise and gratitude, and the more concentrated the attention drawn to the giver, and the greater the welling of self-esteem within him."[58]

Tribal unity remained elusive, however, because the wealth that enabled Osages to be impressively generous was also a magnet for people who conducted economic affairs with other ends in mind. Outsiders' attraction to Osage wealth was not new. The tribal population in 1870 included people Mathews described as "descendants of the jolly, *laissez faire coureurs de bois* and the *voyageurs* and traders. They not only retained their ancient respect for the bourgeois and the official . . . , they liked to walk in reflected glory of great enterprises." After the 1870s, the number of enterprising and acquisitive new reservation residents rose rapidly. Some were White; some were offspring of Whites and Indians; all expected to benefit materially from relationships with Osages.[59]

Even before the oil boom, historian Terry Wilson explains, "there was much . . . to account for this steady influx." Osages had pastures and farmland for lease, stands of merchantable timber, and money to spend. On the eve of a distribution from the tribal trust fund, newspapers in neighboring states announced the dollar amount due, inspiring peddlers and covetous connivers to head for Pawhuska, the Osage capital.[60] Bailey found that the prospect of receiving land and cash also drew in "many 'mixed-blood Osages' who had not been on the reservation. . . . Citizenship in the tribe became valuable." As the twentieth century approached, the reservation was "overrun" with newcomers. Although the tribal roll was growing too, tribe members became a minority on their own reservation.[61]

The presence of many Euro-Americans exposed Osages to economic aspirations and strategies at odds with some key values and relations their Osage ancestors had espoused. Federal officials and schoolteachers exhorted Indians to establish self-reliant households by working steadily, being frugal, acquiring property, and generating an ever-growing fund of family wealth by investing in productive private assets.[62] Non-Indian parents and in-laws made self-interested investment and accumulation seem both desirable and normal. By their associations and their reactions to such messages, Osages sorted themselves roughly into two groups with divergent economic agendas. Those who favored the way of life advocated by government agents, educators, and enterprising White relatives were usually identified as "mixed-bloods." For their less receptive cousins and neighbors, the label "full-bloods" was the norm.

Neither ancestry nor economic practices alone determined a person's classification, yet the group names had both racial and cultural connotations. Descendants of interracial couples tended to marry other biracial individuals or Whites, thus begetting a distinct population composed largely of people with White ancestors—in some cases, more White than Indian ancestors. That population absorbed additional Euro-Americans who apparently thought the material benefits of having light-skinned, economically "progressive" Osage kin and neighbors outweighed the stigma among Whites of fraternizing with Indians. In his *History of the Osage Nation*, published the same year as the allotment act, Philip Jackson Dickerson assured respectable prospective White settlers that they would find a congenial society on the reservation. The leading mixed-blood families, he wrote, had "always been allied with some of the best whites in their territory." Many, Dickerson added, "live just as much apart in manner of life, in eating, drinking, dressing, and in finely improved homes, farms and town residences, with education and culture, as the better citizens of New England."[63]

Thus, the division of the Osage tribe into two subcultures—a division rooted in divergent economic ideologies—proceeded apace. By many accounts, antipathy between the groups grew with the mixed-blood population. Mixed-bloods and full-bloods focused much of their disdain on each other's manners, dress, and social habits. To John Joseph Mathews's fellow mixed-bloods, for instance, "the full bloods appeared as stupid, stubborn, 'blanket Indians.' They were 'uncivilized' and had 'no get up and go.'"[64] Tension between the groups took a clear political turn, however, when federal officials pressed Osages to allot and privatize their land. A so-called mixed-blood or progressive faction coalesced in favor of allotment, and a full-blood faction rallied to resist it. The two parties vied for years to control the governing council that would decide whether to authorize allotment.

Contrary to common mixed-blood claims, opponents of allotment did not necessarily lack the desire or capacity for material gain.[65] Indeed, a longtime full-blood leader reportedly had an abundance of "get up and go." Chief James Bigheart amassed a significant fortune as a cattle rancher, merchant, and bank director. According to a biographer, he was "the wealthiest man of his tribe prior to the discovery of oil." But he spoke for people who were not accustomed to viewing individual economic circumstances solely as an individual or nuclear family responsibility. Nor were his constituents inclined to distinguish principles of economic life from the mores of spiritual or social life.[66] Bigheart himself assumed a role like that of an old-time leading man, symbolically taking responsibility for his people's material well-being and symbolizing their prosperity with his largesse. He "entertained often and lavishly at the ranch"; he "gave many large and elaborate dances and feasts." Among his followers, a sense of interdependence and an expectation of mutual support were apparently still strong.[67] Typical proponents of allotment, in contrast, must have hoped for some relief from the duty to share. Estranged from old school Osage leaders, they expected to fare better on their own than by casting their lot with a tribal collective.

Demographic change effectively decided the contest about allotment. Due in part to federal administrators' addition of many mixed-bloods to the Osage roll, the mixed-blood and full-blood populations reached parity by 1899. Six years later, mixed-bloods were in the majority, 1,156 to 838.[68] Meanwhile, the commissioner of Indian affairs withdrew his recognition of the gridlocked tribal government, which the embattled full-bloods had dominated since its establishment in 1881. The commissioner then put the question of allotment to a smaller council of his own creation. By 1904, when proallotment candidates won six of the seven seats on the new council, half of eligible Osages had already heeded federal officials' admonition to claim homesteads on the tribal domain. Further resistance to allotment was obviously useless.[69]

Bowing to political reality, Bigheart and other full-blood leaders dedicated themselves to negotiating the most advantageous possible plan. They also campaigned to maximize the value of each tribe member's allocation by purging the tribal roll of impostors, but that campaign failed. The Office of Indian Affairs (OIA) approved the enrollment of several hundred persons over full-blood protests, including a few individuals who did not even claim Osage descent.[70] More than 1,300 people on the final roster of 2,229 allottees had substantial Euro-American ancestry. Although that statistical breakdown was hardly a precise measure of tribe members' cultural alignment, it has served many government officials, Osages, and historians as a way to express an undisputed fact: the Osage tribe by 1906 was a culturally diverse, divided population. During a visit that year, a federal inspector saw many mixed-bloods who were "apparently white people and act[ed] like white people, well educated and intelligent." No doubt he also saw tribe members who fit a description penned by the agency superintendent three years earlier: "The full-blood Osage Indian takes pride in mimicking the ancient traditions and customs of his tribe, dressing in bright and rich colored costumes, consisting of leggings, gee-string, and blanket; the squaws with a loose blouse-like shirt and skirt with leggings and moccasins. The older men keep their hair nicely roached and powdered."[71] Clearly, no single description of Osage economic traditions would have applied to all the people on the new Osage tribal roll.

Although U.S. policymakers justified the allotment of tribal lands as a means of teaching Indians to think like "civilized" people about economic relations, the act of Congress that privatized Osage land tacitly conceded that some tribe members would be recalcitrant pupils. It left three tracts in communal ownership, probably to serve as sites for encampments where traditional dancing, feasting, and gift-giving would take place. Otherwise, however, the allotment act treated all Osages alike despite their different degrees of enthusiasm and preparation for American-style private property ownership. Everyone on the Osage roll would make three successive selections of land— 160 acres each time—and designate one of them a homesite. Any leftover reservation land would then be divided equally among members. The United

States would hold the homesites in trust, inalienable and immune from taxation, for a twenty-five-year period that Congress could shorten or lengthen. The Indian office had authority to approve early termination of trusts for tracts other than homesites. Allottees could also ask for certificates of competency, which entitled them to lease or sell their surplus parcels without supervision.[72]

In providing for the distribution of oil and gas income, the federal legislation likewise made no distinction among tribe members based on adaptation to the modern market economy. Although the allotment act left the reservation's subterranean resources in tribal ownership, it instructed federal officials to collect royalties on mineral leases and pay them out to allottees pro rata. In effect, each allottee had a right to 1/2,229th of such revenue—a so-called headright. The stated intent of this arrangement was to minimize oil companies' costs while maximizing Osages' aggregate income and allocating it equitably. But the arrangement was a short-sighted way of trying to achieve equity. Indeed, it was a recipe for eventual economic inequality, albeit less extreme than the disparities that would have resulted from giving allottees title to the minerals beneath their individual tracts.[73]

Like an allotted tract of land, an oil and gas headright was a permanent private property interest. Anyone added to the tribal roll after allotment could share in the oil revenue only by inheriting all or part of a headright. Because some people inherited more headrights than others, the income that flowed initially to 2,229 people in equal amounts was soon collecting in pools of very different sizes. A man named E-gron-kah-shin-kah emphasized this in 1923 when urging congressmen to approve quarterly disbursements greater than $1,000. As interpreter John Abbott explained to the lawmakers, "He . . . wants to tell the committee . . . that the Osages are not equal in the way of finances, because some of them have a good many thousands of dollars while some of them do not draw so much. . . . He says that he is one who does not draw so much; that he has no inherited money. . . . He has not as much money as the newspapers say."[74]

Racial ideology justified the inclusion of mixed-bloods on a tribal allotment roster: as of 1907, it was common to assume that certain innate traits came with Indian ancestry. But the allotment of Osage land and money to mixed-bloods also served political and economic objectives, tribal as well as federal. The larger the tribal roll, the less cause Whites had to complain that the government was leaving Indians in possession of more acres than they could use. However, the enrollment of numerous mixed-bloods also put much of the Osage wealth in the hands of people who associated primarily with Whites, and it was a good bet that their share of Osage land or capital would move into Euro-American hands by inheritance, sale, or investment. Whether or not lawmakers intended that result, it was the result they got. According to a written statement in the record of a 1920 Senate hearing, just thirty-nine of the 1,300-some mixed-blood allottees had more than one-fourth Osage blood; the rest had degrees of Osage ancestry ranging from one-eighth to one-sixty-fourth or lower. Because such people often married Whites, their estates often passed to Whites. Of the 494 estates left by allottees who died between 1906 and 1920, approximately 190 went to Whites in whole or in part. Ninety-six full-bloods and 596 mixed-bloods were then married to Whites, the statement concluded, "making a total of about 882 white persons now participating in the Osage annuity payments."[75]

In sum, when federal agents put people of remote Osage descent on the same allotment roll as Osages with no White kin, they were not ignorant of the tribe's contrasting cultures; nor were they trying to close or paper over the rift between full- and mixed-bloods. On the contrary, they administered the allotment act as if they were intent on widening the rift to the point of complete separation. For the twenty-five years following allotment, OIA personnel were far more likely to bestow certificates of competency on people of mixed ancestry than on other Osages.[76] The practice was not unique to Osages; it was in line with federal action elsewhere as early as 1906. By a "Declaration of Policy" in 1917, the commissioner of Indian affairs made it a national rule and clarified that race would count more than culture in identifying the people who could manage property on their own. All persons of less than half Indian "blood" were deemed competent and would receive unrestricted patents to their land immediately.[77] Thus, it was no surprise when, in 1921, Congress ended the federal trust for land belonging to adult Osages who had more non-Indian than Indian ancestors.[78] The tribe's attorney told a House committee three years later, "We have been always taught . . . that it is the desire of Congress to release from their supervision what we call the 'white Indians,' who have a small quantum of Indian blood."[79]

The oil boom tested the supposition that "blood quantum" was a reliable predictor of a tribe member's economic common sense and money management skills. Lawmakers, bureaucrats, and some Osages showed little interest in the test results, however. In the face of considerable evidence to the contrary, many professed a continuing belief that economic aptitude correlated with ascribed race. While advocating that "supervision . . . be thrown around some full-bloods," a former U.S. agent on the reservation declared in 1920, "I regard a mixed-blood Indian as I regard myself." Others in the government conceded that "white blood" was no guarantee of fiscal prudence, yet they advocated or accepted a financial management scheme that classed full-bloods as incompetent and mixed-bloods as competent. J. George Wright, who began a long tenure as Osage agency superintendent in 1915, saw the arbitrariness of the scheme and endorsed it nonetheless. "Some of the half bloods are as improvident as the full bloods," Wright told congressmen, "though I would not recommend supervising payments of adult mixed bloods."[80]

Wright had a hand in persuading Congress to limit the amount of money the OIA would mete out to "noncompetent" headright holders. "No other Indians on the face of the earth" were as "improvident" as Osages, Wright said at the 1920 hearings, because none had such outlandishly large payments from their trust funds. While an Osage received over $8,000 a year, a government-supervised full-blood in one of the Civilized Tribes received no more than $200, had to "work for a living," and consequently was "far more provident." Along with Wright's testimony, congressmen had the scandalized Inspector Traylor's report from 1918 to consider:

> Every white man in Osage County will tell you that the Indians are now running wild, not only spending their incomes in full but going hundreds of thousands of dollars in debt each year. . . . John Hunter, of Greyhorse, a young Indian, is one of the great spenders. He has had in the last two years four or five good cars, and recently, while drunk, deliberately tried to cross the Arkansas River by fording it and left his car in the middle of the channel. . . . He spends his money as fast as he can get his hands upon it and owes absolutely every one who would trust him in the past. . . . The above dissipations are typical to . . . all of the Osage full bloods [who] spend money in like amounts and for like purposes. They seemingly know no restraint, and will buy and borrow anything and any amount which the merchants and bankers will intrust to them.[81]

Anecdotes about other Indians who apparently "knew no restraint" lent credibility to Traylor's sweeping claims. So did a federal agency estimate that Osages, despite a collective annual income topping $8 million, had run up debts totaling nearly $1 million in short order. Most lawmakers required no further proof of the need to rein in the Indians' spending. Such irresponsibility was unacceptable. After voting to withhold all but $4,000 of every "noncompetent" Osage's annuity, Representative Homer Snyder explained: "The Osages are getting at this time $12,000 to $13,000 apiece and we found they were squandering their money and were throwing it away, and that they were being robbed in every possible direction. . . . It was with a view of putting that money away so that when this oil ran out, if it ever did, the Indians would have sufficient money to take care of them forever."[82]

Snyder and his colleagues in Congress acted without seeking Osage approval. They tacked the provision for reduced disbursements onto a bill the tribal council requested—a bill extending the time the United States would hold Osage oil in trust. According to the tribe's attorney, Osages wanted the trust extended beyond 1931 in order to prevent covetous Whites from robbing them of "this big opportunity to get vast sums of money for distribution among the tribe."[83] However, for the following decade, whenever a congressional committee took testimony on Osage matters, some tribe members were there to plead for repeal of the added provision that unilaterally prohibited full distribution of those vast sums.

In rebuffing the Osage entreaties, legislators implied that there was but one standard of economic good sense, and they would not dream of questioning its wisdom. Probably because the validity of the standard seemed obvious to them, they did not deign to explain it. Some thoughtful Americans had expressed doubt in print that it was possible to agree on a definition of excessive consumption, but members of Congress did not even think the issue worth discussing.[84] They simply expected Osages to understand the folly of spending as if there were no tomorrow to plan for. Osages, on the other hand, vacillated between implying that they subscribed to the same standard of economic prudence as the lawmakers and claiming the right to live by a different one.

Having no desire to understand economic objectives or principles other than their own, the congressmen did not pause to reflect when presented with evidence that some Osages still moved to the beat of a different drum—the drumbeat of community feasts and giveaways. Lawmakers received an agency report praising the prominent full-blood Wah-sho-sha for staying out of debt, but they apparently missed the significance of an added comment: "His greatest failing is his desire for popularity, which he aims to increase by extensive entertaining, evidently realizing that the shortest way to a man's heart is through his stomach." On hearing about lavish Osage funeral feasts, some lawmakers briefly speculated that persistent tribal tradition was at work, but they did not seem to care whether the logic of Osage economic relations prompted and justified such a seemingly senseless use of wealth.[85] Indeed, they talked as if the Indians' problem was not so much a wrongheaded culture as lack of an economic culture. They viewed conservative full-bloods as children, unschooled in the rational management of assets and unprepared for the wiles of Americans who coveted their assets. When Superintendent Wright declared that "the non-English speaking blanket Indians in most instances do not re-

To many Osages, hosting feasts for large numbers of people was an appropriate use of the generous income they derived from oil leases. To agents of the U.S. government and members of Congress, the lavish feasts were evidence of the untutored Indians' improvidence, which necessitated a law limiting the amount of money distributed to them. Courtesy of Research Division of the Oklahoma Historical Society, image 16336.

alize the value of money," he articulated the principal government rationale for rationing Osage funds.[86] The idea that money might have a different but rational value to "blanket Indians" was not one he would entertain.[87]

Whether they thought of Osage full-bloods as economic primitives or as children, congressmen expressed few doubts about their own right to exercise paternalistic control of Osage funds, even though the practice was relatively new. The federal government had begun holding funds in trust for Indian tribes a century earlier, when officials and chiefs or headmen noticed that much of the money paid for tribal land cessions "immediately found its way into the pockets of the designing white traders."[88] But agreements with self-governing tribes to establish trust accounts did not give the United States a legal basis to control the separate property of tribe members. The progression from consensual U.S. custody of tribal funds to unbidden federal guardianships for individual Indians came later with the tribes' drastic loss of power. In 1886, the Supreme Court, citing only the de facto shift of the power balance and an illustrative analogy from an 1831 opinion, declared that Indians were now wards of the federal government, which had a duty to protect them by extending to individual Indians the benefits of American law. A year later, Congress mandated the allotment of tribal lands nationwide, and the Court subsequently condoned such unilateral changes in the status of Indian property. Thus in 1905, when a lawyer for the Osage Tribe argued that Congress could not dictate the terms of land allotment, Representative Charles Curtis shot back, "The Supreme Court has decided that we may do whatever we desire."[89]

A campaign to apportion all tribal funds as well as tribal lands did not succeed until 1918, partly because of fears in Congress that Indians would squander personal cash payments.[90] But there was nothing new by then about federal employees managing individual Indians' money. Under the General Allotment Act of 1887, the government held income from allotted lands in trust for allottees. That the Indian office could therefore control their wards' access to, and use of, the money seemed obvious to bureaucrats and judges. When Congressman Homer Snyder said in a hearing on Osage funds, "I do not think it is quite the competency question there, but it is a question of the frugality of the Indian," he indicated the assumption behind that meddling: government officials should substitute their judgment for the economic judgment of Indians.[91]

Snyder said he saw no sense in giving Osages additional cash if they were going to squander it "and become more useless citizens than they are to-day." Reasoning the same way, the OIA's Osage agency acted to restrict some tribe members' access to their money even before Congress did. Superintendent Wright sought a private guardian for an Osage whenever that person was apparently not conserving "and could not tell anything about how much he got or where it went to."[92] To an Indian service officer such as Wright, it was irrelevant that some White people were no better than such Indians at conserving or tracking their expenditures. By custom and law, the daily affairs of Indians were their federal caretakers' business.

To explain why they took command of Osage purse strings, lawmakers and administrators mentioned the Indians' allegedly naïve extravagance and the United States' responsibility to safeguard Indian resources. But Indians were not the only audience, or even the most important audience, for those explanations. The rhetoric of federal guardianship was also a tactic in a tug-of-war between Whites, some of whom hoped to limit federal power so they could siphon off Osage wealth for themselves.

There were 40,000 people in Osage County, George Wright told lawmakers in 1924, virtually all of them expecting a chance to make money. Their motivation did not discredit them, Wright hastened to add; but Senator Lynn Frazier retorted, "If they take advantage of the Indians, I think that would be a discredit to them."[93] Frazier should have said "when" rather than "if." He had reason to know that people—non-Indians—were taking advantage of Osages in myriad ways. Some types of exploitation were blatantly, cruelly illegal. Indians by the score had reportedly fallen under the spell of bootleggers' and drug dealers' wares, and it took little imagination for con artists to defraud drunken or drugged Indians of their money.[94] Bilking sober Indians who did not speak or read English could be nearly as easy. And the most rapacious predators were not above murdering Osages for their money. By 1923, the Federal Bureau of Investigation (FBI) was following up rumors of a connection between the violent deaths of several rich Indians and the growing fortune of a swaggering local cattleman named William K. Hale.[95]

To more legitimate businesspeople as well, Osages represented valuable fruit ripe for the picking. Some went after that fruit with less concern for propriety than others, but even law-abiding merchants or moneylenders charged what the inflated local market would bear—many times what their products or services would bring outside oil country. An FBI investigator concluded, "The 'better class' of white people are mainly engaged in grafting the Indians, etc. as far as possible, so as to make a pile."[96] But rather than bringing the grafters, usurers, bootleggers, drug dealers, and con artists under control, Congress acted to limit the amount of Osage money that circulated and excited the non-Indians' greed.

The Osage-area Whites whose businesses garnered the most attention in Congress were private guardians and lawyers. Congress had given its blessing to private guardians for Osages in 1912, when it granted Oklahoma state courts jurisdiction to declare allottees incompetent and appoint caretakers for their property. Until 1921, that law provided the only way the Indian agency could avoid paying an Osage the full amount due under the tribe's allotment act. After 1921, some Osages applied on their own to county courts for private guardians, reportedly in the belief that such caretakers were not bound by the new federal allowance plan and would release more spending money than the Indian agent. County judges also declared many unwilling Osages incompetent.[97] As soon as an Indian went into debt, a tribal attorney alleged, someone would petition for appointment of a guardian. Would-be guardians even colluded with merchants to lure Indians into debt because private guardians and their lawyers could make comfortable livings from fees. In addition, guardians could skim money from their charges' accounts with an ease too tempting for many to resist. By 1924, the business of helping "helpless" Osages had become a mainstay of the Osage county bar, economy, and political patronage system.[98] Testimony made that plain even to the densest congressman. When one witness began, "This guardianship business," the committee chair finished the sentence with "is an institution." "One of the industries of the State," a colleague chimed in.[99]

The tribe's lawyers joined Indian agency personnel in portraying the private guardian "industry" as a racket that needlessly cost Osages thousands of dollars. Their testimony had the desired effect on many members of Congress. Representative Snyder, for example, could think of no honorable reason for a Pawhuska lawyer's opposition to the federal method of rationing Osages' income. "He wants to put them back in the same position they were before we enacted the act of 1921," Snyder snapped, "where they will have all their money and lead riotous lives."[100] If the act were repealed, Snyder suspected, a "riotous" Indian's money would find its way into the hands of the lawyer's pals one way or the other. Although congressmen from Oklahoma defended their White constituents' honor and denied that federal intervention would serve Indians' interest, a majority of lawmakers thought otherwise.

However, the debate among Whites about Osage money was not a simple contest between local interest groups and advocates of federal protection for Indians. On one hand, the White people of Osage county were hardly a united bloc, since their various moneymaking schemes were not all compatible. Some had reason to portray Indians as helpless; others found it convenient to say the Indians were capable of managing without federal guidance, and not always because they hoped to preserve the private guardianship business. Oilmen did not take a position on the management of individual Osages' cash, but they did prefer federal to local jurisdiction over Indian resources. They strengthened federal officials' hand and irked some locals by arguing forcefully, in 1905, that minerals should remain tribal property. Although their real aim was to simplify the leasing process, oil company representatives emphasized the injustice to individual Indians of allotting a resource that was unevenly distributed beneath the land. They looked to lawmakers to prevent such an injustice, one spokesman said, because they assumed "that Congress . . . stands in very much the same capacity or relation as guardian of the Indians as the courts do in the distribution of property among minor children."[101]

On the other hand, as is evident from the decision in 1912 to let Oklahoma set up Osage guardianships, people in federal government did not make a precise, inflexible distinction between federal and local interests. They sympathized with White Oklahomans' desire for economic opportunities.[102] Some employees of the Indian office, current and former, were White Oklahomans with a stake in promoting and exploiting local business activity.[103] Furthermore, some congressmen from states other than Oklahoma were wary of measures that would increase executive involvement in the affairs of individual Osages. Officially, the government's aim was still to "turn Indians loose" and get out of the "Indian business." So when legislators remarked that Indians and Whites were equally prone to extravagance, they may have been signaling their desire to minimize the number of people for whom the Indian office acted as money manager, lest the burgeoning federal bureaucracy continue to grow.[104]

Even so, a majority in Congress eventually voted to give federal personnel more power over Osages' individual funds, knowing that the change could cost local judges and private citizens some power and money. Perhaps the vote reflected genuine concern for Indians' welfare; perhaps it was also, or instead, a reaction against the extreme position taken by some White Oklahomans. From the vantage point of the twenty-first century, at least, the argument of one county representative does seem extreme. He said,

> Any man with good judgment would know that this is a white man's country and progress and civilization depends upon the white man and the white civilization; Osage County is an empire in area and the richest plot of ground on the globe so far as wealth-producing resources is concerned, and we do believe that the people who are attempting to make this county a fit place in which to live should be considered in the matter of the distribution of the wealth of this country. . . . With $40,000,000 of money hoarded some place outside of the Treasury of the United States, some person or set of persons will undertake to exploit that money and the way it will get away from the Indian will be just too bad.[105]

A spokesman for the local Republican Party was not of a mind to nominate anyone in the Osage money-management debate for sainthood. "I believe the Indian Office and the bar association are both working from entirely selfish motives," he wrote; "neither of them cares a hoot what becomes of the Indian personally."[106] His letter raises the question of whether federal officers should go on the list of Whites with their hands in the Osage till. The answer is affirmative in one above-board respect. Thanks to a clause of the allotment act, Osage oil money entirely covered the costs of maintaining a government agency on the reservation and handling Osage affairs. The superintendent and his staff drew their salaries from Osage funds.[107]

At times, tribe members voiced a conviction that federal agents were as bent as other outsiders on diverting the money from Osage oil wells into non-Indian bank accounts. A resolution of the tribal council in 1917 complained, without specific details, that Superintendent Wright was "more greatly concerned about and . . . favorable to the interests of big oil companies and men of large financial means and political influence than . . . to the interests of the Osage people." It also requested an investigation "into the matter of conducting the Osage Indian Agency, with the object of reducing all unnecessary costs and eliminating all extravagance." The resolution concluded with a charge that "vast sums of Osage money" were "expended under the direction of the Department of the Interior without regard to the views of the Osage people."[108]

In the 1990s, the Interior Department acknowledged that it had an abysmal record of managing individual Indian trust accounts dating back to the General Allotment Act.[109] It is possible, if not likely, that some Osage funds were among those "lost" since the 1880s in that bureaucratic Bermuda Triangle. It would be astonishing if every civil servant in charge of Osage accounts resisted the temptation to take an illicit cut. Nevertheless, when agents of the Indian service said that the solution for Osage extravagance and non-Indian greed was a federal guardian's firm hand, they were not necessarily engaged in devious self-dealing. Their desire to keep other Whites from fleecing Osages may have been as genuine as their ethnocentrism and their low estimation of Indians' abilities. Most congressmen, at least, did expect the Interior department to conserve the Indians' money, if for no other reason than to save the government from having to support bankrupt Osages in the future. Thus, in 1924, a House committee peppered Osage county bar members with question after skeptical or hostile question about why they favored paid private guardianships for Osages when federal agents would perform the same service without charge.[110]

For their part, vocal Osages reasonably concluded that living under the U.S. eagle's eye was safer, on balance, than living alone in a henhouse surrounded by local foxes. Despite their dissatisfaction with particular federal laws and practices, they did not seek to end the guardianship entirely. Chief Bacon Rind declared a typically ambivalent willingness to accept some United States authority. He repeatedly asked Congress to rescind the quarterly payment plan adopted in 1921, and he complained more than once that the local agency's expenses were excessive; but he also told lawmakers, "Those [private] guardians are robbing the Indians. We want the commissioner to educate those Indians. . . . The agent is the proper guardian under the law." John Abbott, a younger full-blood, expressed similar contradictory sentiments more succinctly. "We want protection," he testified in 1928. "These old men are asking more liberty."[111]

It is no wonder that federal laws and policies elicited ambivalent statements from Osages. The considerations shaping their public responses to federal actions were as complex as those that weighed on their federal overseers' minds. By all accounts, Osages were proud people. To be ruled by others—to be told whether and how they could spend their own money, no less—was galling. Yet they knew, as Bacon Rind said, that "everybody wants to get in here and get some of this money that belongs to the tribe."[112] Many representatives of the U.S. government spoke piously about their duty to preserve the money from such predators. Understandably, numerous Osages wanted to believe them. But given their bewildering circumstances and their own diversity, Osages were bound to differ and sometimes to dither about whether and how much they should rely on the Whites with federal badges for protection from other Whites.

Ambiguous and variable though their public statements were, most of the Osages who lobbied Congress during the 1920s had a single, constant aim: more opportunity to control and use their personal funds. The question implicit in this quest was why federal protection should take the form of sequestering their money. It was usually full-bloods who pleaded for unrestricted access to individual income, because mixed-bloods could often achieve the same end by obtaining certificates of competency. While keeping their eyes on their goal, however, the full-bloods varied their rhetorical tactics considerably.[113] Occasionally, they argued that they could be trusted to manage money sensibly because they had seen the error of their extravagant ways.[114] At other times, without confessing to past folly, they implied that they had come to share the lawmakers' notions of good economic practices. John Abbott, who had a certificate of competency, denied that his people were ignorant or prone to abusive alcohol consumption. Before the act of 1921, he claimed, he had told other Osages, "'When you get a lot of money, let us use better judgment; let us not spend so much money; let us go slowly; and let us save something for a rainy day.'" Although he admitted that some "did not pay any attention," Abbott defended the judgment of his elders. "These old fellows are very good men, considering," he asserted, "and they are probably better able to take care of their money than the younger ones."[115]

On other occasions, full-bloods tried the opposite tack, asking Whites to let them live by values peculiar to Osage society. A few dared to disagree forthrightly with White officials' judgment that Osage liberality amounted to improvidence. They tried to explain that Indians saw economic affairs differently. Perhaps the most daring was Henry Tallchief, whose explication of the Indian way came during a tribal council meeting with agency employees in 1923. "Some have high ideas," Tallchief said. "They want to compete with the people surrounding them, or do more. Consequently they spend more money

The chief whose Osage name was most often translated as Bacon Rind appeared at least twice before congressional committees to request repeal of a 1921 law that put a "noncompetent" Osage headright holder on a $4,000 annual allowance. He acknowledged that lawmakers would consider him an ignorant "blanket Indian" and admitted that he could not refuse his children the many things they wanted, but he nevertheless questioned why a man with his history of work and his eminent status in the tribe was involuntarily subject to financial guardianship. Courtesy of Denver Public Library, Western History Collection, Love Studio photograph, image X-32576.

and they spend more money on their children. . . . They do not want their children to do anything, which as you take it in your own condition it is wrong. At the same time the Indian thinks it is right. . . . I think it is right he should think that and I honor him for it."[116] More often, Osages seemed to say that the older Indians' unwillingness or inability to change was reason to take pity on them and allow them to them do as they pleased. Even young men who abjured the old ways spoke in defense of their elders' right to be extravagant. "They can not understand these laws," Abbott explained. "They think they ought to have more money. . . . I want them to quit worrying concerning this. Pay more money to them because they want to live like kings; they do not want to make millions out of their money; they want to have an easy time to live while they are living."[117]

Full-bloods such as Bacon Rind sometimes played the ignorant Indian card in the hope of gaining lawmakers' sympathy, but they were not as naïve as their statements suggested.[118] Like their less traditional fellow tribesmen, they recognized the extent of United States power, saw the resistance in Congress to rescinding the act of 1921, and made back-up or compromise proposals. John Abbott, while continuing to insist that the old people deserved to get all their money, opined, "It's good to put a young man under supervision if he throws his money away and drinks and neglects his family." This position was consistent with that of the tribal council, a mixed-blood stronghold, which asked both for more say in tribal financial affairs and for continuing government protection. Not only did the tribe need a federal shield against conniving private parties and local officials, councilmen said, but also government guidance was appropriate for those individual Indians who would otherwise take a self-destructive course.[119] A rambling speech by Eves Tall Chief summed up the balance that many hoped to strike.

> As far as working and being industrious people, we are not as a rule,
> but they are very attentive to their families and their home life; very
> good. And I would like to see them encouraged in that line. I am speak-
> ing for the tribe, not just for myself. I am still restricted. I do not know
> why I should be in there, but I just happened to be caught in there and
> I am in there, and I have acquired education that I thought would carry
> me along in life well, but still I am not very well qualified in business
> ways. You will find these others are worse than I am. For that reason we
> would like to say [sic] by the agency rule; but there is so much in the out-
> side world that we are not able to compete with or cope with for lack of
> education. . . . I tried to learn the white people's way myself, and I would

like for the rest of our people to be taught that way, so they can in time be taught to manage their affairs in a business way.[120]

Lawmakers and officials could cite testimony such as this to support their interpretation of the federal government's duty in the Osage case. They could also claim, with hardly a hint of hypocrisy, that they endorsed a strict federal fiscal guardianship because of their desire to rectify some truly dismaying problems. Having cash in extraordinary amounts had wreaked havoc with the lives of many Osages, directly and indirectly. As a modern chronicler of the Oklahoma oil frenzy has noted, the scent of money had attracted "purveyors of every vice known to man." Even for law enforcement officers in the few local jurisdictions that employed them, the stampede of unruly humanity was overwhelming. Bootleg liquor, drug sales, prostitution, and violence "became accepted as a part of boomtown life."[121] A highly visible minority of Osages lost the ability to make safe choices in such an environment. In many cases, alcoholic drink or narcotics damaged their health and judgment.[122] The predicaments of such debilitated Indians were numerous and notorious enough to overshadow the accomplishments of Osages like James Bigheart, who used their new wealth to enhance their own and their kinfolks' health, comfort, and good reputations.[123] Even for the clear-headed, federal supervision could be a refuge from the boomtown free-for-all, not to mention a way to avoid some taxes.[124]

Three years after Congress put the "noncompetent" Osages on a $4,000 annual allowance, committee members coaxed testimony from the tribe's attorney that reinforced their commitment to strict fiscal guardianship. There was no question, lawyer A. T. Woodward conceded, that the Indians were better off financially in 1924 than they had been in 1921. In place of a total indebtedness close to $1 million, the adults under supervision had savings of more than $4 million. Four years later, according to Superintendent Wright, the amount in trust for individual Osages had reached $36 million, although the size of individual accounts ranged from $200,000 to only $20,000. These figures were misleading because Indians, with the illegal encouragement of merchants, had continued to run up debts, which Congress eventually allowed the superintendent to pay from the restricted individual accounts.[125] Nonetheless, if the fiscal guardianship was primarily intended to save Osages' money for a rainy day, it was a modest success. An independent commission, charged with evaluating the administration of Indian affairs in 1928, found that the Osages' situation improved "wonderfully" after Congress authorized the Indian service to invest everything except what the Indians needed for living expenses. As a whole, Osages under government supervision were richer in 1930—that is, they were the trust beneficiaries of more banked and invested money—than those who had been freed from supervision since allotment.[126]

Notably, such facts did not prompt lawmakers to wonder aloud why Indians alone—and mostly full-blood Indians at that—should benefit in this way from the government's fiscal paternalism. Certainly there were oil-rich non-Indians and Osage mixed-bloods who spent as frivolously, drank up as much of their income, or gave as much to con men as any full-blood, yet the U.S. government acted to staunch only the outflow of money belonging to tribe members identified as Indian by race and by their social practices.[127] Even when witnesses at hearings alluded with implicit disapproval to the racial selectivity of the federal guardianship, congressmen did not feel compelled to explain it. They seemed untroubled by the implication that a race-based double standard was responsible for Indians' special treatment. As members of a society structured to confirm the inferiority of Indians and other "colored races," they had no qualms about condescending to Indians.

To congressmen and administrators, the government's self-appointed role as Indians' guardian or trustee was explanation enough for their special treatment of Osages. But that explanation begs a central question in the Osage case: why did Congress change the Osage allotment act in the first place, giving the United States new fiscal responsibility for individual Indians at a time when the government's ostensible goal was to free individual Indians from such oversight? If Congress had not mandated the Osage allowance plan in 1921, federal officials would have had no more legal obligation to help Osages save their money than they had to help spendthrift Whites. Once the tribal oil revenues moved from a federal trust account for the tribe into individual Indians' hands, as specified in the allotment act, the money was property as private as that belonging to non-Indians who struck oil. Without neglecting their duties as trustees for Osage tribal funds, U.S. officials could have allowed all sane adult Osages to make their own economic choices, even choices that most Whites and Indians alike regarded as rash. Osages did not contend that Congress had an obligation, legal or moral, to amend the allotment act in 1921. Quite the contrary. Nevertheless, the amendment passed, with the consequence that many Osages lost their fiscal autonomy.

It is tempting to suggest that Congress and federal officials took charge of Indians' money simply because they had the power to do it. Privately, some of them may have thought that extravagance was endangering White Americans as well as Indians. Like many middle-class Whites, they may have feared for their country's moral fiber as the virtue of thrift seemingly became rarer by the day.[128] But for political reasons, they could not have imposed their personal values or economic moral code on fellow non-Indians. In the case of Indians, however, they could do that without provoking effective Indian resistance or suffering adverse political consequences.

There is some truth to the aphorism that money is power. Certainly money has the power to transform itself into countless desirable things, both tangible and intangible. When people spend money, they do exercise power of a sort. But by the same token, money not spent—money accumulated and conserved instead—also represents power. Spending, therefore, can be either a demonstration of power or a dissipation of power.[129]

It is useful to have this paradox in mind when contemplating reactions to Osage Indian spending in the years following World War I. Osages' pell-mell conversion of their abundant money into automobiles, fur coats, pianos, airplane joyrides, and sumptuous meals unsettled many non-Indian observers in part because it was a display of power that Indians were not supposed to have. Yet it also seemed an irresponsible squandering of power. The Indians' perceived extravagance showed their ignorance of the need in a capitalist market economy to gain security by accumulating and strategically using financial power. It was evidence of their vulnerability to the stratagems of people who had a more complete understanding of power in the modern world. In the name of long-term security for the ignorant Indians, U.S. lawmakers insisted on creating and controlling an Osage saving plan; but their ostensible benevolence also betrayed their reluctance to concede power to Indians.

Osages were not the first or the only Indians in the early twentieth century to learn that money in plentiful amounts was no assurance of power to conduct economic and political relations as they saw fit. Having lost power relative to the United States during the nineteenth century and having conceded that they could preserve a distinct territory and political existence only with American consent, Osages by 1900 had limited means to resist American meddling in the management of their reserved resources, no matter how valuable those resources were. The meddling even extended to defining an Osage Indian. Consequently, at the time of the great oil frenzy, Osages who adhered to a venerable culture of reciprocity and generosity found themselves sharing power with Osages who conceived of economic relations as competition and the object of economic activity as accumulating wealth.

Power relative to other people (the ability to work one's will) is a complex equation.[130] One important factor in the equation is control of information dissemination and public image–making. In that respect, too, Osages were at a disadvantage. With the exception of opportunities to speak at congressional committee hearings (often through interpreters), or to project an image of confidence and good sense in *American Indian* magazine, Osages had little influence in the forums where other Americans gleaned much of their information about contemporary Indians. The people who did have access to those forums viewed Osages through a prism of presumptions about Indians, especially the presumption that Indians were economically inept. The distorted images they said they saw had a power to influence federal actions that defenders of Osage competency could not match.

Power also depends in part on moral suasion. And even though members of Congress and OIA officials explained their management of Osages' money primarily as a pragmatic hedge against future scarcity, they said they acted on moral concerns as well. There again, they largely controlled the terms of discussion. They voiced concern for the moral state of Osages who were drunk on bootleggers' booze and Osages who were metaphorically drunk on free-flowing cash. They deplored the immoral behavior that the Osages' dazzling wealth incited from so many non-Indians. But they made little or no effort to determine whether Osages agreed with them on the moral considerations that should govern responses to the Indians' exceptional affluence. It appears from the written record that Osages made only feeble efforts of their own to initiate such discussions. Indeed, when Osages said they saw nothing wrong with using their money to live in comfort or indulge their children's desires, the standard of acceptability they most often cited was not a distinctive Osage ethic but the example set by avid non-Indian consumers.

Had Osages clearly and more completely communicated the reasons for their "Olympian indifference" to saving up personal wealth, they might have articulated a somewhat different moral code. That is, some of them might have referred to conceptions of right or virtuous conduct passed down from distant Osage ancestors. If so, they would have emphasized the importance of generosity or unselfishness and the importance of loyalty to the tribe. They might have explained that members of a prosperous community in which those were cardinal virtues had no fear of destitution, no matter how freely they disposed of personal wealth. Osages might have said, in essence, that the social capital earned through generous acts was their best assurance of security in the future.

But the problem for Osages who lived by that model of economic relations was that it could work as intended only in relations with like-minded people. An economy in which personal status and security are contingent on liberal sharing requires mutual reliance and unanimous commitment to ensuring the well-being of all community members. In relations with people who declined to make such a commitment and favored an ethic of separate accumulation instead, Osages imbued with the traditional ethos of liberality were bound to be disappointed. They could not count on reciprocity. Even the prodigious spending that demonstrated their prosperity and liberality did not have the power to command the respect that Osage ancestors had earned by similar conduct. Rather, to people more powerful than they, it was proof of their weakness and moral inferiority.

Riches Reclaimed

In May 1928, the *New York Times* announced that most American Indians, unlike those renowned for their oil wealth, were miserably poor. This revelation came in news of a special report that assessed the effectiveness of the government's performance as Indians' guardian. At the request of the Interior Department secretary, independent investigators had visited Indian communities across the country and discovered pervasive poverty. Although the investigators concluded that faulty implementation of federal policy bore much of the responsibility for Indians' impoverishment, the *Times* chose to highlight another explanation in the report: Indians had "never in the past been accustomed to those comforts and conveniences demanded by most whites" and therefore lacked "desire for a higher standard of living."[1]

For the next five decades, public discourse about Indians' economic circumstances and aspirations focused most of the time on their extreme poverty. During Franklin Roosevelt's presidency, the government tried to promote Indian prosperity with a New Deal. After World War II, ascendant conservatives promised better results with a contrary approach, but during the 1960s, national leaders acknowledged that widespread poverty persisted in Indian communities and undertook the most intensive remediation effort to date. These mid-twentieth century events gave Americans compelling cause to think of Indians as the nation's poorest people, trapped in a cycle of economic failure despite years of special federal aid.

By the late 1970s, however, neither the *Times* nor its readers would have lent much credence to the premise that Indians were poor because they were unaware of missing out on "comforts and conveniences." In numerous well-publicized instances, Indians were demanding and securing the means to attain a higher standard of living. To the Indians' chagrin, many Americans disapproved of those demands and achievements. Tribal claims to a variety of economic resources had incited a grassroots opposition movement of people who thought Indians were bent on gaining too much wealth. By reclaiming land, minerals, water, fisheries, and the political power to control such valuable resources, Indians had unsettled their pathetic public image and provoked intense controversy.

In contrast to prior discourse about Indian poverty, which focused mainly on whether federal policy or practice served a goal of Indian self-sufficiency, the controversy of the 1970s and 1980s was largely about core social and political ideals. At issue was the justice or morality of Indians' economic strategy. As people debated Indians' aims, entitlements, and place in American society, they proposed divergent measures of justice, while insisting that their primary objective *was* justice, not material gain. Whether disputing or defending the basis of the tribal claims, they had to indicate their conceptions of fair economic relations. Some non-Indians charged that Indians had an unfair advantage in the competition for economic assets because they did not have to play by all the same rules as other Americans. Indians responded by citing history as justification for their prerogatives and historical injustice as a moral bar to rescinding them. The objectors contended that historical change had invalidated those prerogatives.

This debate took place in major news media, activist publications, Congress, and courts. It reached the U.S. Supreme Court in 1979, via litigation aimed at clarifying Indian fishing rights under nineteenth-century treaties. When a majority of the justices ruled that the treaties imposed a continuing obligation on non-Indians to leave half the available fish for Indians, tribes gained considerable pull in the larger tug-of-war over resources. But the ruling included a surprising caveat: the treaty right should not be worth more than a moderate living, and the Indians' access to a coveted commodity could therefore be limited if they would otherwise receive an unreasonably generous share. The practical implications of that proviso have yet to unfold, but it appears to deviate from a venerable tradition in American law—reverence for contractual rights. Like many of their fellow citizens, several justices were evidently reluctant to honor a negotiated division of resources if it would bring about Indians' "unfair" enrichment.

In retrospect, it seems implausible that politically aware Americans were taken aback in 1928 when the Institute for Government Research reported extensive privation among Indians.[2] Well-informed people—even those who had not seen the dismal conditions on reservations—should at least have suspected that Indians' geographical isolation and powerlessness made hardship likely. Besides, word of the destitution in Indian country was already circulating. From the American Indian Defense Association (AIDA), members of Congress and major periodicals had received tracts challenging rosy statistical profiles issued by the Indian office, calling them a smokescreen to hide Indians' gaunt poverty and widespread hunger. Other government figures showed a significant shrinkage of Indian property since the 1880s—the consequence of federal practices that facilitated a massive transfer of land from Indians to Whites.[3]

Nonetheless, according to the *New York Times*, the research institute's findings contrasted "poignantly with the prevalent slant on the American Indian," which evoked an image of someone "either as driving in luxurious limousines purchased with revenue from valuable oil lands or leading a complacent life on a reservation." The Office of Indian Affairs had promoted that image by maintaining that its charges' prospects for a comfortable "civilized" life were good and steadily improving, and by publicizing without elucidation the great aggregate value of Indian lands, mineral reserves, and timber. Most federal legislators had chosen to believe claims that the longstanding policy of privatizing tribal property was successfully fostering Indian economic advancement.[4]

The voluminous report from the Institute for Government Research, often identified by the name of survey director Lewis Meriam, seems consciously designed to shatter politicians' illusion and rebut the sanguine publicity about Indians. The opening sentence declared, "An overwhelming majority of Indians are poor, even extremely poor, and they are not adjusted to the economic and social system of the dominant white civilization." Many pages of statistics substantiated that assertion. Two-thirds of Indians had assets valued at less than $2,000; nearly 50 percent did not own property worth even $500; and almost three-fourths had annual incomes under $200—not even half the national norm.[5]

Meriam's crew of researchers had help bringing Indian poverty to light. While their inquiry was under way, the Senate—prodded to act by relentless AIDA criticism of the Indian bureau—launched its own survey of Indians' circumstances. A specially constituted committee made a fact-finding tour of the West and Great Plains. In August 1929, committee member Burton Wheeler of Montana went on the radio to share what he had learned with the audiences of two dozen stations. His observations corroborated parts of the Meriam report. Wheeler emphasized the high incidence of deadly disease among Indians and linked it to their penury. "The [Indian] family," he said, "invariably lived in a one-room shack." "It is a disgrace," he added, "to think that this, the wealthiest of all governments, should permit such a sordid condition." To a nation with a booming economy and a president who said he could foresee "the day when poverty will be banished," the news of Indians' dire straits was an embarrassment.[6]

The Meriam report described conditions that would continue to hinder Indian wealth production for years to come: low-grade land, implementation of the land allotment policy in a manner that frustrated self-interested industry, lack of economic education, insufficient funding of federal services that could promote prosperity, and miscellaneous problems associated with "the encroachment of white civilization." On one hand, the report said the typical Indian was not yet economically competent and needed continuing federal guardianship; on the other hand, it complained that Indians were "depending too largely on unearned income from the use or sale of their property, managed for them as a rule by the national government."[7] Three changes of federal policy between 1928 and 1978 did little to eliminate the environmental handicaps, educational deprivation, government paternalism, and resource poaching that had drained Indians of economic power. Consequently, media coverage of Indians in those years tended to confirm that most were persistently poor.

Poor Indians lost news value for a while when the Great Depression toppled millions of other Americans into poverty. From 1929 to 1934, neither the *New York Times* nor magazines in nationwide circulation troubled readers much with Indians' economic woes.[8] But the man who orchestrated the federal response to the depression in Indian country wanted Americans to know and care about Indians' "incredible poverty." John Collier became commissioner of Indian affairs in 1933. Before that, as executive secretary of the AIDA, he had been the Indian bureau's most prominent critic, barraging Congress with accusations that the government was pauperizing Indians while claiming to set them on firm economic ground. Once in office, Collier warned that "the always-poor Indian population" faced a "desperate situation . . . even worse . . . than the whites." That desperation was a principal reason to demand a "new deal" for Indians.[9]

As commissioner, Collier oversaw a two-part Indian New Deal. He proposed legislation to halt and reverse the attrition of Indian land, sanction tribal self-government, authorize tribal business corporations, and establish an economic development loan fund. Even before Congress approved a modified version of his bill—the Indian Reorganization Act of 1934—Collier secured separate emergency relief funds for Indians. Then he personally generated a stream of optimistic publicity about his economic stimulus programs. To tax-payers as well as Indians, Collier held out hope that work relief projects—by paying Indians to improve and conserve reservation forests, farmland, and range—would lay a foundation for long-term prosperity while filling empty pockets in the short term.[10] Collier simultaneously touted the power of the Indian Reorganization Act to raise Indians from poverty. Revived tribal govern-ments would manage stable or expanded landholdings, federal loans would seed the ventures of tribal corporations, and individual Indians would benefit from preferential hiring in the Bureau of Indian Affairs (BIA). When the act's Senate sponsor had a change of heart and sought to repeal it after three years, Collier protested that the new federal commitment to reservation develop-ment had already increased Indians' land base by 2.1 million acres and more than quintupled their income from livestock. In 1942, he exulted that Indians were flush enough to spend $2 million on war bonds and stamps. And in 1945, as he prepared to resign, he announced that Indians' average personal earn-ings were 300 percent higher than in 1935.[11]

Overall, however, Indian economic gains from 1935 to 1945 were modest, and many were temporary. Progress was hard to sustain without more finan-cial aid and changes in the law than Congress could bring itself to approve. Thrift-conscious legislators cut funding for the BIA after 1936, declined to fi-nance much land acquisition, and restricted eligibility for loans. Legal, en-vironmental, and demographic factors also continued to frustrate develop-ment.[12] Hence, the income growth that Collier celebrated in 1945 owed little to New Deal programs. The golden goose was actually World War II, which pro-vided thousands of Indians with military pay and many more with war-related civilian jobs. Even then, by the BIA's estimate, one-third of reservation house-holds had income far below what an average family needed to feed, clothe, and house itself adequately. Moreover, the trend in Indian earnings reversed soon after the war when government dependency allowances ceased, employment opportunities vanished, and demobilized soldiers returned to reservations that offered few means of support.[13] Stories about "poverty-stricken primi-tives" reappeared in periodicals that had recently hailed Indians' economic contributions to the war effort.[14]

Not that poor Indians were prominent media subjects in the 1940s. Atten-tion to their hardship was sporadic until late in the decade, and some of it focused on signs that the First Americans might share in the surging national wealth. A Young Women's Christian Association spokeswoman said optimisti-cally that Indians' wartime work and ongoing migration to urban areas were evidence of "earnest ambition" and an ability to be "self-supporting citizens."

Congressional critics of the BIA favored this reasoning because it bolstered their contention that the bureau was dispensable. If Indians had found work in defense plants without BIA help, nothing should prevent their participation in the postwar boom that was assuring America's status as the world's richest country.[15] More often, though, Indians were said to be in serious economic trouble. Sometimes it was Indians and their allies, seeking federal aid, who publicized the "dire needs" of reservation residents. At other times, the talk of poverty and disease came from people who blamed the Indian New Deal's retarding effects.[16]

By 1950, Americans who followed the news could readily imagine the poverty most Indians endured. Due to recent developments, they probably pictured grimy, sloe-eyed children beside hovels in the desert. Indian hunger and suffering had become a national scandal in 1947–48 when a summer drought depleted food supplies on the Navajo and Hopi Reservations and then gave way to immobilizing winter snowstorms. The spotlight lingered on Navajos and Hopis because Secretary of State George Marshall proposed to combat "hunger, poverty, desperation, and chaos" in postwar Europe with copious economic assistance, and critics of the plan responded that the same problems at home should have first claim on the nation's charity, starting with the Southwest Indians' predicament. Publicized responses to that predicament kept the image of destitute Indians in the public eye. When novelist Oliver La Farge referred to Navajos as "half-starved herdsmen" in a 1948 essay for the *New York Times*, he did not feel a need to explain.[17]

La Farge hoped his essay would influence ongoing political discussion of Indians' peculiar status under law. At the urging of lawmakers who had long agitated for federal withdrawal from Indian affairs, Congress was moving toward a policy that La Farge, president of the Association on American Indian Affairs, regarded as rash and irresponsible. House Concurrent Resolution 108 made the policy shift official in 1953: Congress intended "as rapidly as possible to make the Indians within the territorial limits of the United States subject to the same laws and entitled to the same privileges and responsibilities as are applicable to other citizens . . . , to end their status as wards of the United States, and to grant them all of the rights and prerogatives pertaining to American citizenship."[18] The goal of ending the federal guardianship for Indians and their property gave the new policy its most common name—termination.

Public discourse about termination reflected and reinforced the common association of Indians with poverty and the inclination to blame government for that poverty. Talk of eliminating legal obstacles to Indian prosperity, often paired with an assertion that reservations could not support burgeoning tribal

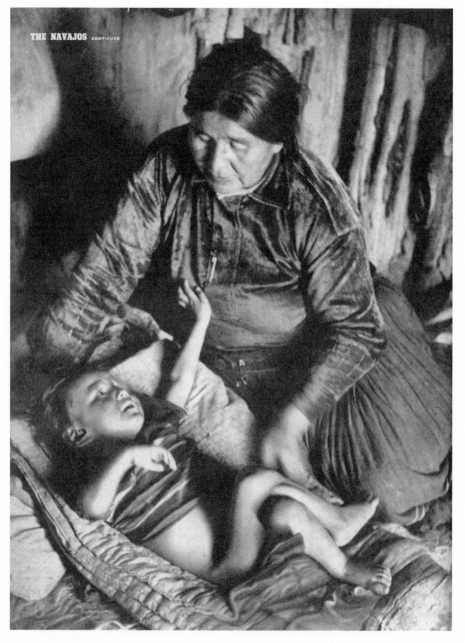

In 1948, having "rediscovered the plight of the Navajos," *Life* magazine reporters and photographers joined the national press in publishing "heart-rending reports of starvation and disease" on that reservation. Such depictions of Indian poverty could serve the cause of Americans who urged an end to the federal guardianship that was supposedly thwarting Indian economic advancement and the cause of those who argued that government aid to Indians was a continuing moral obligation. "The Navajos," *Life*, 1 March 1948, 75–83.

populations, figured prominently in early arguments for the termination policy. The Senate and House of Representatives produced separate reports alleging that federal services were perpetuating Indian dependence and underdevelopment. Other critics of government growth piled on with charges that the swollen Roosevelt/Collier BIA had limited Indians' freedom to pursue the American economic dream.[19]

People who opposed or tried to stall the policy change also spoke often of Indians' poverty. Some depicted it as a handicap that needed correction, with government help, before Indians could function on their own in a capitalist system. Others characterized federal aid for Indians as a continuing moral obligation—as recompense for past deprivation. While deploring the Indian bureau's over-protective paternalism, La Farge maintained that the country owed Indians a debt on which there was still much to pay. Besides continuing to defend Indians from "the raids, in Congress and within the states . . . started yearly against their remaining property," an honorable government would spend substantially more to create opportunities for economic advancement and security.[20]

Advocates of termination appealed to notions of right and wrong as well, but their emphasis was on political rather than economic principles. By the time they had crafted House Concurrent Resolution 108 and whisked it through Congress, they had subordinated their economic arguments to rhetoric that identified legal equality as their objective. They spoke of repealing discriminatory laws and freeing Indians from oppressive government supervision. In a 1957 article explaining the policy he doggedly promoted, Utah senator Arthur Watkins referred to termination of the federal guardianship as "decontrol"; he said almost nothing about Indian poverty or its antidotes.[21] But if Watkins and his confederates hoped that "decontrol" would take the issue of Indian poverty off the government agenda, they faced disappointment. The drive to end the guardianship played out in ironic ways, and one was an increase in federal spending to improve Indians' economic prospects. Administrators said that many Indians, divested of their government life jackets too soon, were likely to flounder in the free market sea. So Congress, after balking at first, funded services meant to prepare Indians to swim rather than sink. Appropriations for BIA development programs rose steeply in the 1950s. A university researcher found that the agency's 1957 budget included "the largest expenditures ever authorized for the social and economic benefit of Indians."[22]

The effort to stimulate reservation economies before termination was spurred and followed by even more exposure of Indian poverty. While promising a payoff, proponents of the effort had to show that Indians still struggled to feed, shelter, and clothe themselves. It was not hard to do. More than once during Dwight Eisenhower's presidency, BIA surveys revealed that Indians' circumstances had not improved appreciably since the war. Critics of termination mustered evidence that BIA-approved bargain-rate sales of reservation land, timber, and minerals were making matters worse, reducing the value of tribal assets to be divided among members when guardianship ended. Impatient advocates of termination likewise directed attention to Indians' persistent poverty with their complaints that the government had little to show for its expensive reservation development projects.[23]

Eisenhower's second BIA commissioner tried in vain to shift the public gaze from "Indian families huddled together in miserable tar paper shacks on the outskirts of . . . western towns" to successful Indian wage earners. In defense of a program that sponsored Indians' relocation to major cities, Commissioner Glenn Emmons said that three-fourths of the relocated people were earning "far more money than they ever did previously."[24] However, poor Indians were still more visible than prospering ones. In 1957, the year Emmons made his claim, an economic slump stifled demand for the labor most Indians could supply, and migration to the cities ebbed. Meanwhile, shortcomings of the relocation program came to the attention of social scientists and journalists, whose critical reports indicated that city-dwelling Indians were as likely to live in squalor as those on reservations.[25]

Even so, the visibility of poor Indians in the 1950s did not reach nearly the height that it attained the following decade when President Lyndon Johnson challenged the nation to help its impoverished people. Johnson was responding to a recent rediscovery of poverty in the United States—privation the nation had largely ignored while a majority of Americans enjoyed the high employment rates, rising incomes, and abundant consumer goods of the postwar period. A few liberal politicians and intellectuals in the 1950s did notice that some population groups had not benefited from the economy's expansion, but their findings got little media play until John F. Kennedy and other Democrats aired them in the election campaign of 1960.[26] Three years later, shortly after inheriting the presidency from Kennedy, Johnson exhorted citizens to turn their eyes toward "the one-fifth of all American families with incomes too small to even meet their basic needs." Picking up a banner that Kennedy was preparing to raise when an assassin's bullet struck him down, Johnson declared unconditional war on poverty.[27]

Data on Indians played little part in awakening the interest in poverty,[28] but that interest soon led to, and fed on, exposés of the distress on reservations. Indians and their sympathizers caught candidate Kennedy's ear in 1960 and elicited a private promise that his policies would foster tribal economic development.[29] Soon after the election, the private Commission on the Rights, Liberties, and Responsibilities of the American Indian—a creation of the nonprofit Fund for the Republic—capped a four-year survey with a report announcing, "The economic position of the Indians is less favorable than that of any other American minority group. In most Indian communities the pattern is one of bare subsistence . . . , [and] some of the nation's worst slums are to be found on Indian reservations."[30] Interior Secretary Stewart Udall responded by appointing a task force on Indian affairs.

Task force members were present a few months later when more than 450 Indians from ninety tribes gathered at the University of Chicago for a well-publicized week-long conference. In a closing statement conveyed to the president, conference participants lamented the end of New Deal efforts to preserve remaining Indian lands, recommended policies and programs to meet Indians' economic needs, and concluded, "When we go before the American people, as we do in this Declaration, and ask for material assistance in developing our resources and developing our opportunities, we pose a moral problem which cannot be left unanswered."[31]

Whether or not he deemed the problem a moral one, Kennedy's successor did not intend to leave it unanswered. Indians were on Lyndon Johnson's list of people in thrall to poverty when he declared a war of economic liberation in January 1964. Two weeks later, a large delegation of tribal leaders extracted an assurance that Johnson would keep them in mind as he plotted his strategy. The president replied that he hoped to put the "first Americans first" in the campaign, because they had suffered more than any other people in the country.[32] Indians felt betrayed, however, when Johnson created the Office of Economic Opportunity (OEO) to direct efforts on behalf of the non-Indian poor but proposed to let the BIA conduct the fight against poverty in Indian country. Rallying to demand a different plan, a coalition of tribal and non-Indian organizations summoned hundreds of people to a National Capital Conference on American Indian Poverty. There, Robert Burnette, outgoing director of the National Congress of American Indians (NCAI), urged the president to come see the "almost indescribable conditions" on reservations, such as "shoeless children in rags, even . . . in the winter." Burnette later recalled that the size of the assembly and delegates' ardent lobbying "really made an impression on the political system of this country. We were soon made a part of the OEO."[33]

Being "made a part of the OEO" had momentous consequences for Indians, though not the consequences the new agency expected. The OEO named tribal governments as the local agencies that would receive federal funds to battle poverty on reservations. Historians agree with the perception of Indians on the front line that this delegation of responsibility was a catalyst of the tribes' ensuing political revitalization, which would eventually change their economic fortunes and precipitate a national controversy about the fairness of Indians' unique legal status. Looking back in 1983, Sioux lawyer Philip S. "Sam" Deloria said, "It was through these Great Society programs that Indian tribes became widely recognized by federal agencies as legitimate governments. . . . It was a milestone of self-determination."[34]

Self-government flourished more than economic conditions when OEO money flowed directly to cash-parched reservations and tribal organizations could channel it as they saw fit. Wherever the money went, jobs, houses, health care services, and other economic essentials sprang up. But the war on Indian poverty did not end in victory; the need was too great, the resources committed too meager, and the time devoted too short for rooting out the enemy. More than five years into the campaign, the census showed that Indians still had not gained on other Americans financially. Indian men's median personal income remained less than half that of White men, and nearly 40 percent of Indians were still classified as poor.[35]

A junior OEO administrator opined in 1967 that the agency's "greatest single service . . . was to stimulate a national dialogue" about the poor and convince other Americans of their existence. In fact, rather than substituting images of prospering Indians for the pathetic pictures that motivated the fight, Johnson's nonviolent war gave Indian poverty its most extensive exposure yet. It is as if policy analysts, journalists, social reformers, and scholars heard the president's battle cry, deigned to look in Indians' direction, saw the destitution there, and were moved to bear witness. All their talk reminded Francis McKinley, a Ute, of something he had read years before. "So I started looking around in our library," McKinley said, "and I came across the Meriam Report of 1928 . . . , and the first thing I read was some statement that went like this: 'The Indian is in extreme poverty. . . .['] I bet you could take sections of it and nobody would ever know this report was made 36 years ago; they'd think you were talking about the present poverty program." A partial transcript of McKinley's own talk on the subject appeared in the Indian Rights Association newsletter, joining a multitude of publications that prompted more such discussion in meeting rooms, classrooms, and living rooms around the country.[36]

The federal attack on poverty worked in tandem with research on the incidence of poverty to raise the visibility of poor Indians further. Government staffers and independent investigators assembled mounds of data on Indians' plight. Their grim profiles reached the general public through politicians and a variety of media. At the Capital Conference on Indian Poverty, Robert Burnette ticked off figures he had heard from the president, and the *New York Times* passed them on: family incomes less than one-third the national average, reservation unemployment rates averaging 50 percent and ranging up to 85 percent, nine out of ten Indians in substandard housing. Once OEO warriors were on duty, alternately claiming some victories and trying to scare up more money with shocking statistics, their efforts inspired or required even more surveys of Indians' circumstances.[37]

Soon, Americans could find books on the subject in shopping malls. *The Indian, America's Unfinished Business*, emphasized how "incredibly poor" the overwhelming majority of Indians were. *The New Indians* declared that "ills of the tribal Indian cannot be measured by even poverty standards" but went on to recite unemployment, income, and substandard housing figures as proof of those ills. It took ten years, author Stan Steiner noted, for average Indian family income to grow from $1,200 to $1,500 while White income increased as much in one year, to $7,170. Although Steiner speculated that the cruelty of such comparisons had "frightened off the statisticians of poverty," uncowed statisticians were busy preparing more figures for publication. People with no time for books saw the data in news magazines or on television.[38] No wonder editors of *The Christian Century* considered their question rhetorical when they wrote in 1965, "His average income is one-half the amount which has been determined to be the general level for the poor in the United States. He can expect to live to age 42. His segregation from the rest of society makes the Negro's degree of acceptance look good. The level of unemployment among his people is seven or eight times that of his nation's average unemployment. . . . Who is he? Any American school child should know that the American Indian and only the American Indian answers to this description."[39]

By 1970, the basic "fact" of Indian poverty must indeed have been common knowledge.[40] In a word-association game, the responses to "Indian" would likely have included "poor" or its synonyms, even from Indian players. On the reasons for Indians' sorry state, however, American thinking was less uniform. Opinion was divided about the causes of any persistent poverty and also about the causes of Indians' predicament in particular.

On one hand, the extension of poverty-fighting government programs to Indians reflected and encouraged a belief that they were poor due to conditions shared by Whites in West Virginia's mountains or Blacks in major cities. An Agriculture Department summary of those conditions bordered on the self-evident: "Limited job opportunities, generally low income, relatively poor education, and unskilled occupations offer little opportunity for rising above the poverty level. Moreover, discrimination often closes the doors to upward social and economic mobility."[41] *The Other America*, a best-selling book, popularized the theory that a "culture of poverty" evolved in such circumstances. The poor acquired fatalistic attitudes and self-defeating habits that condemned them to perpetuate their misery.[42] According to an Indian newspaper editor in Seattle, Washington, that was the case for Indians. As schoolchildren, they were "handicapped" not only because they experienced "squalid poverty . . . , malnutrition and unsanitary conditions" at home but also because they sensed their parents' low aspirations and apathy toward education.[43]

On the other hand, many analysts pointed out special factors that could explain why Indians clustered at the base of the national economic ladder below other poor people.[44] One researcher observed that rural Indians—isolated on reservations with few resources, remote from hubs of modern commerce, subject in property matters to a historically corrupt and incompetent bureaucracy, hamstrung by unique landownership tangles, inadequately educated, and often committed to ancestral values at odds with the competitive American economy—had "been in poverty for a very long time." President Johnson and Secretary Udall, advocating a new policy of "self-determination" for Indians, said a framework of restrictive federal law was to blame for holding Indians back economically.[45]

Some Indians, deeming it time to voice their righteous anger, said the finger of blame should point solely at the United States for denying tribes the rights and resources needed to reverse the cycle of poverty that U.S. actions had caused. At a Senate hearing in 1966, National Indian Youth Council Director Mel Thom testified, "The Federal Government's Indian poverty program is over 100 years old. Under this Indian poverty program the Federal Government had had total economic responsibility for the welfare of Indians . . . The result is an Asiatic-type poverty."[46] Sioux activist and scholar Vine Deloria Jr., having caught media attention with his provocative new book on Indian/White relations, alleged in a 1969 essay for the *New York Times* that "there was no poverty on the reservations" before "allotment was forced on the tribes" with the Dawes Act of 1887. Deloria and others also stressed the ill effects of more recent federal action. They argued that Indians, having surrendered the lands that sustained their ancestors, had a right to expect support from their ostensible government guardian. But the unrepudiated policy of terminating the guardianship had pushed relatively prosperous communities into penury, and fear of termination was still paralyzing Indians who might otherwise have had their hands on their bootstraps, pulling upward.[47]

Indians were not alone in drawing damning conclusions from the history of federal policy. The White editors of *Our Brother's Keeper, the Indian in White America*, had a particularly acerbic reading of the relationship between U.S. policy and Indian poverty: "With the riches of America all around him, the Indian lives in the poverty of an underdeveloped nation. The Federal Government and the Bureau of Indian Affairs keep it that way." Edgar Cahn and David Hearne accused the BIA of being "worse than sluggish about investigating new resources on Indian land," stripping Indians of their land "for their own good," and rarely resisting demands from states for access to Indian resources. *The Christian Century*'s explanation of Indian poverty was even more pointed: Whites had "conquered, dispossessed and abandoned" Indians.[48]

An alternative contention was that aboriginal culture, distinct from the culture engendered by poverty elsewhere, kept Indians poor.[49] Several scholarly studies, aiming to influence the strategy of federal attacks on reservation poverty and perhaps to change the definition of success, portrayed Indians as averse to capitalist values. *The Indian, America's Unfinished Business* elaborated on an argument that Indians esteemed service to community rather than wealth: "The merging of self in the group tends to deter competitiveness or a pride in material possessions for their monetary worth. Indian values have not customarily included the amassing of valuables for private benefit because of the ingrained tradition of sharing. These attitudes perhaps account in part for the improvidence often attributed to Indians." Another research report ascribed Indians' poor showing in the cities to a traditional pattern of "compulsive hospitality and sharing."[50]

Some Indians seemed to corroborate this analysis when they voiced fear that the war on poverty would bring pressure to conform to an alien capitalist culture; but most tribal officials, while saying vaguely that traditional Indian values necessitated Indian self-government and that self-government was essential for preserving Indian values, played up their willingness and ability to become entrepreneurs. Vine Deloria, Burnette's successor as NCAI director, spoke of a need "to beat the white man at his own economic game." When several large western tribes staged an exhibition of their economic potential in New York City, hoping to snag private investment, NCAI president Wendell Chino boasted to a reporter that culture was no barrier to success. "Our increasing proficiency at industrial tasks, our growing inventory of industrial parks and improved transportation links, and most of all our desire to help ourselves, will enable us to meet this goal," Chino declared.[51]

Despite the ongoing exposure of tribal poverty, Deloria's 1969 manifesto, *Custer Died for Your Sins*, described Indians as "invisible." The previous year, both the president's message to Congress and a CBS television feature on Indians bore the title "The Forgotten American," and *Time* magazine ran a major article about Indians under the headline "The Forgotten & Forlorn." By 1970, however, there were notable grounds for disputing that Indians were out of sight and out of mind in the United States. They had moved to a conspicuous spot in the public arena thanks partly to Deloria's book. Vine's brother later recalled that the tremendous impact of *Custer Died for Your Sins* prompted an enthusiastic reviewer to say "the American Indian had finally found his voice." But the reviewer had it backward, Sam Deloria said; "America had simply found its ears."[52]

American ears pricked up because Indians demanded to be heard in novel, hard-to-ignore ways. While Vine Deloria was still on the lecture circuit talking about his book, a band of young Indians elbowed their way into the spotlight by occupying the mothballed federal prison on Alcatraz Island in California. There they issued a proclamation that evoked Indians' historical mistreatment with ironic humor. As network television cameras rolled, instigators of the takeover solicited sympathy for the "invisible American" by enumerating the ways that Alcatraz resembled impoverished Indian reservations: it lacked fertile land, marketable resources, industry, health care services, and employment opportunities. One of the many youths who flocked to the camp on the Rock told a reporter, "We're just asking for some of the things stolen from us so we can govern ourselves."[53]

In the ensuing decade, Indians not only asked for things, they also received. They asked for more and received more than at any time since the United States had become powerful enough to decide unilaterally what it would give Indians. In diverse ways and forums during the 1970s, Indians sought and gained a significant expansion of tribal self-rule, recognition or restoration of rights to some cherished lands, payment for other expropriated territories, and access to, or control over, resources such as water, minerals, and fish. Writers have variously dubbed their endeavors and successes a "tribal renaissance," "modern tribalism," "reborn Indian sovereignty," "American Indian political resurgence," and "the modern tribal sovereignty movement."[54]

Few academic historians have yet analyzed the reasons for Indian gains of the 1970s, but collectively, chroniclers have produced a credible list of contributing factors. Near the top, by general agreement, is the increased assertiveness of Indians themselves. Even before the seizure of Alcatraz, National Indian Youth Council activists and members of Pacific Northwest tribes used civil disobedience tactics to challenge state regulation of Indian fishing as a violation of nineteenth-century treaties. After the Alcatraz exploit, militant Indians dramatized their discontent by taking over several historic sites that could symbolize indigenous peoples' dispossession.[55] Days before the 1972 national election, hundreds of Indians converged on Washington, D.C., for a teach-in and carried out a spontaneous, destructive occupation of BIA offices instead. Meanwhile, tribal officials and older intertribal organizations, working in ways ordained by American law and political custom, also pressed bold demands. Besides federal financial aid, they sought compensation for resources lost, an end to further losses, better returns on assets they were willing to lease or sell, clarification of Indians' status under U.S. law, and above all, greater leeway to govern their tribal communities and reserved territories.[56]

This upsurge in defiant and assertive Indian behavior requires explanation itself. Without reaching consensus on precise causal relationships, historians and eyewitnesses have agreed on some developments that deserve mention. One is a boomerang effect of the termination policy. When the federal government began abandoning responsibilities it had assumed as Indians' guardian, many Indians saw with greater clarity the relationship they wanted with the United States: a guardianship whose purpose was to preserve the tribal entities and protect their autonomy. They mounted a coordinated campaign against termination that prepared them, as one textbook put it, "to make a powerful new case for the value of Indian traditions and the viability of Indian communities in modern society."[57] United States treaty promises were central to their conception of the federal-tribal relationship, for several reasons. Some Indians recalled that John Collier's legal advisors had characterized the treaties as agreements with inherently sovereign tribes. Treaties were also on the minds of Indians who had cases pending in the Indian Claims Commission, many of them concerning broken U.S. promises.[58]

In addition, Americans of African descent were challenging a discriminatory legal system with increasing audacity, and many watching Indians could envision their own crusade for justice. The Indians saw a crucial distinction, however, between their aspirations and the goals of the Black civil rights movement. More than desegregation and legal equality as individuals, Indians wanted restoration of their unique historical autonomy and acknowledgment of their right to maintain distinct societies. As Vine Deloria put it, "Indians were keenly aware that they had been virtually independent nations only a century before, and many young Indians felt that the movement should concern itself with regaining their former status." Successful independence movements in foreign colonies, vociferous Black nationalist groups, and anti-imperialist critiques of ongoing U.S. intervention in a Vietnamese civil war served as added inspiration for Indians' dream of self-determination and new militancy.[59]

In contradictory ways, Indians' growing combativeness was also a product of the campaign to end poverty. First, the campaign educated them about the severity of the privation in their communities; then, the flood of federal money into those communities, the BIA's loss of clout when the OEO became the conduit for aid, the delegation of responsibility to tribal governments, and Lyndon Johnson's talk of tribal self-determination raised Indian expectations of empowerment and a better standard of living. President Richard Nixon encouraged those expectations with a 1970 message to Congress that renounced termination and committed his administration to a policy of self-determination. The hopes of many Indians turned to anger, however, when some lawmakers and bureaucrats subsequently resisted the change in policy, federal funding did not rise as expected, and the government's course remained unclear.[60]

The war on poverty also expanded the arsenal available to tribes in their fight for resources and autonomy, as legal scholar Charles Wilkinson explains: "By the early 1970s tribes had at their disposal an emerging litigation capability, something they had never before possessed. OEO legal services programs served clients in much of Indian country and had good communication with one another." Program lawyers found they could invoke treaty provisions and nineteenth-century court opinions to protect some interests of indigent Indians. With foundation funding, young attorneys also created the Native American Rights Fund, a nonprofit law firm with a national reach, which initiated and assisted efforts to strengthen Indian self-governance and property rights. The firm's Pawnee director and several staff lawyers exemplified another factor in the tribal resurgence—Indians with college degrees and professional training, made possible in many cases by the easing of racist discrimination during the 1960s. A few of those college and law school graduates landed strategic congressional staff positions from which they could promote the self-determination policy. The educated young Indians "developed an agenda based on history, culture, and law" that dovetailed, in Wilkinson's view, with the aims of some "determined tribal chairmen."[61]

Insurgent Indians recognized a need for coordination, and new pan-tribal organizations appeared alongside older ones; but agreement on an Indian agenda was harder to achieve than Wilkinson suggests. Militants in the National Indian Youth Council and American Indian Movement faulted the NCAI for practicing the usual politics of compromise, while many in the NCAI establishment took issue with the militants' tactics. Nevertheless, the ideals of self-determination and sovereignty—hard as they were to define—won endorsement across the spectrum of mobilized Indians. Those ideals inspired tribal government decisions and NCAI resolutions as well as demands of the youth council and American Indian Movement. By 1973 or so, it was a rare Indian activist or tribal official who had not embraced the once-radical goal of reviving and extending tribal sovereignty.[62]

In claiming or aspiring to sovereignty, Indians did not identify economic power as their primary desideratum, but they plainly expressed an understanding that sovereign powers encompassed economic affairs and had the potential to enrich tribal communities. "Apart from the question of land control," Vine Deloria wrote, "the most urgent arguments for restoring Indian sovereignty as the basis for future Indian-U.S. relations are in the economic area." That statement appeared in a summary of the aims that Indians hoped to explain when they converged on Washington in 1972, calling their pilgrimage the Trail of Broken Treaties. They sought to open negotiations with federal officials on twenty points, the great majority of which called for government-to-government relations between tribes and the United States but did not mention economic concerns. The lengthy tenth point, however, demanded land reform, restoration of 110 million acres severed from reserved Indian lands, consolidation of the tribes' natural and economic resources, cancellation of leases to non-Indians, and use of the power of eminent domain to eliminate non-Indian-owned tracts within reservations. Another item urged protection for Indian commerce and tax immunities. According to Deloria, drafters of the twenty points wanted clarification of Indians' relationship to the federal government, but they also "wanted a clear definition of what it was they owned."[63]

Indians who already exercised a measure of self-government understood that their governments would remain limited and vulnerable so long as tribes were unsure what they owned, owned little of economic value, and had few means to generate revenue or provide members with opportunities for self-support. Efforts to secure, protect, and control economic resources, broadly defined, were therefore a fundamental feature of the Indian political revival. While building their capacity for self-government, tribes also sought the elements of economic prosperity. In many instances, that involved laying claim to assets or privileges worth large sums, and those claims succeeded in a significant number of high-profile cases. Editors of a document compendium entitled *Red Power* noted dryly, if a bit obscurely, in 1991, that the United States' history of using treaties with Indians to achieve political and economic purposes had "manifested itself in the past three decades in a variety of legislative and court decisions upholding and expanding tribal rights to develop and control resources and economic development."[64]

Land was foremost among the resources on Indian wish lists, especially land lost to non-Indians in memorable, galling ways. Tribes had sought redress for such losses before, with less than satisfying results. Prior to World War I, a number had tried their luck in the Court of Claims, which could award only money and often cited technical grounds for refusing to do that. After 1946, tribes pressed their cases in the Indian Claims Commission, a tribunal created to consider various grievances against the United States and grant recompense as appropriate. But so protracted were the commission's adjudications that the bulk of the judgments—many for sums that seemed insultingly small—did not come until the 1970s; and by then, Indians had startled the country with more ambitious claims for acreage as well as money.[65]

The first of the new, extraordinary claims exorcised a specter haunting the state of Alaska: aboriginal land rights. Since the 1867 purchase of Russia's interest in Alaska, the United States had exerted sovereignty and allowed new settlements there, even though it had not obtained indigenous people's consent or compensated them for their displacement. The statehood act of 1958 prohibited interference with Native occupancy but incongruously allowed the state to select more than a million acres of "public" lands and specified no procedure for reconciling that privilege with Native rights. The deferred issue finally came to a head in the late 1960s after prospectors struck oil on Alaska's North Slope. Eskimo villages, backed by a statewide Native coalition, raised their unextinguished rights in the area as a bar to drilling, and the secretary of the Interior Department responded with a freeze on state land selections, thwarting oil company plans.[66] Corporations and politicians then felt an urgent need to resolve Native claims. The eventual result was the Alaska Native Claims Settlement Act (ANCSA) of 1971, a federal law that entitled Indians, Aleuts, and Eskimos to 40 million acres of their choice, $462.5 million from the U.S. treasury, and the greater of $500 million or 2 percent of revenues from mineral extraction on public lands. The United States had never paid indigenous people more, in money or land set-asides, to legitimize its takeover of territory.[67]

ANCSA's unique scheme for distributing and managing the settlement money conceived of Native people as modern, wealth-motivated economic actors, but the act also reflected congressional resistance to the incipient shift from a federal policy of assimilating Indians to a policy of tribal self-determination. The money would go neither to Native governments nor directly to individual Natives; it would go instead to new regional Native corporations charged with making profitable investments and spending the returns on civic projects or services. Each Native person would receive a share or shares in a corporation and freedom to sell those assets, even to non-Natives, after a twenty-year period of inalienability.[68]

In light of the furor that followed later Indian land claims, public reactions to Alaska Natives' demands and ANCSA seem restrained. Although conservation groups and some "American settlers" in Alaska grumbled beforehand that Natives were asking too much, it was relatively easy for state and federal negotiators to swallow the final deal because it disturbed no land titles and tapped no private bank accounts. It was harder for local politicians to agree that Natives could siphon off a portion of state oil revenues, even though the portion was miniscule. But rather than charging Natives with greed, most commentators portrayed them as extremely poor people whose requests had moral sanction and were remarkably moderate.

Noting that "there is no state in the nation where the social and economic gap between the races is greater," a *New York Times* article alleged that Whites were enjoying wealth stolen from indigenous Alaskans and implied that the cost of absolving that guilt should be high. Some other observers, believing North Slope oil to be "the richest treasure trove in American history," characterized initial settlement offers to the Natives as stingy. Few outsiders challenged Native leaders' statements that they were "on a mission of unselfish venture," seeking only a secure place in a beloved landscape and "a decent, comfortable life" for their descendants.[69] Indeed, rather than begrudging Natives their mammoth final settlement, some analysts fretted that the land and money would not be enough to make a meaningful difference in Alaska Natives' bleak economic circumstances, especially if federal aid dropped as ANCSA took effect. From startup capital averaging only $500,000 each, how could the Native corporations generate income enough to meet their people's overwhelming needs? Besides, ANCSA's corporate implementation scheme was obviously a gamble. Although Native spokesmen expressed pleasure at the prospect of venturing into the business world, many other people doubted that Natives had the experience, habits, and values required for success in the complex capitalist economy of the 1970s.[70]

Lawmakers and taxpayers in the lower forty-eight states could make sense of a settlement acknowledging Native rights to land in Alaska, where the non-Native toehold was recent and limited. Indian claims to land on the other side of the country were a different matter. Professions of desire to see Indians treated justly, which were commonplace by the 1970s, faced a stiff test when tribes on the East Coast sought to invalidate their distant ancestors' land sales. Suddenly a few hundred Indians, their territory restricted since the eighteenth century to small state reservations, appeared poised to regain tracts where non-Indians had long since established cities and businesses. Some easterners who had expressed no qualms about turning remote Alaska tundra over to Eskimos found themselves feeling less generous toward nearby Indians.

First to jolt their neighbors with an unexpected land claim were the Passamaquoddy and Penobscot Tribes, who sued the state of Maine because a state purchase of tribal land in 1794 did not have the federal approval required by the Indian Trade and Intercourse Act of 1790. Maine officials shrugged off a lower court ruling for the tribes in a related dispute with the Justice Department, but their attitude changed when that ruling survived appeal. The appellate judges agreed in May 1976 that the Trade and Intercourse Act applied to the old land sale and the United States had a duty to enforce it. A *New York Times* article on this decision began, "The Indians may legally own two-thirds of Maine." Fear and anger coursed through the state's non-Indian population. (After news stories pegged the value of the tribes' claim at $25 billion, however, many people asked to be counted in the Indian ranks. Most claimed aboriginal ancestry they had not previously celebrated or documented.)[71] By autumn of that year, local jurisdictions were not issuing bonds, and the real estate business was in turmoil.[72] The Passamaquoddy case had also inspired copycat suits elsewhere, with similar repercussions. Massachusetts, New York, Rhode Island, Connecticut, and South Carolina citizens found themselves looking down the barrels of tribal guns loaded with legal ammunition fashioned for Indians in Maine.[73]

To officials in affected states, waiting for a court to resolve the land title crisis was out of the question. Like Alaskans before them, they appealed for federal help defending their non-Indian constituents from the Indian offensive. Aghast at the idea of relinquishing land, and aware that Congress would have no stomach for extinguishing the Indian claims without compensation, state leaders urged a simple buyout with federal dollars.[74] The resolution of the Maine case was more complex than that, but Congress did come through with the monetary bargaining chips. As news media and many Americans watched with bated breath, negotiators hammered out an agreement that became law in October 1980. The Maine Indian Claims Settlement Act established a trust fund of $27 million for the tribes. A second fund of more than $54 million for land acquisition netted the Indians nearly 300,000 acres, most of them former paper company holdings.[75] Consequently the Passamaquoddy Tribe, neglected by the U.S. government since the Revolutionary War, began the 1980s with one of Maine's largest asset portfolios: land, a cement factory, radio stations, a blueberry farm, retail outlets, and timber.[76] A few other eastern land claims settled in similar ways, with the tribes receiving sizable bundles of federal money and real estate in modest amounts.[77]

The Maine settlement came on the heels of another monumental win for Indians who had contested a long-past reduction of their territory. The Court of Claims ordered the United States to pay the Sioux Nation more than $100 million and interest for confiscating the Black Hills in 1877, nine years after a treaty reserved that area for the Indians' exclusive use. The Sioux case was big news when it ended in "the largest court settlement ever awarded American Indians," and again when Sioux spokesmen subsequently said they wanted more than money. Eight tribal chairmen declared that the government "should not only pay . . . for trespassing on Indian lands since 1877, but should also return the western half of South Dakota to the Sioux," with mineral rights.[78] Uttering the words "mineral rights" assured the chairmen of an attentive audience, and not only because the Black Hills held the Western Hemisphere's largest gold mine and new allure for uranium prospectors. Indian claims to valuable ores warranted close attention by 1979 because tribes across the West had emerged that decade as shrewd competitors for access to mineral and petroleum wealth.

Efforts to take control of underground resources became a conspicuous and controversial feature of the tribal renaissance after some tribes learned that their income from BIA-negotiated mining contracts compared poorly with the resources' market values. In 1972, Indian country buzzed with news that Consolidation Coal had offered an eye-popping sum for mining rights on the Northern Cheyenne Reservation. On other reservations with known deposits of coal, oil, gas, and uranium, partisans of the struggle for self-determination soon put those substances high on the lists of assets they wanted to manage. Their motivation intensified in 1973, when an embargo by the Organization of Petroleum Exporting Countries (OPEC) triggered an energy crisis for the United States, enhancing the importance of domestic resources. Tribes became aware of the potential to earn more from their oil and ores but also realized their vulnerability in the face of escalating non-Indian demand for those riches. By 1975, they had formed the Council of Energy Resource Tribes (CERT) to help them hire expert advisors, train their own managers, and renegotiate flawed leases. Some consortium members were as intent on protecting natural environments and appeasing development-averse constituents as on raising tribal income; but encouraged by consultants, most did hope for more money from existing mines and wells.[79]

In the context of the OPEC embargo, gasoline shortages, and public breast-beating about dependence on foreign oil, the creation of CERT and the moratoriums that some tribes imposed on drilling and mining struck many non-Indians as provocative moves, especially when Indians impertinently likened

CERT to OPEC. At a time when a foreign cartel could disconnect the country's oil feeding tube and leave America gasping for an infusion of domestic petroleum, Indians had seemingly formed a mercenary cartel of their own. According to *Business Week*, CERT's chairman said defiantly, "We are going to get our share for our energy resources, or we aren't going to share at all." Framed in reports that Indian land held an outsized portion of America's total energy resources—30 percent of coal in the West, 37 percent of potentially extractable uranium, and 3 percent of known oil and gas—such a declaration carried more weight with powerful capitalists and bureaucrats than any Indian ultimatum since the nineteenth-century wars for the Great Plains.[80]

Another resource that Indians reclaimed was both an energy producer and a necessity of life. Across the arid West where most reservations were located, water was arguably the most important of nature's marketable substances. In addition to driving turbines and releasing energy as steam in coal-burning plants, it made agricultural enterprise and accelerating urban development possible. And like the land in Maine, the water that Indians sought had to be wrested in many instances from non-Indian users who thought they had superior rights.

The chance that Indians could recapture much of the West's water increased substantially in 1963 when the U.S. Supreme Court, applying principles it had articulated in a much earlier opinion, held that tribes were entitled to a significant share of the Colorado River's coveted flow. The subsequent tribal renaissance and additional lawsuits made the implications of that decision clearer to non-Indian farmers, developers, and utility managers. By 1975, among other things, Paiutes in Nevada had won a ruling that threatened the water supply of a large off-reservation irrigation system, and tribes in Montana were pressing claims to water that state and federal governments had already sold to power companies. In 1978, it seemed to a team of *Newsweek* reporters that Whites and Indians were "battling over the supreme issue of water rights in virtually every Western state" and Indians had the edge in the fight.[81]

In the Nevada Paiute case, the tribe brought suit because the diversion of water from Pyramid Lake feeder streams was endangering fish in the lake, which had long been "the Tribe's principal source of livelihood."[82] Elsewhere, from Michigan and Minnesota to the Columbia River and Puget Sound, non-Indian dominance and activity had thwarted Indians' reliance on fish in waters on or near tribal homelands. Efforts to recover those historic fisheries were some of the most significant battles from which Indians emerged victorious in the 1970s.

The first and most consequential victory came on 12 February 1974 with a long-awaited federal court ruling in Washington State. After decades of disputes about the meaning of a nineteenth-century treaty clause that preserved Indians' right to fish at customary places, fourteen tribes and the U.S. government had faced off against state agencies in a trial before Judge George Boldt, hoping for a resolution of outstanding issues. The principal aim of the case, *United States v. State of Washington*, was to clarify state power over Indian fishing at off-reservation sites. Rejecting the position of the Washington Department of Game, the judge held that the "right of taking fish in common with citizens" meant more for Indians than simply the chance to fish as outnumbered individuals in competition with non-Indians, who could catch migrating salmon and steelhead trout before they reached "accustomed" tribal fishing grounds. The most reasonable and historically accurate interpretation of the treaty language, Judge Boldt concluded, was that the tribes had agreed to share the resource equally with non-Indians as a population. The state of Washington therefore had a duty to regulate its citizens so that Indians would have access to half the harvestable fish.[83]

This conclusion required a hefty cutback in non-Indian fishing. From 1970 through 1973, on average, non-treaty fishers had taken home 95 percent of the salmon harvest in the *United States v. Washington* case area. With roughly five times as many boats as Indians had, non-Indians caught over 85 percent of the salmon in 1974. Therefore, to comply with the judge's ruling, the state had to reduce its licensees' total catch. For reasons that included vigorous state and citizen resistance, the reallocation of opportunity took time to achieve. Treaty fishers did not immediately go from famine to feast. By 1983, however, Indian nets were filling with fish that non-Indians had once expected to land.[84]

Judge Boldt's decision and its repercussions were front-page news for years in the Pacific Northwest, but they also got ample national press, as did tribal wins in other contests for resources and power. The U.S. Civil Rights Commission, reporting in 1981 on its investigation of reactions to the Indian gains, observed that the preceding decade's "dramatic" judgments in Indians' favor had been "major news events and their implications were speculated about with regularity in both the print and electronic media."[85] Thus, while government surveys and other research continued to show that poverty among Indians was extensive and tenacious, Americans were hearing about successful Indian claims to wealth of various kinds. Within a few short years, the belief that many Indians were rich or growing rich had more currency than it had had for half a century.

For some Americans, memories from earlier times lent plausibility to the idea that many Indians had a surfeit of wealth. As common as was the identification of Indians with poverty by the 1970s, it had never completely displaced images of Indians in contrary circumstances. "To hear some people talk," Vine Deloria wrote in 1969, "Indians are simultaneously rich from oil royalties and poor as church mice."[86] He did not exaggerate by much. Throughout the postwar years, while tribal representatives and concerned Whites repeatedly described Indians as poor, mass media kept the contrasting stereotype on life support. In 1947, for instance, a Hollywood producer entertained moviegoers with a romanticized version of the rich Indian image. They chose Mexican Anthony Quinn to portray what a derisive reviewer called "a simple American Indian of the poor, reservation variety" and his "innocent acceptance of great wealth, acquired from an oil well on his land grant."[87] During the 1950s, journalists occasionally went to reservations for the spectacle of Indians scooping up windfall wealth from mining contracts or court awards. One report in 1956 carried the title "Lo! The Rich Indian" and a subheading that told readers, "A Colorado tribe, after collecting for old land claims, is learning to live with money." The article recited difficulties that ensued—"carousing," "brawls," and "pitchmen" who "descended in droves"—after a court bestowed a fortune exceeding $31 million on Utes who had previously lived in "haphazard manner" on "a few head of livestock" and federal handouts. Oil and natural gas finds aggravated the problem, according to the reporter.[88] In the heyday of the termination policy, the press also took an interest in predictions that Indians would get and squander fat rolls of cash when guardianship ended and tribe members received their shares of liquidated tribal assets.[89]

However, before the flurry of lucrative tribal claims in the 1970s, the point of stories about flush Indians was not to suggest that Indians were commonly rich, acquisitive, or entrepreneurial. Instead, as in the Ute case, such Indians attracted attention because they were presumably anomalous and poorly equipped to cope with prosperity. That presumption motivated and colored press coverage even after tribal enterprises sprouted on many reservations in the 1960s. Take, for example, a 1973 *New York Times* article about California Natives who collected several million dollars a year from leases on their land in Palm Springs. The "Agua Caliente tribe of 170 members is no motley impoverished band of Indians," the article began. Sandwiched between paragraphs about the Indians' six-digit incomes, luxurious cars, swimming pools, and exclusive club memberships were clichéd observations that most tribe members had no jobs or job skills and some had "lost the bulk of their wealth through extravagance or speculation, to unscrupulous business advisers or as a result of drinking or gambling."[90]

The occasion for the story about the Agua Caliente Band was their appeal from an adverse ruling in their lawsuit challenging the city's annexation and zoning of tribal land. Information about the litigation came late in the article, however. The opening paragraphs said simply, "The town is under attack by Indians . . . , probably the wealthiest Indians in the United States, many of them millionaires, who have begun a new uprising in the Federal courts to defend the huge economic stake they have in this prosperous winter resort." For city leaders' view of the alleged uprising, the reporter turned to the planning director, who predicted "that an Indian victory . . . would produce 'utter chaos,' destroy the attractiveness of Palm Springs and place its 31,000 permanent residents at the mercy of . . . a handful of Indian agitators."[91]

Such fear and hostility characterized the responses of many people on the receiving end of Indian legal actions during the 1970s. In the Northwest, non-Indian fishers and state officials, including Washington's governor, pronounced Judge Boldt's interpretation of the treaties a disaster. The court-ordered reapportionment of the salmon "completely demolished the fish industry of our state," said a state senator who was apparently unwilling to count Indian fishing as a Washington industry. The U.S. Civil Rights Commission chose the word "extreme" to describe reaction in Maine after the Passamaquoddy and Penobscots won a critical round in court. "Political figures filled the media with prophecies of doom," the commission noted, citing a Bangor newspaper editorial as an example of Maine public opinion. "Unless this country is prepared to destroy itself in the name of justice," *Daily News* editors wailed, "it is madness to foresee 1,500 or so Maine citizens, of any color, creed or ancestral origin, getting 10 or 12 million acres of land and billions of dollars. . . . If Maine's Indian case has merit, then . . . no land in any state in the country is safe."[92]

Words such as "war," "bitter battle," "threat," and "financial ruin" peppered discourse about Indian claims on resources. In 1977, a *Time* magazine headline asked, "Should We Give the U.S. Back to the Indians?" and the article that followed began ominously: "They have been . . . the least conspicuous and most docile of minorities—until recently. Now they are on a warpath of sorts again, armed this time with old treaties and new court writs and led by sharpshooting lawyers whose allies include, to the chagrin of many non-Indians, the U.S. government. Their stated aim: to recover huge swatches of land and some of the rights they yielded during the inexorable sweep of expanding American civilization." Such ambitions inevitably stirred hostility, the reporter warned. From the West Coast, another reporter surveyed Indians' increasing assertiveness and similarly construed the resultant conflict as a "new round of Indian

Members of the U.S. Civil Rights Commission characterized negative reactions to Indian legal victories of the 1970s as "extreme" and permeated by economic considerations. Among the reactions they condemned was the widespread personal vilification of George Boldt, a federal judge whose interpretation of nineteenth-century treaties obliged Washington State to reduce the share of salmon and steelhead its licensees caught so that half the fish would be available to Indian treaty beneficiaries. University of Washington Libraries, Special Collections, Kenneth McLeod Papers, Box 3, Folder 13.

wars, a non-violent variety." This time, he added, "the Indians appear to be winning."[93]

The talk of warfare may have originated with non-Indians, but Indians and their allies readily adopted the same terminology. Those on the tribes' side insisted, however, that the blame for bellicose relations lay with their adversaries, who would not concede anything of value to Indians without a fight. "The whites are on the warpath," announced an essay in the *Nation* titled "Still Scalping the Indians." A writer who identified himself as a descendant of Native people declared in the early 1980s, "There is a war going on right now over Indian resources—a war not too different from the Indian wars of the 1700s or 1800s. The motivation for such wars has always been the same: the exploitation of this continent's resources."[94]

Another term for the angry reactions to Indian gains was "backlash." The label was ubiquitous by 1977, when a western Washington newspaper headline proclaimed, "Indian Successes Could Lead to White Backlash." The Civil Rights Commission explained the inquiry it completed in 1981 as a response to a "backlash . . . against Indians and Indian interests" in "the second half of the seventies." Signs of the backlash included "anti-Indian editorials and articles . . . in both the local and the national media" as well as bills in state and federal legislatures to overturn judicial determinations of Indians' rights, restrict Indian access to water and other resources, and quash some eastern land claims.[95]

By 1977, the backlash had an institutional home. Assorted local and regional groups had coalesced to wage a national campaign against "special rights" for Indians. Their umbrella organization—the Interstate Congress for Equal Rights and Responsibilities (ICERR)—claimed chapters in eighteen states with memberships totaling more than 10,000 people.[96] Aiming to stem a perceived legal trend "that allows the small Indian minority to have special benefits," ICERR sent a lobbyist to Washington, D.C., where bills that it favored vied for votes in the ninety-fifth Congress with bills furthering the tribes' self-determination agenda. House Resolution 9054—an ICERR-backed proposal from a Washington State representative—would have abolished reservations and the BIA, directed the president to abrogate all Indian treaties, and required tribes to choose between converting to private corporations or dividing common property among their members. The Interstate Congress and constituent groups also initiated or intervened in numerous lawsuits.[97]

In response to accusations that their campaign was racist, coalition leaders said their purpose was actually to combat legalized racism, as evidenced by stated ICERR objectives: "'that the constitutional rights of all Americans must supercede treaty rights of some Americans,' that Indian reservations not be enlarged, that tribal governments should not have jurisdiction over non-Indians who have no voice in tribal government, and that grants of public funds to any group of people based on race be prohibited." ICERR organizers contended that court decisions and legislation perpetuating Indians' peculiar status as quasi-sovereign nations were inconsistent with Indians' American citizenship, with other Americans' individual rights, and with the country's commitment to racial equality. "It's minority rule, it's a kind of apartheid," said the group's executive director. As sociologist Jeffrey Dudas observed, ideologues of the backlash claimed credit for mounting "a rousing defense of the American way of life itself."[98]

The effort to craft an image as champions of legal and racial equality included names—not only ICERR's full name with its appeal to equal rights and the names of constituent groups such as South Dakotans for Civil Liberties or Montanans Opposed to Discrimination but also the name of H.R. 9054, the Native American Equal Opportunity Act. This self-styling effort was lost on most journalists, who generally identified ICERR and its backers as overtly anti-Indian.

Supporters of the tribal renaissance, equally unimpressed with their critics' professions of concern for equality, identified themselves as the ones hewing to core American ideals—ideals such as reliance on the legal system for conflict resolution, respect for precedent, and belief in the sanctity of contracts. Treaty rights "are owed by the United States to the Indians as in any contractual obligation," Sam Deloria explained. Indians and their defenders argued further that the only action needed to correct racial discrimination was deference to established law—something Judge Boldt showed in the treaty fishing rights case. A clergyman warned that nullifying Boldt's judgment by legislation would actually undermine basic rights. Two legal scholars agreed: if the backlash were to reverse the gains Indians had won in court and in Congress, Indians could reasonably conclude that "the white man's law" was not a "reservoir of rights," but an instrument of their domination.[99]

However, in public replies to ICERR activists and their ilk, Indians seemed less intent on pressing the racism charge than on painting their critics as stingy or greedy for begrudging Indians a decent share of national wealth. Mel Tonasket, chair of the Colville Confederated Tribes, told a *Business Week* reporter in 1976, "The backlash is not racially, but economically, motivated."[100] His was a view heard often in tribal and intertribal political circles. At a gathering to plan a coordinated Indian response to the backlash, Navajo chairman Peter MacDonald emphasized the disgruntled non-Indians' preoccupation with Indian economic gains. "If you believe what you read," he mused, "we are all millionaires. We are taking back the whole Eastern United States, starting with Maine and working our way down the Eastern Seaboard. We are destroying tourism in the Northwest by asserting our fishing rights. We are holding the entire Southwest hostage with our water rights and energy resources. Americans find it useful and convenient to believe that Indians are rich . . . ; it provides a justification for taking our resources, destroying our tribal sovereignty and ignoring our problems."[101] A 1978 NCAI issue paper described the "'backlash' phenomenon" as "a direct result of fear, misunderstanding, and concern for the loss of resources and markets by non-Indians."[102]

Neutral analysts voiced similar perceptions. The Civil Rights Commission found that obvious economic considerations permeated the positions of resentful non-Indians in the controversies it investigated. *Newsweek* reporters had previously made the same observation about the "paleface uprising." After quoting ICERR spokesmen who purported to care above all about legal equality, the reporters catalogued the economic assets at stake in disputes with Indians and concluded, "Aside from the constitutional arguments . . . , many ICERR leaders are clearly irked at what they think are the Indians' unfair financial advantages." A *Progressive* magazine essay on the treaty fishing contro-

Are We Giving America Back To the Indians?

EQUAL
RIGHTS AND
RESPONSIBILITIES

CURRENT
FEDERAL
INDIAN
POLICY

Interstate Congress For Equal Rights And Responsibilities

Publications of the Interstate Congress for Equal Rights and Responsibilities, established in 1977, promoted the idea that ordinary, innocent non-Indian Americans stood to lose property as well as power if courts and lawmakers conceded the justice of Indian claims to resources such as land, fish, and water on the basis of anachronistic nineteenth-century treaties and laws. University of Washington Libraries, Special Collections, Kenneth McLeod Papers, Box 4, Folder 9.

versy, while acknowledging that Whites as well as Indians esteemed salmon and treaty rights for some non-economic reasons, attributed the fury at Judge Boldt's ruling to the fact that "powerful interests" would lose a share of "the salmon's enormous economic value."[103]

The economic animus for the campaign against "special" Indian rights was indeed obvious. Although ICERR and its constituent groups denied that material self-interest was their primary motivation, members frequently mentioned specific economic concerns and said that resolving the issue of Indians' legal status would determine whether non-Indians lost or retained access to tangible wealth. "There's little question," wrote two of the movement founders, "that long-range goals of activist Indian groups today include control of timber, minerals and oil, and the payment of huge sums of money as indemnities." Claiming to perceive an Indian "frame of mind that continually asks for more," the writers urged dismayed citizens to respond by seeking repeal of treaties and statutes that gave Indians rights denied to other Americans, not only in political matters but also in economic relations.[104]

Pacific Northwest opponents of "special" Indian rights were as adamant as any that protecting non-Indian property or income would merely be an ancillary effect of success in their quest for legal equality. A ruling such as Judge Boldt's offended them, they explained, because it sanctioned an outdated legal status for Indians, which was increasingly the basis for denying non-Indians their civil rights. This disavowal of economic motives might have had more plausibility if the only rights denied were recreational fishing opportunities, but disgruntled people also complained of threats to significant non-Indian wealth from Boldt's ruling. A lawyer who represented the state at trial wrote, "An annually renewable resource worth millions of dollars is 'up for grabs,' and the federal government is doing all it can to encourage Indian exploitation of these resources at the expense of all other citizen users." Even sport fishers argued their case in economic terms. One wrote in an essay for *Field & Stream*, "The Indians are demanding a lion's share of commercial and recreational fisheries that, in the case of Washington State alone, have a wholesale value of more than $150,000,000 per year. . . . Salmon and steelhead in the Pacific Northwest owe their very existence to the license fees paid" by non-Indian fishers.[105] Kenneth McLeod, a sportsman and journalist who raged against Judge Boldt in print and in private correspondence, once drafted a bitterly sarcastic "contract" whose signers would have pledged half their income after 12 February 1974 "to the Indian people," in order to atone for the "White Man's" wrongs.[106]

Economic envy also permeated a book-length publication titled *Indian Treaties, American Nightmare*. The authors—sport fishing enthusiasts Herb Williams and Walt Neubrech—saw Judge Boldt's decision as the keystone of a rapidly rising legal edifice that would sequester much of the nation's wealth for Indians. "Claims, lawsuits and court decisions across the nation are granting ever-increasing control of America's fish, game and other resources to a handful of its citizens," they wrote; "Indian sovereignty sought for reservations would mean control over water, coal and other mineral resources. This control would be over non-Indian as well as Indian-owned land."[107]

Opponents of tribal sovereignty and treaty rights could depict their cause as resistance to odious discrimination because of Indians' common identification as a racial group. Their movement tapped into a broader current of discontent with the perceived unfairness to Whites of government measures countering racism and its impoverishing effect. They shared the belief of many Whites that they were losing economic opportunities to a "minority group" and federal "reverse discrimination" was to blame. Thus, in an interview for a television broadcast about the Passamaquoddy land claim, a Maine homeowner lodged a general protest that measures to help minorities were victimizing White, middle-class Americans. A Temple University religion professor thought the root cause of such protests was the stagnation of middle-class incomes—a result of tax and estate laws benefiting the well-to-do. He lamented that the unhappy people were not directing their envy "upward" at those who held an increasing portion of national wealth but instead, with the encouragement of some politicians, sought to silence the clamor coming from people behind them in the race for resources.[108] Although some analysts were less pessimistic than the professor about income trends, most agreed that middle-class anxiety about economic conditions was acute by the mid-1970s, and some of the anxious people thought they were hurting because they had been made to shoulder the costs of compensatory efforts to reduce inequalities, especially between racial groups.[109]

From the vantage point of 1991, journalist Nicholas Lemann saw the 1970s, beginning with the OPEC oil embargo, as a time when Americans lost their postwar faith that growth and opportunity for all would henceforth be perpetual features of the national economy. "As it slowly began to sink in that everybody wasn't going to be moving forward together anymore, the country became more fragmented, more internally rivalrous," and "the middle class began to define its interests in terms of a rollback of government programs aimed at helping other groups." Ironically, this reaction showed the influence of the minority groups' struggles for justice: White people who would not previously have considered any Americans "oppressed" began representing themselves in the 1970s as victims of government oppression and racial discrimination. An anonymous "petition" protesting Judge Boldt's decision illustrates Lemann's point. "The real tragedy," it said, "lies in the nightmarish reality that all citizens other than Treaty Indians are now forced into a posture of Second Class Citizenship. When Boldt elevated the Indians to a position of super-citizens with super rights, he automatically placed all others in the lower class and said in effect, 'Move to the back of the bus.'"[110]

The economic frustration that Lemann described was apparent in 1978 to legal scholars Jill Shattuck and Petra Norgren, who saw a direct connection to the backlash against Indian rights. Nonetheless, Shattuck and Norgren pleaded for an altruistic response to Indian demands. Instead of objecting that justice for Indians would impose "burdens" on Whites, Whites should acknowledge that their interests had always prevailed in the past and act, for a change, to ameliorate Indians' "longstanding and very real economic and social plight." Published in the *Nation*, a periodical that few of the resentful Whites would see, this plea was quixotic.[111] When Indian victories seemed to come at other Americans' expense, Indians' well-known plight lost much of its power to stir non-Indian sympathy.

As Indian victories accumulated, images of greedy rich Indians did not supplant images of neglected poor ones. The Navajo chairman was indulging in hyperbole when he said, "If you believe what you read, we are all millionaires." But opponents of special Indian rights did challenge the association of Indians with poverty by claiming that great wealth was a not-so-secret goal of nationalist Indians, and one they were well on their way to attaining. In his introduction to *Indian Treaties, American Nightmare*, the National Wildlife Federation vice president mentioned that many tribes, not satisfied with the "hundreds of millions of taxpayer dollars . . . paid to settle" Indian Claims Commission cases, had "returned to the Congress or gone to the courts to ask for land titles as well." The book itself included the obligatory statement that "of all the ethnic minorities in America today, Indians have been near the bottom in terms of income"; but otherwise it discussed Indians and wealth as if they increasingly went hand in hand. Authors Williams and Neubrech alleged that tribes hoped to double their existing land base. Success would make Indians "one of the wealthiest groups in America today, in terms of land ownership."[112] Even before the tribes won their suit in Judge Boldt's court, adversaries claimed that some Indians deviously cultivated an image of poverty as a cover for greed. A *Nation* magazine correspondent reported hearing "the charge that a few off-reservation Indians have made as much as $60,000 to $80,000 in a single year, an obvious impropriety for a red man. Speaking of such a capitalist Indian, a Department of Fisheries officer was quoted as saying recently: 'He's out there preaching the gospel and getting all the liberals to shed tears over the Indians, and all the time he's cleaning up.'"[113]

Some media coverage probably abetted this challenge to long-prevalent ideas about Indians' economic ethos and circumstances. A *New York Times* headline — "Maine Indian Tribes Confronting Era of Abundance" — surely had that effect. So did the title of a 1976 *U.S. News & World Report* story — "Energy-Rich Indians" — and the story's introductory declaration that Indian lands "contain some of the nation's richest reserves of gas, oil, coal and uranium. In a fuel-hungry society, ownership of such property is worth billions." When reporting on the value of energy sources under Navajo land, *Business Week* also recited dollar figures in the billions, then concluded, "The Indians are beginning to think they are selling their resources to the white man too cheaply." Another newspaper article speculated, "Water rights cases . . . along with mineral rights issues could lead the tribes to a powerful economic position in the West."[114] BIA and tribal personnel tried to remind Americans that tribes with mineral resources were few and that most Indians remained abysmally poor, but the president himself counteracted their efforts. During a 1980 trip to the

Soviet Union, Ronald Reagan, sensing criticism of U.S. policy in a Russian student's question about Native Americans, stated that Indians had become "very wealthy" from oil. American news media duly relayed that remark to people at home.[115]

In the face of such publicity, pity for Indians could waver and even transmute to contempt. Some people now pronounced Indians' pursuit of their economic interests unpatriotic and greedy. The tribes' determination to glean greater benefit from their minerals prompted a mining company spokesman to bark, "Those dumb Indians ought to be shot for not letting us dig on their lands. Everything . . . ought to be exploited." For their part, ICERR activists exploited a common perception that the country had already responded generously to Indians' needs, making Indians' dissatisfaction seem like avarice. *Indian Treaties, American Nightmare* charged, "Indian claims to an expanded land base ignore the vast acreages Indians already own," and "each demand that is met is followed by new and greater demands." The authors also chided, "As Indians drive the automobiles, watch the television sets, fly in the aircraft, and use the thousands of things produced by modern industrial society, they are attacking this same society and asking indemnities. It's a case of wanting one's cake and eating it too." Such complaints resonated with a sportsman who condemned "the drive by Indian attorneys to wrest every last advantage from the ancient treaties."[116]

Except during the energy crisis, when consumers suspected oil companies of pocketing excessive profits, criticisms of this sort seldom dogged White Americans who tried to wrest every possible advantage from their economic assets and opportunities.[117] The distinctive critique of Indian ambitions drew on contradictory conceptions of Indian character and values. Some of the disapproval stemmed from a belief that enterprising Indians were either betraying their own noble values or revealing their antimaterialist image to be a deception. In 1982, as Peter MacDonald prepared to relinquish leadership of the Council of Energy Resource Tribes, he observed that the organization had challenged common beliefs about Indians' aversion to, or disengagement from, capitalist culture. It had done so of necessity, because "poverty was no longer fashionable, and hunger was no longer fashionable." But, for trying to make the most of tribal resources, MacDonald said, "We were charged with capitalism in the first degree."[118] To many Indians, MacDonald's quip was no joke. All too often non-Indians had damned them for lacking ambition (and damned them to poverty) if they did not embrace America's competitive economic culture, but damned them for greed or hypocrisy if they did.

For the idea that economic ambition was contrary to Indian mores, non-Indian critics could find support in the words of Indians themselves. Ambivalence and controversy about the importance of striving for wealth were at least as common in Indian country as in the nation at large. Events of the 1970s obliged Indians to examine and rearticulate their economic aspirations and principles. Disagreements were integral and necessary to the long-term and probably utopian project of formulating a position everyone could endorse.

Some Indians disagreed with tribal business plans because of concerns that paralleled and interacted with other Americans' unease about the social and environmental costs of economic development. Across the United States during the 1970s, proponents of development met new resistance from people bent on forestalling damage to the natural environment or serving noneconomic needs. Similarly, many Indians worried that proposed ventures would require land use at odds with essential tribal ideals or obligations. In several of the CERT tribes, factions formed to insist that money could not justify defiling the earth and air. According to *Business Week*, "One survey indicated that Navajos opposed to coal development outnumber[ed] those in favor by nearly 2 to 1." Dissenting from the Hopi tribal council's inclination to authorize coal mining, an elderly tribe member reportedly said, "Just leave it alone. . . . We don't want them to take our Mother Earth." And in 1978, a Sioux spiritual leader at a rally against backlash legislation spoke sorrowfully of corporations raping "the sacred land." In these and many other instances, opponents of plans to cash in on reservation resources characterized them as incompatible with Indian spiritual traditions, with a prescribed human relation to the rest of creation, and with Indians' customary preference for social comforts over possessions.[119]

To accommodate constituents with this mindset and often to honor their own values, tribal officials did consider foregoing the exploitation of some natural resources; but in many cases, they opted nonetheless for action that promised income for their tribes. Speaking of mineral leases that tribal governments approved in 1975, a Native American Rights Fund lawyer said, "There was never any doubt they would sign. . . . They were going to get some money, and money was a good thing."[120] Signing reflected a view of economic enterprise that was more complex and more favorable to gain-oriented pursuits than Peter MacDonald implied when he explained the new tribal capitalism as a necessary alternative to poverty and hunger. Few, if any, tribal leaders thought voluntary austerity was the "Indian way." In fact, many were the descendants of indigenous people who respected the ability to acquire wealth. The taboo for their ancestors was not economic ambition; it was amassing wealth at the expense of kin or sustainability and failing to share what one acquired with relatives and friends in a community network.[121]

How simplistic in comparison is the conception of Indian economic culture promoted in *Indian Treaties, American Nightmare*. Claiming to have heard Indian activists say they did not want to meet the dominant culture on its own terms, authors Williams and Neubrech deemed it hypocritical that Indians had also staged "publicity stunts equal to the best of Madison Avenue or Hollywood" and hired some of the nation's best lawyers.[122] To counter this kind of argument, enterprising Indians had to show that their cultures were dynamic and sophisticated enough to thrive in the modern economic world without sacrificing ideals such as generosity, reciprocity, and stewardship of the natural world. They may have had no need for Madison Avenue when it came to planning publicity stunts, but projecting an image appealing to skeptical Americans was a stiffer challenge.

When soliciting support for their bids to control reservation resources, tribal officials often found it fitting to emphasize that the incidence of Indian poverty remained high, even in tribes with substantial corporate wealth. To charges of greed, they could reply that Indians were still far from economic parity with Whites and then insist that the real issue was Whites' insatiability. To those who questioned whether the new drive for wealth was compatible with Indian values, tribal leaders could reply that grinding poverty was a greater threat to their traditions and moral integrity than doing what was necessary to end poverty.[123]

Still, some people said they could not reconcile Indians' purported concern for the poor or appeals for justice with tribal efforts to take control of wealth at the expense of ordinary non-Indian fishers, farmers, landowners, or reservation residents. How could tribes in good conscience try to dispossess or disempower people whose only apparent sin was assuming that the law made no distinction between Indian citizens and other citizens? What would be unfair about expecting Indians to meet the same responsibilities under law as other Americans? How was it fair for Indians to enjoy both American citizenship and separate sovereignty? The authors of *Indian Treaties, American Nightmare* proposed that true tribal sovereignty would mean complete separation from mainstream America. Because that would be foolish, Indians should eschew sovereignty and instead "should be a part of the economic mainstream. . . . They should pay taxes, contributing to the prosperity of the United States, as well as benefiting from that prosperity."[124]

Indians had good reason to scoff at this advice, betraying as it did the writers' ignorance that Indians were paying taxes, filling jobs, and continuing in many instances to hand their resources and income over to non-Indians. More maddening and morally dubious, in the view of many Indians, was to be told that they should pursue wealth like other Americans and then—after they did so as provided by U.S. law—to hear demands for changes in the law that would nullify the few rights they had salvaged when surrendering to colonial rule.

Neither the Native American Equal Opportunity Act nor other attempts to pull the legal rug out from under resurgent tribes won congressional approval during the 1970s, but the tribes' win-loss ratio in the courts changed for the worse after 1980. Legal scholar David Getches found that a new subjectivity characterized the Supreme Court's approach to contests between Indians and non-Indians, and the justices proved increasingly deferential to the interests of non-Indian litigants.[125] That tendency was not yet apparent in 1979 when the court finally reviewed Judge Boldt's ruling in the fishing case and upheld it in nearly all respects. However, the justices added a word about the treaty right that may have signaled the change to come. They showed some uneasiness at the prospect of Indians having more resources than their marginal place in American society warranted.

After approving Boldt's conclusion that it was equitable to divide the fish harvest into "approximately equal treaty and nontreaty shares," the Supreme Court majority provided for a reduction in the treaty share "if tribal needs may be satisfied by a lesser amount." "The 50% figure imposes a maximum but not a minimum allocation," they explained.

> The central principle here must be that Indian treaty rights to a natural resource . . . secures so much as, but no more than, is necessary to pro-vide the Indians with a livelihood—that is to say, a moderate living. . . . If, for example, a tribe should dwindle to just a few members, or if it should find other sources of support that lead it to abandon its fisheries, a 45% or 50% allocation of an entire run that passes through its custom-ary fishing grounds would be manifestly inappropriate because the livelihood of the tribe under those circumstances could not reasonably require an allotment of a large number of fish.[126]

Two years later, the Civil Rights Commission observed perceptively though vaguely that this paragraph "added some confusion to the determination of the appropriate" fish allocation.[127]

The new qualification, inserted without prompting from any of the liti-gants, also added confusion to the broader issues swirling around Indians' quest for wealth. Did justices in the majority have the broader issues in mind and intend to weigh in on them? Were they uncomfortable with the economic implications of "special" rights for Indians in general? Did they foresee (and not regret) that non-Indians might invoke the "moderate living" limitation to restrict the value Indians could derive from resources other than fish? Neither the Court's published opinion nor the justices' internal correspondence answers these questions. But letters and memoranda do show that the opinion's author, John Paul Stevens, proposed the limitation in order to meet the concerns of colleagues who were balking at a fifty-fifty division of the fish because they thought the Indian share would be too great for the size of the Indian population. David Getches calls the proposal a "solution to the possibility that some Indians, especially in small tribes, could use the percentage entitlement to get rich."[128]

Justice Stevens took two approaches to winning other justices' support for his proposal. One approach was to assure them—citing the case record—that Indians had a limited number of customary places to set nets and were therefore likely to continue taking less than half the salmon and steelhead harvest. In effect, Stevens played to the common conception of Indians as people whose historical behavior restricted their ability to gain wealth. His other tactic was to liken the moderate living cap to a principle from water rights cases that Indian reservations came with a tacit inclusion of water in amounts adequate for their habitation and self-support. These lines of reasoning suggest that Stevens was inclined to limit the value of treaty rights beyond the two eventualities of sharply decreased tribal membership and decreased fishing. Some legal scholars think the language of his opinion lends itself to an argument that changed circumstances can provide a rationale for restricting the value of any resources reserved for Indians. As one scholar proposed, and a lower court subsequently said, it could even mean "that a division of treaty-secured resources may be predicated by increased non-Indian demand for that resource."[129]

In several subsequent contests over resources, Indians' adversaries have taken heart at the language Justice Stevens composed.[130] A few have seen it as a basis for minimizing Indian economic opportunities and even as a bar to Indians accumulating wealth or saving for the future. Whether or not judges ultimately accept such extreme interpretations, the moderate living concept could present tribes with a dilemma. As legal scholar Dana Johnson noted understatedly, the new doctrine "may operate as a disincentive to economic growth and development by foreclosing the possibility of significant economic success." However "moderate" is ultimately construed, it is apt to mean something less than indisputably wealthy or unusually affluent. And if judges rule that Indians do not have the right to grow rich from resources vested in them by law, Indians will face "constraints upon tribal economic endeavors which are not placed on non-Indian enterprises."[131]

Back in 1968, who could have foreseen that thousands of resentful Americans would soon have reason to call for constraints on tribal economic endeavors? As government agencies and news media documented persistent Indian privation, who could have imagined the next decade's successful tribal claims to land, minerals, water, and fish worth many millions of dollars? Four years into the federal war on poverty, the identification of Indians with poverty seemed unquestionable and enduring. Then-middle-aged Americans had been exposed during their lifetimes to disclosure after disclosure that Indians were poorer than any other demographic group in the United States. Occasional reports of rich Indians merely proved the rule by depicting their wealth as serendipitous, unearned, and squandered. The stereotypical rich Indian and poor Indian were flip sides of the same coin. Both validated an idea as old as Europe's discovery of the Americas—a conception of Indians as Europeans' converse in key respects, including economic culture. Many Indians as well as non-Indians assumed that Indian practices would contrast with the ambition and ever-increasing wealth production attributed to Euro-Americans. Both of the common explanations for Indians' poverty—a traditional Indian mindset and government failure to bring Indians into the American mainstream—depended on this conception of Indianness.

From the 1920s through the 1960s, Americans debated successive strategies for reducing Indian poverty, and some occasionally declared that government aid was a moral obligation; but the usual issue was whether government policy and practice was suited to achieving an uncontested goal—Indians' economic normalization. Indian poverty caused concern because it was inconsistent with expectations fostered by reformers and government agents, or it was a sign that the federal government, in its emerging role as a referee of the economic game, had failed to prevent strong players from hurting weaker ones.

When Indian tribes did get in the game and score major victories in the 1970s, public discourse changed character. Moral concerns—talk of greed, injustice, and disloyalty to core American ideals—became a prominent feature of the discourse. Indian poverty had confirmed and reinforced a common belief that Indians, by tradition or disposition, were less mercenary than other Americans; so when tribes sought to control and profit from valuable resources, many non-Indians and even fellow Indians said they saw signs of aberration, including avarice. The enterprising Indians also met objections that their gains were achieved by unfair means. The loudest protests came from non-Indians who cast themselves as victims of injustice, at a disadvantage because the federal government granted Indians rights and powers beyond those that other Americans enjoyed. The protesters named Indians' political prerogatives as their primary concern but left no doubt about their objection to the economic leverage that would follow from tribal power. Without billing themselves explicitly as moralists, they hoped to excite moral indignation about Indians' "special" rights. They portrayed such rights as a betrayal of the American economic ethic as they conceived it—an ethic that defined fairness as uniform individual opportunity for all citizens.

These hostile responses to Indian economic ambitions were ironic and distinctive consequences of Indians' historical dispossession and racialization. They were grounded in a paradoxical pairing of beliefs that had long influenced Indian/non-Indian relations. On one hand, they reflected a conviction as old as the American republic that Indians were not destined to survive the creation and expansion of the United States as autonomous peoples; their only alternative to eradication was absorption on Euro-American terms. On the other hand, the arguments also reflected a conception of Indians as a distinct race defined in significant part by ancestry. Once equality and desegregation of the races became the ostensible American norm in the 1960s, opponents of a special status for Indians could object to it either as contrary to that norm or as contrary to the premise of granting Indians all the benefits of citizenship.

When contemplating threatening reactions to tribal gains, Indians had cause to feel damned if they did not get rich and damned if they did. Despite a continuing and notorious high rate of Indian indigence, the reactions exposed widespread uneasiness about the tribes' pursuit or control of additional wealth. Confronted with assertions that it was unjust, racially discriminatory, and greedy to preserve and enforce the few legal and economic concessions that tribes had wrung from their conquerors, Indians tried to articulate alternative conceptions of morality, fairness, and decency. The principles they appealed to were the sanctity of promises and the obligation of the wealthy and powerful to show benevolence toward the weak. Those were principles of economic relations that earlier generations of Indians had also endorsed and had pleaded with Euro-Americans to observe.

Gambling Money

"American Indians Discover Money Is Power." With that headline in 1993, *Fortune* magazine announced its own discovery of Indians who deserved coverage in a publication for and about American business. Over the next decade, enterprising Indians caught the attention of many other magazines and newspapers. Stories ran under headings such as "Oneida Indian Nation Businesses Worth $1,000,000,000," "Indian Tribes Enjoy Big Payoff from Casinos," "Tribes Looking to Share the Wealth With Other Indian-Run Companies," "Tribes Fear Backlash to Prosperity," and "A Business Empire Transforms Life for Colorado Tribe." As of 2005, media interest in lucrative tribal ventures showed no sign of abating.[1] Thus, as the twenty-first century approached and then got under way, the press documented and contributed to a new round of national discourse about Indians' economic status and aims. Because the focus was on developments that put more money in Indian hands than ever before and had direct impacts on millions of non-Indians, commentary was profuse. Indians were prominent among those airing their views, both in forums of their own and in media under others' control. Never had so many Americans engaged for so long in public debate about enterprising and affluent Indians.

This instance of Indian affluence differed from earlier ones in other notable ways. Its causes, extensive geographical reach, and impact on non-Indians had no historical equivalents. Most of the discourse concerned Indians who were making money as business owners—specifically, as owners of gambling casinos. Tribes with lavish casino revenues could be found at all four corners of the United States and many places in between, usually near urban areas. Since the great majority of casino patrons were non-Indians, Indians appeared to profit, for the first time in history, by siphoning cash out of other Americans' wallets faster than other Americans could extract wealth from Indian country. But money was not only flowing to Indians in unprecedented ways and amounts; it was flowing from Indians to non-Indians for novel purposes. Indians were paying multitudes of non-Indians to work for them, subsidizing government services in neighboring jurisdictions, supporting diverse charitable causes, and funding state and nationwide political campaigns.

Although the tribal casino phenomenon broke new ground in some respects, many of the issues it raised were not new. Commentators revisited questions discussed in past times when Indians had substantial wealth. Was it correct to characterize the Indians as rich? Was the wealth justly distributed? Were the prospering people actually Indians? Was the money disorienting or corrupting Indian recipients? Did the new affluence reflect and foster practices that would subvert Indian culture, or would traditional values determine its effects on the Indians? And could the money secure power for Indians, or would non-Indians expropriate the wealth?

If the ghosts of long-dead Powhatan chiefs, Cherokee slaveowners, Creek ranchers, or Osage headright holders were hovering near, taking in the discourse on tribal casinos, they heard some familiar themes. They heard the disapproval of non-Indians who attributed Indians' economic fortunes both to cultural or political otherness and to the manipulations of non-Indians. They heard Indians debate the morality and point out the irony of efforts to preserve their cultural and legal autonomy by adopting economic practices learned from Euro-Americans. In sum, they witnessed yet another phase of discussion on the centuries-old challenge of reconciling Indian economic aims and practices with those of other Americans. But the eavesdropping spirits may also have noticed something unfamiliar—a rise in the power of Indian wealth to influence the direction and consequences of the discussion.

Indians first saw commercial gambling houses as a potential source of revenue in the 1970s, particularly after the U.S. Supreme Court affirmed that reservations were distinct jurisdictions where federally protected tribal sovereignty could preempt state law.[2] Seminoles counted on immunity from state control when they opened a bingo hall with bigger prizes and longer hours of operation than Florida-regulated games. A federal court order forbidding the state to interfere inspired other tribes to try similar ventures.[3] Among them was the Cabazon Band of Mission Indians, whose full-fledged casino did not comply with California law. In 1987, the Supreme Court sanctioned the Cabazon enterprise, even though Congress had previously granted California civil jurisdiction on all reservations in the state. A majority of justices held that the earlier legislation simply allowed state courts to adjudicate civil disputes arising in Indian country; it did not confer broad regulatory power on the state government. Therefore, the tribe, rather than the state, could set the terms of gambling on its land. The Court's decision opened the door to tribal casinos in any state that did not flatly prohibit gambling.[4]

Officials from many states, together with foes of gambling, promptly stepped up pressure on Congress for legislation subjecting tribes to state gambling regulations. The lawmakers weighed that pressure and their professed desire to discourage organized crime against the tribes' hardship at a time of federal funding cuts, and they devised a compromise. The Indian Gaming Regulatory Act of 1988 approved tribe-owned bingo, punchcard, and pull-tab gambling overseen by a National Indian Gaming Commission. It also authorized tribes to offer casino games, but only as provided in compacts with state officials.[5] Although some state governments initially responded to proposals for tribal casinos by stonewalling, twenty-eight states and 224 tribes had negotiated 249 compacts by 2005.[6]

When gauging whether Indians were rich as a result of these events, interested parties did not have to cope with cultural differences like those between Powhatans and English colonists in 1607. Long exposed to American capitalist culture, modern Indians spoke dollars and cents as well as English. U.S. currency was a common medium of exchange; everyone knew what it could buy. Even so, because "rich" derives its meanings from comparisons, disagreement about the propriety of pinning that label on Indians was as common in 2005 as in the seventeenth century.[7]

Press coverage of tribal casinos did not habitually link the adjective "rich" or "wealthy" to Indians, but it did encourage that association. Many stories highlighted facts and figures suggesting wealth on a grand scale. *Fortune* calculated in 2000 that the Indian sector of the gambling industry was growing three times faster than the non-Indian sector, referred to the Mississippi Choctaws' casino as "a cash machine that grosses more than $100 million a year," and repeated hearsay that a Mashantucket Pequot casino was paying dividends "in the high five figures" to all tribe members.[8] News services announced Indian receipts from commercial gambling as enormous aggregate sums. The Associated Press reported that the 2004 take of all tribal casinos in the United States, from Maine to California and Minnesota to Louisiana, was $19.4 billion—15 percent more than the previous year and almost twice as much as the total for Nevada's famous gambling businesses.[9]

After years of such publicity, readers of the *Los Angeles Times* probably nodded knowingly at this sentence in a 2004 op-ed piece: "Indians, at least the ones with the land and leverage to set up casinos, are raking in great honking piles of money . . . , coining new millionaires every month—in short, acting like the all-American capitalists we always said we wanted them to become."[10] By then, the belief that casinos were making Indians rich was common enough that a satirical television show could cast Indians as arrogant gambling moguls and expect viewers to get the point. In a 2003 episode of *South Park* titled "Red Man's Greed," tribal owners of the Three Feathers Casino planned to acquire a swath of land through town so they could run a highway to their establishment's front door. South Park's working class residents were modern-day Davids facing Indian Goliaths armed with piles of money.[11]

Nevertheless, depictions of Indians as rich and powerful were no less likely to meet with disbelief or dispute after 1990 than in the 1690s or the 1960s. Journalists, scholars, and Indian leaders routinely paired news of tribal income growth with evidence of continuing hardship in Indian communities. The *Fortune* article of 1993 noted, "Nearly one-third of [American Indians and Alaska Natives] are still below the poverty line vs. 13% of the total U.S. population." Seven years later, the magazine punctuated a feature on thriving Indian enterprises with a reference to contrasting conditions on the Pine Ridge Sioux Reservation, "the poorest county in the nation, an economic dead zone where tribal unemployment hovers around 80%."[12] Reciting such dismal statistics was still common in 2005 when a Harvard University researcher said at a reservation economic summit that Indians' income rose faster in the 1990s than the income of other Americans, but bracketed that news with a sobering observation. "All of us are aware that American Indians are among the poorest identifiable groups in the nation," he pointed out. "American Indians have incomes about 40 percent lower than the U.S. average."[13]

While touting the power of casinos to reduce Indian poverty, the National Indian Gaming Association (NIGA) likewise hastened to deny that "wealthy" was an accurate description of its constituents. Tribal spokesmen concurred. After listing the benefits accruing to Eastern Cherokees from a casino, Chief Leon Jones remarked, "We're still not rich here." The head of a Minnesota tribe with a very profitable casino said, "Simply put, we are self-sufficient again."[14] Other Indian leaders stressed that Indian poverty remained "unacceptably high." Ron Allen, president of the National Congress of American Indians, said in 1997, "Indians are at the bottom of almost every category for poverty or social ills, yet there's this perception now that we're all getting rich. . . . The truth is that the majority of Indian casinos are really just marginal operations."[15]

History worked in concert with human diversity and psychology to promote disparate assessments of Indians' circumstances. Perceptions varied according to observers' vantage points but also reflected contradictory, historically conditioned expectations about Indians. Americans had inherited images of rich and freeloading Indians as well as pitifully poor ones, and both images influenced interpretations of the gaming boom. Reports of per capita distributions from casino profits seemed to corroborate the belief of some non-Indians that many tribe members lived well without laboring, thanks to special income sources. Conversely, people who expected Indians to be poor might react to the fuss about casinos either by marshaling evidence that Indians' economic problems persisted or by overcorrecting their assumption.

Since the notoriety of Indian poverty gave the casino phenomenon much of its news value, there was also lively interest in whether the new wealth was reaching poor Indians. Many analysts found that a majority of Indians had seen little or none of the money gambled at tribal casinos. For every Indian who had scooped thousands of dollars from a tribal jackpot, there were scores of others whose hands remained empty, and the discrepancy seemed to grow. As in the 1890s, the divide between poor and prospering Indians was the subject of much commentary—some indignant, some concerned, some defensive—reactions that were inseparable from commentators' concepts of Indians. One issue was whether the inequitable distribution of the new wealth contravened Indian values and thus discredited commercial gambling as a tribal economic development strategy.

A 2000 Associated Press investigation reportedly revealed that only a tiny minority of Indians were banking significant income from any source. Some tribes with the most successful gaming operations paid "each member hundreds of thousands of dollars a year," but two-thirds of Indians belonged to tribes "locked in poverty." Of the tribal casinos, "only a few near major population centers . . . thrived." From such data a *Fortune* writer concluded, "While mega-resorts like [the Pequots'] billion-dollar-a-year Foxwoods (currently the largest casino on the planet) may be the symbols of Indian gaming, they are also its anomalies." The chairwoman of the Hualapai Tribe made the same point in plainer terms: "Everybody thinks that tribes are getting rich from gaming, and very few of them are."[16]

Two years later, *Time* magazine used statistics from undisclosed sources to make a case for the casino boom's unfairness:

Revenue from gaming is so lopsided that Indian casinos in five states with almost half the Native American population—Montana, Nevada, North Dakota, Oklahoma and South Dakota—account for less than 3% of all casino proceeds. On average, they produce the equivalent of about

$400 in revenue per Indian. Meanwhile, casinos in California, Connecticut and Florida—states with only 3% of the Indian population—haul in 44% of all revenue, an average of $1,000,000 per Indian. In California, the casino run by the San Manuel Band of Mission Indians pulls in well over $100 million a year. That's about $900,000 per member.[17]

According to the same article, the federal government compounded these inequities by conferring money on tribes without regard to economic means, giving more to some wealthy casino tribes than to needy Indians. By 2004, *Washington Post* writer Blaine Harden counted forty-one tribes (out of 562) "raking in 65 percent of all revenue" from casinos. Harden ventured that Lakotas at Pine Ridge, "mired in the old pattern of poverty," had no basis to imagine the clout of the Mashantucket Pequots, "with their stupendously profitable . . . casino." Then he made a rare, provocative comparison: "Income distribution in Indian Country—thanks to gambling—looks more and more like the American mainstream in the 21st century, with increasing wealth concentrated in fewer hands."[18]

University of North Dakota researchers Steven Andrew Light and Kathryn Rand were suspicious of non-Indians who deplored the disparate profitability of tribal casinos. "Indian gaming's detractors, particularly policy makers, contend that they are concerned about the welfare of all Native Americans and merely seek to avoid injustice," Light and Rand noted. "Yet the proposed legislative and administrative responses to the perceived problems associated with tribes like the Pequots are likely to undo the tenuous gains achieved by many gaming tribes at the other pole of the spectrum of success. . . . By failing to adequately take into account the varying circumstances, experiences, and goals of tribes, critics are able to conclude that tribes are either too poor or too rich and thus that Indian gaming works for no tribe."[19] Light and Rand did not compare the critics to Americans in the 1890s who proposed to rectify the Five Civilized Tribes' inequitable land allocation while failing to correct the same problem in the States, but the analogy was arguably apt.

Some disapproving twenty-first-century observers did what the nineteenth-century "reformers" had done: turned the spotlight toward Indians who seemed bent on hogging the moneymaking opportunities that tribal enclaves afforded. The supposed new Indian monopolists were not in the gaming business as private citizens, however; they were officeholders in entrepreneurial tribal governments, maneuvering to block competing Indian businesses. Nowhere was this fight to control the gambling market fiercer, according to the *New York Times*, than San Diego County, where the Viejas Band of Kumeyaay

Indians operated "the state's most lucrative casino" in 2003, and sought to prevent "cousins" in the rival Ewiiaapaayp Band from building one a mile away. The *Times* reporter heard Ewiiaapaayp "spiritual leader" Tony Pinto remark, "They don't want to share. It keeps going this way and there won't be any Indian people before too long."[20]

Pinto may have meant that selfishness was a sign of Indians becoming non-Indian by culture. He could instead have had in mind the efforts of some Indians to limit or trim their tribes' membership rolls, presumably with the aim of minimizing the number of people who would share casino revenues. In moves reminiscent of attempts to purge the Osage roll of gold diggers with dubious tribal ties, factions in several California tribes were blocking or trying to revoke other individuals' membership. Similarly, some groups seeking federal recognition as Indian tribes blamed the opposition of recognized tribes on a desire to corner the local market for gambling.[21]

Charges that greed motivated tribal membership applications, expulsions, and recognition controversies were particularly common in states like California and Connecticut, where the receipts of strategically located casinos were immense, and Indians' history of forced dispersal and federal neglect made it difficult to document tribal lineage. A *Washington Post* report on the subject concluded with the words of a woman dropped from a California band's rolls: "We all got along and the tribe was going good until the casino came up. . . . Everybody started turning ugly. . . . It's like banishment for something we did wrong, but we didn't do anything wrong." "Banished" people traded accusations of avarice with remaining tribe members, and both expressed contempt for opportunists who now wanted to exploit a tribal affiliation they had formerly regarded as a liability.[22] The rising popularity of tribal membership must have seemed familiar to Passamaquoddy Indians who remembered the surge of applications for enrollment that followed their successful land claim in the 1970s.

Arguments also erupted about the allocation of casino receipts within tribes, reflecting a mistrust of centralized political power with antecedents as far back as Creek resentment of Alexander McGillivray's influence. Under the Indian Gaming Regulatory Act, a tribe could spend net gains from gambling enterprises on just five things—government operations, economic development, charitable activities, services from other local governments, or general tribal welfare. Dividing the money equally among members required Interior Department approval of a plan meeting specific statutory criteria, and most tribes chose instead to put all or the vast majority of their profits into public projects.[23] Members often preferred per capita payments, in part because they doubted that their governments would allocate benefits evenhandedly. A Pawnee Business Council candidate wanted 75 percent of casino income meted out; otherwise, he said, officials would "find some way to blow it."[24] Such proposals divided some tribes into distrustful camps, each accusing the other of greed.[25]

As in the 1800s, when chiefs faced accusations of venality, outsiders joined Indians in questioning the integrity and public-mindedness of tribal officers who controlled tribal wealth. After tracing the cash-lubricated connections of several tribes to lobbyists and non-Indian politicians, a journalist took two Seminole leaders to task for living in luxury while tribe members struggled with unemployment and debt. A *Seattle Times* columnist offered criticism similar to that leveled at nineteenth-century Cherokee leaders who financed frequent trips to Washington, D.C., from tribal accounts. If "crippling economic conditions" still prevailed on most reservations, Collin Levey argued, the reason probably lay in the tribal elite's obsession with preserving their special privileges instead of addressing their people's problems. "At the very least," she asked, "shouldn't more of the casino proceeds be flowing back to reinvest in jobs and services for Native Americans instead of spending millions on lobbying and campaign donations?"[26]

Critics cited other reasons to doubt enterprising Indians' concern for equity. Since the poor spent proportionally more than the rich on gambling, they said, tribes with casinos made their money by taking it from customers who could ill afford to use it frivolously.[27] Some people also pronounced it regrettable, even reprehensible, that tribes opted to better their economic condition by diverting money that might otherwise "create jobs and tax revenue elsewhere." In addition, non-Indian politicians said they saw a selfish streak and disdain for the general welfare in negative tribal responses to state requests for hefty portions of casino receipts. When California tribes asked voters to approve a ceiling on the amount of casino profits the state could demand, the governor railed, "The Indians are ripping us off."[28]

Indians who profited from the gambling bonanza were neither deaf to concerns about the tribes' widely varying fortunes nor insensitive to accusations of avarice. Like Cherokee and Creek champions of common landownership in the Gilded Age, they depicted tribal ownership of the new businesses as the best means to perpetuate an Indian tradition of inclusion and sharing. Casino revenue, they said, was financing amenities to which all members of a tribe had equal rights—not only per capita allowances, but also such entitlements as a computer for each family and a scholarship for every member admitted to college. Tribes with abundant gaming income also showed their concern for less fortunate fellow Indians. Some invested in the ventures of poorer tribes or voluntarily passed a portion of their earnings to tribes with less profitable casinos. The NIGA report for 2004 listed several revenue-sharing arrangements among tribes. More than seventy California bands with small-scale operations or none at all received up to $1.1 million each that year from a fund composed of other tribes' receipts.[29]

NIGA spokesmen, perhaps mindful of protesters in the 1970s who equated Indians' unique legal rights with reverse racism, stressed that fortunate tribes were sharing their wealth with non-Indians as well. Chairman Ernest Stevens Jr. elaborated at length on the tribes' contributions to charity in 2004—more than $70 million worth. Stevens's "favorite examples . . . of Tribal generosity" included the small Morongo Band's gift of several thousand Thanksgiving turkeys to nearby needy families and Mdewakanton Sioux subsidies of medical research, substance abuse treatment, a dialysis center, college facilities, and water lines to benefit the general public. "Gaming," Stevens declared on a different occasion, "is bringing prosperity to Indian and non-Indian communities alike nationwide." A NIGA impact report for 2003 supplied figures to back that broad claim, including estimates that casino-linked tribal businesses had generated $5.5 billion in federal revenues and "a windfall" of $1.8 billion for state governments. The NIGA also announced that non-Indians made up approximately 75 percent of the half million people employed in tribal gambling operations.[30]

Other commentators cast a less flattering light on the rewards reaped from tribal casinos. A few were Indians who regretted that much of the money pouring into tribal tills leaked out again because Indian consumers and businesses had to buy supplies and services from non-Indians. Both Indians and non-Indians could also be heard to grumble that many of the gaming boom's direct beneficiaries were Whites, and for sinister reasons. In some cases, they alleged, the ostensible Indian identity of casino owners was fraudulent. And everywhere, predatory Whites, in the Euro-American tradition, were sinking their talons into as much of the new Indian wealth as they could.

Roughly one hundred years earlier, many people said the Civilized Tribes' rich citizens were not Indians but Whites, and Osages complained that people with no Osage ancestry had gained access to the tribe's wealth by finagling their way onto the allotment roll. In the twenty-first century as well, suspicions were rife that tribal gambling business proceeds accrued in many instances to phony Indians. The idea gained traction from the fact that two spectacularly successful casinos in Connecticut belonged to people whose histories and physical appearance did not match common expectations about Indians. During three centuries without federal protection for their communities, many descendants of Mohegans and Pequots had married non-Indians, conformed substantially to Euro-American culture, relinquished most of their lands, and dispersed. Yet in the 1980s, some of those descendants persuaded the U.S. government to acknowledge them and their tribal organizations as successors of the historic tribes—a prerequisite to casino operation on tribal territory.

A *New York Times* critic seemed more bemused than appalled to think that dreams of wealth could rouse blue-eyed blondes and dark-skinned people with nappy hair to claim Indian ancestry and a tribal identity imperceptible to other New Englanders. In a generally positive review of the Mohegan casino's Indian-themed aesthetics, he remarked, "The result may be synthetic, but no more so than the current constitution of the Mohegan tribe itself. Several years ago, Sun International assembled the tribe's scattered descendants and financed their application for recognition by the Federal Government."[31] Other analysts insinuated or flatly asserted that greed-driven deception and self-deception explained the nationwide increase in bids for legal Indian status. Journalist Jeff Benedict, galvanized by personal distaste for the Pequots' grandiose casino, undertook a muckraking probe of their unusual path to federal recognition and concluded there was plenty of reason to doubt the tribe's authenticity. Benedict's book, *Without Reservation*, inspired a segment on the CBS television show *Sixty Minutes*, after which a 2002 *Time* magazine cover story on tribal casinos referred with minimal explanation to the Pequot case as "perhaps the most notorious example" of a tribe's resurrection long after it had ceased to exist.[32]

Wherever lineage could entitle a person to share in casino bounty, there were people on the lookout for non-Indians willing to invent an Indian ancestor or claim a long-disowned one.[33] The ambiguous meaning of "Indian"— the varying mixes of race, culture, descent, and political affiliation that could mark individuals as Indian—contributed to suspicions that White and Black gold diggers were faking Indian identity. *Time*'s cover story promoted that belief by opening with a photo and tale of a dark-skinned woman "raised in Los Angeles in an African-American family" who learned at age twenty-two that her late mother was the last survivor of a Cahuilla Indian band. After two brothers died, she was the only "certified" member of "America's smallest tribe," yet she contracted with a Las Vegas company to build and manage a tribal casino. *Time* underscored its point with a provocative adjective: "Tribal leaders are free to set their own *whimsical* rules for admission, without regard to Indian heritage."[34] Non-Indian gaming mogul Donald Trump, anticipating that Foxwoods would lure customers away from his casinos in New Jersey, insisted that the proof of the Pequots' phoniness was their physical appearance. "I have seen these Indians," Trump told a reporter, "and *you* have more Indian blood than they have."[35] It was virtually the same tactic Georgia governor Wilson Lumpkin used to impugn Cherokee Nation leadership in the early 1800s.

Indians had mixed reactions to disparaging characterizations of the grounds on which people were identified as Indian.[36] Implications that tribal membership criteria were arbitrary discredited Indian sovereignty, and sovereignty's champions reacted sharply, telling outsiders they had no business questioning the tribes' standards for enrollment or their tribal history. Editors of *Indian Country Today* declared, "For all the claims that casino interests are corruptly pushing to 'create' new tribes, the questionable influences we have seen in the recognition process all come from the other direction. . . . Some cynics have even suggested that federally recognized tribes are somehow trying to protect their gaming markets against new entrants. We refuse to believe it. The termination spirit [reflected in criticism of the federal recognition process] is a clear threat to everyone."[37]

Other Indians protested that tribal rolls and the list of recognized tribes were indeed swelling with people who had only economic reasons to claim Indian status. The protesters rarely betrayed a concern that their own share of the gambling market or per capita payments would shrink as born-again Indians cut in. Rather, they warned that recognizing mercenary "wannabes" as Indian would corrupt the meaning and endanger the nonmaterial rewards of Indian identity. The public face of Connecticut Indians seemed all wrong to Delphine Red Shirt, an Oglala Lakota teaching at Yale and Connecticut College in 2001. Red Shirt vented her exasperation in a letter to the *Hartford Courant*. To her, the Pequots, Mohegans, and others looked like they were of European and African stock. "These are not Indians," she declared. "The federal recognition process has become a new arena for profit-making," where "speculators are willing to bankroll these questionable 'tribes' for mutual gain." "What I am witnessing in this casino-made state," Red Shirt concluded, "is a corruption of my heritage. I am outraged by it."[38]

Dubious Indians were not the only profiteers *Time* magazine promised to unmask when exhorting on its cover, "Look Who's Cashing in at Indian Casinos. Hint: It's not the people who are supposed to benefit." The article inside was largely devoted to showing that non-Indians were "extracting hundreds of millions of dollars . . . from casinos they helped to establish, either by taking advantage of regulatory loopholes or cutting backroom deals." Similarly, the *Nation* reported in 1998 that the smell of money on reservations had drawn a school of non-Indian sharks who were taking mighty bites out of casino proceeds. It listed thirteen men getting rich from the tribal casino industry, all but two of them outsiders.[39] Such exposés were a time-honored feature of discourse about Indian wealth. In 1828, 1898, and 1928 as well, people professed disgust at mercenary Whites who insinuated themselves into affluent Indian communities.

To cash in on the tribal gambling business, non-Indians did not have to defraud, steal from, or marry into a tribe, as some White Americans did in the heyday of Indian Territory development. Most people on the *Nation*'s list earned cuts of casino cash by selling services needed to keep the money coming, particularly legal representation, legislative advocacy, and advertising. Over the following years, many other non-Indian lawyers, lobbyists, and media advisors pulled chairs up to tribal tables, expecting a feast.[40] And as in the past, some of the diners bit the Indian hands that fed them. For instance, evidence surfaced in 2004 that a prominent lobbyist and his partner, a public relations consultant, accepted $4.2 million from the Tigua Tribe to wage a campaign in defense of its casino and did not reveal that they had a concurrent contract to help two other tribes thwart the Tigua effort. The incident brings to mind corrupt guardians for oil-rich Osages.[41]

However, it was harder in 2004 than 1924 to find Indians stripped of wealth because they were economically naïve or inexperienced. Aided by collective historical memory, most twenty-first-century Indians were as alert as muckraking journalists or federal overseers to the likelihood that their money would attract predators. Indeed, they were quick to spot wolves at the door. Generally, the wolves they decried were not hucksters or con men hoping to make a killing from vulnerable individuals as so many had done during the Osage oil frenzy. Instead, the packs on the prowl were non-Indian politicians, hungry for public funds.[42]

In 2002, budget troubles prompted Washington State legislators to consider a bill authorizing the expansion of non-Indian-owned gaming enterprises, from which they could collect taxes that tribes did not have to pay. Realizing that the move would undercut tribal businesses, Brian Cladoosby, chairman of the Swinomish Tribe, condemned it as "a repeat of history." "The non-Indians came here and saw all these resources—land, fish—well, those resources are just about destroyed, and now they see gaming. And they want that too." Cladoosby was one of many Indians who sounded the alarm during years when state revenues fell short of budgets and politicians openly salivated for a chunk of the fattening tribal calf. *Indian Country Today* issued a hyperbolical warning in 2004: "States of the Union pull off the surgical gloves and grasp for the butcher knife as governors come after Indian financial gains with

In 2004, when governors in several states pressed Indian tribes for new or increased contributions to state coffers from the tribes' casino proceeds, *Indian Country Today* editorial cartoonist Marty Two Bulls expressed visually the conviction of many Indians that they were witnessing the latest instance in a long historical series of greedy non-Indian schemes to appropriate the best part of Indian wealth. Courtesy of Marty Two Bulls Sr.

a greed lust not seen since the Termination Era of the 1950s." The governor of Pojoaque Pueblo told a congressional committee, "Revenue sharing has become a smokescreen for extortion."[43]

Indians also detected a recurrence of White avarice and treachery when members of Congress showed interest in slowing the growth of the tribal gambling business. Talk of amending the Indian Gaming Regulatory Act prompted tribal leaders to remind lawmakers of "countless compacts . . . written then disregarded in Washington." "We've had 200 years of that process," snapped Timothy Wapato, the NIGA's executive director. A White lawyer for a successful gaming tribe added, "History shows that any time Indians have anything of value there's been people on the non-Indian side ready to take it away."[44] Similar reactions greeted a proposal from Senator Slade Gorton to allocate federal funds for tribes according to need, as indicated by their business ledgers. Tribal spokesmen told the *Seattle Times* that history was the best indicator of Gorton's purpose. "Once Congress knows exactly how much money is made at American Indian casinos, it's only a matter of time before that source of wealth is taken away, just as lands were taken away in the 19th century."[45] They did not mention a more recent sign of reluctance to leave "excessive" wealth in Indian hands—the Supreme Court's imposition in 1979 of a "moderate living" limit on the value of a treaty-reserved resource.

To many Indians, the betrayal they expected seemed imminent by 2004. Non-Indians were objecting to the local impacts of several new and proposed casinos, and Congress was seriously considering legislation that would discourage tribal casinos' proliferation.[46] Was the long history of Whites dispossessing Indians in fact repeating itself? While tribal representatives suggested as much, some opponents said the problem instead was that Indians and non-Indians had reversed their historical roles, and non-Indians had become the victims of Indian greed. This claim rested on the same reasoning as criticism of Indian legal victories in the 1970s: it was unjust to let tribes operate outside laws that constrained everyone else, especially now that Indians were U.S. citizens and the nation was committed to racial equality. "Since when is it the sole right of one group in this case Native Americans to reap the profits of gambling?" asked a supporter of a 2004 Washington State ballot measure that would have eliminated the jurisdictional disadvantage of non-Indian gaming enterprises.[47]

In the century leading up to 2004, Indians' legal status *had* changed significantly, and not only because Congress had conferred citizenship on all Indians born in the United States.[48] Yet Whites at both ends of that time span identified Indians' special treatment under federal law as an injustice to non-Indians. They all complained of losing economic opportunities because the law gave Indians exclusive access to coveted sources of wealth. In the nineteenth and early twentieth centuries, many Americans deemed it unjust to reserve large tracts of real estate for Indians who were not realizing the land's full wealth-generating potential. A century later, when some of the lands remaining to Indians did become sites of significant wealth production, many non-Indians again felt cheated. The apparent incongruity of Indian citizenship and autonomy merely aggravated their resentment—a resentment that Indian sovereignty and control of economic resources had so often aroused in non-Indians since 1492.[49]

Another old habit of thought that retained some vitality in the new millennium was belief in wealth's power to corrupt. Believers watched the suddenly affluent tribal communities for signs that would validate their conviction. The vigil was also a continuation of a long-running deathwatch for Indian culture. Under the influence of the venerable idea that Indians were not traditionally materialistic, non-Indians as well as some Indians readily construed reports of trouble among newly rich Indians as evidence of cultural decline.

A lot of people expected soaring Indian income to be as much a jinx as a joy. Even though Americans were far more inclined in 2000 than in 1800 to measure their personal success in monetary terms, platitudes about money's power to demoralize were part of their philosophical and folkloric heritage, springing easily to mind when problems accompanied a dramatic rise in personal or group wealth. The proverbial association of money with evil also underlay some opposition to gambling. Moralists believed that the siren song issuing from casinos would all too often drown out the voice of conscience. They were not alone in their concern that commercial gambling created many temptations to do wrong. "Both liberal and conservative gambling foes have argued that the spread of casinos has a corrupting effect on politics because so much money is at stake," columnist E. J. Dionne remarked. Some Indian elders advised against casinos for similar reasons, warning that corruption and organized crime could lurk in the shadows of the gambling houses.[50]

Fear of easy money's threat to morals and political ethics merged in many minds with worries about a loss of spiritual bearings. In 2000, believing that preoccupation with material desires was incompatible with piety, the congregation of a small Georgia church gave away most of a $60-million bequest, lest the money "cheapen their faith." Where Indians were concerned, that way of thinking was entwined with belief in an essential link between spirituality and Indian identity, if not Indians' physical survival. One commentator wrote that elderly Indians regarded "the proliferation of gaming" as "a spiritual cancer eating away at what is left of the soul of Native American communities."[51] Navajo Armando Roanhorse worried, "Casinos—with their enormous parking lots, blinding street lamps, and flashy billboards. It seems so misplaced. . . . The beautiful landscapes, skylines, and vegetation are made possible by the frequent prayers and sacrifices of our elders. Giving way to commercialization, urbanization, and above all, capitalism will only prove fatal to us."[52]

Like Roanhorse, Anishinaabe writer Marty Firerider identified the principal threat to Indians in 2005 as an invasive non-Indian value system. "Gaming has brought in the dominant culture's disease of greed," Firerider declared. That analysis had other advocates as well. Apropos of a controversy about economic strategy in the Oneida Nation, self-described Mohawk traditionalist Doug George-Kanentiio told a reporter, "We were given a series of warnings about what would happen to us—the Iroquois people—if we adopted European attitudes toward wealth. . . . It would lead to chaos and corruption and conflict." The views of these three men would have made sense to Creek traditionalists a century earlier. Regarding the scramble for wealth in the Indian Territory then, a character created by Creek satirist Alexander Posey commented simply, "Injuns was not like that."[53]

Many non-Indians also subscribed to the notion that property accumulation was a Euro-American culture trait whose appearance among Indians portended the disintegration of the indigenous societies. Journalists—always interested in conflict—crafted stories that reflected and reinforced this assumption. It was rare for a reporter to cover a tribe's economic triumphs without mentioning "dark twists" in the "road to riches" and quoting community members who felt that their compatriots, succumbing to greed, had abandoned the Indian way. A *Texas Monthly* writer judged that a feud about Tigua tribal membership was at heart "a fight for the soul of the tribe, which some believe has been corrupted by sudden, wild wealth."[54]

In contrast, and in line with the sentiments of many a historical Cherokee and Osage, some Indians had no patience with assertions that it was un-Indian and unseemly to embrace commercial activity and affluence. The *Denver Post* ran a letter from one of them under the heading "Can't Indians Be Successful?" Novelist, poet, and filmmaker Sherman Alexie was a trenchant critic of the idea that Indians should prefer poverty to casino revenues. After describing (with tongue in cheek) a visit to the casino on the Spokane Reservation, his boyhood home, Alexie wrote, "I've heard it said that Indians shouldn't become involved in high-stake gambling because it tarnishes our noble heritage. Personally, I've never believed in the nobility of poverty. Personally, I believe in the nobility of breakfast, lunch and dinner. Indians need money." His words conveyed the same idea expressed by Navajo leader Peter MacDonald in 1985: tribal capitalism was a necessary antidote to hunger and chronic poverty.[55]

Indians did need money, many agreed, and needed it partly so they could preserve their cultural heritage. Anthropologist Jessica Cattelino found that Florida Seminoles did not see themselves sacrificing tradition on the altar of economic exigency when they established casinos; they saw their business income as a means to underwrite the preservation of their distinctive lifeway.[56] Other Indians likewise expected casino money to help them fend off threats to their culture, not the least of which was poverty. Yavapai president Patricia McGee impressed a *Wall Street Journal* reporter with her understanding "that economic development and a healthy private sector reinforce rather than undermine traditional tribal values. Economic freedom fosters pride and independence and brings in precious dollars for language programs, schools, and museums." Prosperity also bolstered tradition by enticing self-exiled tribe members back to reservations where they could take part in community activities.[57] According to the NIGA, because the new businesses made tribal philanthropy possible, they also perpetuated an Indian tradition of measuring people's wealth "not by how much they have, but by how much they give away." Even gambling was an Indian tradition, said NIGA's Timothy Wapato, whereas reservation poverty was the product of government policies in the modern era.[58]

These arguments did not assuage the doubts of Indians such as Marty Firerider, who agreed that "numerous tribes have preserved their culture and language due to gaming monies" but lamented nonetheless that affluence had corrosive effects on Indian values and solidarity. "The elders rarely meet anymore," he claimed, and some young adults forget that "without the bonds of family and community, an individual has no worth." Shaunna McCovey's radical position on the issue reflected her equation of Indian identity with economic otherness. "I would like to . . . look at poverty and inequality as necessary for us to continue as Indian peoples," the Yurok/Karuk scholar wrote. "Had we been granted lives of upper- or middle-class luxury would we have continued to be as strong culturally as we are today? . . . Being labeled poor has allowed us to remember how to dance and sing in a traditional way, and for this we are rich. Being thought of as unequal has forced us to rely on our knowledge of culture to survive, and this knowledge is wealth."[59]

Did Firerider correctly perceive that affluence was weakening Indians' commitment to shunning or sharing material wealth? Some observers detected no appreciable erosion of that ethos even after enthusiasm for tribal casinos had taken hold. In 1999, an academic researcher described Indian economic culture in terms remarkably similar to studies from the 1960s, when scholars were trying to account for the tribes' stubbornly high rates of poverty. He found that "value systems on reservations remain[ed] markedly different" from those in the Euro-American world, except among off-reservation civil servants and acculturated mixed-bloods who negotiated with outsiders on the tribes' behalf. Largely because of "a highly developed collective consciousness," income and property still garnered a person little admiration. Instead, a "mutual willingness to give help and to share material goods was . . . an important measure" of an individual's or family's prestige.[60]

Yet in operating twenty-first-century businesses, Indians were performing a culture unknown in America before 1492. When they established and ran casinos, they necessarily observed some norms that originated with Europeans and deviated in key respects from the stated value systems of many tribal communities. If the number of Indian-owned businesses climbed from "less than a handful" in 1969 to 360,000 in 2005, as estimated by the National Center for American Indian Enterprise Development, then thousands of Indians in 2005 had adopted behavior they did not learn from observing an older generation of Indians.[61] For them, that could mean more than dealing blackjack instead of fishing or raising corn as grandfathers and grandmothers did. It could effectively rearrange personal and social priorities. The manager of the Swinomish Tribe's casino told a *Seattle Times* reporter, "There are things I have to do, culturally, that I give up because I have to get to work. . . . Service to the community is a huge cultural value. . . . It is a way of life. It takes priority over everything. If a family member needs you, you help them. . . . This (gaming) industry has changed that dramatically." And a Mohawk business owner told the *Detroit News* she was trying to strike a balance between an Indian prohibition against taking more than she needed and the capitalist precept that more is always better.[62]

Whether or not they strived for such a balance, Indians who presided over their tribes' lucrative new ventures appeared to understand and embrace essential aspects of capitalist culture. A professional stock analyst pronounced the tribes' "ability to adapt to gambling 'nothing short of overwhelming,'" and an employee of the Washington State gambling commission described Muckleshoot tribal negotiators as "very businesslike." When four gaming-rich tribes announced plans to open a hotel in Washington, D.C., they explained the move in the language of corporate America: the aim was to maximize the tribes' resources both on and off reservation by capitalizing on their growing business expertise.[63] Furthermore, as tribe members became mindful of the habits, knowledge, and hierarchy of values required for success in commercial ventures, many committed themselves to train and socialize their offspring accordingly. An Oneida man, pleased with the income from his job at the tribe's casino in Wisconsin, said his children would "probably need master's degrees in business. . . . Law degrees wouldn't hurt either." In tribe after tribe with gambling profits to spend, making it financially feasible for members to get college and professional degrees became a priority.[64]

Thus, tribal capitalism had the potential to reverse the relationship between economic activities and tradition. In the past, as Cattelino found in the Seminole case, Indians could adopt alien economic practices and quickly refigure them as tribal tradition. Whether the same would be true of practices adopted in the twenty-first century was unclear when Cattelino published her findings in 2004. Would the newest activities change the core of the tribe's identity instead? Like many other Indians, Seminoles had long been taught to "despise the man who lives rich"; but if their soaring incomes deprived that saying of meaning, would other defining aspects of Seminole society lose meaning and salience as well?[65] By 2005, questions such as these were nagging at many other Indians communities. Would capitalist culture or exponential increases in wealth overpower an ethos that had served Indians well in ages gone by, when the material abundance of the twenty-first century was unimaginable? Could the teachings of elders or the exhortations of tribal officials inspire adherence to Indian ancestors' spiritual and social priorities if the success of tribal businesses depended on conformity in many respects to a materialistic ethos? In the dialectic between the profit-oriented mainstream

American culture and an inherited Indian culture that valued social solidarity over material wealth, which would ultimately prove dominant? Which would define Indian societies?

The business ventures and the vast tribal revenues that raised these questions were new for most Indians, but the questions, in essence, were not. Think, for instance, of the nineteenth-century Americans who predicted that the experience of improving and farming private allotments would effect a wholesale change in Indians' culture. Those American reformers presumed that Indians would adapt their values and ultimately their conception of human relations to their restructured economic relations and, with that adaptation, become something other than Indian. The growth of tribal gaming enterprises promised to test once again that belief about the relationship of culture and identity to economic practice.

Some people maintained that each Indian tribe would meet the test in its own way—in other words, that every tribe's economic strategy would by definition be an Indian strategy. Historically, after all, strategic adaptation was as much "the Indian way" as honoring age-old traditions.[66] But no matter how confidently the enterprising tribes represented their rapidly changing societies as Indian, they would face doubters. They would face questions like the one noted by Paul Pasquaretta, author of *Gambling and Survival in Native North America*: "In the new tribal world of consumer economics, federal subsidies, and wage labor, what can be recognized as authentically Indian?" Upon reading in *Fortune* that Indians were increasingly "determined to regain their independence and dignity by . . . working hard, raising capital, and getting not mad but rich," some people would wonder whether Indian culture was coming to be defined by what money could buy. If certain distinctive economic tendencies long attributed to Indians were no longer evident, some observers would also question the rationale for delimiting Indian societies with special laws and lands. And when Indians asserted, as Ernest Stevens did, that money from tribal gaming enterprises gave them "a chance to grab onto the 'American dream,'" they would surely hear non-Indians ask why Indians should have a legal status unlike that of other American dreamers.[67] If such questioners became numerous and vocal, tribes in the twenty-first century—like Creek ranchers of the 1890s or tribes slated for termination in the 1950s—might find themselves fighting off efforts to topple the protective legal fence around Indians so that non-Indians could more easily get at the wealth accumulating there.

The possibility of such an assault prompted tribes to adopt political tactics as paradoxical and potentially subversive of tradition as their economic initiatives. To protect the right of self-government that enabled them to underwrite tribal culture with profits from corporate enterprises, many Indians stepped up their participation in politics outside Indian country. Like enterprising members of the Civilized Tribes in the 1820s, they reached the conclusion that their hope of preserving separate governments and economic resources rested on influencing governments other than their own. But this time, Indians had unprecedented means to exert influence.

As tribes climbed the ranks of American entrepreneurs, they realized that their swelling treasuries could enable them to gain on non-Indians in another domain as well. At state and national levels, Indians proved willing to spend casino profits for political favors and campaigns, thereby jumping into another sort of high-stakes game. "Native Americans have come of age politically," the *Albuquerque Journal* declared in coverage of a National Congress of American Indians conference in 2003. "At the top of the [NCAI] agenda was protection of tribal sovereignty. But the horsepower pushing this platform is the profit from Indian casinos used to leverage newfound political clout. . . . Tribes are shelling out millions in political campaign contributions. . . . And money may well talk louder than the potential ballots of an estimated 1.5 million Native American voters. . . . Ignoring their needs and aspirations isn't a choice for politicians anymore."[68] In the following years, tribes boosted their donations to campaigns, and media attention kept pace.[69] After Washington State tribes gave twenty-one times more in 2004 than in 2002, a local business journal solicited comments from David Wilkins, a university professor and Lumbee Tribe member. Wilkins replied that gaming revenue was "changing the landscape fundamentally," enabling Indians to throw their weight around as never before "and on a scale that is completely unique." A spokesman for California Common Cause said, "The tribes were invisible until they started writing checks. There is no better illustration of the power of money in politics."[70]

In some instances, the tribes' contributions to political causes and candidates were meant specifically to protect gaming profits, but often they reflected interest in broader issues. Tribal money helped substantially with the cost of a successful campaign to deny Washington senator Gorton reelection in 2000, not because of his stance on casinos, but because he had shown a desire to curtail tribes' governmental powers. A Suquamish spokesman explained that Indians, whose voting rate was heading steeply upward, sought candidates supportive of their sovereignty.[71] Other tribal representatives confirmed that the overriding aim of their political expenditures was to protect sovereignty, which was a prerequisite of operating casinos and the ultimate purpose of the casinos. "The real issue is not gaming, and tribal leaders know this in a profound way," said a veteran of tribal politics in California. "The issue is that Native American tribes are governments and gaming is hooked up to the . . . right to self-government."[72] Tribes were using their money to gain power in state, local, and national political arenas, but they wanted that power in order to maintain governments of their own that were largely insulated from state, local, or federal interference. UCLA professors Carole Goldberg and Duane Champagne pronounced this strategy a success in California as of 2002. "In attaining political power through gaming," they wrote, "California tribes may have developed a stronger conception of their sovereignty" while creating an economic base that made it "easier to implement their sovereignty, establishing sovereign realities 'on the ground' that change[d] options for both state and federal governments."[73]

There was a caveat to the tribes' achievement, however—a reason to wonder whether the changes in state and federal options would be permanent. Indians felt the need for involvement in politics outside their tribes because the United States had the power to curtail tribal sovereignty and even abolish tribes altogether. People who resented the tribes' agenda could press national lawmakers for changes in the very legal status that made casinos and their tax-free profits possible. David Wilkins was one of many analysts who warned of such a possibility. Indians' new assertiveness, he cautioned, "might come back to haunt us." The legal foundation of the tribes' newfound political influence might come under attack from people convinced "that we're all bronze-skinned Donald Trumps."[74] In that event, would Indians' cash-fueled strength hold? Money had boosted their political power significantly, but was that power now great and secure enough to protect its own source? After nearly two centuries of vulnerability to U.S. power, did Indians finally have the means to deflect assaults on their coveted sovereign status and economic resources?

Opposition to the tribes' growing clout had already surfaced when Wilkins spoke of it. By 2004, tribal power to affect regional conditions angered neighbors of Indians from California to Connecticut. Plans to expand a Chumash casino precipitated a collision with other residents of the Santa Ynez Valley. The clash appeared extraordinary to a *Los Angeles Times* reporter "in part because the Chumash, once impoverished and powerless, can now match the political and financial muscle of their adversaries." But the casino's original manager said, "I saw the [surrounding] community's attitude change from one of contempt to respect to jealousy. . . . The feeling was, it's OK for them to be successful. Just don't be too successful."[75] Muckleshoot Indians drew the same conclusion from their neighbors' attempt to block the tribe's construction of a major music performance venue. Tribe members quipped that "it was much easier to like the Indians . . . when they were visible only at annual salmon ceremonies." After a Tulalip Indian won election to the Washington State legislature in 2003, the defeated non-Indian opined that the tribes had too much money and thus too much power. That fall, the *Los Angeles Times* spotlighted a woman bent on persuading the public that "'fundamentalist tribal leaders' armed with an antique notion of sovereignty and huge gambling profits" wielded "undue influence" over state politics, their ultimate goal being to "seize control of California public policy and retake lands lost more than a century ago."[76]

Once again, as in the 1970s, the word "backlash" peppered public discourse about Indians. A San Francisco reporter predicted a backlash "against California's latest gold rush: Indian gaming." Tribes and "local communities across the state" were "butting heads . . . over issues of sovereignty, ethics, regulatory power and Big Money." The tribes' "clout and arrogance" seemed to mushroom along with their wealth, the writer commented, but they would be well advised not to forget that "Indian sovereignty is limited by Congress and the U.S. Supreme Court." *Indian Country Today* editors also sensed a backlash "emboldened" by recent Supreme Court rulings. The Court in turn had "abandoned legal principle because of emotional fears whipped up by . . . anti-sovereignty propaganda." As the "cash flow from gaming . . . allowed tribes to repurchase a land base and give substance to their sovereignty," a common reaction was "to wish Indians out of existence as self-governing peoples."[77]

Many complaints about excessive tribal power were not addressed to the tribes. Instead, as was often true from the 1820s through the 1970s, non-Indians argued with each other about Indian policy, revealing an assumption that Indians were pawns in others' rivalries. "In the theater of the absurd known as California Indian gaming," one commentator wrote, "Native Americans have become little more than human props in the high-stakes battle involving real estate developers, powerful consultants, and out-of-state gaming interests." Syndicated columnist Rich Lowry implied that the tribes' access to the corridors of power depended on devious non-Indians who were building their own power base. "GOP politicians and lobbyists now milk casino-hungry Indians in turn," he alleged.[78] These were updated versions of an old refrain. Non-Indians still found it is easy to believe that Indians were greedy but hard to believe that they were smart enough to engineer sophisticated ways of satisfying their greed.

Lowry's comment pointed to questions that could ultimately decide whether casino proceeds and the wealth they begot would represent decisive, lasting power for Indians—power sufficient to foil outsiders' designs on that wealth. Did or could the tribes' economic activity earn them non-Indian allies likely to help them keep what they had? Could numerous voters and politicians be convinced that enterprising tribes were a force for the well-being of non-Indian Americans? Would a critical mass of Americans finally see wealthy Indians not as a problem but as welcome benefactors?

Indians had reason to foresee affirmative answers to these questions. Many casinos were major employers, recreational attractions, and donors to local governments and nonprofits. The Oneida Nation's mammoth operation rescued the surrounding area of upstate New York from economic doldrums. As of 2005, the tribe employed 4,200 people, 97 percent of them non-Indian. By then, the Siletz tribal casino was the biggest employer in Lincoln County, Oregon, and the small Muckleshoot Tribe's diverse workforce of 2,550 was the second largest in south King County, Washington, outnumbered only at Boeing aircraft assembly plants. Four tribal casinos near Minnesota cities provided more jobs than any other employers in their respective vicinities. Facts such as these went a long way toward explaining why tribes secured the blessing of state officials and voters for their casinos. California voters, for example, approved ballot measures legalizing slot machines in tribal establishments. According to Professors Goldberg and Champagne, the tribes "gained considerable support from local groups and organizations through significant redistribution of gaming profits."[79]

Here and there, non-Indians with power of their own corroborated that assessment, prompting *Fortune* reporter Jerry Useem to call them a "fan base" for tribes whose enterprises were reviving local economies. The mayor of Philadelphia, Mississippi, for one, proclaimed, "Our best industry by far is the Choctaw Nation. . . . If the tribe went bankrupt, we'd go into a depression." Several California counties acknowledged their dependence on distributions from Indian casino proceeds to meet acute local needs. Banks acquired a stake in tribes' success when they financed ancillary businesses serving visitors to Indian reservations, and universities warmed to Indian entrepreneurship when prospering tribes contributed money for professorships and programs in fields of interest to them.[80]

Surveying such developments at the end of 2004, *Indian Country Today* began on a positive note:

American Indians, always on the media margins, grow in relevance with the growth of financial means. The concept of Native tribal rights has been projected into the public discourse as tens of millions of mainstream Americans visit and spend both time and money at Native-owned casinos.

American Indian tribal political power, for decades a mere concept, now asserts itself with economic clout. This is new. Indian people, the most fiercely independent of Americans because of their inherent and pre-existing governmental sovereignty, are now found among the country's economic power brokers.

But the editorial changed course abruptly. Be forewarned, it said, that "the tribes are being recast again as America's enemies in a manipulated, and sometimes compliant, media as despicable 'rip-offs' and greedy 'special interests.'" Opposition groups are "more sophisticated than ever and tied in to larger political machines."[81] Casinos had brought wealth so great that the balance of power was tipping farther in Indians' favor than they had known for many generations, but the new balance was precarious. To understand how insecure their control of wealth could be, Indians had only to think of their history.

This book considers a handful of episodes in that long history. Indigenous North Americans have experienced instances of significant affluence besides those featured here, and a bigger book might have examined several more. It might have focused on the Pacific Northwest Coast, where native people increased their ceremonial distributions of accumulated wealth as trade with Europeans and Euro-Americans enriched them. It might have analyzed a class of Navajos who prospered in an economy based on the sheep and horses that Europeans introduced. Even with those additions or others, however, a collection of discrete case studies could not be the basis for general conclusions about the changing role of wealth among the diverse peoples now known as American Indians. Nor would it tell a comprehensive story of Euro-American responses to affluent Indians, notwithstanding its 400-year time scope. Rather, additional studies would heighten the challenge of finding a narrative thread in a long, multifaceted history.

On one hand, then, the lessons this book can impart are necessarily limited and provisional. On the other hand, the central lesson to be learned is an important one. These seven stories confirm that Indians' possession of substantial wealth has repeatedly prompted both Indians and non-Indians to define, debate, and take action on some of the most vexing issues of their intertwined histories, and in particular, to address moral issues that underlie economic relations. The stories also show why those issues have endured into the twenty-first century.

Controversies triggered by Indian wealth have been freighted with moral questions because of their origin in the morally debatable European colonization of North America. In early encounters of Europeans and indigenous Americans—despite differences in the forms and sources of their wealth and their ways of organizing economic relations—both peoples readily identified many of each other's possessions as riches and sought relations that would afford opportunities to acquire riches from each other. However, because colonization could not proceed without appropriation of local resources, the presence of native people who might need or want the same resources put the righteousness of the colonial project at issue. Belief in the moral superiority of European economic culture enabled colonists to rationalize what they did. As they devised justifications for systematically helping themselves when possible to New World wealth, their relations with "Indians" took on an offensive character. Indians then had corresponding reasons to denigrate and demonize the intruders' economic culture.

Perceptions of difference between the economic cultures sharpened and took firm hold in both populations as a consequence of their struggles for wealth. Some perceptions reflected differences we can verify—differences in whether and how Europeans and Indians encouraged the accumulation or redistribution of wealth, and differences in wealth's social functions. But the competition to control vital resources prompted people to believe, or say they believed, in greater disparities between the economic cultures than the evidence probably justified. By attributing moral significance to those ascribed differences and to the colonial takeover, both non-Indians and Indians gave themselves reasons to embrace some differences and reasons to be uneasy at times when differences seemed to narrow.

Although some Euro-Americans gave full rein to their lust for Indian wealth, usually justifying such actions with bald claims of White superiority, Euro-Americans as a whole have not necessarily intended by their quests for wealth to make Indians poor. However, the creation and growth of profitable colonies was premised on subordinating Indians to colonial interests. In the long run, that objective could be achieved only by suppressing or restricting indigenous sovereignty, and sovereignty was the basis for Indian control of vital resources. Controlling vital resources was in turn a requisite of Indian sovereignty.[82] Various Indians—from Joseph Brant and John Ross in the early nineteenth century to those who formed the Consortium of Energy Resource Tribes in the 1970s—concluded that their nations' or tribes' existence depended on the acquisition, generation, or preservation of substantial wealth.

That conclusion raised a provocative question: whether the goal of economic strength could best or only be realized by adopting an economic ethos akin to the dominant, profit-oriented ethos of Euro-Americans.

Thus, at the heart of discourse about wealthy and wealth-seeking Indians have been two interrelated issues: Indian sovereignty and the role of economic culture in Indians' survival as distinct peoples. Even when couched in moral terms, much of the commentary on affluent Indians has been about power. Hostility to accumulations of wealth in Indian hands has often reflected fear of excess power, and not only non-Indian fear. In Native societies with a tradition of diffuse political leadership conditioned on generosity and reciprocity, some Indians have been apprehensive or resentful when individuals gained unprecedented influence by amassing wealth, thereby presenting difficult new questions about the relationship of power to wealth.

Settler colonists achieved control over Indian resources through a mutually reinforcing interplay of power and wealth, with power as the decisive factor. In the face of Euro-American power based on overwhelming population numbers, centralized and institutionalized political governance, and an ideology of superiority that justified forceful suppression of nonconformity, Indians could not retain wealth coveted by colonizers. Although many Indian nations did win grudging acknowledgment of their sovereignty from the United States, they eventually had insufficient power to prevent the American republic from imposing limits on that sovereignty. Their access to wealth came to depend on laws that Euro-Americans made and that Euro-Americans could change. Until the late twentieth century, most U.S. law concerning American Indians served to bring tribal economic resources under non-Indian ownership or control, with the result that Indian societies were impoverished. To preserve or gain wealth in those circumstances, Indians had to appeal to principles that Euro-Americans espoused and purported to serve by their laws, including the principle of honoring solemn agreements.

From Euro-American perspectives, promoting Indian adoption of an economic culture based in Euro-American principles was an alternative to tolerating Indian sovereignty. Converts to a culture of individual self-sufficiency and private property accumulation could presumably be enticed or made to disperse and find personal roles in the colonial economy. Because economic culture was an essential element of the moral superiority that Euro-Americans claimed for their civilization, conversions could also validate that claim while bringing Indian labor and wealth more directly and securely under Euro-American control. Ironically, however, if Indians resisted domination and incorporation—and most did—they offered opportunities to prove Euro-

American superiority in another way: by forcible conquest. Even more ironically, the material success of Indians who did copy Euro-American economic practices could stimulate the colonial appetite for wealth, and thus perpetuate the inclination to rationalize Indians' dispossession by characterizing their economic practices as unacceptably aberrant. At the same time, however, successful enterprising Indians effectively held a mirror to Euro-American economic culture, and in that event, they could prompt some non-Indians to doubt the supposed virtues of economic individualism.

For Indians, emulating or participating in the colonial economy has sometimes been an onerous necessity and sometimes a response to attractive opportunities. But whatever its motivation, that course of action has been subject to challenge as endangering Indian societies, and not only from Indians concerned about betrayal of aboriginal ideals such as reciprocity and generosity. Some Euro-Americans have also lamented Indians' apparent renunciation of those ideals. Acculturation has been problematic because of its contradictory implications for Indian autonomy. Tribes were hard-pressed to generate the resources necessary for effective sovereignty without some concessions to Euro-American economic culture. United States acceptance of Indian autonomy, however, was premised in part on Indians' cultural otherness, and diminished cultural differences could trigger Euro-American denials of Indian sovereignty. Cherokees in the nineteenth century and many tribal governments in the late twentieth century adopted methods of generating wealth recommended by Euro-Americans and experienced rising prosperity as a result, but this did not forestall objections from Euro-Americans who recognized the new wealth's power to underwrite sovereignty.

Thus, by conspicuous gains in wealth, Indians have not only triggered normative comparisons of Indian and Euro-American economic practices; they have also raised questions about the morality of making, inducing, or forcing culture change that could threaten a people's very existence as a distinct society. Due to Euro-Americans' frequent praise for an ethic of private wealth accumulation, and their insistence that Indians abandon Indian ways, tribe members who appeared to emulate Euro-American economic practices have faced doubts about their Indianness. In either justifying or renouncing the systematic pursuit of significant wealth, Indians have had to articulate not only their ethical and social ideals but also their conceptions of Indian identity.

Indian identity became ambiguous and debatable in large part because of relations occasioned by quests for economic opportunity, and economic conduct in turn became one possible marker of Indian identity. As a consequence of relations linking Indian and colonial economies, racial and cultural distinctions blurred in places, especially where there was significant wealth to be had. In several of the cases considered here, the race and culture of enterprising tribe members were ambiguous due to their dual Indian and Euro-American ancestry—the result of unions that secured economic advantages to the partners and their kin. Many people attributed the economic ambition of those bicultural individuals to their White ancestry or questioned their Indianness because of their aspirations. Emerging class differentiations between more and less enterprising tribe members reinforced this tendency to see economic culture as an indicator of identity. In the 1820s, when southeastern tribes counted on their adoption of "civilized" economic practices to appease White neighbors' hostility, the contrast between a tiny minority of rich tribe members and a large majority of poor ones was fuel for Whites' argument that most members remained "real" Indians, devoted to an economic culture incompatible with civilization.

For non-Indians who expected Indians to disappear as distinct, autonomous peoples after forsaking their traditional culture, it has been confounding to see Indians adopt "civilized" economic practices in order to bolster their autonomy and prevent their disappearance. That has been a major reason for eruptions of controversy concerning affluent Indians. It partially explains the movement to reverse Indians' late-twentieth-century economic gains, for example. The movement tapped into two related assumptions—an assumption that cultural distinctiveness was a basis for the "special" rights that made Indian economic gains possible, and an assumption that wealth-seeking was not a characteristic of traditional Indian culture. Having apparently lost their distinctive economic culture, modern wealth-seeking Indians faced the contention that they should have lost their special rights as well. The opposition to those rights was grounded in the additional belief that Indian tribal autonomy was obsolete, not only because of culture change, but also because of Indians' admission to American citizenship and its assurance of legal equality.[83] These ideas combined to infuse the controversy about Indian economic aims with distinctive moral content.

In sum, ambivalence has been a continual hallmark of reactions to enterprising Indians. There have been people with reason to regard Indian economic conduct as aberrant rather than admirable whether the Indians were poor or prosperous. Both Indians and non-Indians have vacillated in their approach to perceived differences in the two peoples' economic cultures, sometimes trying to narrow the differences, sometimes displaying unease with the consequences of doing so. At bottom, it is this ambivalence that accounts for the persistence of controversies about rich Indians. Dogged by criticism or poverty when they have not been enterprising, some Indians have taken the alternate course, only to meet with other criticism and threats, internal as well as external. From many chapters of their history, Indians could reasonably conclude that they were damned if they did get rich and damned if they did not.

It is no wonder that doubts about the compatibility of Indian and non-Indian economic aims have persisted into the present. Contrasting characterizations of Indian and Euro-American economic cultures have had staying power and have sometimes been self-fulfilling, not only because of their moral connotations, but also because they have served economic and political interests and psychological needs. Whether Euro-Americans worked at converting Indians to a Euro-American economic ethic or declared that Indians were incapable of such a conversion, it was with an expectation of serving their own material interests and validating their own culture. As they appropriated resources that Indians required to prosper, many Euro-Americans interpreted Indians' widespread impoverishment as confirmation of cultural or racial deficiencies. Federal guardianship and services necessitated by Indians' poverty then reinforced the image of Native Americans as anomalous economic actors.

To Indians, meanwhile, their impoverishment became proof of White people's greed and disdain for the life-sustaining ethic of reciprocity. Some Euro-Americans, uneasy with the adverse effects of their society's greater materialism, agreed; they interpreted Indians' poverty as evidence of adherence to more admirable ideals, such as spirituality and generosity. Many Indians have taken satisfaction in the implication that their humble material circumstances reflected values at odds with the self-interested accumulation of Euro-Americans. At times, Indian appeals for economic aid have exploited Euro-Americans' discomfort with this implication.

The ideology of race that gained widespread acceptance by the 1800s also worked to perpetuate beliefs in a fundamental conflict between Indian and Euro-American economic ethics. It reinforced a tendency to think of the two peoples' behavior patterns as innate and enduring. Once "race" came to denote a person's inescapable propensities, capabilities, and limitations grounded in lineage and the human body, most Euro-Americans and many Indians imagined a link between Indian ancestry and a particular economic orientation. They were inclined to explain the acquisitiveness of some Indian tribe members as a trait that came with White ancestry or as evidence of the Indians' manipulation by Whites. Due in large part to this conflation of economic culture with racial identity, it became common to assume or pretend either that race was a predictor of enterprise or that economic conduct and status were markers of race. Whenever putative Indians underwent scrutiny for their economic conduct, other Indians as well as non-Indians judged them in light of their of their ascribed racial identity and its supposed implications.

Given the substantial stakes in controversies about Indian economic practices, it is unsurprising that many moral pronouncements on the subject have been of dubious sincerity. Ulterior motives are easy to detect in the historical record, particularly when self-righteous speakers obviously disregarded pertinent information or when their conduct did not conform to their own professed standards. The record of hypocrisy and greed is especially clear and extensive for Euro-Americans. The deprivation that their colonization and expansion ultimately visited on Indians is reason enough to subject their statements about wealthy Indians to skeptical examination.

Indians have done that, of course, calling Euro-Americans on their hypocrisy many a time. And unlike Euro-Americans, who have had fewer incentives to understand Indian economic morality than to demonize it, Indians have had a practical need to understand the ideals of the people wielding power over them. Endorsing and appealing to Euro-American ideals has been a significant part of Indian strategies to protect tribal resources. Yet Indians have also defended or promoted their own interests with disingenuous arguments at times, or they have let contests for resources distract them from the difficult task of honestly assessing their adherence to their own principles. As the Five Civilized Tribes learned in the Gilded Age, Indians have had little chance to reevaluate their economic ideals and practices in isolation, without regard to Euro-American aims. From at least the time of the United States' creation, Euro-American presence and power compelled Indians to strike a balance between honestly critiquing their own economic morality and defending their economic choices against attacks by any available means. For this reason if no other, taking Indian commentary at face value is inadvisable.

The history of reactions to Indians with substantial wealth is far from a simple morality tale of voracious Whites and their Indian victims. Granted, non-Indians who schemed to get control of Indian wealth make appearances in every chapter of this book, whereas only the sixth chapter describes concerted Indian action with the arguable objective of dispossessing non-Indians. But these stories also feature some non-Indians who looked at Indians' circumstances, saw things that made them anxious about their own society's wrongdoing, and announced their commitment to economic justice for Indians. Indians have even gained or retained a little wealth through the operation of Euro-American institutions, often with the help of Euro-Americans themselves. Conversely, some Indians have opened themselves to charges of greed even as they directed such charges at non-Indians. Acknowledging pervasive Euro-American greed or hypocrisy does not absolve those Indians who may have committed the same sins, whether or not they lost the struggle for wealth. No group in these stories had a monopoly on avarice, and no group was a band of selfless idealists. However, present-day Indians who fear losing wealth to Whites can cite a historical record that Whites who warn of grasping Indians cannot match. In light of the fact that Euro-Americans have wielded their power far more often to Indians' economic detriment than to their advantage, non-Indian expressions of alarm about recent tribal gains seem greatly exaggerated.

Hypocrisy and self-deception notwithstanding, controversies about Indian wealth have been dignified at times by meaningful discourse on important moral issues. Issues have included the virtues and perils of the private profit motive; the responsibilities of the powerful and wealthy to others in their community, nation, or power; the measures of fair economic opportunity and reward; the moral obligations arising from historical injustice; and the relative importance of such common American ideals as affording all citizens of a nation the same civic rights, honoring old promises, and respecting different beliefs. For every position on one of these issues that was cynically calibrated to serve selfish interests, there has been someone willing to contest it, and the ensuing debates reveal efforts on both sides to quiet uneasy consciences. Inherent in every debate—intercultural or intracultural— has been a possibility of finding common ideological or moral ground between Indians and non-Indians. Neither Indians nor non-Indians could judge the others' economic dreams without also judging their own dreams.

Notes

Abbreviations

AP	Associated Press
ARCIA	U.S. Department of the Interior, *Annual Report of the Commissioner of Indian Affairs*. Washington, D.C.: Government Printing Office.
BIA	U.S. Bureau of Indian Affairs
CNP	Cherokee Nation Papers (microform)
CRSC	*Colonial Records of South Carolina: Documents Relating to Indian Affairs*
CRSG	*Colonial Records of the State of Georgia*
ICT	*Indian Country Today*
NYT	*New York Times*
U.S. House	House of Representatives
WHC	Western History Collections, University of Oklahoma, Norman

Introduction

1. Andrew Hacker, "Good or Bad, Greed Is Often Beside the Point," *NYT*, 8 June 1997, p. 43.

2. Krugman, *Great Unraveling*, 220–21; David Brooks, "Voters Don't Resent the Rich," *Seattle Post-Intelligencer*, 17 Jan. 2003, p. B7 (emphasis in original).

3. Marty Firerider, *ICT*, 25 May 2005, p. A3.

4. "Indians as Thieves," *ICT*, 3 Nov. 2004, p. A2. See also Susannah Rosenblatt, *Los Angeles Times*, 10 July 2003, p. A21.

5. "Indians as Thieves," *ICT*, 3 Nov. 2004, p. A2; Timothy Egan, "Now, a White Backlash against Rich Indians," *NYT*, 7 Sept. 1997, p. 43. I capitalize "White" when it designates a category equivalent to "Indian" or "Native American"—a racial or ethnic category that has never been self-defining, static, or identified by skin that is/was actually white. The designation became common by the late 1700s, as did "Indian" as a term for various descendants of America's original inhabitants.

6. David Cournoyer, "Can't Indians Be Successful?," *Denver Post*, 7 June 2000, p. B11; Dave Palermo, "Hopi Forgo Gaming to Preserve Way of Life," *ICT*, 18 Aug. 2004, p. A5.

7. One result of research to answer those questions: Alexandra Harmon, "American Indians and Land Monopolies."

8. Berkhofer, *White Man's Indian*; Pearce, *Savagism and Civilization*; Philip J. Deloria, *Playing Indian*.

9. For example, Raibmon, *Authentic Indians*; Alexandra Harmon, *Indians in the Making*; Denson, *Demanding the Cherokee Nation*.

10. Wolfe, *Settler Colonialism*, 3. See also Usner, *Indian Work*.

11. This book does not, of course, present an exhaustive survey, but rather a series of case studies; there have been many Indians besides those featured here with wealth enough to prompt comment and controversy.

12. Clifford, *Predicament of Culture*; Axtell, "Ethnohistory," 6; Gudeman, *Economics as Culture*.

13. For example, Boxberger, *To Fish in Common*; Lewis, *Neither Wolf Nor Dog*; Meyer, *White Earth Tragedy*; Pickering, *Lakota Culture, World Economy*; Richard White, *Roots of Dependency*; Fixico, *Invasion of Indian Country*; Johansen, *Encyclopedia of Native American Economic History*, xv.

14. Notable exceptions: Saunt, *New Order of Things*; Terry Wilson, *Underground Reservation*; Thorne, *World's Richest Indian*.

15. Philip J. Deloria, *Indians in Unexpected Places*, particularly the introduction.

16. Galbraith, Rodriguez, and Stiles, "False Myths and Indigenous Entrepreneurial Strategies," 6–7; Barrington, *Other Side of the Frontier*, 4.

17. The paradigm reflects anthropologists' assertion that aboriginal tribal relations generally functioned more as networks for wealth redistribution than for accumulation. Forde and Douglas, "Primitive Economics," 22.

18. Trigger, "Early Native North American Responses"; Mervyn Rothstein, "Getting a Tale of 80's Avarice on Screen," *NYT*, 31 Oct. 1990, p. C15.

19. Whatever the biological basis of "human possessive behaviour," no one experiences "unmediated instincts. . . . Consciousness is transformed and interpreted through signs learned in our cultures." Dittmar, *Social Psychology*, 37–38.

20. Fraser and Gerstle, *Ruling America*, 2, 4; Beckert, *Monied Metropolis*, 9.

21. Yorgason, *Transformation of the Mormon Culture Region*, 79.

22. Some social and labor histories are Appleby, *Economic Thought and Ideology*; Horn, *Adapting to a New World*; Innes, *Creating the Commonwealth*; Kulikoff, *From British Peasants to Colonial American Farmers*; Glickman, *Living Wage*; Mercier, *Anaconda*; Hodgson, *How Economics Forgot History*, 223, 232.

23. Philip J. Deloria, *Indians in Unexpected Places*, especially 52–108 and 183–223; Raibmon, *Authentic Indians*; Moses, *Wild West Shows*. See also Alexandra Harmon, *Indians in the Making*; Hanson, "Ethnicity and the Looking Glass"; O'Nell, "Telling about Whites."

24. For a similar argument regarding Indian political thought, see Denson, *Demanding the Cherokee Nation*.

25. Rosier, "Crossing the Narrative Tracks"; Barrington, *Other Side of the Frontier*, ix, x; Usner, *Indian Work*, 73–76.

26. Plattner, *Economic Anthropology*, 12–13; Albers, "Labor and Exchange," 274. An emphasis on culture, Albers notes, also caused many anthropologists to overlook or understate impacts of broader forces and conditions on tribal economies. See also Sahlins, *Culture and Practical Reason*, 211.

27. Hodgson, *How Economics Forgot History*, 176, 6, 30, 232, 235. See also Bourdieu, *Social Structures of the Economy*, 210, on economists' claim that they describe forces and behavior subject to scientific laws.

28. Plattner, *Economic Anthropology*, 12.

29. Matson, "House of Many Mansions," 69.

30. Axtell, "Ethnohistory of Native North America," 2.

31. Hoxie, "Ethnohistory for a Tribal World." For an argument that ethnohistorians have neglected economics, see Trosper, "That Other Discipline."

32. Bloch and Parry, *Money and the Morality of Exchange*, 1; Zelizer, *Social Meaning of Money*.

33. *American Heritage Dictionary of the English Language*, 4th ed. (Boston: Houghton Mifflin, 2000); *Random House College Dictionary*.

34. This paragraph draws from Dalton, *Tribal and Peasant Economies*; Dittmar, *Social Psychology*, 28; Graeber, *Toward an Anthropological Theory of Value*; Gudeman, *Economics as Culture*, vii; Hann, *Property Relations*; Hunt and Gilman, *Property in Economic Context*; Plattner, *Economic Anthropology*; Sahlins, *Stone Age Economics*.

35. Manning Nash, *Cauldron of Ethnicity*; Roosens, *Creating Ethnicity*, 156–57.

36. Sahlins, *Culture and Practical Reason*, 211; Plattner, *Economic Anthropology*, 11–13.

37. Manning Nash, "Organization of Economic Life," 7, 9; Dittmar, *Social Psychology*, 8; Bloch and Parry, *Money and the Morality of Exchange*, 26.

38. Gudeman, *Economics as Culture*, vii, 1, 40.

39. Gudeman, *Anthropology of Economy*, 2; Bourdieu, *Social Structures of the Economy*, 211.

40. Benjamin Heber Johnson, "Red Populism?," 20.

41. Gudeman, *Economics as Culture*, 39, viii; Gudeman, *Anthropology of Economy*, 19.

42. Graeber, *Toward an Anthropological Theory of Value*, 86.

43. Sahlins, *Historical Metaphors and Mythical Realities*.

44. Feelings of moral obligation often run contrary to accepted policies. Povinelli, *Cunning of Recognition*, 4–5.

45. Robert Williams, *Like a Loaded Weapon*, 33–34, citing Omi and Winant, *Racial Formation*, 62. See also Wolfe, "Land, Labor, and Difference"; Chaplin, "Race"; Smedley, *Race in North America*.

Chapter 1

1. Beverley, *History and Present State of Virginia*, 227, 233 (emphasis in original).

2. Lederer, *Discoveries of John Lederer*, 12; Michel, "Report of the Journey," 129.

3. Lawson, *New Voyage to Carolina*, 9, 17.

4. In April 1606, James I licensed four men to claim up to 20,000 square miles and plant a colony in "Virginia," an area larger than the present state. The venture was a privately funded public joint-stock company under ultimate Crown control. McCarthy, "Influence of 'Legal Habit,'" 40, 53.

5. Rountree, *Powhatan, Pocahontas, Opechancanough*.

6. Smith, *Complete Works*, 1:206. Powhatan was a town. Like the colonists, historians apply the name to the confederation of towns or tribes ruled by the man who also assumed that name. Scholars identify indigenous people of the larger region and their language family as Chesapeake or Middle Atlantic Algonquian. Mallios, *Deadly Politics of Giving*, 9; Rountree, *Powhatan, Pocahontas, Opechancanough*, 37; Gleach, *Powhatan's World*. Common early English terms for all native people were "savages" and "Indians."

7. Rountree, *Powhatan Indians of Virginia*, 15. John Smith and William Strachey recorded just 264 Powhatan words. Hranicky, "Virginia Algonquian Language," 19–20.

8. Chaplin, *Subject Matter*, 26–27.

9. Rountree, *Powhatan Indians*; Rountree, *Powhatan, Pocahontas, Opechancanough*; Rountree and Davidson, *Eastern Shore Indians*; Rountree and Turner, *Before and After Jamestown*.

10. Rountree, *Powhatan Indians*, 32, 57; Rountree and Davidson, *Eastern Shore Indians*, 45.

11. Gleach, *Powhatan's World*, 25–26; Rountree, *Powhatan Indians*, 55, 109, 51, 146; Turner, "Socio-Political Organization," 203.

12. Gleach, *Powhatan's World*, 10, 58; Potter, *Commoners, Tribute, and Chiefs*, 169, 18. There is evidence of similar beliefs among other Algonquians. Trigger, "Early Native North American Responses," 1204–6; Miller and Hamell, "A New Perspective," 315, 317.

13. Murray, *Indian Giving*, 67–68; Gleach, *Powhatan's World*, 54–55. A similar ethos prevailed in aboriginal societies throughout eastern North America. Dickason, *Myth of the Savage*, 97; Main, *Peoples of a Spacious Land*, 14–16; Starna, "Pequots in the Early Seventeenth Century," 42.

14. Sahlins, *Stone Age Economics*, 41–42, 130, 132, 140, 170. See also Turner, "Socio-Political Organization," 195; Sahlins, *Culture and Practical Reason*, 212, 217; Allen Johnson, "Horticulturalists," 74; Main, *Peoples of a Spacious Land*, 14, 15.

15. Smith, *Complete Works*, 1:173, 69.

16. Strachey, *Historie of Travell Into Virginia*, 87; Smith, *Captain John Smith's History*, 18. The thirty-plus weroances, Strachey wrote, "all . . . haue their precincts, and bowndes, proper . . . , that no one intrude vpon the other . . . , and for the grownd wherein each one soweth . . . , he tythes to the great king of all the Commodityes growing in the same, or of what ells his shiere brings forth . . . a peremptory rate sett downe." *Historie of Travell*, 63.

17. Gibb, *Archaeology of Wealth*, 41, 53; Musgrave, *Early Modern European Economy*, 5, 191, 194; Miskimin, *Economy of Later Renaissance Europe*, 22, 47, 51, 132.

18. Kulikoff, *From British Peasants to Colonial American Farmers*, 71; Bell, "Social Relations of Property and Efficiency," 29–30.

19. Brace, *Idea of Property*, 79.

20. Cornwall, *Wealth and Society*, 11, 154; Appleby, *Economic Thought and Ideology*, 25; Musgrave, *Early Modern European Economy*, 6; Strachey, *Historie of Travell*, xx, 23. Many arguments for colonial enterprises were couched in moral terms. Quinn, *New American World*, 168–69.

21. Notestein, *English People*, 20; Youings, *Sixteenth-Century England*, 19, 304, 310, 325; Kupperman, *Settling with the Indians*, 8; Quitt, "Trade and Acculturation," 229.

22. Notestein, *English People*, 109; Musgrave, *Early Modern European Economy*, 6; Sheehan, *Savagism and Civility*, 4; Mildred Campbell, "Social Origins of Some Early Americans," 65–66; Appleby, *Economic Thought and Ideology*, 20, 25, 129; Cornwall, *Wealth and Society*, 154.

23. Kupperman, *Jamestown Project*, 237.

24. McCarthy, "Influence of 'Legal Habit,'" 40, 53; Kupperman, *Settling with the Indians*, 189–95.

25. Kulikoff, *From British Peasants to Colonial American Farmers*, 57; Billings, Selby, and Tate, *Colonial Virginia*, 13; Kupperman, *Settling with the Indians*, 9. On the status of account writers, see Smith, *Captain John Smith's History*, xiii–xiv. On emerging criteria of gentility, see Cornwall, *Wealth and Society*, 13.

26. De la Ware, Smith, Cope, and Waterson, "Rationale for Settlement," 14–15; Smith, *Captain John Smith's History*, 42.

27. Force, *Tracts and Other Papers*, 2:23; De la Ware, Smith, Cope, and Waterson, "Rationale for Settlement," 14–15; Robert Johnson, *Nova Britannia*, n.p. See also Arber, *First Three English Books*, especially 189–97, 343; Sheehan, *Savagism and Civility*, 14; Holifield, *Era of Persuasion*, 23; Dorfman, *Economic Mind*, 15, 16; Philip Bruce, *Economic History of Virginia*, 1:13; Quinn, *New American World*, 1:227. Cf. Bridenbaugh, *Jamestown*, 6.

28. Wright, *Elizabethans' America*, 55–57; Sheehan, *Savagism and Civility*, 15; Dorfman, *Economic Mind*, 16. Early English colonizers "paid particularly close attention to Richard Hakluyt's *The Principal Navigations: Voyages and Discoveries of the English Nation*. The Virginia Company owned the work, which contained several accounts describing the process by which the Spanish conquered their American territories and appropriated indigenous tribute systems." Hatfield, "Spanish Colonization Literature," 257, 258–59.

29. Quinn, *Roanoke Voyages*, 2:102; Tyler, *Narratives of Early Virginia*, 14; Holifield, *Era of Persuasion*, 25.

30. Smith, *Captain John Smith's History*, 42; Smith, *Complete Works*, 1:227–28.

31. Hatfield, "Spanish Colonization Literature," 265. The first contingent of colonists neglected trade in favor of seeking precious metals and a passage to the Orient. Rountree, "Powhatans and the English," 180.

32. Robert Johnson, *Nova Britannia*, n.p.

33. Wright, *Elizabethans' America*, 30. See also Billings, *Old Dominion*, 14–15.

34. Strachey, *Historie of Travell*, 17; Murray, *Indian Giving*, 3. Not until his fourth voyage did Columbus reach a coast where "rich clothing" and other "good things" prompted him to describe the natives as wealthy. Few Europeans saw that report. Bodmer, *Armature of Conquest*, 33.

35. Deep-rooted myths influenced this perception of indigenous Americans. Author Pietro Martire [Peter Martyr] drew on them in 1515 when he likened New World "savages" to people in an imagined prehistoric Golden Age who lived simply in the midst of plenty, their basic needs met from nature's cornucopia. Innocent of the avarice infecting civilized peoples, they assigned no economic values to resources around them. As Europeans probed the Americas, writer after writer echoed Martire. Moffitt and Sebastian, *O Brave New People*, 301, 70; Brandon, *New Worlds for Old*, 6, 8; Dickason, *Myth of the Savage*, 54, 65. Extensive scholarship analyzes the intellectual traditions, mythologies, yearnings, and pragmatic objectives that fostered and perpetuated a disposition to see many indigenous Americans as voluntarily poor. Baudet, *Paradise on Earth*; Gary Nash, "Image of the Indian," 199–201.

36. Barbour, *Jamestown Voyages*, 93.

37. Ibid., 101.

38. De Bry, *Thomas Hariot's Virginia*, 25. Hariot saw towns in the vicinity of Roanoke Island, now in North Carolina but then within the area designated "Virginia" by the company charter. Billings, Selby, and Tate, *Colonial Virginia*, 15.

39. Purchas, *Hakluytus Posthumus*, 108.

40. Strachey, *Historie of Travell*, 115.

41. Barbour, *Jamestown Voyages*, 151; Kupperman, *Settling with the Indians*, 192; Quinn, *Roanoke Voyages*, 260.

42. Hatfield, "Spanish Colonization Literature."

43. Of Wahunsonacock, Smith wrote, "In all his ancient inheritances, hee hath houses . . . some 30 some 40 yardes long, and at every house provision for his entertainement." *Complete Works*, 1:173.

44. Illustration 7, de Bry, *Thomas Hariot's Virginia*. Smith, *Complete Works*, 1:160–61 stated that the "common sort" of Indians, in contrast to the "better sort," had "scarce to cover their nakednesse but with grasse, the leaves of trees, or such like." For the English, "Clothes were the single most important indicator of status and identity as well as the best boundary maintainer." Kupperman, *Settling with the Indians*, 37.

45. Strachey, *Historie of Travell*, 65.

46. Smith, *Travels and Works*, 24, 26; Rountree, *Powhatan Indians*, 106–7.

47. Smith, *Captain John Smith's History*, 40.

48. Smith, *Complete Works*, 1:161.

49. Strachey, *Historie of Travell*, 60; Rountree and Davidson, *Eastern Shore Indians*, 42.

50. Potter, *Commoners, Tribute, and Chiefs*, 11.

51. Purchas, *Hakluytus Posthumus*, 63.

52. Smith, *Captain John Smith's History*, 93. See also Kupperman, *Jamestown Project*, 278, quoting John Chamberlain.

53. Quinn, *Roanoke Voyages*, 105.

54. Quinn, *New American World*, 216, 215.

55. Tyler, *Narratives of Early Virginia*, 20–21. Colonists dubbed the period from October 1609 to June 1610 "the starving time." Smith attributed the famine to colonists' improvidence, lack of industry, and bad governance, not to the country's barrenness. Smith, *Captain John Smith's History*, 118. On the abundance of Indian food stores and English reactions, see Gleach, *Powhatan's World*, 90–91; Philip Bruce, *Economic History of Virginia*, 1:179, 181.

56. Smith, *Complete Works*, 1:251, 256; Strachey, *Historie of Travell*, 84, 107; Smith, *Captain John Smith's History*, 86, 92; Quinn, *New American World*, 292, 185–86; Sheehan, *Savagism and Civility*, 104–6.

57. Tyler, *Narratives of Early Virginia*, 284–85, 441, 444; Kupperman, *Settling with the Indians*, 173.

58. De Bry, *Thomas Hariot's Virginia*, 25.

59. John Pory asked a man named Wamanato "if he desired to bee great and rich; he answered, They were things all men aspired unto." Tyler, *Narratives of Early Virginia*, 353. But did Wamanato understand what Pory meant by "rich"? Pory did not say whether the conversation was in English. Several colonists learned the native language, but "European words, with all of their culturally specific associations, may not do justice to . . . native terms." Bruce White, "Encounters with Spirits," 372. Another document identifies Wamanato as an important man who traded beaver skins for English goods and took the goods with him to the grave. Purchas, *Hakluytus Posthumus*, 168.

60. Strachey, *Historie of Travell*, 115. Hariot claimed that English technology convinced

the natives of English superiority: de Bry, *Thomas Hariot's Virginia*, 27. Rountree speculates that Indians saw the first settlers as "odd but 'rich' people." However, she also alludes to evidence that they often "felt the invaders were subhuman"—neither good nor high-status. *Powhatan, Pocahontas, Opechancanough*, 55, 5.

61. Tyler, *Narratives of Early Virginia*, 135; Smith, *Complete Works*, 1:215.

62. Smith, *Travels and Works*, Part 1, cvii; Rountree and Davidson, *Eastern Shore Indians*, 40.

63. Rountree, *Pocahontas, Powhatan, Opechancanough*, 149.

64. Kupperman, *Jamestown Project*, 227; Smith, *Complete Works*, 1:247, 261; Bridenbaugh, *Jamestown*, 45; Earle, "Environment, Disease, and Mortality," 96–125. Estimates vary for the number of colonists who arrived in 1607. Kupperman's figure is 108. *Jamestown Project*, 217.

65. Tyler, *Narratives of Early Virginia*, 188. Indians elsewhere asked why the supposedly powerful god of the Europeans did not give his people riches and necessities so they would not risk the dangers of coming to America to take riches from native unbelievers. Dickason, *Myth of the Savage*, 134.

66. Purchas, *Hakluytus Posthumus*, 119; Kupperman, *Jamestown Project*, 232. Smith thought Namontack did tell Wahunsonacock about the military "greatnesse" of England's rulers. Smith, *Complete Works*, 1:57, 236. Of another Indian who went to England in 1616, Sheehan says, "He seems to have discovered that he could not count the English population single-handedly but learned little more." *Savagism and Civility*, 134. See also Axtell, "Through Another Glass Darkly," 141.

67. A frigid winter aggravated effects of the drought, which lasted five years and recurred briefly in the early 1620s. Kupperman, *Jamestown Project*, 223, 251, 303. Estimates of the native population in 1607 range from Smith's guess of 5,000 to 170,000 or more. Billings, Selby, and Tate, *Colonial Virginia*, 20; Mallios, *Deadly Politics of Giving*, 9. Most scholars agree that Powhatan numbers dropped shortly before the English arrived, perhaps due to the combined effects of crop failures, warfare, and introduced diseases. Fitzhugh, *Cultures in Contact*, 189; Barker, "Powhatan's Pursestrings." Cf. Rountree *Powhatan, Pocahontas, Opechancanough*, 42, 14.

68. Philip Bruce, *Economic History of Virginia*, 1:176; Bridenbaugh, *Jamestown*, 50.

69. Strachey, *Historie of Travell*, 115; Quinn, *New American World*, 292, 297; Smith, *Captain Smith's History*, 66, 72; Tyler, *Narratives of Early Virginia*, 33, 37, 50, 167.

70. Strachey, *Historie of Travell*, 107; Kupperman, *Indians and English*, 213; Hantman, "Between Powhatan and Quirank." No doubt, Powhatans had diverse thoughts about these developments, but there is little evidence of the new wealth's repercussions in Powhatan society. Weroance control of imports such as copper could have accelerated social stratification and power concentration, provoking resentment in some native hearts. But commoners could get prestigious items directly from Englishmen, thus offsetting the tendency to stratification and undermining weroance influence. There is English testimony suggesting both effects. Smith understood that native commoners tendered their valuable acquisitions—stolen items, at least—to the weroance. But Strachey said some Indians hid such items, suggesting that the English presence encouraged them to be selfish, contrary to the ethic of generosity and reciprocity. Smith, *Complete Works*, 1:81; Strachey, *Historie of Travell*, 115; Barbour, *Jamestown Voyages*, 87.

71. George Percy claimed that when "Savages murmured" at the colonists' plan to occupy a small tract, "this Werowance made answere againe very wisely of a Savage. Why should you be offended with them as long as they hurt you not, nor take any thing away by force. They take but a little waste ground, which doth you nor any of us any good." Tyler, *Narratives of Early Virginia*, 18. The site chosen for Jamestown was hunting territory for residents of Paspahegh, however, and the English occupation did not sit well with them. Billings, Selby, and Tate, *Colonial Virginia*, 29–30; Mallios, *Deadly Politics of Giving*, 81.

72. Philip Bruce, *Economic History of Virginia*, 1:490; Sheehan, *Savagism and Civility*, 149. According to Rountree, Powhatans still had territory enough as late as the 1630s, by which time the English occupied the James River below the falls, lower York Valley, and large areas of Virginia's Eastern Shore. "Powhatans and the English," 192–93.

73. Under the charter, land claimed for the colony was company property until 1616, when it would be apportioned among original settlers. Smith, *Captain John Smith's History*, xiv.

74. Kingsbury, *Records of the Virginia Company*, 3:245 and 4:522; Morgan, "First American Boom," 169–71, 177; Billings, Selby, and Tate, *Colonial Virginia*, 38; Bridenbaugh, *Jamestown*, 41; Axtell, "Rise and Fall of the Powhatan Empire."

75. Gary Nash, "Image of the Indian," 217; Rountree, "Powhatans and the English," 174.

76. Philip Bruce, *Economic History of Virginia*, 1:487, 489; McCarthy, "Influence of 'Legal Habit,'" 53–54; Banner, *How the Indians Lost Their Land*, 15.

77. Banner, *How the Indians Lost Their Land*, 12–13; Philip Bruce, *Economic History of Virginia*, 1:488.

78. Quoted in Townsend, *Pocahontas and the Powhatan Dilemma*, 35.

79. Strachey, *Historie of Travell*, 22, 26.

80. Banner, *How the Indians Lost Their Land*, 20–21, 24; Kingsbury, *Records of the Virginia Company*, 3:304; Strachey, *Historie of Travell*, 56. In early dealings with Wahunsonacock, Smith promised to trade weapons for "corne and ground." Smith, *Complete Works*, 1:65. In 1615, when some Indian towns were short on provisions, their chiefs "mortgaged to the English, for four of five hundred bushels of corn, divisions of country as extensive as an English shire. A large body of land at Wyanoke was, in 1617, presented to Sir George Yeardley by Opechancanough, and this gift was confirmed by the Company." Philip Bruce, *Economic History of Virginia*, 1:490.

81. Rountree, *Powhatan, Pocahontas, and Opechancanough*, 149, 191, 192, 200; Vaughan, "'Expulsion of the Salvages,'" 73.

82. Rountree, *Powhatan, Pocahontas, Opechancanough*, 116–17; Smith, *Complete Works*, 2:222.

83. Strachey, *Historie of Travell*, 75, 115; Barbour, *Jamestown Voyages*, 87; Tyler, *Narratives of Early Virginia*, 63.

84. Strachey, *Historie of Travell*, 87, 107.

85. Smith, *Captain John Smith's History*, 53, 14; Strachey, *Historie of Travell*, 62; Smith, *Complete Works*, 1:59; Rountree and Davidson, *Eastern Shore Indians*, 42; Smith, *Travels and Works*, cv.

86. McCarthy, "Influence of 'Legal Habit,'" 54; Seed, *American Pentimento*, chaps. 1–2; Purchas, *Hakluytus Posthumus*, 232; Horn, *Adapting to a New World*, 127.

87. Townsend, *Pocahontas and the Powhatan Dilemma*, 90, 35–36. European lawyers agreed that settlers had a right to unoccupied land, but the meaning of "occupied" was disputed. "In Virginia, contemporary accounts suggest that the English simply fenced in land that did not seem to be in use." Banner, *How the Indians Lost Their Land*, 30–31. Robert Johnson argued in 1609 that the king could claim dominion over the Indians because the English had been in Virginia for years without interruption. Pagden, *Lords of All the World*, 90. "Perhaps the land belonged to the natives, perhaps not; Englishmen were undecided on that point. But they were certain that the Indians had misused their territory." Vaughan, "'Expulsion of the Salvages,'" 61.

88. Tyler, *Narratives of Early Virginia*, 99; McCarthy, "Influence of 'Legal Habit,'" 54–55. Locke's labor theory of property, which would provide a rationale for English land appropriation elsewhere in North America by the eighteenth century, was developing but inchoate in the early 1600s. Banner, *How The Indians Lost Their Land*, 46.

89. Strachey, *Historie of Travell*, 116; Smith, *Captain John Smith's History*, 5, 93.

90. In 1622, a Virginia Company employee published an unrebutted argument that colonists had a natural right to enslave and command Indians because they "know no industry, no Arts, no culture, nor no good use of this blessed Country heere, but are meere ignorance, sloth, and brutishnesse, and [are] an unprofitable burthen." Quoted in Vaughan, "'Expulsion of the Salvages,'" 79.

91. Banner, *How the Indians Lost Their Land*, 20–21.

92. Company directors warned colonists that it would be virtually impossible to prevent Indian discontent with the English presence. Kupperman, *Jamestown Project*, 215.

93. Mallios, *Deadly Politics*, 107. Other Algonquians approached trade with Europeans in the same manner. Richard White, *Middle Ground*, 99–102.

94. Smith, *Captain John Smith's History*, 36; Rountree, *Powhatan, Pocahontas, Opechancanough*, 83.

95. Tyler, *Narratives of Early Virginia*, 57, 135; Quitt, "Trade and Acculturation," 250; Gleach, *Powhatan's World*, 125.

96. Quitt, "Trade and Acculturation," 245, 246; Smith, *Captain John Smith's History*, 36; Quinn, *New American World*, 217, 330. "If the English failed to reciprocate a gift of land or corn, Indians expected the English to recognize them as superiors; the English, viewing the gift as a sale, refused. . . . Indians viewed the colonists' behavior as selfish." Kulikoff, *From British Peasants to Colonial American Farmers*, 94.

97. Tyler, *Narratives of Early Virginia*, 167, 329.

98. Townsend, *Pocahontas and the Powhatan Dilemma*, 57, 58, 60–61; Vaughan, "'Expulsion of the Salvages,'" 65. See also Kupperman, *Jamestown Project*, 228.

99. Smith soon understood the Powhatan model of relations and invoked it when convenient. When the mamanitowock for his part grasped the colonists' vision of trade and began demanding that they pay for corn with an equivalency of English goods, Smith reacted angrily. Quitt, "Trade and Acculturation," 250, 254.

100. Smith, *Captain John Smith's History*, 53; Smith, *Complete Works*, 1:67.

101. Quinn, *New American World*, 5:215.

102. Mallios, *Deadly Politics of Giving*, 94.

103. Quoted in Bridenbaugh, *Jamestown*, 50. Drought contributed to the conflict because colonists demanded corn at a time of scarcity in native towns. Rountree, *Powhatan, Pocahontas, Opechancanough*, 14.

104. Kingsbury, *Records of the Virginia Company*, 4:468.

105. Vaughan, "'Expulsion of the Salvages,'" 57, 77, 78; Billings, *Old Dominion*, 209; Kupperman, *Jamestown Project*, 310.

106. Billings, *Old Dominion*, 208; Gary Nash, "Image of the Indian," 215.

107. Vaughan, "'Expulsion of the Salvages,'" 73–74.

108. Bridenbaugh, *Jamestown*, 51.

109. Fausz, "Patterns of Anglo-Indian Aggression and Accommodation," 250; Fausz, "Present at the 'Creation,'" 9; Fausz, "Merging and Emerging Worlds," 53–56.

110. Kupperman, *Settling with the Indians*, 19. Fausz sees the tobacco boom as the result of the new oligarchs' success more than the reason for it, "since the Powhatan war provided them with the monopoly on servants, ships, and political authority that launched their careers as merchant-planters." "Merging and Emerging Worlds," 53–56.

111. Philip Bruce, *Economic History of Virginia*, 1:491.

112. Rountree, *Powhatan, Pocahontas, Opechancanough*, 231–37; Craven, *White, Red, and Black*, 56; Force, *Tracts and Other Papers* 2: book 8, pp. 13, 7.

113. Force, *Tracts and Other Papers* 2: book 8, p. 5.

114. Craven, *White, Red, and Black*, 55–60; Billings, *Old Dominion*, 210; Kulikoff, *From British Peasants to Colonial American Farmers*, 96; Philip Bruce, *Economic History of Virginia*, 1:487–89, 491, 493, 494; Sheehan, *Savagism and Civility*, 178. In 1622, a court in England ruled that only the company, acting through the court, could grant land titles. The judges objected to a grant by George Yeardley, made on the condition "that he compounded for the same with Opachankano . . . whereby a Soveraignity in that heathen Infidell was acknowledged." Kingsbury, *Records of the Virginia Company*, 2:94–95.

115. Rountree, *Pocahontas's People*, 129.

116. McIlwaine, *Journals of the House of Burgesses*, 64.

117. Ibid., 16.

118. McIlwaine, *Executive Journals of the Council*, 1:136.

119. Philip Bruce, *Economic History of Virginia*, 1:498, 499, 495; Rountree, *Pocahontas's People*, 87, 89, 128. See also Rountree, "Powhatans and the English," 193, 198.

120. Fausz, "Present at the 'Creation,'" 14; Philip Bruce, *Economic History of Virginia*, 2:385–89.

121. Fausz, "Merging and Emerging Worlds," 49, 84.

122. Ibid., 84, 97, 90.

123. Durand of Dauphiné, *Huguenot Exile in Virginia*, 111–12.

124. Ibid., 153, 157.

125. Pargellis, "'Account of the Indians,'" 236. The author was probably John Clayton.

126. Billings, *Old Dominion*, 290; Carr, "Emigration and the Standard of Living," 280–81; Tyler, *Narratives of Early Virginia*, 414. Just surviving was difficult for colonists throughout the seventeenth century. Carr, "Emigration and the Standard of Living," 272. Not until the 1680s or 1690s did life expectancy rise to the point that the colony could

maintain or increase population without immigration. Billings, Selby, and Tate, *Colonial Virginia*, 126.

127. Michel, "Report of the Journey," 130, 132; Rountree, *Pocahontas's People*, 89, 128, 132, 144–49. In 1680, the English king sent "four rich Coronets with Robes Silver badges, and sev[ll] other presents to four Indian Kings and Queens," drawing a protest from the colonial council, which labeled them "mean persons" who should be managed by fear, "not kindness." McIlwaine, *Executive Journals of the Council*, 1:4.

128. Michel, "Report of the Journey," 129, 131, 134; Rountree, *Pocahontas's People*, 128, 133.

129. Jones, *Present State of Virginia*, 51, 54.

130. Fausz, "'Present at the Creation,'" 16, 18.

131. Rountree and Davidson, *Eastern Shore Indians*, 76–77.

132. Berkeley, *Reverend John Clayton*, 4, 27; Pargellis, "'Account of the Indians,'" 230.

Chapter 2

1. Quoted in Halsey, *Old New York Frontier*, 321–22. See also Stone, *Life of Joseph Brant*, 2:257.

2. P. Campbell, *Travels in the Interior*, 165, 163; Kelsay, *Joseph Brant*, 240, 390–91. The land grant was not to Brant personally, but to the Indians on whose behalf he ostensibly acted. Johnston, "Joseph Brant, the Grand River Lands, and the Northwest Crisis," 270. Wanting a buffer zone on the U.S. border, the English discouraged most Iroquois from withdrawing to Canada after the war. They made an exception for Mohawks, partly in hopes of controlling the "prodigious talents and volatile charisma of Joseph and Molly Brant." For the same reason, Mohawks were their only Indian allies to receive compensation for war losses. Alan Taylor, *Divided Ground*, 119–21.

3. P. Campbell, *Travels in the Interior*, 165; Kelsay, *Joseph Brant*, 523, 527, 535–36, 601. Johnson quoted in Stone, *Life of Joseph Brant*, 2:xliv [Appendix], 481.

4. Johnston, "Joseph Brant, the Grand River Lands, and the Northwest Crisis," 270–75.

5. Wood, *Radicalism of the American Revolution*, 89, 38, 60. See also Alan Taylor, *William Cooper's Town*, 13, 14; Bushman, *Refinement of America*, 182.

6. Wood, *Radicalism of the American Revolution*, 26, 27, 30, 32; Rozbicki, *Complete Colonial Gentleman*, 128, 135.

7. On whether Brant had White ancestry, see Huey and Pulis, *Molly Brant*, 13, 71; Stone, *Life of Joseph Brant*, 2:3–4; Pooley narrative, 136.

8. Quoted in Stone, *Life of Joseph Brant*, 2:458, 457; Alan Taylor, *Divided Ground*, 52, 127.

9. Rozbicki, *Complete Colonial Gentleman*, 87. Burr quoted in Stone, *Life of Joseph Brant*, 2:456. On eighteenth-century colonial measures of gentility, see Wood, *Radicalism of the American Revolution*, 31–33, 36.

10. Holton, *Forced Founders*, 84.

11. Alexander Hamilton, *Gentleman's Progress*, 98. I thank Richard R. Johnson for bringing this source to my attention.

12. Michael Green, "Alexander McGillivray," 41–42.

13. Greene, *Imperatives, Behaviors, and Identities*, 149, 150, 158, 160. See also Wood, *Radicalism of the American Revolution*, 126, 128, 229, 340; Dunaway, *First American Frontier*, 15; Perkins, *Economy of Colonial America*, 70.

14. Kulikoff, *From British Peasants to Colonial American Farmers*, 100. See also Chapter 1 and sources cited there.

15. Dunaway, *First American Frontier*, 25, 27; Hatley, *Dividing Paths*, 29; Perkins, *Economy of Colonial America*, 9; Furstenberg, "Significance of the Trans-Appalachian Frontier." On the trade in Indian captives, see Gallay, *Indian Slave Trade*.

16. Snapp, *John Stuart and the Struggle for Empire*, 8, 15; Corkran, *Creek Frontier*, 49; Mereness, *Travels in the American Colonies*, 95.

17. Corkran, *Creek Frontier*, 49–50; McDowell, *CRSC 1754–1765*, xii. The English applied the name "Creek" to communities stretching across much of present-day Georgia and Alabama. Saunt, *New Order of Things*, 13–14.

18. Atkin, *Indians of the Southern Colonial Frontier*, 17; Brickell, *Natural History of North-Carolina*, v–vi; Cashin, "Gentlemen of Augusta," 8; Cashin, "From Creeks to Crackers," 70; Hahn, "Mother of Necessity," 95; Adair, *Adair's History*, 394, n. 216.

19. Richard White, *Middle Ground*, 15, 180–82; Hatley, *Dividing Paths*, 44; Perdue, *"Mixed Blood" Indians*, 9.

20. Reid, *Better Kind of Hatchet*, 35.

21. McDowell, *CRSC May 21, 1750–August 7, 1754*, 208.

22. Cashin, *Lachlan McGillivray*, 22; Greene, *Imperatives, Behaviors, and Identities*, 122; Perkins, *Economy of Colonial America*, 124. See also Wolf, *As Various as Their Land*, 19.

23. Bartram, *Travels*, 194–95. See also Cashin, *Lachlan McGillivray*, 19.

24. Perdue, *"Mixed Blood" Indians*, 25; Corkran, *Creek Frontier*, 53–54. Traders residing in Indian towns did not have high status in the colonies. Reid, *Better Kind of Hatchet*, 141–42. Indians, seeing them as a source of wealth, may not have known this.

25. As of June 1739, an estimated 600 Whites lived by trade in Indian nations. Adair, *Adair's History*, 394, n. 216.

26. Quoted in Greene, *Imperatives, Behaviors, and Identities*, 98.

27. "Deerskins . . . were the most stable economic product of the southern colonies before the Revolutionary War, and the Indian trade was the chief instrument of southern economic expansion during the early colonial period." Dunaway, *First American Frontier*, 14, see also 33. See also Hatley, *Dividing Paths*, 70; Reid, *Better Kind of Hatchet*, 14, 34; Greene, *Imperatives, Behaviors, and Identities*, 75, 81; Philip Brown, "Early Indian Trade," 118.

28. Hahn, "Mother of Necessity," 92, 94. Women also traded baskets and produce for British goods. Hatley, *Dividing Paths*, 33; Dunaway, *First American Frontier*, 41.

29. Corkran, *Creek Frontier*, 53. See also Hahn, "Mother of Necessity," 98; Shoemaker, *Strange Likeness*, 53, 54; Reid, *Better Kind of Hatchet*, 14.

30. Mereness, *Travels in the American Colonies*, 192; McDowell, *CRSC: Journals of the Commissioners*, 11; Corkran, *Creek Frontier*, 50–51; Philip Brown, "Early Indian Trade," 121; Dunaway, *First American Frontier*, 38. See also McDowell, *CRSC May 21, 1750–August 7, 1754*, 196, 197; Hahn, "Mother of Necessity," 98.

31. Quoted in Corkran, *Creek Frontier*, 190. Indians could even construe their indebtedness as an asset. Hatley, *Dividing Paths*, 48. Colonial spokesmen also urged them to

see the trade as a source of unprecedented wealth. McDowell, *CRSC May 21, 1750–August 7, 1754*, 45.

32. Bartram, *Travels*, 211. See also Corkran, *Creek Frontier*, 114.

33. Hatley, *Dividing Paths*, 42; Philip Brown, "Early Indian Trade," 125, 127–28; Perkins, *Economy of Colonial America*, 137.

34. Michael Morris, *Bringing of Wonder*, 43; McDowell, *CRSC 1754–1765*, 72.

35. Greene finds "ever greater divergence between behavior and values" in the economic realm of colonial life. *Imperatives, Behaviors, and Identities*, 151, 153. Churchmen did not hinder materialism but exhorted the elite to consider its effects and "provide society with spiritual goods." Sachs and Hoogenboom, *Enterprising Colonials*, 53.

36. Adair, *Adair's History*, 18, 7; Brickell, *Natural History of North-Carolina*, 282, 353; [first name?] Bolzius, "Extract of the Reverend Mr. *Bolzius*'s Journal," in Reese, *Our First Visit in America*, 61; Lane, *General Oglethorpe's Georgia*, 2:504; Shoemaker, *Strange Likeness*, 52; Saunt, *New Order of Things*, 39. Colonists saw Cherokees pool their commodities to meet traders' prices, then share their acquisitions. Dunaway, *First American Frontier*, 41. On Indian reactions to wealth and poverty in colonial society, see Johansen, "Native American Societies and the Evolution of Democracy," 288; Alan Taylor, *Divided Ground*, 17.

37. McDowell, *CRSC 1754–1765*, 259; Hatley, *Dividing Paths*, 68.

38. Dunaway, *First American Frontier*, 27; McDowell, *CRSC May 21, 1750–August 7, 1754*, 151; Reese, *Our First Visit in America*, 61; Saunt, *New Order of Things*, 44; Perdue, *"Mixed Blood" Indians*, 50, 52–53.

39. McDowell, *CRSC May 21, 1750–August 7, 1754*, 161, 162.

40. Mereness, *Travels in the American Colonies*, 132.

41. Reid, *Better Kind of Hatchet*, 135–36; Hatley, *Dividing Paths*, 67; Mereness, *Travels in the American Colonies*, 109. Ability to deal with Europeans became a source of influence. Reid, *Better Kind of Hatchet*, 62–63. Some Indians concluded that controlling wealth was a surer basis for status than hunting or war exploits. Saunt, *New Order of Things*, 47.

42. Quoted in Saunt, *New Order of Things*, 34.

43. Atkin, *Indians of the Southern Colonial Frontier*, 29.

44. Coleman and Ready, *CRSG*, 20:271–72. Tomochichi may have been distributing gifts selectively, not hoarding them. Juricek, *Georgia Treaties*, 48.

45. Saunt, *New Order of Things*, 44, 45; McDowell, *CRSC May 21, 1750–August 7, 1754*, 367. See also Candler, *CRSG*, 6:283.

46. Adair, *Adair's History*, 178, 179.

47. Hatley, *Dividing Paths*, 10; Holton, *Forced Founders*, 5.

48. Adair, *Adair's History*, 186; Hatley, *Dividing Paths*, 48; Saunt, *New Order of Things*, 43.

49. Hatley, *Dividing Paths*, 11, 45, 46. In the view of Indians, colonists' gifts to a headman "displayed his special ability to extract resources from a colonial patron." Alan Taylor, *Divided Ground*, 27.

50. Adair, *Adair's History*, 463.

51. Coleman and Ready, *CRSG*, 27:197; Saunt, *New Order of Things*, 39.

52. McDowell, *CRSC 1754–1765*, 116; McDowell, *CRSC May 21, 1750–August 7, 1754*, 391; Alan Taylor, *Divided Ground*, 27.

53. Juricek, *Georgia Treaties*, 140–41; Mereness, *Travels in the American Colonies*, 215. Baine, "Notes and Documents," says Coosaponakeesa falsified details of her genealogy and biography. If he is correct that she was not born a Creek aristocrat, her story adds evidence that access to wealth could raise an Indian's social rank.

54. Michael Green, "Mary Musgrove," 29, 31; Corkran, *Creek Frontier*, 63.

55. Juricek, *Georgia Treaties*, 4, 11, 142; Reese, *Our First Visit in America*, 124; Coleman and Ready, *CRSG*, 20:13 and 27:68, 216; Corkran, *Creek Frontier*, 69, 80, 82.

56. Juricek, *Georgia Treaties*, 141–42; Coleman and Ready, *CRSG*, 20:16, 122. See also Coulter, "Mary Musgrove," 2.

57. Juricek, *Georgia Treaties*, 6; Corkran, *Creek Frontier*, 89, 84, 99, 114; Michael Morris, *Bringing of Wonder*, 43; Coulter, "Mary Musgrove," 4.

58. Coleman and Ready, *CRSG*, 20:439 and 27:5–6, 9, 12, 16.

59. Ibid., 27:16, 8. Coulter thinks Heron, Mary, and her husband conspired to manipulate Indians and colonists for profit and power. "Mary Musgrove," 12–13.

60. Reese, *Our First Visit in America*, 125. See also Cashin, *Lachlan McGillivray*, 27–28, 109.

61. Juricek, *Georgia Treaties*, 89–90, 3, 4, 11, 29.

62. Davis, *Fledgling Province*, 168, quoting Stephens's journal; Todd, *Mary Musgrove*, 84–85.

63. Michael Green, "Mary Musgrove," 33. By the late 1740s, Mary claimed the original Musgrove plantation, 500 acres received for service to Georgia trustees, the Yamacraw grant from Tomochichi, other land where she had a trading post, and three islands that Malatchi gave her. Cashin, *Lachlan McGillivray*, 115; Michael Morris, *Bringing of Wonder*, 46. See also Coleman and Ready, *CRSG*, 27:194–95.

64. Candler, *CRSG*, 6:269; Juricek, *Georgia Treaties*, 157–62, 115; Corkran, *Creek Frontier*, 126; Coleman and Ready, *CRSG*, 27:15.

65. Coleman and Ready, *CRSG*, 27:215, 216. Creek positions on the title issue were contradictory and vacillating, due perhaps to differences between towns or to puzzlement about the nature of property rights under English law.

66. Corkran, *Creek Frontier*, 220. Gillespie, "Sexual Politics," 194–95, argues that Mary lost clout with Georgians in 1747 when, seeking personal gain, she "reclaimed" Creek identity and renounced the status she had attained by converting to Christianity and marrying a clergyman. But Governor Ellis wanted to settle her claims in the belief that regaining her goodwill would foster Indian support in war with the French and that a colonial jury would not return a verdict against her. See also Corry, "Some New Light on the Bosomworth Claims," 220–21; Juricek, *Georgia Treaties*, 233.

67. Cashin, *Lachlan McGillivray*, 109; Corkran, *Creek Frontier*, 99, 124, 126; Candler, *CRSG*, 6:262.

68. Corkran, *Creek Frontier*, 139, 170–71, 190.

69. Candler, *CRSG*, 6:270–71; McDowell, *CRSC May 21, 1750–August 7, 1754*, 405.

70. Candler, *CRSG*, 6:262–63, 272.

71. McDowell, *CRSC May 21, 1750–August 7, 1754*, 397. By Creek custom, common descent from Brim through their mothers made Mary and Malatchi siblings, and siblings were obliged to support each other. Reid, *Better Kind of Hatchet*, 21.

72. Reese, *Our First Visit in America*, 63 (italics in original).

73. Ibid., 48; Coleman and Ready, *CRSG*, 27:7, 12. In the 1740s, European sexism was a greater hindrance than racism to a strategy of biculturalism. Had Mary accepted English gender roles and gendered law, Creek ancestry would likely have been a negligible barrier to high status in colonial society.

74. Perdue, *"Mixed Blood" Indians*, 39; Reid, *Better Kind of Hatchet*, 21–22.

75. Michael Green, "Mary Musgrove," 38.

76. Hahn, *Invention of the Creek Nation*, 205.

77. Adair, *Adair's History*, 187. Each of Mary's first two husbands bequeathed her property by will. Todd, *Mary Musgrove*, 54, 77.

78. Quoted in Hahn, *Invention of the Creek Nation*, 188.

79. Malatchi's decision probably had precedents among Southeastern Indians. Hudson, *Southeastern Indians*, 187–88.

80. For example, Todd, *Mary Musgrove*, 81, 86, 96–97.

81. Wortman, *Women in American Law*, 1:14; Hoffer, *Law and People in Colonial America*, 105; Corry, "Some New Light on the Bosomworth Claims," 196.

82. Perdue, *"Mixed Blood" Indians*, 25.

83. A Bosomworth petition, likely penned by Thomas, implicitly protested officials' preference for English law, with its gender bias, over the rights of women in Creek society. Coleman and Ready, *CRSG*, 27:68.

84. Molly also carried the names Degonwadonti and Konwatsi'tsiaienni or Gonwatsijayenna. Thomas, *Three Faces of Molly Brant*, 17.

85. Calloway, "Continuing Revolution in Indian Country," 16.

86. O'Toole, *White Savage*, 51, 57, 234; Alan Taylor, *Divided Ground*, 17, 22.

87. Alan Taylor, *Divided Ground*, 16, 37–38.

88. O'Toole, *White Savage*, 57; Alan Taylor, *Divided Ground*, 17.

89. Thomas, *Three Faces of Molly Brant*, 20, 23; Gretchen Green, "Molly Brant, Catharine Brant, and their Daughters," 236; James Taylor Carson, "Molly Brant," 51; Huey and Pulis, *Molly Brant*, 13, 19–21; Kelsay, *Joseph Brant*, 45, 53–54; O'Toole, *White Savage*, 170. On the Brants' alleged "noble blood," see Stone, *Life of Joseph Brant*, 1:3–4, 18. See also Jean Johnson, "Ancestry and Descendants of Molly Brant," 86–87.

90. Thomas, *Three Faces of Molly Brant*, 15–16, 31; Kelsay, *Joseph Brant*, 58.

91. Milton Hamilton, *Papers of Sir William Johnson*, 13:724; Mullin, "Personal Politics," 351; Danvers, "Gendered Encounters," 188–92.

92. Musgrave, *Early Modern European Economy*, 182–83; Greene, *Pursuits of Happiness*, 127, 128; Alan Taylor, *William Cooper's Town*, 44, 58, 14; Wood, *Radicalism of the American Revolution*, 89; O'Toole, *White Savage*, 220.

93. Milton Hamilton, *Papers of Sir William Johnson*, 12:652; Huey and Pulis, *Molly Brant*, 29–31; Sweeney, "High-Style Vernacular," 2, 5, 11.

94. O'Toole, *White Savage*, 57, 234; Mullin, "Personal Politics," 351; Milton Hamilton, *Papers of Sir William Johnson*, 13:206.

95. Milton Hamilton, *Papers of Sir William Johnson*, 12:124, 288, 800; 13:112. See also P. Campbell, *Travels in the Interior*, 226.

96. Milton Hamilton, *Papers of Sir William Johnson*, 12:96, 204–5; 13:192. On Johnson's dealings with Indian land grantors, see Alan Taylor, *Divided Ground*, 40. On his landholdings, see Halsey, *Old New York Frontier*, 153.

97. On the basis for Johnson's designation both as a ritual Mohawk sachem and as a "chief of the more pragmatic kind," see O'Toole, *White Savage*, 68–69, 164–65.

98. Milton Hamilton, *Papers of Sir William Johnson*, 3:707–8; 2:80; 13:112; 10:87.

99. "Influence of the Mohawk Women," in Johnston, *Valley of the Six Nations*, 30–31; Milton Hamilton, *Papers of Sir William Johnson*, 4:50–58; James Taylor Carson, "Molly Brant," 48–50.

100. Mullin, "Personal Politics," 354; O'Toole, *White Savage*, 176.

101. Huey and Pulis, *Molly Brant*, 25–29; James Taylor Carson, "Molly Brant," 52; Thomas, *Three Faces of Molly Brant*, 44, 50; Gretchen Green, "Molly Brant, Catharine Brant, and Their Daughters" 238–39; Milton Hamilton, "Sir William Johnson," 278. See also Danvers, "Gendered Encounters," 199. "Johnson's homes, after 1756, had a ritual significance for the Iroquois as places where the council fire burned, and Molly is . . . accurately regarded as a co-keeper of that fire." O'Toole, *White Savage*, 172–73.

102. Kelsay, *Joseph Brant*, 120; O'Callaghan, *Documents Relative to the Colonial History of the State of New-York*, 8:725; Danvers, "Gendered Encounters," 199; Huey and Pulis, *Molly Brant*, 10, 27.

103. Huey and Pulis, *Molly Brant*, 81, 31, 33–34; Gretchen Green, "Molly Brant, Catharine Brant, and Their Daughters," 237; Tilghman, *Memoir*, 87; O'Toole, *White Savage*, 176.

104. Milton Hamilton, *Papers of Sir William Johnson*, 13:1062–75, 647.

105. "Estimate of the Losses sustained by the Mohawk Indians & others of the Six United Nations . . . Valued in the Year 1775," transcription, 1784, National Archives of Canada, MG 11 Q Series; O'Callaghan, *Documents Relative to the Colonial History of the State of New-York*, 725. See also Kelsay, *Joseph Brant*, 390–91.

106. Tilghman, *Memoir*, 83, 86–87; Gretchen Green, "Molly Brant, Catherine Brant, and Their Daughters," 239; Claus to Knox, in O'Callaghan, *Documents Relative to the Colonial History of the State of New-York*, 725; Huey and Pulis, *Molly Brant*, 44, 49.

107. Quoted in James Taylor Carson, "Molly Brant," 54–57. See also Huey and Pulis, *Molly Brant*, 63, 65; Gretchen Green, "Molly Brant, Catharine Brant, and Their Daughters," 241.

108. James Taylor Carson, "Molly Brant," 57; Huey and Pulis, *Molly Brant*, 75, 77, 79, 81, 84–89; Alan Taylor, *Divided Ground*, 96; Milton Hamilton, *Papers of Sir William Johnson*, 13:636.

109. Huey and Pulis, *Molly Brant*, 61, 66, 79; O'Toole, *White Savage*, 174.

110. Roberts, "Freemasonry," 466; Halsey, *Old New York Frontier*, 159–60, 248; Kelsay, *Joseph Brant*, 113; Stone, *Life of Joseph Brant*, 1:22–23; Wallace, *Thirty Thousand Miles*, 362.

111. Alan Taylor, *Divided Ground*, 52, 127.

112. Johnson deeded 512 acres to Joseph Brant, who had acquired eighty other acres by the 1760s, perhaps by purchase from fellow Mohawks. Kelsay, *Joseph Brant*, 116.

113. William Dummer Powell cited in Johnston, *Valley of the Six Nations*, 103; John Norton, *Journal*, 285.

114. Stone, *Life of Joseph Brant*, 2:418–19; William Palmer, *Memoir of the Distinguished Mohawk*, 58–59, 81; Johnston, "Joseph Brant, the Grand River Lands, and the Northwest Crisis," 270–72. Brant acted as business agent for Iroquois nations. Klinck and Talman,

editors of John Norton's *Journal*, claim he "netted" 5,000 acres in the disposal of one Grand River tract (p. lvii).

115. Wallace, *Thirty Thousand Miles*, 362; Kelsay, *Joseph Brant*, 639. Brant offered Whites large Grand River tracts, expecting the rent to support the Indians and the Whites to show Indians how to develop farms. "Emulating his mentor . . . , Brant wanted to build an interest in the colonial world by developing a network of dependent white men." Alan Taylor, *Divided Ground*, 124. He was not alone in hoping to protect Indian land by recruiting White tenants who would then have a stake in the Indians' survival. So did Andrew Montour. Merrell, "'Cast of His Countenance,'" 30–32.

116. Perdue, *"Mixed Blood" Indians*, 34–35; Bartram, *Travels*, 449.

117. Sehoy's father was a French officer whose role in her upbringing is undocumented. Caughey, *McGillivray of the Creeks*, 11.

118. On uncertainty about McGillivray's schooling, see Caughey, *McGillivray of the Creeks*, 13, 15; Cashin, *Lachlan McGillivray*, 73; Saunt, *New Order of Things*, 67.

119. Quoted in Saunt, *New Order of Things*, 75.

120. Cashin, *Lachlan McGillivray*, 73, 156, 158, 209–10, 252, 257, 260, 263, 313; Caughey, *McGillivray of the Creeks*, 16.

121. Michael Green, "Alexander McGillivray," 42, 45.

122. Debo, *Road to Disappearance*, 44–45.

123. Abbott and Twohig, *Papers of George Washington*, 3:556, 124.

124. Saunt, *New Order of Things*, 26.

125. Michael Green, "Alexander McGillivray," 51; Caughey, *McGillivray of the Creeks*, 24–25, 31. On McGillivray's arrangement with Panton, Leslie and Company, see Saunt, *New Order of Things*, 78–79.

126. Caughey, *McGillivray of the Creeks*, 40, 44, 47, 55.

127. Ibid., 45, 55; Milfort, *Memoirs*, 92; Chappell, *Miscellanies of Georgia*, 15; Michael Green, "Alexander McGillivray," 56.

128. Chappell, *Miscellanies of Georgia*, 32; Milfort, *Memoirs*, 22; Pope, *Tour through the Southern and Western Territories*, 46–47, 49; Cashin, *Lachlan McGillivray*, 77, 304, 306; Saunt, *New Order of Things*, 70–73, 79.

129. Caughey, *McGillivray of the Creeks*, 83, 86, 263, 274–75; Saunt, *New Order of Things*, 80.

130. Caughey, *McGillivray of the Creeks*, 55–56, 47; Michael Green, "Alexander McGillivray," 56–57; Saunt, *New Order of Things*, 79.

131. Saunt, *New Order of Things*, 79, 81.

132. Kulikoff, *From British Peasants to Colonial American Farmers*; Wolf, *As Various as Their Land*, 173.

133. Furstenberg, "Significance of the Trans-Appalachian Frontier," 675.

134. Wood, *Radicalism of the American Revolution*, 83, 104. Like Brant and McGillivray, the courtly and rich George Washington denied that money motivated him to accept a leadership role. Nordham, *George Washington and Money*, 85, 31. See also Rozbicki, *Complete Colonial Gentleman*, 1, 157; Bartram, *Travels*, 4, 313–14; Calvert, "Function of Fashion," 260, 271. Many White witnesses reported that eminent Indians were seldom rich, but always liberal and hospitable. Adair, *Adair's History*, 18.

135. Whites with "sufficient aristocratic status . . . could scorn commercial profiteer-

ing as greedy and ungenteel and yet . . . exploit every possible means to increase their wealth without any sense of contradiction." Wood, *Radicalism of the American Revolution*, 36. In theory, a wealthy gentleman's economic security enabled him to rise above personal interests and act for the greater public good. Dorfman, *Economic Mind*, 445.

136. Saunt, *New Order of Things*, 87–88; Champagne, *Social Order and Political Change*, 82–83.

137. Champagne, *Social Order and Political Change*, 29, 34.

138. Wood, *Radicalism of the American Revolution*, 26, 32, 33, 196; Rozbicki, *Complete Colonial Gentleman*, 135.

139. Wood, *Radicalism of the American Revolution*, 195, 236–37.

140. Chaplin, "Race," 154. Horsman dates the emergence of pervasive racialism to the nineteenth century. "Indian Policy of an 'Empire for Liberty,'" 59.

141. Wood, *Radicalism of the American Revolution*, 24, 415; Bushman, *Refinement of America*, xix; Rozbicki, *Complete Colonial Gentleman*, 138; Ingersoll, "'Riches and Honor Were Rejected by Them,'" 59; Liebersohn, *Aristocratic Encounters*, 37, 72; Wolf, *As Various as Their Land*, 69.

142. Alan Taylor, *Divided Ground*, 17.

143. Brant said he would not accept too much in compensation or material favors from British officials, as he "should be sorry to raise jealousies" among the Indians. Quoted in Halsey, *Old New York Frontier*, 322.

144. For a similar argument that racial ideology was muted when colonizers could not overpower Indians, see Barr, *Peace Came in the Form of a Woman*, particularly 289, 291.

145. On indigenous conceptions of land as sovereign territory and group property, see Shoemaker, *Strange Likeness*, 18.

146. Alan Taylor, *Divided Ground*, 37–39.

147. The long-term sovereignty of the new United States "would hinge on the outcome of the indigenous resistance to European settlement and claims of sovereignty." "One had to fail for the other to succeed." Furstenberg, "Significance of the Trans-Appalachian Frontier," 663.

148. Calloway, "Continuing Revolution," 3, 26, 32–33. The United States initially claimed full rights to the Indians' land by virtue of the treaty confirming its victory over Britain. Horsman, "Indian Policy of an 'Empire for Liberty,'" 40.

Chapter 3

1. Jackson, "To the Cherokee Tribe of Indians," ⟨http://dlg.galileo.usg.edu/z/nà/ id:pamo13⟩.

2. Ross, "Our Hearts are Sickened," ⟨http://historymatters.gmu.edu/d/6598⟩.

3. Burstein, *Passions of Andrew Jackson*, 25, 27, 50, 120, 230; Rogin, *Fathers and Children*, 55, 188; Moulton, *John Ross*, 33, 202, 197; Malone, *Cherokees of the Old South*, 55.

4. Rogin, *Fathers and Children*, 171; Burstein, *Passions of Andrew Jackson*, 187; Feller, *Jacksonian Promise*, 182; Kohl, *Politics of Individualism*, 22, 24, 69–70.

5. Sellers, *Market Revolution*; Stokes and Conway, *Market Revolution in America*. On businessmen's pursuit of "wealth beyond the minimum needed for a comfortable existence," see Sheriff, *Artificial River*, 130.

6. Saunt, *New Order of Things*; James Taylor Carson, "Native Americans, the Market Revolution," 1–18; Champagne, *Social Order and Political Change*; McLoughlin, *Cherokee Renascence*; Perdue, *Slavery and the Evolution of Cherokee Society*; Perdue, "Conflict Within"; Perdue, "Cherokee Planters"; Saunt, "Taking Account of Property."

7. Champagne, *Social Order and Political Change*, 127; Fogelson and Kutsche, "Cherokee Economic Cooperatives," 98–99; Rogin, *Fathers and Children*, 299; Cumfer, *Separate Peoples, One Land*, 208.

8. Rogin, *Fathers and Children*, 33; Vickers, "Competency and Competition," 11, 12.

9. Kohl, *Politics of Individualism*, 4; Cochran and Miller, *Age of Enterprise*, 2; Burstein, *Passions of Andrew Jackson*, 184; Rogin, *Fathers and Children*, 102.

10. Rogin, *Fathers and Children*, 13.

11. Matson, "Capitalizing Hope," 273, 277. See also Handlin and Handlin, *Wealth of the American People*, 46.

12. Colden quoted in Carey, *Appeal to the Wealthy*, Appendix, 36; Gilmer, *Sketches*, 349; Startup, *Root of All Evil*, 21.

13. Huston, *Securing the Fruits of Labor*, 83; Scott, *In Pursuit of Happiness*, 75; Cochran and Miller, *Age of Enterprise*, 70; Michael Morrison, *Human Tradition*, xiii.

14. Pessen, *Jacksonian America*, 109–10; Rogin, *Fathers and Children*, 252; Bloom, "Acculturation of the Eastern Cherokee," 344.

15. See chapter 2 on the development of commercial trade in deerskins.

16. Perdue, *"Mixed Blood" Indians*, 61; Wilms, "Cherokee Land Use," 2; Champagne, *Social Order and Political Change*, 91; James Taylor Carson, "Native Americans, the Market Revolution," 9. For a contemporary Cherokee account of the transition, see Boudinot, "Address to the Whites."

17. John Ridge to Albert Gallatin, 27 Feb. 1826, Payne Papers, 8:104, Ayer Ms. 689, Newberry Library.

18. Thos. L. McKenney quoting David Brown, *American State Papers*, 2:651–52, CIS microform 231, ASP 08.

19. Mr. Kingsbury, "Choctaws," *Cherokee Phoenix* (from *Missionary Herald*), 27 May 1829, pp. 1–2; Nutt, "Diary of a Tour," 41–44.

20. Pessen, *Jacksonian America*, 91, 110. Missionaries in the Cherokee Nation noted the "rich clothing" and "many ornaments" worn by the son and daughter of a chief. The editors of David Brainerd's journal identify them as Major Ridge's children. Phillips and Gary, *Brainerd Journal*, 34 and 443, n. 32.

21. Bass, *Cherokee Messenger*, 101. For a description of Major Ridge's "elegant" two-story house, see Shadburn, *Cherokee Planters in Georgia*, 127–28.

22. John Norton, *Journal*, 60, 68.

23. McLoughlin, *Cherokee Renascence*, 73.

24. Moulton, *Papers of Chief John Ross*, 1:433; Shadburn, *Cherokee Planters*, 262; Malone, *Cherokees of the Old South*, 125.

25. Moulton, *John Ross*, 80; Moulton, *Papers of Chief John Ross*, 2:56; Spring, *Cultural Transformation*, 189.

26. Soltow, "Economic Inequality," 838.

27. Shadburn, *Cherokee Planters*, 12; Perdue, "Cherokee Planters," 118; Spring, *Cultural Transformation*, 43.

28. Soltow, "Economic Inequality," 825; Daniel Butrick to Mr. J. P. Northrup, *Religious Intelligencer* 10 (Oct. 1825): 280–81; Thurman Wilkins, *Cherokee Tragedy*, 188.

29. Cass, *Considerations on the Present State of the Indians*, 57.

30. Baird, *Peter Pitchlynn*, 45–46; Spring, *Cultural Transformation*, 43; Gibson, *Chickasaws*, 101; Nutt, "Diary of a Tour," 48, 56.

31. Mildred Campbell, "Social Origins of Some Early Americans," 65–66; Appleby, *Economic Thought and Ideology*, 32, 248.

32. Bailyn, *New England Merchants*, 16, 22, 103; Cary Carson, "Consumer Revolution," 556; Crowley, *This Sheba, Self*, 6, 77.

33. Appleby, "Consumption in Early Modern Social Thought," 163.

34. Hudson, *Southeastern Indians*, 310–12; Champagne, *Social Order and Political Change*, 22, 24; Reid, *Law of Blood*, 236; Bloom, "Acculturation of the Eastern Cherokee," 340.

35. Stiggins, "Historical Narration," 34, 141–42. For eighteenth-century sources on the economic ethos of southeastern Indians, see chapter 2. Payne heard Whites blame Indians' "corruption" on learning promoted by missionaries. Payne Papers 9:54–55, Newberry Library.

36. For instance, Wilms, "Cherokee Land Use," 1–5.

37. Hudson, *Southeastern Indians*, 312, 187–88; Perdue and Green, *Columbia Guide to American Indians*, 62; Gibson, *Chickasaws*, 10; Thurman Wilkins, *Cherokee Tragedy*, 28. Daniel Butrick praised the Cherokee language for having pronouns "to express . . . the real possession of something as property." Butrick Journal, 1825, Harvard Library.

38. Perdue, *"Mixed Blood" Indians*, 61. See also Hatley, *Dividing Paths*, 10.

39. Reid, *Law of Blood*, 262.

40. Perdue, *"Mixed Blood" Indians*, 4; McLoughlin, *Cherokee Renascence*, 69; Thurman Wilkins, *Cherokee Tragedy*, 188.

41. Malone, *Cherokees of the Old South*, 14; Benjamin Hawkins, "A Sketch of the Creek Country," 51–52; Benjamin Hawkins, *A Combination of a Sketch of the Creek Country*, 29–31.

42. McLoughlin, *Cherokee Renascence*, 69; Perdue, *"Mixed Blood" Indians*, 34–36; Champagne, *Social Order and Political Change*, 54.

43. Wade, "Greenwood LeFlore," 44–45; Baird, *Peter Pitchlynn*, 7, 18; Moulton, *John Ross*, 2–4, 6, 8; Perdue, *"Mixed Blood" Indians*, 58.

44. John Norton, *Journal*, 116–17. Some Indian children also saw their White fathers seize the opportunity to own large tracts of land under treaties that provided individual reservations in ceded territory. Perdue, *"Mixed Blood" Indians*, 29.

45. Perdue, *"Mixed-Blood" Indians*, 23; Benjamin Hawkins, "Sketch of the Creek Country," 85–86; Hawkins, *A Combination of a Sketch of the Creek Country*, 70.

46. Quoted in McLoughlin, *Cherokee Renascence*, 143. See also Payne Papers, 9:53–54, Newberry Library. Cherokee leaders also credited their nation's growing prosperity in part to U.S. officials' helpful advice. Hemphill, *Papers of John C. Calhoun*, 8:488.

47. Hemphill, *Papers of John C. Calhoun*, 8:552; Rogin, *Fathers and Children*, 184, 175.

48. James Taylor Carson, *Searching for the Bright Path*, 71; Champagne, *Social Order and Political Change*, 91. See also Bass, *Cherokee Messenger*, 233.

49. "On the State of the Indians," 42; Andrew, *From Revivals to Removal*, 115; *American State Papers*, 2:651–52, microform 231, ASP 08.

50. Oliphant, *Through the South and the West*, 21, 23; Berkhofer, *Salvation and the Savage*, 69–70, 81.

51. "Choctaws," *Cherokee Phoenix*, 27 May 1829, pp. 1–2.

52. Cyrus Kingsbury to Elias Cornelius, 15 Feb. 1820, Papers of the American Board of Commissioners for Foreign Missions, Harvard University, microfilm reel 780.

53. James Taylor Carson, *Searching for the Bright Path*, 84; Moulton, *John Ross*, 7; Bass, *Cherokee Messenger*, 91; Phillips and Gary, *Brainerd Journal*. Choctaw headmen came to regard mission schools "as 'goods' that could be distributed throughout the nation . . . [and] would confer great prestige on the chiefs who sponsored them." James Taylor Carson, *Searching for the Bright Path*, 90.

54. Spring, *Cultural Transformation*, 71; Wilms, "Cherokee Land Use," 146.

55. Hemphill, *Papers of John C. Calhoun*, 6:660; Berkhofer, *Salvation and the Savage*, 81; McLoughlin, *Cherokee Renascence*, 386; Bass, *Cherokee Messenger*, 28.

56. Andrew, *From Revivals to Removal*, 127, citing *Missionary Herald* 20 (Apr. 1824): 131–32; John Norton, *Journal*, lv.

57. McLoughlin, *Cherokee Renascence*, 173, 351, 359–61; Saunt, *New Order of Things*, 20; Champagne, *Social Order and Political Change*, 149; Oliphant, *Through the South and the West*, 37–38.

58. Quoted in Champagne, *Social Order and Political Change*, 92, 148, 158; Perdue, "Rising from the Ashes," 211; Faiman-Silva, *Choctaws at the Crossroads*, 27; McLoughlin, *Cherokee Renascence*, 363. The concept of class as a social category based in economic wherewithal was just then taking root. The *Oxford English Dictionary* gives several early nineteenth-century usages that equate "class" with economic rank, although the word could also denote social groups based on other characteristics.

59. McLoughlin, *Cherokee Renascence*, 330, quoting R. J. Meigs to Benjamin Hawkins, 13 Feb. 1805; Butrick Journal, Jan. 1821 and 7 Nov. 1832, Harvard Library.

60. Oliphant, *Through the South and the West*; "How to Be Rich," *Cherokee Phoenix*, 4 Nov. 1829, p. 4.

61. Saunt, *New Order of Things*, 255, 265; Moulton, *Papers of Chief John Ross*, 1:37.

62. Samuel Wells, "Role of Mixed-Bloods," 47–48; Andrew, *From Revivals to Removal*, 200; McLoughlin, *Cherokee Renascence*, 301, 363.

63. Champagne, *Social Order and Political Change*, 112, 127; McLoughlin, *Cherokee Renascence*, 125. Norton implied that covetous outsiders gave the tribe's subsistence farmers and large-scale planters reason to unite. *Journal*, 131.

64. Gibson, *Chickasaws*, 126; Perdue, *"Mixed Blood" Indians*, 90.

65. Samuel Wells, "Role of Mixed-Bloods," 42; Champagne, *Social Order and Political Change*, 112; Young, "John Ross," 116.

66. Evarts, "Letter from the Treasurer," 338–39.

67. Saunt, *New Order of Things*, 205–6, 214, 220.

68. Michael Green, *Politics of Indian Removal*, 39.

69. Perdue, *"Mixed Blood" Indians*, 49–50, 52–53; James Taylor Carson, *Searching for the Bright Path*, 90; Faiman-Silva, *Choctaws at the Crossroads*, 25; Debo, *Road to Disap-*

pearance, 91. On McGillivray's agreement with the United States in 1790, see chapter 2. Carson relates in *Searching for the Bright Path* (p. 88) that "a prosperous stockman and slaveowner" named Mushulatubbee participated "comfortably and successfully in the marketplace economy" but also "adhered to an ancient ideology predicated on divisional autonomy and redistribution of prestige goods."

70. Champagne, *Social Order and Political Change*, 105–6; R. J. Meigs to Gen. Dearborn, 3 Dec. 1807, *American State Papers*, 1:753, ASP 07; McLoughlin, *Cherokee Renascence*, 109.

71. James Taylor Carson, *Searching for the Bright Path*, 97; D. S. Butrick to J. H. Payne, 29 Dec. 1840, Payne Papers 4:105, Newberry Library.

72. John Ridge to Wilson Lumpkin, 2 Nov. 1836, cited in Thurman Wilkins, *Cherokee Tragedy*, 294; Moulton, *John Ross*, 203; Ray, *Chieftain Greenwood Leflore*, 68; Perdue, *"Mixed Blood" Indians*, 49.

73. McLoughlin, *Cherokee Renascence*, 92; Thurman Wilkins, *Cherokee Tragedy*, 165. Creeks also redistributed wealth by seizing property from the rich. Saunt, *New Order of Things*, 175, 255.

74. McLoughlin, *Cherokee Renascence*, 116, 96. See also Rogin, *Fathers and Children*, 226.

75. Ridge to Gallatin, 27 Feb. 1826, Payne Papers 8:104, Newberry Library. See also Boudinot, *Cherokee Editor*, 27; *Cherokee Phoenix*, 2 July 1828.

76. McLoughlin, *Cherokee Renascence*, 289.

77. Hemphill, *Papers of John C. Calhoun*, 8:591.

78. *Constitutions and Laws of the American Indian Tribes*, 5:3, 52–53 (Cherokee Nation); 9:69–70 (Choctaw Nation); McLoughlin, *Cherokee Renascence*, 285, 289; Woodward, *Cherokees*, 145; Moulton, *John Ross*, 29; Baird, *Peter Pitchlynn*, 26; Gibson, *Chickasaws*, 137.

79. Huston, *Securing the Fruits*, 83.

80. Gibson, *Chickasaws*, 129–30; Saunt, "Taking Account of Property," 748, 750; Perdue, "Conflict Within," 62–63; Shadburn, *Cherokee Planters*; Champagne, *Social Order and Political Change*, 128, 148; Wilms, "Cherokee Land Use," 16.

81. Quoted in McLoughlin, *Cherokee Renascence*, 300.

82. Startup, *Root of All Evil*, 49; Evarts, "Letter from the Treasurer," 344. Adams quoted in Thurman Wilkins, *Cherokee Tragedy*, 157.

83. Evarts, "Letter from the Treasurer," 338; Evarts, *Cherokee Removal*, 175.

84. Malone, *Cherokees of the Old South*, 137–38; Rogin, *Fathers and Children*, 299; Lebergott, *Americans*, 193; Scott, *In Pursuit of Happiness*, 75; Cumfer, *Separate Peoples*, 217.

85. Rogin, *Fathers and Children*, 175; Abernethy, *From Frontier to Plantation*, 227.

86. Andrew, *From Revivals to Removal*, 87; Burstein, *Passions of Andrew Jackson*, xiii, 87, 93, 121, 161.

87. Moulton, *John Ross*, 31, 37, 84, 201; Moulton, *Papers of Chief John Ross*, 1:9.

88. Jackson himself speculated in Indian land. Rogin, *Fathers and Children*, 84, 165.

89. Moulton, *John Ross*, 25. About the bribe attempt, Ross wrote: "An honorable and honest character is more valuable than the filthy lucre of the whole world; . . . I would prefer to live as poor as the worm . . . than to gain the world's wealth and have my repu-

tation as an honest man tarnished by the acceptation of a pecuniary bribery for self aggrandizement." Moulton, *Papers of Chief John Ross*, 1:54.

90. Baird, *Peter Pitchlynn*, 40, 42, 70; Ray, *Chieftain Greenwood Leflore*, 74; Michael Green, *Politics of Indian Removal*, 39; Waring, "Laws of the Creek Nation," 3; Hemphill, *Papers of John C. Calhoun*, 5:618–19; McLoughlin, *Cherokee Renascence*, 90.

91. Champagne, *Social Order and Political Change*, 110; Gibson, *Chickasaws*, 134, 137; Bassett, *Correspondence of Andrew Jackson*, 2:399–400.

92. Cayton, "Senator John Smith," 68–69.

93. Startup, *Root of All Evil*, 13, 14, 21; Cawelti, *Apostles of the Self-Made Man*, 54; Kohl, *Politics of Individualism*, 88; Rogin, *Fathers and Children*, 14–15.

94. Elson, *Guardians of Tradition*, 215, 217, 218, 252, 262–63; Startup, *Root of All Evil*, 30.

95. For examples, see Sheriff, *Artificial River*, 4, 96, 131.

96. Handlin and Handlin, *Wealth of the American People*, 42–43. See also Andrew, *From Revivals to Removal*, 5, on Evarts's concern about Americans' focus on gain.

97. Startup, *Root of All Evil*, 61; Kornblith, "Hiram Hill," 61; Kohl, *Politics of Individualism*, 17.

98. Welter, *Mind of America*, 78, 99, 106; Startup, *Root of All Evil*, 56; Hershberger, "Mobilizing Women," 33; Burstein, *Passions of Andrew Jackson*, 183; Huston, *Securing the Fruits*, 65; Pessen, *Riches, Class, and Power*, 308–9.

99. Piomingo, *Savage*, 178–79, 18, 76.

100. Quoted in Perdue, *"Mixed Blood" Indians*, 29.

101. Waring, "Laws of the Creek Nation," 3; Champagne, *Social Order and Political Change*, 92; McLoughlin, *Cherokee Renascence*, 90. A grievance of some Creeks who fought a civil war in 1812–13 was headmen who received salaries and emoluments from agent Benjamin Hawkins and became more responsive to him than to constituents. Michael Green, *Politics of Indian Removal*, 41.

102. Bassett, *Correspondence of Andrew Jackson*, 2:399–400; Bass, *Cherokee Messenger*, 168–69.

103. "A Good Conscience," *Cherokee Phoenix*, 21 Feb. 1828; Sir Richard Phillips, "Golden Rules," ibid., 11 Feb. 1829; A Cherokee, "Money and Principles," ibid., 28 Feb. 1828, and 20 Mar. 1828. See also *Cherokee Phoenix*, 30 July 1828, cited in Boudinot, *Cherokee Editor*, 19. "Buying and Selling," an essay on page 2 in the *Phoenix*'s 4 Mar. 1829 issue, argued that commercial exchange was unjust if undertaken with the aim of getting more than an equivalent for one's merchandise.

104. Elson, *Guardians of Tradition*, 271; Andrew, *From Revivals to Removal*, 68; Oliphant, *Through the South and the West*, 80.

105. *Cherokee Phoenix*, 18 June 1828.

106. Advocates of self-help preached that men must "pursue individual economic advancement, but they must do so without wishing to be rich or to rise dramatically in social status." Cawelti, *Apostles of the Self-Made Man*, 54.

107. For example, see "Removal of the Indians," 400.

108. Andrew, *From Revivals to Removal*, 7, 151, 171, 183.

109. Evarts, *Cherokee Removal*, 178–79, 127, 175.

110. "Removal of the Indians."

111. Evarts, *Cherokee Removal*, 194, 214, 235, 240, 222–23.

112. Andrew, *From Revivals to Removal*, 156; Debo, *Rise and Fall*, 52.

113. Startup, *Root of All Evil*, 18; Gabriel, *Elias Boudinot*, 92.

114. Phillips and Gary, *Brainerd Journal*, 180; Bass, *Cherokee Messenger*, 54; Butrick Journal, Jan. 1821, Harvard Library.

115. Berkhofer, *Salvation and the Savage*, 2, 7; Oliphant, *Through the South and the West*, 17; Noll, "Protestant Reasoning," 271; Cawardine, "'Antinomians' and 'Arminians,'" 287, 292, 294.

116. Oliphant, *Through the South and the West*, 79; Dorfman, *Economic Mind*, 2:765, 759.

117. Butrick Journal, Jan. 1821, Harvard Library.

118. McLoughlin, *Cherokee Renascence*, 248; Oliphant, *Through the South and the West*, 80.

119. Startup, *Root of All Evil*, 43; Butrick Journal, 1826, Harvard Library; Bass, *Cherokee Messenger*, 234, 237; Phillips and Gary, *Brainerd Journal*, 126.

120. Handlin and Handlin, *Wealth of the American People*, 67; Berkhofer, *Salvation and the Savage*, 2; Oliphant, *Through the South and the West*, 21–22.

121. Bass, *Cherokee Messenger*, 91; D. S. B. to Mr. J. Ridge, 24 June 1836, Payne Papers, 9:28–29, Newberry Library; Butrick Journal, 1833, Harvard Library. Charges that missionaries had more interest in economic gain than in converts came mostly from southerners, but word that missionaries used slaves led some New Englanders to suspect greed. Bass, *Cherokee Messenger*, 234.

122. Butrick Journal, 1830–31 and June 1838, Harvard Library; D. S. B. to Mr. J. Ridge, 24 June 1836, Payne Papers 9:28–30, Newberry Library.

123. Butrick Journal, 11 Jan. 1832, and 1825, 1830–31, 1832, Harvard Library.

124. Cawelti, *Apostles of the Self-Made Man*, 5; Startup, *Root of All Evil*, 24; Andrew, *From Revivals to Removal*, 176.

125. Lumpkin, *Removal of the Cherokee Indians*, 1:129.

126. Cass, *Considerations on the Present State of the Indians*, 12, 9, 13, 20; Gilmer, *Sketches*, 246–48, 296; Elson, *Guardians of Tradition*, 69.

127. Gilmer, *Sketches*, 249, 273–74. See also Young, "John Ross," 115.

128. Cass, *Considerations on the Present State of the Indians*, 11. See also Young, "Indian Removal and Land Allotment."

129. Horsman, "Indian Policy of an 'Empire for Liberty,'" 57; Cherokees of Aquohee District to Elias Boudinot, *Religious Intelligencer* 13 (May 1829): 822–23. Georgians feared the discovery of gold in Cherokee country would make the wealthy Indians even more reluctant to leave. Gilmer, *Sketches*, 269.

130. Hemphill, *Papers of John C. Calhoun*, 7:351.

131. *American State Papers*, 2:248, 709, 717–18. See also McLoughlin, *Cherokee Renascence*, 237, 303; Young, "Indian Removal," 33.

132. Lumpkin, *Removal of the Cherokee Indians*, 1:187, 189. See also Oliphant, *Through the South and the West*, 73–74.

133. Hemphill, *Papers of John C. Calhoun*, 6:618–19; Bassett, *Correspondence of Andrew Jackson*, 2:303–4, and 5:324, 350; Payne Papers 7:345, Newberry Library; Cass, *Consid-*

erations on the Present State of the Indians, 57–58. See also McLoughlin, *Cherokee Rena-scence*, 269, 402; Andrew, *From Revivals to Removal*, 213–14; James Taylor Carson, *Search-ing for the Bright Path*, 87. On U.S. bribes and material incentives for chiefs' cooperation, see Debo, *Rise and Fall*, 51, 54; Gibson, *Chickasaws*, 101; McLoughlin, *Cherokee Rena-scence*, 89; Bassett, *Correspondence of Andrew Jackson*, 2:399–400.

134. Rogin, *Fathers and Children*, 182–83. On Jacksonians' conception of aristocrats, see Welter, *Mind of America*, 78, 96. See also Kohl, *Politics of Individualism*, 24, 26, 31; Scott, *In Pursuit of Happiness*, 78.

135. Lumpkin, *Removal of the Cherokee Indians*, 1:280, 304.

136. Feller, *Jacksonian Promise*, 178–79; Lumpkin, *Removal of the Cherokee Indians*, 2:196; Bass, *Cherokee Messenger*, 163.

137. Moulton, *Papers of Chief John Ross*, 1:433, 442, 443; Rogin, *Fathers and Children*, 229; Burstein, *Passions of Andrew Jackson*, 186; Gilmer, *Sketches*, 269, 282; Bass, *Cherokee Messenger*, 108; Gibson, *Chickasaws*, 136; Woodward, *Cherokees*, 212.

138. Butrick Journal, June 1838, Harvard Library. See also Moulton, *John Ross*, 105.

139. Michael Green, *Politics of Indian Removal*, 26; Plea of unnamed chief, *Religious Intelligencer* 4 (26 Feb. 1820): 617; Moulton, *Papers of Chief John Ross*, 1:433; Moulton, *John Ross*, 42; Phillips and Gary, *Brainerd Journal*, 355.

140. McLoughlin, *Cherokee Renascence*, 377–78; Payne Papers 9:28–29, Newberry Library; Phillips and Gary, *Brainerd Journal*, 230; Hemphill, *Papers of John C. Calhoun*, 8:335; Butrick Journal, 1833, Harvard Library.

141. Champagne, *Social Order and Political Change*, 145.

142. Baird, *Peter Pitchlynn*, 63.

143. Champagne, *Social Order and Political Change*, 127; Faiman-Silva, *Choctaws at the Crossroads*, 32; Spring, *Cultural Transformation*, 97; Moulton, *Papers of Chief John Ross*, 1:442; Hemphill, *Papers of John C. Calhoun*, 8:382.

144. Baird, *Peter Pitchlynn*, 40–42; Gibson, *Chickasaws*, 174; Michael Green, *Politics of Indian Removal*, 149; Debo, *Rise and Fall*, 52. Moulton doubts that John Ross profited on contracts to supply Cherokee emigrants. *Papers of Chief John Ross*, 1:9.

145. "From Our Correspondent," *Cherokee Phoenix*, 4 Mar. 1829, p. 2; McLoughlin, *Cherokee Renascence*, 239.

146. Agent H. Montgomery to Lewis Cass, Oct. 1832, Records of the Cherokee Agency in Tennessee, 1801–35, Record Group 75, M-208, Roll 10, National Archives, Washing-ton, D.C.; Boudinot, *Cherokee Editor*, 27; Lumpkin, *Removal of the Cherokee Indians*, 2:94; Moulton, *John Ross*, 76; Thurman Wilkins, *Cherokee Tragedy*, 250, 300.

147. Young, "John Ross," 122.

148. Thurman Wilkins, *Cherokee Tragedy*, 244, 253.

149. Boudinot, [Letter to Mr. John Ross], 28–29, ⟨http://dlg.galileo.usg.edu/z/na/id:pam012⟩; Boudinot, *Cherokee Editor*, 201–2.

150. Moulton, *Papers of Chief John Ross*, 1:438; Woodward, *Cherokees*, 183.

151. Gabriel, *Elias Boudinot*, 160–63. For Ross's response to other charges of greed by John Ridge and Boudinot, see Moulton, *Papers of Chief John Ross*, 1:454, 637.

152. Boudinot, *Cherokee Editor*, 210–24, 69.

153. Boudinot, *Cherokee Editor*, 26–27; Champagne, *Social Order and Political Change*, 144.

154. Moulton, *Papers of Chief John Ross*, 1:456, 283.

155. Andrew, *From Revivals to Removal*, 224–25.

156. Rogin, *Fathers and Children*, 251.

157. Moulton, *John Ross*, 71. Missionary Samuel Worcester deemed Boudinot's decision to sign a treaty "entirely unjustifiable" but "dictated by good motives." Bass, *Cherokee Messenger*, 218.

158. Butrick Journal, 19 Aug. 1832 and 26 May 1838, Harvard Library. See also Young, "John Ross," 117.

159. Rogin, *Fathers and Children*, 171, 177, 202, 220; Gilmer, *Sketches*, 285; Lumpkin, *Removal of the Cherokee Indians*, 1:165, 182.

160. Feller, *Jacksonian Promise*, 182.

161. Lumpkin, *Removal of the Cherokee Indians*, 1:182. See also Bassett, *Correspondence of Andrew Jackson*, 5:351.

Chapter 4

1. Dale, "Some Letters of General Stand Watie," 56. See also Sarah Watie to Stand Watie, 4 Sept. 1864, roll 38, CNP.

2. Dale, "Letters of the Two Boudinots," 345–46; Franks, "Watie, Stand."

3. Cornelius to Aunt Sallie, 28 Jan. 1878, roll 40, folder 4316, CNP; ibid., 23 Apr. 1877, roll 40, folder 4315, CNP; E. C. Boudinot to James M. Bell, 17 May 1874, roll 41, folder 4886, CNP; E. C. Boudinot to Aunt Sally, 18 Oct. 1879, roll 40, folder 4330, CNP; Hewes, *Occupying the Cherokee Country*, 30, n. 66.

4. McLoughlin, *After the Trail of Tears*, 265, 308.

5. J. M. Bell to Mrs. S. C. Watie, Spencer S. Stephens, Rin Duncan, Thos. Howie & others, 21 May 1879, roll 40, folder 4382, CNP; Sarah Watie to "My dear brother," 31 Jan. 1872, roll 40, folder 4347, CNP; ibid., 7 Feb. 1879, folder 4379; ibid., 26 May 1879, folder 4383; ibid., 2 Sept. 1877, folder 4377.

6. Bays, *Townsite Settlement and Dispossession*, 60; Colbert, "Visionary or Rogue?," 273; Dale, "Letters of the Two Boudinots."

7. Madeleine Shelton to Aunt Sallie, 15 May 1876, roll 40, folder 4522, CNP.

8. Sarah Watie to My dear brother, 5 July 1880, roll 40, folder 4406, CNP; McLoughlin, *After the Trail of Tears*, 265; Bays, *Townsite Settlement and Dispossession*, 59. See also "Cherokee Cities," *Cherokee Advocate*, 7 Sept. 1872, p. 2.

9. See chapter 3.

10. Hays, *Response to Industrialism*, 20.

11. "The Cherokees," *Cherokee Advocate*, 6 Oct. 1882, p. 2. On conditions in the tribes after the Civil War, see Miner, *The Corporation and the Indian*, 4–5.

12. Annual message of Chief Perryman, *Muskogee Phoenix*, 6 Oct. 1892, editorial page; Alfred Williams, "Civilized Indian," 272; McLoughlin, *After the Trail of Tears*, 245.

13. Champagne, *Social Order and Political Change*, 210; McLoughlin, *After the Trail of Tears*, 245; James Morrison, "Problems in the Industrial Progress," 77. By 1899, over 25,000 of the 45,505 farms in Indian Territory produced 1.8 percent of U.S. cotton. Fite, "Development of the Cotton Industry," 352. In 1900, 75–80 percent of Cherokees and Creeks were farming, 4.5 percent were in a trade, and 1.8 percent were in professions. May, *African Americans and Native Americans*, 204–5.

14. Trachtenberg, *Incorporation of America*, 20; Ginger, *Nationalizing of American Life*, 10, 11; Nell Painter, *Standing at Armageddon*, xix.

15. Bays, *Townsite Settlement and Dispossession*, 33; James Morrison, "Problems in the Industrial Progress," 71; U.S. Senate, *Condition of the Indians in the Indian Territory*, xix. A Creek humorist remarked on Whites' desire to marry Indian women who had money and property. Posey, *Fus Fixico Letters*, 27.

16. Jenness, "Indian Territory," 446; *ARCIA* (1869), 397.

17. Wardell, *Political History*, 262; Travis, "Life in the Cherokee Nation," 27–28.

18. U.S. Senate, *Five Civilized Tribes*, 624–25.

19. Mr. Robinson to Stand Waitie [*sic*], 18 Apr. 1871, roll 40, folder 4304, CNP; Ben Hamilton to Stand Watie, 11 Mar. 1870, roll 40, folder 4292, CNP; Debo, *Road to Disappearance*, 286.

20. *ARCIA* (1889), 201; Debo, *Still the Waters Run*, 8; Debo, *Rise and Fall*, 26–27; Debo, *Road to Disappearance*, 235; Travis, "Life in the Cherokee Nation," 25.

21. Hoping to control and profit from rail lines while retaining sovereignty, the Cherokee and Choctaw nations created railroad stock corporations, but the U.S. government, citing the treaties, vetoed them. Miner, *The Corporation and the Indian*, 24–27.

22. The 1890 census showed that U.S. industrial output had finally surpassed farm and ranch products in value. May, *African Americans and Native Americans*, 204; Wrobel, *End of American Exceptionalism*, 30.

23. Debo, *Rise and Fall*, 114; James Morrison, "Problems in the Industrial Progress," 90; McLoughlin, *After the Trail of Tears*, 264; Denson, *Demanding the Cherokee Nation*, 177; Miner, *The Corporation and the Indian*, 9–11.

24. Galpin, "Some Administrative Difficulties," 310.

25. McAdam, "Indian Commonwealth," 894; Debo, *Rise and Fall*, 127, 131; Debo, *Still the Waters Run*, 16; James Morrison, "Problems in the Industrial Progress," 84. See also "The Indian Question Discussed by Spencer S. Stevens of the Cherokee Nation," *Titusville Morning Herald Print*, 1882, p. 27, roll 38, CNP.

26. Bryce, *American Commonwealth*, 2:600. See also Editorial, *NYT*, 3 June 1880, p. 4; Ginger, *Nationalizing of American Life*, 10; Nell Painter, *Standing at Armageddon*, xix–xx; Debo, *Rise and Fall*, 110–12; Debo, *Still the Waters Run*, 16.

27. McAdam, "Indian Commonwealth," 887.

28. Bryce, *American Commonwealth*, 2:600, 603; Trachtenberg, *Incorporation of America*, 80, 86–87, 5. See also Cable, *Top Drawer*, 10, 89.

29. Editorial, *NYT*, 20 June 1880, p. 6.

30. Gideon, *Indian Territory*, 261, 343. See also Debo, *Still the Waters Run*, 16; John Bartlett Meserve, "Chief Wilson Nathaniel Jones," 423.

31. "Shall the Indian Territory Be Modernized?—Shall It Be the Indian's?," *Chicago Daily Tribune*, 9 Dec. 1873, p. 2. On Jones's wealth, see Michael Bruce, "'Our Best Men are Fast Leaving Us,'" 295–96; Spring, *Cultural Transformation*, 117, 172.

32. *Indian Chieftain*, 20 Nov. 1884, pp. 1–2. On Severs and other rich Creek ranchers, see Debo, *Road to Disappearance*, 286.

33. Miner, *The Corporation and the Indian*, 70, 104, 106, 117.

34. Reprint, *Cherokee Advocate*, 20 Apr. 1883, p. 1. See also Editorial with excerpt from *Texas Live Stock Journal*, *Cherokee Advocate*, 5 Jan. 1883, p. 2.

35. "Wealthy Indians," *Cherokee Advocate*, 26 Aug. 1893, p. 1; Allen Wright, "A Visit to the Mansion of the Chickasaw Governor," *Oklahoma Star*, 23 May 1876. For other evidence of interest in the rich, see "Personal Reminiscences of Robert B. Ross, Sr.," 3 Nov. 1928, Ayer Ms. 46.5, 9, Ballenger Papers, Newberry Library, and Indian-Pioneer History entries, Susie Ross Martin, 34:160–173; Caroline Everett, 3:406–7; Mora M. Duncan, 23:69; Nathan E. Harrison, 28:156; James R. Padgett, 38:441, 445; A. A. McReynolds, 106:463; Levina R. Beavers, 104:39; Edward Nail, 7:386–87; J. L. Griffin, 26:453; Lucinda Hickey, 29:33; Millard (Bud) House, 85:232; R. R. Meigs, 108:213–16.

36. Nell Painter, *Standing at Armageddon*, xlii–xliii; Trachtenberg, *Incorporation of America*, 72.

37. Ginger, *Nationalizing of American Life*, 31–32; U.S. House, *Argument of Hon. John H. Reagan of Texas*; Moody, *Land and Labor in the United States*; Desmond, "America's Land Question."

38. Shearman, "Owners of the United States"; Spahr, *Essay on the Present Distribution of Wealth*, 55, 69; Pomeroy, "Concentration of Wealth"; Taubeneck, "Concentration of Wealth"; Collins, *Distribution of Wealth*; Ashley, "Distribution of Wealth." Cf. Carnegie, *Gospel of Wealth*, 50–53. In 1890, "the richest one percent earned more than the total income of the poorest 50 percent, and commanded more wealth than the remaining 99 percent." Trachtenberg, *Incorporation of America*, 99.

39. Garraty, *New Commonwealth*, 123, 310–11; Ginger, *Nationalizing of American Life*, 204; Bruce Palmer, *"Man over Money,"* 21; Trachtenberg, *Incorporation of American Life*, 99; Sumner, *What Social Classes Owe to Each Other*, 40.

40. Advocate, "Allotment," *Indian Chieftain*, 5 Sept. 1895. The author was DeWitt Clinton Duncan. Littlefield and Parins, *Biobibliography of Native American Writers*.

41. "What Would it Avail a Man If He Should Gain the Whole Cherokee Nation, and Lose All Excep [*sic*] His 160 Acres," *Cherokee Advocate*, 28 Mar. 1874, p. 2; Charles Thompson's Annual Message, *Cherokee Advocate*, 11 Nov. 1876, p. 1.

42. Wardell, *Political History*, 274; Letter of Samuel Mayes, *The Telephone*, 14 June 1895, p. 1; S. S. Stephens, "The Cherokee Lands," *Indian Chieftain*, 26 Aug. 1886.

43. Trachtenberg, *Incorporation of America*, 71, 166–67; Nell Painter, *Standing at Armageddon*, 70; Hays, *Response to Industrialism*, 37. "Class" was taking on a socioeconomic connotation, but Populists still "used the term . . . as a synonym for 'interest,'" often invoking it to deride legislation favoring one group's economic interests. Postel, *Populist Vision*, 224, 285–86. See Joseph E. Worcester's *Dictionary of the English Language* (Philadelphia: Lippincott, 1881).

44. Trachtenberg, *Incorporation of America*, 77.

45. Hays, *Response to Industrialism*, 73–74; Trachtenberg, *Incorporation of America*, 73; Nell Painter, *Standing at Armageddon*, xxix; Cawelti, *Apostles of the Self-Made Man*, 133; Bruce Palmer, *"Man over Money,"* 11, 21.

46. Champagne, *Social Order and Political Change*, 210–12.

47. Robert C. Childers, "Honest Indian Views," *Muskogee Phoenix*, 9 Apr. 1891, p. 1. See also message of Principal Chief C. J. Harris, *Cherokee Advocate*, 11 Nov. 1893, pp. 1–2.

48. Wilson Locke, Indian-Pioneer History 6:292, 297–98; Lavinia Murray Harkins, Indian-Pioneer History 27:431; Champagne, *Social Order and Political Change*, 233; McLoughlin, *After the Trail of Tears*, 239, 242, 294, 324; *ARCIA* (1888), 134.

49. Dawes, "Unknown Nation," 601; William W. West to J. M. Bell, n.d., roll 42, folder 5116, CNP. See also *ARCIA* (1885), 108.

50. Champagne, *Social Order and Political Change*, 212, 233; Hewes, *Occupying the Cherokee Country*, 37–38; Nick Comingdeer, Indian-Pioneer History 20:314–15; Roff, "Reminiscences of Early Days," 178. McLoughlin describes tensions between rich and poor Cherokee "classes" but maintains that Cherokee "populism" had a cultural and ethnic character missing from American populism. *After the Trail of Tears*, 238, 242, 294, 315.

51. Dawes, "Unknown Nation," 604.

52. John Bartlett Meserve, "Plea of Crazy Snake," 904; Este Makoke, "The Allotment of Our Lands," *Indian Chieftain*, 28 Nov. 1889; Ooh la nee ter, "A Fullblood's View," *Indian Chieftain*, 18 Oct. 1900, p. 3.

53. Denson, *Demanding the Cherokee Nation*, 179, 185–86; Zissu, *Blood Matters*, 10, 13.

54. Robert C. Childers, "Honest Indian Views," *Muskogee Phoenix*, 9 Apr. 1891, p. 1; Homeless Citizen, "Favor Allotment," *Indian Chieftain*, 23 Aug. 1895; C. C. Robards to Hon. A. S. McKennon, 2 Feb. 1894, box 51, Dawes Papers, Library of Congress; Alfred Williams, "Among the Cherokees," 195; Too Qua Stee, "Difficulties Galore," *Indian Chieftain*, 28 Jan. 1897.

55. McLoughlin, *After the Trail of Tears*, 313; "Shall the Indian Territory Be Modernized?," *Chicago Daily Tribune*, 9 Dec. 1873, p. 2. According to McLoughlin, "the old Watie-Boudinot faction" exemplified ambitious Cherokees who felt that the tribal legal system did not promote their property interests. *After the Trail of Tears*, 341, 307, 312–24, 328.

56. Debo, *Still the Waters Run*, 17; Wardell, *Political History*, 341–42; John Thompson, *Closing the Frontier*, 30.

57. Robert C. Childers, "Honest Indian Views," *Muskogee Phoenix*, 9 Apr. 1891, p. 1; An Indian, "Two Vital Questions," *Muskogee Phoenix*, 6 Oct. 1892.

58. Committee of Safety to James Bell Esq., 12 Sept. 1881, roll 43, folder 5691, CNP; Miner, *The Corporation and the Indian*, 81–83.

59. On American workers' general devotion to private property and individualism, see Garraty, *New Commonwealth*, 140, 146.

60. "Capital and Labor," *Cherokee Advocate*, 11 Oct. 1873, p. 2.

61. "To the Cherokee People," roll 38, CNP; McLoughlin, *After the Trail of Tears*, 324, 327–28.

62. Quoted in Debo, *Road to Disappearance*, 215–16.

63. Message of Coleman Cole, 1878 (typescript), OHS 19437, Cole Collection, Choctaw Nation, WHC. See also Este Makoke, "Allotment of Our Land Question," *Muskogee Phoenix*, 7 Nov. 1889.

64. Quoted in McLoughlin, *After the Trail of Tears*, 369–70.

65. Bruce Palmer, *"Man Over Money,"* 10–11; Fine, *Laissez Faire*, 118; Garraty, *New Commonwealth*, 140, 146, 310; Hays, *Response to Industrialism* 2, 22.

66. [No headline], *NYT*, 10 Oct. 1895, p. 4, c. 5; Cawelti, *Apostles of the Self-Made Man*, 46.

67. Quoted in Trachtenberg, *Incorporation of America*, 75. See also Fine, *Laissez Faire*, 53–54, 249; Sumner, *What Social Classes Owe*, 144–45; David Wells, *Recent Economic Changes*, 430.

68. Bryce, *American Commonwealth*, 2:604. See also Trachtenberg, *Incorporation of America*, 73; Garraty, *New Commonwealth*, 321.

69. Bowen, *Principles of Political Economy*, 505–6; Conwell, *Acres of Diamonds*, 19–20, 25–26; Russell Sage, "Wealth—A Decree of Justice," *Independent*, 1 May 1902, p. 1027; Emerson, "Give the Rich Man a Chance," 501. See also Trachtenberg, *Incorporation of America*, 80; Hofstadter, *Social Darwinism*, 10.

70. Bowen, *Principles of Political Economy*, 20; Sumner, *What Social Classes Owe*, 47–48; Phelps, "Irresponsible Wealth," 528, 533.

71. David Wells, *Recent Economic Changes*, 725; Mallock, "Who Are the Chief Wealth-Producers?," 649–50; Charles R. Flint, "Centralization and Natural Law," *Independent*, 1 May 1902, 1027. See also Cashman, *America in the Gilded Age*, 41; Cable, *Top Drawer*, 166.

72. Excerpt from Henry George and David Dudley Field, "Land and Taxation: A Conversation," *North American Review* 141 (July 1885) in Ginger, *Nationalizing of American Life*, 49, 52.

73. *ARCIA* (1888), 134; Robert C. Childers, "Honest Indian Views," *Muskogee Phoenix*, 9 Apr. 1891, p. 1.

74. Cf. Clark, *Philosophy of Wealth*, v, 35, 172.

75. Quoted in Garraty, *New Commonwealth*, 25. See also Trachtenberg, *Incorporation of America*, 151.

76. Hays, *Response to Industrialism*, 38; David Wells, *Recent Economic Change*, 431; Phelps, "Irresponsible Wealth," 525; Patterson, *America's Struggle against Poverty*, 8.

77. "Mr. Beecher's Lecture," *NYT*, 11 Dec. 1881, p. 7. See also Charles Elliot Norton, "Poverty of England," 153; Gibbons, "Wealth and Its Obligations"; Phelps, "Irresponsible Wealth," 530; Hamer, "Money and the Moral Order," 141.

78. Garraty, *New Commonwealth*, 122; Bruce Palmer, *"Man over Money,"* xv, xvii, 9, 23; Postel, *Populist Vision*, 4–5; Fine, *Laissez Faire*, 249.

79. Ashley, "Distribution of Wealth," 727, 729; David Wells, *Recent Economic Changes*, 437. See also Garraty, *New Commonwealth*, 318; Hays, *Response to Industrialism*, 41. Henry George did advocate a major legal change—abolition of private land title—but also argued that abundance would kill people's appetite for extreme wealth. *Progress and Poverty*, 445–46, 465.

80. Walter Thompson Adair, "Bread Money," *Cherokee Advocate*, 3 Mar. 1882; Sa-loo, "Ah-Dah-Lv Kah-too," ibid., 17 Mar. 1882, p. 2; W. T. Adair, "Bread Money," ibid., 12 May 1882; ibid., 13 May 1882, p. 2; "Childers Station Items," ibid., 31 Mar. 1882, p. 2: Saline, "Bread-Stuff," ibid., 14 Apr. 1882.

81. Cherokee Commission to U.S. Commissioners, 28 Oct. 1897, Dawes Papers, box 52, Library of Congress; U.S. Senate, *Relations between the United States and the Five Civilized Tribes*, 7.

82. "Wire Fencing and Other Fencing," *Cherokee Advocate*, 20 Oct. 1882, p. 2. Editors later criticized private uses of undivided common property that took advantage of others' "indisposition or inability" to use the land. "Wire Fencing East of Ninety-Six," *Cherokee Advocate*, 17 Nov. 1882, p. 2.

83. *Indian Champion*, 17 May 1884, p. 3. See also Este Makoke, "Allotment of Our Land Question," *Indian Chieftain*, 28 Nov. 1889.

84. S. S. Stephens [also spelled Stevens], "The Cherokee Lands," *Indian Chieftain*, 26 Aug. 1886.

85. "Bushyhead's Letter of Acceptance," *Cherokee Telephone*, 11 June 1891 (clipping), box 3, no. 156, D. W. Bushyhead Papers, WHC; Pleasant Porter to Isparhecher, 18 June 1891, *Purcell Register*, 26 June 1891 (clipping), box 1, no. 4, Porter Collection, WHC; First Annual Message of Hon. Joel B. Mayes, 4 Nov. 1891, Adair Papers, Oklahoma Historical Society.

86. Miner, *The Corporation and the Indian*, 116.

87. "Monopoly," *Cherokee Advocate*, 6 July 1892; W. P. Boudinot, "What Is Monopoly?," *Cherokee Advocate*, 27 July 1892, and responses of C. C. Robards and the editors; W. P. Boudinot, "Monopoly of Lands," *Cherokee Advocate*, 26 Oct. 1892.

88. W. P. Boudinot, "What Is Monopoly?," *Cherokee Advocate*, 27 July 1892.

89. An Indian, "Two Vital Questions," *Muskogee Phoenix*, 6 Oct. 1892; "Speech of M. M. Edmiston," *Purcell Register*, 7 July 1893 (clipping), box 1, folder 6, Porter Collection, WHC; Advocate, "Allotment," *Indian Chieftain*, 5 Sept. 1895; "'Too-Qua-Stee' on Monopoly," ibid., 9 Sept. 1895; Too Qua Stee, "Difficulties Galore," ibid., 28 Jan. 1897.

90. Pleasant Porter to Isparhecher, 18 June 1891, *Purcell Register*, 26 June 1891 (clipping), box 1, no. 4, Porter Collection, WHC.

91. Champagne, *Social Order and Political Change*, 211; McLoughlin, *After the Trail of Tears*, 296, 348–49; A. S. McKennon to H. L. Dawes, 25 July 1895, box 51, Dawes Papers, Library of Congress. For the most part, the tribes' remedial laws banned or set limits on practices that enabled some people to claim big tracts by proxy. *Constitutions and Laws of the American Indian Tribes*, 1:90; 2:148, 199–200; 5:45; 6:24; 11:74; 12:238, 240, 281; 18:115, 117, 118–20.

92. Moore, *Political Condition of the Indians*, 44.

93. U.S. House, *Re-organization of the Indian Territory*.

94. Prucha, *Great Father*, 2:738; Bays, *Townsite Settlement and Dispossession*, 123.

95. U.S. House, Hayt, "Proposal for a General Allotment Law"; Denson, *Demanding the Cherokee Nation*, 198; Miner, *The Corporation and the Indian*, 10–12, 45–47, 82, 87–88, 118–19, 139. On tribe members' earlier demands for allotment, see Champagne, *Social Order and Political Change*, 224–27; McLoughlin, *After the Trail of Tears*, 310, 312–13.

96. Benjamin Heber Johnson, "Red Populism?," 29. Proponents of allotment also had Whites' desires in mind; they expected that Indian lots of eighty to 160 acres would leave excess reservation land available for non-Indian purchasers. Hoxie, *Final Promise*, 71.

97. When Congress did authorize allotment of reservations in the General Allotment Act of 1887, it exempted the Civilized Tribes, and debate about proposals to subdivide and privatize the lands of those tribes continued for several years.

98. Moore, *Political Condition of the Indians*, 17–18, 32; *Proceedings of the Annual Lake Mohonk Conference* (1891), 82; M. H. Kidd to H. L. Dawes, 4 Sept. 1894, Dawes Papers, box 51, Library of Congress; Bays, *Townsite Settlement and Dispossession*, 153; Denson, *Demanding the Cherokee Nation*, 187, 198; "Report of C. C. Painter," part 5, "Civilized Nations," in Indian Rights Association, *Eighth Annual Report*, 37; *ARCIA* (1886), vi.

99. McAdam, "Indian Commonwealth," 887; *Proceedings of the Annual Lake Mohonk Conference* (1894), 30; H. L. Dawes, "The Indian Territory," in *Proceedings of the Annual Lake Mohonk Conference* (1896), 98–99; Platt, "Problems in the Indian Territory," 200. See also U.S. Senate, *Report of Select Committee on the Five Civilized Tribes of Indians*, 12; J. R.

Trott to A. S. McKennon, 13 July 1895, box 51, Dawes Papers, Library of Congress; Charles Meserve, "The Five Nations," *Proceedings of the Annual Lake Mohonk Conference* (1897), 48; Charles Meserve, "Dawes Commission and the Five Civilized Tribes," 18–19.

100. "Hear! Hear!," *Cherokee Advocate*, 18 Nov. 1876; Pitchlynn, *Letter of Peter P. Pitchlynn*, 5, 13; "Proclamation by the Principal Chief," *Cherokee Advocate*, 22 Oct. 1870, p. 2; Jenness, "Indian Territory," 450; Principal Chief C. J. Harris to Messrs. Kidd & McKennon, 25 Aug. 1894, Dawes Papers, box 51, Library of Congress; Debo, *Still the Waters Run*, 29.

101. Bays, *Townsite Settlement and Dispossession*, 123.

102. Pitchlynn, *Letter of Peter P. Pitchlynn*, 1–2, 11–13.

103. Cherokee by Blood, "Allotment," *Indian Chieftain*, 25 Mar. 1886; *Objections of the Chickasaw, Choctaw, Seminole, Creek, and Cherokee Indians.*

104. Some maverick Americans saw virtues in the Indian system, or at least saw a reason to let Indians run their "political experiment . . . in order that they might demonstrate the feasibility or impracticability" of preventing the inequality that was emerging in the United States. "The Cure for Monopoly," *Indian Chieftain*, 5 Sept. 1895; "Land Monopoly" (from the *Washington Chronicle*), *Cherokee Advocate*, 28 Mar. 1874, p. 1; Benjamin Heber Johnson, "Red Populism?," 31–32.

105. Many Americans by then conceived of race as a biological category that entailed character traits, including economic tendencies and abilities. A prominent social scientist agreed that the "value-perceiving sense or faculty . . . differs widely in different races and families." David Wells, *Recent Economic Changes*, 453.

106. It was common to blame Indians' alleged backwardness on tribes' "peculiarly homogeneous character" and tribe members' conformity. Galpin, "Some Administrative Difficulties," 309.

107. U.S. House, Hayt, "Proposal for a General Allotment Law," 2–3; Miner, *The Corporation and the Indian*, 56–57, 78–80.

108. Trachtenberg, *Incorporation of America*, 36; Bowen, *Principles of Political Economy*, 1, 65; Benjamin Heber Johnson, "Red Populism?," 5; Alice C. Fletcher, "The Allotted Indian's Difficulties," *Outlook*, 11 Apr. 1896, 660.

109. Bushyhead et al., *Summary of the Census*, 4. See also Cherokee Commission to U.S. Commissioners, 28 Oct. 1897, Dawes Papers, box 52, Library of Congress; Denson, *Demanding the Cherokee Nation*, 225; Testimony of Roley M'Intosh [Creek], U.S. Senate, *Relations between the United States and the Five Civilized Tribes*, 66.

110. Michael Bruce, "'Our Best Men Are Fast Leaving Us,'" 795–96; *Objections of the Chickasaw, Choctaw, Seminole, Creek, and Cherokee Indians*, 11.

111. *Remonstrance of the Cherokee, Creek, Choctaw and Seminole*; First Annual Message of Hon. Joel B. Mayes, 4 Nov. 1891, Adair Papers, Oklahoma Historical Society. See also Charles Meserve, "Dawes Commission and the Five Civilized Tribes," 22–23; Cherokee Commission to U.S. Commissioners, 28 Oct. 1897, Dawes Papers, box 52, Library of Congress; "The Cherokees," *Cherokee Advocate*, 6 Oct. 1882, p. 2; U.S. Senate, *Relations between the United States and the Five Civilized Tribes*, 85.

112. James W. Duncan, "Our Land-Tenure: The Cherokee Nation's Vital Question," *Indian Chieftain*, 25 Aug. 1892, p. 2; Zissu, *Blood Matters*, 16.

113. Quoted in Benjamin Heber Johnson, "Red Populism?," 33–34. See also Denson, *Demanding the Cherokee Nation*, 191, 228; Pitchlynn, *Letter of Peter P. Pitchlynn*, 5.

114. B. W. Williams, "Evils of Land Monopoly," 538; Desmond, "America's Land Question," 157; Taubeneck, "Concentration of Wealth," 462; Collins, *Distribution of Wealth*, 3–4.

115. Porter to Isparhecher, 18 June 1891, Porter Collection, WHC; "Speech of M. M. Edmiston," ibid.; Letter of Samuel Mayes, *The Telephone*, 14 June 1895, p. 1; C. C. Robards to A. S. McKennon, 2 Feb. 1894, Dawes Papers, box 51, Library of Congress.

116. Jenness, "Indian Territory," 445.

117. McAdam, "Indian Commonwealth," 886; Hinton, "The Indian Territory," 458.

118. U.S. Senate, *Condition of the Indians in the Indian Territory*, xix. See also "The Indian Lobby," *NYT*, 17 Jan. 1879, quoted in Hays, *Response to Industrialism*, 194. A belief that Indians could not prosper because they were not modern prompted many Euro-Americans to look for Whites behind wealthy persons of obvious Indian ancestry.

119. An Indian, "Two Vital Questions," *Muskogee Phoenix*, 6 Oct. 1892; Editorial, *Indian Chieftain*, 29 Aug. 1895. See also C. C. Robards to A. S. McKennon, 2 Feb. 1894, box 51, Dawes Papers, Library of Congress. Describing Indians as "more like a child" than Whites and not "as good a judge of humanity," Pleasant Porter said, "We are all the creatures of inherited tendencies and capacities, that descend to us through numberless generations." U.S. Senate, *Five Civilized Tribes*, 623, 627.

120. Platt, "Problems in the Indian Territory," 196.

121. 27 *U.S. Statutes at Large* 645–46 (1893); Loren Brown, "Dawes Commission," 73; Loren Brown, "Establishment of the Dawes Commission," 171–81.

122. U.S. Commission to the Five Civilized Tribes, *Annual Report* (1894), 17, 20; ibid. (1895), 78.

123. 29 *U.S. Statutes at Large* 339–40 (1896); 30 *U.S. Statutes at Large* 505–13 (1898).

124. *ARCIA* (1886), 82–84; Charles Painter, *Proposed Removal of Indians*, 3; H. L. Dawes to Secretary, 20 Sept. 1897, Dawes Papers, box 52, Library of Congress; Prucha, *Great Father*, 2:746–53; Hays, *Response to Industrialism*, 194. Senators expressed doubt that they could constitutionally change the status of the Five Tribes' lands, but they finessed the problem by requiring allotment agreements with tribes, then creating circumstances obliging tribes to agree. U.S. Senate, *Condition of the Indians in the Indian Territory*, xx.

125. Benjamin Heber Johnson, "Red Populism?," 6, 25, 31; Debo, *Still the Waters Run*, 22.

126. Julian Ralph, "The Unique Plight of the Five Nations," *Harper's Weekly*, 18 Jan. 1896, 10–15. Some other Americans slammed their countrymen for habitually robbing Indians — for example, Gen. Rush Hawkins, "Brutality and Avarice Triumphant," 665.

127. William R. Draper, "The Reconstruction of Indian Territory," *Outlook*, 22 June 1901, 444.

128. Hendricks, "Land of the Five Tribes," 674–75.

129. "Mohonk Indian Conference."

130. Editorial, *Indian's Friend* 8 (Aug. 1896): 6.

131. Denson, *Demanding the Cherokee Nation*, 198. The Knights of Labor constitution preamble asked rhetorically how Americans could justify taking Indians' land "by physical power, by robbery or fraud," driving them from land that was "originally common

property" to force its surrender to individual proprietors. Trachtenberg, *Incorporation of America*, 99.

132. Between 1889 and 1891, Congress did supplement public land laws so as to discourage monopolization more effectively, but it did not order the dispossession of people who had already assembled huge estates from the public domain, as it did for the tribes. Alexandra Harmon, "Indians and Land Monopolies," 121, 129.

133. Berkhofer, *White Man's Indian*; Philip J. Deloria, *Playing Indian*.

134. *Proceedings of the Annual Lake Mohonk Conference* (1901), 39.

135. Hays, *Response to Industrialism*, 82–83; Sheriff, *Artificial River*, 80.

136. W. A. Duncan, "Allotment 5," *Cherokee Advocate*, 26 Oct. 1892; *Objections of the Chickasaw, Choctaw, Seminole, Creek, and Cherokee*, 11, 21–22; Debo, *Still the Waters Run*, 29.

137. Debo, *Still the Waters Run*, 91.

138. Kidd to Dawes, 4 Sept. 1894, Dawes Papers, box 51, Library of Congress.

139. Zissu, *Blood Matters*, 10.

140. Debo, *Rise and Fall*, 255–64; Isparhecher to Muskogee Nation Council, 24 Aug. 1897, flap folder 7, file 26, Grayson Family Papers Collection, WHC.

141. Tension worsened as thousands of people from the States tried to gain Indian Territory land by claiming Indian ancestry. Debo, *Road to Disappearance*, 370.

142. Full-bloods of the different tribes were reportedly in constant communication. A. S. McKennon to Gen. Frank C. Armstrong, 24 Aug. 1897, Dawes Papers, box 52, Library of Congress; Zissu, *Blood Matters*, 28.

143. Debo, *Still the Waters Run*, 57, 95.

144. U.S. Senate, *Five Civilized Tribes*, 94–95, 92–93.

145. Posey, *Fus Fixico Letters*, 164; Debo, *Still the Waters Run*, 53–54; Zissu, *Blood Matters*, 28–29.

146. U.S. Senate, *Five Civilized Tribes*, 107.

147. "Reflections upon Crazy Snake," *Indian Journal* (clipping), box 1, folder 50, Porter Collection, WHC.

148. Debo, *Still the Waters Run*, 27; "Letter of J. F. Brown," *Muskogee Phoenix*, 31 May 1894 (clipping), folder 9, John F. Brown Collection, WHC; U.S. Senate, *Five Civilized Tribes*, 180–87.

149. Hewes, *Occupying the Cherokee Country*, 49; Debo, *Still the Waters Run*, 98, 126–27.

150. Debo, *Still the Waters Run*, 98–99, 92, 95–96, 106; William E. Curtis, "New Era for Red Men," *Springfield Daily* (clipping, n.d., 1903), Dawes Papers, box 56, Library of Congress; Bays, *Townsite Settlement and Dispossession*, 157–60; U.S. Senate, *Five Civilized Tribes*, 300–301.

151. "Editorial on Chickasaw Nation," *South McAlester News*, 2 Apr. 1903 (clipping), folder 22, Chickasaw Nation Papers, WHC.

152. Kenny Brown, "Progressive from Oklahoma," 235.

153. Quoted in Debo, *Still the Waters Run*, 172.

154. Also, there is little evidence that wealthy tribe members distributed wealth as eighteenth-century chiefs had.

155. Postel, *Populist Vision*, 288.

Chapter 5

1. 41 *U.S. Statutes at Large* 1249 (1921); BIA, *Osage People*, viii.

2. U.S. House, *Modifying Osage Fund Restrictions*, 67th Cong., 2d sess., Feb. 1922, serial 1, 60.

3. Ibid., Jan. 1923, serial 3, 4–5.

4. 43 *U.S. Statutes at Large* 1008 (1925); BIA, *Osage People*, ix; U.S. House, *Modifying Osage Fund Restrictions*, 68th Cong., 1st sess., 1924, 152.

5. U.S. Senate, *Osage Fund Restrictions*, 68th Cong., 1st sess., Mar.–Apr. 1924, 81, 76.

6. U.S. House, *Modifying Osage Fund Restrictions*, 68th Cong., 1st sess., 25 Jan.–7 Feb. 1924, 23–24.

7. By then, Osages were already "widely heralded as the richest people per capita in the world." Dickerson, *History of the Osage Nation*, 41, 55.

8. Thompson, Vehik, and Swan, "Oil Wealth and the Osage Indians," 40–46; Baird, *Osage People*, 55–58, 66, 71; BIA, *Osage People*.

9. After 1921, personal income rose every year until 1929. Patterson, *America's Struggle against Poverty*, 15. Due to advances in technology and labor efficiency, the 60 percent gain in production far outstripped population gain. Mowry, *The Twenties*, 3. See also U.S. Federal Trade Commission, *National Wealth and Income*, 2–3.

10. Noggle, *Into the Twenties*, 168; Benson, "Gender, Generation, and Consumption," 224; Horowitz, *Morality of Spending*, 134. Arguments that a small upper-income group was responsible for increased consumption appear in Holt, "Who Benefited from the Prosperity?," 277–89; Cochran, *Challenges to American Values*, 86.

11. Albert W. Atwood, "Are You Rich or Poor?," *Saturday Evening Post*, 23 Oct. 1920, 19. See also "Our 11,000 Millionaires," *Literary Digest*, 25 Sept. 1926, 14; "Ours Again a Land of Plenty," *Literary Digest*, 26 Aug. 1922, 15. For a less sanguine view, see Lewis Corey, "Who Owns the Nation's Wealth?," *New Republic*, 10 Aug. 1927, 300–303.

12. Allen, *Only Yesterday*, 160, 167.

13. Ibid., 172, 182, 166, 168, 169, 176; Matt, *Keeping Up with the Joneses*, 2, 3, 17, 47, 50; Noggle, *Into the Twenties*, 168; Albert W. Atwood, "Are We Extravagant?," *Saturday Evening Post*, 3 Jan. 1920, 16; Carter, *Twenties in America*, 32, 37. On organized labor's contribution to this ideological shift, see Glickman, *Living Wage*, 6, 79.

14. Allen, *Only Yesterday*, 7, 163; Horowitz, *Morality of Spending*, 143; Albert W. Atwood, "Are You Rich or Poor?," *Saturday Evening Post*, 23 Oct. 1920, 19.

15. Albert W. Atwood, "What Becomes of the Rich Man's Income?," *Saturday Evening Post*, 6 Sept. 1924, 14, 154; Allen, *Only Yesterday*, 81, 187, 189; Carter, *Twenties in America*, 27–28, 32.

16. For periodical coverage of American wealth and consumption not otherwise cited herein, see Laurence Todd, "Government by Millionaires," *The Nation*, 27 Mar. 1929, 367–68; "Pitiful Rich," ibid., 6 Aug. 1930, 42; "Sorrows of the Recently Rich," *Living Age*, 21 Aug. 1920, 491–94; "Old Rich and New Rich," ibid., 8 Oct. 1921, 103–5; "Our 11,000 Millionaires," *Literary Digest*, 25 Sept. 1926, 14; "Our Million-A-Year Men," ibid., 10 May 1930, 73–74; "Housekeeping for the Richest Rich," *Saturday Evening Post*, 31 Jan. 1920, 18, 177–78, 181–82; "Rich Man's Dilemma," ibid., 3 Dec. 1921, 12, 78, 80–82; "Millions," ibid., 6 Feb. 1926, 33, 132, 137–38; Cornelius Vanderbilt Jr., "It's Hard to Be a Rich Man's Son," ibid., 4 Dec. 1926, 8–9, 56–60.

17. Albert W. Atwood, "What Becomes of the Rich Man's Income?," *Saturday Evening Post*, 6 Sept. 1924, 154; Stuart Chase, "Park Avenue," *New Republic*, 25 May 1927, 9–11. See also Allen, *Only Yesterday*, 6.

18. Miley, "Overnight Millions," 84.

19. Albert W. Atwood, "What Becomes of the Rich Man's Income?," *Saturday Evening Post*, 6 Sept. 1924, 154; Albert W Atwood, "Are We Extravagant?," ibid., 3 Jan. 1920, 119.

20. "Too Much Money," *Saturday Evening Post*, 31 Mar. 1923, 26; Miley, "Overnight Millions," 15, 84. See also Morgan and Strickland, *Oklahoma Memories*, 217; Ida M. Tarbell, "'Save the Rich!,'" *New Republic*, 21 Dec. 1921, 100.

21. BIA, *Osage People*, vii, 16; McAuliffe, *Bloodland*, 48; Thompson, Vehik, and Swan, "Oil Wealth and the Osage Indians," 46; Holt, "Who Benefited from the Prosperity?," 278. Headright payments from oil peaked in 1923 and 1925 at $12,400 and $13,200, respectively. McAuliffe, *Bloodland*, 19. In 1920, the Brookings Institution estimated that 60 percent of American families had income under $2,000—the amount needed for basic necessities. Patterson, *America's Struggle against Poverty*, 16, 17, 29.

22. "Richest People Per Capita on Earth Get $8,290,100," 740–41; Shepherd, "Lo, the Rich Indian!," 724. See also Burwell, "Richest People," 88–96; Sherman Rogers, "Red Men in Gas Buggies," *Outlook*, 22 Aug. 1923, 629–32; Estelle Brown, "Our Plutocratic Osage," 19–22, 34, 36; E. T. Peterson, "The Miracle of Oil," *Independent and Weekly Review*, 26 Apr. 1924, 229, 234; "Other Folks, Also, Are Extravagant," *NYT*, 6 July 1920, p. 14; "Indians Lavish Spenders," *NYT*, 14 Nov. 1920, sec. 2, p. 20; Dill, "Portraits in Red and Black," 99, 138, 142, 143, 155, 156.

23. W. Irwin, "Richest People on Earth," *Collier's*, 22 Aug. 1925, 6; Estelle Brown, "Our Plutocratic Osage," 20; "'Black Curse' of the Osages," *Literary Digest*, 3 Apr. 1926, 44; Stuart Chase, "Park Avenue," *New Republic*, 25 May 1927, 9–11.

24. "American Aristocracy," 139.

25. [Illegible] Moran, "A Few of the Troubles of Filling 'Meanest Job in Civil Service,'" [unknown newspaper], 27 June 1926, [page numbers illegible], reel 10, I-300, no. 699, Collier Papers, University of Washington; E. T. Peterson, "The Miracle of Oil," *Independent and Weekly Review*, 26 Apr. 1924, 229; "'Black Curse' of the Osages," *Literary Digest*, 3 Apr. 1926, 44; Glasscock, *Then Came Oil*, 148; Burchardt, "Osage Oil," 265; Dill, "Portraits in Red and Black," 157, 99.

26. "'Black Curse' of the Osages," *Literary Digest*, 3 Apr. 1926, 42; E. T. Peterson, "The Miracle of Oil," *Independent and Weekly Review*, 26 Apr. 1924, 229; Shepherd, "Lo, the Rich Indian!," 734; William R. Draper, "Depression in the Osage," *Outlook*, 27 Jan. 1932, 114; Estelle Brown, "Our Plutocratic Osage," 22; Institute for Government Research, *Problem of Indian Administration*, 433.

27. On the origin of Indians as "Poor Lo," see Alexander Pope, *Essay on Man*, cited at ⟨http://www.Bartleby.com/100/203.10.html⟩. By the twentieth century, "Poor Lo" was a common allusion to Indians' expected decline and disappearance in the face of civilization. "Lo, the Poor Indian in Industry," 411; McKenzie, "Lo! the Poor Indian."

28. Charles de Young Elkus, "Prosperity of the American Indian a Bureau Smoke Screen," *American Indian Life* supplement (May 1927), reprint from *San Francisco Chronicle*, 22 Apr. 1927, reel 9, Collier Papers, University of Washington; George H. Dacy, "Washingtonians Guard and Direct Billionaire Indian Business," *Washington*

Star, 13 Mar. 1927 (clipping), reel 10, frame 726, Collier Papers, University of Washington; E. E. Slosson, "Lo! The Rich Indian," *Independent and Weekly Review*, 18 Sept. 1920, 37. Citing an Interior secretary's report that Indians owned property valued at more than $1.5 million, Slosson calculated they were "worth on the average $5,600 apiece." See also James O'Donnell Bennett, "That 'Vanishing Race' Is Gaining 1,000 Each Year," *Chicago Tribune*, 21 Dec. 1924, part 1, 14; "Remnant of Senecas Lives a Modern Life," *New York World*, 1 May 1926 (clipping), reel 10, Collier Papers, University of Washington.

29. "Indian Welfare Attracting Attention," *Harlow's Weekly*, 16 Jan. 1918, 6–7; E. T. Peterson, "The Miracle of Oil," *Independent and Weekly Review*, 26 Apr. 1924, 229; "Chief Two Moon" photograph, lot 12297, vol. 6, card 95509530, Library of Congress; Thorne, *World's Richest Indian*; Wishart, "Wealthiest Navajo," 13; Rosier, *Rebirth of the Blackfeet Nation*, 41.

30. American Indian Defense Association publications blaming Indian destitution on the Office of Indian Affairs in Collier Papers, University of Washington: reel 10, I-274, nos. 387, 389, 472; I-301, no 812; I-355, no. 1216; I-276, no. 684; I-280, no. 941. See also remarks of Rep. M. Clyde Kelly, *Congressional Record*, 64th Cong., 4th sess., 29 Dec. 1922, 1089; Vera L. Connolly, "The Cry of a Broken People"; Blanchard, "Deplorable State of Our Indians"; "Lo, the Poor Indian in Industry."

31. Estelle Brown, "Our Plutocratic Osage," 19; William R. Draper, "Depression in the Osage," *Outlook*, 27 Jan. 1932, 113; McAuliffe, *Bloodland*, 44.

32. Sherman Rogers, "Red Men in Gas Buggies," *Outlook*, 22 Aug. 1923, 629.

33. E. T. Peterson, "The Miracle of Oil," *Independent and Weekly Review*, 26 Apr. 1924, 229; "To Stomp Dance in Aeroplane," *Harlow's Weekly*, 14 May 1920, 11; W. Irwin, "Richest People on Earth," *Collier's*, 22 Aug. 1925, 6; "Richest Indians," *Literary Digest*, 12 Dec. 1936, 14.

34. E. E. Slosson, "Lo! The Rich Indian," *Independent and Weekly Review*, 18 Sept. 1920, 337.

35. Syndic, "An Apology for Murder," *Independent*, 20 Feb. 1926, 227–28.

36. In the survey histories of the 1920s cited herein, I found no mention of Osages, Indian oil and mineral development, or other Indian experiences of the period.

37. Board of Indian Commissioners, *Annual Report* (1920), 116–17; Estelle Brown, "Our Plutocratic Osage," 19. See also Terry Wilson, *Underground Reservation*, 127; U.S. House, *Indians of the United States*, 201, 174; DeBerry, "Ethos of the Oklahoma Oil Boom Frontier," 100.

38. Stuart Chase, "Park Avenue," *New Republic*, 25 May 1927, 9–11; "Negro Oil Magnates Visit City," *Los Angeles Daily Times*, 24 May 1922, sec. 2, p. 7.

39. McAuliffe, *Bloodland*, 43–44; W. Irwin, "Richest People on Earth," *Collier's*, 22 Aug. 1925, 6; Estelle Brown, "Our Plutocratic Osage," 22; Glasscock, *Then Came Oil*, 263; Franks, *Osage Oil Boom*, 111, 112. See also "Indians Lavish Spenders," *NYT*, 14 Nov. 1920, sec. 2, p. 20, c. 4; E. T. Peterson, "The Miracle of Oil," *Independent and Weekly Review*, 26 Apr. 1924, 229; Terry Wilson, *Underground Reservation*, 128.

40. Shepherd, "Lo, the Rich Indian!," 725–26; E. T. Peterson, "The Miracle of Oil," *Independent and Weekly Review*, 26 Apr. 1924, 229; Franks, *Osage Oil Boom*, 111; McAuliffe, *Bloodland*, 233.

41. Dittmar, *Social Psychology of Material Possessions*, 155, 30, 66; McCracken, *Culture and Consumption*, 60.

42. Frederick Palmer, "You Cannot Buy It All," 305; Horowitz, *Morality of Spending*, 69; Glickman, *Living Wage*, 86, 80; Cable, *Top Drawer*, 66, 70.

43. Shepherd, "Lo, the Rich Indian!," 727, 728; E. T. Peterson, "The Miracle of Oil," *Independent and Weekly Review*, 26 Apr. 1924, 229.

44. Westbrook, "And 'Twas the Night Before Christmas,'" 8.

45. Mathews, *The Osages*, 775.

46. On the scarcity of Osage scholarship, see Bailey, *Changes in Osage Social Organization*, 1. A well-educated man of predominantly White ancestry and cultural orientation, Mathews was not a trained ethnographer. Bailey, "John Joseph Mathews," 204–14.

47. "Making the Best of Luxury," *Saturday Evening Post*, 30 July 1921, 20. On Osage love of adornment, see Speck, "Notes on the Ethnology of the Osage Indians," 163.

48. Mathews, *Sundown*, 243.

49. Rollings, *The Osage*, 18, 80; Bailey, "Changes in Osage Social Organization," 23; Mathews, *Wah'kon-tah*, 183; Bailey, *Osage and the Invisible World*, 49, 53, 220; Nett, "Historical Changes in the Osage Kinship System," 176–77.

50. Mathews, *Wah'kon-tah*, 31.

51. Bailey, *Osage and the Invisible World*, 6, 31, 277; Bailey, "Changes in Social Organization," 24; Rollings, *The Osage*, 28, 29.

52. Bailey contends, however, that "basic social norms and values, as well as the general concepts of the world expressed in the teaching of the old priests, were alive and well in the collective minds of members of the contemporary Osage community." *Osage and the Invisible World*, 6.

53. Rollings, *The Osage*, 6; Bailey, "Changes in Osage Social Organization," 33, 67. See also Wayne Morris, "Auguste Pierre Chouteau"; Nett, "Historical Changes," 180.

54. Rollings, *The Osage*, 11, 43, 83.

55. Ibid., 259. Changes between 1870 and 1900 included the establishment of a tribal council on an Anglo-American model, the decline of Osage clans, disappearance of the most prestigious priesthood (the Non-hon-zhin-ga), and disintegration of the extended family household. Bailey, *Changes in Osage Social Organization*, 78, 86.

56. Bailey, "Changes in Osage Social Organization," 85. Speck, "Notes on the Ethnology of the Osage," 165, found secret societies in 1907 with some characteristics of the old priesthoods, including a fee and a feast as the price of entrance.

57. Terry Wilson, *Underground Reservation*, 34; Bailey, "Changes in Osage Social Organization," 88.

58. Mathews, *The Osages*, 727–28.

59. Ibid., 772; Terry Wilson, *Underground Reservation*, 13, 17, 60.

60. Terry Wilson, *Underground Reservation*, 49, 50. Periodicals publicized Osages' great wealth as early as 1903. Sweet, "Richest People in the World."

61. Bailey, "Changes in Osage Social Organization," 84, 85; Terry Wilson, *Underground Reservation*, 75; Terry Wilson, "Osage Indian Women," 192; Nett, "Historical Changes," 180.

62. Adams, *Education for Extinction*, 22–23, 149.

63. Dickerson, *History of the Osage Nation*, 5, 49, 93. White men needed little encour-

agement to seek rich Osages as brides. Terry Wilson, "Osage Women," 194. On the segregation of full-blood and mixed-blood populations, see U.S. Senate, *Enrollment of Osage Indians*, 184.

64. Mathews, *The Osages*, 772.

65. Any ideological sketch of the factions is likely to oversimplify. Lewis, "Reservation Leadership and the Progressive-Traditional Dichotomy," 124–48.

66. Mathews implied that spiritual matters motivated Osages more than economic practicalities. *Wah'kon-tah*, 41. But a 1932 Osage dictionary contains numerous terms relating to money, credit, debt, ownership, prosperity, economic planning, and consumer goods. La Flesche, *Dictionary of the Osage Language*.

67. Russell, "Chief James Bigheart," 390, 389. At a council meeting, through an interpreter, William Pryor said, "We admit we are too big-hearted. We give away too much money, we keep broke feeding people and giving away to other people." Records of the Osage Agency, Record Group 75, Miscellaneous, Box 2 of E-39, Records of the Field Solicitor, National Archives, Southwestern Region, Fort Worth, Tex.

68. Terry Wilson, *Underground Reservation*, 75.

69. For an account of this political history, see ibid., 24–44, 84–91; Berlin Chapman, "Dissolution of the Osage Reservation," 244–54, 375–77.

70. Berlin Chapman, "Dissolution of the Osage Reservation," 382. The U.S. government historically deemed persons of mixed descent entitled to share in property reserved for their Indian progenitors' tribe, but Bailey believes that agents improperly added many such people to the Osage annuity roll. Bailey, "Osage Roll," 26–27.

71. *ARCIA* (1906), 312; *ARCIA* (1903), 271.

72. 34 *U.S. Statutes at Large* 539 (1906), secs. 2, 3; Berlin Chapman, "Dissolution of the Osage Reservation," 378–80.

73. Regarding inequities expected from allotting oil along with land, see U.S. House, *Division of Lands and Moneys of the Osage Tribe*, 55, 81.

74. U.S. House, *Modifying Osage Fund Restrictions*, 67th Cong., 2d sess., serial 3, 24–25. See also Terry Wilson, *Underground Reservation*, 173.

75. U.S. Senate, *Osage Extension*, 137. Pursuant to federal laws and regulations, one-third of reservation acreage passed into non-Indian ownership by 1922. U.S. House, *Modifying Osage Fund Restrictions*, 67th Cong., 2d sess., serial 1, 4. In 1925, Congress prohibited Whites from inheriting restricted land, money, or minerals from Osages of half or more Indian blood. 43 *U.S. Statutes at Large* 1008 (1925), sec. 7.

76. U.S. House, *Modifying Osage Fund Restrictions*, 68th Cong., 1st sess., 6, 14.

77. Meyer, *White Earth Tragedy*, 153; Hoxie, *Final Promise*, 181.

78. 41 *U.S. Statutes at Large* 1249 (1921). By eliminating a tax exemption for lots not designated homesteads, the same act probably speeded land transfers to non-Indians. By 1928, certificates of competency covered more than 600,000 of the reservation's 1.5 million acres. U.S. House, *Hearings on H.R. 9294*, 4.

79. U.S. House, *Modifying Osage Fund Restrictions*, 68th Cong., 1st sess., 19.

80. U.S. Senate, *Osage Extension*, 68; U.S. House, *Indians of the United States*, part 3, 175, 203, 341–42. An act of March 1929 mandated competency certificates for adults of less than half-Indian blood, even though Wright testified that many such people had "little or nothing" left shortly after receiving payments of $40,000 to $60,000. U.S. House, *Bill*

Relating to the Tribal and Individual Affairs, 10; BIA, *Osage People*, 24. Some persons of more non-Indian than Indian ancestry were also declared incompetent. Records of the Osage Agency, Record Group 75, Boxes 1–3, E 37, Transcript of Hearings, 1920–24, Records of the Field Solicitor, National Archives, Southwest Region, Fort Worth, Tex.

81. U.S. House, *Indians of the United States*, 174, 204–5.

82. U.S. House, *Modifying Osage Fund Restrictions*, 67th Cong., 2d sess., serial 1, 5, 6; U.S. House, *Modifying Osage Fund Restrictions*, 68th Cong., 1st sess., 126.

83. U.S. Senate, *Osage Extension*, 24, also reporting the Osage council's fear that oil moneys would not be equitably distributed after the trust expired. See also U.S. House, *Indians of the United States*, 281.

84. "Making the Best of Luxury," *Saturday Evening Post*, 30 July 1921, 20; Albert W. Atwood, "Are We Extravagant?," ibid., 3 Jan. 1920, 17; Stewart, "Ethics of Luxury and Leisure," 257.

85. U.S. House, *Indians of the United States*, part 3, 341–42; U.S. House, *Modifying Osage Fund Restrictions*, 67th Cong., 2d sess., serial 1, 103–4.

86. U.S. House, *Modifying Osage Fund Restrictions*, 68th Cong., 1st sess., 33; U.S. House, *Modifying Osage Fund Restrictions*, 67th Cong., 2d sess., serial 1, 9; Schmeckebier, *Office of Indian Affairs*, 113.

87. Fungible and neutral though money may seem, people use it to express diverse, culturally-specific moral categories. Zelizer, *Social Meaning of Money*, 24.

88. George Harmon, "Indian Trust Funds," 23.

89. U.S. House, *Division of Lands and Moneys*, 165.

90. Prucha, *Great Father*, 2:870–72.

91. U.S. House, *Modifying Osage Fund Restrictions*, 67th Cong., 2d sess., serial 3, 15. On court cases and legal opinions affirming the federal guardianship of "backward" individual Indians and their money, see Hoxie, *Final Promise*, 211–19, and notes.

92. U.S. House, *Modifying Osage Fund Restrictions*, 67th Cong., 2d sess., serial 3, 7; serial 1, 9.

93. U.S. House, *Osage Fund Restrictions*, 73. It is unclear whether Wright was counting Indians among the 40,000 people.

94. Wilbur Corbet married full-blood Mary Elkins, who had eight and a half headrights, after getting her too drunk to understand the ceremony; he then kept her in a stupor while he rapidly spent her money. Mary's guardian proved that Corbet was working for people who conspired to fleece Mary. Corbet accepted $1,000 to have the marriage annulled. Frank, *Osage Oil Boom*, 114; Terry Wilson, "Osage Women," 194–95.

95. FBI File on the Osage Indian Murders, Newberry Library.

96. Ibid., report of J. R. Burger, 31 Dec. 1923, 3, and report of T. F. Weiss, 13; Franks, *Osage Oil Boom*, 111; McAuliffe, *Bloodland*, 232; BIA, *Osage People*, 64.

97. U.S. Senate, *Osage Fund Restrictions*, vol. 216, no. 3, 49, 66; BIA, *Osage People*, x, 55; U.S. House, *Modifying Osage Fund Restrictions*, 67th Cong., 2d sess., serial 3, 19.

98. Statement of George W. Hewitt, 26 June 1925, FBI File on Osage Murders, Newberry Library; U.S. House, *Modifying Osage Fund Restrictions*, 67th Cong., 2d sess., serial 2, 17; serial 1, 8–11; U.S. House, *Osage Fund Restrictions*, 66; U.S. House, *Modifying Osage Fund Restrictions*, 68th Cong., 1st sess., 6–8, 11, 46, 48.

99. U.S. House, *Modifying Osage Fund Restrictions*, 68th Cong., 1st sess., 40.

100. Ibid., 126.

101. U.S. House, *Division of Lands and Moneys*, 55, 81.

102. U.S. House, *Osage Fund Restrictions*, 245; U.S. House, *Modifying Osage Fund Restrictions*, 68th Cong., 1st sess., 117. In 1929, Congress ordered the Indian bureau to cover Osage debts to local businesses with trust account money despite evidence that merchants and guardians had extended credit to Indians in defiance of federal regulations. Terry Wilson, *Underground Reservation*, 141–42.

103. A former Osage agency head argued on behalf of county homeowners against more federal supervision. U.S. Senate, *Osage Extension*, 68–69, 74.

104. U.S. House, *Modifying Osage Fund Restrictions*, 67th Cong., 1st. sess., serial 1, 10.

105. U.S. House, *Osage Fund Restrictions*, 44.

106. Ibid., 41–42.

107. U.S. House, *Modifying Osage Fund Restrictions*, 67th Cong., 2d sess., serial 1, 6.

108. U.S. Senate, *Relief of Osage Indians*, 9–10. See also U.S. House, *Modifying Osage Fund Restrictions*, 68th Cong., 1st sess., 99.

109. Louis Sahagun, "Tribal Trust Funds in Disarray, U.S. Admits," *Seattle Times*, 10 Nov. 1996, p. A10; Robert Gehrke, "Trust Reform Will Cost Hundreds of Millions, Norton Tells Committee," AP State and Local Wire, 7 Feb. 2002.

110. U.S. House, *Modifying Osage Fund Restrictions*, 68th Cong., 1st sess. See also U.S. House, *Osage Fund Restrictions*, 5–6.

111. U.S. House, *Hearings on H.R. 9294*, 13, 11.

112. U.S. House, *Indians of the United States*, part 3, 281. Bacon Rind also testified that half of Pawhuska's residents were lawyers "trying to get money from the Indians. If an Indian dies they go and make a law suit, or an Indian makes a will giving the money to another one and they kill the Indian about a week afterwards." U.S. House, *Hearings on H.R. 9294*, 13. See also Raymond Wilson, "Dr. Charles A. Eastman's Report," 345.

113. U.S. House, *Modifying Osage Fund Restrictions*, 67th Cong., 2d sess., serial 1, 25; U.S. House, *Osage Fund Restrictions*, 86.

114. U.S. House, *Modifying Osage Fund Restrictions*, 67th Cong., 2d sess., serial 3, 5.

115. Ibid., 25.

116. Records of the Osage Agency, Record Group 75, Minutes, 9 Oct. 1923, Osage Tribal Council Minutes and Proceedings, 1891–1950, E-24, microfilm 7RA-172, roll 3, National Archives, Southwest Region, Fort Worth, Tex.

117. U.S. House, *Hearings on H.R. 9294*, 12. Bacon Rind said, "We are unable at this time to follow the ways of civilization. . . . We have grown up a different way and do not know anything else." Wah-shoh-shah concurred. Bacon Rind added, "The full blood is extravagant. He does not know the value of money. I myself do not know the value of a dollar to this day." U.S. House, *Indians of the United States*, part 3, 281, 283, 286.

118. By precisely reciting the history of laws governing Osage property, Bacon Rind belied his own statement that he was not competent to live under U.S. law. U.S. House, *Hearings on H.R. 9294*, 12, 13, 22. See also U.S. Senate, *Osage Extension*, 17.

119 U.S. House, *Division of Lands and Moneys*, 168; U.S. House, *Modifying Osage Fund Restrictions*, 68th Cong., 1st sess., 157–59; BIA, *Osage People*, x.

120. U.S. House, *Modifying Osage Fund Restrictions*, 68th Cong., 1st sess., 93.

121. Franks, *Osage Oil Boom*, 77, 96, 97; McAuliffe, *Bloodland*, 232; Terry Wilson, *Underground Reservation*, 132–47; Burchardt, "Osage Oil," 253–69.

122. U.S. House, *Modifying Osage Fund Restrictions*, 67th Cong., 2d sess., serial 2, 8, 16; Boutwell, "Adjustment of Osage Indian Youth," 54–59.

123. Franks, *Osage Oil Boom*, 142, 145. In contrast to most journalists and his colleagues in the Indian bureau, Charles Eastman said of the Osages in 1924 "that their moral condition is better than any people would be in similar situation." Raymond Wilson, "Dr. Charles Eastman's Report," 345. For an independent investigator's mixed review, see Parman, "Lewis Meriam's Letters," 365–66.

124. U.S. House, *Modifying Osage Fund Restrictions*, 68th Cong., 1st sess., 95. See also U.S. House, *Hearings on H.R. 9294*, 12, 13–14, 22; Tallchief testimony, U.S. Senate, *Survey of Conditions of the Indians*, 6871; Boutwell, "Adjustment of Osage Indian Youth," 95.

125. U.S. House, *Modifying Osage Fund Restrictions*, 68th Cong., 1st sess., 4; BIA, *Osage People*, viii–ix, 65.

126. Institute for Government Research, *Problem of Indian Administration*, 18, 485; U.S. House, *Hearings on H.R. 9294*, 9.

127. Lawmakers' solution to Osages' alleged economic folly contrasts with a concurrent trend among social workers, who thought that American consumers—even those unused to having money—should be allowed to learn how to make wise choices by doing. Zelizer, *Social Meaning of Money*, 31–32, 144, 147–48, 150.

128. Horowitz, *Morality of Spending*, 74, 78.

129. Graeber, *Toward an Anthropological Theory of Value*, 100.

130. Foucault, *Power/Knowledge*, 98.

Chapter 6

1. "Survey of Indians Shows Many in Want," *NYT*, 21 May 1928, p. 39; William Atherton Du Puy, "The Plight of the Listless American Indians," *NYT*, 27 May 1928, p. 124; Institute for Government Research, *Problem of Indian Administration*, 3, 6–8, 108.

2. On staffing and methods of the Institute survey, see Prucha, *Great Father*, 2:809.

3. Charles de Young Elkus, "Prosperity of the American Indian a Bureau Smoke Screen," *American Indian Life* supplement, May 1927, reel 9, I-274, Collier papers, University of Washington; AIDA circular, 15 Jan. 1927, I-276, no. 684, ibid.; *Congressional Record*, 64th Cong., 4th sess., 29 Dec. 1922, 1089, reel 10, I-290, ibid.; Collier, "Vanquished Indian," 11 Jan. 1928, I-335, no. 1216, ibid.; Prucha, *Great Father*, 2:805, 811; Philp, "Indian Reorganization Act," 16.

4. "Rich Indian Bride Wins," *NYT*, 18 Aug. 1923, p. 9; "Tells the Troubles of Rich Indians," *NYT*, 23 Nov. 1926, p. 18; "Rich Indian Heiress Again Disappears," *NYT*, 29 Mar. 1927, p. 14; "Red Men Take Up Civilized Ways," *NYT*, 18 Apr. 1926, p. X15. See also Institute for Government Research, *Problem of Indian Administration*, 437.

5. Institute for Government Research, *Problem of Indian Administration*, 3.

6. Prucha, *Great Father*, 2:812; Vine Deloria Jr., *Behind the Trail of Broken Treaties*, 193. Wheeler quoted in "Says Government Neglects Indians," *NYT*, 11 Aug. 1929, p. 11. Coolidge quoted in Patterson, *America's Struggle against Poverty*, 15.

7. Investigators did not assign ultimate or primary blame for Indians' poverty. Problems interact in a "vicious circle," they wrote, and "causes cannot be differentiated from

effects." Institute for Government Research, *Problem of Indian Administration*, 3, 5, 7, 14, 89, 100, 430, 442–43, 445–46, 449–50, 452–53, 455–56. See also Parman, *Indians and the American West*, 84–85; Gerald Nagel, "Economics of the Reservation," 247.

8. Online, I searched *Readers' Guide Retrospective* (H. W. Wilson Co., 2009) for articles about Indians in these years. I found just three emphasizing economic plight, plus one on the Senate investigation and two referring to Indian poverty in connection with federal policy. They are Salamanca, "Helping the First Americans"; William R. Draper, "Depression in the Osage," *Outlook*, 27 Jan. 1932, 113–14; "Poor Lo Rich No Longer," *Literary Digest*, 12 Aug. 1933, 33; Fergusson, "Senators Investigate Indians"; Dupuy, "New Policy of Aiding the American Indian"; John Collier, "Indian Bureau's Record," *The Nation*, 5 Oct. 1932, 303–5.

9. AIDA circular, 15 Jan. 1927, Collier Papers, University of Washington; John Collier, "Indian Bureau's Record," *The Nation*, 5 Oct. 1932, 303–5; John Collier, "The Vanquished Indian," *The Nation*, 11 Jan. 1928, 38–41; John Collier, "A Lift for the Forgotten Red Man, Too," *NYT*, 6 May 1934, p. SM10.

10. John Collier, "Indian Family Camps Do Conservation Work," *NYT*, 27 Aug. 1933, p. XX12; John Collier, "Our Indian Policy Has Definite Aims," *NYT*, 10 June 1934, p. E5; "New Deal for the American Indian," *Literary Digest*, 7 Apr. 1934, 21; John Collier, *Indians at Work* 1 (July 1933): 1–4; "Indians Get Federal Aid," *NYT*, 6 Jan. 1935, p. E6. See also Parman, *Indians and the American West*, 93; "Rebuilding Indian Country," ⟨http://video .google.com/videoplay?docid=516613933821682208⟩.

11. Frank Ernest Hill, "A New Pattern of Life for the Indian," *NYT*, 14 July 1935, p. SM110; "Two Camps Form Over Indian Law," *NYT*, 28 Mar. 1937, p. 63; John Collier, "Indians Improve State," *NYT*, 12 Apr. 1942, p. E8; "11,000 Indians Join Our Armed Forces," *NYT*, 22 Dec. 1942, p. 17; "A Panorama of American Indian Life Today," *NYT*, 7 Sept. 1941, p. 93; "Indian Fighter," *Time*, 19 Feb. 1945, 18–19.

12. Parman, *Indians and the American West*, 97, 105, 106; Philp, "Indian Reorganization Act," 19; Graham Taylor, *New Deal and American Indian Tribalism*, 120–24; Bernstein, *American Indians and World War II*, 17–18; Burt, "Western Tribes and Balance Sheets," 477.

13. Bernstein, *American Indians and World War II*, 59, 67–68, 71–73, 141; Parman, *Indians and the American West*, 105, 107, 117; Prucha, *Great Father*, 2:1074; Philp, "Indian Reorganization Act," 20.

14. Allan Spalding, "The Poor Are Still Poor," *New Republic*, 1 Nov. 1943, 617; Oliver La Farge, "A Plea for a Square Deal for the Indians," *NYT*, 27 June 1948, p. SM14.

15. "Indian Girls Now at War Jobs," *NYT*, 6 Feb. 1943, p. 16; "Navajos Prosper in Uranium Hunt," *NYT*, 4 Nov. 1951, p. 75. On postwar American prosperity, see Heilbroner, "Who Are the American Poor?"; Patterson, *America's Struggle against Poverty*, 79.

16. Gladwin Hill, "Delegates of U.S. Indian Tribes Gather to Stress Their Problems," *NYT*, 6 Apr. 1949, p. 34; "Midwest Indians Found in Squalor," *NYT*, 1 Sept. 1949, p. 17; "Papago Indians Ask Help," *NYT*, 19 Aug. 1950, p. 14; Oliver La Farge, "Not an Indian, but a White-Man Problem," *NYT*, 30 Apr. 1950, p. SM4; "U.S. Indians Seen Going Downgrade," *NYT*, 26 Apr. 1950, p. 31; "Indian Jobs Sought Off Reservations," *NYT*, 26 Sept. 1950, p. 35; Harold E. Fey, "Most Indians Are Poor," *Christian Century*, 18 May 1955, 592–94; "Health of Navajos Fails to Improve," *NYT*, 10 Aug. 1951, p. 14; Gladwin Hill, "15 States Seek End of U.S. Indian Rule," *NYT*, 13 May 1950, p. 17.

17. Bernstein, *American Indians and World War II*, 151–57; Remarks of Mr. Bow, *Congressional Record*, 82d Cong., 1st sess. 97:8 (14 Aug. 1951), 9993; N. R. Johnson, "Solution: Assimilation"; Oliver La Farge, "Plea for a Square Deal," *NYT*, 27 June 1948, p. SM14. See also Rosier, "'They Are Ancestral Homelands,'" 1311.

18. Watkins, "Termination of Federal Supervision," 50.

19. Kelly, "Economic Basis of Indian Life," 76; Fixico, *Termination and Relocation*, 55, 67; Remarks of Sen. Malone, *Congressional Record*, 82d Cong., 1st sess., 97:9 (22 Sept. 1951), 11911; Prucha, *Great Father*, 2:1000–1001; Herbert Corey, "Lo! The Poor Indian Bureau," 31–32, 69–70; Bess Furman, "Program to 'Free' Indians Advances," *NYT*, 18 July 1954, p. 25.

20. "Indian Bills Opposed," *NYT*, 26 Mar. 1954, p. 9; "Indians Get Pledge," *NYT*, 14 Dec. 1954, p. 44; "Responsibility to the Indian," *NYT*, 4 Apr. 1954, p. E8; "Indian Bill Called 'Signal for Chaos,'" *NYT*, 26 Feb. 1954, p. 8; Nevill Joyner, "Indian Bill Opposed," *NYT*, 23 Mar. 1952, p. E8; Oliver La Farge, "Not an Indian, but a White Man Problem," *NYT*, 30 Apr. 1950, p. SM4; Prucha, *Great Father*, 2:1023.

21. Watkins, "Termination of Federal Supervision."

22. Fixico, *Termination and Relocation*, 59, 67, 108, 146, 158–59, 160, 163, 174, 181; Prucha, *Great Father*, 2:1077; Kelly, "Economic Basis of Indian Life," 78.

23. Fixico, *Termination and Relocation*, 148, 103, 167; "Indian Land Sale Is Eased by U.S.," *NYT*, 27 June 1955, p. 21; William Zimmerman Jr., "Indian Ownership of Land," *NYT*, 12 July 1955, p. 24; Harold E. Fey, "Most Indians Are Poor," *Christian Century*, 18 May 1955, 592–94; "Health of Navajos Fails to Improve," *NYT*, 10 Apr. 1951, p. 14; Parman, *Indians and the American West*, 144–45.

24. Quoted in "Jobs in Industry Aid Indian's Lot," *NYT*, 22 Apr. 1957, p. 25.

25. On 4 March 1957, *Time* brought attention to a *Minneapolis Tribune* series detailing the misery of the city's Indians and tracing the roots of their poverty. ⟨http://www.time.com/time/magazine/article/0,9171,862,467,00.html⟩. See also Robert W. Fenwick, "America's Lost People," a 12-part *Denver Post* series, 3–15 Jan. 1960, reprint in *Congressional Record*, 86th Cong., 2d sess. (22 Jan. 1960), 947–58; NBC Television, "An American Stranger," 15 Nov. 1958, ⟨http://www.nbcnewsarchives.com/nass/AssetDetailHandler.do?signal=guestAssetDetails⟩; John P. Shanley, "Report on Indians," *NYT*, 17 Nov. 1958, p. 63.

26. Brauer, "Kennedy, Johnson, and the War on Poverty," 101; Marjorie Hunter, "Kennedy Began War on Poverty," *NYT*, 10 Jan. 1964, p. 17; Marjorie Hunter, "To Help the Poor," *NYT*, 19 Jan. 1964, p. E7.

27. Johnson quoted in Brauer, "Kennedy, Johnson, and the War on Poverty," 99–100, 117. See also Patterson, *America's Struggle against Poverty*, 78–79; Zarefsky, *President Johnson's War on Poverty*, 24–28; Horowitz, *Anxieties of Affluence*, 145, 148–49; Meissner, *Poverty in the Affluent Society*, 39.

28. Indians went unmentioned in *The Other America* (1962), a book on poverty in the United States that caught the Kennedy team's attention and became a best seller when Johnson launched his anti-poverty campaign. Patterson, *America's Struggle against Poverty*, 99; Zarefsky, *President Johnson's War*, 24–25; Brauer, "Kennedy, Johnson, and the War on Poverty," 103; Horowitz, *Anxieties of Affluence*, 148–49. The report from a 1962 national conference on poverty also ignored Indians. Steiner, *New Indians*, 202.

29. "Indian Aid Pledged," *NYT*, 1 Nov. 1960, p. 22; "Indian Aid Pledged," *NYT*, 18 Nov. 1960, p. 26; Prucha, *Great Father*, 2:1087; Philp, *Indian Self-Rule*, 226.

30. Brophy and Aberle, *The Indian*, 62, vii; Prucha, *Great Father*, 2:1088.

31. "Parley of Indians Urges Wider Role," *NYT*, 22 June 1961, p. 12; Donald Janson, "Gains for Indians in U.S. Predicted," *NYT*, 16 June 1961, p. 34; American Indian Chicago Conference, *Declaration of Indian Purpose*, 4, 26, 16, 6–8, 19. See also Prucha, *Great Father*, 2:1089; Philp, *Indian Self-Rule*, 211. On Kennedy administration responses to Indian poverty, see "More Funds Asked for Indian Affairs," *NYT*, 28 Feb. 1962, p. 12; Donald Janson, "U.S. Moves to Spur Tribal Economies," *NYT*, 5 Sept. 1962, p. 61; Burt, "Western Tribes and Balance Sheets," 480, 381; Prucha, *Great Father*, 2:1091, 1092; Philp, *Indian Self-Rule*, 211; Clarkin, *Federal Indian Policy*, 72. Attorney General Robert Kennedy implied that Indian poverty was a moral test for the federal guardian. "Indian Victims, R. F. Kennedy Says," *NYT*, 14 Sept. 1963, p. 11.

32. Clarkin, *Federal Indian Policy*, 105; "Johnson Pledges Help for Tribes," *NYT*, 21 Jan. 1964, p. 15. Johnson quoted in Steiner, *New Indians*, 201.

33. Donald Janson, "U.S. Asked to Ease Poverty of Tribes," *NYT*, 10 May 1964, p. 83; Philp, *Indian Self-Rule*, 212; Burnette, *Tortured Americans*, 88; *The Amerindian* 12 (Mar.–Apr. 1964): 3; *Indian Truth* 4 (June 1964): 13; Clarkin, *Federal Indian Policy*, 113, 114. See also Cobb, "Philosophy of an Indian War," 73–74; Burt, "Western Tribes and Balance Sheets," 481.

34. Philp, *Indian Self-Rule*, 199–200; Clarkin, *Federal Indian Policy*, 72, 110, 132; Cobb, "Philosophy of an Indian War," 74–75, 93; Burt, "Western Tribes and Balance Sheets," 483; Castile, *To Show Heart*, 34; Joseph A. Loftus, "Indians Acclaim Poverty Agency," *NYT*, 25 Apr. 1967, p. 31.

35. Clarkin, *Federal Indian Policy*, 2–3, 72; Cobb, "Philosophy of an Indian War," 91.

36. Nicolau, "War on Poverty," 79, 82; McKinley, "Federal Indian Policy," 1–2.

37. "Johnson Pledges Help for Tribes," *NYT*, 21 Jan. 1964, p. 15; Donald Janson, "U.S. Asked to Ease Poverty," *NYT*, 10 May 1964, p. 83; Donald Janson, "Udall Promises 'New Approach' to End Poverty of Indian Tribes," *NYT*, 16 Apr. 1966, p. 1; Donald Janson, "Sioux Reclaiming Land in Dakotas," *NYT*, 21 Mar. 1965, p. 81.

38. Brophy and Aberle, *The Indian*, 62, 87; Steiner, *New Indians*, 198, 211; Cahn and Hearne, *Our Brother's Keeper*; Levitan and Hetrick, *Big Brother's Indian Programs*; "Where the Real Poverty Is," *U.S. News & World Report*, 25 Apr. 1966, 104, 106; "Forgotten and Forlorn," *Time*, 15 Mar. 1968, 20; Jack Gould, "TV: Hunger amid Plenty," *NYT*, 22 May 1968, p. 95; Robert Browning, "The Plight of Our Indians," *Seattle Post-Intelligencer*, 20 Apr. 1964, p. 1; Don Hannula, "Poverty on Indian Reservations Is Evident at Port Gamble," *Seattle Times*, 12 Feb. 1967, p. 33; Don Hannula, "The Indian Problem," *Seattle Times*, 30 June 1968, p. 92.

39. "Help the Neediest First," *Christian Century*, 27 May 1965, 693. See also Thomas E. Connolly, "The Indian and the Poverty War," *America*, 12 Sept. 1964, 260–61.

40. President Nixon recited the facts in a special message on Indian affairs: "Unemployment among Indians is ten times the national average . . . 80 percent on some of the poorest reservations. Eighty percent of reservation Indians have an income which falls below the poverty line." Quoted in Josephy, Nagel, and Johnson, *Red Power*, 111.

41. Clarkin, *Federal Indian Policy*, 72; Burt, "Western Tribes and Balance Sheets," 479; U.S. Department of Agriculture, *American Indians in Transition*, 7.

42. Zarefsky, *President Johnson's War*, 107–8; Robert Coles, "The Poor Don't Want to Be Middle-Class," *NYT*, 19 Dec. 1965, p. SM 7.

43. Mrs. Robert G. Fleagle, "State Indian Children Still Handicapped," *Seattle Times*, 20 Feb. 1958, p. 8. See also Robert Browning, "Plight of Our Indians," *Seattle Post-Intelligencer*, 20 Apr. 1964, p. 1.

44. Brophy and Aberle, *The Indian*, 62–63; Levitan and Hetrick, *Big Brother's Indian Programs*, 125–26, 138; Levitan and Johnston, *Indian Giving*, 14, 21; Hough, *Development of Indian Resources*, xiii, 17; Cahn and Hearne, *Our Brother's Keeper*, 9, 74–75, 93; Ablon, "American Indian Relocation," 367; Don Hannula, "Poverty on Indian Reservations Is Evident at Port Gamble," *Seattle Times*, 12 Feb. 1967, p. 33.

45. U.S. Department of Agriculture, *Rural Indian Americans in Poverty*, 12; William M. Blair, "President Urges Broad Tribal Aid," *NYT*, 17 May 1967, p. 30; William M. Blair, "Senators Attack Bill to Aid Indians," *NYT*, 12 July 1967, p. 22.

46. Statement of Melvin Thom, U.S. Senate, *Federal Role in Urban Affairs*, 2602. Chippewa Roger Jourdain said, "Where did you get the money for your government programs? And your riches? From us! . . . You acquired the richest resource we had. It was our land that made you rich." Quoted in Steiner, *New Indians*, 197. For Indian complaints of inadequate federal aid, see ibid., 133; Chino, "Indian Affairs."

47. Vine Deloria Jr., "The War Between the Redskins and the Feds," *NYT*, 7 Dec. 1969, p. SM47; U.S. Senate, *Examination of the War on Poverty*, 1082–84; Vine Deloria Jr., *Custer Died for Your Sins*, 86; Hough, *Development of Indian Resources*, 17, 161–68.

48. Cahn and Hearne, *Our Brother's Keeper*, 92, 69, 74–75, 90, 164 (italics omitted). See also Earl Caldwell, "Kennedy Urges Wide Reform on Policy for Indians," *NYT*, 8 Oct. 1969, p. 29; John Leonard, "Red Powerlessness," *NYT*, 18 Nov. 1969, p. 45.

49. Patterson, *America's Struggle against Poverty*, 117; Peter MacDonald testimony, U.S. Senate, *Examination of the War on Poverty*, 1137; Don Hannula, "The Indian Problem," *Seattle Times*, 30 June 1968, p. 92.

50. Brophy and Aberle, *The Indian*, 4; Ablon, "American Indian Relocation," 363, 364; Steiner, *New Indians*, 194–195; Cahn and Hearne, *Our Brother's Keeper*, 171; U.S. Department of Agriculture, *Rural Indian Americans in Poverty*, 13; Clarkin, *Federal Indian Policy*, 72. Vine Deloria Jr. asserted, "Indian society is founded on status and social prestige" but competition is "confined . . . to inter-personal relationships instead of allowing it to run rampant in economic circles. . . . A holder of great wealth is merely selfish unless he has other redeeming qualities." *Custer Died for Your Sins*, 233.

51. Deloria quoted in Steiner, *New Indians*, 172. Chino quoted in Robert A. Wright, "Indians Hold 'Red Capitalism' Meeting," *NYT*, 19 June 1969. See also Nakai, "Inaugural Address," 54; Vine Deloria Jr., *Custer Died for Your Sins*, 262–63.

52. Vine Deloria Jr., *Custer Died for Your Sins*, 12; Lyndon Johnson, "The Forgotten American: President's Message to the Congress on Goals and Programs for American Indians," 6 Mar. 1968, ⟨http://www.eric.ed/gov/ERICDOCS/data/ericdocs2sql/content_storage_01/0000019b/80/32/7a/ac.pdf⟩; CBS and Carousel Films, "The Forgotten American"; Philp, *Indian Self-Rule*, 203–4.

53. "Indians Rally behind Seizure of Alcatraz Island," *NYT*, 30 Nov. 1969, p. 80; Earl

Caldwell, "Determined Indians Watch and Wait on 'the Rock,'" *NYT*, 10 Dec. 1969, pp. 37, 43; Edmunds, Hoxie, and Salisbury, *The People*, 422.

54. Ambler, *Breaking the Iron Bonds*, 32; Robert H. Mottram, "Tribal Renaissance Stunning Society," *Tacoma News Tribune*, 14 June 1977, p. 1; Wunder, *"Retained by the People,"* 149; Ben A. Franklin, "Indian Sovereignty Is Reborn in U.S.," *NYT*, 27 Mar. 1977, p. 151; Cornell, *Return of the Native*; Wilkinson, *Blood Struggle*, xiii; Joane Nagel, *American Indian Ethnic Renewal*; Getches, "Conquering the Cultural Frontier," 1591–93.

55. Edmunds, Hoxie, and Salisbury, *The People*, 425.

56. Wallace Turner, "Eskimos Press Land Claims in Alaska," *NYT*, 29 June 1969, p. 1; Earl Caldwell, "Indians Discern a 'Turning Point,'" *NYT*, 12 Oct. 1969, p. 41; Nancy Hicks, "Indian Links Gain for His People to Recognition of Tribal Power," *NYT*, 29 Mar. 1970, p. 45; Homer Bigart, "Indians Voice Alarm on Shrinking Resources," *NYT*, 27 Feb. 1972, p. 57; "California Indians Sue for $15-Billion," *NYT*, 13 Sept. 1972, p. 8; Richard J. Margolis, "A Long List of Grievances," *NYT*, 12 Nov. 1972, p. E5; Grace Lichtenstein, "Indian Tribes Are Using the System to Win Rights," *NYT*, 21 Dec. 1975, p. 1; National Congress of American Indians, *Resolutions Adopted by 23rd Annual Convention*.

57. Edmunds, Hoxie, and Salisbury, *The People*, 415, 418; Josephy, "Modern America and the Indian," 207–8; Wilkinson, *Blood Struggle*, 107.

58. Josephy, Nagel, and Johnson, *Red Power*, 69–71, 76–77.

59. National Congress of American Indians, *Resolutions Adopted by 25th Annual Convention*, No. 6; Vine Deloria Jr., *Behind the Trail of Broken Treaties*, 34, 37, 40; CBS Evening News, 12 Apr. 1978, Vanderbilt University Television News Archive, Record 257329; Wilkinson, *Blood Struggle*, 107.

60. Vine Deloria Jr., *Behind the Trail of Broken Treaties*, 33, 45, 249; William M. Blair, "Indian Leader Sees 'Typical Snow Job' in Federal Efforts," *NYT*, 22 Jan. 1972, p. 59; William M. Blair, "Indians Charge Administration Is Attempting to Divide Tribes," *NYT*, 11 Nov. 1972, p. 14; James Sterba, "Indian Militants Appeal for Unity," *NYT*, 1 Nov. 1973, p. 12; Alvin M. Josephy Jr., "What the Indians Want," *NYT*, 18 Mar. 1973, p. 260; Richard J. Margolis, "Long List of Grievances," *NYT*, 12 Nov. 1972, p. E5; Earl Caldwell, "Indians Discern a 'Turning Point,'" *NYT*, 12 Oct. 1969, p. 41; U.S. Commission on Civil Rights, *Indian Tribes*, 4; Wilkinson, *Blood Struggle*, 128, 196; Josephy, Nagel, and Johnson, *Red Power*, 78.

61. Wilkinson, *Blood Struggle*, 242, 112, 125, 195; Castile, *To Show Heart*, 35; Native American Rights Fund, ⟨http://www.narf.org/about/history.htm⟩; U.S. Commission on Civil Rights, *Indian Tribes*, 4.

62. Vine Deloria Jr., *Behind the Trail of Broken Treaties*, 38; Josephy, "Modern America and the Indian," 210; National Congress of American Indians, *Resolutions Adopted by 25th Annual Convention*, No. 1; James P. Sterba, "Indian Militants Appeal for Unity," *NYT*, 1 Nov. 1973, p. 12.

63. Vine Deloria Jr., *Behind the Trail of Broken Treaties*, 174, 50; Akwesasne Notes, *Trail of Broken Treaties*, 63.

64. Josephy, Nagel, and Johnson, *Red Power*, 4, 77, 146.

65. Olson and Wilson, *Native Americans in the Twentieth Century*, 194; David Wilkins, *American Indian Sovereignty*, 215–16.

66. 72 *U.S. Statutes at Large* 339 (1958); Public Land Order 4582, 34 *Federal Register* 1025 (1969).

67. 85 *U.S. Statutes at Large* 688 (1971); Wilkinson, *Blood Struggle*, 235; Wunder, *"Retained by the People,"* 165; Daniel Henninger, "Alaska: Share the Oil," *New Republic*, 28 June 1969, 15; Mary Clay Berry, "Oil Gumming Up Alaskan Dispute," *Washington Post*, 31 Aug. 1969, pp. D1, D2; Thomas Richards Jr., "State Lease Sale $900 Million while Few Natives Protested," *Tundra Times*, 12 Sept. 1969, p. 1; Robert Zelnick, "The Oil Rush of '70," *NYT*, 1 Mar. 1970, pp. 27, 54, 61, 68; Chris Carlson, "The Nixon Claims Bill Introduced," *Anchorage Daily News*, 7 Apr. 1971, p. 1; William M. Blair, "Congress Votes Alaska Land Bill," *NYT*, 15 Dec. 1971, p 9; U.S. Commission on Civil Rights, "How to Exploit and Destroy."

68. 43 *United States Code* 1606, 1607, 1613. A 1988 amendment prohibited sales of shares without corporation approval. Wunder, *"Retained by the People,"* 165.

69. Daniel Henninger, "Alaska: Share the Oil," *New Republic*, 28 June 1969, 15; Wallace Turner, "Eskimos Press Land Claims in Alaska," *NYT*, 29 June 1969, p. 1; Native testimony quoted in ⟨http://www.alaskool.org/PROJECTS/ANCSA/testimony/ancsa_hearings⟩. See also Lewis Lapham, "Alaska: Politicians and Natives, Money and Oil," *Harper's Magazine* (May 1970), ibid.; U.S. Commission on Civil Rights, "How to Exploit and Destroy"; "'Take Our Land, Take Our Life,'" *NYT*, 28 Feb. 1971, p. E12; "Chamber Backs Native Claims for $1 Billion," *Anchorage Daily Times*, 26 Mar. 1971, p. 1.

70. Trahant, "The 1970s," 240; "Land Selection Problems Confront Alaskan Natives," *NYT*, 24 Dec. 1972, p. 22.

71. "Judge Backs Indians in Maine Land Suit," *NYT*, 25 June 1972, p. 45; *Joint Tribal Council of the Passamaquoddy Tribe v. Morton*, 528 Fed. 2d 370 (1st Cir. 1976); "Maine Municipalities in Turmoil Over Land Suit Filed by Indians," *NYT*, 5 Oct. 1976, p. 14; "Indians Rush to Join Legal Fight for Land," *NYT*, 12 Dec. 1976, p. 32; West and Gover, "Struggle for Indian Civil Rights," 230. The Supreme Court approved the lower courts' reasoning in *County of Oneida v. Oneida Indian Nation*, 470 U.S. 226 (1985).

72. NBC Evening News, 5 May 1976, Vanderbilt Archive, Record 488553; NBC Evening News, 11 Oct. 1976, ibid., Record 485693; CBS Evening News, ibid., Record 250658; John Kifner, "Maine Indian Suit for Land Halts Bond Sales and Endangers Titles," *NYT*, 24 Oct. 1976, p. 1.

73. U.S. Commission on Civil Rights, *Indian Tribes*, 107–18; "Mashpee, Mass. Fights Suit by Indians to Recover 16,000 Acres Owned by Ancestors," *NYT*, 15 Nov. 1976, p. 20; CBS Evening News, 9 Dec. 1976, Vanderbilt Archive, Record 244198; "Oneidas File a Suit for Upstate Tract," *NYT*, 9 Dec. 1979, p. 71; "Indians Hope to Win Land," *NYT*, 7 Aug. 1977, p. CN1.

74. "Who Owns Maine?," *NYT*, 28 Jan. 1977, p. 17; Joseph E. Brennan, "'More at Stake' than One Indian Lawsuit," *NYT*, 18 July 1977, p. L27; "Maine Proposals Offered to End Indian Land Suit," *NYT*, 10 Feb. 1977, p. 18.

75. Wunder, *"Retained by the People,"* 168; John Kifner, "2 Maine Tribes Would Get $25 Million and 100,000 Acres in Proposal," *NYT*, 16 July 1977, p. 45; "Panel Urges Settlement of Tribal Claims in Maine," *NYT*, 10 Feb. 1978, p. A16; "Proposal on Indian Claim Shocks Officials in Maine," *NYT*, 12 Feb. 1978, p. 20; "Indian Settlement Is Likely to Create Jobs,"

NYT, 17 Feb. 1978, p. A14; "Maine to Seek Settlement of Indians' Claim to Land," *NYT*, 27 Apr. 1978, p. A21; Michael Knight, "Accord on Indian Claims Is Believed Near in Maine," *NYT*, 10 Feb. 1980, p. 28; "Maine Signs Settlement of Indians' Land Claims," *NYT*, 4 Apr. 1980, p. A8.

76. 94 *U.S. Statutes at Large* 1785 (1980); Robert White, *Tribal Assets*, 12; David Wilkins, *American Indian Sovereignty*, 216; Josephy, Nagel, and Johnson, *Red Power*, 4.

77. Bruce DeSilva, "First Eastern Indian Land Claim Is Settled," *Washington Post*, 10 May 1979, p. A5; "Catawba Indians to Ask Congress to Settle Land Claim in Carolina," *NYT*, 5 Apr. 1977, p. 12; Michael Knight, "Rhode Island and Owners Agree to Return 1,800 Acres to Tribe," *NYT*, 3 Mar. 1978, p. A8.

78. *United States v. Sioux Nation of Indians*, 448 U.S. 371 (1980); "Court Awards $100 Million to Indians in Land Claim," *NYT*, 14 June 1979, p. A20; "Sioux Leaders to Appeal U.S. Offer on Lost Lands," *NYT*, 3 Oct. 1979, p. A18; Ann Crittenden, "In the Braves' New World, Indians Like Land, Not Cash," *NYT*, 2 Nov. 1980, p. E8; David Wilkins, *American Indian Sovereignty*, 217.

79. Ambler, *Breaking the Iron Bonds*, 29, 32, 59, 64, 65, 67, 70, 78, 79, 93, 97; Parman, *Indians and the American West*, 170; Josephy, "Modern America and the Indian," 210; NBC Evening News, 16 July 1974, Vanderbilt Archive, Record 477761; NBC Evening News, 18 Aug. 1979, ibid., Record 505836; Judith Cummings, "Indian Tribes Seek to Increase Income in Mineral Leases," *NYT*, 8 June 1978, p. A11; Ann Crittenden, "Tribes Tap Iranian's Fuel Expertise," *NYT*, 7 Aug. 1979, pp. D1, D14; "Indians Discuss Uses of Resources That They Own," *NYT*, 24 Aug. 1980, p. A37; Wilkinson, *Blood Struggle*, 113.

80. Ambler, *Breaking the Iron Bonds*, 129; Gladwin Hill, "Study Says Coal Lessees Await Speculative Profit," *NYT*, 21 May 1974, p. 55; "Indians Want a Bigger Share of Their Wealth," *Business Week*, 3 May 1976, 100; Grace Lichtenstein, "Indian Tribes Are Using the System to Win Rights," *NYT*, 21 Dec. 1975, p. 1; "Energy-Rich Indians," *U.S. News & World Report*, 2 Aug. 1976, 29; Ann Crittenden, "Coal: The Last Chance for the Crow," *NYT*, 8 Jan. 1978, pp. F1, F11.

81. Richard Boeth, Jeff B. Copeland, Mary Hager, and Phyllis Malamud, "A Paleface Uprising," *Newsweek*, 10 Apr. 1978, 39; Grace Lichtenstein, "Indian Tribes Are Using the System to Win Rights," *NYT*, 21 Dec. 1975, p. 1; Hobbs, Goldstein, and Friedman, "Review of Developments in Indian Law," 11.

82. *Pyramid Lake Paiute Tribe of Indians v. Morton*, 354 Fed. Supp. 252 (D.D.C., 1973).

83. *United States v. State of Washington*, 384 Fed. Supp. 312 (W.D. Wash. 1974).

84. Cohen, *Treaties on Trial*, 155, 84.

85. U.S. Commission on Civil Rights, *Indian Tribes*, 4–5. See also Josephy, Nagel, and Johnson, *Red Power*, 215.

86. Vine Deloria Jr., *Custer Died for Your Sins*, 25.

87. Bosley Crowther, "Lo! The Rich Indian," *NYT*, 5 Sept. 1947, p. 16. A best-selling satirical novel's characters included Chief White Halfoat "a handsome, swarthy Indian from Oklahoma . . . out to revenge himself upon the white man" because, "'Every place we pitched our tent, they sank an oil well. Every time they sank a well, they hit oil. And every time they hit oil, they made us pack up our tent and go someplace else. . . . We were a walking business boom.'" Heller, *Catch-22*, 44–45.

88. "Navajos Prosper in Uranium Hunt," *NYT*, 4 Nov. 1951, p. 75; Seth S. King, "Lo! The Rich Indian," *NYT*, 2 Dec. 1956, p. SM55; "Ute Indians Hit a $31.7 Million Jackpot," *Life*, 24 July 1950, 37–38.

89. Lawrence E. Davies, "Indians in Oregon Give U.S. a Riddle," *NYT*, 10 Feb. 1957, p. 46; "Indian Bill Called 'Signal for Chaos,'" *NYT*, 26 Feb. 1954, p. 8. See also "Indians on Coast Get Rich on Land," *NYT*, 26 Nov. 1961, p. 147.

90. Everett R. Holless, "Wealthy Indian Tribe Suing over Its Palm Springs Land," *NYT*, 29 Dec. 1973, pp. 27, 47.

91. Ibid.

92. Frank Zoretich, "Fishermen Face Disaster—Evans," *Seattle Post Intelligencer*, 26 Oct. 1974, pp. A1, A14; "Innocent Hurt By Fishing Order, Evans Declares," *Seattle Post-Intelligencer*, 29 Oct. 1975, p. A9; Parfit, "Fishermen at Sea in Puget Sound," 60; U.S. Commission on Civil Rights, *Indian Tribes*, 118, 119; Faller, "Washington's Fish War," 53.

93. Frank Trippett, "Should We Give the U.S. Back to the Indians?," *Time*, 11 Apr. 1977, 51–52; Robert H. Mottram, "Tribal Renaissance Stunning to Society," *Tacoma News Tribune*, 14 June 1977, pp. A1, A3. See also Parfit "Fishermen at Sea in Puget Sound."

94. Peter Kovler, "Still Scalping the Indians," *The Nation*, 17 Sept. 1977, 233; Jorgensen, *Native Americans and Energy Development*, 7.

95. Jim Haley, "Indian Successes Could Lead to White Backlash," *Everett Herald*, 24 Feb. 1977, p. 3A; Petra Shattuck and Jill Norgren, "Indian Rights," *The Nation*, 22–29 July 1978, 71; "Backlash Stalks the Indians," *Business Week*, 11 Sept. 1978, 153; Basinger, Anderson, Marks, and Stoebner, "Review of Indian Legislation"; U.S. Commission on Civil Rights, *Indian Tribes*, 1. See also Trahant, "1970s," 249.

96. Bruce Johansen, "Anti-Treaty Group Fights 'Judicial Oligarchy,'" *The Daily of the University of Washington*, 30 Nov. 1977, p. 9; William Chapman, "Native Americans' New Clout."

97. ICERR quoted in Peter Kovler, "Still Scalping the Indians," *The Nation*, 17 Sept. 1977, 234. See also U.S. Commission on Civil Rights, *Indian Tribes*, 9–10, 12–13; Basinger, Anderson, Marks, and Stoebner, "Review of Indian Legislation"; Ben A. Franklin, "For Indians, The Militancy Is Muted," *NYT*, 16 July 1978, p. E8.

98. U.S. Commission on Civil Rights, *Indian Tribes*, 9–10; "Anti-Indian-Rights Group Meets Saturday," *Seattle Times*, 24 Nov. 1977, p. A7; CBS Evening News, 12 Apr. 1978, Vanderbilt Archive, Record 257329; Peter Kovler, "Still Scalping the Indians," *The Nation*, 17 Sept. 1977, 234; Richard Boeth, Jeff B. Copeland, Mary Hager, and Phyllis Malamud, "A Paleface Uprising," *Newsweek*, 10 Apr. 1978, 39; "Backlash Stalks the Indians," *Business Week*, 11 Sept. 1978, 153; Parfit, "Fishermen at Sea in Puget Sound," 61; Dudas, "In the Name of Equal Rights," 757. Opponents of Indian rights also protested a "judicial oligarchy's" excessive power. Bruce Johansen, "Anti-Treaty Group Fights 'Judicial Oligarchy,'" *The Daily of the University of Washington*, 30 Nov. 1977, p. 9.

99. Richard Boeth, Jeff B. Copeland, Mary Hager, and Phyllis Malamud, "A Paleface Uprising," *Newsweek*, 10 Apr. 1978, 39; Joseph B. Delacruz, "Senator Debates Indians on Steelhead Issue," *Seattle Post-Intelligencer*, 10 July 1981, p. A9; Ross Anderson, "Indians, Fishermen Clash on Steelhead," *Seattle Times*, 30 June 1981, p. 1; Petra Shattuck and Jill Norgren, "Indian Rights," *The Nation*, 22–29 July 1978, 71; "Foes Call Fishing Initiative Racist Act," *Seattle Times*, 14 June 1984, p. A26.

100. "Backlash Stalks the Indians," *Business Week*, 11 Sept. 1978, 153.

101. Quoted in Molly Ivins, "120 Tribes Form New Group to Block Anti-Indian Moves," *NYT*, 16 Apr. 1978, p. 24.

102. United Indian Planners Association, "Indian Reservation Development," in National Congress of American Indians, *American Indian Issue Papers*, 3. See also Howell Raines, "American Indians Struggling for Power and Identity," *NYT*, 11 Feb. 1979, p. SM6. About a Washington State ballot initiative to nullify Boldt's decision, one Indian official said the issue was not race-based privilege but property rights. "Foes Call Fishing Initiative Racist Act," *Seattle Times*, 14 June 1984, p. A26.

103. U.S. Commission on Civil Rights, *Indian Tribes*, 1, 11, 47, 71, 73; Richard Boeth, Jeff B. Copeland, Mary Hager, and Phyllis Malamud, "A Paleface Uprising," *Newsweek*, 10 Apr. 1978, 39; Faller, "Washington's Fish War." See also William Chapman, "Native Americans' New Clout."

104. Williams and Neubrech, *Indian Treaties*, 76. See also Francis G. Hutchins, "Righting Old Wrongs," *New Republic*, 30 Aug. 1980, 14–17; Faller, "Washington's Fish War," 53.

105. Williams and Neubrech, *Indian Treaties*, 72–75; Reiger, "Bury My Heart at the Western District Court"; Ross Anderson, "Indians, Fishermen Clash," *Seattle Times*, 30 June 1981, p. 1; U.S. Commission on Civil Rights, *Indian Tribes*, 73.

106. McLeod Papers, box 3, folder 14, University of Washington. McLeod was also Washington State ICERR director.

107. Williams and Neubrech, *Indian Treaties*, 1, 62.

108. John C. Raines, "Middle America: Up against the Wall and Going Nowhere," *Christian Century*, 2 May 1973, 504–7.

109. CBS Evening News, 28 Feb. 1977, Vanderbilt Archive, Record 250658; "Equality; American Dream—or Nightmare?," *U.S. News & World Report*, 4 Aug. 1975, 26; Jencks, "Hidden Prosperity of the 1970s"; Dudas, "In the Name of Equal Rights," 30.

110. Lemann, "How the Seventies Changed America," 41, 42, 44; McLeod Papers, Correspondence of Others File, University of Washington.

111. Petra Shattuck and Jill Norgren, "Indian Rights," *The Nation*, 22–29 July 1978, 71–72.

112. Williams and Neubrech, *Indian Treaties*, xii, 84.

113. Robert C. Lee, "Dick Gregory Goes Fishing," *The Nation*, 25 Apr. 1966, 488. I thank Paul Rosier for sharing this item.

114. "Maine Indian Tribes Confronting Era of Abundance," *NYT*, 22 Apr. 1979, p. 57; "Energy-Rich Indians," *U.S. News & World Report*, 2 Aug. 1976, 29; "Indians Want a Bigger Share of Their Wealth," *Business Week*, 3 May 1976, 100; Michael Knight, "Gains Affirm Indians' Rights Demands," *NYT*, 9 July 1979, p. A10. See also Jorgensen, *Native Americans and Energy Development*, 8. Parfit, "Fishermen at Sea," 59, 67, reported that Bob Satiacum, one of the first "modern" Indians to challenge Washington's regulation of treaty fishers, "is a millionaire now, grown rich on the profits of reservation liquor and tobacco sales and gambling operations. He owns a $200,000 covered swimming pool, and he wears a gold arrowhead at his throat."

115. Reagan quoted in Ambler, *Breaking the Iron Bonds*, 99. On the tribes' potential wealth and actual poverty, see American Indian Policy Review Commission, *Final Re-*

port, 1, 7, 305, 347, and *Report on Reservation and Resource Development and Protection*, 12, 127.

116. Josephy, Nagel, and Johnson, *Red Power*, 154; Williams and Neubrech, *Indian Treaties*, 76, 77, 83; Reiger, "Bury my Heart at the Western District Court," 102.

117. Michael C. Jensen, "Attacks on Oil Industry Grow Fiercer," *NYT*, 3 Feb. 1975, p. 47. For concurrent coverage of other rich people, see Marilyn Bender, "Oil, Some Cats and Dogs in Rockefeller Portfolio," *NYT*, 24 Sept. 1974, p. 149; John Corry, "About New York: Where the Rich Go Browsing," *NYT*, 3 May 1974, p. 44; Michael Fedo, "A Millionaire in the Unmaking," *NYT*, 8 Apr. 1979, p. F7.

118. Quoted in Ambler, *Breaking the Iron Bonds*, 72, 91, 96, 99, 107.

119. "Indians Want a Bigger Share of Their Wealth," *Business Week*, 3 May 1976, 100; Jorgensen, *Native Americans and Energy Development*, 9; Ben A. Franklin, "For Indians, the Militancy Is Muted," *NYT*, 16 July 1978, p. E8; Jim Haley, "Are Better Times Ahead for the Indians?," *Everett Herald*, 24 Feb. 1977, p. 3A; Howell Raines, "American Indians Struggling for Power and Identity," *NYT*, 11 Feb. 1979, p. SM6. See also Vine Deloria Jr., "Land and Natural Resources," 187.

120. "Indians Want a Bigger Share of Their Wealth," *Business Week*, 3 May 1976, 100.

121. For example, Oberg, *Social Economy of the Tlingit*, 35; Lamphere, *To Run After Them*; Rollings, *The Osage*, 31, 80–81; Stern, *Klamath Tribe*, 16.

122. Williams and Neubrech, *Indian Treaties*, 22.

123. Jim Haley, "Are Better Times Ahead for the Indians?," *Everett Herald*, 24 Feb. 1977, p. 3A.

124. Williams and Neubrech, *Indian Treaties*, 85.

125. Getches, "Conquering the Cultural Frontier," 1574–76, 1594–95; Wunder, *"Retained by the People,"* 179–80. See also National Indian Law Library, "Indian Law Cases Before the United States Supreme Court 1988–1998."

126. *Washington v. Washington State Commercial Passenger Fishing Vessel Association*, 443 U.S. 658 (1979), 685–87. The case was not titled *United States v. Washington* because the Court declined to review that decision. It later agreed to review the same issues in a case from Washington's high court, which held that state officials could not legally comply with federal court implementation orders.

127. U.S. Commission on Civil Rights, *Indian Tribes*, 98.

128. Getches, "Conquering the Cultural Frontier," 1637–38. I thank David Getches for sharing copies of relevant materials in the papers of Justices Thurgood Marshall and William J. Brennan from the Manuscript Division, Library of Congress.

129. Dana Johnson, "Native American Treaty Rights to Scarce Natural Resources," 567, 573. However, water rights cases peg Indian entitlement not to population or non-Indian demand, but to reservation acreage. Indians do not forfeit water by failing to use it. *United States v. Winters*, 207 U.S. 564 (1908); *Arizona v. California*, 373 U.S. 546 (1963).

130. In *United States v. State of Washington*, 157 F. 3d 630 (9th Cir. 1998), some adversaries tried unsuccessfully to win a reduction in treaty fishing, citing Stevens's language and new tribal revenue.

131. Dana Johnson, "Native American Treaty Rights," 570, 574–75, 583. Although courts have construed the treaty as an Indian grant to non-Indians, the Supreme Court did not say that the grant limited non-Indian fishers to a moderate living.

Chapter 7

1. Andrew E. Serwer, "American Indians Discover Money Is Power," *Fortune*, 19 Apr. 1993, 136–40; Glenn Coin, "Oneida Indian Nation Businesses Worth $1,000,000,000," *Post-Standard* [Syracuse, N.Y.], 15 Feb. 2005, p. A1; Erica Werner, "Indian Tribes Enjoy Big Payoff from Casinos," *Seattle Post-Intelligencer*, 16 Feb. 2005, p. 3; Lolita C. Baldor, "Tribes Looking to Share the Wealth with Other Indian-Run Companies," AP State and Local Wire, 20 Sept. 2004; Louis Sahagun, "Tribes Fear Backlash to Prosperity," *Los Angeles Times*, 3 May 2004, p. B1; Ianthe Jeanne Dugan, "A Business Empire Transforms Life for Colorado Tribe," *Wall Street Journal*, 13 June 2003, p. A1.

2. *McClanahan v. Arizona State Tax Commission*, 411 U.S. 164 (1973); *Bryan v. Itasca County*, 426 U.S. 373 (1976).

3. *Seminole Tribe of Florida v. Butterworth*, 658 Fed. 2d 310 (5th Cir. 1981).

4. *California v. Cabazon Band of Mission Indians*, 480 U.S. 202 (1987).

5. 25 *U.S. Code* 2701–21.

6. National Indian Gaming Association, Gaming Facts, ⟨http://indiangaming.org/library/⟩.

7. Graeber, *Toward an Anthropological Theory of Value*, 86.

8. Jerry Useem, "The Big Gamble," *Fortune*, 2 Oct. 2000, 222.

9. Ken Ritter, "Commission Reports Tribal Casinos Earned $19.4 Billion in 2004," AP State and Local Wire, 14 July 2005; Jim Doyle, "California Ka-Ching!," *San Francisco Chronicle*, 1 June 2003, p. D1; National Public Radio business report by Matthew Algeo, 16 Feb. 2005, ⟨http://www.npr.org/template/story/story.php?storyId=4501670⟩; William Booth, "Tribes Ride a Casino Dream," *Washington Post*, 9 May 2000, p. A1; Gillian Flaccus, "Membership Disputes Roil Indian Tribes," *Washington Post*, 11 Apr. 2004, p. A05.

10. Patt Morrison, "Oh, for the Bad Old Days When Gambling Was Illegal," *Los Angeles Times*, 23 June 2004, p. B13.

11. "Red Man's Greed," *South Park*, Comedy Central, aired 28 Apr. 2003. Other programs had similar Indian characters. Light and Rand, *Indian Gaming and Tribal Sovereignty*, 1, 121.

12. Andrew E. Serwer, "American Indians Discover Money is Power," *Fortune*, 19 Apr. 1993, 136–40; Jerry Useem, "The Big Gamble," *Fortune*, 2 Oct. 2000, 222. See also Timothy Egan, "Hunting 'The New Buffalo': Now a White Backlash against Rich Indians," *NYT*, 7 Sept. 1997, p. 43; Peter T. Kilborn, "For Poorest Indians, Casinos Aren't Enough," *NYT*, 11 June 1997, p. A1.

13. "Reservation Economic Summit (RES) 2005," U.S. Newswire, 9 Feb. 2005, p. 1, quoting Joseph Kalt. See also Rick Green, "Native American Casinos Are Significant Economic Force for Tribes, Study Shows," *Hartford Courant*, 21 May 2003, p. 1; Brad Knickerbocker, "Indians Making Big Strides Apart from Casinos, Too," *Seattle Times*, 16 Feb. 2005, p. A12; Lynda V. Mapes and Justin Mayo, "Indians Making Gains with Games," *Seattle Times*, 22 Sept. 2002, p. A1; and Blaine Harden, "Walking the Land with Pride Again," *Washington Post*, 19 Sept. 2004, p. A01.

14. "Tribes Have Paid their Fair Share," *Native Voice*, 15–19 Apr. 2005, p. 1; Andrew Mollison, "Cherokees' Casino Hits the Jackpot," *Atlanta Journal-Constitution*, 27 Apr. 2003, p. B1, quoting Jones; Jerry Reynolds, "NIGA Tribal Gaming Impact Analysis," *ICT*, 2 Mar. 2005, p. C1, quoting Doreen Hagen.

15. "Tribal Gaming: The Native American Success Story," *Native Voice*, 1–15 Apr. 2005, p. 1D; Bob Anez, "Cheyenne Leader: Economic Growth Top Priority," AP State and Local Wire, 27 June 2005; "Indian Leader Cites Poverty and Pleads for Aid," *NYT*, 1 Feb. 2003, p. A17. Allen quoted in Timothy Egan, "Hunting 'The New Buffalo,'" *NYT*, 7 Sept. 1997, p. 43. See also Jacob L. Coin, "Fighting the Myth of the Rich Indian," *ICT*, 3 Mar. 2004, p. A5; Mark Fogarty, "Casino Analysis Still in its Infancy," *ICT*, 24 Dec. 2003, p. C1.

16. "Indians Losing in Gambling Business," *Seattle Post-Intelligencer*, 4 Sept. 2000, pp. A1, A6, quoting the Hualapai chairwoman; Jerry Useem, "The Big Gamble," *Fortune*, 2 Oct. 2000, 222. See also Jim Barnett, "The Great Casino Hope," *Seattle Times*, 20 Feb. 2000, p. B9; Lynda V. Mapes and Justin Mayo, "Indians Making Gains with Games," *Seattle Times*, 22 Sept. 2002, p. A1; Michael Rezendes, "Few Tribes Share in Casino Windfall," *Boston Globe*, 11 Dec. 2000, p. A1.

17. Donald L. Barlett and James B. Steele, "Wheel of Misfortune," *Time*, 16 Dec. 2002, 47.

18. Blaine Harden, "Walking the Land with Pride Again," *Washington Post*, 19 Sept. 2004, p. A01.

19. Light and Rand, *Indian Gaming and Tribal Sovereignty*, 139–40.

20. Charlie LeDuff, "With Riches at Stake, Two Tribes Square Off," *NYT*, 2 Feb. 2003, pp. 1, 16. See also "Coushattas Bought Rival Casino Tribe Land for Reservation," AP State and Local Wire, 17 Feb. 2002; Steven Ritea, "Choctaw Casino Pact Rattles the Competition," *Times-Picayune*, 17 Feb. 2002, p. 1; Doug George-Kanentiio, "New York Hearings Reveal Deep Divisions among Iroquois," *News from Indian Country*, 4 Apr. 2005, p. 12.

21. Rob Carson, "Membership in Indian Tribes Becomes Increasingly Important, Divisive Issue," *Tacoma News Tribune*, 17 Feb. 2002; Marty Firerider, "The Red Path Has Turned Green for Some," *ICT*, 25 May 2005, p. A3; Chris T. Nguyen, "American Indians Meet in SoCal for Tribal Disenrollment Protest," AP State and Local Wire, 21 May 2005; Tim O'Leary and Michelle Dearmond, "Second Pechanga Family Faces Ouster; Financial Blow," *Press-Enterprise* [Riverside, Calif.], 21 Mar. 2006.

22. Mike Adams, "Banking on Indian Identity," *Baltimore Sun*, 8 Apr. 2004, p. 2A; Gillian Flaccus, "Membership Disputes Roil Indian Tribes," *Washington Post*, 11 Apr. 2004, p. A05; Harlan McKosato commentary, National Public Radio, 20 May 2005, ⟨http://www.npr.org/template/story/story.php?storyID=4660784⟩.

23. 25 *U.S. Code* 2710, paras. 2(B) and 3(A).

24. Lynda V. Mapes, "A New Welfare State? Tribes Call Puyallups' Plan a Gamble," *Seattle Times*, 15 May 2002, pp. A1, A13; "Reservations with Casinos Gain Ground on Poverty," *NYT*, 3 Sept. 2000, p. 19; "Political Candidate: Give Casino Profits Directly to Tribal Members," *Native American Times*, 23 Mar. 2005, p. 5; "Casino Payments at Issue in Mille Lacs Election Race," AP State and Local Wire, 9 May 2000.

25. Lynda V. Mapes, "Hitting the Jackpot and Raising the Stakes," *Seattle Times*, 19 May 2002, pp. A1, A18; Christine Clarridge and Steve Miletich, "Each Tulalip to Get $10,000 Payment from Casino Profits," *Seattle Times*, 19 May 2002, p. A18. On Indians' use of the word "greed" to connote usurpation of power, self-importance, and dishonesty in politics, see Lurie, "Money, Semantics, and Indian Leadership," 57–59.

26. Ken Silverstein, "Cashing In," *The Nation*, 6 July 1998, 20–21; Collin Levey, "Democrats Roll the Dice with Their Tribal Buddies," *Seattle Times*, 25 Sept. 2003, p. B7.

27. Mark Fogarty, "Casino Analysis Still in its Infancy," *ICT*, 24 Dec. 2003, p. C1; Jerry Useem, "The Big Gamble," *Fortune*, 2 Oct. 2000, 222; Lora Abaurrea, "Native Americans are Cashing-In with Gambling Casinos on the Reservation," *Take Pride! Community Magazine* [Los Angeles], 15–21 Nov. 2004, i. See also Light and Rand, *Indian Gaming and Tribal Sovereignty*, 103.

28. William E. Schmidt, "Bingo Boom Brings Tribes Profit and Conflict," *NYT*, 29 Mar. 1983, p. A1; Andrew Mollison, "Cherokees' Casino Hits the Jackpot," *Atlanta Journal-Constitution*, 27 Apr. 2003, p. B1; "Indians as Thieves," *ICT*, 3 Nov. 2004, p. A2.

29. Roxana Hegeman, "Connecticut Tribe Wants to Spread the Casino Wealth," *Tulsa World*, 15 Apr. 2005, p. A16; Tom Wanamaker, "Let the Games Begin; Indians Helping Indians, and Others," *ICT*, 11 Aug. 2004, p. C1; Michelle Breidenbach, "Wealthy Tribes Return Government Payment," *Seattle Times*, 10 Dec. 2000, p. B2; Lolita C. Baldor, "Tribes Looking to Share the Wealth with Other Indian-Run Companies," AP State and Local Wire, 20 Sept. 2004; Light and Rand, *Indian Gaming*, 71.

30. Ernest L. Stevens Jr., "Tribal Government Gaming: There are Only 'Positives,'" *Native Voice*, 22 Feb. 2004, p. C5; "Campbell: Tribes Have Paid their Fair Share," *Native Voice*, 15–29 Apr. 2005, p. 1.

31. Herbert Muschamp, "A Primal Phantasmagoria Not Just for Gamblers," *NYT*, 21 Oct. 1996, p. C13.

32. Benedict, *Without Reservation*; Jeff Benedict's website, ⟨http://www.jeffbenedict.com/about.cfm⟩; Donald L. Barlett and James B. Steele, "Wheel of Misfortune," *Time*, 16 Dec. 2002, 46–47. See also Light and Rand, *Indian Gaming and Tribal Sovereignty*, 61; Jerry Useem, "The Big Gamble," *Fortune*, 2 Oct. 2000, 222; Mike Adams, "Banking on Indian Identity," *Baltimore Sun*, 8 Apr. 2004, p. 2A; Eisler, *Revenge of the Pequots*.

33. Brett Marte, "Rags-to-Riches Louisiana Tribe Besieged by Relatives It Didn't Know It Had," AP State and Local Wire, 28 July 2001; Rob Carson, "Membership in Indian Tribes Becomes Increasingly Important, Divisive Issue," *Tacoma News Tribune*, 17 Feb. 2002; Paul Nowell, "North Carolina's Cherokees Battle over Bloodlines—and Money," AP Press and Local Wire, 27 Mar. 2004.

34. Donald L. Barlett and James B. Steele, "Wheel of Misfortune," *Time*, 16 Dec. 2002, 46–47. Emphasis added.

35. Francis X. Clines, "The Pequots," *NYT*, 27 Feb. 1994, p. SM49.

36. Jack Hitt, "The Newest Indians," *NYT*, 21 Aug. 2005, p. SM36.

37. "Termination at the Times?," *ICT*, 25 May 2005, p. A2.

38. Dahleen Glanton, "More Americans Want to Be Counted Native," *Seattle Times*, 7 Apr. 2001; Delphine Red Shirt, Letter to *Hartford Courant*, 8 Dec. 2002. I am indebted to Colleen Boyd for sharing this source.

39. Donald L. Barlett and James B. Steele, "Wheel of Misfortune," *Time*, 16 Dec. 2002, 47–58; Ken Silverstein, "Cashing In," *The Nation*, 6 July 1998, 20–21. See also Ron Russell, "Jackpot; How Four Tiny Indian Tribes, with Help from Powerful Gambling Interests, Are Trying to Transform the Bay Area into a Slot Machine Mecca," *S.F. Weekly*, 27 Oct. 2004, n.p.

40. Marty Firerider, "The Red Path Has Turned Green for Some," *ICT*, 25 May 2005, p. A3; William Claiborne, "A Stake in Indian Country," *Washington Post*, 1 Sept. 1999, p. A21; Susan Schmidt, "Jackpot From Indian Gaming Tribes," ibid., 22 Feb. 2004, p. A1;

E. J. Dionne Jr., "Rolling the Dice on a GOP Rift," ibid., 15 Mar. 2005, p. A23; Rich Lowry, "Making Money Off the BIA," *Seattle Post-Intelligencer*, 5 July 2005, p. B6.

41. "Abramoff 'Totally in Bed' with Anti-Gaming Forces," Indianz.Com in Print, 29 Nov. 2004, citing "Double-Dealing Cost Tiguas Casino $4.2 Million," *El Paso Times*, 18 Nov. 2004, ⟨http://www.indianz.com/News/2004/005527.asp⟩.

42. Lynda V. Mapes, "A New Welfare State?," *Seattle Times*, 15 May 2002, pp. A1, A13; Mark Trahant, "When Tribes Become Successful, It's Time to Change the Rules," *Seattle Post-Intelligencer*, 31 Aug. 2003, p. B6.

43. Lynda V. Mapes, "State Ponders Taking Exclusive Rights to Slot Machines Away from Tribal Casinos," *Seattle Times*, 6 Oct. 2002; John M. Broder and Charlie LeDuff, "Cash-Strapped California Might Expand Gambling," ibid., 2 Feb. 2003; Susannah Rosenblatt, "Tribes with Casino Profits Averse to Aiding Strapped States," *Los Angeles Times*, 10 July 2003, p. A1, quoting Poqoaque governor.

44. Francis X. Clines, "The Pequots," *NYT*, 27 Feb. 1994, p. SM49.

45. Jim Barnett, "Great Casino Hope," *Seattle Times*, 20 Feb. 2000, p. B29; See also Timothy Egan, "Hunting 'The New Buffalo,'" *NYT*, 7 Sept. 1997, p. 43.

46. Louis Sahagun, "Tribes Fear Backlash to Prosperity," *Los Angeles Times*, 3 May 2004, p. B1; "Indians as Thieves," *ICT*, 3 Nov. 2004, p. A2; Jim Adams, "Anti-Indian Groups Fail at Ballot Box," *ICT*, 7 Apr. 2004, p. A1; Glenn F. Bunting, "Casino's Success Breeds Tension," *Los Angeles Times*, 25 Dec. 2004, pp. A1, A38–39; Steve Chawkins, "Casino Fuels Prosperity, Fears," ibid., 20 May 2001, p. A1.

47. John Hieger, "Level the Playing Field, Cut Taxes," *Seattle Times*, 3 Oct. 2004, p. D4.

48. Before the American Indian Citizenship Act of 1924, many Indians became citizens pursuant to the General Allotment Act of 1887 or other special legislation.

49. On stereotypes of indigent Indians who drain local government resources and of rich Indians whose undeserved wealth derives from federal coffers, see O'Nell, "Telling about Whites, Talking about Indians," 97.

50. E. J. Dionne Jr., "Rolling the Dice on a GOP Rift," *Washington Post*, 15 Mar. 2005, p. A23.

51. Russ Bynum, "Congregation Spurns Root of All Evil," *Seattle Times*, 10 Dec. 2000, p. B1; Lora Abaurrea, "Native Americans are Cashing-In with Gambling Casinos on the Reservation," *Take Pride! Community Magazine* [Los Angeles], 15–21 Nov. 2004, i.

52. Armando Roanhorse, "Casinos Herald a Culture of the Past," *Navajo Times*, 7 Apr. 2005, p. A6. See also Vizenor, "Gambling on Sovereignty," 412; Cattelino, "Casino Roots," 67; Pasquaretta, *Gambling and Survival in Native North America*, 111.

53. Marty Firerider, "The Red Path Has Turned Green for Some," *ICT*, 25 May 2005, p. A3; Beverly Gage, "Indian Country, NY," *The Nation*, 27 Nov. 2000, 11, 16; Posey, *Fus Fixico Letters*, 70.

54. Colloff, "Blood of the Tigua," 112; Ianthe Jeanne Dugan, "A Business Empire Transforms Life for Colorado Tribe," *Wall Street Journal*, 13 June 2003, p. A1; William Booth, "Tribes Ride a Casino Dream," *Washington Post*, 9 May 2000, p. A1. See also Gonzales, "Gaming and Displacement."

55. David Cournoyer, "Can't Indians Be Successful?," *Denver Post*, 7 June 2000, p. B11; Sherman Alexie, "Love, Hunger, Money, and Other Not-So-Facetious Reasons Why the

Spokane Indians Want to Bet on Casinos," *High Country News*, 19 Sept. 1994, at ⟨http://www.english.uiuc.edu/maps/poets/a_f/alexie/casinos.htm⟩.

56. Cattelino, "Casino Roots," 84.

57. McGee quoted in Andrew E. Serwer, "American Indians Discover Money is Power," *Fortune*, 19 Apr. 1993, 136–40. See also Jerry Reynolds, "NIGA Tribal Gaming Impact Analysis," *ICT*, 2 Mar. 2005, p. C1; "Through the Eyes of the Mississippi Choctaw," ⟨http://www.choctaw.org/culture/expression.htm⟩; Goldberg and Champagne, "Ramona Redeemed?," 58; Light and Rand, *Indian Gaming*, 100; Gerdes, Napoli, Pattea, and Segal, "Impact of Indian Gaming on Economic Development," 26–28.

58. Frank J. King III, "The Trials and Tribulations of Indian Gaming, Part I," *Native Voice*, 28 Jan.–11 Feb. 2005, p. C5; "Tribal Gaming: The Native American Success Story," *Native Voice*, 1–15 Apr. 2005, p. 1D.

59. Marty Firerider, "The Red Path Has Turned Green for Some," *ICT*, 25 May 2005, p. A3; McCovey, "Ascending Poverty and Inequality in Native America," 86–87.

60. Frantz, "'Economic Spirit' and Economic Structure of Indian Reservations," 157, 164–65, 170. See also Dave Palermo, "Hopi Forgo Gaming to Preserve Way of Life," *ICT*, 18 Aug. 2004, p. A5.

61. U.S. Newswire, 9 Feb. 2005, ⟨http://proquest.umi.com/pqdweb?did=790836051&FMT=3&clientId=8991&RQT=309&VName=PQD⟩.

62. Lynda V. Mapes and Justin Mayo, "Indians Making Gains with Games," *Seattle Times*, 22 Sept. 2002, p. A1; "Native Americans Balance Traditional, Capitalist Cultures," *Detroit News*, 23 Mar. 1999, p. B2.

63. Francis X. Cline, "The Pequots," *NYT*, 27 Feb. 1994, p. SM49.; Lynda V. Mapes, "Once Invisible, Muckleshoots Are Now an Economic Force," *Seattle Times*, 27 Nov. 2002, pp. A1, A12; Editorial, *ICT*, 14 Oct. 2002.

64. Francis X. Cline, "The Pequots," *NYT*, 27 Feb. 1994, p. SM49; Lynda Y. Mapes, "The Education Jackpot," *Seattle Times*, 3 Nov. 2002, pp. A1, A16.

65. Cattelino, "Casino Roots," 84–85.

66. Charles Strinz, "Let Indians Decide for Themselves on Reservation Gambling," *NYT*, 4 Feb. 1992, p. A20.

67. Pasquaretta, *Gambling and Survival*, 112; Andrew E. Serwer, "American Indians Discover Money Is Power," *Fortune*, 19 Apr. 1993, 136–40; Ernest L. Stevens Jr., "Tribal Government Gaming," *Native Voice*, 22 Feb. 2004, p. C5.

68. Ben Neary, "Gaming Gives Indians Political Edge," *Santa Fe New Mexican*, 3 Oct. 2004, p. B-1; "Indian Gathering Marks New Political Power," *Albuquerque Journal*, 26 Nov. 2003, p. A12. See also George Weeks, "Indian Political Activism Grows," *Detroit News*, 26 Sept. 2004, p. A22.

69. A sampling: "Campaign 2000/The Donors: Gambling Riches Give Indian Tribes New Clout," *Boston Globe*, 20 Oct. 2000, p. A28; Jim Lynch, "Native American Tribes Invest Record Cash in Oregon Politics," *Knight Ridder Tribune Business News*, 15 Jan. 2003, 1; Emily Heffter, "Tribes Becoming Political Players with Casino Cash," *Seattle Times*, 17 Nov. 2003, pp. A1, A12; Mark Fogarty, "Indian Gaming Money Tilts to Dems—Barely," *ICT*, 4 Feb. 2004, p. B1; Deirdre Gregg, "Increasing Clout; Tribes Exert Power over Elections," *Puget Sound Business Journal*, 1–7 Oct. 2004, 1, 76; Michael Kranish, "Antitax Activist Says He Got $1.5M From Tribes, Set Up Policy Talks With President," *Boston Globe*,

13 May 2005, p. A1. See also Goldberg and Champagne, "Ramona Redeemed?"; Darian-Smith, *New Capitalists*, 106.

70. Deirdre Gregg, "Increasing Clout," *Puget Sound Business Journal*, 1–7 Oct. 2004, 1, 76; Glenn F. Bunting and Dan Morain, "Tribes Take a Wait-and-See Recall Stance," *Los Angeles Times*, 17 Aug. 2003, p. B1.

71. Emily Heffter, "Tribes Becoming Political Players with Casino Cash," *Seattle Times*, 17 Nov. 2003, pp. A1, A12; Deirdre Gregg, "Increasing Clout," *Puget Sound Business Journal*, 1–7 Oct. 2004, 1, 76; Brad Cain, "Tribe Says It May Run More Anti-Kulongoski Ads," AP State and Local Wire, 28 May 2006.

72. Goldberg and Champagne, "Ramona Redeemed?," 57, quoting Ioana Patringenaru, "Tribes Come of Age," *California Journal* 30 (1999): 14. See also Jerry Useem, "The Big Gamble," *Fortune*, 2 Oct. 2000, 222.

73. Goldberg and Champagne, "Ramona Redeemed?," 57–58.

74. Deirdre Gregg, "Increasing Clout," *Puget Sound Business Journal*, 1–7 Oct. 2004, 1, 76.

75. Glenn F. Bunting, "Casino's Success Breeds Tension," *Los Angeles Times*, 25 Dec. 2004, pp. A1, A38–39. See also Patt Morrison, "Oh, for the Bad Old Days When Gambling Was Illegal," *Los Angeles Times*, 23 June 2004, p. B13.

76. "When Tribal Law and Others Collide," *NYT*, 8 Mar. 1998, p. 24; Emily Heffter, "Tribes Becoming Political Players with Casino Cash," *Seattle Times*, 17 Nov. 2003, pp. A1, A12; Eric Bailey, "In Casino Wars, She's a Player," *Los Angeles Times*, 3 Nov. 2003, p. A1.

77. Jim Doyle, "California Ka-Ching!," *San Francisco Chronicle*, 1 June 2003, p. D1; "Termination at the Times?," *ICT*, 25 May 2005, p. A2. See also Thomas W. Donovan, "Indian Tribes Should Be Wary of Supreme Court Justices Scalia and Thomas," *Ojibwe News*, 23 Apr. 2004, p. 4.

78. Ron Russell, "Jackpot," *S.F. Weekly*, 27 Oct. 2004, n.p.; Rich Lowry, "Making Money off the BIA," *Seattle Post-Intelligencer*, 5 July 2005, p. B6.

79. Tom Wanamaker, "The Economic Impact of Indian Gaming," *ICT*, 9 Mar. 2005, p. C1; "Siletz Tribes Celebrate 25 Years of Reunification," AP State and Local Wire, 17 Nov. 2002; Lynda V. Mapes, "Once Invisible, Muckleshoots Are Now an Economic Force," *Seattle Times*, 27 Nov. 2002, pp. A1, A12; Lora Abaurrea, "Native Americans Are Cashing-In with Gambling Casinos on the Reservation," *Take Pride! Community Magazine* [Los Angeles], 15–21 Nov. 2004, i; John K. Wiley, "Casinos Helping Tribes, Leader Says," *Seattle Post-Intelligencer*, 3 Dec. 2001, p. B-4.

80. Jerry Useem, "The Big Gamble," *Fortune*, 2 Oct. 2000, 222; Sarah Jimenez, "Tulare Co. Dips in Casino Pot Again," *Fresno Bee*, 3 Apr. 2006; "Indian Casinos Prompt Changes in Banking Market," AP State and Local Wire, 10 Dec. 2000; "Indian Tribes Funding School Projects, Endeavors," *Los Angeles Times*, 11 Apr. 2004.

81. Editorial, *ICT*, 29 Dec. 2004, p. A2.

82. As Cattelino observes, "Sovereignty is material and money is political," *High Stakes*, 199.

83. Ibid., 201.

Selected Sources

Archival Records

Harvard University Library, Cambridge, Mass.

    American Board of Commissioners for Foreign Missions Papers, Unit 6:
        Missions on the American Continents and to the Islands of the Pacific,
        1813–1883 (microform)

    Journal of D. S. [Daniel Sabin] Butrick, 1819–45 (microform)

Library of Congress, Washington, D.C.

    Henry Laurens Dawes Papers

    Photographs

National Archives, Washington, D.C.

    Record Group 75, Records of the Cherokee Agency in Tennessee, 1801–35

National Archives, Southwest Region, Fort Worth, Tex.

    Record Group 75, Records of the Osage Agency

National Archives of Canada, Ottawa, Ont.

    MG 11 Q Series

Newberry Library, Chicago, Ill.

    Thomas Ballenger Papers

    Federal Bureau of Investigation (FBI) File on the Osage Indian Murders,
        Microfilm 813

    John Howard Payne Papers, Typescripts

Oklahoma Historical Society, Oklahoma City

    John T. Adair Papers, Accession 81.101

    Indian-Pioneer History Collection

University of Oklahoma Western History Collections, Norman

    John F. Brown Collection

    D. W. Bushyhead Papers

    Cherokee Nation Papers (microform)

    Chickasaw Nation Papers

    Coleman Cole Collection

    Creek Nation Papers

    Grayson Family Papers

    Pleasant Porter Collection

University of Washington Libraries, Seattle

John Collier Papers (microform)

Kenneth McLeod Papers, 1934–85, Accession 2487-005.

Congressional Hearings and Documents

U.S. Congress. *American State Papers: Documents, Legislative and Executive, of the Congress of the United States*, Class 2, *Indian Affairs*, edited by Walter Lowrie and Walter S. Franklin. 2 vols. Washington, D.C.: Gales and Seaton, 1832–34. CIS microform set.

———. *Congressional Record*. Washington, D.C., 1920–60.

U.S. House of Representatives. *Argument of Hon. John H. Reagan of Texas before the Committee on Commerce of the House of Representatives on the Railroad Problem*. 47th Cong., 1st sess., 28–30 March 1882. Published Hearing HInt 47-A.

———. Committee on Indian Affairs. *Modifying Osage Fund Restrictions: Hearing before the Committee on Indian Affairs*, 67th Cong., 2d sess. February 1922–January 1923. Serials 1–3. Published Hearing H. 320-8 A,B,C.

———. Committee on Indian Affairs. *Modifying Osage Fund Restrictions: Hearing on H.R. 5726*. 68th Cong., 1st sess. 25 January–7 February 1924. CIS H. 342-8-A.

———. Ezra Hayt, "Proposal for a General Allotment Law." 45th Cong., 3d sess., 24 January 1879. H. Rept. 165. Serial 1866.

———. *Re-organization of the Indian Territory*. Resolution of the National Commercial Convention, Memorializing Congress. 42d Cong., 3d sess., 14 January 1873. H. Misc. Doc. No. 42. Serial 1572.

———. Subcommittee of the Committee on Indian Affairs. *Division of Lands and Moneys of the Osage Tribe of Indians: Hearings on H.R. 1478*. 58th Cong., 3d sess., 20 January 1905. HIn 58-A-1 and 2.

———. Subcommittee of the Committee on Indian Affairs. *Hearings on H.R. 9294*. 70th Cong., 1st sess., 17 and 19 January 1928. Published Hearing H. 477-3.

———. Subcommittee of the Committee on Indian Affairs. *Indians of the United States: Investigation of the Field Service*. 66th Cong., 2d sess., 1920. Published Hearing H. 231, part 3.

U.S. Senate. Collins, J. A. *Distribution of Wealth in the United States*. 55th Cong., 2d sess., 19 January 1898. S. Doc. 75.

———. Committee on Indian Affairs. *Enrollment of Osage Indians*. 60th Cong., 2d sess., 1 March 1909. S. Doc. 744.

———. Committee on Indian Affairs. *Osage Extension*. 66th Cong., 3d sess., 17–18 December 1920. Hearing on S. 4039.

———. Committee on Indian Affairs. *Relief of Osage Indians in Oklahoma: Hearings on S. 7027*. 64th Cong., 2d sess., 13 and 26 January 1917. U.S. Congressional Hearings, vol. 92, no. 2.

———. *Condition of the Indians in the Indian Territory, and other Reservations, etc.* 49th Cong., 1st sess., 4 June 1886. S. Rept. 1278. Serial 2362.

———. *Five Civilized Tribes*. Report to the Senate from the Select Committee to Investigate Matters Connected with Affairs in the Indian Territory. 16 January 1907. 59th Cong., 2d sess. S. Rept. 5013. CIS Serial 5062, 5063.

———. *Osage Fund Restrictions.* 68th Cong., 1st sess., 28–29 March and 1 April 1924. CIS H-216, No. 3.

———. *Report of Select Committee on the Five Civilized Tribes of Indians.* 53d Cong., 2d sess., 1894. S. Rept. 377. Serial 3183.

———. Subcommittee of the Committee of Indian Affairs. *Relations between the United States and the Five Civilized Tribes of Indians.* 1892. 52d Cong., 1st sess., 7 May–9 June 1892. Congressional Hearings Supplement SIn 52 C.

———. Subcommittee of the Committee on Indian Affairs. *Survey of Conditions of the Indians in the United States.* 71st Cong., special sess., 18 November 1930. Senate Library, vol. 545-5, pp. 6739 et seq.

———. Subcommittee on Employment, Manpower, and Poverty of the Committee on Labor and Public Welfare. *Examination of the War on Poverty.* 90th Cong., 1st sess., 24 April 1967. CIS No.: 90 S.1812-3-C.

———. Subcommiteee on Executive Reorganization of the Committee on Government Operations. *Federal Role in Urban Affairs.* 89th Cong., 2d sess., 9 and 12 December 1966. CIS No: 89-S.1813-3-C.

Selected Newspapers and Weekly Magazines

Business Week, 1960–2005

Cherokee Advocate [Tahlequah, Cherokee Nation], 1870–1900

Fortune, 1950–2005

Harper's and *Harper's Weekly*, 1880–1970

Independent (and Weekly Review)

Indian Chieftain [Vinita, Cherokee Nation], 1880–1900

Indian Country Today [Oneida, N.Y.], 2002–8

Literary Digest, 1920–40

Los Angeles Times, 1960–2005

Muskogee Phoenix [Creek Nation], 1880–1900

The Nation, 1900–2005

New Republic, 1920–2005

New York Times, 1879–2005

Newsweek, 1960–2005

Outlook, 1890-1940

Saturday Evening Post, 1920–60

Seattle Post-Intelligencer, 1960–2005

Seattle Times, 1950–2005

Time, 1960–2005

U.S. New and World Report, 1960–2005

Washington Post, 1960–2005

Books and Published Articles

Abbott, W. W., and Dorothy Twohig, eds. *The Papers of George Washington, Presidential Series.* 9 vols. Charlottesville: University Press of Virginia, 1989.

Abernethy, Thomas Perkins. *From Frontier to Plantation in Tennessee: A Study in Frontier Democracy.* Chapel Hill: University of North Carolina Press, 1932.

Ablon, Joan. "American Indian Relocation: Problems of Dependency and Management in the City." *Phylon* 26:4 (1965): 362–71.

Adair, John. *Adair's History of the American Indians.* Edited by Samuel Cole Williams. Johnson City, Tenn.: Watauga Press, 1930.

Adams, David Wallace. *Education for Extinction: American Indians and the Boarding School Experience, 1875–1928.* Lawrence: University Press of Kansas, 1995.

Akwesasne Notes. *Trail of Broken Treaties: B.I.A. I'm Not Your Indian Anymore.* Mohawk Nation, Rooseveltown, N.Y.: Akwesasne Notes, 1976.

Albers, Patricia. "Labor and Exchange in American Indian History." In *Companion to Native American History*, edited by Philip J. Deloria and Neal Salisbury, 269–86. Malden, Mass., and Oxford, U.K.: Blackwell Publishers, 2002.

Allen, Frederick Lewis. *Only Yesterday: An Informal History of the Nineteen-Twenties*. New York: Blue Ribbon Books, 1931.

Ambler, Marjane. *Breaking the Iron Bonds: Indian Control of Energy Development*. Lawrence: University Press of Kansas, 1990.

"American Aristocracy." *World's Work* 34 (June 1917): 139–40.

American Indian Chicago Conference. *Declaration of Indian Purpose: The Voice of the American Indian*. Chicago: University of Chicago, 1961.

American Indian Policy Review Commission. *Final Report*. Washington, D.C.: Government Printing Office, 1977.

———. *Report on Reservation and Resource Development and Protection*. Washington, D.C.: Government Printing Office, 1976.

Andrew, John A., III. *From Revivals to Removal: Jeremiah Evarts, the Cherokee Nation, and the Search for the Soul of America*. Athens: University of Georgia Press, 1992.

Appleby, Joyce. "Consumption in Early Modern Social Thought." In *Consumption and the World of Goods*, edited by John Brewer and Roy Porter, 162–73. London and New York: Routledge, 1993.

———. *Economic Thought and Ideology in Seventeenth-Century England*. Princeton, N.J.: Princeton University Press, 1978.

Arber, Edward, ed. *The First Three English Books on America, 1511?–1555 A.D.* Birmingham: Turnbull and Spears, 1885.

Ashley, Charles S. "The Distribution of Wealth." *Popular Science Monthly* 29 (October 1886): 721–33.

Atkin, Edmond. *Indians of the Southern Colonial Frontier: The Edmond Atkin Report and Plan of 1755*. Edited by Wilbur R. Jacobs. Columbia: University of South Carolina Press, 1954.

Axtell, James. "The Ethnohistory of Native North America." In *Natives and Newcomers: The Cultural Origins of North America*, 1–14. New York: Oxford University Press, 2001.

———. "Ethnohistory: An Historian's Viewpoint." In *The European and the Indian: Essays in the Ethnohistory of Colonial North America*, 3–15. New York: Oxford University Press, 1981.

———. "Through Another Glass Darkly: Early Indian Views of Europeans." In *After Columbus: Essays in the Ethnohistory of Colonial North America*, 125–43. New York: Oxford University Press, 1988.

———. "The Rise and Fall of the Powhatan Empire." In *After Columbus: Essays in the Ethnohistory of Colonial North America*, 182–221. New York: Oxford University Press, 1988.

Bailey, Garrick Alan. *Changes in Osage Social Organization: 1673–1906*. University of Oregon Anthropological Papers No. 5. Eugene: University of Oregon, 1973.

———. "John Joseph Mathews." In *American Indian Intellectuals*, edited by Margot Liberty, 204–14. St. Paul, Minn.: West Publishing, 1978.

———, ed. *The Osage and the Invisible World, From the Works of Francis La Flesche*. Norman: University of Oklahoma Press, 1995.

————. "The Osage Roll: An Analysis." *The Indian Historian* 5 (Spring 1972): 26–29.

Bailyn, Bernard. *The New England Merchants in the Seventeenth Century.* Cambridge, Mass.: Harvard University Press, 1955.

Baine, Rodney M. "Notes and Documents: Myths of Mary Musgrove." *Georgia Historical Quarterly* 76 (Summer 1992): 428–35.

Baird, W. David. *The Osage People.* Phoenix: Indian Tribal Series, 1972.

————. *Peter Pitchlynn: Chief of the Choctaws.* Norman: University of Oklahoma Press, 1989.

Banner, Stuart. *How the Indians Lost Their Land: Law and Power on the Frontier.* Cambridge, Mass.: Belknap Press of Harvard University Press, 2005.

Barbour, Philip L., ed. *Jamestown Voyages under the First Charter, 1606–1609.* 2 vols. Cambridge: Cambridge University Press for the Hakluyt Society, 1969.

Barker, Alex W. "Powhatan's Pursestrings: On the Meaning of Surplus in a Seventeenth Century Algonkian Chiefdom." In *Lords of the Southeast: Social Inequality and the Native Elites of Southeastern North America,* edited by Alex W. Barker and Timothy R. Pauketat, 61–80. Archaeological Papers of the American Anthropological Association No. 3. Washington, D.C.: American Anthropological Association, 1992.

Barr, Juliana. *Peace Came in the Form of a Woman: Indians and Spaniards in the Texas Borderlands.* Chapel Hill: University of North Carolina Press, 2007.

Barrington, Linda. *The Other Side of the Frontier: Economic Explorations into Native American History.* Boulder, Colo.: Westview Press, 1999.

Bartram, William. "Observations on the Creek and Cherokee Indians, 1789." Facsimile of *Transactions of the American Ethnological Society* 3 (1853): 1–81. In *A Creek Source Book,* edited by William C. Sturtevant, not paginated. New York: Garland Publishing, Inc., 1987.

————. *Travels through North and South Carolina, Georgia, East and West Florida, the Cherokee Country, the Extensive Territories of the Muscogulges, or Creek Confederacy, and the Country of the Chactaws.* Philadelphia: James & Johnson, 1791.

Basinger, Douglas, Terry Anderson, Patty Marks, and Kerry Stoebner. "Review of Indian Legislation During the 95th Congress." *American Indian Journal* (November 1978): 16–28, bound with National Congress of American Indians, *American Indian Issue Papers,* 25th Annual Convention, September 18–22, 1978.

Bass, Althea. *Cherokee Messenger.* Norman: University of Oklahoma Press, 1936.

Bassett, John Spencer, ed. *Correspondence of Andrew Jackson.* 7 vols. Washington: Carnegie Institute of Washington, 1926–33.

Baudet, Henri. *Paradise on Earth: Some Thoughts on European Images of Non-European Man.* Translated by Elizabeth Wenthold. New Haven, Conn.: Yale University Press, 1965.

Bays, Brad A. *Townsite Settlement and Dispossession in the Cherokee Nation, 1866–1907.* New York: Garland, 1998.

Beckert, Sven. *The Monied Metropolis: New York City and the Consolidation of the American Bourgeoisie, 1850–1896.* New York: Cambridge University Press, 2001.

Bell, Duran. "The Social Relations of Property and Efficiency." In *Property in Economic Context,* edited by Robert C. Hunt and Antonio Gilman, 29–45. Monographs in Economic Anthropology No. 14. Lanham, Md., and New York: University Press of America, 1998.

Benedict, Jeff. *Without Reservation: How a Controversial Indian Tribe Rose to Power and Built the World's Largest Casino*. New York: Harper Collins, 2000.

Benson, Susan Porter. "Gender, Generation, and Consumption in the United States: Working-Class Families in the Interwar Period." In *Getting and Spending: European and American Consumer Societies in the Twentieth Century*, edited by Susan Strasser, Charles McGovern, and Matthias Judt, 223–40. Washington, D.C.: German Historical Institute and Cambridge University Press, 1998.

Berkeley, Edmund, and Dorothy Smith Berkeley, eds. *The Reverend John Clayton, a Parson with a Scientific Mind: His Scientific Writings and Other Related Papers*. Charlottesville: University Press of Virginia, 1965.

Berkhofer, Robert F., Jr. *Salvation and the Savage: An Analysis of Protestant Missions and American Indian Response, 1787–1862*. Lexington: University of Kentucky Press, 1965.

———. *The White Man's Indian: Images of the American Indian from Columbus to the Present*. New York: Vintage Books, 1978.

Bernstein, Alison R. *American Indians and World War II: Toward a New Era in Indian Affairs*. Norman: University of Oklahoma Press, 1991.

Beverley, Robert. *The History and Present State of Virginia*. London, 1705. Reprint, edited by Louis B. Wright, Chapel Hill: University of North Carolina Press, 1947.

Billings, Warren M., ed. *The Old Dominion in the Seventeenth Century: A Documentary History of Virginia, 1606–1689*. Chapel Hill: University of North Carolina Press, 1975.

Billings, Warren M., John E. Selby, and Thad W. Tate. *Colonial Virginia: A History*. White Plains, N.Y.: KTO Press, 1986.

Blanchard, Frances A. "The Deplorable State of Our Indians." *Current History* 18 (July 1923): 630–36.

Bloch, Maurice, and Jonathan Parry, eds. *Money and the Morality of Exchange*. Cambridge, U.K.: Cambridge University Press, 1989.

Bloom, Leonard. "The Acculturation of the Eastern Cherokee: Historical Aspects." *North Carolina Historical Review* 19 (October 1942): 323–58.

Bodmer, Beatriz Pastor. *The Armature of Conquest: Spanish Accounts of the Discovery of America, 1492–1589*. Translated by Lydia Longstreth Hunt. Stanford, Calif.: Stanford University Press, 1992.

Boudinot, Elias. "Address to the Whites." *North American Review* 33 (October 1826): 470.

———. *Cherokee Editor: The Writings of Elias Boudinot*. Edited by Theda Perdue. Knoxville: University of Tennessee Press, 1983.

Bourdieu, Pierre. *The Social Structures of the Economy*. Translated by Chris Turner. Cambridge, U.K.: Polity Press, 2005.

Bowen, Francis. *The Principles of Political Economy Applied to the Condition, the Resources, and the Institutions of the American People*. Boston: Little, Brown, 1856.

Boxberger, Daniel L. *To Fish in Common: The Ethnohistory of Lummi Indian Salmon Fishing*. Lincoln: University of Nebraska Press, 1989.

Brace, Laura. *The Idea of Property in Seventeenth-Century England: Tithes and the Individual*. Manchester and New York: Manchester University Press, 1998.

Brandon, William. *New Worlds for Old: Reports from the New World and their Effect on the Development of Social Thought in Europe, 1500–1800*. Athens: Ohio University Press, 1986.

Brauer, Carl M. "Kennedy, Johnson, and the War on Poverty." *Journal of American History* 69 (June 1982): 98–119.

Brickell, John. *The Natural History of North-Carolina*. Dublin: James Carson, 1737.

Bridenbaugh, Carl. *Jamestown, 1544–1699*. New York: Oxford University Press, 1980.

Brophy, William A., and Sophie D. Aberle. *The Indian: America's Unfinished Business*. Norman: University of Oklahoma Press, 1966.

Brown, Estelle Aubrey. "Our Plutocratic Osage Indians." *Travel* 39 (October 1922): 19–22.

Brown, Kenny L. "A Progressive from Oklahoma: Senator Robert Latham Owen, Jr." *Chronicles of Oklahoma* 62 (Fall 1984): 232–65.

Brown, Loren N. "The Dawes Commission." *Chronicles of Oklahoma* 9 (Spring 1931): 71–105.

———. "The Establishment of the Dawes Commission for Indian Territory." *Chronicles of Oklahoma* 18 (Summer 1940): 171–81.

Brown, Philip M. "Early Indian Trade in the Development of South Carolina: Politics, Economics, and Social Mobility during the Proprietary Period, 1670–1719." *South Carolina Historical Magazine* 76 (July 1975): 118–28.

Bruce, Michael L. "'Our Best Men Are Fast Leaving Us': The Life and Times of Robert M. Jones." *Chronicles of Oklahoma* 66 (Fall 1988): 294–305.

Bruce, Philip Alexander. *Economic History of Virginia in the Seventeenth Century*. 2 vols. New York: Macmillan, 1896.

Bryce, James. *The American Commonwealth*. Vol. 2. London: Macmillan, 1889.

Burchardt, Bill. "Osage Oil." *Chronicles of Oklahoma* 41 (Fall 1963): 253–69.

Burnette, Robert. *The Tortured Americans*. Englewood Cliffs, N.J.: Prentice-Hall, 1971.

Burstein, Andrew. *The Passions of Andrew Jackson*. New York: Alfred E. Knopf, 2003.

Burt, Larry. "Western Tribes and Balance Sheets: Business Development Programs in the 1960s and 1970s." *Western Historical Quarterly* 23 (November 1992): 475–95.

Burwell, Kate P. "Richest People in the World." *Sturm's Oklahoma Magazine* 2 (December 1924): 89–93.

Bushman, Richard L. *The Refinement of America: Persons, Houses, Cities*. New York: Vintage Books, 1993.

Bushyhead, D. W., P. N. Blackstone, and George Sanders. *Summary of the Census of the Cherokee Nation . . . , in the Year of 1880*. Washington, D.C.: Gibson Brothers, 1881.

Cable, Mary. *Top Drawer: American High Society from the Gilded Age to the Roaring Twenties*. New York: Atheneum, 1984.

Cahn, Edgar S., and David W. Hearne, eds. *Our Brother's Keeper: The Indian in White America*. New York and Cleveland: New Community Press, 1969.

Calloway, Colin G. "The Continuing Revolution in Indian Country." In *Native Americans and the Early Republic*, edited by Frederick E. Hoxie, Ronald Hoffman, and Peter J. Albert, 3–33. Charlottesville: University Press of Virginia, 1999.

Calvert, Karin. "The Function of Fashion in Eighteenth-Century America." In *Of Consuming Interests: The Style of Life in the Eighteenth Century*, edited by Cary Carson, Ronald Hoffman, and Peter J. Albert, 252–83. Charlottesville: University Press of Virginia, 1994.

Campbell, Mildred. "Social Origins of Some Early Americans." In *Seventeenth-Century*

America: Essays in Colonial History, edited by James Morton Smith, 63–89. Chapel Hill: University of North Carolina Press, 1959.

Campbell, P. Travels in the Interior Inhabited Parts of North America in the Years 1791 and 1792 by P. Campbell. [1793]. Reprint, edited by H. H. Langton, Toronto: Champlain Society, 1937.

Candler, Allen D., ed. Colonial Records of the State of Georgia. Vol. 6. Atlanta: Franklin Printing and Publishing, 1906.

Carey, Mathew. Appeal to the Wealthy of the Land, Ladies As Well As Gentlemen, on the Character, Conduct, Situation, and Prospects of Those Whose Sole Dependence for Subsistence Is on the Labour of Their Hands. Philadelphia: L. Johnson, 1833.

Carnegie, Andrew. The Gospel of Wealth and Other Timely Essays. Edited by Edward C. Kirkland. Cambridge, Mass.: Belknap Press of Harvard University Press, 1962.

Carr, Lois Green. "Emigration and the Standard of Living: The Seventeenth Century Chesapeake." Journal of Economic History 52 (June 1992): 271–91.

Carson, Cary. "The Consumer Revolution in Colonial British America: Why Demand?" In Of Consuming Interests: The Style of Life in the Eighteenth Century, edited by Cary Carson, Ronald Hoffman, and Peter J. Albert, 483–697. Charlottesville: University Press of Virginia, 1994.

Carson, James Taylor. "Molly Brant: From Clan Mother to Loyalist Chief." In Sifters: Native American Women's Lives, edited by Theda Perdue, 48–59. New York: Oxford University Press, 2001.

———. "Native Americans, the Market Revolution, and Culture Change." Agricultural History 71 (Winter 1997): 1–18.

———. Searching for the Bright Path: The Mississippi Choctaws from Prehistory to Removal. Lincoln: University of Nebraska Press, 1999.

Carter, Paul A. The Twenties in America. New York: Thomas Y. Crowell Company, 1968.

Cashin, Edward J., ed. Colonial Augusta: "Key of the Indian Countrey." Macon, Ga.: Mercer University Press, 1986.

———. "From Creeks to Crackers." In The Southern Colonial Backcountry: Interdisciplinary Perspectives on Frontier Communities, edited by David Colin Crass, Steven D. Smith, Martha A. Zierden, and Richard D. Brooks, 69–75. Knoxville: University of Tennessee Press, 1998.

———. Lachlan McGillivray, Indian Trader: The Shaping of the Southern Colonial Frontier. Athens: University of Georgia Press, 1992.

Cashman, Sean Dennis. America in the Gilded Age: From the Death of Lincoln to the Rise of Theodore Roosevelt. 3d ed. New York: New York University Press, 1993.

Cass, Lewis. Considerations on the Present State of the Indians, and Their Removal to the West of the Mississippi. Boston: Gray and Bowen, 1828. Reprint, New York: Arno Press, 1975.

Castile, George Pierre. To Show Heart: Native American Self-Determination and Federal Indian Policy, 1960–1975. Tucson: University of Arizona Press, 1998.

Cattelino, Jessica R. "Casino Roots: The Cultural Production of Twentieth-Century Seminole Economic Development." In Native Pathways: Economic Development and American Indian Culture in the Twentieth Century, edited by Brian Hosmer and Colleen O'Neill, 66–90. Boulder: University of Colorado Press, 2003.

———. *High Stakes: Florida Seminole Gaming and Sovereignty*. Durham, N.C.: Duke University Press, 2008.

Caughey, John W. *McGillivray of the Creeks*. Norman: University of Oklahoma Press, 1938.

Cawardine, Richard. "'Antinomians' and 'Arminians': Methodists and the Market Revolution." In *The Market Revolution in America: Social, Political, and Religious Expressions, 1800–1880*, edited by Melvyn Stokes and Stephen Conway, 282–307. Charlottesville: University Press of Virginia, 1996.

Cawelti, John G. *Apostles of the Self-Made Man*. Chicago and London: University of Chicago Press, 1965.

Cayton, Andrew R. L. "Senator John Smith: The Rise and Fall of a Frontier Entrepreneur." In *The Human Tradition in Antebellum America*, edited by Michael A. Morrison, 67–81. Wilmington, Del.: Scholarly Resources, 2000.

Champagne, Duane. *Social Order and Political Change: Constitutional Governments among the Cherokee, the Choctaw, the Chickasaw, and the Creek*. Stanford, Calif.: Stanford University Press, 1992.

Chaplin, Joyce E. "Race." In *The British-American World, 1500–1800*, edited by David Armitage and Michael J. Braddick, 154–72. New York: Palgrave Macmillan, 2002.

———. *Subject Matter: Technology, the Body, and Science on the Anglo-American Frontier, 1500–1676*. Cambridge, Mass.: Harvard University Press, 2001.

Chapman, Berlin B. "Dissolution of the Osage Reservation." *Chronicles of Oklahoma* 20 (Fall/Winter 1942): 244–54, 376–86; 21 (Spring/Summer 1943): 78–88, 171–82.

Chapman, William. "Native Americans' New Clout." *Progressive* 41 (August 1977): 30–32.

Chappell, Absalom H. *Miscellanies of Georgia, Historical, Biographical, Descriptiive, etc.* Atlanta: J. F. Meegan, [1874].

Chino, Wendell. "Indian Affairs—What Has Been Done and What Needs to Be Done." In *Representative American Speeches: 1969–1970*, edited by Lester Thonssen, 181–83. New York: H. W. Wilson Company, 1970.

Clark, John B. *The Philosophy of Wealth: Economic Principles Newly Formulated*. Boston: Ginn & Company, 1894.

Clarkin, Thomas. *Federal Indian Policy in the Kennedy and Johnson Administrations, 1961–1969*. Albuquerque: University of New Mexico Press, 2001.

[Clayton, John]. "An Account of the Indians in Virginia," edited by Stanley Pargellis. *William and Mary Quarterly*, 3d series, 16 (April 1959): 228–43.

Clifford, James. *The Predicament of Culture: Twentieth-Century Ethnography, Literature, and Art*. Cambridge, Mass.: Harvard University Press, 1988.

Cobb, Daniel M. "Philosophy of an Indian War: Indian Community Action in the Johnson Administration's War on Indian Poverty, 1964–1968." *American Indian Culture and Research Journal* 22:2 (1998): 71–102.

Cochran, Thomas C. *Challenges to American Values: Society, Business, and Religion*. New York: Oxford University Press, 1985.

Cochran, Thomas C., and William Miller. *The Age of Enterprise: A Social History of Industrial America*. New York: Harper & Brothers, 1961.

Cohen, Fay G. *Treaties on Trial: The Continuing Controversy over Northwest Indian Fishing Rights*. Seattle: University of Washington Press, 1986.

Colbert, Thomas Burnell. "Visionary or Rogue?: The Life and Legacy of Elias Cornelius Boudinot." *Chronicles of Oklahoma* 65 (Fall 1987): 268–81.

Coleman, Kenneth, and Milton Ready, eds. *Colonial Records of the State of Georgia*, Vol. 20, *Original Papers, Correspondence to the Trustees, James Oglethorpe, and Others, 1732–1735*. Athens: University of Georgia Press, 1982.

———. *Colonial Records of the State of Georgia*, Vol. 27, *Original Papers of Governor John Reynolds, 1754–1756*. Athens: University of Georgia Press, 1977.

Colloff, Pamela. "The Blood of the Tigua." *Texas Monthly* (August 1999): 112–16, 128–33.

Connolly, Vera L. "The Cry of a Broken People—A Story of Injustice and Cruelty That Is as Terrible as It Is True." *Good Housekeeping*. Reprint, *Congressional Record*, 70th Cong., 2d sess., 26 January 1929, vol. 70, 1–4.

Constitutions and Laws of the American Indian Tribes. Vols. 1, 2, 5–8, 9, 12, 18, 19. Wilmington, Del.: Scholarly Resources Inc., 1973.

Conwell, Russell H. *Acres of Diamonds*. New York: Harper & Brothers, 1915.

Corey, Herbert. "Lo! The Poor Indian Bureau." *Nation's Business* 33 (February 1945): 31–32, 69–70.

Corkran, David H. *The Creek Frontier, 1540–1783*. Norman: University of Oklahoma Press, 1967.

Cornell, Stephen. *The Return of the Native: American Indian Political Resurgence*. New York: Oxford University Press, 1988.

Cornwall, J. C. K. *Wealth and Society in Early Sixteenth Century England*. London: Routledge & Kegan Paul, 1988.

Corry, John Pitts. "Some New Light on the Bosomworth Claims." *Georgia Historical Quarterly* 25 (September 1941): 195–224.

Coulter, E. Merton. "Mary Musgrove, 'Queen of the Creeks': A Chapter of Early Georgia Troubles." *Georgia Historical Quarterly* 11 (March 1927): 1–30.

Craven, Wesley Frank. *White, Red, and Black: The Seventeenth-Century Virginian*. Charlottesville: University Press of Virginia, 1971.

Crowley, J. E. *This Sheba, Self: The Conceptualization of Economic Life in Eighteenth-Century America*. Baltimore: Johns Hopkins University Press, 1974.

Cumfer, Cynthia. *Separate Peoples, One Land: The Minds of Cherokees, Whites, and Blacks on the Tennessee Frontier*. Chapel Hill: University of North Carolina Press, 2007.

Dale, Edward E. "Letters of the Two Boudinots." *Chronicles of Oklahoma* 6 (September 1928): 328–47.

———. "Some Letters of General Stand Watie." *Chronicles of Oklahoma* 1 (March 1921): 30–59.

Dalton, George, ed. *Tribal and Peasant Economies: Readings in Economic Anthropology*. Garden City, N.Y.: Natural History Press, 1967.

Danvers, Gail D. "Gendered Encounters: Warriors, Women, and William Johnson." *Journal of American Studies* 35 (August 2001): 187–202.

Darian-Smith, Eve. *New Capitalists: Law, Politics, and Identity Surrounding Casino Gaming on Native American Land*. Belmont, Calif.: Thomson Wadsworth, 2004.

Davis, Harold E. *The Fledgling Province: Social and Cultural Life in Colonial Georgia, 1733–1776*. Chapel Hill: University of North Carolina Press, 1976.

Dawes, Anna Laurens. "An Unknown Nation." *Harper's Magazine* 76 (1887–88): 598–605.

Debo, Angie. *And Still the Waters Run*. Princeton, N.J.: Princeton University Press, 1940.

———. *The Rise and Fall of the Choctaw Republic*. Norman: University of Oklahoma Press, 1934; 2d ed., 1961.

———. *The Road to Disappearance: A History of the Creek Indians*. Norman: University of Oklahoma Press, 1941.

De Bry, Theodore. *Thomas Hariot's Virginia*. 1590. Reprint, March of America Facsimile Series, No. 15. Ann Arbor, Mich.: University Microfilms, 1966.

De la Ware, Lord Thomas, Sir Thomas Smith, Sir Walter Cope, and Master Waterson. "The Rationale for Settlement." In *The Old Dominion in the Seventeenth Century: A Documentary History of Virginia, 1606–1689*, edited by Warren M. Billings, Doc. 1. Chapel Hill: University of North Carolina Press, 1975.

Deloria, Philip J. *Indians in Unexpected Places*. Lawrence: University Press of Kansas, 2004.

———. *Playing Indian*. New Haven: Yale University Press, 1998.

Deloria, Vine, Jr. *Behind the Trail of Broken Treaties: An Indian Declaration of Independence*. New York: Dell Publishing, 1974.

———. *Custer Died for Your Sins: An Indian Manifesto*. New York: Macmillan, 1969.

———. "Land and Natural Resources." In *Minority Report: What Has Happened to Blacks, Hispanics, American Indians, and Other Minorities in the Eighties*, edited by Leslie W. Dunbar, 152–90. New York: Pantheon Books, 1984.

Denson, Andrew. *Demanding the Cherokee Nation: Indian Autonomy and American Culture, 1830–1900*. Lincoln: University of Nebraska Press, 2004.

Desmond, A. J. "America's Land Question." *North American Review* 142 (1886): 153–58.

Dickason, Olive Patricia. *The Myth of the Savage and the Beginnings of French Colonialism in the Americas*. Edmonton: University of Alberta Press, 1984.

Dickerson, Philip Jackson. *History of the Osage Nation: Its People, Resources and Prospects; the Last Reservation to Open in the New State*. Pawhuska, Okla.: N.p., 1906. (microform)

Dittmar, Helga. *The Social Psychology of Material Possessions: To Have Is To Be*. New York: St. Martin's Press, 1992.

Dorfman, Joseph. *The Economic Mind in American Civilization, 1606–1865*. New York: Viking, 1953.

Dudas, Jeffrey R. "In the Name of Equal Rights: 'Special' Rights and the Politics of Resentment in Post–Civil Rights America." *Law and Society Review* 39 (December 2005): 723–58.

Dunaway, Wilma A. *The First American Frontier: Transition to Capitalism in Southern Appalachia, 1700–1860*. Chapel Hill: University of North Carolina, 1996.

Dupuy, W. A. "New Policy of Aiding the American Indian." *Current History* 32 (September 1930): 1138–43.

Durand of Dauphiné. *A Huguenot Exile in Virginia, Or Voyages of a Frenchman Exiled for His Religion, with a Description of Virginia and Maryland*. Translated by Gilbert Chinard. 1687. Reprint, New York: Press of the Pioneers, 1934.

Earle, Carville V. "Environment, Disease, and Mortality in Early Virginia." In *The Chesapeake in the Seventeenth Century: Essays on Anglo-American Society*, edited by Thad W. Tate and David L Ammerman, 96–125. Chapel Hill: University of North Carolina Press, 1979.

Edmunds, David, Frederick E. Hoxie, and Neal Salisbury. *The People: A History of Native America*. Boston and New York: Houghton Mifflin Company, 2007.

Eisler, Kim Isaac. *Revenge of the Pequots: How a Small Native American Tribe Created the World's Most Profitable Casino*. Lincoln: University of Nebraska Press, 2002.

Elson, Ruth. *Guardians of Tradition: American Schoolbooks of the Nineteenth Century*. Lincoln: University of Nebraska Press, 1964.

Emerson, Elizabeth. "Give the Rich Man a Chance." *Chatauquan* 13 (July 1891): 500–501.

Evarts, Jeremiah. *Cherokee Removal: The "William Penn" Essays and Other Writings*. Edited by Francis Paul Prucha. Knoxville: University of Tennessee Press, 1981.

———. "Letter from the Treasurer of the American Board." *Panoplist and Missionary Herald* 14 (July 1818): 338–47.

Faiman-Silva, Sandra. *Choctaws at the Crossroads: The Political Economy of Class and Culture in the Oklahoma Timber Region*. Lincoln: University of Nebraska Press, 1997.

Faller, Nancy. "Washington's Fish War: Who Will Harvest the Salmon?" *Progressive* 44 (September 1980): 51–53.

Fausz, J. Frederick. "Merging and Emerging Worlds: Anglo-Indian Interest Groups and the Development of the Seventeenth-Century Chesapeake." In *Colonial Chesapeake Society*, edited by Lois Green Carr, Philip D. Morgan, and Jean B. Russo, 47–98. Chapel Hill: University of North Carolina Press, 1988.

———. "Present at the 'Creation': The Chesapeake World That Greeted the Maryland Colonists." *Maryland Historical Magazine* 79 (Spring 1984): 7–20.

———. "Patterns of Anglo-Indian Aggression and Accommodation along the Mid-Atlantic Coast, 1584–1634." In *Cultures in Contact: The Impact of European Contacts on Native American Cultural Institutions, A.D. 1000–1800*, edited by William W. Fitzhugh, 225–61. Washington, D.C.: Smithsonian Institution Press, 1985.

Feller, Daniel. *The Jacksonian Promise: America, 1815–1840*. Baltimore: Johns Hopkins University Press, 1995.

Fergusson, E. "Senators Investigate Indians." *American Mercury* 23 (August 1931): 464–68.

Fine, Sidney. *Laissez Faire and the General-Welfare State: A Study of Conflict in American Thought, 1865–1901*. Ann Arbor: University of Michigan Press, 1956.

Fite, Gilbert C. "Development of the Cotton Industry by the Five Civilized Tribes in Indian Territory." *Journal of Southern History* 15 (August 1949): 342–53.

Fixico, Donald. *The Invasion of Indian Country in the Twentieth Century: American Capitalism and Tribal Natural Resources*. Niwot: University Press of Colorado, 1998.

———. *Termination and Relocation: Federal Indian Policy, 1945–1960*. Albuquerque: University of New Mexico Press, 1986.

Fogelson, Raymond D., and Paul Kutsche. "Cherokee Economic Cooperatives: The Gadugi." In *Symposium on Cherokee and Iroquois Culture*, edited by William N. Fenton and John Gulick, 87–123. Bureau of American Ethnology *Bulletin* 180. Washington, D.C.: Smithsonian Institution, 1961.

Force, Peter, comp. *Tracts and Other Papers, Relating Principally to the Origin, Settlement, and Progress of the Colonies in North America, from the Discovery of the Country to the Year 1776*. Vol. 2. Gloucester, Mass.: Peter Smith, 1963.

Forde, Daryll, and Mary Douglas. "Primitive Economics." In *Tribal and Peasant Economies: Readings in Economic Anthropology*, edited by George Dalton, 330–44. Garden City, N.Y.: Natural History Press, 1967.

Foucault, Michel. *Power/Knowledge: Selected Interviews and Other Writings by Michel Foucault, 1972–1977*. Edited by Gordon Colin. New York: Pantheon Books, 1980.

Franks, Kenny A. *The Osage Oil Boom*. Oklahoma City: Oklahoma Heritage Association, 1989.

———. "Watie, Stand (De-Ga-Ta-Ga)." In *Encyclopedia of North American Indians*, edited by Frederick E. Hoxie, 679–80. Boston: Houghton Mifflin, 1996.

Frantz, Klaus. "The 'Economic Spirit' and Economic Structure of Indian Reservations: American Indian Value Systems and other Regulating Factors." In *Indian Reservations in the United States*, edited by Klaus Frantz, 156–88. Chicago: University of Chicago Press, 1999.

Fraser, Steve, and Gary Gerstle, eds. *Ruling America: A History of Wealth and Power in a Democracy*. Cambridge, Mass.: Harvard University Press, 2005.

Furstenberg, François. "The Significance of the Trans-Appalachian Frontier in Atlantic History." *American Historical Review* 113 (June 2008): 647–77.

Gabriel, Ralph Henry. *Elias Boudinot, Cherokee, and His America*. Norman: University of Oklahoma Press, 1941.

Galbraith, Craig S., Carlos L. Rodriguez, and Curt H. Stiles. "False Myths and Indigenous Entrepreneurial Strategies." In *Self-Determination: The Other Path for Native Americans*, edited by Terry L. Anderson, Bruce L. Benson, and Thomas E. Flanagan, 4–28. Stanford, Calif.: Stanford University Press, 2006.

Gallay, Alan. *The Indian Slave Trade: The Rise of the English Empire in the American South, 1670–1717*. New Haven, Conn.: Yale University Press, 2002.

Galpin, S. A. "Some Administrative Difficulties of the Indian Problem." *New Englander and Yale Review* 46 (April 1887): 305–18.

Garraty, John A. *The New Commonwealth 1877–1890*. New York: Harper & Row, 1968.

George, Henry. *Progress and Poverty: An Inquiry into the Cause of Industrial Depressions and of Increase of Want with Increase of Wealth. The Remedy*. New York: H. George, 1879.

Gerdes, Karen, Maria Napoli, Clinton M. Pattea, and Elizabeth A. Segal. "The Impact of Indian Gaming on Economic Development." In *Pressing Issues of Inequality and American Indian Communities*, edited by Elizabeth A. Segal and Keith M. Kilty, 17–30. New York and London: Haworth Press, 1998.

Getches, David H. "Conquering the Cultural Frontier: The New Subjectivity of the Supreme Court in Indian Law." *California Law Review* 84 (December 1996): 1573–1656.

Gibb, James G. *The Archaeology of Wealth: Consumer Behavior in English America*. New York and London: Plenum Press, 1996.

Gibbons, [James] Cardinal. "Wealth and Its Obligations." *North American Review* 152 (April 1891): 385–94.

Gibson, Arrell M. *The Chickasaws*. Norman: University of Oklahoma Press, 1971.

Gideon, D. C. *Indian Territory, Description, Biographical and Genealogical, Including the Landed Estates, County Seats, etc.* New York and Chicago: Lewis Publishing, 1901.

Gillespie, Michele. "The Sexual Politics of Race and Gender: Mary Musgrove and the Georgia Trustees." In *The Devil's Lane: Sex and Race in the Early South*, edited by Catherine Clinton and Michele Gillespie, 187–201. New York: Oxford University Press, 1997.

Gilmer, George R. *Sketches of Some of the First Settlers of Upper Georgia, of the Cherokees, and the Author*. New York, 1855; 1926. Reprint, Baltimore: Genealogical Publishing Company, 1970.

Ginger, Ray, ed. *The Nationalizing of American Life, 1877–1900*. New York: Free Press, 1965.

Glasscock, C. B. *Then Came Oil: The Story of the Last Frontier*. Indianapolis and New York: Bobbs-Merrill, 1938.

Gleach, Frederic W. *Powhatan's World and Colonial Virginia: A Conflict of Cultures*. Lincoln: University of Nebraska Press, 1997.

Glickman, Lawrence B. *A Living Wage: American Workers and the Making of Consumer Society*. Ithaca, N.Y.: Cornell University Press, 1997.

Goldberg, Carole, and Duane Champagne. "Ramona Redeemed? The Rise of Tribal Political Power in California." *Wicazo Sa Review* 17 (Spring 2002): 43–64.

Gonzales, Angela A. "Gaming and Displacement: Winners and Losers in American Indian Casino Development." *International Social Science Journal* 55 (March 2003): 123–33.

Graeber, David. *Toward an Anthropological Theory of Value: The False Coin of Our Own Dreams*. New York: Palgrave, 2001.

Green, Gretchen. "Molly Brant, Catharine Brant, and Their Daughters: A Study in Colonial Acculturation." *Ontario History* 81 (September 1989): 235–50.

Green, Michael D. "Alexander McGillivray." In *American Indian Leaders: Studies in Diversity*, edited by R. David Edmunds, 41–63. Lincoln: University of Nebraska Press, 1980.

———. "Mary Musgrove: Creating a New World." In *Sifters: Native American Women's Lives*, edited by Theda Perdue, 29–47. New York: Oxford University Press, 2001.

———. *The Politics of Indian Removal: Creek Government and Society in Crisis*. Lincoln: University of Nebraska Press, 1982.

Greene, Jack P. *Imperatives, Behaviors, and Identities: Essays in Early American Cultural History*. Charlottesville: University Press of Virginia, 1992.

———. *Pursuits of Happiness: The Social Development of Early Modern British Colonies and the Formation of American Culture*. Chapel Hill: University of North Carolina Press, 1988.

Gudeman, Stephen. *Economics as Culture: Models and Metaphors of Livelihood*. London, Boston, and Henley: Routledge & Kegan Paul, 1986.

———. *The Anthropology of Economy: Community, Market, and Culture*. Malden, Mass.: Blackwell, 2001.

Hahn, Steven C. *The Invention of the Creek Nation, 1670–1763*. Lincoln: University of Nebraska Press, 2004.

———. "The Mother of Necessity: Carolina, the Creek Indians, and the Making of a New Order in the American Southeast, 1670–1763." In *The Transformation of the Southeastern Indians, 1540–1760*, edited by Robbie Ethridge and Charles Hudson, 79–114. Jackson: University Press of Mississippi, 2002.

Halsey, F. W. *The Old New York Frontier; Its Wars with Indians and Tories; Its Missionary Schools, Pioneers and Land Titles, 1614–1800*. New York: Charles Scribner's Sons, 1901.

Hamer, John H. "Money and the Moral Order in Late Nineteenth and Early Twentieth-Century American Capitalism." *Anthropological Quarterly* 71 (July 1998): 138–49.

Hamilton, Alexander. *Gentleman's Progress: The Itinerarium of Dr. Alexander Hamilton, 1744*. Edited by Carl Bridenbaugh. Chapel Hill: University of North Carolina Press, 1948.

Hamilton, Milton W. "Sir William Johnson: Interpreter of the Iroquois." *Ethnohistory* 10 (Summer 1963): 270–86.

——, ed. *The Papers of Sir William Johnson*. Albany: University of the State of New York, 1921–1962.

Handlin, Oscar and Mary F. *The Wealth of the American People: A History of American Affluence*. New York: McGraw-Hill, 1975.

Hann, C. M., ed. *Property Relations: Renewing the Anthropological Tradition*. Cambridge, U.K.: Cambridge University Press, 1998.

Hanson, Jeffery R. "Ethnicity and the Looking Glass: The Dialectics of National Indian Identity." *American Indian Quarterly* 21 (Spring 1997): 195–208.

Hantman, Jeffrey L. "Between Powhatan and Quirank: Reconstructing Monacan Culture and History in the Context of Jamestown." *American Anthropologist* 92 (December 1990): 676–90.

Harmon, Alexandra. "American Indians and Land Monopolies in the Gilded Age." *Journal of American History* 90 (June 2003): 106–33.

——. *Indians in the Making: Ethnic Relations and Indian Identities around Puget Sound*. Berkeley and Los Angeles: University of California Press, 1998.

Harmon, George D. "The Indian Trust Funds, 1797–1865." Institute of Research Circular 105. *Lehigh University Publication* 8:12 (December 1934): 23–30.

Harrington, Michael. *The Other America: Poverty in the United States*. Baltimore: Penguin, 1964.

Hatfield, April Lee. "Spanish Colonization Literature, Powhatan Geographies, and English Perceptions of Tsenacommacah/Virginia." *Journal of Southern History* 69 (May 2003): 245–82.

Hatley, Tom. *The Dividing Paths: Cherokees and South Carolinians through the Era of Revolution*. New York: Oxford University Press, 1993.

Hawkins, Benjamin. *A Combination of a Sketch of the Creek Country, in the Years 1798 and 1799; and, Letters of Benjamin Hawkins, 1796–1806*. Spartanburg, S.C.: The Reprint Company, 1974.

Hawkins, Rush C. "Brutality and Avarice Triumphant." *North American Review* 152 (December 1891): 656–81.

Hays, Samuel P. *The Response to Industrialism, 1885–1914*. Chicago: University of Chicago Press, 1957.

Heilbroner, Robert L. "Who Are the American Poor?" *Harper's Magazine* 200 (June 1950): 27–33.

Heller, Joseph. *Catch-22*. 2d ed. New York: Dell, 1961.

Hemphill, W. Edwin, ed. *The Papers of John C. Calhoun*. Columbia: University of South Carolina Press, 1972.

Hendricks, Allan. "The Land of the Five Tribes." *Lippincott's Magazine* 58 (1896): 670–76.

Hershberger, Mary. "Mobilizing Women, Anticipating Abolition: The Struggle against Indian Removal in the 1830s. " *Journal of American History* 86 (June 1999): 15–40.

Hewes, Leslie. *Occupying the Cherokee Country of Oklahoma*. Lincoln: University of Nebraska, 1978.

Hinton, Richard J. "The Indian Territory,—Its Status, Development, and Future." *American Monthly Review of Reviews* 23 (April 1901): 451–58.

Hobbs, Charles A., Jerry R. Goldstein, and Robin A. Friedman. "Review of Developments in Indian Law in the Courts." *American Indian Journal* (November 1978); reprint, NCAI, *American Indian Issue Papers*, 25th Annual Convention, 18–22 September 1978.

Hodgson, Geoffrey M. *How Economics Forgot History: The Problem of Historical Specificity in Social Science*. London and New York: Routledge, 2001.

Hoffer, Peter Charles. *Law and People in Colonial America*. Rev. ed. Baltimore: Johns Hopkins University Press, 1998.

Hofstadter, Richard. *Social Darwinism in American Thought, 1860–1915*. Philadelphia: University Pennsylvania Press, 1945.

Holifield, E. Brooks. *Era of Persuasion: American Thought and Culture, 1521–1680*. Boston: Twayne Publishers, 1989.

Holt, Charles F. "Who Benefited from the Prosperity of the Twenties?" *Explorations in Economic History* 14 (July 1977): 277–89.

Holton, Woody. *Forced Founders: Indians, Debtors, Slaves, and the Making of the American Revolution in Virginia*. Chapel Hill: University of North Carolina Press, 1999.

Horn, James. *Adapting to a New World: English Society in the Seventeenth-Century Chesapeake*. Chapel Hill: University of North Carolina Press, 1994.

Horowitz, Daniel. *The Anxieties of Affluence: Critiques of American Consumer Culture, 1939–1979*. Amherst and Boston: University of Massachusetts Press, 2004.

———. *The Morality of Spending: Attitudes toward the Consumer Society in America, 1875–1940*. Baltimore: Johns Hopkins University Press, 1985. Reprint, Chicago: Elephant Paperbacks, Ivan R. Dee, 1992.

Horsman, Reginald. "The Indian Policy of an 'Empire for Liberty.'" In *Native Americans and the Early Republic*, edited by Frederick E. Hoxie, Ronald Hoffman, and Peter J. Albert, 37–61. Charlottesville: University Press of Virginia, 1999.

Hough, Henry W. *Development of Indian Resources*. Denver: World Press, 1967.

Hoxie, Frederick E. "Ethnohistory for a Tribal World." *Ethnohistory* 44 (Autumn 1997): 595–615.

———. *A Final Promise: The Campaign to Assimilate the Indians, 1880–1920*. Lincoln: University of Nebraska, 1984.

Hranicky, William Jack. "The Virginia Algonquian Language." *The Chesopiean* 20 (June–August 1982): 19–20.

Hudson, Charles M. *The Southeastern Indians*. Knoxville: University of Tennessee Press, 1976.

Huey, Lois M., and Bonnie Pulis. *Molly Brant: A Legacy of Her Own*. Youngstown, N.Y.: Old Fort Niagara Association, 1997.

Hunt, Robert C., and Antonio Gilman, eds. *Property in Economic Context*. Monographs in Economic Anthropology No. 14. Lanham and New York: University Press of America, 1998.

Huston, James L. *Securing the Fruits of Labor: The American Concept of Wealth Distribution, 1765–1900.* Baton Rouge: Louisiana State University Press, 1998.

Indian Rights Association. *Eighth Annual Report of the Executive Committee of the Indian Rights Association.* Philadelphia: Office of the Indian Rights Association, 1891.

The Indian's Friend 8:12 (August 1896): 6.

Ingersoll, Thomas N. "'Riches and Honor Were Rejected by Them as Loathsome Vomit': The Fear of Leveling in New England." In *Inequality in Early America*, edited by Carla Gardina Pestana and Sharon V. Salinger, 46–66. Hanover: University Press of New England, 1999.

Innes, Stephen. *Creating the Commonwealth: The Economic Culture of Puritan New England.* New York: W. W. Norton & Company, 1995.

Institute for Government Research [Lewis Meriam, et al.]. *The Problem of Indian Administration: Report of a Survey Made at the Request of Honorable Hubert Work, Secretary of the Interior, and Submitted to Him, February 21, 1928.* 1928. Reprint, New York: Johnson Reprint Corporation, 1971.

Jencks, Christopher. "The Hidden Prosperity of the 1970s." *Public Interest* 77 (Fall 1984): 37–61.

Jenness, Theodora R. "The Indian Territory." *Atlantic Monthly* 43:4 (1879): 444–52.

Johansen, Bruce E. *The Encyclopedia of Native American Economic History.* Westport, Conn.: Greenwood Press, 1999.

———. "Native American Societies and the Evolution of Democracy in America, 1600–1800." *Ethnohistory* 37 (Summer 1990): 279–90.

Johnson, Allen. "Horticulturalists: Economic Behavior in Tribes." In *Economic Anthropology*, edited by Stuart Plattner, 49–77. Stanford, Calif.: Stanford University Press, 1989.

Johnson, Benjamin Heber. "Red Populism? T. A. Bland, Agrarian Radicalism, and the Debate over the Dawes Act." In *The Countryside in the Age of the Modern State: Political Histories of Rural America*, edited by Catherine McNicol and Robert D. Johnston, 15–37. Ithaca: Cornell University Press, 2001.

Johnson, Dana. "Native American Treaty Rights to Scarce Natural Resources." *UCLA Law Review* 43 (December 1995–96): 547–85.

Johnson, Jean. "Ancestry and Descendants of Molly Brant." *Ontario History* 63 (July 1971): 87–92.

Johnson, N. R. "Solution: Assimilation." *Rotarian* 85 (August 1954): 29.

[Johnson, Robert]. *Nova Britannia: Offering Most Excellent Fruites by Planting in Virginia.* London: Samuel Macham, 1609. (microform)

Johnston, Charles M. "Joseph Brant, the Grand River Lands, and the Northwest Crisis." *Ontario History* 55 (December 1963): 267–82.

———, ed. *The Valley of the Six Nations: A Collection of Documents on the Indian Lands of the Grand River.* Toronto: Champlain Society, 1964.

Jones, Hugh. *The Present State of Virginia, from Whence Is Inferred a Short View of Maryland and North Carolina.* Edited by Richard L. Morton. Chapel Hill: University of North Carolina Press, 1956.

Jorgensen, Joseph G., ed. *Native Americans and Energy Development II*. Boston: Anthropology Resource Center and Seventh Generation Fund, 1984.

Josephy, Alvin M., Jr. "Modern America and the Indian." In *Indians in American History: An Introduction*, edited by Frederick E. Hoxie and Peter Iverson, 198–217. Wheeling, Ill.: Harlan Davidson, 1998.

Josephy, Alvin M., Jr., Joane Nagel, and Troy Johnson. *Red Power: The American Indians' Fight for Freedom*. 2d ed. Lincoln: University of Nebraska Press, 1991.

Juricek, John T., ed. *Georgia Treaties, 1733–1763*. Vol. 11 of *Early American Indian Documents: Treaties and Laws, 1607–1789*. Frederick, Md.: University Publications of America, 1989.

Kansas City Star. "Report on the Five Civilized Tribes, 1897." *Chronicles of Oklahoma* 48 (Winter 1970): 416–30.

Kelly, William H. "The Economic Basis of Indian Life." *Annals of the American Academy of Political and Social Science* 311 (May 1957): 76.

Kelsay, Isabel Thompson. *Joseph Brant, 1743–1807: Man of Two Worlds*. Syracuse, N.Y.: Syracuse University Press, 1984.

Kingsbury, Susan Myra, ed. *The Records of the Virginia Company of London*. Vols. 1–4. Washington, D.C.: United States Government Printing Office, 1906–1935.

Kohl, Lawrence Frederick. *The Politics of Individualism: Parties and the American Character in the Jacksonian Era*. New York: Oxford University Press, 1989.

Kornblith, Gary J. "Hiram Hill: House Carpenter, Lumber Dealer, Self-Made Man." In *The Human Tradition in Antebellum America*, edited by Michael A. Morrison, 53–65. Wilmington, Del.: Scholarly Resources, 2000.

Krugman, Paul. *The Great Unraveling: Losing Our Way in the New Century*. New York: W. W. Norton, 2003.

Kulikoff, Allan. *From British Peasants to Colonial American Farmers*. Chapel Hill: University of North Carolina Press, 2000.

Kupperman, Karen Ordahl. *Indians and English: Facing Off in Early America*. Ithaca: Cornell University Press, 2000.

———. *The Jamestown Project*. Cambridge, Mass.: Belknap Press of Harvard University Press, 2007.

———. *Settling with the Indians: The Meeting of English and Indian Cultures in America, 1580–1640*. Totowa, N.J.: Rowman and Littlefield, 1980.

LaFlesche, Francis. *A Dictionary of the Osage Language*. Bureau of American Ethnology Bulletin No. 109. Washington, D.C.: Smithsonian Institution, 1932.

Lamphere, Louise. *To Run After Them: Cultural and Social Bases of Cooperation in a Navajo Community*. Tucson: University of Arizona Press, 1977.

Lane, Mills, ed. *General Oglethorpe's Georgia: Colonial Letters, 1733–1743*. 2 vols. Savannah: Beehive Press, 1975.

Lanman, Charles. "Peter Pitchlynn, Chief of the Choctaws." *Atlantic Monthly* (April 1870): 486.

Lawson, John. *A New Voyage to Carolina*. Edited by Hugh Talmage Lefler. Chapel Hill: University of North Carolina Press, 1967.

Lebergott, Stanley. *The Americans: An Economic Record*. New York: W. W. Norton, 1984.

Lederer, John. *The Discoveries of John Lederer*. Compiled and translated by Sir William

Talbot Baronet. London: 1672. Facsimile reprint, Ann Arbor, Mich.: University Microfilms, 1966.

Lemann, Nicholas. "How the Seventies Changed America." *American Heritage* (July/ August 1991): 39–49.

Levitan, Sar A., and Barbara Hetrick. *Big Brother's Indian Programs—With Reservations.* New York: McGraw-Hill, 1971.

Levitan, Sar A., and William B. Johnston. *Indian Giving: Federal Programs for Native Americans.* Baltimore: Johns Hopkins University Press, 1975.

Lewis, David Rich. *Neither Wolf nor Dog: American Indians, Environment, and Agrarian Change.* New York: Oxford University Press, 1999.

———. "Reservation Leadership and the Progressive-Traditional Dichotomy: William Wash and the Northern Utes, 1865–1928." *Ethnohistory* 38 (Spring 1991): 124–48.

Liebersohn, Harry. *Aristocratic Encounters: European Travelers and North American Indians.* Cambridge, U.K.: Cambridge University Press, 1998.

Light, Steven Andrew, and Kathryn R. L. Rand. *Indian Gaming and Tribal Sovereignty.* Lawrence: University Press of Kansas, 2005.

Littlefield, Daniel F., Jr., and James W. Parins. *A Biobibliography of Native American Writers, 1772–1924.* Metuchen, N.J.: Scarecrow Press, 1981.

"Lo, the Poor Indian in Industry." *Current Opinion* 72 (March 1922): 411–12.

Lumpkin, Wilson. *The Removal of the Cherokee Indians from Georgia.* 2 vols. 1852. Reprint, Savannah, Ga.: Savannah Morning News Print, 1907.

Lurie, Nancy Oestreich. "Money, Semantics, and Indian Leadership." *American Indian Quarterly* 10 (Winter 1986): 47–63.

Main, Gloria L. *Peoples of a Spacious Land: Families and Cultures in Colonial New England.* Cambridge, Mass.: Harvard University Press, 2001.

Mallios, Seth. *The Deadly Politics of Giving: Exchange and Violence at Ajacan, Roanoke, and Jamestown.* Tuscaloosa: University of Alabama Press, 2006.

Mallock, W. H. "Who Are the Chief Wealth-Producers?" *North American Review* 156 (December 1893): 648–60.

Malone, Henry Thompson. *Cherokees of the Old South: A People in Transition.* Athens: University of Georgia Press, 1956.

Mathews, John Joseph. *The Osages: Children of the Middle Waters.* Norman: University of Oklahoma Press, 1961.

———. *Sundown.* New York: Longmans, Green, and Co., 1934.

———. *Wah'kon-tah: The Osage and the White Man's Road.* Norman: University of Oklahoma Press, 1932.

Matson, Cathy D. "Capitalizing Hope: Economic Thought and the Early National Economy." *Journal of the Early Republic* 16 (Summer 1996): 273–91.

———. "A House of Many Mansions: Some Thoughts on the Field of Economic History." In *The Economy of Early America: Historical Perspectives and New Directions*, edited by Cathy Matson, 1–70. University Park: Pennsylvania State University, 2006.

Matt, Susan J. *Keeping Up with the Joneses: Envy in American Consumer Society, 1890–1930.* Philadelphia: University of Pennsylvania Press, 2003.

May, Katja. *African Americans and Native Americans in the Creek and Cherokee Nations, 1830s to 1920s: Collision and Collusion.* New York: Garland, 1996.

McAdam, Rezin W. "An Indian Commonwealth." *Harper's New Monthly Magazine* 87 (November 1893): 884–97.

McAuliffe, Dennis, Jr. *Bloodland: A Family Story of Oil, Greed and Murder on the Osage Reservation*. San Francisco and Tulsa: Council Oak Books, 1999.

McCarthy, Finbarr. "The Influence of 'Legal Habit' on English-Indian Relations in Jamestown, 1606–1612." *Continuity and Change* 5 (May 1990): 39–64.

McCovey, Shaunna. "Ascending Poverty and Inequality in Native America: An Alternative Perspective." In *Pressing Issues of Inequality and American Indian Communities*, edited by Elizabeth A. Segal and Keith M. Kilty, 85–87. New York and London: Haworth Press, 1998.

McCracken, Grant. *Culture and Consumption: New Approaches to the Symbolic Character of Consumer Goods and Activities*. Bloomington and Indianapolis: Indiana University Press, 1990.

McDowell, William L., Jr., ed. *Colonial Records of South Carolina: Documents Relating to Indian Affairs, May 21, 1750–August 7, 1754*. Columbia: South Carolina Archives Department, 1958.

———. *Colonial Records of South Carolina: Documents Relating to Indian Affairs, 1754–1765*. Columbia: University of South Carolina Press, 1970.

———. *Colonial Records of South Carolina: Journals of the Commissioners of the Indian Trade, September 20, 1710–August 29, 1718*. Columbia: South Carolina Archives Department, 1955.

McIlwaine, H. R., ed. *Executive Journals of the Council of Colonial Virginia*, Vol. 1. Richmond: Virginia State Library, 1925.

———, ed. *Journals of the House of Burgesses of Virginia, 1659/60–1693*. Vols. 1–13. Richmond: Virginia State Library, 1914.

McKenzie, Fayette Avery. "Lo! the Poor Indian: Calls for the Attention of the American Public." [New York: Society of American Indians], 1914.

McKinley, Francis. "Federal Indian Policy as It Affects Local Indian Affairs." *Indian Truth* 41 (June 1964): 1–2.

McLoughlin, William G. *After the Trail of Tears: The Cherokees' Struggle for Sovereignty, 1839–1880*. Chapel Hill: University of North Carolina Press, 1993.

———. *Cherokee Renascence in the New Republic*. Princeton, N.J.: Princeton University Press, 1986.

Meissner, Hanna H. *Poverty in the Affluent Society*. New York: Harper & Row, 1966; rev. ed., 1973.

Mercier, Laurie. *Anaconda: Labor, Community, and Culture in Montana's Smelter City*. Urbana and Chicago: University of Illinois Press, 2001.

Mereness, Newton D., ed. *Travels in the American Colonies*. New York: Macmillan Company, 1916.

Merrell, James H. "'The Cast of His Countenance': Reading Andrew Montour." In *Through a Glass Darkly: Reflections on Personal Identity in Early America*, edited by Ronald Hoffman, Mechal Sobel, and Fredrika J. Teute, 13–39. Chapel Hill: University of North Carolina Press, 1997.

Meserve, Charles F. "The Dawes Commission and the Five Civilized Tribes of Indian Territory." *Bulletin of the Indian Rights Association* 33 (1896): 18–19.

Meserve, John Bartlett. "Chief Wilson Nathaniel Jones." *Chronicles of Oklahoma* 14 (Winter 1936): 419–33.

————, ed. "The Plea of Crazy Snake (Chitto Harjo)." *Chronicles of Oklahoma* 11 (September 1933): 899–911.

Meyer, Melissa L. *The White Earth Tragedy: Ethnicity and Dispossession at a Minnesota Anishinaabe Reservation*. Lincoln: University of Nebraska Press, 1994.

Michel, Francis Louis. "Report on the Journey of Francis Louis Michel from Berne, Switzerland, to Virginia, October 2, 1701–December 1, 1702," Part 2, edited and translated by William J. Hinke. *Virginia Magazine of History and Biography* 24 (1916): 1–43, 113–41, 275–303.

Miley, Cora. "Overnight Millions." *American Magazine* (May 1931): 15–17, 84–85.

Milfort, Leclerc. *Memoirs or A Quick Glance at my Various Travels and my Sojourn in the Creek Nation*. Edited and translated by Ben C. McCary. Kennesaw, Ga.: Continental Book Company, 1959.

Miller, Christopher L., and George R. Hamell. "A New Perspective on Indian-White Contact: Cultural Symbols and Colonial Trade." *Journal of American History* 73 (September 1986): 311–28.

Miner, H. Craig. *The Corporation and the Indian: Tribal Sovereignty and Industrial Civilization in Indian Territory, 1865–1907*. Norman: University of Oklahoma Press, 1976.

Miskimin, Harry A. *The Economy of Later Renaissance Europe, 1460–1600*. Cambridge, U.K.: Cambridge University Press, 1977.

Moffitt, John F., and Santiago Sebastian. *O Brave New People: The European Invention of the American Indian*. Albuquerque: University of New Mexico Press, 1996.

"Mohonk Indian Conference." *The Indian's Friend* 6 (November 1894): 7; 9 (November 1896): 8.

Moody, William G. *Land and Labor in the United States*. New York: Charles Scribner's Sons, 1883.

Moore, J. H. *The Political Condition of the Indians and the Resources of Indian Territory*. St. Louis: Southwestern Book and Publishing Co., 1874.

Morgan, Anne Hodges, and Rennard Strickland, eds. *Oklahoma Memories*. Norman: University of Oklahoma Press, 1981.

Morgan, Edmund S. "The First American Boom: Virginia, 1618–1630." *William and Mary Quarterly*, 3d series, 28 (January 1971): 169–98.

Morris, Michael P. *The Bringing of Wonder: Trade and the Indians of the Southeast, 1700–1783*. Westport, Conn.: Greenwood Press, 1999.

Morris, Wayne. "Auguste Pierre Chouteau, Merchant Prince at the Three Forks of the Arkansas." *Chronicles of Oklahoma* 48 (Summer 1970): 155–63.

Morrison, James D. "Problems in the Industrial Progress and Development of the Choctaw Nation, 1865 to 1907." *Chronicles of Oklahoma* 32 (Spring 1954): 70–91.

Morrison, Michael A., ed. *The Human Tradition in Antebellum America*. Wilmington, Del.: Scholarly Resources, 2000.

Moses, L. G. *Wild West Shows and the Images of American Indians, 1883–1933*. Albuquerque: University of New Mexico Press, 1996.

Moulton, Gary E. *John Ross, Cherokee Chief*. Athens: University of Georgia Press, 1978.

————, ed. *The Papers of Chief John Ross*. 2 vols. Norman: University of Oklahoma Press, 1985.

Mowry, George E., ed. *The Twenties: Fords, Flappers and Fanatics*. Englewood Cliffs, N.J.: Prentice-Hall, 1963.

Mullin, Michael J. "Personal Politics: William Johnson and the Mohawks." *American Indian Quarterly* 17 (Summer 1993): 350–58.

Murray, David. *Indian Giving: Economies of Power in Indian-White Exchanges*. Amherst: University of Massachusetts Press, 2000.

Musgrave, Peter. *The Early Modern European Economy*. New York: St. Martin's Press, 1999.

Nagel, Gerald S. "Economics of the Reservation." *Current History* 67 (December 1974): 245–49, 278–79.

Nagel, Joane. *American Indian Ethnic Renewal: Red Power and the Resurgence of Identity and Culture*. New York: Oxford University Press, 1996.

Nakai, Raymond. "Inaugural Address." In *Representative American Speeches, 1963–64*, edited by Lester Thonssen, 54. New York: H. W. Wilson Company, 1964.

Nash, Gary B. "The Image of the Indian in the Southern Colonial Mind." *William and Mary Quarterly*, 3d series, 29 (April 1972): 197–230.

Nash, Manning. *The Cauldron of Ethnicity in the Modern World*. Chicago: University of Chicago Press, 1989.

————. "The Organization of Economic Life." In *Tribal and Peasant Economies: Readings in Economic Anthropology*, edited by George Dalton, 3–11. Garden City, N.Y.: Natural History Press, 1967.

National Congress of American Indians. *American Indian Issue Papers*, 25th Annual Convention, September 18–22, 1978.

————. *Resolutions Adopted by 23rd Annual Convention*. Oklahoma City, 1966.

————. *Resolutions Adopted by 25th Annual Convention*. Omaha, Neb., 1968.

Nett, Betty R. "Historical Changes in the Osage Kinship System." *Southwestern Journal of Anthropology* 8 (Summer 1952): 164–81.

"News and Notes." *The Indian's Friend* 7 (January 1895): 2.

Nicolau, George. "The War on Poverty." In *Dialogue on Poverty*, edited by Paul Jacobs, Arthur McCormack, Bayard Rustin, Leon H. Keyserling, Robert Theobald, Nat Hentoff, and Don Benson, 77–90. Indianapolis and New York: Bobbs-Merrill, 1967.

Noggle, Burl. *Into the Twenties: The United States from Armistice to Normalcy*. Urbana: University of Illinois Press, 1974.

Noll, Mark A. "Protestant Reasoning about Money and the Economy, 1790–1860: A Preliminary Probe." In *God and Mammon: Protestants, Money, and the Market, 1790–1860*, edited by Mark A. Noll, 265–94. New York: Oxford University Press, 2002.

Nordham, George Washington. *George Washington and Money*. Washington, D.C.: University Press of America, 1982.

Norton, Charles Elliot. "The Poverty of England." *North American Review* 109 (July 1869): 122–54.

Norton, John. *The Journal of Major John Norton, 1816*. Edited by Carl F. Klinck and James J. Talman. Toronto: The Champlain Society, 1970.

Notestein, Wallace. *The English People on the Eve of Colonization, 1603–1642*. New York: Harper, 1954.

Nutt, Rush. "Diary of a Tour through the Western and Southern Parts of the United States in America." *Journal of Mississippi History* 9 (January 1947): 41–44.

Oberg, Kalervo. *The Social Economy of the Tlingit Indians*. Seattle: University of Washington Press, 1973.

Objections of the Chickasaw, Choctaw, Seminole, Creek, and Cherokee Indians to the Bill for the Organization of the Territory of Oklahoma (H.R. 315) pending in the House of Representatives of the United States. Washington, D.C.: 1885. (microfiche)

O'Callaghan, E. B., ed. *Documents Relative to the Colonial History of the State of New-York; Procured in Holland, England and France*. Albany: Weed, Parsons and Company, 1857.

Oliphant, Orin J., ed. *Through the South and the West with Jeremiah Evarts in 1826*. Lewisburg, Pa.: Bucknell University Press, 1956.

Olson, James S., and Raymond Wilson. *Native Americans in the Twentieth Century*. Urbana and Chicago: University of Illinois Press, 1984.

Omi, Michael, and Howard Winant. *Racial Formation in the United States: From the 1960s to the 1990s*. 2d ed. New York: Routledge, 1994.

"On the State of the Indians." *North American Review* 7 (January 1823): 30–45.

O'Nell, Theresa D. "Telling about Whites, Talking about Indians: Oppression, Resistance, and Contemporary American Indian Identity." *Cultural Anthropology* 9 (February 1994): 94–126.

O'Toole, Fintan. *White Savage: William Johnson and the Invention of America*. New York: Farrar, Straus and Giroux, 2005.

Pagden, Anthony. *Lords of All the World: Ideologies of Empire in Spain, Britain and France c. 1500–c. 1800*. New Haven: Yale University Press, 1995.

Painter, Charles C. *The Proposed Removal of Indians to Oklahoma*. Philadelphia: Indian Rights Association, 1888.

Painter, Nell Irvin. *Standing at Armageddon: The United States, 1877–1919*. New York: W. W. Norton & Company, 1987.

Palmer, Bruce. *"Man over Money": The Southern Populist Critique of American Capitalism*. Chapel Hill: University of North Carolina Press, 1980.

Palmer, Frederick. "You Cannot Buy It All." *Harper's Monthly Magazine* 149 (August 1924): 305–10.

Palmer, William E. *Memoir of the Distinguished Mohawk Indian Chief, Sachem and Warrior, Capt. Joseph Brant*. Brantford, Ontario: C. E. Stewart & Co., 1872.

Parfit, Michael. "Fishermen at Sea in Puget Sound War of the Salmon." *Smithsonian* 9 (February 1979): 56–67.

Parman, Donald L. *Indians and the American West in the Twentieth Century*. Bloomington and Indianapolis: Indiana University Press, 1994.

————, ed. "Lewis Meriam's Letters during the Survey of Indian Affairs, 1926–1927." *Arizona and the West* 24 (Autumn and Winter 1982): 253–80, 341–70.

Pasquaretta, Paul. *Gambling and Survival in Native North America*. Tucson: University of Arizona Press, 2003.

Patterson, James T. *America's Struggle against Poverty, 1900–1980*. Cambridge: Harvard University Press, 1981.

Pearce, Roy Harvey. *Savagism and Civilization: A Study of the Indian and the American Mind*. Berkeley and Los Angeles: University of California Press, 1988.

Perdue, Theda. "Cherokee Planters: The Development of Plantation Slavery before Removal." In *The Cherokee Indian Nation: A Troubled History*, edited by Duane H. King, 110–28. Knoxville: University of Tennessee Press, 1979.

———. "The Conflict Within: Cherokees and Removal." In *Cherokee Removal: Before and After*, edited by William L. Anderson, 55–74. Athens: University of Georgia Press, 1991.

———. *"Mixed Blood" Indians: Racial Construction in the Early South*. Athens: University of Georgia Press, 2003.

———. "Rising from the Ashes: The *Cherokee Phoenix* as an Ethnohistorical Source." *Ethnohistory* 24 (Summer 1977): 207–18.

———. *Slavery and the Evolution of Cherokee Society, 1540–1866*. Knoxville: University of Tennessee Press, 1979.

Perdue, Theda, and Michael D. Green. *The Columbia Guide to American Indians of the Southeast*. New York: Columbia University Press, 2001.

"Perfect Description of Virginia." [1649]. In *Tracts and Other Papers Relating Principally to the Origin, Settlement, and Progress of the Colonies of North America, from the Discovery of the Country to the Year 1776*, edited by Peter Force. Vol. 2. 1837. Reprint, Gloucester, Mass.: Peter Smith, 1963.

Perkins, Edwin J. *The Economy of Colonial America*. 2d ed. New York: Columbia University Press, 1988.

Pessen, Edward. *Jacksonian America: Society, Personality, and Politics*. Rev. ed. Urbana and Chicago: University of Illinois Press, 1985.

———. *Riches, Class and Power before the Civil War*. Lexington, Mass.: D. C. Heath, 1974.

Phelps, J. Edward. "Irresponsible Wealth." *North American Review* 152 (November 1891): 523–33.

Phillips, Joyce B., and Paul Gary, eds. *The Brainerd Journal: A Mission to the Cherokees, 1817–1823*. Lincoln: University of Nebraska Press, 1998.

Philp, Kenneth R., ed. *Indian Self-Rule: First-Hand Accounts of Indian-White Relations from Roosevelt to Reagan*. Logan: Utah State University Press, 1995.

Pickering, Kathleen. *Lakota Culture, World Economy*. Lincoln: University of Nebraska Press, 2003.

Piomingo [pseudo.]. *The Savage*. Philadelphia: printed for Thomas S. Manning, [1810].

Pitchlynn, Peter. *Letter of P. P. Pitchlynn to the People of the Choctaw and Chickasaw Nations upon the Question of Sectionizing and Dividing Their Land in Severalty*. Washington, D.C., 1870. Reprint, *The Gilcrease-Hargrett Catalogue of Imprints*, edited by Lester Hargrett. Norman: University of Oklahoma Press, 1972.

Platt, Orville H. "Problems in the Indian Territory." *North American Review* 160 (February 1895): 195–202.

Plattner, Stuart, ed. *Economic Anthropology*. Stanford, Calif.: Stanford University Press, 1989.

Pomeroy, Eltweed. "The Concentration of Wealth." *Arena* 85 (December 1896): 82–96.

Pooley, Sophia. [Untitled narrative.] In *The Refugee: or The Narratives of Fugitive Slaves in Canada*, edited by Benjamin Drew, 135–36. 1856. Reprint as *Four Fugitive Slave Narratives*, Reading, Mass: Addison-Wesley, 1969.

Pope, John. *A Tour through the Southern and Western Territories of the United States of*

North-America. Facsimile reproduction of 1792 edition, with introduction by J. Barton Starr. Gainesville: University Presses of Florida, 1979.

Posey, Alexander. *The Fus Fixico Letters.* Edited by Daniel F. Littlefield, Jr., and Carol A. Petty Hunter. Lincoln: University of Nebraska Press, 1993.

Postel, Charles. *The Populist Vision.* New York: Oxford University Press, 2007.

Potter, Stephen R. *Commoners, Tribute, and Chiefs: The Development of Algonquian Culture in the Potomac Valley.* Charlottesville: University Press of Virginia, 1993.

Povinelli, Elizabeth. *The Cunning of Recognition: Indigenous Alterities and the Making of Australian Multiculturalism.* Durham, N.C.: Duke University Press, 2002.

Proceedings of the Annual Lake Mohonk Conference of Friends of the Indian. Lake Mohonk, N.Y.: N.p., 1885–1901.

Prucha, Francis Paul, ed. *Americanizing the American Indians: Writings by the "Friends of the Indian," 1880–1900.* Cambridge, Mass.: Harvard University Press, 1973.

———. *The Great Father: The United States Government and the American Indian.* 2 vols. Lincoln: University of Nebraska Press, 1984.

Purchas, Samuel. *Hakluytus Posthumus or Purchas His Pilgrimes.* Vol. 19. Glasgow: James MacLehose and Sons, 1905–7.

Quinn, David Beers, ed. *New American World: A Documentary History of North America to 1612.* Vol. 5. New York: Arno Press and Hector Bye, 1979.

———, ed. *The Roanoke Voyages, 1584–1590.* Vol. 1. London: For the Hakluyt Society, 1955.

Quitt, Martin H. "Trade and Acculturation at Jamestown, 1607–1609: The Limits of Understanding." *William and Mary Quarterly,* 3d series, 52 (April 1995): 227–258.

Raibmon, Paige. *Authentic Indians: Episodes of Encounter from the Late-Nineteenth-Century Northwest Coast.* Durham, N.C.: Duke University Press, 2005.

Ray, Florence Rebecca. *Chieftain Greenwood Leflore and the Choctaw Indians of the Mississippi Valley (Last Chief of Choctaws East of Mississippi River).* Memphis, Tenn.: C. A. Davis Printing Company, 1936.

Reese, Trevor R., ed. *Our First Visit in America: Early Reports from the Colony of Georgia, 1732–1740.* Savannah: Beehive Press, 1974.

Reid, John Phillip. *A Better Kind of Hatchet: Law, Trade, and Diplomacy in the Cherokee Nation during the Early Years of European Contact.* University Park: Pennsylvania State University Press, 1976.

———. *A Law of Blood: The Primitive Law of the Cherokee Nation.* New York: New York University Press, 1970.

Reiger, George. "Bury my Heart at the Western District Court." *Field & Stream* 80 (June 1975): 38, 102, 104.

Remonstrance of the Cherokee, Creek, Choctaw and Seminole Delegations against the Organization of the Indian Territory into a Territory of the United States. Washington, D.C.: John L. Ginck, 1876.

"Removal of the Indians." *North American Review* 31 (October 1830): 396–442.

"Richest People Per Capita on Earth Get \$8,290,100 for Oil Leases." *Current Opinion* 74 (June 1923): 740–41.

Roberts, Timothy M. "Freemasonry." In *Dictionary of American History,* edited by Stanley I. Kutler. 3d ed. Vols. 3, 10. New York: Charles Scribner's Sons, 2003.

Roff, Joe T. "Reminiscences of Early Days in the Chickasaw Nation." *Chronicles of Oklahoma* 13 (June 1935): 169–90.

Rogin, Michael Paul. *Fathers and Children: Andrew Jackson and the Subjugation of the American Indian.* New York: Alfred A. Knopf, 1975.

Rollings, Willard H. *The Osage: An Ethnohistorical Study of Hegemony on the Prairie-Plains.* Columbia: University of Missouri Press, 1992.

Roosens, Eugeen E. *Creating Ethnicity: The Process of Ethnogenesis.* Newbury Park and London: Sage Publications, 1989.

Rosier, Paul C. *Rebirth of the Blackfeet Nation, 1912–1954.* Lincoln: University of Nebraska Press, 2001.

———. "'They Are Ancestral Homelands': Race, Place, and Politics in Cold War Native America." *Journal of American History* 92 (March 2006): 1300–1326.

Rountree, Helen C. *Pocahontas's People: The Powhatan Indians of Virginia through Four Centuries.* Norman: University of Oklahoma Press, 1990.

———. *Powhatan, Pocahontas, Opechancanough: Three Indian Lives Changed by Jamestown.* Charlottesville: University of Virginia Press, 2005.

———. "The Powhatans and the English: A Case of Multiple Conflicting Agendas." In *Powhatan Foreign Relations, 1500–1722*, edited by Helen C. Rountree, 173–205. Charlottesville: University of Virginia Press, 1993.

———. *The Powhatan Indians of Virginia: Their Traditional Culture.* Norman: University of Oklahoma Press, 1989.

Rountree, Helen C., and E. Randolph Turner III. *Before and After Jamestown: Virginia's Powhatans and Their Predecessors.* Gainesville: University of Florida Press, 2002.

Rountree, Helen C., and Thomas E. Davidson. *Eastern Shore Indians of Virginia and Maryland.* Charlottesville: University Press of Virginia, 1997.

Rozbicki, Michal J. *The Complete Colonial Gentleman: Cultural Legitimacy in Plantation America.* Charlottesville: University Press of Virginia, 1998.

Russell, Orpha B. "Chief James Bigheart of the Osages." *Chronicles of Oklahoma* 32 (Winter 1954–55): 384–94.

Sachs, William S., and Ari Hoogenboom. *The Enterprising Colonials: Society on the Eve of the Revolution.* Chicago: Argonaut, 1965.

Sahlins, Marshall. *Culture and Practical Reason.* Chicago: University of Chicago Press, 1976.

———. *Historical Metaphors and Mythical Realities: Structure in the Early History of the Sandwich Islands Kingdom.* Ann Arbor: University of Michigan Press, 1981.

———. *Stone Age Economics.* Chicago and New York: Aldine-Atherton, Inc., 1972.

Salamanca, L. "Helping the First Americans." *National Republic* 18 (July 1930): 18–19, 40.

Saunt, Claudio. *A New Order of Things: Property, Power, and the Transformation of the Creek Indians, 1733–1816.* New York: Cambridge University Press, 1999.

———. "Taking Account of Property: Stratification among the Creek Indians in the Early Nineteenth Century." *William and Mary Quarterly*, 3d series, 57 (October 2000): 733–60.

Schmeckebier, Laurence F. *The Office of Indian Affairs: Its History, Activities, and Organization,* Baltimore: Johns Hopkins University Press, 1927.

Scott, William B. *In Pursuit of Happiness: American Conceptions of Property from the Seventeenth to the Twentieth Century*. Bloomington: Indiana University Press, 1977.

Seed, Patricia. *American Pentimento: The Invention of Indians and the Pursuit of Riches*. Minneapolis and London: University of Minnesota Press, 2001.

Sellers, Charles. *The Market Revolution: Jacksonian America, 1815–1846*. New York: Oxford University Press, 1991.

Shadburn, Don L. *Cherokee Planters in Georgia, 1832–1838: Historical Essays on Eleven Counties in the Cherokee Nation of Georgia*. Roswell, Ga.: W. H. Wolfe Associates, 1990.

Shearman, Thomas G. "The Owners of the United States." *Forum* 8 (1889): 262–73.

Sheehan, Bernard W. *Savagism and Civility: Indians and Englishmen in Colonial Virginia*. New York: Cambridge University Press, 1980.

Sheriff, Carol. *The Artificial River: The Erie Canal and the Paradox of Progress, 1817–1862*. New York: Hill and Wang, 1996.

Shepherd, William G. "Lo, the Rich Indian." *Harper's Monthly Magazine* 141 (November 1920): 723–34.

Shoemaker, Nancy. *A Strange Likeness: Becoming Red and White in Eighteenth-Century North America*. New York: Oxford University Press, 2004.

Smedley, Audrey. *Race in North America: Origin and Evolution of a Worldview*. Boulder, Colo.: Westview, 1999.

Smith, John. *Captain John Smith's History of Virginia: A Selection*. Edited by David Hawke. Indianapolis and New York: Bobbs-Merrill, 1970.

———. *The Complete Works of Captain John Smith*. Edited by Philip L. Barbour. 3 vols. Chapel Hill: University of North Carolina Press, 1986.

———. *Travels and Works of Captain John Smith, President of Virginia, and Admiral of New England, 1580–1631*. Edited by Edward A. Arber. New York: B. Franklin, 1910.

Snapp, J. Russell. *John Stuart and the Struggle for Empire on the Southern Frontier*. Baton Rouge: Louisiana State University Press, 1996.

Soltow, Lee. "Economic Inequality in the United States in the Period from 1790 to 1860." *Journal of Economic History* 31 (December 1971): 822–39.

Spahr, Charles B. *An Essay on the Present Distribution of Wealth in the United States*. New York: Thomas Y. Crowell & Company, 1896.

Speck, F. G. "Notes on the Ethnology of the Osage Indians." *Transactions* 2, Part 2. Department of Archaeology, University of Pennsylvania, 1907: 159–71.

Spring, Joel. *The Cultural Transformation of a Native American Family and Its Tribe, 1763–1995: A Basket of Apples*. Mahwah, N.J.: Lawrence Erlbaum Associates, 1996.

Starna, William A. "The Pequots in the Early Seventeenth Century." In *The Pequots in Southern New England: The Fall and Rise of an American Indian Nation*, edited by Laurence M. Hauptman and James D. Wherry, 33–47. Norman: University of Oklahoma Press, 1990.

Startup, Kenneth Moore. *The Root of All Evil: The Protestant Clergy and the Economic Mind of the Old South*. Athens: University of Georgia Press, 1997.

Steiner, Stan. *The New Indians*. New York: Harper & Row, 1968.

Stern, Theodore. *The Klamath Tribe: A People and Their Reservation*. Seattle: University of Washington Press, 1965.

Stewart, Herbert L. "The Ethics of Luxury and Leisure." *American Journal of Sociology* 24 (November 1918): 241–59.

Stiggins, George. "A Historical Narration of the Genealogy, Traditions and Downfall of the Ispocaga or Creek Tribe of Indians," edited by Theron A. Nunez, Jr. In *A Creek Source Book*, edited by William C. Sturtevant, [not paginated]. New York: Garland, 1987.

Stokes, Melvyn, and Stephen Conway, eds. *The Market Revolution in America: Social, Political, and Religious Expressions, 1800–1880*. Charlottesville: University Press of Virginia, 1996.

Stone, William L. *Life of Joseph Brant-Thayendanegea, Including the Indian Wars of the American Revolution*. 2 vols. 1838. Reprint, New York: Kraus Reprint, 1969.

Strachey, William. *The Historie of Travell into Virginia Britania* [1612]. Edited by Louis B. Wright and Virginia Freund. 1953. Reprint, Nendeln/Liechtenstein: Kraus Reprint, 1967.

Sumner, William Graham. *What Social Classes Owe to Each Other*. 1883. Reprint, Caldwell, Idaho: Caxton Printers, 1966.

Sweeney, Kevin M. "High-Style Vernacular: Lifestyles of the Colonial Elite." In *Of Consuming Interests: The Style of Life in Eighteenth-Century America*, edited by Cary Carson, Ronald Hoffman, and Peter J. Albert, 1–58. Charlottesville: University Press of Virginia. 1994.

Sweet, Evander M. "Richest People in the World." *World To-Day* 5 (November 1903): 1454–58.

Taubeneck, Herman E. "The Concentration of Wealth, Its Cause and Results." *Arena* 18 (September 1897): 289–301, 452–69.

Taylor, Alan. *The Divided Ground: Indians, Settlers, and the Northern Borderland of the American Revolution*. New York: Alfred A. Knopf, 2006.

———. *William Cooper's Town: Power and Persuasion on the Frontier of the Early American Republic*. New York: Alfred A. Knopf, 1995.

Taylor, Graham D. *The New Deal and American Indian Tribalism*. Lincoln: University of Nebraska Press, 1980.

Thoburn, Joseph B. *A Standard History of Oklahoma; an Authentic Narrative of its Development from the Date of the First European Exploration Down to the Present Time, Including Accounts of the Indian Tribes, Both Civilized and Wild, of the Cattle Range, of the Land Openings and the Achievements of the Most Recent Period*. Chicago and New York: American Historical Society, 1916.

Thomas, Earle. *The Three Faces of Molly Brant*. Kingston, Ontario: Quarry Press, 1996.

Thompson, John. *Closing the Frontier: Radical Response in Oklahoma, 1889–1923*. Norman: University of Oklahoma Press, 1986.

Thompson, Stephen I., Susan C. Vehik, and Daniel C. Swan. "Oil Wealth and the Osage Indians." In *Affluence and Cultural Survival*, edited by R. F. Salisbury and E. Tooker, 12–25. Washington, D.C.: American Ethnological Society, 1984.

Thorne, Tanis C. *The World's Richest Indian: The Scandal over Jackson Barnett's Oil Fortune*. New York: Oxford University Press, 2003.

Tilghman, Tench. *Memoir of Lieut. Col. Tench Tilghman*. Albany: J. Munsell, 1876.

Todd, Helen. *Mary Musgrove: Georgia Indian Princess*. Chicago: Adams Press, 1981.

Townsend, Camilla. *Pocahontas and the Powhatan Dilemma*. New York: Hill and Wang, 2004.

Trachtenberg, Alan. *The Incorporation of America: Culture and Society in the Gilded Age*. New York: Hill and Wang, 1982.

Trahant, Mark N. "The 1970s: New Leaders for Indian Country." In *Indians in American History: An Introduction*, edited by Frederick E. Hoxie and Peter Iverson, 235–52. Wheeling, Ill.: Harlan Davidson, 1998.

Travis, V. A. "Life in the Cherokee Nation a Decade after the Civil War." *Chronicles of Oklahoma* 4 (March 1926): 16–30.

Trigger, Bruce G. "Early Native North American Responses to European Contact: Romantic versus Rationalistic Interpretations." *Journal of American History* 77 (March 1991): 1109–29.

Trosper, Ronald L. "That Other Discipline: Economics and American Indian History." In *New Directions in American Indian History*, edited by Colin G. Calloway, 199–222. Norman: University of Oklahoma Press, 1988.

Turner, E. Randolph. "Socio-Political Organization within the Powhatan Chiefdom and the Effects of European Contact, A.D. 1607–1646." In *Cultures in Contact: The Impact of European Contacts on Native American Cultural Institutions, A.D. 1000–1800*, edited by William W. Fitzhugh, 193–224. Washington, D.C.: Smithsonian Institution, 1985.

Tyler, Lyon Gardiner, ed. *Narratives of Early Virginia, 1606–1825*. New York: Barnes & Noble, 1907.

U.S. Bureau of Indian Affairs, Anadarko Area Office, Osage Agency. *The Osage People and Their Trust Property*. Washington, D.C.: Department of the Interior, 1953.

U.S. Commission on Civil Rights. "How to Exploit and Destroy a People: The Case of the Alaskan Native." *Civil Rights Digest* 2 (Summer 1969): 6–13.

———. *Indian Tribes: A Continuing Quest for Survival*. [n.p.] June 1981.

U.S. Commission to the Five Civilized Tribes. *Annual Report*. Washington, D.C., 1894 and 1895.

U.S. Department of Agriculture, Economic Research Service [Helen W. Johnson]. *Rural Indian Americans in Poverty*. Agricultural Economic Report No. 167. Washington, D.C., 1969.

———. *American Indians in Transition*. Agricultural Economic Report No. 283. Washington, D.C., 1975.

U.S. Department of the Interior. *Annual Report of the Commissioner of Indian Affairs*. Washington: Government Printing Office, 1851–1932.

U.S. Federal Trade Commission. *National Wealth and Income*. Washington, D.C.: Government Printing Office, 1926.

Usner, Daniel H., Jr. *Indian Work: Language and Livelihood in Native American History*. Cambridge, Mass.: Harvard University Press, 2009.

Vaughan, Alden T. "'Expulsion of the Salvages': English Policy and the Virginia Massacre of 1622." *William and Mary Quarterly*, 3d series, 35 (January 1978): 57–84.

Vizenor, Gerald. "Gambling on Sovereignty." *American Indian Quarterly* 16 (Summer 1992): 411–13.

Vickers, Daniel. "Competency and Competition: Economic Culture in Early America." *William and Mary Quarterly*, 3d series, 47 (January 1990): 3–29.

Wade, Emmie Ellen. "Greenwood LeFlore: Farsighted Realist." In *Mississippi Heroes*, edited by Dean Faulkner Wells and Hunter Cole, 43–65. Jackson: University Press of Mississippi, 1980.

Wallace, Paul A. W., ed. *Thirty Thousand Miles with John Heckewelder*. Pittsburgh: University of Pittsburgh Press, 1958.

Wardell, Morris L. *A Political History of the Cherokee Nation, 1838–1907*. Norman: University of Oklahoma Press, 1938.

Waring, Antonio J., ed. "Laws of the Creek Nation." In *A Creek Source Book*, edited by William C. Sturtevant [not paginated]. New York: Garland, 1987.

Watkins, Arthur V. "Termination of Federal Supervision: The Removal of Restrictions over Indian Property and Persons." *Annals of the American Academy of Political and Social Science* 311 (May 1957): 49.

Wells, David A. *Recent Economic Changes and Their Effect on the Production and Distribution of Wealth and the Well-Being of Society*. New York: D. Appleton and Company, 1896.

Wells, Samuel J. "The Role of Mixed-Bloods in Mississippi Choctaw History." In *After Removal: The Choctaw in Mississippi*, edited by Samuel J. Wells and Roseanna Tubby, 42–55. Jackson: University of Mississippi Press, 1986.

Welter, Rush. *The Mind of America, 1820–1860*. New York: Columbia University Press, 1975.

West, W. Richard, Jr., and Kevin Gover. "The Struggle for Indian Civil Rights." In *Indians in American History: An Introduction*, edited by Frederick E. Hoxie and Peter Iverson, 218–34. Wheeling, Ill.: Harlan Davidson, 1998.

Westbrook, Harriet Johnson. "And 'Twas the Night before Christmas' with Osages: by O-Jan-Jan-Win." *American Indian* 4 (1929): 8.

White, Bruce M. "Encounters with Spirits: Ojibwa and Dakota Theories about the French and Their Merchandise." *Ethnohistory* 41 (Summer 1994): 369–405.

White, Richard. *The Middle Ground: Indians, Empires, and Republics in the Great Lakes Region, 1650–1815*. New York: Cambridge University Press, 1992.

————. *The Roots of Dependency: Subsistence, Environment, and Social Change among the Choctaws, Pawnees, and Navajos*. Lincoln: University of Nebraska Press, 1983.

White, Robert H. *Tribal Assets: The Rebirth of Native America*. New York: Henry Holt and Company, 1990.

Wilkins, David E. *American Indian Sovereignty and the U.S. Supreme Court: The Masking of Justice*. Austin: University of Texas Press, 1997.

Wilkins, Thurman. *Cherokee Tragedy: The Story of the Ridge Family and the Decimation of a People*. 2d ed. Norman: University of Oklahoma Press, 1986.

Wilkinson, Charles. *Blood Struggle: The Rise of Modern Indian Nations*. New York: W. W. Norton, 2005.

Williams, Alfred M. "Among the Cherokees." *Lippincott's Magazine* 31 (February 1881): 195–203.

————. "The Civilized Indian." *Lippincott's Magazine* 31 (March 1883): 271–79.

Williams, B. W. "Evils of Land Monopoly." *Arena* 16 (1896): 538–42.

Williams, C. Herb, and Walt Neubrech. *Indian Treaties: American Nightmare*. Seattle: Outdoor Empire Publishing, 1976.

Williams, Robert A. *Like a Loaded Weapon: The Rehnquist Court, Indian Rights, and the Legal History of Racism in America*. Minneapolis: University of Minnesota Press, 2005.

Wilms, Douglas C. "Cherokee Land Use in Georgia Before Removal." In *Cherokee Removal: Before and After*, edited by William L. Anderson, 1–28. Athens: University of Georgia Press.

Wilson, Raymond, ed. "Dr. Charles A. Eastman's Report on the Economic Conditions of the Osage Indians in Oklahoma, 1924." *Chronicles of Oklahoma* 55 (Fall 1977): 343–45.

Wilson, Terry P. "Osage Indian Women during a Century of Change, 1870–1980." *Prologue* 14 (Winter 1982): 185–201.

———. *The Underground Reservation: Osage Oil*. Lincoln: University of Nebraska Press, 1985.

Wishart, Chas. A. "The Wealthiest Navajo." *American Indian* (February 1929): 13.

Wolf, Stephanie Grauman. *As Various as Their Land: The Everyday Lives of Eighteenth-Century Americans*. New York: Harper Collins, 1993.

Wolfe, Patrick. "Land, Labor, and Difference: Elementary Structures of Race." *American Historical Review* 106 (June 2001): 866–905.

———. *Settler Colonialism and the Transformation of Anthropology: The Politics and Poetics of an Ethnographic Event*. London and New York: Cassell, 1999.

Wood, Gordon S. *The Radicalism of the American Revolution*. New York: Alfred A. Knopf, 1992.

Woodward, Grace Steele. *The Cherokees*. Norman: University of Oklahoma Press, 1963.

Wortman, Marlene Stein, ed. *Women in American Law*. 2 vols. New York: Holmes and Meier, 1985–1991.

Wright, Louis B., ed. *The Elizabethans' America: A Collection of Early Reports by Englishmen on the New World*. Cambridge, Mass.: Harvard University Press, 1969.

Wrobel, David M. *The End of American Exceptionalism: Frontier Anxiety from the Old West to the New Deal*. Lawrence: University Press of Kansas, 1993.

Wunder, John R. *"Retained by the People": A History of American Indians and the Bill of Rights*. New York: Oxford University Press, 1994.

Yorgason, Ethan R. *Transformation of the Mormon Culture Region*. Urbana: University of Illinois Press, 2003.

Youings, Joyce. *Sixteenth-Century England*. London: Allen Lane (Penguin Books), 1984.

Young, Mary. "Indian Removal and Land Allotment: The Civilized Tribes and Jacksonian Justice." *American Historical Review* 64 (October 1958): 31–45.

———. "John Ross: Cherokee Chief and Defender of the Nation." In *The Human Tradition in Antebellum America*, edited by Michael A. Morrison, 115–30. Wilmington, Del.: Scholarly Resources, 2000.

Zarefsky, David. *President Johnson's War on Poverty: Rhetoric and History*. Tuscaloosa: University of Alabama Press, 1986.

Zelizer, Viviana A. *The Social Meaning of Money*. New York: Basic Books, 1994.

Zissu, Erik M. *Blood Matters: The Five Civilized Tribes and the Search for Unity in the Twentieth Century*. New York and London: Routledge, 2001.

Online Sources

Alexie, Sherman. "Love, Hunger, Money, and Other Not-So-Facetious Reasons Why the Spokane Indians Want to Bet on Casinos." *High Country News*, September 19, 1994. ⟨www.hcn.org/1994/sep19/dir/essay.html⟩. 3 July 2009.

Boudinot, Elias. [Letter to Mr. John Ross, New Echota, November 25, 1836.] In *Documents in Relation to the Validity of the Cherokee Treaty of 1835 . . .: Letters and Other Papers Relating to Cherokee Affairs; Being a Reply to Sundry Publications Authorized by John Ross*, 26–31. Georgia's Virtual Library, GALILEO, Southeastern Native American Documents, 1730–1842. ⟨http://dlg.galileo.usg.edu/z/na/id:pam012⟩. June 20, 2008.

Choctaw Nation of Mississippi. "Through the Eyes of the Mississippi Choctaw." ⟨http://www.choctaw.org/culture/expression.htm⟩.

Indianz.com in Print ⟨http://www.indianz.com/News/⟩.

Jackson, Andrew. "To the Cherokee Tribe of Indians East of the Mississippi River," March 16, 1835. Galileo Digital Library of Georgia, Southeastern Native American Documents, 1730–1842, ⟨http://dlg.galileo.usg.edu/z?na/id:pam013⟩. June 20, 2008.

National Indian Gaming Association. *Gaming Facts.* ⟨http://indiangaming.org/library?⟩.

National Indian Law Library. Indian Law Bulletins, U.S. Supreme Court. "Indian Law Cases before the United States Supreme Court, 1988–1998—Chronology of a Decade." ⟨http://www.narf.org/nill/bulletins/sct/sctdecade.htm⟩. July 9, 2009.

National Public Radio Archives, ⟨http://www.npr.org⟩.

Ross, John. "Our Hearts are Sickened." 1836. ⟨http://historymatters.gmu.edu/d/6598/⟩. June 20, 2008.

U.S. Bureau of Indian Affairs. "Rebuilding Indian Country" (National Archives and Records Administration film, [1937]). ⟨http://www.youtube.com/watch?v=zz5MaXQv3U⟩.

United States Commission on Civil Rights. *Civil Rights Digest* 2 (Summer 1969): 6–13, ⟨http://www.alaskool.org.PROJECTS/ANCSA/articles/crd1969/dest_ak_native.htm⟩.

Vanderbilt University Television News Archive. ⟨http://tvnews.vanderbilt.edu/⟩.

Unpublished Manuscripts

Boutwell, Ruth. "Adjustment of Osage Indian Youth to Contemporary Civilization." M.S.W. thesis, University of Oklahoma, 1936.

DeBerry, Drue Lemuel. "The Ethos of the Oklahoma Oil Boom Frontier." M.A. thesis, University of Oklahoma, 1970.

Dill, Robert Leland. "Portraits in Red and Black: Racial Stereotypes in Oklahoma Newspapers, 1900–1925." M.A. thesis, Texas Christian University, 1979.

O'Brien, Greg. "'To Live by Labor Like the White Men': Changing Notions of Power among Choctaw Elites in the 1790s." Paper presented at the Western Historical Association annual meeting, 2000.

Rosier, Paul. "Crossing the Narrative Tracks: Native American Capitalisms and American History." 2009.

Webb-Storey, Anna. "Culture Clash: A Case Study of Three Osage Native American Families." Ed.D. dissertation, Oklahoma State University, 1998.

Index

Abbott, John, 201; favors supervision of trust funds, 203

Aboriginal land rights, 227

Acquisitive Indians, Whites blamed for, 102

Adair, James: on contrasting economic values of Indians and Whites, 63; on Indians not coveting riches, 65

Adair, W. T., proposes national relief fund, 151

Adams, Abigail, on McGillivray's appearance, 83

Advertising, rise of mass, 174–75

Agricultural development on tribal lands: and export economy, 137; rapid increases of, in Gilded Age, 137

Alaska, gap between Native and White economic status in, 228

Alaska Native Claims Settlement Act (ANCSA), 227–29; distribution of funds from, 227–28

Albuquerque Journal, on growing Indian power, 268

Albers, Patricia, on anthropologists and Indian economies, 11

Alcatraz, occupation of, 223

Alcohol abuse, 204

Alexie, Sherman, on casino revenue preferable to poverty, 264

Allen, Frederick Lewis, on American prosperity in 1920s, 174

Allen, Ron, on Indian economic status, 252

Allotment of Indian land, 136, 158–64; as antidote to avarice, 155; and Civilized Tribes, 136; debates over, contrasted with removal debates, 163; framing debate over as choice between economic systems, 160; Knights of Labor support for, 164; mandated by Congress, 195–96; motives for, 162; obstacles to, 155–56; opposition to, 162–64; Osage demographics and, 189–90; Osage resistance to, 173; paired with dissolution of Indian governments, 156; power of Congress over, 196; as solution to concentrated wealth, 164; as vindication of American ideals, 164–65

American Board of Commissioners for Foreign Missions, 107, 119; financial support from rich Whites to, 121

American Indian (magazine), on images of Osages, 184 (ill.), 207

American Indian Defense Association, 211

American Indian Movement (AIM), 225

Archer, Capt. Gabriel, on visit to Pamunkey, 27

Argall, Samuel, on Powhatan inability to pay tribute, 47

Atkin, Edmond, on complaints from headmen about being bypassed, 65

Atwood, Albert, on automobiles and prosperity, 174–75

Augusta, Ga.: Chickasaw band relocates to, 60; as trade center with Creeks, 60

Automobiles: Indian ownership of, 174, 177; as symbol of prosperity, 174

Axtell, James, defines culture, 7

Backlash, White, 235–36; to Indian political power, 270; Interstate Congress

Deerskin trade, 66; dependence on goods purchased with, 97; Yamacraw post, 67

Deloria, Philip, on reconsidering expectations regarding Indians, 9

Deloria, Vine, Jr.: blames government for Indian poverty, 221; manifesto, 222–23

Dickerson, Philip Jackson, *History of Osage Nation*, 188–89

Dionne, E. J., on opposition to gambling, 263

Discrimination, Indian response to contrasted with African American, 224

Drought: Jamestown, 36; southwestern United States, 214

Duncan, D. W. C., loses out on allotment, 167

Durand of Dauphiné, on contrast between English and Indian economic culture, 50

Economic behavior, reactions to as reflecting norms, 14

Economic culture: assumptions identical between White and Indian, 148; balancing traditional and modern, 266; as cause for poverty, 222; changes among Civilized Tribes, 135; changes in Osage, 186–87; colonial view of inferior Indian, 19, 34; contrasts between Indian and White, 277; differences in, 273; of English in colonies, 50, 51; gambling and, 251, 255, 262; identity and, 276; of Indians, 50; Indians showing dynamic, 244; morality and, 7, 10; of Powhatan Indians, 20, 51; Powhatan view of English, 35; presumed absence of, 194; relation between White and Indian, 137; in removal debate, 131–32; revolutions in Indian, 96; and schisms in tribes, 136; sovereignty and, 274; support for traditional, 203; threats from gambling on, 263; traditional Osage, 186; wealth and, 274

Economic ethics/morality, 207, 273, 278; argument by opponents to removal based on, 118; Boudinot and Ross on, 129–30; as central issue in 1970s, 210; debates over, 3, 160; economic justice

and, 14; in removal debates, 130–31; wealth and, 243

Economic gains: ambivalence toward Indian, 276–77; hostility toward Indian, 248; Indian loss and colonial, 17

Economic history: anthropologists and Indians in, 11; exclusion of Indians from, 12; Indians in, 11, 12

Economic individualism, 96, 146–47; accepting logic of, 150; advocates of discourage selfish choices, 118; allotments and, 205; approval of some Indians for, 15; blaming Whites for Indian, 102; Five Tribes contemplate problems with, 135; Indian turns toward, 102; as justification for scramble for wealth, 96; linked to race, 161; missionaries' role in bringing Indians, 121; Osage balance between unity and, 187; promoted, 139; stimulating, 216–17; teaching Indians, 103

Economic rationality: anthropologists' arguments on, 13; cultural variation in, 13; debates over, 9; far-reaching influence of "Western," 13

Economic risk, Virginia Company and, 25

Economic values: changes in Creek, 102; colonist views of Indian, 17, 22, 27; comparing Indian with primitive Christian, 63; competing, 18; contrasting English and Indian, 53; Creek Indian, 63; differences among Cherokee classes, 109; of English goods among Indians, 33; English view of Indian, 28, 41, 53, 54; evidence of Indian, 101–2; evolution of Indian, 103; held by Jackson and Ross, 93; incompatibility of, 94; investor views of, 34; Powhatan assessment of English, 34–35; in relocation debate, 95; roots of White and Indian, 101; similarity of southern Indian and American, 94; variations among colonies, 54

Education: as basis for rise to economic elite, 104; from government agents, 105; of Indian children of White men, 82; of Johnson's children, 80, 82–83; as means of gaining gentility, 89; mission schools, 106–8

Egalitarianism: myth of, 9; view of Indian, 63

Elites: likeness between Indian and White, 114; rise of New York, 10; rise of tribal, 136, 144

Elkus, Charles de Young, on notion of rich Indians, 178

Ellis, Henry, settles with Coosapona-keesa, 71

Emmons, Glenn, on urban Indians, 217

Estate tax, lack of opposition to, 2

Ethnohistorians: Indians as subjects of, 12; views of Powhatan Indian economic culture, 20

Everts, Jeremiah: compares Indian and White cabins, 114; on emerging Cherokee class divisions, 110; moral code, 130; opposes Indian removal on moral grounds, 119–20

Eves Tall Chief, on federal guardianship, 203–4

Exchanges: commercial contrasted with kinship, 43; English tactics during, 32–33; Indian initial advantages in, 32; Powhatan and English, 32, 37

Exploitation: Powhatan deficiencies as excuses for, 41; reciprocity and, 22

Farming, Indian: in market economy, 98; transition from hunting to, 98

Farming, subsistence: prevalence in Jacksonian America, 96

Fausz, Frederick, on warfare dooming fur trade benefits, 49–50

Federal Bureau of Investigation, investigates murder of Osages, 197

Firerider, Marty, 2; on gambling as threat to Indian value system, 263, 264–65; on Indian disunity, 2

Fishing rights: Boldt decision, 232; litigation over, 210, 232

Fitch, Tobias, on Creeks urging continued British trade, 61–62

Five Tribes: accused of avarice, 156; defend land ownership system, 158; division of lands of, 161; governments dissolve, 168; growth of non-Indian populations among, 152; on restraining greed through allotments, 165;

role of government in allocating wealth, 151

Florida, reports of Indians wearing gold in, 25

Folsom, David: in Choctaw governance, 112; slave ownership, 101

Food: English theft of Powhatan, 40; Indian advantage in production of, 18; as measure of wealth, 35, 36–37; as product for exchange, 33

Fortune (magazine), on Indian power, 249

Four Mothers Society, opposes allotments, 166

Fraser, Steve, on wealth and ideology, 10

Frazier, Lynn, on people taking advantage of Osages, 196–97

Freemasonry, Joseph Brant acceptance into, 80

Friends of the Indian, 155, 156, 163, 164–65

Full-bloods: characterizations, 189; economic strategies of, 144–45; as term, 144, 188

Fund for the Republic report, 218

Fur trade: advantages of, for Indians, 49; Indian wealth and, 29, 33, 49; as pillar of colonial economy, 49; as provocation for war, 49–50

Gambling and Survival in Native North America, 267

Gambling enterprises, 249–77; as change to economic culture, 267; and media coverage, 251; non-Indians benefiting from, 259–60; operated by tribes, 249; opposition to, 263, 269; perceptions of wealth from, 252–53; questions on corrupting influence of, 250; revenues used to gain political power, 268; tribal control confirmed by courts, 251

Gaming. *See* Gambling enterprises

Gates, Thomas: instructed on exchange tactics, 32–33; instructed to rule Indians, 45–46

General Allotment Act, Five Tribes exempted from, 156

Generosity, as Osage characteristic, 187

Gentility: ability of Indians to achieve, 89–90; concepts of, 89

George, Henry, on rich enjoying fruits of rented land, 149

George-Kanentiio, Doug, on Iroquois prophecies, 263

Georgia: colony established, 67; and Indian removal, 126

Gerstle, Gary, on wealth and ideology, 10

Gift exchanges: differing interpretations of, 60; between Johnson and Mohawks, 77

Gift-giving, 60, 66–67; to communicate intentions, 66; distinguished from bribery, 64; and Indian concepts of value, 67; as means of influencing Indian support, 64; Osages and, 185, 187, 190; as social obligation, 42–43; White disapproval of, 107–8

The Gilded Age, 140

Gilmer, George: defends removal policy, 123, 131; distinguishes among Indians, 123–24

Ginger, Ray, on Gilded Age prosperity, 138

Gleach, Frederic, on Powhatan beliefs about wealth, 21

Glen, James, on Indian complaints of gifts to headmen, 65

Gold: English hopes to discover, 25; Florida Indians and, 25; reports of Indians accumulating, 25

Goldsberg, Carole, on tribal sovereignty, 269

Gorton, Slade: advocates federal funds to tribes based on balance sheets, 261; on cutting aid to tribes, 2; Indian role in loss of election, 268; redistributing federal funds, 3

Gould, Jay: owner of rail lines through Indian country, 141; reviled for greed, 142; wealthy Indian compared to, 141

Government, Indian: corruption, 162; coupling allotment with dissolution of, 156; debate over role in allocating wealth, 151; moral obligation to feed poor, 151; protecting poor through, 159; regulation of land ownership, 154

Gray, Robert, on taking Indian land, 39

Grazing commons, proprietary interest in, 152

Grearson, Robert, relations with Creeks, 104

Great Depression, distracts national attention from Indian poverty, 212

Greed, 1, 134, 135, 159, 199; accusations of, by Indians, 95–96; in allotment process, 168; considered American trait, 157; criticisms of, 142; critics of Indian, 117–18; English perception of Powhatan, 40–41; European assumptions of Indian, 63; evidence of Indian, 65; images depicting Indian, 241; imperial strategy appealing to, 63; Indian and non-Indian responses to, 6; Jacksonian accusations of, 95; McGillivray charged with, 86; and media focus on gambling, 254–55; missionary appeal to student, 108; motivates fraud and corruption, 255; as motivation for Indian removal, 119, 122, 126–27, 130; noted among Cherokees, 143; Powhatan concepts of, 21; restraint of, through allotments, 165; role in removal, 130–31; and states pressing for share of revenues from Indian casinos, 261, 261 (ill.); warnings from clergy about, 116

Green, Michael: on Indian name for Whites, 126; on McGillivray's clan connections, 84; on McGillivray's motivations, 86

Guardians, private, as unscrupulous, 197, 198

Guardianship, federal, 200, 204, 205, 224; conflicting views of value of, 199; considered a duty to Indians, 172, 205, 216; drive to end, 216; for Osages, 172, 195; Osage preference for over state guardianship, 200

Hacker, Andrew, on rich getting richer, 1

Hakluyt, Richard, on trade with Indians, 26

Hale, William K., and Osage murders, 197

Hamilton, Alexander, describes home of wealthy Indian, 58

Handlin, Oscar and Mary, on contrast of sermons and actions, 116

Hariot, Thomas: advice on determining Indian status, 29; comment on display of wealth, 34; comparing Indian wealth to English, 28

Hastings, W. W., on Osage guardianship, 172

Hatley, Tom, on traders' wealth, 62

Hawkins, Benjamin: reports on Indian trader, 104; wealth as incentive to others, 105

Headmen, status affected by English wealth distribution, 65

Heckewelder, John, on Joseph Brant's land sales, 82

Heron, Alexander, proclaims Coosaponakeesa's importance, 68

Hicks, Charles (chief), 115

Hide trade, 61, 63

Hierarchy: clothing as emblems of Indian, 29, 31; colonist hope for Indian, 29; in English population, 24; identifying Indian, through types of possessions, 29; among Powhatans, 21, 30

History of the Osage Nation, 188

Homesteads: National Commercial Convention urges for Indians, 155; Osage, 190

Hospitality: concepts of, 112; as sign of wealth, 30

House Committee on Indian Affairs, 171

House Concurrent Resolution 108, 214, 216

Ideals, American, 237

Income: disparities, 2; generated by gambling, 256–57; generated by oil, 175–76; Indian, 220, 240–41

Incompetency, judicial determination, 197

The Indian, America's Unfinished Business, 220, 222

Indian ancestry, inventing to gain from tribal revenues, 258

Indian Champion, defends property ownership, 152

Indian Chieftain, on Indian traits, 161

Indian Claims Commission, 224, 227

Indian Country Today: on criticism of tribal recognition, 259; on greedy state governments, 260; on growing Indian

power, 271–72; on resistance to Indian sovereignty, 270

Indian ethos, Brant statement of, 56

Indian Gaming Regulatory Act, 251

Indian ideas, historians' consideration of, 11

Indian Journal, on resistance to "progress," 167

Indian New Deal, 212

Indian Reorganization Act, 212

Indian Rights Association, 155

Indians: beliefs in wealth of, 179; businesses owned by, 265; causes for economic gains of, 223–24; colonial attitudes about Indian economics, 16; demand better way of life, 210; demand reform, 226–27; depictions in film, 233; envy over wealth of, 181–82; gambling revenues, 255–57; poverty, 217–20; reliance on commercial hunting tracts, 98; role in generating common images, 10–11; second-class citizenship, 240; viewed as resistant to change, 158; wealth accumulation by, 96. *See also specific tribes*

Indian Treaties, American Nightmare, 239, 241, 242, 244

Indian-White relations, 59; economic values as structuring, 56; mutual desire for cordial, 59, 60

Individualism. *See* Economic individualism

Information, control over, 206–7

Institute for Government Research. *See* Meriam report

Intermediaries: self-interest of, 91; value, 89–90

Interstate Congress for Equal Rights and Responsibilities (ICERR), 236; constituent groups, 236; exploits envy of Indian resources, 242; lobbies against Indian rights, 236, 238 (ill.)

Inventions, Powhatan awe of English, 36

Investments, by non-Indians on Osage lands, 188

Iroquois nations: consumer economy, 75; economic relations with English, 75

Isparhecher, Chief, 153–54, 166

Jackson, Andrew: advocates racial separation, 94; ancestry compared to John Ross, 93; antagonism toward missions, 125–26; argues removal policy positive for poor Indians, 125; beliefs in common with John Ross, 93; motivation for removal policy, 131; nationalism of, 93; political rise in common with John Ross, 114; urges Indians to move west, 92

Jamestown: attacked, 46; colonist perceptions of Wahunsonacock, 23; death rate, 35; quality of initial site for, 35; questions about economic effects on Indians, 18; wealth of Indians in proximity to, 18

Johnson, Benjamin Heber, on capitalism as a force, 13

Johnson, Jeromus, on meeting with Brant, 55–56

Johnson, Lyndon B.: declares war on poverty, 217, 218–19; establishes OEO, 218

Johnson, Robert, recruits colonists by promising wealth, 26

Johnson, William: accumulates wealth, 76; death, 78; granted titles, 76; marriage to Molly Brant, 75, 76, 78; reciprocal gift-giving with Mohawks, 77; respect for Indian economic rules, 77; social status, 88; teaches Joseph Brant importance of land, 81; trade acumen, 76; wealth, 76–77, 88

Johnson Hall, 78

Jones, Hugh, comments on Indian society, 52, 53

Jones, Leon (chief), 252

Jones, Robert M., comments on Indian traits, 159

Kecoughtan: English attack on, 31; lack of wealth, 32

Kelsay, Isabel, on Molly Brant's benevolence, 78

Kingsbury, Cyrus: on dispensing charity, 108; praises Choctaws for seeking wealth, 107

Kinship bonds: McGillivray-Creek, 84; as prerequisite for trade, 60

Kinship relations: trade and, 43; wealth and, 22

Knights of Labor, support allotment policy, 164

Knox, Henry, on McGillivray's power among Creeks, 84

Krugman, Paul, on acceptance of inequality, 1–2

LaFarge, Oliver: on Indians as half-starved herdsmen, 214; on U.S. debt to Indians, 216

Lakota, Black Hills litigation, 230

Land: accumulation by English, 39; allocation debates within Five Tribes, 151; allotment system, 136, 146, 163; Choctaw trade of Mississippi for western, 127; colonial government efforts to preserve Powhatan, 48–49; English occupation of Powhatan, 40; exchanges for English goods, 48; as factory for raw materials, 97; as focus of Indian political revival, 226–27; given to English, 38, 39; greed for, 143, 160; Indian wealth from leasing, 233–34; as insurance against poverty, 97; justifications for English seizure of Powhatan, 40, 41–42, 46–47, 48; leases for minerals, 243; loss of Powhatan base, 38; and measure of wealth, 19, 23, 57, 141; as motivation for Indian removal, 119, 126; possibility of huge holdings of, 151–52; power derived from, 81, 86; Powhatans cede, as result of war, 48; removal from, motivated by development, 123; requirement for commercial hunting, 98; role in changing exchange balance, 32; rumor of missionary exchanges of, for education, 126; sale of private, by Chickasaw, 101; sales as basis for Virginia Company success, 38; shrinkage of Indian, 97; speculation, 97; traditions respecting acquisition of, 88–89; valued for game animals, 97–98

Land ownership/title: absentee, 160; chiefs dispute British ability to confer, 71; in common, 113, 156–57; dispute

McLoughlin, William: on Cherokee middle class, 146; on traders raising Indian children as Whites, 104

McMinn, Joseph, allows corruption, 105

Media: coverage of gambling, 251, 263–64; depictions of Indian greed, 241; depictions of Indian poverty and casinos, 252–53; on popularity of Indian casinos, 272

Meigs, Return J., 105, 124; on Cherokee views of class, 109; on influence of speculators and Indian elites, 124

Mekahwahtiankah, urges release of trust funds, 172

Meriam report, 210–12

Mineral wealth, tribal, 230, 241–42. *See also* Resources

Missionaries, 106–7; economic interests in opposing removal, 126; preaching economic values, 107; rumored to exchange education for land, 126; subordinates economic agenda to religious agenda, 120; tolerating Indians holding slaves, 121

Missions: Jackson's suspicions of, 125–26; role in American expansion, 121; role in drive for wealth, 121–22

Mission schools: as attraction for travelers, 107; discouraging charity, 107; economic opportunity provided by, 107; paid employment from, 107; promote American economic culture, 106–7; sort children by class status, 108; student numbers, 108

Mississaugas, ask Joseph Brant to serve as spokesman for, 82

Mohawks: prosperity, 75; receive gifts from Johnson, 77; respect for William Johnson, 77; sell lands, 75; trade goods, 75–76

Money-making, inconsistency with Indianness, 3

Moody, William, exposé on land monopoly, 142

Morality, 205–6, 207, 278; contrasting views of trade, 44; defined, 8; federal action as motivated by, 207; gambling and debates over, 250; Indian removal and, 130, 132; Osage, 186; questions of associated with colonization, 273; of wealth, 4, 8

Moravian missions, 106–7

Muckleshoot Indians, 269

Multicultural societies, creation of tribal, 110

Murray, David, on chiefs' control of wealth, 21–22

Musgrove, Johnny: as Coosaponakeesa's husband, 62; death, 68; opens trading house, 67; settles on South Carolina plantation, 67

Musgrove, Mary. *See* Coosaponakeesa

Mushulatubbee, 106

Muskogee Phoenix, on monopolization of land ownership, 153

Namontack, travels to England, 36

Narcotics abuse, 204

Nash, Manning, on economic activity, 13

The Nation (magazine), readership, 240; on White backlash, 235

National Capital Conference on Indian Poverty, 218, 220

National Commercial Convention, urges Indian homesteads, 155

National Indian Gaming Association (NIGA), 252

National Indian Youth Council, 223, 225

Nationalism, as factor in Cherokee removal, 93

Native American Equal Opportunity Act, 245

Native American Rights Fund, 225

Necotowance, forced to sign treaty with English, 48

New Deal, relation with Indians, 209

The New Indians, 220

Newport, Capt. Christopher: on Powhatan hospitality, 30; stages coronation, 37; trade with Wahunsonacock, 43; Wahunsonacock assessment of status of, 35, 46

Newsweek, on Indian water rights, 231; on White backlash, 237

New York Times: coverage of Indian poverty, 212; on Indian material

Perdue, Theda: on evolving Indian economic values, 103, 104; on raising children as Indians, 104

Peterson, Elmer, on wasteful Osage spending, 183

Petroleum. *See* Oil

Piomingo (author's pseudonym), 117

Pitchlynn, John, educates children, 104

Pitchlynn, Peter: opposes sectionalizing lands, 157; slave ownership and purchases, 101; and Treaty of Dancing Rabbit Creek, 127; wealth, 101

Platt, Orville, urges allotment, 156

Pocahontas (Matoaka), 31 (ill.); marriage to John Rolfe, 46

Political power: deriving wealth from, 114; effect of wealth on, 116; evidenced by election victories, 270; gambling and, 268; goal for Jackson and Ross, 93; opposition to tribal, 269–70; relation to wealth, 172, 206; wealth as requisite for, 56

Populism, 142

Porter, Peter B., comment on Joseph Brant, 57

Porter, Chief Pleasant, 154 (ill.); on competition among Whites, 160; promotes opportunities in Indian country, 138–39; uses public land, 153–54; on White cattle in Indian country, 138

Pory, John, on colonist wealth, 34

Potter, Stephen, on Powhatan channeling of resources, 21

Poverty, Indian, 210–11, 216–17, 219–20; campaign to end, 225; comparing colonial poverty to, 53; contrasting colonial prosperity with, 18; contrasting public perception of Indian wealth with, 211; contrasting richness of land with, 27; contrasting with colonial perceptions of, 51, 52; explanations of by experts, 221; federal government blamed for, 221, 222; federal government discloses extent of, 209; media comparisons of casinos with, 252; media depictions of, 247; Navajo, 215 (ill.); public perceptions of, 220; Senate survey of, 211; strategies to reduce, 247–48; White

colonists' conceptions of, as fate, 19, 54; White conceptions of, 18, 51

Powhatan Indians, 5, 6, 20; attack Jamestown, 46; daily life described, 20; dependence on English sources for knowledge about, 20; erosion of wealth, 47; material culture, 20; population decline, 52; poverty among, 52; rights to land, 39; scant evidence of, 20; tribute payments among, 21; war with English, 46, 47; wealth measures, 20; working as servants in English homes, 52–53

The Principal Navigations, 25

Progressive (magazine), on opposition to Indian fishing, 237–38

Progressives, Indian, and allotments, 167

Promotion, economic, 28, 139

Property. *See also* Land; Land ownership/title

—Indian: colonists on lack of, 19; redistribution approved by Congress, 169–70

—private: missionaries not allowed to own, 120; missions promoting ideas of, 106; as reason to resist removal, 124; removal required to develop, 123; tribes pass laws protecting, 110, 113

—rights: changes made in Indian, 136; comparing Indian and White systems of, 164; granted by Five Tribes, 151; as necessary for progress, 147

Prosperity. *See* Wealth; Wealth accumulation

Purchas, Samuel, defends English colonization, 41

Pyramid Lake water case, 231

Racism, 89; invoked by removal proponents, 131

Railroads, 138; bolster migration, 138; built across Indian lands, 139; rights-of-way for, 155

Ranching, Whites in Indian country, 138

Rand, Kathryn, on criticism of tribal casinos, 254

Rationality, wealth accumulation and, 10

Reagan, John H., denounces monopolies, 142

Reciprocity, exploitation and, 22

Seminole Indians, casino revenues as preserving lifeway, 264, 266

Settler-colonial economy, 4; meaning for Indians, 14

Severs, F. B., compared to Jay Gould, 141

Shattuck, Jill, on White response to Indian plight, 240

Shell beads, as objects of sacred power, 21

Shelton, Madeleine, on ambition for wealth, 134

Shepherd, William, on wasteful Osage spending, 177, 183

Sioux, Black Hills litigation, 230

Slaves: Cherokee ownership of, 100; Choctaw ownership of, 101; Creek bequest of, 100–101; owned by Mc-Gillivray, 85; ownership as measure of wealth, 100; wealth gained from ownership, 61

Slosson, Edwin, on Indian wealth as lesson in chance, 180–81

Smith, John: blames Indians for colony failures, 32; captivity story, 43; on colonist ambitions for gold, 26; on colonist dependence on Indian food, 35; on coronation of Wahunsonacock, 37; on criticism from Wahunsonacock, 44; on English stealing Indian corn, 40; on Indian food supplies, 33; intentions questioned, 44; on kinship ethic, 45; on necessity for gift-giving, 41; on Powhatan deceptions, 44; on Powhatan views of barter and kinship, 43; social status, 25; understanding Powhatan ethics, 45

Snyder, Homer, 193; complains about Osage debt, 193–94; on unscrupulous guardians, 198

Social merger, between leading Whites and Indians, 59

Social relationships, as facilitating trade, 60–61

Social status: accumulating trade goods as symbol of, 66; colonial, 57; comparing wealthy Osage to White, 183, 184; connection of wealth to, 183; Indians in colonies, 57, 88; land as measure of, 71; Osage women, 184; White difficulty determining Indian, 64, 183

Soltow, Lewis, on slave ownership as measure of wealth, 100

Sources, historical, differing types of, 8

South Dakota, Sioux claims to, 230

South Park, Indian gambling television episode, 252

Spanish expansion, English preemption of, 25

Speculation, 133–34; in Cherokee Nation, 134–35; Jacksonian era real estate, 97

Spelman, Henry: on Powhatan polygamy, 35; sees weroance fling beads, 21

Status. *See* Social status

Stephens (also spelled Stevens), S. S.: condemns land greed, 143; demands government limit property accumulation, 153

Stephens, William, on marriage of Coosaponakeesa, 69

Stereotypes: Indian exploitation of, 11; of Indians, 206; Osage wealth and, 184–85

Stevens, Justice John Paul: on Boldt decision, 246; new doctrine on Indian economic opportunity, 246–47

Stiggins, George: on changes in Creek economic culture, 102; on Indian wealth acquisition, 101–2

Strachey, William: on determining Indian hierarchy by clothing, 29–30; expectations about Indians, 27; perception of Wahunsonacock, 23; pledges purchase of Powhatan land, 39–40; on Powhatan accumulation of copper, 37; on Powhatan food supplies, 33; on Powhatan greed, 41; on Powhatan numbers, 36; on value of Indian commodities, 28; view on wealth accumulation, 24

Strong, Josiah, on gulf between employees and employers, 144

Supreme Court of the United States: on Indians as U.S. wards, 195; ruling on Boldt decision, 246

Symonds, William, denies Indian land ownership, 41–42

Tallchief, Henry, urges release of trust funds, 201–2

Tax, Cherokee head, 153

Taylor, Alan, on Joseph Brant's wealth, 81

requisite for political power, 56; ritual dismantling of, 66; of rulers, 22, 23; significance among societies, 12; as sign of strong character, 149; social utility of disparities in, 148–49; sovereignty and, 274; tracing interrelationships of culture and, 10, 15; transfer by Indians, 102–3; Virginia precedent for loss of Indian, 18; wasteful use of, 175, 181–83; weakening tribal culture through, 265

Wealth accumulation, 4; from agriculture, 139; colonist views of Indian, 19, 29; from deer hide trade, 61; explanations, 9; from gambling, 249, 255–60; generosity and, 66; and ideologies of race, 4; Indian, as lesson in chance, 180–81; by Indians and Whites, 96; legislation to discourage, 148, 150–51; luck as factor in, 179–80; origins of American drive for, 101; probing explanations for Indian, 9; rapid increases in Indian territory of, 137; rationale rooted in Indian culture, 66

Wealthy class: expected to aid less fortunate, 110–12, 151; prominence of, 140; resemblance of Indian to White, 113–14; as successors to headmen, 111

Weroances (Powhatan rulers), 21; as figures of bounty, 22

West, Capt. Francis, receives land from Wahunsonacock, 40

Wheeler, Burton, on Indian poverty, 211–12

Wilkins, David: on growing Indian power, 268; on risk of backlash, 269

Wilkinson, Charles, on Indian poverty, 225

Williams, Robert A., on Indians as "other," 16

Wilson, Terry, on Osage oil boom, 188

Wire fences, preempting land with, 152

Without Reservation, 258

Wolfe, Patrick, on words as defense of indigenous identity, 4

Women: Cherokee urge censure of wealthy, 117; control over property, 74, 77; as measure of Powhatan wealth, 35; Mohawks seek approval for land sales from, 77; presence at war councils, 77; role in building trade relationships, 61; role in furthering husbands' wealth, 78

Women's National Indian Association, 155, 163

Wood, Gordon, on connection between wealth and political power, 56

Woodward, A. T., 204

Worcester, Samuel: on Cherokee wealth, 99; on private property of missionaries, 120

World War II, influence on Indian poverty, 213

Wright, J. George, 196; advocates for limits on payments to Osage, 193; as ally of oil companies, 199–200; on Osage financial irresponsibility, 194–95; on supervising payments to Osages, 193, 196

Yamacraw trading post, 67

Yeardley, George, receives land from Powhatans, 38

Yorgason, Ethan, on economy as system of meaning, 10

Youings, Joyce, on rising English wealth, 24

Zissu, Erik, on competition for tribal land, 165